The SuperCollider Book

The SuperCollider Book

edited by Scott Wilson, David Cottle, and Nick Collins

The MIT Press
Cambridge, Massachusetts
London, England

For information about special quantity discounts, please e-mail special_sales@mitpress.mit .edu

This book was set in Sabon on InDesign by Asco Typesetters, Hong Kong. Printed and bound in the United States of America.

Library of Congress Cataloging-in-Publication Data

The SuperCollider book / edited by Scott Wilson, David Cottle, and Nick Collins.
    p.   cm.
Includes bibliographical references and index.
ISBN 978-0-262-23269-2 (hardcover : alk. paper)
1. SuperCollider (Computer file) 2. Software synthesizers. 3. Computer composition.
I. Wilson, Scott, 1969 Nov. 26–. II. Cottle, David. III. Collins, Nick (Nicholas).
ML74.4.S86S86 2011
781.3'45133—dc22

10 9 8 7 6 5 4 3 2 1

Contents

Foreword

James McCartney

Why use a computer programming language for composing music? Specifically, why use SuperCollider? There are several very high-level language environments for audio besides SuperCollider, such as Common Music, Kyma, Nyquist, and Patchwork. These all demonstrate very interesting work in this area and are worth looking into. SuperCollider, though, has the unique combination of being free, well supported, and designed for real time. It is a language for describing sound processes. SuperCollider is very good at allowing one to create nice sounds with minimal effort, but more important, it allows one to represent musical concepts as objects, to transform them via functions or methods, to compose transformations into higher-level building blocks, and to design interactions for manipulating music in real time, from the top-level structure of a piece down to the level of the waveform. You can build a library of classes and functions that become building blocks for your working style and in this way make a customized working environment. With SuperCollider, one can create many things: very long or infinitely long pieces, infinite variations of structure or surface detail, algorithmic mass production of synthesis voices, sonification of empirical data or mathematical formulas, to name a few. It has also been used as a vehicle for live coding and networked performances. Because of this open-endedness, early on, I often felt it difficult to know how best to write the documentation. There were too many possible approaches and applications.

Thus, I am pleased that there will now be a book on SuperCollider, and the best part of it for me is that I have not had to do much of the hard work to get it done. Since I made SuperCollider open source, it has taken on a life of its own and become a community-sustained project as opposed to being a project sustained by a single author. Many people have stepped up and volunteered to undertake tasks of documentation, porting to other operating systems, interfacing to hardware and software, writing new unit generators, extending the class library, maintaining a Web site, mailing lists, and a wiki, fixing bugs, and, finally, writing and editing the chapters of this book. All of these efforts have resulted in more features, better documentation, and a more complete, robust, and bugfree program.

SuperCollider came about as the latest in a series of software synthesis languages that I have written over the years. I have been interested in writing software to synthesize electronic music ever since I was in high school. At that time, I had written on a piece of notebook paper a set of imaginary subroutine calls in BASIC for implementing all of the common analog synthesizer modules. Of course, doing audio synthesis in BASIC on the hardware of that time was completely impractical, but the idea had become a goal of mine. When I graduated college, I went to have a look at E-mu in California and found that it was operating out of a two-story house. I figured that the synthesizer industry was a lot smaller than I had imagined and that I should rethink my career plans.

The first software synthesizer I wrote was a graphical patching environment called Synfonix that generated samples for the Ensoniq Mirage sampling keyboard using a Macintosh computer. I attempted to sell this program but sold only two copies, one to Ivan Tcherepnin at Harvard and another to Mark Polishook. A business lesson I learned from this is not to sell a product that requires purchasers to already own two niche products. The intersection of two small markets is near zero.

In 1990, I wrote a program called Synth-O-Matic that I used personally but never meant to distribute, even though one copy I gave to a friend got circulated. I created this program after learning CSound and deciding that I never wanted to actually have to use CSound's assembly-language-like syntax. Synth-O-Matic had a more expression-oriented syntax for writing signal flow graphs and a graphical user interface for editing wave tables. I used this program on and off, but it was quite slow so I stopped using it, for the most part, in favor of hardware synthesizers.

It wasn't until the PowerPC came out that it became practical to do floating-point signal processing in real time on a personal computer. At the time I had been working on music for a modern dance piece, using Synth-O-Matic to do granular synthesis. It was taking a long time to generate the sound, and I was running behind schedule to get the piece done. On the day in March 1994 when the first PowerPC-based machine came out, I went and bought the fastest one. I recompiled my code, and it ran 32 times faster. I was then able to complete the piece on time. I noticed that my code was now running faster than real time, so I began working on a program designed to do real-time synthesis. Around this time I got a note in the mail from Curtis Roads, who had apparently gotten one of the circulating copies of Synth-O-Matic, encouraging me to further develop the program. So I took the Synth-O-Matic engine and combined it with the Pyrite scripting language object which I had written for MAX. This became SuperCollider version 1, which was released in March 1996. The first two orders were from John Bischoff and Chris Brown of The Hub.

The name "SuperCollider" has an amusing origin. During the early 1990s I worked in the Astronomy Department of the University of Texas at Austin on the Hubble Space Telescope Astrometry Science Team, writing software for data analysis and telescope observation planning. On the floors below my office was the Physics Department, some of the members of which were involved in the Superconducting Super Collider project. In 1993, Congress cut the funding for the project, and there were many glum faces around the building after that. I had been thinking about this merging, or "collision," if you will, of a real-time synthesis engine with a high-level garbage collected language, and it seemed to me that it was an experiment that would likely fail, so I named it after the failed Big Science project of the day. Except that the experiment didn't fail. To my surprise, it actually worked rather well.

The version 1 language was dynamically typed, with a C-like syntax, closures borrowed from Scheme, and a limited amount of polymorphism. After using version 1 for a couple of years, and especially after a project on which I was invited by Iannis Zannos to work on a concert in an indoor swimming pool in Berlin, I realized that it had severe limitations on its ability to scale up to create large working environments. So I began working on version 2, which borrowed heavily from Smalltalk. It was for the most part the same as the language described in this book except for the synthesis engine and class library, which have changed a great deal.

The goal of SuperCollider version 2 and beyond was to create a language for describing real-time interactive sound processes. I wanted to create a way to describe categories of sound processes that could be parameterized or customized. The main idea of SuperCollider is to algorithmically compose objects to create sound-generating processes. Unit generators, a concept invented by Max Matthews for his Music N languages, are very much like objects and are a natural fit for a purely object-oriented Smalltalk-like language.

In 2001 I was working on version 3 of SuperCollider, and because of the architecture of the server, it was looking like it really should be open source, so that anyone could modify it however they liked. I was (barely) making a living at the time selling SuperCollider, so the decision to give it away was a difficult one to make. But financially it was looking like I would need a "real" job soon, anyway. I was also worried that the period of self-employment on my résumé would begin looking suspect to potential employers. Ultimately, I did get a job, so I was able to open source the program. On the day that I made all of my previously copyright-protected programs free, my Web site experienced an eightfold increase in traffic. So obviously there was a lot of interest in an open source audio language and engine, especially one that is free.

I hope that this book will enable and inspire the reader to apply this tool in useful and interesting ways. And I hope to hear and enjoy the results!

Introduction

Scott Wilson, David Cottle, and Nick Collins

Welcome to *The SuperCollider Book*. We're delighted to present a collection of tutorials, essays, and projects that highlight one of the most exciting and powerful audio environments. SuperCollider (SC to its friends) is a domain-specific programming language specialized for sound but with capabilities to rival any general-purpose language. Though it is technically a blend of Smalltalk, C, and ideas from a number of other programming languages, many users simply accept SuperCollider as its own wonderful dialect, a superlative tool for real-time audio adventures. Indeed, for many artists, SuperCollider is the first programming language they learn, and they do so without fear because the results are immediately engaging; you can learn a little at a time in such a way that you hardly notice that you're programming until it's too late and you're hooked! The potential applications in real-time interaction, installations, electroacoustic pieces, generative music, audiovisuals, and a host of other possibilities make up for any other qualms. On top of that, it's free, powerful, and open source, and has one of the most supportive and diverse user and developer communities around.

Pathways

This book will be your companion to SuperCollider; some of you will already have experience and be itching to turn to the many and varied chapters further on from this point. We'll let you follow the book in any order you choose! But we would like to take care to welcome any newcomers and point them straight in the direction of chapter 1, which provides a friendly introduction to the basics. For those on Windows or Linux it may be read together with chapter 11 or 12, respectively, which cover some of the cross-platform installation issues. From there we suggest beginners continue through until chapter 4, as this path will provide you with some basic skills and knowledge which can serve as a foundation for further learning.

For more advanced users, we suggest you look at the more "topics"-oriented chapters which follow. These chapters aren't designed to be read in any particular order, so proceed with those of particular interest and relevance to you and your pursuits. Naturally we have referred to other chapters for clarification where necessary and have tried to avoid duplication of materials except where absolutely crucial for clarity.

These "topics" chapters are divided into sections titled Advanced Tutorials, Platforms and GUI, and Practical Applications. They begin with chapter 5, "Programming in SuperCollider," which provides a detailed overview of SuperCollider as a programming language. This may be of interest to beginners with a computer science background who'd rather approach SC from a language design and theory perspective than through the more user-friendly approach in chapter 1. Chapters on a variety of subjects follow, including sonification, spatialization, microsound, GUIs, machine listening, alternative tunings, and non-real-time synthesis.

Following these chapters is a section for intermediate and advanced users titled Projects and Perspectives. The material therein provides examples of how Super-Collider has been used in the real world. These chapters also provide some philosophical insight into issues of language design and its implications (most specifically in chapter 23, "Dialects, Constraints, and Systems-Within-Systems"). This sort of intellectual pursuit has been an important part of SuperCollider's development; SC is a language that self-consciously aims for good design, and to allow and encourage elegance, and even beauty, in the user's code. Although this might seem a little abstract at first, we feel that this sets SC apart from other computer music environments and that as users advance, awareness of such things can improve their code.

Finally, there is a section titled Developer Topics, which provides detailed "under the hood" information on SC. These chapters are for advanced users seeking a deeper understanding of the SC and its workings and for those wishing to extend SC, for instance, by writing custom unit generator plug-ins.

Code Examples and Text Conventions

Initially SuperCollider was Mac only, but as an open source project since 2001, it has widened its scope to cover all major platforms, with only minor differences between them. Most code in this book should run on all platforms with the same results, and we will note places where there are different mechanisms in place; most of the time, the code itself will already have taken account of any differences automatically. For instance, SC includes cross-platform GUI classes such as View, Slider, and Window. These will automatically redirect to the correct GUI implementation, either Cocoa (on Mac OSX; see chapter 9) or SwingOSC (on all platforms; see chapter 10). However, there are some differences in the programming editor environments (such as available menu items) and the keyboard shortcuts. You are referred as well to the extensive Help system that comes with the SuperCollider application; a Help file on keyboard Shortcuts for the various platforms is prominently linked from the main Help page.

Just to note, when you come across keyboard shortcuts in the text, they'll appear like this: [enter] designates the "enter" (and *not* the "return") key, [ctrl+a] means the control key plus the "a" key, and so on. Furthermore, all text appearing in the code font will almost always be valid SuperCollider code (very occasionally there may be exceptions for didactic purposes, such as here). You will also encounter some special SuperCollider terms (e.g., Synth, SynthDef, and Array) that aren't in code font and are discussed in a friendly manner; this is because they are ubiquitous concepts and it would be exhausting to have them in the code font every time. You may also see them appearing with a capital letter (i.e., Synths), or all lower case (synths), depending again on how formal we are being. Anyway, if you're new to SuperCollider, don't worry about this at all; chapter 1 will start you on the righteous path, and you'll soon be chatting about Synths and UGens like the rest of us.

The Book Web Site

This brings us to the accompanying Web site for the book (<http://supercolliderbook .net>), which contains all the code reproduced within, ready to run, as well as download links to the application itself, its source code, and all sorts of third-party extras, extensions, libraries, and examples. A standardized version of SuperCollider is used for the book, SuperCollider 3.4, for which all book code should work without trouble. Of course, the reader may find it productive to download newer versions of SuperCollider as they become available, and it is our intention to provide updated versions of the example code where needed. Although we can make no hard promises, in this fast-paced world of operating system shifts, that the code in this book will remain eternally correct—the ongoing development and improvement of environments such as SuperCollider are a big part of what makes them so exciting—we've done our best to present you with a snapshot of SuperCollider that should retain a core validity in future years.

Final Thoughts

Please be careful with audio examples; there is of course the potential to make noises that can damage your hearing if you're not sensible with volume levels. Until you become accustomed to the program, we suggest you start each example with the volume all the way down, and then slowly raise it to a comfortable level. (And if you're not getting any sound, remember to check if you've left the monitors off or the computer audio muted.) Some examples may use audio input and have the potential to feedback unless your monitoring arrangements are correct. The easiest way to deal with such examples is to monitor via headphones.

We couldn't possibly cover everything concerning SuperCollider, and there are many online resources to track down new developments and alternative viewpoints, including mailing lists, forums, and a host of artists, composers, technology developers, and SuperCollider maniacs with interesting pages. We have provided a few of the most important links (at the time of writing) below, but Wikigoopedigle, or whatever your contemporary equivalent is, will allow you to search out the current SuperCollider 15.7 as necessary.

We're sure you'll have fun as you explore this compendium, and we're also sure you'll be inspired to some fantastic art and science as you go. Enjoy exploring the SuperCollider world first charted by James McCartney but since expanded immeasurably by everyone who partakes in this infinitely flexible open source project.

Primary Web Resources
Main community home page: <http://supercollider.sourceforge.net>
Application download and project site: <http://sourceforge.net/projects/supercollider>
James McCartney's home page: <http://www.audiosynth.com>
The venerable swiki site: <http://swiki.hfbk-hamburg.de:8888/MusicTechnology/6>

Acknowledgments

We owe a debt of gratitude to the chapter contributors and to the wider SuperCollider community, who have supported this project. SC's community is one of its greatest strengths, and innumerable phone calls, e-mails, chats over cups of tea at the SC Symposium, and many other interactions, have contributed to making this book and SC itself stronger. We apologize to all who have put up with our insistent editing and acknowledge the great efforts of the developers to prepare a stable SuperCollider 3.4 version for this book. A thousand thank-yous:

```
1000.do{"domo arigato gozaimashita".postln};
```

Thanks to all at MIT Press who have assisted in the handling of our proposal and manuscript for this book.

Thank you to friends, family, and colleagues who had to deal with us while we were immersed in the lengthy task of organizing, editing, and assembling this book. Editing may seem like a solitary business, but from their perspective we're quite sure it was a team effort!

Many thanks to our students, who have served as guinea pigs for pedagogical approaches, tutorial materials, experimental developments, and harebrained ideas. Now back to your exercise wheels!

Finally, the editors would like to thank each other for support during the period of gestation. At the time of writing, we've been working on this project for 2 years to bring the final manuscript to fruition. Though Scott and Nick have met on many occasions (and were co-organizers of the 2006 SuperCollider Symposium at the University of Birmingham), neither has ever met David in person (we sometimes wonder if he really exists!); but you should see the number of e-mails we've sent each other. For many months, in the heat of the project, David modified his routine to include a 3 A.M. e-mail check to keep up with those using GMT, which imparts a celestially imposed 8-hour advantage. In any case, although it has at times been exhausting, seeing this book through to fruition has been a pleasure, and we hope it brings you pleasure to read it and learn about SC.

Tutorials

1 Beginner's Tutorial

David Michael Cottle

1.1 Hello World

This chapter will be your guide on an initial journey through the amazing, complex, esoteric, and sometimes confusing SC environment. It does not assume prior programming experience but does assume basic computer skills and some synthesis background; that is, you won't be surprised by terms such as voltage control, envelope, oscillator, or LFO. (We will look at examples in subtractive synthesis, additive synthesis, phase modulation, and physical modeling.) You may also have some background in music and may be familiar with music software such as trackers and sequencers.

Meeting these criteria is not a prerequisite, but you may have to do some work on these topics to fill in the blanks. On the other hand, if you're an experienced programmer and trained musician, you might skim this material and move as quickly as possible to chapter 2.

The goal is getting interesting sounds as quickly as possible. To that end we'll often take liberties with the terms of object-oriented programming and the internal structure of SC, occasionally leaving out details so as to focus better on the topic at hand. Other chapters of this book will fill in the gaps.

This tutorial refers first and foremost to the Mac OSX version of the program (on which it was originally developed), but all the material should be directly applicable across platforms. Take a look at chapters 11 and 12 for installation and coding differences if you're using Windows or Linux. There's also a handy Shortcuts file included in SC's Help.

You may become a little lost during some of this discussion, but don't panic. This chapter is intended to push the envelope and set you up for later discussions. Just keep treading water, focus on the interesting sounds and the topics at hand, and your questions should be resolved further on.

Assuming you have downloaded and installed SC, now start it up.

As the program starts, a post window will spout a barrage of cryptic lines. You can ignore them, but keep the window visible; it will print useful data as we move along.

Open a new window (File/New menu item or [cmd+N] Mac, [ctrl+N] Windows) and type the line of code below, including quotes. (All examples of code intended to be typed and executed in SC will appear in the following font.)

```
"Hello world"
```

Select the entire line and press the [enter] key ([shift+return] or [fn+return] on Mac laptops, [ctrl+enter] for Windows, [ctrl+c, ctrl+c] for Linux-Emacs) to evaluate the code. Voilà! "Hello world" appears in the post window. Congratulations! You've just written and executed your first SC program.

Or, if you're like most new users, voilà, the line disappears. That's because you pressed the [return] key rather than [enter]. There's a difference. (On a full-size keyboard, [enter] is the one on the number pad.) If the disappearing line happens to you, choose Edit/Undo to bring the text back, select again, and keep pecking until you get the right key and see "Hello world" in the post window.

The example we just ran came by way of the client side of SC, which essentially consists of the windows where you type and evaluate lines of code (i.e., commands for making sounds). Audio comes from the server side (on most platforms the 2 windows named *internal server* and *localhost server*), a separate program that takes the client commands and turns them into sounds. We didn't need the server for the first example, which produced no sounds, but for the next one we do, so let's get it running. Replace "Hello world" with the following line (it's case sensitive), select, and evaluate. (Alternatively, you can start the server by clicking the boot button in the server window.)

```
Server.default = s = Server.internal.boot
```

This boots the internal server, makes it the default server, and assigns it to the variable s. (You will have to do this each time you launch SC, but only once per session.) In this chapter we will always use the internal server, and we will assume you have it running from here on. (On Windows there is no internal server, so instead of the above line, just use s.boot.)

Before we start some sound, it's probably best if we explain how to stop it. To stop all sound, press these keys: OSX [cmd+.], Windows [alt+.]; on Linux it depends on your choice of editor (see the Shortcuts file and chapter 12). Now delete everything (or open a new window) and type this line:

```
play({SinOsc.ar(LFNoise0.kr(12, mul: 600, add: 1000), 0.3)})
```

Once you've done this, select that line and press [enter].

You should hear, as an appropriate introduction to SC, a sci-fi computer sound effect. If, on the other hand, you're enjoying Cage's "4'33"" (i.e. silence), check for an error blurb in the post window, something like this:

```
• ERROR: Parse error
    in file 'selected text'
    line 1 char 48:
play({SinOsc.ar(LFNoise0.kr(12, mul: 600, add: 1000) 0.3•)})
-----------------------------------
• ERROR: Command line parse failed
nil
```

Error messages are a common occurrence in SC, so it's important to learn how to read them. In this case it's a parse error, which is usually just a typo. The large dot after the 0.3 indicates where the program stopped understanding (couldn't parse). The mistake is usually somewhere before that. Check for a missing comma (in this example, the comma before 0.3 is missing), brace instead of bracket, or incorrect case; any of them would cause an error.

Proof, change, and try it again until you get the correct result. If you didn't get an error, try introducing one so you can get some practice reading them.

In this next example we'll look at changing some parameters.

```
play({RLPF.ar(Dust.ar([12, 15]), LFNoise1.ar(1/[3, 4], 1500, 1600), 0.02)})
```

Stop the sound and experiment by replacing the numbers 12 and 15 with values between 1 and 100. Change the 3 and/or 4 to numbers between 1 and 10 and start it again. See if you can discern what aspect of the sound each number is controlling. (Hint: This example is *subtractive synthesis*; a resonant low-pass filter applied to low-frequency random impulses.) You can stop each sound between trials or pile them one on top of the other.

Figure 1.1 shows an example spread out and indented into several lines, so be sure to select everything before evaluating. You can use Edit/Select All if it's the only thing in the file. It takes about 30 seconds to hear the full effect of this example.

After the sound fades, stop the patch and try replacing 5 with 10, then start it again. Try values between 1 and 40. Stop again and change the speed (6) to values between 1 and 40, stopping and running between each value. Replace LFNoise1 with LFNoise0. Swap the +1 and –1 to reverse the fade. Put everything except the –1 and +1 back to its original state (use undo), then replace x+1*100 with exprand(100, 10000). Next—and this will start to demonstrate some of SC's power—increase the number of sine waves (where it says sines) from 5 to 10, 20, 40, 100. Finally, mix and match any of these changes.

```
play({
    var sines = 5, speed = 6;
    Mix.fill(sines,
        {arg x;
            Pan2.ar(
                SinOsc.ar(x+1*100,
                    mul: max(0,
                        LFNoise1.kr(speed) +
                        Line.kr(1, -1, 30)
                    )
                ), rand2(1.0))})/sines})
```

Figure 1.1
Example of additive synthesis.

Figure 1.1 illustrates *additive synthesis* (in which individual sine waves are summed) in a way that is audibly apparent in the actual sound; rich, complex, yet you hear the individual frequencies emerge as the whole sound fades in or out. It shows how this method, impossible (or at least difficult) on many software or hardware synths, can be accomplished with just a dozen lines of code in SC. And, finally, it shows how quickly, with strategic changes, you can layer sounds that evolve from a few undulating tones to something very complex.

You probably did not understand everything in the code above. If these examples look like Greek, it's because SC is, to you, a foreign language that you're going to have to learn. If you're patient, you will soon be able to read and write SC code as you would any language. Look again at the additive synthesis example and see if you can recognize a few of the words with the help of this translation: This example tells the server to play a sound that is filled with a Mix of 5 panned SineOscillators tuned to multiples of 100, which are flashed on and off as a Low-Frequency Noise source pops up above a maximum of itself and 0, all slowly following a Line of attenuation over 30 seconds. Once you have learned the SC language, you can tell it what to do, using commands or messages.

1.2 Messages and Arguments

A message is a lowercase word followed by a pair of parentheses containing a list of arguments. Arguments are lists of items separated by commas, inside parentheses, next to a message. Together they look something like this: message(arg1, arg2, arg3). Sometimes messages appear on their own, such as max(arglist) or rand2(arglist), and sometimes they are connected to an uppercase word (discussed later) with a dot

(for example .ar or .fill in constructions such as SinOsc.ar(arglist) and Mix.
fill(arglist)). Scan the examples given so far and identify messages and argument
lists. (Each argument list is terminated by a closing parenthesis.)

Messages are commands such as jump, bake, or sing. Arguments are qualifications
to these commands: jump 3 feet to the right, bake a pizza at 500° for 30 minutes,
sing "Daisy, Daisy, Give Me Your Answer, Do." These commands, written in SC,
might look like this:

```
jump(3, right)
bake(pizza, 500, 30)
sing("Daisy, Daisy, Give Me Your Answer, Do.")
```

SC understands a number of synthesis- and composition-related commands. Let's
try a few starting with rand, which takes a single argument. The argument sets the
upper limit of a random number selection. Type and evaluate the line below. But
first, here is a trick that can be used with single-line examples. First, don't start a new
line (by pressing [return]) after the last parenthesis. That will leave the cursor at the
end of the code example. This does two things. First, you don't have to select the
entire line to evaluate it. That's because pressing [enter] will execute selected code or,
if nothing is selected, it will execute the entire line where the cursor sits. Second, if
there is no vacant line below what you are evaluating, the cursor will remain on the
last line of the selection you just evaluated. This allows you to run that one line over
and over without repositioning the cursor.

```
rand(100)
```

Check the post window. You should see integers between 0 and 99.

Replace 100 with 100.0 and note the difference. As a general rule, if you use a
float (short for floating point, e.g., 1.298, 178.287, 0.3) as an argument, a float is
returned. Integers (e.g., 4, –55, 7, –11982, 1235) will return integers. (Also note that
in SC both positive and negative floats smaller than 1 must have a leading zero: 0.1,
–0.125, 0.003, 0.75.)

Here is another type of random message with 2 arguments. Can you guess the difference between rand and exprand and what the 2 arguments indicate? You may have
to run it quite a few times to see a pattern.

```
exprand(1.0, 100.0)
```

The exprand message returns values from an exponential range (i.e., biased toward
lower numbers). Notice that about half the choices are between 1 and 10, and the
others between 10 and 100. Exponential random choices are useful for frequency,
since successive musical intervals perceived by humans to be equal are in reality exponentially larger frequencies (for example, A4, A5, A6 are 440, 880, 1760).

In case you thought computers did anything truly random, try this line repeatedly, which chooses 10 "random" numbers. (The semicolons, braces, and exclamation point will be explained later.)

```
thisThread.randSeed = 666; {rand(10.0)} ! 10;
```

This is called *seeding* the random number generator, and 666 is the random seed. Try a less satanic number (66, 3, 7, 9, 12, 40, etc.). When you use a given seed, even on different computers (with the same OS), you will get the same "random" results (deus ex machina).

Here are some more messages. Try them 1 line at a time.

```
dup("echo", 20)
round([3.141, 5.9265, 358.98], 0.01)
sort([23, 54, 678, 1, 21, 91, 34, 78])
round(dup({exprand(1, 10)}, 100), 0.1)
sort(round(dup({exprand(1, 10)}, 100), 0.1))
```

You might guess from the name of each message what it does, but can you guess the significance of each argument? (Hint: Change the arguments and run them again.)

The first message is a duplicator. Its first argument, "echo", is duplicated the number of times specified by the second argument. The round rounds the first argument (the numbers inside the brackets) to the precision of the second argument. sort takes a single argument—a collection of numbers—and sorts them. The next picks 100 random numbers and rounds them. The last does all that, then sorts them. Notice that the exprand and dup, previously on their own, are inside the argument list for round, which is inside sort. This is called nesting.

1.3   Nesting

To further clarify the idea of nesting, consider a hypothetical example in which SC will make you lunch. To do so, you might use a serve message. The arguments might be salad, main course, and dessert. But just saying serve(lettuce, fish, banana) may not give you the results you want. So to be safe you could clarify those arguments, replacing each with a nested message and argument.

```
serve(toss(lettuce, tomato, cheese), bake(fish, 400, 20), mix(banana, ice
cream))
```

SC would then serve not just lettuce, fish, and banana, but a tossed salad with lettuce, tomato, and cheese, a baked fish, and a banana sundae. These inner commands can be further clarified by nesting a message(arg) for each ingredient: lettuce, to-

```
serve(
    toss(
        wash(lettuce, water, 10),
        dice(tomato, small),
        sprinkle(choose([blue, feta, gouda]))
    ),
    bake(catch(lagoon, hook, bamboo), 400, 20),
    mix(
        slice(peel(banana), 20),
        cook(mix(milk, sugar, starch), 200, 10)
    )
)
```

Figure 1.2
Nested commands for fortuitous robot.

mato, cheese, and so on. Each internal message produces a result that is in turn used as an argument by the outer message.

When the nesting has several levels, we can use new lines and indents for clarity, as you saw in figure 1.1. Some messages and arguments are left on 1 line, some are spread out with 1 argument per line—whichever is clearer. Each indent level should indicate a level of nesting. (Note that you can have any amount of white space—new lines, tabs, or spaces—between bits of code.)

In figure 1.2 the lunch program is now told to wash the lettuce in water for 20 minutes and to dice the tomato into small pieces before tossing them into the salad bowl and sprinkling them with cheese. You've also specified where to catch the fish and to bake it at 400° for 20 minutes before serving, and so on.

To "read" this style of code you start from the innermost nested message and move out to each successive layer. Here is an example aligned to show how the innermost message is nested inside the outer messages.

```
                        exprand(1.0, 1000.0)
               dup({exprand(1.0, 1000.0)}, 100)
          sort(dup({exprand(1.0, 1000.0)}, 100))
round(sort(dup({exprand(1.0, 1000.0)}, 100)), 0.01)
```

Figure 1.3 makes use of nesting. Execute it, and then test your understanding by answering the questions that follow.

1. What is the second argument for LFNoise1.ar?
2. What is the first argument for LFSaw.ar?
3. What is the third argument for LFNoise1.ar?

```
(
play(
    {
        CombN.ar(
            SinOsc.ar(
                midicps(
                    LFNoise1.ar(3, 24,
                        LFSaw.ar([5, 5.123], 0, 3, 80)
                    )
                ),
                0, 0.4),
            1, 0.3, 2)
    }
)
)
```

Figure 1.3
Fortuitous futuristic nested music.

4. How many arguments are in midicps?
5. What is the third argument for SinOsc.ar?
6. What are the second and third arguments for CombN.ar?
7. What is the only argument for play?

See this chapter's notes for the answers.[1]

1.4   Receiver.message, Comments

In the sound examples we've seen above, the uppercase words attached to messages with a dot, such as SinOsc in SinOsc.ar and LFNoise1 in LFNoise1.kr, are UGens ("unit generators"), which produce a stream of numbers suitable for digital audio. In more general terms, however, they are receivers. Messages are what to do. Arguments are how to do it. A receiver performs the action indicated by a message with 0 or more arguments.

There are many types of receivers (UGens, numbers, strings). When linked to a message, they can generate output, sometimes individual values or collections. When a UGen is messaged, it may set up a process on the synthesis server to generate audio number streams. The dot between receiver and message loosely means "do this." The argument list describes how the receiver should complete the command. So LFNoise1.kr(10, 100) means "make a low-frequency noise generator of type 1, which will produce a random number between –100 and 100, ten times per second."

Numbers, functions, arrays, and strings (text inside quotes) can also be told what to do by way of a dot and message.

In the next examples we'll slip in a new convention: comments. Text that falls between two slashes and the end of a line is ignored during evaluation. This allows short explanations inside code. Comments are sometimes on a separate line but often are placed at the end of a line. Try this: select all the lines below and choose the syntax colorize option on your system (Mac OSX menu item under Format, but usually automatic for the Windows and Linux editors). The comments turn red, and the text string, gray.

```
[45, 13, 10, 498, 78].sort // collection of items, do this; sort yourself
"echo".dup(20) // echo, do this; repeat yourself 20 times
50.midicps // the number 50, do this; convert yourself into Hz
444.cpsmidi // 444, do this; convert yourself into a midi number
100.rand // 100, do this; pick a number between 0 and yourself
{100.rand}.dup(50) // random picking function, do this; repeat 50 times
[1.001, 45.827, 187.18].round(0.1) // collection of items; round to 0.1
// Mac users only, sorry
"I've just picked up a fault in the AE35 unit".speak // Hal; plot to kill
me
```

Earlier we saw dup("echo", 20) and rand(100), but here we use "echo".dup(20) and 100.rand. What is the difference? Nothing (in terms of results). 100.rand is receiver notation. rand(100) is functional notation. The first argument of a message can be placed in front of the message, separated by a dot; message(arg) and arg.message, or message(arg1, arg2) and arg1.message(arg2) are precisely the same.

Which should you use when? It's a matter of style. Things that begin with uppercase letters (Mix, SinOsc, Pan2, Array) are nearly always written as receiver.messages. Numbers, arrays, and text can be written either way, depending on whichever is clearer in a given context. For example, receiver notation can be used to string together a series of messages as an alternative to nesting, as shown below. The result of each receiver.message pair becomes the receiver for the next message. Note the subtle but important distinction between the periods in 1000.0.rand. The first is a floating point, indicating that the number is a float. The second is a dot that sends the message rand to 1000.0.

```
1000.0 // a number
1000.0.rand // choose a number between 0 and 1000
1000.0.rand.round(0.01) // choose a number and round it
1000.0.rand.round(0.01).post // choose, round, then post
{1000.0.rand.round(0.01).postln}.dup(100).plot // choose, round, dup, plot
{1000.0.rand.round(0.01).postln}.dup(100).postln.sort.plot // choose etc.,
sort, plot
```

```
//Mac only
1000.0.rand.round(0.01).postln.asString.speak // convert to string and
speak
```

1.5   Enclosures

There are four types of enclosures in the examples above: (parentheses), [brackets], {braces}, and quotation marks ("some text"). It is important to keep these pairs matched or "balanced" as you write code. Nesting can make balancing difficult and confusing. Later in the chapter we'll see other (often clearer) methods, such as assigning items to variables, but the SuperCollider language editor has some tools to help you keep track. These range from automatic indication of matching brackets when you complete a pair of parentheses or double clicking on a parenthesis to select everything within, to menu items such as Format/Balance (on Mac OSX). Balancing is a quick way to select large sections of code for evaluation, deletion, or copy/paste operations.

Quotation marks are used to enclose a string of characters (including spaces) as a single unit. These are aptly called strings. Single quotes create symbols, which are similar to strings. You can also make a symbol by preceding some txt with a backslash. Thus `'aSymbol'` and `\aSymbol` are equivalent. Symbols are often used as labels for parameters and are sometimes, but not always, interchangeable with strings. See the Symbol and String help files for more information.

We've already used parentheses to enclose argument lists. They can also force precedence, which is the order in which things get done. For example; what is 5 + 10 * 4? Are you sure? Try this line to find out:

```
5 + 10 * 4
```

In normal mathematics it would be 45, but in SC it's 60. That's because precedence with binary operators (+, –, *, /, etc.) in SC is left to right, regardless of operation. The equation above calculates 5 + 10, then that result is multiplied by 4. That is, unless you use parentheses to force precedence: (5 + 10) * 4 = 60, but 5 + (10 * 4) = 45.

Precedence can also be forced when combining binary operations and messages, where messages normally take precedence. For example, 5 + 10.squared results in 105 (10 squared + 5), whereas (5 + 10).squared results in 5 + 10, which is then squared: 225.

The next enclosure, already used in several patches, is a bracket. Brackets define a collection of items. An `Array` (one type of collection) can contain numbers but also text, functions, or entire patches. You can even mix data types within an array. Arrays can receive messages such as `reverse`, `scramble`, `mirror`, `rotate`, `midicps`, choose, and permute, to name a few. You can also perform mathematical operations on arrays:

```
[0, 11, 10, 1, 9, 8, 2, 3, 7, 4, 6, 5].reverse // retrograde of a 12-tone
row
12 - [0, 11, 10, 1, 9, 8, 2, 3, 7, 4, 6, 5].reverse // retrograde
inversion
[0, 2, 4, 5, 6, 7, 9, 11].scramble // diatonic scale
[60, 62, 64, 67, 69].mirror // pentatonic
[1, 2, 3, 4, 5, 6, 7, 8, 9, 10, 11].rotate
[60, 62, 64, 65, 67, 69, 71].midicps.round(0.1) // convert midi to
frequency in Hz
[1, 0.75, 0.5, 0.25, 0.125].choose // maybe durations?
0.125 * [1, 2, 3, 4, 5, 6, 7, 8].choose // multiples of a smallest
quantize value
[1, 2, 3, 4, 5, 6, 7, 8, 9, 10, 11].permute(6)
```

More on arrays later.

Braces, the last enclosure, define functions. Functions perform specific tasks that are usually repeated, often millions of times and often with different results. Try these lines, one at a time.

```
exprand(1, 1000.0)
{exprand(1, 1000.0)}
```

The first line picks a random number, which is displayed in the post window. The second prints a very different result: a function. What does the function do? It picks a random number. How can that difference affect code? Consider the lines below. The first chooses a random number and duplicates it. The second executes the random-number-picking function 5 times and collects the results in an array.

```
dup(rand(1000.0), 5) // picks a number, duplicates it
dup({rand(1000.0)}, 5) //duplicates the function of picking a number
// essentially, this (which has a similar result)
[rand(1000.0), rand(1000.0), rand(1000.0), rand(1000.0), rand(1000.0)]
```

Functions understand a number of messages: plot, play, scope, and dup, to list a few.

```
{LFNoise0.ar}.play //play a series of random numbers
{LFNoise0.ar(10000)}.plot // plot those numbers
{LFNoise0.ar(10000)}.scope // play and show on a scope
{100.rand}.dup(10) // pick 10 random numbers
{100.rand} ! 10 // same as above
{100.rand}.dup(10).postln.plot // pick 10 numbers, post, then plot them
{100.rand}.dup(100).sort.plot // pick 100 numbers, sort them, then plot
```

Take a moment to scan all the examples in this chapter, maybe even venture into other chapters, and see if you can identify these key elements of code:

Receivers, messages, and argument lists   object.message(arglist)
Collections   [list of items]
Functions   {often multiple lines of code}
Strings   "words inside quotes"
Symbols   "words inside single quotes" or preceded by a backslash (\)

For a more detailed discussion of SuperCollider's syntax, you'll probably eventually want to delve into chapter 5.

1.6   Multichannel Expansion

Arrays have many applications, but multichannel expansion is one that borders on voodoo. If an array is used as any argument in a UGen, the entire patch is duplicated. The first copy is sent to channel 1, using the first value of the array in that patch; the second copy goes to channel 2 with the second value of the array. Note that the only difference between the lines below is the array for the first argument of the LFNoise.kr.

```
{Blip.ar(25, LFNoise0.kr(5, 12, 14), 0.3)}.play // single channel
{Blip.ar(25, LFNoise0.kr([5, 10], 12, 14), 0.3)}.play // stereo
{Blip.ar(25, LFNoise0.kr([5, 10, 2, 25], 12, 14), 0.3)}.play // quad
{Blip.ar(25, LFNoise0.kr([5, 4, 7, 9, 5, 1, 9, 2], 12, 14), 0.3)}.play //
8 channel
```

The first example is in mono, generating random pitches at a rate of 5 times per second. The next is stereo with a rate of 5 times a second in the left channel while the right is playing at 10. The next is (yes, it's that easy) quad; 5 in front left, 10 in front right, 2 in back left (depending on your setup), 25 in back right. If your interface supports 2 channels only, as most do, the last 2 examples will run, but you won't hear beyond the second incarnation. The last line produces 8 discrete audio signals, each with a different LFO rate.

If the other arguments are arrays, the values are matched up accordingly. For example, if one argument has [45, 32, 66, 19], and another has [5.3, 35.1], then channel 1 will use 45 and 5.3, channel 2 will use 32 and 35.1, channel 3 will be 66 and 5.3, and channel 4, 19 and 35.1.

Assignment: Go back through all the mono patches and make them stereo by replacing any argument in any ar or kr message list with an array containing 2 numbers.

Multichannel expansion illustrates one of the ways in which SC is both powerful and economical. Simply adding an array gives you multiple channels, whereas in a graphical patching language like Max or PD, you would have to duplicate all of the objects and patch cords by hand. But in SC it's just a few lines of code. Duplicate that for 4 speakers? Type 6 extra characters and press [enter].

Naturally, to make the most of SC it is important to know what objects are available, what messages they understand, what argument lists accompany the messages, and what kind of output they produce. Where can one find a message's list of arguments and a description of what they do?

1.7   Help!

Items with capital letters (SinOsc, LFSaw, LFNoise, PMOsc, Array, Mix) and many messages (midicps, max, loop, randomSeed) have Help[1,2] files. Double click on any of these (to select) and ask for help (Mac: [cmd+d], Windows: [F1], Linux: see chapter 12 and the Shortcuts Help file). A Help file appears with a description, a list of arguments, and a few examples.

Let's test this using a new UGen: PMOsc. Type that word into any window, select, open, and read the Help file. Just skip over the terms you don't know. Most important, try the examples.

PMOsc, as the name implies and the Help file confirms, is a phase modulation oscillator, the more efficient cousin of frequency modulation. The gist of amplitude, frequency, and phase modulation is achieving rich harmonic spectra (i.e., an interesting sound) at very little cost. In the days of modular synthesis even top electronic studios had, at best, a dozen oscillators for experiments. FM synthesis required only two, so it was an effective procedure back then. But even today phase modulation can be an efficient path to complex sounds.

```
{PMOsc.ar(440, 550, 7)}.play // like an FM radio
```

The Help file reveals that arguments for PMOsc.ar are carrier wave, modulator, index, modulator phase, then mul and add. In the next example try values between 100 and 1000 for arguments 1 (carrier) and 2 (modulator), and values between 1 and 8 for the third (index). In this example we don't supply arguments for modphase, mul, or add. In most cases a UGen will use defaults if no values are given.

Now let's make this example more interesting by nesting. As we've seen, an argument can be a single static number (e.g., 440, 550, 7) or a complete nested UGen, such as LFNoise1, Line, or, better yet, MouseX or MouseY. These are mouse controls that understand the kr message with minval, maxval, warp, and lag as arguments (read each Help file for details). MouseX and MouseY generate a continuous output between low and high arguments. In the example below, their output is being used as the second and third arguments in PMOsc, allowing you to explore how each argument in these ranges affects the sound.

```
{PMOsc.ar(440, MouseY.kr(1, 550), MouseX.kr(1, 15))}.play
```

Arguments have to be in the correct order to work properly. If you mix them up or skip one, bad (or, occasionally, unexpected and exciting) things happen. There are situations, however, where it is convenient to skip or reorder arguments. In these cases we use keyword assignment. If you precede an argument with its keyword (listed in the Help file) and a colon, you identify that argument explicitly, regardless of its position in the argument list. To illustrate, all of the following lines have precisely the same meaning and result.

```
{PMOsc.ar(100, 500, 10, 0, 0.5)}.play // all arguments listed in order
{PMOsc.ar(carfreq: 100, modfreq: 500, pmindex: 10, mul: 0.5)}.play //
keywords
{PMOsc.ar(carfreq: 100, mul: 0.5, pmindex: 10, modfreq: 500)}.play //
mixed
```

This has a number of advantages. First, it's a type of documentation similar to comments. Second, it sometimes makes the argument list more portable. When experimenting, you may want to swap out UGens. The argument lists for each UGen may be interchangeable, but usually they are not. For example, in Blip.ar(400, 10, 0.5), 400 is the frequency, 10 is the number of harmonics, and 0.5 is the mul. But if we used that same argument list in LFNoise1.ar(400, 10, 0.5), 400 is frequency, but 10 is now mul, and 0.5 is the add: a very different result. (Don't try it.) But using keywords—Blip.ar(freq: 400, mul: 0.5), SinOsc.ar(freq: 400, mul: 05), and LFNoise1.ar(freq: 400, mul: 0.5)—will have similar results because the arguments are explicitly identified. The worst that could happen is a warning if the UGen has no such keyword.

Finally, we can list arguments in any order, or even leave them off (to illustrate mul in a simple SinOsc, for example) without all that typing. Note that if you mix ordered and keyword arguments, the ordered ones must come first.

```
{SinOsc.ar(mul: MouseX.kr(0, 1.0))}.scope
```

mul can do some very clever things, depending, for instance, on what its UGen is plugged into, but in this context it controls the volume of the sound we hear.

Using the MouseX in these examples illustrates how parameters such as amplitude, carrier frequency, modulation index, and phase can be manually controlled. You can also build patches in which parameters are modified using an automated process, for example, a Line.kr. (This is technically different from, but analogous to, voltage control.) Look up the Line Help file, note its arguments, and try the examples. Then, based on your experiments with PMOsc and the mouse controls, write a patch that uses 3 Line.kr UGens inside a PMOsc, one for each of the first 3 arguments in the PMOsc.

```
(
{
    Blip.ar(
        TRand.kr( // frequency or VCO
            100, 1000, // range
            Impulse.kr(Line.kr(1, 20, 60))), // trigger
        TRand.kr( // number of harmonics or VCF
            1, 10, // range
            Impulse.kr(Line.kr(1, 20, 60))), // trigger
        Linen.kr( // mul, or amplitude, VCA
            Impulse.kr(Line.kr(1, 20, 60)), // trigger
            0, // attack
            0.5, // sustain level
            1/Line.kr(1, 20, 60)) // trigger
    )
}.play
)
```

Figure 1.4
VCO, VCF, VCA.

One solution appears in the notes section.[3] Remember, this very complex sound is essentially just 2 oscillators.

Use the code in figure 1.4 to practice getting help. It is modeled after a classic voltage-controlled oscillator (VCO), a voltage-controlled filter (VCF; though in Blip, it's not technically a filter), and voltage-controlled amplifier (VCA). If you like, use multichannel expansion to make it stereo.

Here's the example explained from the inside out: 3 instances of Line.kr send a number to the 3 Impulse UGens, which send triggers to both Linen and TRand. At each trigger the two TRand UGens generate values between 100 and 1000 and between 1 and 10, the first being used for the freq argument in Blip (frequency), and the other for the second argument of Blip, numharm (number of harmonics).

Both the kr and ar messages tell a UGen to send a stream of numbers produced in a given fashion: a sine wave for SinOsc, a triangle wave for LFTri, or a saw wave, or a pulse, or a noise (something random) in the case of TRand. The Blip generates sounds we actually hear, so the stream of numbers needs to be produced at an audio rate (e.g., 44.1 kHz, depending on your sound card settings). The TRand, Impulse, and Line are controls and need to supply only a dozen or so values per second, so their resolution doesn't need to be as fine. The ar message generates values at an audio rate, and kr generates them at a control rate. Using kr requires fewer calculations and saves on processing.

Another `Impulse` sends a trigger to the `Linen`, which is an envelope. It shapes the `mul` (amplitude) of each event. The arguments for `Linen` are trigger (or gate), attack time, sustain level, and decay. At each trigger (the rate of which is controlled by a `Line`) the `mul` argument of the `Blip` will move from 0 amplitude to a held level of 0.5 (out of a maximum of 1) in 0 seconds (attack time), then decay back to 0 in 1/`Line` second (decay time).

What is meant by 1/`Line` second? The `Impulse` is sending a series of triggers to `Linen`. The rate of those triggers is controlled by `Line`, which begins at 1, then increases to 20 times per second over a period of 60 seconds. The duration between each event is the reciprocal of the trigger rate. When the trigger is 20, the time period between each trigger is 1/20 of a second. It would make sense, then, for the duration of each envelope to be the same as the time between each trigger. Since attack time is 0, we can just focus on the decay, so decay time = duration. Using 1/`Line` links the two so that duration will always be the reciprocal of trigger rate. As the triggers change, so does the duration of the envelope for each event (e.g., 5 per second, each one a fifth of a second in duration, 2 times per second, each one half a second long; that is, when `Line` = 2, 1/`Line` = 1/2).

Notice the redundancy in this code with the duplicated UGens. We've created 9 UGens where 3 would do. Since the 3 Impulses, 2 TRands, and 4 Line UGens are identical, wouldn't it be easier to use one of each, somehow linking them all?

Yes, but to do that we need to learn about something else: variables.

1.8   Variables

The default set of SC variables is just what you remember from algebra: the lower-case letters from a through z that were used in expressions like x ∗ y = 60 and if x = 10, y must be 6.

You can store numbers, words, UGens, functions, or entire patches in any of these variables, using the equal (=) sign (though by convention a few are reserved; for example, the variable s is always used for the server). That variable then can be spread around the patch, linking important functions. Here is a simple math example:

```
(
a = 440;
b = 3;
c = "math operations";
[c, a, b, a*b, a + b, a.pow(b), a.mod(b)]
)
// same as
["math operations", 440, 3, 440*3, 440 + 3, 440.pow(3), 440.mod(3)]
```

These examples are a collection of statements (lines of code ending with a semi-colon). Pages and pages of code are usually broken up into a series of statements. They are executed in order, such as saying "do this; then this; now do this; and finally this (and return the result)." The order of the steps is important because we have to give variables a value before we use them.

If the last 2 examples have the same result, what is the point? First, efficiency. We can make 1 change to the variable b, and that change is carried over to all the subsequent operations. The second reason is to link related parts of code, for example, a trigger and an envelope duration.

Here is an example using the variable r to hold a MouseX UGen.

```
(
{
r = MouseX.kr(1/3, 10);
SinOsc.ar(mul: Linen.kr(Impulse.kr(r), 0, 1, 1/r))
}.play
)
```

Using the variable r, we link the trigger rate for Impulse to the duration of each envelope. When r is 1/3 (one every 3 seconds), the duration of the envelope is 3 seconds (and if r is 1/3, then 1/r is 3). When r is 10, then the decay rate is 1/10. To illustrate the difference, change 1/r to a static number (e.g., 1).

Figure 1.5 shows a more complex synthesis example with variables and statements. Notice the commented alternatives. When you remove the comment marks

```
(
// run this first
p = { // make p equal to this function
r = Line.kr(1, 20, 60); // rate
// r = LFTri.kr(1/10) * 3 + 7;
t = Impulse.kr(r); // trigger
// t = Dust.kr(r);
e = Linen.kr(t, 0, 0.5, 1/r); // envelope uses r and t
f = TRand.kr(1, 10, t); // triggered random also uses t
// f = e + 1 * 4;
Blip.ar(f*100, f, e) // f, and e used in Blip
}.play
)

p.free;  // run this to stop it
```

Figure 1.5
Synthesis example with variables and statements.

from in front of a line, say, r = LFTri.kr(1/10)*3 + 7, that line replaces the r = Line.kr(1, 20, 60) above it, swapping the line control for a low-frequency triangle wave. For clarity and efficiency you should probably also "comment out" the first line, but in short examples or demonstrations it's not necessary.

This version is more efficient, because the variable t—a single Impulse—operates in 3 different places and the variable r—a single Line—is used in 2 places. The TRand, stored in f, is generating values between 1 and 10. It is used by itself as the numHarm argument, and when multiplied or scaled by 100, it will work for frequency, too: 100 to 1000. (See the discussion on scale and offset below.) The first version of this patch uses 10 UGens. The second, with variables, uses only 4, a 60% reduction. That is significant.

In addition to efficiency, we have linked all three triggers, and hence the duration of each event, together. This is possible only when using a common variable.

There are many situations in which you want to link 1 parameter with another. Phase modulation is one. In PM, 2 frequencies are combined as modulator and carrier. Sidebands emerge from the blended waves and contribute to the quality of the sound. We can provide independent values or controls for each, and that's interesting, but if we describe the modulator as a function of the carrier, the composition of sidebands will remain constant (relative to the carrier) when the carrier changes. This ensures a consistent timbre, and our ears track the fundamental frequency better. In other words, if the modulator is expressed as a ratio of the carrier, we hear pitch changes with the same timbre. In the second example in figure 1.6, a MouseX controls the modulator ratio. Use the mouse to fish for an interesting timbre, but note that once you settle on 1 position, the timbre is consistent, even though the carrier frequency changes.

There is one problem with the default variables a through z. As single letters it's hard to know what their function is. For this reason one should use them only for short examples and tests. For larger patches you should *declare* your own variables with names that better reflect their functions in the patch. Variable names must begin with the lowercase letters a through z (you can use numbers or underscores within the name, just not as the first character), and they must be contiguous (no spaces or punctuation). Note that you can assign a value to a variable at declaration (var rate = 4).

Time for a practical test. Beginning with figure 1.6,

1. Make it stereo.
2. Add a Line.kr to move the index (now 12) from 1 to 12.
3. Identify the arguments for each receiver.message pair.
4. Control the rate, using another Line with a range of 1 to 20.
5. Add keywords to all argument lists.

```
(
{ // carrier and modulator not linked
    r = Impulse.kr(10);
    c = TRand.kr(100, 5000, r);
    m = TRand.kr(100, 5000, r);
    PMOsc.ar(c, m, 12)*0.3
}.play
)


(
{

    var rate = 4, carrier, modRatio; // declare variables
    carrier = LFNoise0.kr(rate) * 500 + 700;
    modRatio = MouseX.kr(1, 2.0);
    // modulator expressed as ratio, therefore timbre
    PMOsc.ar(carrier, carrier*modRatio, 12)*0.3
}.play
)
```

Figure 1.6
Phase modulation with modulator as ratio.

6. Add a new variable called env, and assign it to Linen (an envelope) with an attack of 1/rate and a decay of 0 to control the mul of the PMOsc (use keyword assignment).
7. Figure out what the * 500 + 700 are doing. Just 1 hint: the LFNoise0 is a bipolar UGen, meaning that it generates values between –1 and +1.

See the notes section for one version.[4]

This assignment, if completed correctly, will give an error: WARNING: keyword arg 'index' not found in call to Meta_PMOsc:ar. The Help file says the third argument is index, but that's incorrect. With all the advantages of an open source project, there is this flaw—changes (this keyword was changed) don't always make it into the documentation. For that reason, we'll share 3 other snooping methods found under the Lang menu: Open Class Def, Implementations of, and References to. They are a good supplement to the Help files, and in this case, Open Class Def will take you to the actual source code for PMOsc. You will see there that the Help file is incorrect, and the third argument is actually pmindex.

1.9   Synth Definitions

With each example you probably noticed the text Synth("temp_number") : 1000), which appeared in the post window. Each set of interconnected UGens is packaged into a SynthDef (i.e., a Synth Definition), which describes which UGens are used and how they are plugged together. The server can then use this definition to make running Synths based on that synthesis recipe. When you use {}.play, SuperCollider does the work for you under the surface, such as autonaming the associated Synth-Def and using it straight away to create a running Synth, with the assigned temporary name. We can be more explicit about this process; we specify a name ourselves when wrapping a patch in a `SynthDef`. In addition to the name, we have to explicitly identify the output bus (covered next) with the `Out.ar` message.

```
{SinOsc.ar}.play // generates a temp_number synth
// names the SynthDef and output bus 0 (left) explicitly
SynthDef("sine", {Out.ar(0, SinOsc.ar)}).play // create a synthdef and
play immediately
SynthDef("sine", {Out.ar(1, SinOsc.ar)}).play // right channel
// or
(
SynthDef("one_tone_only", {
    var out, freq = 440;
    out = SinOsc.ar(freq);
    Out.ar(0, out)
}).add // make sure SuperCollider knows about this SynthDef
)
// then use it to create a running Synth
Synth("one_tone_only");
```

Note here two ways of invoking the SynthDef, the first being to `play` it, just like the {}.`play` construction, wrapping up definition and use of definition in one go. The second is to `add` the SynthDef, adding it to the list of SynthDefs that SuperCollider's synthesizer knows about. We then explicitly and separately create a Synth that uses the new SynthDef. In practice, there are a variety of messages for setting up a SynthDef, to pass itself over to the server (`send(s)`), or to write itself to the hard drive ready for future reuse (`writeDefFile`), among others. You may read more about these variants in the SynthDef help file if you're curious, but `add` and `play` will do for now; `add` in particular will be the primary mechanism for creating SynthDefs in this book.

We named this SynthDef "one_tone_only" because the variable for frequency cannot be changed once the SynthDef is established. It will always play 440, not very useful outside of tuning. It is possible to change Synths once they are playing, but to implement that important flexibility, we must use arguments instead of variables for the SynthDef. Arguments allow you to pass different values to a Synth while it is running. They are declared at the start of the function within the SynthDef and should be assigned defaults.

```
SynthDef("different_tones", {
    arg freq = 440; // declare an argument and give it a default value
    var out;
    out = SinOsc.ar(freq)*0.3;
    Out.ar(0, out)
}).play
```

These arguments are similar to the ones we've been using to set and change parameters on UGen message pairs, but the syntax for calling them is a little different.
The first argument for Synth is the name of the SynthDef; the second is an array with
pairs of values matching the synth argument name with the value you want to use,
["arg1", 10, "arg2", 111]. The name can be identified with freq or \freq. (In this
case Symbols and Strings *are* interchangeable.)

```
// Run all four, then stop all
Synth("different_tones", ["freq", 550]);
Synth("different_tones", [\freq, 660]); // same as "freq"
Synth("different_tones", ["freq", 880]);
// If no argument is specified, defaults are used (440)
Synth("different_tones")
```

In the previous example we had to stop all synths at once, using Lang/Stop (a sort
of sledgehammer method). But a synth combined with a variable assignment allows
several instances to be tracked and controlled independently, using commands to
free (stop) or set (change) an argument in flight. Run all of these lines one at a time.

```
a = Synth("different_tones", ["freq", 64.midicps]);
b = Synth("different_tones", ["freq", 67.midicps]);
c = Synth("different_tones", ["freq", 72.midicps]);
a.set("freq", 65.midicps);
c.set("freq", 71.midicps);
a.set("freq", 64.midicps); c.set("freq", 72.midicps);
a.free;
b.free;
c.free;
```

Figure 1.7 shows a PMOsc, configured to produce a crotale-like sound, set inside a
definition with arguments. This one has a few new ideas (such as Env and doneAction)
that are not germane to our discussion. You can read about them in the Help files or
other chapters. Sending the synth definition to the server will not result in any sound.
It adds it to the list of synth types that the server can then make instances of, akin to
calling up a preset on a synthesizer, but possibly with multiple voices. Executing the
last line multiple times creates and plays synths based on that definition, sending different values for midi and index each time.

```
(
//run this first
SynthDef("PMCrotale", {
arg midi = 60, tone = 3, art = 1, amp = 0.8, pan = 0;
var env, out, mod, freq;

freq = midi.midicps;
env = Env.perc(0, art);
mod = 5 + (1/IRand(2, 6));

out = PMOsc.ar(freq, mod*freq,
    pmindex: EnvGen.kr(env, timeScale: art, levelScale: tone),
    mul: EnvGen.kr(env, timeScale: art, levelScale: 0.3));

out = Pan2.ar(out, pan);

out = out * EnvGen.kr(env, timeScale: 1.3*art,
    levelScale: Rand(0.1, 0.5), doneAction:2);
Out.ar(0, out); //Out.ar(bus, out);

}).add;
)

//Then run this a bunch of times:

Synth("PMCrotale", ["midi", rrand(48, 72).round(1), "tone", rrand(1, 6)])
```

Figure 1.7
Synth definition.

Unless explicitly removed or replaced, this definition will stay with the server until it quits, and we can access it anytime. We will use it in some examples later on.

1.10   Buses, Buffers, and Nodes

Buses are used for routing audio or control signals. There are 128 audio buses and 4096 control buses by default, but you can change this if you like (see the Server-Options Help file.) The audio outputs and inputs of your sound hardware are numbered among the audio buses, coming at the start of the numbering with outputs first (recall Out.ar(0), that is, sending to the first audio bus, equivalent to your first output), then inputs (by default beginning with bus 8, though this will depend on the number of output channels set in ServerOptions). The other buses are "private" and are for internal routing purposes such as parallel controls and fx, where you route 1 control source (such as a random wave) to several sounds and/or several sounds to a single effect (such as a delay). There are two advantages to parallel controls and effects: they are more efficient (similar to the variables example), and a single change to a control or effect will change all sounds to which it is connected.

As an example, imagine you have a 5-member band and want to improve their sound with some reverb. You could buy a reverb unit for each musician, but wouldn't it be more efficient to route them all to a mixer that is connected to 1 reverb? That is less expensive, and if you want a longer delay time for everyone, you change that parameter on only 1 unit. How do you connect everyone to a single control or effect in SC? With a bus.

For these experiments let's try a new UGen: PlayBuf. It plays an audio file, allowing complex, real-time concrete treatment such as looping and speed change. First, we have to read a file into a buffer. The files we'll use are in the sounds folder, which is in the SC folder. Feel free to try your own audio files; just change the path accordingly or move them to the sounds folder in the SC folder. (Also see SoundIn, treated in chapter 4, for live audio input.) We'll assign the buffers to environment variables. They are declared using the tilde (~) character and are similar to a through z, but user defined. They will work anywhere in the patch, in other patches, even in other windows. By contrast, the variables in figure 1.7 (env, out, mod, and freq) will work only inside the function where they are declared. (For more on variable scope and environments, see chapters 5 and 8.) We need environment variables for these examples because we'll be using them in lots of places. (We will use these 2 buffers for quite a few of the examples below. So if SC crashes or you are interrupted, run these lines again before continuing.)

```
~houston = Buffer.read(s, "sounds/a11wlk01-44_1.aiff");
~chooston = Buffer.read(s, "sounds/a11wlk01.wav");

{PlayBuf.ar(1, ~houston)}.play; // number of channels and buffer.
{PlayBuf.ar(1, ~chooston)}.play; // number of channels and buffer.
```

Once we've loaded a buffer we can retrieve information such as how many frames it has, and therefore how long it is (see figure 1.8). PlayBuf can be looped using its loop argument (1 = loop, 0 = don't loop), but here a trigger is used to reset the playback, looping only a section of the file (see also TGrains). The trigger for the right channel is slightly later than the left one (by 0.01), allowing the loops to slowly shift and "come out" of phase. The position of the loop is also gradually increased with the Line.kr. The envelope is used to chop off the first and last hundredths of a second for a cleaner transition.

Let's simplify the loop and apply controls for playback speed and direction.

```
[~houston.bufnum, ~houston.numChannels, ~houston.path, ~houston.numFrames];

[~chooston.bufnum, ~chooston.numChannels, ~chooston.path, ~chooston.numFrames];

(  // phasing
{
    var rate, trigger, frames;
    frames = ~houston.numFrames; // or use ~chooston.numFrames

    rate = [1, 1.01];
    trigger = Impulse.kr(rate);
    PlayBuf.ar(1, ~houston, 1, trigger, frames * Line.kr(0, 1, 60)) *
    EnvGen.kr(Env.linen(0.01, 0.96, 0.01), trigger) * rate;
}.play;
)
```

Figure 1.8
Playback buffers.

```
( // speed and direction change
{
    var speed, direction;
    speed = LFNoise0.kr(12) * 0.2 + 1;
    direction = LFClipNoise.kr(1/3);
    PlayBuf.ar(1, ~houston, (speed * direction), loop: 1);
}.play;
)
```

But wait—you have 2 sounds loaded into buffers. What if you want to use 1 control on both PlayBufs? Similarly, what if you would like to switch between several controls (LFNoise1, LFNoise0, and SinOsc) with either PlayBuf, applying them independently? What if you want to apply 2 controls at the same time?

Building separate synths for each of those possibilities is inefficient and limits you to those designs. Better to create the sources and controls as modules (like vintage modular synths) and connect them using buses (like virtual patch cords). For control rate signals, we will use control buses. To connect them we use Out.kr and In.kr. The arguments for Out and In are the bus number (anything up to 4096) and the number of channels. So to connect an output to an input, you would use the same bus number: Out.kr(1950, 2 SomeControl.kr), then SinOsc.ar(In.kr(1950, 2)).

The usual way of doing this is to use a bus object, as shown in figure 1.9, which will get an index for you. If you work this way, you can pass the variable it is as-

```
(
// if these haven't been used they will hold 0
~kbus1 = Bus.control; // a control bus
~kbus2 = Bus.control; // a control bus
{
    var speed, direction;
    speed = In.kr(~kbus1, 1) * 0.2 + 1;
    direction = In.kr(~kbus2);
    PlayBuf.ar(1, ~chooston, (speed * direction), loop: 1);
}.play;
)
(
// now start the controls
{Out.kr(~kbus1, LFNoise0.kr(12))}.play;

{Out.kr(~kbus2, LFClipNoise.kr(1/4))}.play;
)
// Now start the second buffer with the same control input buses,
// but send it to the right channel using Out.ar(1 etc.

(
{
    var speed, direction;
    speed = In.kr(~kbus1, 1) * 0.2 + 1;
    direction = In.kr(~kbus2);
    Out.ar(1, PlayBuf.ar(1, ~houston, (speed * direction), loop: 1));
}.play;
)
```

Figure 1.9
Connecting controls with a bus.

signed to directly, without needing to access its index. It also makes your code more reusable, since you won't need to worry about index conflicts. You won't hear any sound on the first example because it has no control (nothing is connected to the In.kr buses).

We started the two control sources after the first PlayBuf so you could hear there was no sound until they were running. In the next example we start the controls first and show them on scopes. When the scopes appear, they are the frontmost window, so be sure to switch back to the SC code window before running the next example. Try running the last 2 lines on their own to see what it would sound like without the controls.

```
~kbus3 = Bus.control; // a control bus
~kbus4 = Bus.control; // a control bus
    // run these one at a time, (turn down the speakers!)
{Out.kr(~kbus3, SinOsc.kr(3).scope("out3") * 100)}.play;
{Out.kr(~kbus4, LFPulse.kr(1/3).scope("out4") * 200)}.play;
{Out.ar(0, SinOsc.ar(In.kr(~kbus3) + In.kr(~kbus4) + 440).scope("left"))}.
play;
{Out.ar(1, SinOsc.ar(In.kr(~kbus3) + In.kr(~kbus4) + 880).
scope("right"))}.play;
```

When combined with a SynthDef, the routing can be swapped around in real time.

```
~kbus3 = Bus.control; // a control bus
~kbus4 = Bus.control; // a control bus
{Out.kr(~kbus3, SinOsc.kr(3).range(340, 540))}.play;
{Out.kr(~kbus4, LFPulse.kr(6).range(240, 640))}.play;
SynthDef("Switch", {arg freq = 440; Out.ar(0, SinOsc.ar(freq, 0, 0.3)) }).
add
x = Synth("Switch"); // default
x.map(\freq, ~kbus3)
x.map(\freq, ~kbus4)
```

Similarly, an audio signal can be routed through a chain of effects using audio buses. To illustrate, figure 1.10 shows 2 effects for our PlayBufs: a modulator and a delay. (The 2 buffers, ~houston and ~chooston, should still contain the sounds we loaded earlier. If they don't, run that code again.) Try them separately.

In figure 1.11 we break the sources and effects into components (i.e., separate synths) and connect them using audio buses. You won't hear anything until you run the last 2 lines, which start the source. When each synth is executed, it is placed on a *node* on the server. With audio buses, order of execution matters, and therefore the order of the resulting nodes matters. We use *groups* (a grouping of synths and/or other groups) and the arguments for target and addAction to order the chain correctly. These allow you to specify a target node in the chain and a position relative to it (e.g., add just after a particular synth or group). Buses, nodes, and groups can be complicated, so at this point we'll just recommend that you have a look at the Order of Execution Help file, which explores the issue in more detail.

The gate has 2 outputs, [0, ~mod]. This sends the signal directly to the output as well as to the next item in the effects chain. This is a parallel effect send. If you replaced it with just ~mod, you would not hear any of the "dry" signal in the mix.

1.11   Arrays, Iteration, and Logical Expressions

Instructions for playing music are often expressed as collections: a 12-tone row, a series of harmonics, a scale or mode (collection of pitches), a motive, pitch-class

```
(
{
    Out.ar(0,
        Pan2.ar( PlayBuf.ar(1, ~houston, loop: 1) *
            SinOsc.ar(LFNoise0.kr(12, mul: 500, add: 600)),
        0.5)
    )
}.play
)


(
{
var source, delay;
    source = PlayBuf.ar(1, ~chooston, loop: 1);
    delay =  AllpassC.ar(source, 2, [0.65, 1.15], 10);
    Out.ar(0,
    Pan2.ar(source) + delay
    )
}.play
)
```

Figure 1.10
Buffer modulation.

names, and so on. Arrays allow us to manage those collections. Earlier we saw messages that modified an entire array, and we've used an array for stereo signals. But now we will use each item in the collection individually. To use 1 item in an array, we have to retrieve it. This is called referencing and is done using the at message. The argument for at is the index number, starting at 0.

```
a = ["C", "C#", "D", "Eb", "E", "F", "F#", "G", "Ab", "A", "Bb", "B"];
a.at(8);
"Item at index 5 is: ".post; a.at(5).postln; // why didn't it print E?
"Item at index 0 is: ".post; a.at(0).postln; // because we start with 0
do(50, {[0, 2, 4, 5, 7, 9, 11].at(7.rand).postln})
do(50, {["C", "D", "E", "F", "G", "A", "B"].at(7.rand).postln})
```

We've introduced a new message here: do. It is a type of iteration (see also loop, while, for, forBy) which repeats an action. The first argument for do is the number of repetitions (50); the second is the repeated function. A repeated process, such as a do, can be placed inside a Task with a wait time. (Chapter 3 will explore timing and scheduling in more detail.)

```
// Create and name buses
~delay = Bus.audio(s, 2);
~mod = Bus.audio(s, 2);
~gate = Bus.audio(s, 2);
~k5 = Bus.control;

~controlSyn= {Out.kr(~k5, LFNoise0.kr(4))}.play; // start the control

// Start the last item in the chain, the delay
~delaySyn = {Out.ar(0, AllpassC.ar(In.ar(~delay, 2), 2, [0.65, 1.15],
10))}.play(~controlSyn, addAction: \addAfter)

// Start the next to last item, the modulation
~modSyn = {Out.ar(~delay, In.ar(~mod, 2) * SinOsc.ar(In.kr(~k5)*500 +
1100))}.play(~delaySyn, addAction: \addBefore);

// Start the third to last item, the gate
~gateSyn = {Out.ar([0, ~mod], In.ar(~gate, 2) * max(0, In.kr(~k5)))}.play(~modSyn,
addAction: \addBefore);

// make a group for the PlayBuf synths at the head of the chain
~pbGroup = Group.before(~controlSyn);

// Start one buffer. Since we add to the group, we know where it will go
{Out.ar(~gate, Pan2.ar(PlayBuf.ar(1, ~houston, loop: 1), 0.5))}.play(~pbGroup);

// Start the other
{Out.ar(~gate, Pan2.ar(PlayBuf.ar(1, ~chooston, loop: 1), -0.5))}.play(~pbGroup);
```

Figure 1.11
FX routing using buses.

```
Task({
    50.do({
        ["C", "D", "E", "F", "G", "A", "B"].at(7.rand).postln;
        1.wait;
    });
}).play // Cmd-. or equivalent to stop
```

Arrays can be used to map 1 type of data to another, for example, MIDI numbers and note names. Computers are better at handling numbers, but we like to see letters (C, F#, Ab6) when working with music. A referenced array can resolve them both. Consider the random MIDI walk in figure 1.12. It picks a number between 36 and 72, but for our convenience also prints a note name using the wrapAt message, a

```
Task({
a = ["C", "C#", "D",  "Eb", "E", "F", "F#", "G", "Ab", "A", "Bb", "B"];
"count, midi, pitch, octave".postln;
    do(50, {arg count;
        p = rrand(36, 72);
        [count, p, a.wrapAt(p), (p/12).round(1) - 1].postln;
    1.wait;
    })
}).play
```

Figure 1.12
Random MIDI walk.

variation of at that wraps numbers larger than 12 around to the beginning; 12 will return index 0, and 14 will return index 2. It also uses some simple math to print the octave.

The argument inside the do function (count) is similar to the arguments in the synth definition but with a critical difference: we get to name it anything we want, but we can't define what it is. It is always a counter that keeps track of the number of repetitions and is *passed* to the function by the do. Keeping track of iterations is very useful, as we will see later.

We can use the do and Task to make music, stepping through a series of notes with a repeating task to play the synth (be sure you've defined PMCrotale above before running this example) with a wait time between each iteration. In figure 1.13 an infinite do appears, but we must be careful with this. An infinite do with no wait will hang SuperCollider. Save before trying it, if you wish to do so.

Again we've sneaked in a new convention. In this example it is the logical statement if, which is currently disabled but will soon provide rhythmic variety. The syntax is if(condition, {true action}, {false action}). The condition is a Boolean test. If the test returns a true, the true (first) function is executed; otherwise the false function is run. Table 1.1 shows some Boolean operators. Note the important distinction between a single equal sign, which assigns a value to a variable (myVar = 10) and 2 equal signs (myVar == 10), which means "Is myVar equal to 10?" Try running the examples in the true or false column alone, and you will actually see "true" or "false" in the post window.

Following are code examples. The % is a modulo, which wraps a number so it is always within a given range. This is useful when working with scales, arrays, and counters. For example, if a counter variable runs through 0, 1, 2, 3, 4, 5, 6, 7, 8, 9, 10, 11, and so on, then counter%5 will return 0, 1, 2, 3, 4, 0, 1, 2, 3, 4, 0, 1, 2, 3, and so on.

```
// This uses the PMCrotale synth definition
(
a = ["C", "C#", "D",  "Eb", "E", "F", "F#", "G", "Ab", "A", "Bb", "B"];
"event, midi, pitch, octave".postln;
r = Task({
    inf.do({ arg count;
        var midi, oct, density;
        density = 1.0; // 100% of the time. Uncomment below for 70%, etc.
        // density = 0.7;
        // density = 0.3;
        midi = [0, 2, 4, 7, 9].choose;
        // midi = [0, 2, 4, 5, 7, 9, 11].choose;
        // midi = [0, 2, 3, 5, 6, 8, 9, 11] .choose;
        // midi = [0, 1, 2, 3, 4, 5, 6, 7, 8, 9, 10, 11] .choose;
        oct = [48, 60, 72].choose;
        if(density.coin,
            { // true action
                "".postln;
                [midi + oct, a.wrapAt(midi),
                (oct/12).round(1)].post;
                Synth("PMCrotale",
                    ["midi", midi + oct, "tone", rrand(1, 7),
                    "art", rrand(0.3, 2.0), "amp", rrand(0.3, 0.6), "pan",
1.0.rand2]);
            }, {["rest"].post}); // false action
        0.2.wait;
    });
}).start
)

r.stop; // run this to stop
```

Figure 1.13
Random Crotale walk.

```
if(10 == 10, {"10 is indeed equal to 10"}, {"false"})
if((1 < 20).and(1.isInteger), {"1 is less than 20"}, {"false"})
10.do({arg count; [count, if(count.odd, {"odd"}, {"even"})].postln})
(
84.do({arg count; if([0, 4, 7].includes(count%12),
    {count.post; "is part of a C triad.".postln},
    {count.post; "is not part of a C triad".postln})})
)
50.do({if(1.0.rand.round(0.01).post > 0.5, {"> 0.5".postln}, {"< 0.5".
postln})})
```

Table 1.1
Logical Expressions

Symbol	Meaning	True Example	False Example
==	equal to?	10 == 10	10 == 14
!=	not equal to?	10 != 15	10 != 10
>	greater than?	10 > 5	10 > 14
<	less than?	10 < 14	10 < 5
>=	greater than or equal to?	10 >= 10, 10 >= 9	10 > = 14
<=	less than or equal to?	10 <=10, 10 <= 14	10 <= 9
odd	is it odd?	11.odd	10.odd
even	is it even?	10.even	11.even
isInteger	is it an integer?	10.isInteger	10.2345.isInteger
isFloat	is it a float?	10.129.isFloat	10.isFloat
and	both conditions	1.odd.and(2.even)	1.odd.and(3.even)
or	either condition	1.odd.or(1.even)	2.odd.or(3.even)

```
50.do({if(1.0.rand > 0.5, {"play a note".postln}, {"rest".postln})})
50.do({if(0.5.coin, {"play a note".postln}, {"rest".postln})}) // same as
above
if((10.odd).or(10 < 20), {"true".postln}, {"false".postln})
```

In figure 1.13 above, we set up a pulse of 5 events per second (0.2 wait time), with a note at each pulse. The Boolean test uses coin as a condition, but it is currently doing nothing, since the variable density is 1.0. 1.0.coin (100% of the time) will always return true. The true function (playing a crotale note) is always executed. Change density to a value such as 0.3 (30% of the time) or 0.7 (70% of the time) to adjust the density of events.

With a pulse of 0.2, several "rests" in a row will produce silences at lengths of any 0.2 multiple. An alternative method would be to remove the if altogether, placing the synth on its own, then choose different wait times by replacing 0.2.wait with wchoose([0, 0.2, 0.4, 0.8], [0.2, 0.5, 0.1, 0.2]).wait, which chooses a value from the first array according to probabilities in the second array. In this example, that would be 0 20% of the time, 0.2 50% of the time, 0.4 10% of the time, and 0.8 20% of the time. Note that a 0 wait time means "play the next note now," ergo a harmonic rather than a melodic interval. Here is an isolated wchoose example.

```
Array.fill(100, {wchoose([1, 2, 3, 4], [0.5, 0.3, 0.125, 0.075])}).sort
```

Additional if statements could be used for more variety, for example, to choose durations from a different range depending on octave or MIDI note choice, setting the dur arg for each synth like so: "dur", if(oct == 48, {rrand(1, 3)}, {rrand(3, 12)}).

You might also try replacing the `1.0.rand` (pan position) with a short math calculation that will place low notes toward the left (–1), middle notes in the middle (0), and high notes on the right (1).

1.12   How to "Do" an Array

We've seen how a do, when attached to a number, passes a counter to the function being repeated. When do is attached to an array, it passes 2 arguments; the first is each item in the array, and the second is a counter. As before, we name them whatever we want, but they will always be each item and a counter, in that order.

```
[0, 2, 4, 5, 7, 9, 11].do({arg each, count; ["count", count, "each",
each].postln})
// same
[0, 2, 4, 5, 7, 9, 11].do({arg whatever, blech; [blech, whatever].postln})
(
var pc;
pc = ["C", "C#", "D", "Eb", "E", "F", "F#", "G", "Ab", "A", "Bb", "B"];
[0, 2, 4, 5, 7, 9, 11].do({arg each; pc.wrapAt(each).postln;})
)
```

To illustrate *doing* an array, figure 1.14 generates a 12-tone matrix. That is (without dwelling on the details of serialism), it generates an interleaved matrix showing all 48 possible variations of a single nonrepeating series built from all 12 notes of a chromatic scale. If you don't know 12-tone theory (e.g., what RI6 is), you can skip the next 2 paragraphs.

Think of the prime version of a 12-tone set as an array. When building a matrix, the prime, or original, transpositions run from left to right. Each of those transpositions is built on successive pitches from the inversion, which occupies the first column, top to bottom. So you are in practice "doing" the inversion of the row and then, at each pitch from the inversion, "doing" that transposition. (The difference is conceptual. Turn the matrix on its side, and the inversion becomes the original.) So there are 2 do messages, 1 to do each pitch in I0, then a do for the transposition of the prime beginning on that pitch.

You might try to generate the original row by scrambling an array from 0 to 11. The problem is that the prime form of a row starts with 0, and scrambling 0 through 11 would rarely place 0 at the first position. So we cheat by scrambling 1 through 11, then insert a 0 at the first index.

Figure 1.15 breaks down a variation of our earlier patch by using additive synthesis. Additive synthesis blends pure sine waves from a harmonic or inharmonic spectrum into a single sound. This is done with an array filled with sine waves. We'll

```
(
var row, inversion, pitchClass;
row = Array.series(11, 1).scramble.insert(0, 0);
// or enter your own row, e.g. Webern's Op 27
// row = [0, 11, 8, 2, 1, 7, 9, 10, 4, 3, 5, 6];
row.postln;
inversion = 12 - row;
// I add spaces to the strings for a tidy row
pitchClass = ["C  ", "C# ", "D  ", "Eb ",
    "E  ", "F  ", "F# ", "G  ", "Ab ", "A  ", "Bb ", "B  "];
inversion.do({arg eachInv;
    var trans;
    trans = (row + eachInv);
    // prints just pitch class
    trans.do({arg scaleDegree; pitchClass.wrapAt(scaleDegree).post});
    //"".postln; // uncomment these line if you want to do both
    // prints just numbers
    //trans.do({arg scaleDegree; (scaleDegree%12).post; " ".post});
    "".postln;
    });
"".postln
)
```

Figure 1.14
Nested do to generate a 12-tone matrix.

build this additive sound 1 sine wave at a time, each with an LFNoise1 amplitude control. This produces random envelopes for amplitude.

```
{LFNoise1.ar(5000)}.plot // random wave
{max(0, LFNoise1.ar(5000))}.plot // return only positive values
(
{
var ampCont;
ampCont = max(0, LFNoise1.kr(12)); // slow it down for LFO control
SinOsc.ar(440, mul: ampCont)
}.scope
)
```

Then we mix a bunch of them, tuned to multiples, for what sounds like filtering but is additive. The Mix takes as its first argument an array of SinOsc UGens.

As we've seen before, the Array can be paired with the series message to build a set of numbers. That's useful for generating harmonics or 12-tone rows. But we can

```
// Mix down a few of them tuned to harmonics:

(
{
var fund = 220;
Mix.ar(
    [
    SinOsc.ar(220, mul: max(0, LFNoise1.kr(12))),
    SinOsc.ar(440, mul: max(0, LFNoise1.kr(12)))*1/2,
    SinOsc.ar(660, mul: max(0, LFNoise1.kr(12)))*1/3,
    SinOsc.ar(880, mul: max(0, LFNoise1.kr(12)))*1/4,
    SinOsc.ar(1110, mul: max(0, LFNoise1.kr(12)))*1/5,
    SinOsc.ar(1320, mul: max(0, LFNoise1.kr(12)))*1/6
    ]
)*0.3
}.play
)
```

Figure 1.15
Examples of additive synthesis.

also use the fill message to generate an Array of UGens. The first argument is the number of items in the Array, and the second is the function used to fill the Array. It also has a counter, which we use to generate multiples of 110. The entire patch above could have been constructed thus:

The harmonics are calculated using count + 1*110, but we also use the counter to synchronize the SinOsc amplitude control. These undulating LFO sine waves are controlling the amplitude of each harmonic in the series. The frequency for them increases as count increases; it is 1/4 for the first sine, 2/4 for the next, 3/4 for the next, and so on. This means that every 4 seconds we hear all 10 harmonics at full volume, and hence a nice additive saw wave. In a way, the LFO is mimicking the additive process of each sine wave it controls. Figure 1.17 shows a sonogram of the sound.

This example sounds like a filter sweep, but it is not. The difference is that we have independent control over each harmonic and can manipulate them precisely. To illustrate, try these alternatives for the SinOsc.ar(cnt+1/4), SinOsc.kr(rrand(1/4, 5/4)), SinOsc.kr(1/4, 2pi.rand), or, finally, LFNoise1.kr(1) or LFNoise0.kr(rrand(1, 5)).

Figure 1.18 is a collection of bells created with Klank, a resonator useful for physical modeling. It requires arrays to describe the resonances, amplitudes, and rings

```
// Try this first
Array.fill(20, {arg cnt; cnt + 1*110}); // harmonics built on 110

// And a patch
(
{Mix.ar(
    Array.fill(12,
        {arg count;
        var harm;
        harm = count + 1 * 110; // remember precedence; count + 1, then * 110
            SinOsc.ar(harm,
                mul: max([0, 0], SinOsc.kr(count+1/4))
                )*1/(count+1)
        })
)*0.7}.play
)
```

Figure 1.16
Example of additive synthesis.

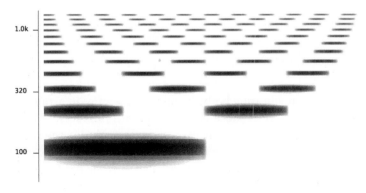

Figure 1.17
Sonogram of additive synthesis example.

```
// Try this first, to illustrate the array of arrays.
Array.fill(3, {Array.fill(10, {rand(1000)})})
// Then this patch.
(
{
var scale, specs, freqs, amps, rings,
    numRes = 5, bells = 20, pan;
scale = [60, 62, 64, 67, 69].midicps;
    Mix.fill(bells, {
        freqs = Array.fill(numRes, {rrand(1, 15)*(scale.choose)});
        amps = Array.fill(numRes, {rrand(0.3, 0.9)});
        rings = Array.fill(numRes, {rrand(1.0, 4.0)});
        specs = [freqs, amps, rings].round(0.01);
        // specs.postln;
        pan = (LFNoise1.kr(rrand(3, 6))*2).softclip;
        Pan2.ar(
            Klank.ar('specs,
                Dust.ar(1/6, 0.03)),
                pan)
    })
}.play;
)
```

Figure 1.18
Physically modeled bells.

(decay) of a virtual vibrating body. Its first argument is an array of arrays (like a box filled with boxes, each of those boxes filled with numbers). The inner three arrays are freqs, amps, and rings, which are gathered together in the specs arg (which is an array of those arrays). Note the tick mark (`) in front of specs in Klank.ar. We saw earlier that using an array as an argument expands the patch into different channels. We don't want that to happen here; the array needs to be mixed down to 2 channels. The tick mark keeps it from expanding into 5 channels.

1.13   Arrays in Sequences

Figure 1.19 uses arrays to play a series of sequences in minimalist style. A new variation is introduced at if(cnt%6 == 0). All 3 variations are reset when cnt gets to 24. That's how many repetitions you have to listen to, entranced, to get the full effect. (And don't you dare change the 12.wait to 2.wait!) There is a new convention: amp = amp - ((midiPitch - 60) * 0.02), that is, a variable made equal to itself

```
( // first define the synth

SynthDef.new("SimpleBlip", {
arg midi = 60, tone = 10, art = 0.125, amp = 0.2, pan = -1;
var out, temper;
out =    Pan2.ar(
            Blip.ar( // play the sequence
                midi.midicps,
                tone
                ) * EnvGen.kr(Env.perc(0.01, art)),
        pan // pan left, center, or right
    );
DetectSilence.ar(out, doneAction:2);
amp = amp - ((midi - 60) * 0.02);
Out.ar(0, out*amp)
    }).add;
)


(
// Then run this Task
~inst = [0, 0, 0]; // Three containers for tasks
~pSeq = [0, 0, 0]; // Three containers for sequences
~scaleAdd = [4, 5, 11, nil, 10, 3, 6, nil]; //
~notes =
[" C", " C#", " D", " Eb", " E", " F",
    " F#", " G", " Ab", " A", " Bb", " B"];
~rout = Task({
    inf.do({
        arg cnt1;
        var steps, durSeq, harmSeq;
        steps = rrand(6, 12);
        if(cnt1%6 == 0, // every sixth iteration, add a degree
            {~scale = ~scale.add(~scaleAdd.wrapAt((cnt1/6).round(1) - 1));});
        "\nIteration: ".post; cnt1.post;
        [" (center) ", " (right) ", " (left) "].wrapAt(cnt1).postln;
        if(cnt1%24 == 0, // reset all three
            {~scale = [0, 2, 7, 9];
            3.do({arg cnt2;
                ~pSeq.wrapPut(cnt2,
                    Array.fill(steps,
                        {~scale.choose + [48, 60].choose}))})}));
        "scale: ".post; ~scale.postln;
```

Figure 1.19
Generative sequences using arrays.

```
        ~pSeq.wrapPut(cnt1, // fill array with scale steps
            Array.fill(steps, {~scale.choose + [48, 60].choose}));
        "MIDI seq: ".post; (~pSeq.wrapAt(cnt1)%12).postln;
        "Sequence (notes): ".post;
        ~pSeq.wrapAt(cnt1).do( // print the sequence using note names
            {arg thisItem; ~notes.at(thisItem%12).post});
        "".postln;
        // create harmonic and duration arrays
        harmSeq = Array.fill(steps, {rrand(1.0, 5.0)});
        durSeq = Array.fill(steps - 1, {rrand(0.01, 0.9)});
        // stop the previous task at this array position
        ~inst.wrapAt(cnt1).stop;
        ~inst.wrapPut(cnt1,
            Task({
                inf.do({arg cnt3; // each sequence
                    Synth("SimpleBlip",
                        [\midi, ~pSeq.wrapAt(cnt1).wrapAt(cnt3),
                        \tone, harmSeq.wrapAt(cnt3),
                        \art, durSeq.wrapAt(cnt3),
                        \amp, rrand(0.1, 0.3),
                        \pan, cnt1.wrap(-1, 2)]);
                    0.125.wait; // tempo of each note
                })}).start;
        );
        12.wait;})
}).start; // time between each new sequence
)

~rout.stop; // stop new sequences
~inst.at(0).stop; // at any time, stop center sequence
~inst.at(1).stop; // stop right sequence
~inst.at(2).stop; // stop center sequence
```

Figure 1.19
(continued)

in some other expression. This line of code tempers the amplitude of pitches above 60, reducing them in increments of 0.02.

The first (environment) variable is ~inst (for instances, not instrument). It is an array used to hold each task. A new sequence is executed, and wrapPut places it in the array at the position pointed to by cnt1. Before each new execution, the previous sequence in that slot is freed. An array is the best way to manage these 3 automated events. If we used garden-variety variables (e.g., seq1, seq2, seq3), then there is no way to free them. If you use seq1.free on 1 iteration, you cannot use seq2.free on the next. But an array can identify each iteration by way of a wrapped number: ~inst.wrapAt(cnt1).free. At the fourth iteration, for example, cnt1 will be 3, and it will free ~inst.wrapAt(3), which when wrapped is 0, or the first sequence.

Arrays are also used to manage additions to the scale, from which the sequence steps are chosen. After 6 repetitions, the next item in scaleAdd is added to the scale array. Finally, though we could have used a local variable for the sequence itself (similar to durSeq and harmSeq), that would preclude resetting all 3 at once at every 24th repetition (cnt1%24). We have to store all 3 in 1 spot so as to access them at that point in the execution.

Each sequence is built by filling an array with between 6 and 10 (whatever value is given to steps) pitches chosen from the scale. That scale step is added to 48 (octave 4) or 60 (octave 5). Calculating the pitches separately from the octaves preserves the scale (whereas rrand(36, 72) would not). That array is used in the task-within-a-task, generating each pitch of the sequence using a Synth call. Using cnt2, the task also rotates through arrays for the number of harmonics and duration (i.e., articulation). Note that the articulation array is one item shorter than the pitch array. This adds phasing to the pattern.

There are a number of variations you can try with this patch. For example, you can start with (and keep throughout) 1 scale. Or change the scaleAdd collection to gradually build different scales (whole tone, chromatic). Try different lengths of sequences for each element, or the same for each. Try different instruments. And here is where a little planning can pay off. Note that the PMCrotale SynthDef we created earlier has the same set of arguments as the SimpleBlip SynthDef. This allows us to swap them without making any changes to the Synth call. Just replace SimpleBlip with PMCrotale. Try setting up another .wait that is less than 12 and turn off a sequence before the next one starts. Add a random pan. Add a sequence for amplitude but include values of 0 (rests).

Logical expressions are what distinguish programs like SC from user-friendly software synths; few of the latter allow for compositional algorithms such as choosing a different 12-tone row after x number of iterations, execution according to probabilities, or Markov chains (which require many, many arrays).

```
(
    {
    var trigger, wave, label, scale, offset;
    trigger = Impulse.kr(10);
    wave = SinOsc.kr(1/10) ; // change to 400
    scale = 1; offset = 0;
//  wave = wave * scale + offset;
    label = "scale = " ++ scale.asString ++ ", offset = " ++ offset.asString;
    wave.round(0.01).poll(label: label);
    }.scope(1)
)
```

Figure 1.20
Offset and scale.

1.14   Scale and Offset

The * 500 and + 1000 (that you've been pondering since figure 1.6) do exactly that; they scale (multiply) and offset (add to or subtract from) the output of LFNoise0. Scale and offset are, typically, the hardest ideas for beginners to grasp, but they are crucial to understanding the way UGens work.

In figure 1.20 we'll use the poll message. It is useful for tracking values while a patch is running. We are also using a scope, so be sure that the internal server is running (as opposed to local), and that it is default (this is necessary for using scope on OSX). Since the SinOsc is running at control rate, you shouldn't hear any sound.

The ++ concatenates 2 strings into one.

Ten times per second, poll is printing the value of the SinOsc, rounded to the nearest multiple of 0.01. As you can see from the post window and the scope, the SinOsc is moving smoothly above and below 0; +1 above, –1 below, once every 10 seconds (a frequency of 1/10, i.e., 1 time in 10 seconds). A wave that oscillates between –1 and +1 is bipolar, because it deviates above and below 0.

What if we changed the SinOsc frequency from 1/10 to 400? Does that change the range of numbers? No; this is a common misunderstanding among beginners. The sine would still be bopping back and forth between –1 and +1, but at a much faster rate. How would that become sound? If it were an audio rate (ar), you could send the stream of numbers to your speakers, which would move forward (+1) and back (–1) 400 times per second, and that's what you would hear. The range hasn't changed, just the frequency at which it moves within that range.

So what would happen if you multiplied (*scaled*) each number in that stream by 0.5? The highest number in the range—1—would become 0.5, and 0.5 would be

0.25, and so on. All the numbers are reduced by 0.5, and hence the speakers move forward and back half as far. In that case the scale is being used to control volume or amplitude. Change scale = 1 to scale = 0.5 and note the difference in the wave and the numbers.

What if, and why would you, scale the SinOsc by numbers greater than 1: 5, 10, 100, 1000? What would the output be? Of greater concern, what would that do to your speakers? Change the scale to these values and note the change. You will see the wave in the scope shoot off and above the visible portion of the window; then, as it moves to negative values, it will fly past again. Notice the stream of numbers move smoothly up to 1000, then down to –1000, and then repeat that range at the frequency of 1 in 10 seconds.

Now change the scale back to 100 and apply an offset (or *add*). What does the stream of numbers (starting at 0, then +/–100) become if added to 600? Change the offset to confirm your hunch. The center value of the deviation becomes 600. Now the stream of numbers is starting at 600 (instead of 0), then moving up 100 to 700, then down 100 below 600, to 500. In short, the wave was +0 and –1; now it's +600 and –100.

Replace the SinOsc with LFSaw and LFNoise1, and carefully watch the results. Each will have the same range of values, but one is in the shape of a ramp and the other is random.

Finally, to see a more graphic representation of a scale and offset on the scope, change the frequency to 100, then change the scale to values between 0.1 and 0.5, and the offset to values between –0.5 and +0.5.

Values this high are not appropriate for amplitude, unless you're using your speakers for booster rockets. But they are useful as controls. In fact, you didn't hear any effect in this patch because the output is sent to a control bus, which we don't hear.

Why would we scale and offset an oscillator that high? Where might we use a smooth, low-frequency sine motion, or ramp motion, or random motion in the range between 500 and 700 in a patch? As we hope is obvious, as a control for another UGen's frequency input, where values that high are expected. This is illustrated in figure 1.21. It uses 2 SinOsc UGens. One is generating the frequency we hear (frequencies between 500 and 700); the other, an LFO (low-frequency oscillator), is providing numbers for the outer SinOsc frequency. This controls the undulation above and below 600 Hz like a slow, wide vibrato. In addition to the poll, which monitors the value of abs(control), we've attached 2 scope messages to the control UGen and the audio UGen.

Change the frequency of the control oscillator from 1 in 4 (1/4) to 1, 2, or 5, for instance—maybe higher for FM? Change the control UGen (SinOsc) to other waveforms, such as LFNoise1, LFNoise0, LFSaw, LFTri, and LFPulse. Change the scale

```
(
    {
    var trigger, control, scale, offset;
    scale = 300; // try other values, but not greater than offset
    offset = 600; // try other values
    trigger = Impulse.kr(10);
    control = SinOsc.ar(1/4).scope("control"); // LFO
    control = control  * scale + offset;
    SinOsc.ar(freq: abs(control).poll).scope("audio")
    }.play
)

// Speaking of vibrato, I can't resist this faux Theremin:

{SinOsc.ar(SinOsc.ar(8, 0, 10, MouseX.kr(440, 1760, 1)))}.play
```

Figure 1.21
SinOsc offset and scaled for control.

and offset, noting how they change the sound. See if you can add a convincing vibrato.

A warning about offset and scale: some UGens will produce unpredictable sounds with negative values (e.g., CombN). A simple error in calculating the scale and offset can yield unwanted negative values. There are 2 simple methods for avoiding this: never use a scale larger than the offset, never nest the control in an abs function.

Offset and scale are used to set a UGen's output to the correct range for controls sent to other UGens. To find the correct range, you have to make this calculation: What range of input do we need for this control? What is the controlling UGen's default output? Therefore, how do we have to scale and offset the default to get the range we want? Try it with the index of a PMOsc. An effective range is 1 to 15. To control it with an LFNoise1, which has a default output of 0, +/−1, you would offset by 8 to make that the center of the range, then scale by 7 so that the range would be 8, +/− 7. This is simple enough, but not all UGens are bipolar. Many (envelopes, lines, LFPulse) are unipolar, with a default output of 0 to 1. (The Help file usually tells you which they are, or you can use the signalRange method to find out, e.g., SinOsc.ar.signalRange.) So to control the same index with a range of 1 to 15, the LFPulse would be scaled by 14 and offset by 1 (0 to 1 * 14 is 0 to 14, then + 1 is 1 to 15).

The following explanations may help to clarify.

For bipolar UGens: The offset is the center of the range, and the scale is the distance it deviates from the center. For example, an offset of 1000 and a scale of 200

Table 1.2
Scale and Offset Examples

Parameter	Example Range	Default	Offset	Scale	Think of It As
MIDI	48 to 72	bipolar	60	12	60 +/– 12
		unipolar	48	24	48 + 24
Amplitude	0 to 0.8	bipolar	0.4	0.4	0.4 +/– 0.4
		unipolar	0	0.8	0 + 0.8
Frequency	200 to 1800	bipolar	1000	800	1000 +/– 800
		unipolar	200	1600	200 + 1600
Harmonics	1 to 23	bipolar	12	11	12 +/– 11
		unipolar	1	22	1 + 22

means the range will be between +1000 and –200, which is 800 to 1200. Also, the scale is half the range. The offset is the lowest value of the range, plus the scale. So if you want a range of 10 to 20, the scale is 5 (half the range), and the offset is 15 (low value plus the scale, or center of the range).

For unipolar UGens: The offset is the lowest value in the range, and the scale is the range. The scale plus the offset is the highest value. For example, an offset of 500 and a scale of 1000 means the range will be 500 to 1500 (500 + 1000).

Table 1.2 shows some examples matching control type, example range, typical UGen defaults, scale, and offset, and how to keep them straight.

That was a lot to take in, but it's essential to everything we will do. So essential that most UGens have arguments for both scale and offset, called `mul` and `add`, respectively. Since these arguments are so common, they usually aren't documented in Help files.

There are some shortcuts. The `range` message will map both unipolar and bipolar UGens to the range specified by their low and high arguments. So `SinOsc.ar.range(500, 1000)` and `LFPulse.ar.range(500, 1000)` will both generate values between 500 and 1000 even though the `SinOsc` is bipolar and the `LFPulse` is unipolar. If you use range, however, make sure that you don't supply values for `mul` and `add`, as that would result in a conflict. There are other similar methods documented (along with `scope`, `poll`, etc.) in the `UGen` Help file, which is a good file to get familiar with.

Now for some real-life examples. Table 1.3 shows the arguments for PMOsc and Blip, how they affect the UGen, and what range of values we could use for that parameter. (Other ranges may work. We're just suggesting these ranges for the next patch.) Remember that the modulator can be a frequency, but to better hear pitch, we use a ratio * carrier frequency.

Test your understanding by filling in table 1.4. Check your answers.[5]

Table 1.3
Two UGens and Their Arguments

PMOsc	What It Changes	Range We Need
carfreq	pitch (frequency or MIDI)	48 to 72 (MIDI)
modfreq	ratio of sidebands	3 to 7 (* carfreq)
index	higher number, more sidebands, brighter timbre	4 to 16
mul	Amplitude	0 to 1
Blip		
freq	pitch in MIDI	100 to 1000 (pitch)
numHarm	number of harmonics	1 to 15
mul	Amplitude	0 to 1

Table 1.4
Test Your Knowledge of mul and add args

Range We Need	Scale and Offset Required for Bipolar UGen (-1 to 1)	Scale and Offset Required for Unipolar UGen (0 to 1)
48 to 72		
100 to 1000		
3.0 to 7.0		
1 to 15		
0 to 1		

Now try your skills on a patch. Figure 1.22 contains a PMOsc with static, garden-variety values for pitch, modulator, and index. We've provided a bipolar control in the form of an LFNoise0, but it's not doing anything right now. Try the following, where "??" indicates numbers you are to provide.

Replace 62 with control * ?? + ?? (a scale and offset) such that those values are in the range of 36 to 84.

Replace 4.125 with control * ?? + ?? (a different scale and offset) such that those values are in the range of 4 to 6.

Do the same with 10, so that those values are between 1 and 15.

Next, create your own controls for modRatio and index, using a SinOsc or LFNoise1 with the correct scale and offset.

Extra credit: Can you round the modulator to 0.125, resulting in clearer pitches?

Try the same examples with control.range.

See the notes section for the answers.[6]

```
(
{
    var carrier, rate, trigger, modRatio, index, control, env;
    rate = 3;
    trigger = Impulse.kr(rate);
    control = LFNoise0.kr(rate);
    carrier = 62;
    modRatio = 4.125;
    index = 10;
    carrier = carrier.midicps;
    carrier.poll(trigger, "carrier");
    index.poll(trigger, "index");
    modRatio.poll(trigger, "modRatio");
    PMOsc.ar(carrier, carrier*modRatio, index)
}.play
)
```

Figure 1.22
Test your skills on a patch.

Figure 1.23 is a similar example in a SynthDef with an envelope. We saw in the last example that a single control source can be applied to multiple points in a patch, each being scaled correctly. Here we'll use a single Linen, which normally generates an envelope between 0 and 1. This can be used as an amplitude control (the mul of the PMOsc). But it is common in phase modulation also to use an envelope to control the index, which in this case we'll supply with values between 4 and 16. Since we want to use it for both, we won't change the mul and add arguments of the Linen, but rather scale and offset it by 12 and 4 just for the index.

Figure 1.24 shows a more complicated example using a classic sample and hold, which strikes a pleasing balance between repetition and variety. Examine each mul and add, calculating the resulting control range.

Do the next one on your own, creating another VCA, VCF, and VCO. Start with the Blip UGen, and insert mouse or line controls on each argument (frequency, harmonics, amplitude) to test which values you want to use. Then insert an LFNoise0 to control pitch (using either frequency or MIDI note values converted to frequency), followed by an LFNoise1 to control the number of harmonics, and finally an LFTri to control amplitude. Try 100 to 1000 for pitch, 1 to 9 for harmonics, and 0 to 1 for amplitude. To start out, set the LFNoise0 frequency to 15, the LFNoise1 frequency to 1, and the LFTri to, say, 1/5.

See the notes section for one version.[7]

```
(
a = SynthDef("PMOsc_ex",
{
    arg left = 10, right = 10, indexLow = 4, indexHigh = 12;
    var pitch, timbre, trigger, env, index, out;
    trigger = Impulse.kr([left, right]); // trigger
    pitch = TRand.kr(36, 72, trigger).round(1); // C2 to C6
    timbre = LFNoise0.kr(1/20, mul: 0.2, add: 2); // mod control
    env = Linen.kr(trigger, releaseTime: 1/[left, right]); // envelope
    index = env * indexHigh + indexLow; // env scaled and offset for index
    pitch = pitch.midicps; // midi converted to freq
    out = PMOsc.ar(pitch, pitch*timbre, index, mul: env);
    Out.ar(0, out);
}).play
)

a.set("left", 4)

a.set("right", 5)

a.set("indexLow", 1)

a.set("indexHigh", 4)
```

Figure 1.23
PMOsc with offset and scale.

1.15   When Bad Code Happens to Good People (Debugging)

Even after years of coding, you will still encounter the occasional error message. When it happens, and it will, try these recovery strategies: proofread, undo, multiple versions, monitor, selectively evaluate, comment out suspect code, use "safe" values.

Let's start with a working patch (figure 1.25) and then introduce some errors. It has a random trigger, so you may have to listen a dozen or so seconds before the first attack strikes. Run it a few times to start several bells.

Introduce the following errors into figure 1.25. First, remove the .kr from the first EnvGen.kr and run it. Notice that this error doesn't even offer a message; the patch runs, but you don't get any sound. This illustrates the most common error: a typo. The first thing you should do, before tearing a patch apart, is to proofread. Another common typo is an unmatched enclosure (e.g., { without }, [without], or " without a closing "). Try removing any of the enclosures and executing the code. You'll see plenty of these innocuous but annoying parse errors. But typos can cause further errors. Select Edit/Undo to restore the original patch, then change Env.perc to

```
(
// run this first
a = SynthDef("Latch_demo",
{
arg rate = 9;
var freq, latchrate, index, ratio, env, out;
latchrate = rate*LFNoise0.kr(1/10, mul: 0.03, add: 1.6);
index = Latch.kr(
    LFSaw.kr(latchrate, mul: 5, add: 6),
    Impulse.kr(rate)
    );
freq = Latch.kr(
    LFSaw.kr(latchrate,
    mul: max(0, LFNoise1.kr(1/5, mul: 24, add: 10)),
    add: LFNoise0.kr(1/7, mul: 12, add: 60)),
    Impulse.kr(rate)
    ).round(1).midicps;

ratio = LFNoise1.kr(1/10, mul: 2.0, add: 5.0);

env = EnvGen.kr(
    Env.perc(0, LFNoise0.kr(rate, mul: 1, add: 1.5)/rate),
    Impulse.kr(rate),
    LFNoise1.kr([5, 5], 2, 1).max(0).min(0.8));
out = PMOsc.ar(
    [freq, freq * 1.5],
    freq*ratio,
    index,
    mul: env
);
Out.ar(0, out);
}
).play
)

a.set("rate", 10)

a.set("rate", 15)

a.set("rate", 6)

a.free;
```

Figure 1.24
PMOsc with sample and hold (latch).

```
(
{ // it's just a bell
var burst, burstEnv, bell, delay, dry,
burstFreq = 500, freqs, amps, rings;
burstEnv = EnvGen.kr(Env.perc(0, 0.05),
             Dust.kr(1/5), 0.1);
// burstEnv.poll(100, "env");
burst = SinOsc.ar(freq: burstFreq,
    mul: burstEnv);
// burst.poll(100, "burst");
freqs = Array.fill(10, {exprand(100, 1000)});
amps = Array.fill(10, {rrand(0.01, 0.1)});
rings = Array.fill(10, {rrand(1.0, 6.0)});
// [freqs, amps, rings].round(0.01).postln;
// "safe" values
// freqs = [100, 200, 300, 400];
// amps = [1, 1, 1, 1];
// rings = [1, 1, 1, 1];

bell = Pan2.ar(
    Klank.ar('[freqs, amps, rings], burst),
    rrand(-1.0, 1.0)
);

delay = AllpassN.ar(bell, 2.5,
    [LFNoise1.kr(7, 1.5, 1.6), LFNoise1.kr(7, 1.5, 1.6)],
    1, mul: 0.8);
bell
+ delay
// + SinOsc.ar(mul: LFPulse.kr(1) * 0.05);
}.play
)
```

Figure 1.25
It's just a bell.

Env.parc and evaluate. These longer, more cryptic messages can be difficult to decipher at first, but they can offer clues even to beginners, especially if you look near the top, where there is a higher density of comprehensible words; you will see "parc not understood," pointing to the typo.

As you develop a patch, you may introduce half a dozen changes into something that ran fine prior to the last evaluation. Then suddenly it's broken. To find out which change caused the crash, you can back out of the error, as we have been doing with this patch, and "undo until it's unbroken." Retrace your steps by repeating Undo/Execute until it is working again. When the error disappears, choose Redo. The code that caused the error will be selected.

Another strategy is to save multiple versions. When a patch is working the way you like, save it, then immediately choose Save As and rename it (e.g., "myPatch 1.13"). You can experiment with this new file worry free. If something breaks, revert to the working version.

One can also proof by following a variable through the patch, noting the values as you read. For this you may have to dig through the junk drawer for a pencil and paper. Write down 2 or 3 variables and record what happens to each variable as you proofread through your code. A common error is to use a variable before it is given a value. As an example, change burstFreq = 500 to just burstFreq (remove the = 500). When that variable arrives at the SinOsc, it has a value of nil, causing an error (nil is a special value in SC that means "nothing").

You can also monitor values using postln. If you put the post on a new line with a collection of values (in an array) such as [freqs, amps, rings].postln, it can be turned on and off by commenting it out, but you can also sneak in a postln at lots of places. For example:

```
Array.series(1, 11).scramble.insert(0, 0) //
```

can become

```
Array.series(1, 11).postln.scramble.postln.insert(0, 0).postln
```

The post can even be made conditional during a repeated process, such as do: if(count%9 == 0, {[count, myVar].postln}). (If you are repeating a process, monitor the counter, too. This will tell you at what step the program failed.)

Similarly, you can isolate and evaluate small sections of code. In the example above, select Array.series(1, 11) only and press [enter]. Next add the .scramble, then the .insert. If the results aren't what you expected or wanted, then the message is not what the program expected or needed.

The poll message can also be used to monitor a UGen's values in real time. The first 2 arguments are rate (how often the UGen is polled) and label (a string that accompanies the posted value). We've included 2 commented examples in figure

1.25. In addition, the scope can be attached to any UGen, as seen in many examples. (See also the `Poll` UGen.)

You can isolate which part of a patch is causing an error by using comments to disable suspect lines, but this can be tricky. In figure 1.25 above, you may suspect the 3 lines beginning with `delay =`. But if you comment out those lines, `bell + delay` will introduce a new error because you've removed `delay`. You would have to comment out both the `delay` chunk and `+ delay`, or give `delay` a safe value such as 0. This, however, may also cause its own set of errors.

Try replacing `exprand(100, 1000)` with 0. This effectively kills the patch. Loading arrays with a complex expression may give unwanted results. To isolate this kind of problem, one can use "safe" values (i.e., values which are known to work). For example, if we suspect the lines that fill `freqs`, `amps`, and `rings`, we can insert safer lines (commented) below. When we uncomment the lower 3 lines, they replace the upper 3 lines, pointing to the faulty section. Indeed, we may develop the patch this way, first putting it together with simple, safe values, then gradually adding more complex processes while keeping the original to fall back on when things go wrong.

A test tone is a type of safe value. For example, you can uncomment the `+ SinOsc` at the bottom. This adds a pulse-controlled test tone that beeps on and off to make sure the patch is indeed running and making sound, thus helping to narrow down what went wrong. If you hear the test tone but not the bells, then the issue is probably not in the code itself (like a typo) but a conceptual error (e.g., a signal at 0 amplitude).

A more wily and destructive gremlin is code that returns NaN (not a number) or inf (infinite) values. What you'll hear is a single pop, followed by no sound from that patch or any other patch, even a simple, isolated `{SinOsc.ar}.play`. In this case you may need to quit the server: `Server.internal.quit`. Restart with `Server.internal. boot`. (Or use `Local` for the local server.) You can also quit and relaunch SC.

Remove all the errors we introduced into our example and try adding some monitoring points using `postln` and `poll`. Of course you need not wait for a disaster for an excuse to poke around. Use these techniques to figure out what is going on in a working patch. Much can be revealed in the examples from this and other chapters with a few well-placed `post`, `scope`, and `Poll` UGens.

Finally, not all errors are errors. Sometimes aberrant values produce interesting results. Exploration in SC can yield serendipitous rewards for the adventurous programmer.

1.16   What Next?

Take a moment to sit back and take in what you've learned. SC is a collection of virtual synthesis modules that can be linked through nesting or with variables to create complex sounds. Using the Help files, you can learn what objects there are and what messages and arguments they understand. You can match the output of one module to the input of another with scale and offset, creating automated controls. These patches can be sent to the server as SynthDefs, with arguments that can be changed for real-time composition and performance. Or you can record the patches to be used in a DAW-style composition. Finally, you've learned some strategies to overcome crashes.

Now that you've done some actual code examples, you will see the value of shortcuts. You'll find a complete list of shortcuts in the Help documentation.

You should also start writing your own personal Help file. When you generate a clever patch or solve a complex problem, paste it into the Help file for future reference.

Read this chapter again. Many of the examples were, out of necessity, more complicated than the accompanying explanation. Now more things will make sense. Although there will still be nebulous sections (encouraging you to dig on your own), you no doubt will be pleasantly surprised at how much more you understand the second time through.

Peruse the Help files. Try the examples. Reverse engineer them (and these examples). Put them together one piece at a time. This is a time-honored way of learning.

And, of course, read the other chapters in this text, written by a cadre of international SC developers.

Join the online community. Answer someone else's question. It's good karma.

Finally, have fun. In the old days one had to go where the equipment was. This often meant getting accepted in a degree program at a distant university, then finding an apartment and moving all your junk to that city just to compete with a dozen other composers for a few hours a week over one machine. You, on the other hand, don't have to be a D.M.A. candidate, and you don't have to move to another town. You can pull out your laptop right now. The worst you'll get is startled pets, a hard reboot from an infinite do, or annoyed glances from a resident significant other. You'd be crazy not to fiddle with it every spare minute. You are obligated to take advantage of such a golden opportunity. Tell your significant other/mom/boss/cat/ iguana this book said so, and get to it.

Notes

1.

24
```
    [5, 5.123] (both numbers and brackets)
    Entire LFSaw line
    1
    0.4
    1 and 0.3
    Everything between the 2 curly brackets.
```

2. SC Help files are "browsable" html. You can open them in SC and also in any browser (even bookmark them), which may have better navigation tools. SC, on the other hand, allows you to run the examples, which is not possible in a browser. You can also write your own Help files and link items in your patches using Edit/Link to Help File (OSX).

3.

```
{PMOsc.ar(Line.kr(10, 1000, 60), Line.kr(1000, 10, 60), Line.kr(1, 30,
60))}.play
```

4.

```
{
    var rate = 4, carrier, modRatio, ind;
    rate = Line.kr(start: 1, end: 12, dur: 60);
    carrier = LFNoise0.kr(freq: rate) * 500 + 700;
    ind = Line.kr(start: 1, end: 12.0, dur: 60);
    modRatio = MouseX.kr(minval: [1, 1], maxval: 2.0);
    PMOsc.ar(carfreq: carrier, modfreq: carrier*modRatio,
        pmindex: ind)*0.3
}.play
```

5. The answers are

1. 48 to 72, 12 and 60, 24 and 48
2. 100 to 1000, 450 and 550, 900 and 100
3. 3.0 to 7.0, 2.0 and 5, 4.0 and 3
4. 1 to 15, 7 and 8, 14 and 1
5. 0 to 1, 0.5 and 0.5, none.

6. The answers are

1. control * 24 + 60
2. control + 5 (note: no scale necessary)
3. control * 7 + 8
4. modRatio = SinOsc.ar(1/5, offset: 5), index = LFNoise1(1/5, mul: 7, add: 8)
5. modRatio = (answers above).round(0.125)

6.

```
{Blip.ar(LFNoise0.kr(13, mul: 500, add: 600), LFNoise1.kr(1, mul: 4, add:
5), LFTri.kr(1/5, mul: 0.5, add: 0.5))}.play
```

7.

```
{
    var rate = 4, carrier, modRatio, ind;
    rate = Line.kr(start: 1, end: 12, dur: 60);
    carrier = LFNoise0.kr(freq: rate) * 500 + 700;
    ind = Line.kr(start: 1, end: 12.0, dur: 60);
    modRatio = MouseX.kr(minval: [1, 1], maxval: 2.0);
    PMOsc.ar(carfreq: carrier, modfreq: carrier*modRatio,
        pmindex: ind)*0.3
}.play
```

2 The Unit Generator

Joshua Parmenter

2.1 Introduction

As you learned in chapter 1, Unit Generators (UGens) are used for generating and processing signals with the SuperCollider synthesis server (hereafter referred to by its application name, scsynth). This chapter will cover the basic functionality of UGens in the standard SuperCollider distribution as well as some of the more common extension libraries. As SuperCollider is a descendant of the Music N family of synthesis programs, UGens in SuperCollider provide an efficient modular system for creating complicated audio networks, which we'll refer to as UGen graphs (Roads, 1996). Examples will demonstrate the efficient creation of SynthDef functions as well as how to group UGen graphs together for dynamic synthesis and audio processing controls. In addition, the examples will offer hints for optimizations that maximize processor efficiency for real-time performance. Event triggering, system debugging, and signal routing will also be demonstrated.

In some cases I will discuss more technical aspects, such as details of the source code for UGens, or use specific technical terms from the field of digital audio. If you've arrived at this chapter as a beginner (having just completed chapter 1), don't worry if not everything immediately makes complete sense. Just trust that some of the information provided is for more technically savvy users and come back to it later if you need to. In some cases I've provided more basic explanations in the notes.

2.2 UGens, scsynth, and SuperCollider

The UGen is the signal-generating and -processing workhorse for the SuperCollider synthesis environment. I use the term "environment" specifically to immediately bring to light the role that UGens themselves play, where they actually exist in the program, and how they are represented inside the SuperCollider language. UGens are defined within libraries, which are written in the C++ programming language and compiled before use. These libraries (plug-ins) are loaded into an instance of scsynth when it is booted and persist until the server quits. Any sound produced by scsynth is the result of a UGen, and UGens are used only inside scsynth. UGens are represented in the SuperCollider language's class system. If you've not encountered classes in programming before, a class is a sort of template that makes objects like UGens or Arrays when it is sent the appropriate message. For example, in the code `SinOsc.ar`, the class is `SinOsc` and `ar` is the message. (This topic is explored in more detail in chapter 5.) It is important to realize that the UGen class itself does not return signal values to the language. The output of a UGen is generally not available to the language unless values are specifically sent from the server to the language. As a result, the role of UGens in the SuperCollider language is restricted to the composition of SynthDefs for the description of a UGen graph. These SynthDefs will be sent to the server, and *only there* can they produce sound.

A number of methods exist to create SynthDefs for you; for example, `Function:play` (`{}.play`) will wrap a signal flow description into a SynthDef. Though some of these language constructs may make it look as though synthesis is happening inside the language, it is important to keep in mind that all synthesis is done on the server, and a SynthDef is always created. To avoid confusion, I will simply refer to both the SuperCollider language objects and the server-side signal-processing units as UGens.[1]

The chief job of the majority of SuperCollider's UGens is the generation of an output signal, but what happens inside the UGen to generate the signal will vary widely. SuperCollider computes this output in blocks of values (called samples) for both audio rate (`ar`) and control rate (`kr`) signals (i.e., calculating several values at a time for each UGen in turn). The default block size is 64 samples, with an ar UGen computing 64 samples and a kr UGen returning a single value for each block. The terms "block" and "control period" should therefore be understood as closely related. The input parameters to a UGen will typically be a scalar value (i.e., a number), a control rate signal, or an audio rate signal. Some UGens require a specific kind of input, such as `BufRd`, where the phase argument must be the same rate as the BufRd UGen itself. Special cases like this are usually noted in the Help file for a given UGen. In cases where a UGen's input is limited to the control rate, audio rate signals are still allowed, but only the first sample in the block will be read. Internally, control rate signals are usually linearly interpolated in cases where a noninterpolated signal would cause noise in the resulting signal. Linear interpolation means that the signal will ramp from the previous control rate value to the value that was sampled at the beginning of the control period.[2] In doing this it will change its value by a constant amount for each sample in the block and would thus appear as a straight line if you graphed it. (This is the *linear* aspect.) In cases where an audio rate input may be more common, the UGen's source code function will check the input parameter's rate and run the appropriate function for you.[3]

Before moving into a more in-depth discussion of the input and output of a typical UGen, I'll briefly expand upon and review some of the discussion from chapter 1, starting with the very common `mul` and `add` parameters. UGens whose output will be used as an audio signal typically output samples with a range of floating-point values between +1.0 and −1.0 (i.e., a *bipolar* range, as noted earlier). For reasons of efficiency, `mul` and `add` are implemented by wrapping a UGen inside a separate `MulAdd` UGen. MulAdd takes the output of a UGen, scales its values by `mul`, and adds `add`. mul defaults to 1.0, and add defaults to 0.0. Although the typical UGen's output is +/−1.0, in reality this works out as +/−mul + add. Using this, output values can have a broad range, so a UGen's output can be much higher than +1.0 or lower than −1.0.[4] Since the mul and add parameters are so common, they will usually be left out of the discussion of a particular UGen's input.

The input to a UGen parameter may also be an Array of values or UGens. As noted in chapter 1, in these cases a UGen will "multichannel expand." Figure 2.1 shows how an Array affects and expands the output of a SinOsc UGen, as well as ways to manipulate the output Array that results. Using the SynthDef \UGen_ex1a, a single SinOsc will be generated and its output will be sent to audio bus 0. If all you have done is started the server and run the scope, your server window should show 12 UGens running. Once \UGen_ex1a is run, you should see 15: the original 12 plus 1 UGen for the SinOsc, 1 UGen for the MulAdd that the SinOsc is wrapped in, and 1 UGen for the Out UGen. The SynthDef \UGen_ex1b shows the multichannel expansion that results from the use of an Array with 4 elements for the freq parameter. The output is spread over output channels 0 through 3, and there are now 9 UGens that are used in this SynthDef. Out accounts for 1 UGen, 4 more for the 4 SinOscs, and 4 more for the MulAdd UGens. The use of Arrays is one of the simplest ways in SuperCollider to create multichannel sound, though each element of the Array is simply output to the corresponding channel (in other words, this isn't really sophisticated panning). (See chapter 14 for a detailed discussion of multichannel synthesis and spatialization.)

In the SynthDef \UGen_ex1c, a 4-element Array is used for the mul argument. As a result, the SinOsc created with the frequency located at index 0 in the freq Array will be joined with the element at index 0 in the mul Array, the elements at index 1 are paired, and so on. No new UGens are added to this example (since the 4 MulAdds were already present in the previous SynthDef). Part d shows 2 concepts, the first exploring what happens when Arrays of different sizes are used. Elements 0, 1, and 2 will match up between the 2 Arrays, with element 3 in the freq Array paired with element 0 from the mul Array. Second, the sum method, when applied to an Array, will return a single value representing the sum of the Array's values, in this case the summing of the output of the 4 SinOscs contained inside the Array. Due to the way that SynthDefs are optimized, there is no additional UGen added as a result of the

```
Server.default = s = Server.internal;

s.boot;

z = s.scope(4);

// a) mono output
(
SynthDef(\UGen_ex1a, {
    Out.ar(0, SinOsc.ar(440, 0, 0.1))
}).add
)

a= Synth(\UGen_ex1a);

a.free;

// b) freq input is an Array of 4 items - outputs to busses 0-3
(
SynthDef(\UGen_ex1b, {
    Out.ar(0, SinOsc.ar([440, 446, 448.5, 882], 0, 0.1))
}).add
)

a= Synth(\UGen_ex1b);

a.free;

// c) Array is added to the 'mul' arg to show mapping
(
SynthDef(\UGen_ex1c, {
    Out.ar(0, SinOsc.ar([440, 446, 448.5, 882], 0, [0.1, 0.2, 0.3, 0.4]))
}).add;
)

a= Synth(\UGen_ex1c);

a.free;
```

Figure 2.1
Arrays and multichannel expansion.

```
// d) The output of the SinOsc above is actually an Array of four SinOscs. Sum them
// together for an additive synthesis example.
(

SynthDef(\UGen_ex1d, {
    Out.ar(0, SinOsc.ar([440, 446, 448.5, 882], 0, [0.1, 0.2, 0.3]).sum);
}).add
)

a= Synth(\UGen_ex1d);

a.free;

z.window.close;
```

Figure 2.1
(continued)

sum method! In the course of building the SynthDef, basic addition like this will be folded into the MulAdd UGens, taking advantage of the addition that already exists.

As mentioned in chapter 1, the output signals of UGens can be used as inputs to another UGen. The output of other synthesis nodes (Synths) themselves can also be accessed. The In UGen will allow access to data written to an audio or control bus. It should be noted that the order of execution for nodes and the difference between audio and control signals need to be taken into account for these signals to be used correctly. To fully understand the power of the In and Out UGens, the nature of the bus system needs to be addressed first.

The number of audio buses available for use is set up at the server's boot time, using its ServerOptions. By default, 128 audio buses are allocated. Of these, the output buses to the system hardware are numbered first, as set by the numOutputBusChannels parameter in ServerOptions. By default, this number is 8, corresponding to audio busses 0–7. The next block of buses is set to read audio from the system inputs and corresponds in number to the numInputBusChannels value. This value again defaults to 8 and corresponds to channels 8–15. The remaining buses can be used for any routing that is not intended for direct input or output to the system, acting like virtual buses in standard audio sequencer software. Even though system input buses are set aside for reading in sound from the computer, these buses, like any other bus, can be written to. The same can be said for the output buses; there is no reason that the signal written to them cannot be read and further manipulated. It is important to understand that in a technical sense buses are nothing more than small areas of memory where samples can be stored. In this sense they are rather like Arrays in the language, which can also be used to store a collection of values. Audio buses are large enough to hold one block's worth of samples; control buses contain a single value.

Every time a block of samples is produced, scsynth will calculate sample values according to its node tree. The node tree gives the running order for working through the Synths; if Synth B's input depends on Synth A's output, it is important to calculate A before B! Every Synth on the server exists as a node in this tree. The other type of node is the Group, which is used to organize a set of Synths into a particular subset (in computer science terms, Groups are internal nodes of a tree, and the Synths are the leaves).

For each synthesis node in the tree, scsynth will evaluate the corresponding Synth-Def's code line by line. In practice this means calculating the output of each UGen in turn, in the order they are specified. If you are using one or more Out UGens in your synthesis process (or if one is created for you, using Function.play, for instance), any specified output from the UGen graph is written to an audio bus. The next node in the tree is then evaluated in the same way. If audio from a previous node has already been written into an audio bus, any node that follows later in the node tree can access it with an In UGen. Through arguments to both the Synth and Group objects, as well as convenience methods such as after and before, you are able to place nodes or groups of nodes anywhere you want in the node tree's order of execution. You can have the server print out its current node tree—showing each group and synth in order, labeled by id and SynthDef name—by executing s.queryAllNodes or by selecting the server's window and pressing "n." (See the Synth, Group, and Order of Execution Help files for more detail on this topic.)

Before any synthesis nodes are calculated for a given block cycle, all audio buses have their samples zeroed out (i.e., are reset to silence). Incoming signal is then filled into the hardware input buses. When an Out UGen is used, signal written to a bus is added to the current signal already on the bus. Out also has some variants. A ReplaceOut UGen will zero out any signal on the bus before writing its output, and the XOut UGen will write a mixture of the UGen's output with what is already on the audio bus according to an xfade (cross-fade) argument. OffsetOut is a special-case Out UGen that can start writing output in the middle of a control block and should be used when sample accurate timing is necessary.

You can write to and read from the control buses with the kr versions of In and Out, respectively.[5] Unlike the audio buses, control bus values are not zeroed out and persist across control blocks. They thus change only when touched. If more than 1 value is written to a control bus within the same control period, the values are added together; otherwise, older values are replaced. There are no control buses associated with system hardware, and since they contain only a single sample, they have a much smaller overhead. By default, 4096 control buses are set up when the Server boots. Examples of using the control buses to control multiple Synths will be shown near the end of the chapter, in the section on optimization tips and tips for taking advantage of the server's order of execution in the node tree.

In addition to signals that are internal to a SynthDef and those that are routed through the In UGen, many UGens are also able to access, write, and share data through the use of memory buffers. As shown in chapter 1, buffers may contain sound file samples but also may be used to store any other data, such as recorded signals, or FFT, or analysis data from a number of other programs (including Csound or Juan Pampin's Analysis-Transformation-Synthesis (ATS data files)).

Now that the basics of the input and output for UGens has been covered, a more in-depth exploration of the tools available can take place, as well as a discussion of creative ways to optimize your usage of UGens.

2.3   UGens Available in SuperCollider

The first place that anyone should look when starting to use SuperCollider is the Tour_of_UGens Help file, accessible from the main Help page. The tour is a mini tutorial on signal creation and processing. This Help file is a wonderful resource for beginners to the SuperCollider language. Even after years of synthesis and DSP experience, I still find new ideas in the basic examples in this file. I make it a point to browse it when I am stuck or between pieces. Though there is very little in the examples that should be used directly, the techniques and use of the SuperCollider language demonstrated here make it one of the gems of the Help file system.

Without going into great detail, the tour of the UGens file will show you many of the basic signal generators that are built into SuperCollider. Oscillators with both band-limited and non-band-limited shapes (i.e., limited or unlimited in terms of the frequency spectrum of their output) are available. Also included are a number of table lookup oscillators—UGens which derive their output by looping through a predetermined table of sample values—that access both internal tables (this is the case with SinOsc and its built-in sine table) and user-supplied tables that allow for the creation of complex periodic signals through the buffer system (the Osc and OscN UGens, for example). Buffers can also be accessed for sound file playback (PlayBuf, BufRd), and sound can be written to memory in real time (using RecordBuf and BufWr as well as a number of buffer-based delay UGens). A wide variety of signal-processing UGens are also available, from the most basic filters (FOS, SOS, OnePole, and OneZero), through user-friendly standard filters[6] (LPF, BPF, HPF, Resonz, MoogFF, for example), to more complex delay- and feedback-based processes (the Comb family of delays and Pluck are examples). An FFT/IFFT-based phase vocoder system is also available. SuperCollider has a large system of random-number generators for the creation of random values ranging in rate from a single sample to periodically inter-polated values and sample-by-sample generators for noise of different colors. The tour also shows examples of numerous distortion techniques that map trigonometry functions onto a signal, various clipping techniques, and advanced waveshaping available through the Shaper UGen.

A number of UGens are also available for spatialization. These typically return an Array of signals corresponding to the number of outputs for a given panner, from the simple equal-power stereo panning of Pan2, through the PanAz UGen for panning across, and up to numerous audio channels. PanB2 and DecodeB2 provide the means for 2-dimensional Ambisonic panning, and a number of extension libraries expand these capabilities to fill 3-dimensional Ambisonics through the 4th order (again, see chapter 14 for more information).

UGens are also available for smoothing control signals (e.g., Lag and Decay smooth by using different shapes). A number of UGens also exist for the creation of enve-lopes (Line, XLine, and the EnvGen UGen in combination with Env to specify an en-velope itself). Though the tour covers most of the techniques just mentioned and provides easy access to the Help files for each UGen shown, the remainder of this chapter will deal with notable omissions from the tour Help file.

One of the questions most commonly asked by new users deals with dynamic processing. Figure 2.2 shows the use of a Compander (SuperCollider's general-purpose dynamics processor) for compressing an incoming signal. Compander is a hard-knee processor that compares the input src signal against the input control signal, then adjusts the src according to the slopes that are described by the remaining parame-ters. This means that the gain can be scaled up or down, depending on whether the input is higher or lower than the control, resulting in *compression* or *expansion* of the dynamic range of the signal. There are parameters for the amount of time used for gain adjustment to take effect on signals that are out of range, as well as for the amount of time the UGen takes for the gain adjustment to relax. Since the attack is so hard, the signal, even when passed through the Compander, may overshoot the maximum output allowed for a 32-bit signal (+/–1.0 in linear amplitude), which can result in clipping (a kind of distortion). To prevent clipping, the output of the Com-pander is then fed into a fast look ahead Limiter. Using the poll method (very handy for debugging), the peak outputs of the compressed values, the compressed and lim-ited values, and the source (src) peak are tracked and printed to the post window to show the difference in the output values. Since Limiter introduces a delay, the com-pressor and src signal are also delayed, so all of the signals line up with the Limiter output.

Figure 2.3 shows one of the uses for triggers inside SuperCollider. In general, a trigger is any signal on the server that changes from a value of 0 or less to a positive

```
Server.default = s = Server.internal.boot;

z = s.scope;
(
SynthDef(\UGen_ex2, {arg freq = 440;
    var src, compressor, limiter, out;
    // 10 SinOsc's, mixed together. Output amplitude is controlled with an Dust UGen
    // wrapped in a Decay2 UGen to create a spike with an Exponential Decay
    src = SinOsc.ar(
        // a harmonic series based on freq
        Array.series(10, freq, freq),
        0, // phase
        Array.fill(10, {Decay2.ar(
            // Dust will create an impulse about every 2 seconds, with values
between 0
            // and 5
            Dust.ar(0.1, 5),
            // Decay2, attach time of 0.01 seconds and a decay time of 5 seconds to
            // allow for a build up of signal
            0.01, 5)});
        ).sum;
    // compress signal about 0.5
    compressor = Compander.ar(src, src, 0.5, 1, 0.1);
    limiter = Limiter.ar(compressor, 0.5);
    // out is the compressed only signal on the left, the compressed and limited on
the
    // right
    out = [DelayN.ar(compressor, 0.02, 0.02), limiter];
    // use Peak and poll to track the highest output values. Updates every second
    Peak.ar(out ++  src, Impulse.kr(1)).poll(1, ["compressed", "limited", "src"]);
    Out.ar(0, out);
}).add;
)
a = Synth(\UGen_ex2, [\freq, 440]);

a.free; z.window.close;
```

Figure 2.2
Dynamics processing.

```
(
SynthDef(\UGen_ex3, {arg gate = 1, amp = 1, rate = 10;
    var trigger, dur, carfreq, modfreq, index, pan, env;
    trigger = Impulse.ar(rate);
    dur = rate.reciprocal;
    carfreq = LFNoise2.kr.range(100, 110);
    modfreq = LFTri.kr(0.1).exprange(200, 840);
    index = LFCub.kr(0.2).range(4, 10);
    pan = WhiteNoise.ar.range(-0.1, 0.1);
    env = EnvGen.kr(
        Env([0, 1, 0], [1, 1], \sin, 1),
        gate,
        levelScale: amp,
        doneAction: 2);
    Out.ar(0,
        GrainFM.ar(2, trigger, dur, carfreq, modfreq, index,
            pan, -1) * env)
}).add;
)
a = Synth(\UGen_ex3, [\rate, 80, \amp, 0.2]);

b = Synth(\UGen_ex3, [\rate, 42, \amp, 0.2]);

c = Synth(\UGen_ex3, [\rate, 121, \amp, 0.2]);

[a, b, c].do({arg thisSynth; thisSynth.set(\gate, 0)});
```

Figure 2.3
Triggering from within the server.

value. In the example, the trigger is used to control the GrainFM UGen. A new grain is created every time a trigger occurs from the signal fed into the trig input parameter. UGens such as Impulse (outputs single samples of value mul at a periodic rate, and 0 the rest of the time) and Dust (random impulses with a density parameter) are excellent for controlling trigger-based UGens. For GrainFM, as well as the other granular synthesis UGens that come with SuperCollider (TGrains, GrainSin, GrainBuf, and GrainIn),[7] the rate of the trigger is important. In this case audio rate trigger UGens will create sample accurate grains, whereas a kr input will create new grains only at the beginning of a block. When a trigger is received by the UGen, the remaining inputs are polled to control each grain's parameters. For more on granular synthesis and SuperCollider, see chapter 16.

Before going on to the use of triggers for sending values from the server to the language client, the range and exprange messages in the above example deserve mention. We've already seen in chapter 1 that the range method can provide a shortcut to setting the range of a UGen's output by computing the necessary mul and add values for both bipolar (normal output between –1.0 and +1.0) and unipolar (output between 0.0 and 1.0) UGens. Range does this in a *linear* fashion (i.e., in a "straight line," as described above in the discussion about interpolation). The use of exprange on the LFTri UGen in figure 2.3 will map the linear output values between 0.0 and 1.0 to an exponential curve between 200 and 440 (exponential mapping is very useful when dealing with a UGen that is controlling frequency, since it is closer to the way our ears perceive it). In this case, not only has the range of the signal changed, but so has the shape!

As noted at the beginning of this chapter, UGens run on the server, and it is not possible for the SuperCollider language to access their output directly. The SendTrig UGen represents one of the few ways for scsynth to send information back to the client language.[8] An OSCresponder (or more commonly, an OSCresponderNode) must be set up inside the language to look for the /tr message sent by the SendTrig UGen. The OSC in OSCresponder is short for Open Sound Control, which is the network protocol SC uses to communicate between the language and the server. An OSC-responder is thus something that responds to an incoming OSC message. The OSC-responder's function will be evaluated when a trigger message is received. (For a more detailed discussion of OSC and OSCresponders, see chapter 4.) It should be noted that these data are communicated through the network and are not suitable for sending audio data from the server to the language. However, a large amount of useful information can still be communicated using a number of the signal analysis and binary operation UGens available. Many of the Boolean operations available in the language (which test if something is true or false, such as greater than or less than) will return 0 when false, and 1 when true, when applied to UGens and can then be used as a trigger signal. The UGen InRange will tell you if a signal's current value is between 2 values. UGens that take a trigger, such as Timer and Latch, can also have their output polled at the time of the trigger, and these values can then be sent back to the language. Figure 2.4 shows a number of SynthDefs that will analyze the audio from the first audio input to the system. We'll use the SoundIn UGen to get the input signal (which is just a shorthand that saves us having to offset to the first hardware input bus), and then we'll send information about it back to the language with various triggers. The OSCresponder function checks for various id values that are sent back with the trigger information and will provide a unique auditory response to the right speaker based on this information. I recommend using headphones and giving the input some sort of musical input. Be varied with pitch, rhythm,

```
(
SynthDef(\UGen_ex4a, {arg id, limit = 1;
    var src, pitch, hasPitch, keynum, outOfTune;
    // read input
    src = SoundIn.ar(0);
    // analyze the frequency of the input
    #pitch, hasPitch = Pitch.kr(src);
    // convert to a midi keynum, but don't round! This value will be used later.
    pitch = pitch.cpsmidi;
    // if you are within an eighth tone of an equal tempered pitch, send a trigger
    outOfTune = (pitch - pitch.round).abs < 0.25;
    // if outOfTune is true, send a trigger. Limit to 1 trigger every 'limit' seconds
    SendTrig.kr(Trig.kr(outOfTune, limit), id, pitch.round);
}).add;

SynthDef(\UGen_ex4b, {arg id1, id2, limit = 1, thresh = 0.5;
    var src, amp, amptrig, timer;
    src = SoundIn.ar(0);
    // analyze the amplitude input, cause a trigger if the output is over the thresh
    amp = Amplitude.kr(src);
    amptrig = Trig.kr(amp > thresh, limit);
    // use amptrig to see how long it is between triggers.
    timer = Timer.kr(amptrig);
    // send the values back with two different ids
    SendTrig.kr(amptrig, id1, amp);
    SendTrig.kr(amptrig, id2, timer);
}).add;

// plays a SinOsc of the pitch you were closest to
SynthDef(\UGen_ex4c, {arg freq;
    Out.ar(1, SinOsc.ar(freq, 0, XLine.kr(0.1, 0.00001, 0.5, doneAction: 2)))
}).add;

// modulated noise to respond to amp spikes
SynthDef(\UGen_ex4d, {arg freq;
    Out.ar(1, LFNoise1.ar(200) * SinOsc.ar(freq, 0,
        XLine.kr(0.1, 0.00001, 0.5, doneAction: 2)));
}).add;

// allocate three unique ids for the trigger ids
a = UniqueID.next;
```

Figure 2.4
Triggers and sending values from the server back to the SuperCollider language.

```
b = UniqueID.next;
c = UniqueID.next;

// an envelope to poll for amp values later
e = Env([440, 880], [1], \exp);

// add the responder
o = OSCresponderNode(s.addr, '/tr', {arg time, responder, msg;
    // the msg is an array with 4 values... post them
    msg.postln;
    // the id sent back from the SendTrig is msg[2]... use it to decide what to do
    case
        // pitch trigger
        {msg[2] == a}
        // msg[3] is the rounded keynum
        {Synth(\UGen_ex4c, [\freq, msg[3].midicps])}
        // amp trigger
        {msg[2] == b}
        // play a noise burst, higher the amp value, higher the freq (polls the
        // Env 'e')
        {Synth(\UGen_ex4d, [\freq, e[msg[3]]])}
        // use the Timer value to play a delayed noise burst at 2000 Hz
        {msg[2] == c}
        {SystemClock.sched(msg[3], {
            Synth(\UGen_ex4d, [\freq, 2000]);
            })}
}).add;

// schedule the start our listening synths...
// then sing or tap away on the input.
SystemClock.sched(1.0, {
    Synth(\UGen_ex4a, [\id, a, \limit, 1]);
    Synth(\UGen_ex4b, [\id1, b, \id2, c, \limit, 0.2, \thresh, 0.25]);
});

// add a command period function to stop the synths and remove the responder
CmdPeriod.doOnce({
    o.remove; "Removed the responder".postln;
})
)
```

Figure 2.4
(continued)

and force of attack. In order to limit the number of triggers that are sent by each process, the Trig UGen is used. In case you need to send back more complicated information to the language, you can use the SendReply UGen, which allows for sending back Arrays of values at the same time and lets you use a custom label (e.g., myArrayMessage).

Generating random values on the server, like any other process, needs to be handled with the use of UGens. The SimpleNumber methods such as rand and rrand do not work properly inside a SynthDef, since they will be evaluated by the language only once, when the SynthDef is built, rather than in a continuous manner once they are running on the server. The WhiteNoise UGen will give you a new random value every sample with a range of +/−mul (similar to the rand2 method in the language) and is suitable for generating a full-spectrum noise signal. At the other extreme are the Rand UGen, which creates a single random floating-point value, and IRand, which will create a single integer value upon the instantiation of a Synth. TRand and TIRand are k-rate UGens that will generate a new random value whenever a trigger occurs. There are also UGens for generating values with different distributions (see LinRand, ExpRand, and NRand). The LFNoise and LFDNoise UGens are excellent for slower-moving random signals, providing a number of different interpolation methods between each random value. Figure 2.5 shows sample uses of a number of these UGens, as well as how randomness in a Synth can be seeded.[9]

FreeVerb and FreeVerb2 (for stereo inputs) and GVerb (an implementation of Juhana Sadeharju's reverb algorithm) are also included in the standard SuperCollider distribution. FreeVerb multichannel expands like any other UGen (and can be useful for wrapping around a Pan UGen's output to localize the reverberation). Both Free-Verb2 and GVerb output stereo. In the case of GVerb, input is mono, and a spread parameter controls the width of the reverb field. FreeVerb2 takes 2 inputs, corresponding to left and right channels. These 3 UGens also have a built-in low-pass filter for high-frequency damping within the reverb feedback loop. GVerb adds controls for reverb time as well as level controls over the dry, early, and tail portions of the signal. Like most other reverbs, each of these UGens has its own color, so tinkering with their controls is essential. Because of the controls given in the GVerb UGen, a number of unusual and interesting effects, beyond what you might expect from a reverb, are possible (figure 2.6).

There are many more useful and powerful UGens available as extensions to the SuperCollider server. The main SuperCollider Web page at SourceForge (<http://supercollider.sourceforge.net>) provides links to these resources. The SuperCollider users' mailing list and archive also provide an enormous resource for UGens as they are developed. If you can't find something you need, asking the community is a good first step. The UGen may already exist, or you may find a developer who is bored at 2 a.m. on a Saturday and willing to do it for you!

```
(
SynthDef(\UGen_ex5, {arg gate = 1, seed = 0, id = 1, amp = 1;
    var src, pitchbase, freq, rq, filt, trigger, env;
    RandID.ir(id);
    RandSeed.ir(1, seed);
    env = EnvGen.kr(Env([0, 1, 0], [1, 4], [4, -4], 1), gate, doneAction: 2);
    src = WhiteNoise.ar;
    trigger = Impulse.kr(Rand.new(2, 5));
    pitchbase = IRand.new(4, 9) * 12;
    freq = TIRand.kr(pitchbase, pitchbase + 12, trigger).midicps;
    rq = LFDNoise3.kr(Rand.new(0.3, 0.8)).range(0.01, 0.005);
    filt = Resonz.ar(src, Lag2.kr(freq), rq);
    Out.ar(0, Pan2.ar(filt, LFNoise1.kr(0.1)) * env * amp)
}).add;
)
a = Synth(\UGen_ex5, [\seed, 123]);

a.release;

// Using the same seed, we get the same gesture
b = Synth(\UGen_ex5, [\seed, 123]);

b.release;

// passing in different seeds
(
r = Routine.run({
    thisThread.randSeed_(123);
    10.do({
        a = Synth(\UGen_ex5, [\seed, 10000.rand.postln, \amp, 3.dbamp]);
        1.wait;
        a.release;
    })
});
)
```

Figure 2.5
Random-number generators and random seeding in the server.

```
(
SynthDef(\UGen_ex6, {arg gate = 1, roomsize = 200, revtime = 450;
    var src, env, gverb;
    env = EnvGen.kr(Env([0, 1, 0], [1, 4], [4, -4], 1), gate, doneAction: 2);
    src = Resonz.ar(
        Array.fill(4, {Dust.ar(6)}),
        1760 * [1, 2.2, 3.95, 8.76] +
            Array.fill(4, {LFNoise2.kr(1, 20)}),
        0.01).sum * 30.dbamp;
    gverb = GVerb.ar(
        src,
        roomsize,
        revtime,
        // feedback loop damping
        0.99,
        // input bw of signal
        LFNoise2.kr(0.1).range(0.9, 0.7),
        // spread
        LFNoise1.kr(0.2).range(0.2, 0.6),
        // almost no direct source
        -60.dbamp,
        // some early reflection
        -18.dbamp,
        // lots of the tail
        3.dbamp,
        roomsize);
    Out.ar(0, gverb * env)
}).add;
)
a = Synth(\UGen_ex6);

a.release;
```

Figure 2.6
GVerb.

```
(
SynthDef(\UGen_ex7a, {arg gate = 1, freq = 440, amp = 0.1, rate = 0.2;
    var src, pos, env;
    src = SinOsc.ar(freq, 0);
    pos = LFNoise2.ar(rate);
    env = EnvGen.kr(
        Env([0, 1, 0], [1, 1], \sin, 1), gate, levelScale: amp, doneAction: 2);
    Out.ar(0, Pan2.ar(src, pos) * env);
}).add;

SynthDef(\UGen_ex7b, {arg gate = 1, freq = 440, amp = 0.1, rate = 0.2;
    var src, pos, env;
    src = SinOsc.ar(freq, 0);
    pos = LFNoise2.kr(rate);
    env = EnvGen.kr(
        Env([0, 1, 0], [1, 1], \sin, 1), gate, levelScale: amp, doneAction: 2);
    Out.ar(0, Pan2.ar(src, pos) * env);
}).add;

SynthDef(\UGen_ex7c, {arg gate = 1, freq = 440, amp = 0.1, rate = 0.2;
    var src, pos, env;
    src = SinOsc.ar(freq, 0);
    pos = LFNoise2.kr(rate);
    env = EnvGen.kr(
        Env([0, 1, 0], [1, 1], \sin, 1), gate, levelScale: amp, doneAction: 2);
    Out.ar(0, Pan2.ar(src * env, pos));
}).add;
)

// 56% on my machine
(
a = Group.new;
250.do({
    Synth(\UGen_ex7a, [\freq, 440.0.rrand(1760.0), \amp, 0.001, \rate, 0.2], a)
});
)
a.release;

// 39%
(
a = Group.new;
250.do({
```

Figure 2.7
Audio rate and control rate comparisons.

```
    Synth(\UGen_ex7b, [\freq, 440.0.rrand(1760.0), \amp, 0.001, \rate, 0.2], a)
});
)
a.release;

// 35%
(
a = Group.new;
250.do({
    Synth(\UGen_ex7c, [\freq, 440.0.rrand(1760.0), \amp, 0.001, \rate, 0.2], a)
});
)
a.release;
```

Figure 2.7
(continued)

2.4   Optimization Tips

UGens are generally the most CPU-intensive part of SuperCollider, with the possible exception of fast-changing GUI processes. Whereas GUI processes are purposely run on a lower-priority thread in the operating system to avoid audio glitches, UGens on scsynth run at the highest priority. This means that although a GUI process may take up lots of CPU, if the server needs the CPU to process audio, the GUI process will take a backseat. But once the server is using all the CPU time available, there is little that the computer can do, and your audio will glitch. Though the UGens themselves tend to be highly optimized, there are still things that you as a user can do to minimize overhead.

The first tip is to use k-rate UGens whenever possible. If you are using a UGen to control a parameter rather than for actual audio output, using the k-rate version can sometimes significantly reduce your CPU usage with no noticeable effect on your sound. Figure 2.7 shows an example of this, where a slow-moving LFNoise2 UGen is used to control the panning of a SinOsc. In the first SynthDef, the UGen is run at audio rate and shows an average CPU usage of about 56% on my machine. Switching the LFNoise2 UGen to kr reduces the load to about 39%. There are probably few optimizations that will reduce your load this highly, but in real-time situations where CPU is becoming an issue, it is worth looking through your SynthDefs to see where you may be using a-rate UGens that aren't needed. If you are working on a fixed piece with scsynth's NRT (non-real-time) mode (see chapter 18), kr UGens can still be very useful for quicker renders while testing. Then, when you are ready to do

```
(
SynthDef(\UGen_ex8a, {arg gate = 1, freq = 440, amp = 0.1, rate = 0.2;
    var w, x, y, out, env, decode;
    #w, x, y = PanB2.ar(
        SinOsc.ar(freq, 0), LFNoise2.kr(rate));
    env = EnvGen.kr(
        Env([0, 1, 0], [1, 1], \sin, 1), gate, levelScale: amp, doneAction: 2);
    decode = DecodeB2.ar(2, w, x, y);
    Out.ar(0, decode * env)
}).add;

SynthDef(\UGen_ex8b, {arg outbus, freq = 440, rate = 0.2;
    var w, x, y;
    #w, x, y = PanB2.ar(
        SinOsc.ar(freq, 0), LFNoise2.kr(rate));
    Out.ar(outbus, [w, x, y])
}).add;

SynthDef(\UGen_ex8c, {arg inbus, gate = 1, amp = 0.1;
    var w, x, y, env, decode;
    #w, x, y = In.ar(inbus, 3);
    env = EnvGen.kr(
        Env([0, 1, 0], [1, 1], \sin, 1), gate, levelScale: amp, doneAction: 14);
    decode = DecodeB2.ar(2, w, x, y) * env;
    ReplaceOut.ar(0, decode);
}).add;
)

(
a = Group.new;
250.do({
    Synth(\UGen_ex8a, [\freq, 440.0.rrand(1760.0), \amp, 0.001, \rate, 0.2], a)
});
)
a.release;

(
a = Group.new;
z = Bus.audio(s, 3);

// the 'catch-all' synth for decoding and enveloping
Synth(\UGen_ex8c, [\inbus, z, \amp, 0.001], a, \addToTail); // add it to the tail of
```

Figure 2.8
Signal routing optimizations.

```
the Group containing the encoding synths

250.do({
    Synth(\UGen_ex8b, [\freq, 440.0.rrand(1760.0), \outbus, z, \rate, 0.2], a)
});
)

a.release;
```

Figure 2.8
(continued)

a final render, the ServerOptions blockSize parameter can be set to 1, in effect turning all of the kr UGens into audio rate ones.[10] This of course will slow compilation time greatly, but your signals will be free of any interpolation noise that would be introduced with the larger control blocks.

The final optimization in this example has to do with the placement of the enveloping multiplier. Note that in the first 2 SynthDefs, the output of Pan2 is multiplied by the envelope. Since Pan2's output is an Array of 2 outputs, the EnvGen also multichannel expands, so 2 EnvGens are actually used! In the third SynthDef, the mono src is multiplied before it is panned, saving additional overhead (note also that the number of UGens to run the last example has fallen from 2000 to 1750). And all of the Synths in this case are using the same envelope shape. Through inter-Synth signal routing, this load could be reduced even more.

Signal routing can also reduce CPU usage, as well as give you global control over a number of Synths. Figure 2.8a shows a sound similar to that in figure 2.7, this time with Ambisonic encoding and decoding.[11] Since each Synth is decoding the Ambisonic signal in the same way and using the same envelope, these 2 aspects can be incorporated into their own SynthDef. All the encoding Synths will be placed into a single Group. The Ambisonic signal will be patched from each individual Synth into a single Synth that will capture all of the output from the Group, and decode and envelop the resulting sound. The UGen usage is reduced from 2250 to 1257, and the CPU usage from 57% to 38%. The trick here is to remember to use the correct addAction for the catchall Synth; by adding it *after* the source Group, we ensure that order of execution is correct. (As you may have gathered, Groups are an excellent way of organizing and ordering your Synths!) This approach to signal routing can also reduce your CPU load when using a limiter or reverb on a large number of Synths, or indeed in any case where a single process can be applied to multiple source Synths. At the same time this approach lets you make a level or parameter change to your synthesis process in a single location rather than in multiple Synths.

```
(
// pass in amp in db
SynthDef(\UGen_ex9a, {arg gate = 1, freq = 440, amp = 0;
    var src, pos, env;
    src = SinOsc.ar(freq, 0, amp.dbamp);
    env = EnvGen.kr(
        Env([0, 1, 0], [1, 1], \sin, 1), gate, doneAction: 2);
    Out.ar(0, Pan2.ar(src * env, Rand(-1.0, 1.0)));
}).add;

// pass in linear amplitude
SynthDef(\UGen_ex9b, {arg gate = 1, freq = 440, amp = 1;
    var src, env;
    src = SinOsc.ar(freq, 0, amp);
    env = EnvGen.kr(
        Env([0, 1, 0], [1, 1], \sin, 1), gate, doneAction: 2);
    Out.ar(0, Pan2.ar(src * env, Rand(-1.0, 1.0)));
}).add;

SynthDef(\UGen_ex9c, {arg gate = 1, freq = 440, amp = -3, pos = 0;
    var src, env;
    src = SinOsc.ar(freq, 0, amp);
    env = EnvGen.kr(
        Env([0, 1, 0], [1, 1], \sin, 1), gate, doneAction: 2);
    Out.ar(0, Pan2.ar(src * env, pos));
}).add;
)

// 45% on my machine
(
a = Group.new;
250.do({
    Synth(\UGen_ex9a, [\freq, 440.0.rrand(1760.0), \amp, -60], a)
});
)
a.release;

// 36%
(
a = Group.new;
250.do({
    Synth(\UGen_ex9b, [\freq, 440.0.rrand(1760.0), \amp, -60.dbamp], a)
```

Figure 2.9
Client-side calculations versus server-side calculations.

```
});
)
a.release;

// 36% (no difference from b)
(
a = Group.new;
250.do({
    Synth(\UGen_ex9c, [\freq, 440.0.rrand(1760.0), \amp, -60.dbamp, \pos,
1.0.rand2], a)
});
)
a.release;
```

Figure 2.9
(continued)

Figure 2.9 shows how certain math operations may benefit from computation on the client side rather than on the server. In the SynthDef \UGen_ex9a, the values that are passed into the Synth are in dB, and the SynthDef takes care of converting the value inside the SynthDef into linear amplitude. However, in every control block this calculation is done on a value that is set only once, when the Synth starts. The second SynthDef expects linear amplitudes, with the conversion done in the language when the parameter is passed to the Synth. The CPU usage in these examples decreases from 45% to 36%. If the value is updated later from the language, you just need to make the conversion only when setting the new value. However, some UGens (such as Rand in these examples) evaluate only once, when the Synth starts. Doing the calculation in the language doesn't yield a significant difference in CPU usage.

One final thing to look out for is UGens with different kinds of interpolation. A number of delay UGens, as well as variable-rate buffer UGens, offer different methods of interpolation. The Comb UGen and its N, L, and C variants are a good example. N, L, and C refer to no interpolation, linear interpolation, and cubic interpolation, respectively.[12] One might imagine that you should always use the CombC UGen because the cubic interpolation version will always give you the "best" delay. If the delay amount is one that would land between samples, this is certainly true. If the delay time is changing, the change of pitch that results will benefit from a smooth, accurate interpolation. However, especially in instances where the delay length is fixed, it will be worth your time to hear if linear interpolation is close enough for your ears, or even if any interpolation is needed at all. Figure 2.10 gives a couple of examples. In it, SynthDefs \Ugen_ex10a, \Ugen_ex10b, and \Ugen_ex10c

```
(
SynthDef(\UGen_ex10a, {arg gate = 1;
    var src, delay, env;
    env = EnvGen.kr(
        Env([0, 1, 0], [1, 1], \sin, 1), gate, doneAction: 2);
    src = Decay.ar(Impulse.ar(1), 1.0, PinkNoise.ar(0.1));
    delay = CombN.ar(src, 0.1, Line.kr(0.0001, 0.001, 10));
    Out.ar(0, (delay * env).dup);
}).add;

SynthDef(\UGen_ex10b, {arg gate = 1;
    var src, delay, env;
    env = EnvGen.kr(
        Env([0, 1, 0], [1, 1], \sin, 1), gate, doneAction: 2);
    src = Decay.ar(Impulse.ar(1), 1.0, PinkNoise.ar(0.1));
    delay = CombL.ar(src, 0.1, Line.kr(0.0001, 0.001, 10));
    Out.ar(0, (delay * env).dup);
}).add;

SynthDef(\UGen_ex10c, {arg gate = 1;
    var src, delay, env;
    env = EnvGen.kr(
        Env([0, 1, 0], [1, 1], \sin, 1), gate, doneAction: 2);
    src = Decay.ar(Impulse.ar(1), 1.0, PinkNoise.ar(0.1));
    delay = CombC.ar(src, 0.1, Line.kr(0.0001, 0.001, 10));
    Out.ar(0, (delay * env).dup);
}).add;
)

a = Synth(\UGen_ex10a); // no interpolation
a.release;

a = Synth(\UGen_ex10b); // linear interpolation
a.release;

a = Synth(\UGen_ex10c); // cubic interpolation
a.release;

(
SynthDef(\UGen_ex10d, {arg gate = 1, deltime = 0.001;
    var src, delay, env;
    env = EnvGen.kr(
        Env([0, 1, 0], [1, 1], \sin, 1), gate, doneAction: 2);
```

Figure 2.10
Interpolation methods in delays, and the processor and sonic differences.

```
    src = Decay.ar(Impulse.ar(1), 1.0, PinkNoise.ar(0.1));
    delay = CombN.ar(src, 0.1, deltime);
    Out.ar(0, (delay * env).dup);
}).add;

SynthDef(\UGen_ex10e, {arg gate = 1, deltime = 0.001;
    var src, delay, env;
    env = EnvGen.kr(
        Env([0, 1, 0], [1, 1], \sin, 1), gate, doneAction: 2);
    src = Decay.ar(Impulse.ar(1), 1.0, PinkNoise.ar(0.1));
    delay = CombL.ar(src, 0.1, deltime);
    Out.ar(0, (delay * env).dup);
}).add;

SynthDef(\UGen_ex10f, {arg gate = 1, deltime = 0.001;
    var src, delay, env;
    env = EnvGen.kr(
        Env([0, 1, 0], [1, 1], \sin, 1), gate, doneAction: 2);
    src = Decay.ar(Impulse.ar(1), 1.0, PinkNoise.ar(0.1));
    delay = CombC.ar(src, 0.1, deltime);
    Out.ar(0, (delay * env).dup);
}).add;
)

// tune to a specific pitch
a = Synth(\UGen_ex10d, [\deltime, 100.midicps.reciprocal]); // no interpolation
a.release;

a = Synth(\UGen_ex10e, [\deltime, 100.midicps.reciprocal]); // linear interpolation
a.release;

a = Synth(\UGen_ex10f, [\deltime, 100.midicps.reciprocal]); // cubic interpolation
a.release;

// a much longer delay
a = Synth(\UGen_ex10d, [\deltime, 0.1]); // no interpolation
a.release;

a = Synth(\UGen_ex10e, [\deltime, 0.1]); // linear interpolation
a.release;

a = Synth(\UGen_ex10f, [\deltime, 0.1]); // cubic interpolation
a.release;
```

Figure 2.10
(continued)

all use a dynamic delay time with the 3 different interpolation methods, and the difference in sound is noticeable. If a large number of these UGens were used, a CPU difference would also be seen. For comparison, SynthDefs \Ugen_ex10d, \Ugen_ex10e, and Ugen_ex10f use a fixed delay length with the 3 different interpolation methods. For feedback delays that result in a resonant pitch (in this example, the pitch "e" should resonate), a difference can be noticed. However, with larger delay times, the sonic difference between the interpolation methods is negligible, if it can be noticed at all.

2.5   Conclusion

UGens are probably the most actively developed area of the SuperCollider program. The fact that SuperCollider gets its signal-processing power from dynamically loaded libraries allows developers and users to create, share, and explore new DSP and signal-creation approaches quickly and easily. This aspect of the program is also wonderful for researchers looking for a flexible way of exploring and manipulating how we perceive sound. It is the creative combination of these basic tools, however, that gives the artist using SuperCollider a great amount of freedom as well as the ability to build the tools needed to create sounds, textures, and structures that don't yet exist.

Reference

Roads, C. 1996. *The Computer Music Tutorial*. Cambridge, MA: MIT Press.

Notes

1. It is possible to communicate with the Server from other applications (called clients) than from the SuperCollider language. I trust that readers who do use other applications will be able to make the distinction between the language classes and UGens on the server.

2. This linear interpolation is one of the features of SuperCollider that I think make it sound so clean. Many other synthesis programs that have a control rate use a sample-and-hold approach to control rate values, keeping a single value for the entire block and possibly introducing more noise into the system than a linearly interpolated signal does.

3. As an example, the SinOsc UGen has 2 inputs, one for the freq argument and another for phase. Both of these inputs can take an audio rate signal (allowing for frequency and phase modulation) or a control rate signal. As a result, inside the source code for the SinOsc UGen there are 4 different functions to handle each specific combination of inputs. One function (labeled in the source next_aa) will compute output values for the SinOsc if both freq and phase are audio rate. The next_ak function will handle the case where freq is ar but phase is kr or slower, and the next_ka handles the reverse case. Finally, next_kk is used when both

inputs are kr or slower. However, it is not uncommon for most UGens to create different calculation functions for every input possibility, especially since many kr inputs would be linearly interpolated. Therefore, in cases where an ar input to a signal does not seem to be responding as you expect it to, this should be one of the first limitations to consider. It could be that the UGen reads the input only at the control rate, and the ar signal is simply having its first sample in each block period taken.

4. The technical name for SC's internal sample format is linear amplitude 32-bit floating point. This allows for a huge range of values.

5. Control buses can also have values written to them with the OSC commands "/c_set" and "/c_setn" and the methods Bus:set and Bus:setn. See the Server-Command-Reference and Bus Help files for more information.

6. Filters remove part of a signal's frequency spectrum. For instance, LPF stands for "low-pass filter," which means it "passes" frequencies below a specified cutoff unchanged, and removes them to an increasing extent as you go above the cutoff. HPF stands for "high-pass filter," which does the opposite. The Tour of UGens file has examples of these which will make this clearer.

7. In addition to the granular UGens mentioned here, a number of third-party UGens are available as extensions by both myself and Bhob Rainey. Bhob's granular UGens are variants of the TGrain UGen that allow for different windowing functions. My granular UGens also offer different windowing functions, as well as the ability to interpolate between 2 different tables containing different envelopes. I also have variants that support Ambisonic output.

8. Poll also broadcasts a "/tr" message and can be used in a similar way.

9. Randomness in computers is never really random, it just seems that way. Technically, it's referred to as "pseudo-random." Because of this, it is possible to "seed" a Synth's random-number generator with a value. The practical upshot of this is that if you do, you will always get the same sequence of pseudo-random values if you provide the same seed.

10. It should be noted that some UGens react badly to block sizes other than 64 samples. For example, many machine-listening ones are dependent on keeping the ServerOption's blockSize at the default 64.

11. Ambisonics is a multichannel spatialization technique. See chapter 14 for further discussion.

12. The Comb UGens are a type of "delay" and involve combining a signal with a delayed version of itself, which results in a kind of filtering. The interpolation here refers to the method used to derive the delayed signal if the delay time does not correspond to an integer multiple of samples.

3 Composition with SuperCollider

Scott Wilson and Julio d'Escriván

3.1 Introduction

The actual process of composing, and deciding how to go about it, can be one of the most difficult things about using SuperCollider. People often find it hard to make the jump from modifying simple examples to producing a full-scale piece. In contrast to Digital Audio Workstation (DAW) software such as Pro Tools, for example, SC doesn't present the user with a single "preferred" way of working. This can be confusing, but it's an inevitable side effect of the flexibility of SC, which allows for many different approaches to generating and assembling material. A brief and incomplete list of ways people might use SC for composition could include the following:

- Real-time interactive works with musicians
- Sound installations
- Generating material for tape music composition (to be assembled later on a DAW), perhaps performed in real time
- As a processing and synthesis tool kit for experimenting with sound
- To get away from always using the same plug-ins
- To create generative music programs
- To create a composition or performance tool kit tailored to one's own musical ideas.

All of these activities have different requirements and suggest different approaches. This chapter attempts to give the composer or sound artist some starting points for creative exploration. Naturally, we can't hope to be anywhere near exhaustive, as the topic of the chapter is huge and in some senses encompasses all aspects of SC. Thus we'll take a pragmatic approach, exploring both some abstract ideas and concrete applications, and referring you to other chapters in this book where they are relevant.

3.1.1   Coding for Flexibility

The notion of making things that are flexible and reusable is something that we'll keep in mind as we examine different ideas in this chapter. As an example, you might have some code that generates a finished sound file, possibly your entire piece. With a little planning and foresight, you might be able to change that code so that it can easily be customized on the fly in live performance, or be adapted to generate a new version to different specifications (quad instead of stereo, for instance).

With this in mind, it may be useful to utilize environment variables which allow for global storage and are easily recalled. You'll recall from chapter 1 that environment variables are preceded by a tilde (~).

```
// some code we may want to use later...
~something = {Pulse.ar(80)*EnvGen.ar(Env.perc, doneAction: 2)};
// when the time comes, just call it by its name and play it!
~something.play
```

Since environment variables do not have the limited scope of normal variables, we'll use them in this chapter for creating simple examples. Keep in mind, however, that in the final version of a piece there may be good reasons for structuring your code differently.

3.2   Control and Structure

When deciding how to control and structure a piece, you need to consider both practical and aesthetic issues: Who is your piece for? Who is performing it? (Maybe you, maybe an SC Luddite . . .) What kind of flexibility (or expressiveness!) is musically meaningful in your context? Does pragmatism (i.e., maximum reliability) override aesthetic or other concerns (i.e., you're a hard-core experimentalist, or you are on tenure track and need to do something technically impressive)?

A fundamental part of designing a piece in SC is deciding how to control what happens when. How you do this depends upon your individual needs. You may have a simple list of events that need to happen at specific times, or a collection of things that can be triggered flexibly (for instance, from a GUI) in response to input from a performer, or algorithmically. Or you may need to combine multiple approaches.

We use the term *structure* here when discussing this issue of how to control when and how things happen, but keep in mind that this could mean anything from the macro scale to the micro scale. In many cases in SC the mechanisms you use might be the same.

3.2.1   Clocks, Routines, and Tasks

Here's a very simple example that shows you how to schedule something to happen at a given time. It makes use of the `SystemClock` class.

```
SystemClock.sched(2, {"foo".postln;});
```

The first argument to the `sched` message is a delay in seconds, and the second is a `Function` that will be evaluated after that delay. In this case the Function simply posts the word "foo," but it could contain any valid SC code. If the last thing to be evaluated in the Function returns a number, SystemClock will reschedule the Function, using that value as the new delay time.

```
// "foo" repeats every second
SystemClock.sched(0, {"foo".postln; 1.0});
// "bar" repeats at a random delay
SystemClock.sched(0, {"bar".postln; 1.0.rand});
// clear all scheduled events
SystemClock.clear;
```

SystemClock has one important limitation: it cannot be used to schedule events which affect native GUI widgets on OSX. For this purpose another clock exists, called `AppClock`. Generally you can use it in the same way as SystemClock, but be aware that its timing is slightly less accurate. There is a shortcut for scheduling something on the AppClock immediately, which is to wrap it in a Function and call `defer` on it.

```
// causes an "operation cannot be called from this Process" error
SystemClock.sched(1, {SCWindow.new.front});
// defer reschedules GUI code on the AppClock, so this works
SystemClock.sched(1, {{ SCWindow.new.front}.defer});
```

GUI, by the way, is short for Graphical User Interface and refers to things such as windows, buttons, and sliders. This topic is covered in detail in chapters 9 and 10, so although we'll see some GUI code in a few of the examples in this chapter, we won't worry too much about the nitty-gritty details of it. Most of it should be pretty straightforward and intuitive, anyway, so for now, just move past any bits that aren't clear and try to focus on the topics at hand.

Another Clock subclass, `TempoClock`, provides the ability to schedule events according to beats rather than in seconds. Unlike the clocks we've looked at so far, you need to create an instance of TempoClock and send sched messages to it, rather than to the class. This is because you can have many instances of TempoClock, each with its own tempo, but there's only one each of SystemClock and AppClock. By varying a TempoClock's tempo (in beats per second), you can change the speed. Here's a simple example.

```
(
t = TempoClock.new; // make a new TempoClock
t.sched(0, {"Hello!".postln; 1});
)
t.tempo = 2; // twice as fast
t.clear;
```

TempoClock also allows beat-based and bar-based scheduling, so it can be particularly useful when composing metric music. (See the TempoClock Help file for more details.)

Now let's take a look at Routines. A Routine is like a Function that you can evaluate a bit at a time, and in fact you can use one almost anywhere you'd use a Function. Within a Routine, you use the yield method to return a value and pause execution. The next time you evaluate the Routine, it picks up where it left off.

```
(
r = Routine({
"foo".yield;
"bar".yield;
});
)
r.value; // foo
r.value; // bar
r.value; // we've reached the end, so it returns nil
```

Routine has a commonly used synonym for value, which is next. Although "next" might make more sense semantically with a Routine, "value" is sometimes preferable, for reasons we'll explore below.

Now here's the really interesting thing: since a Routine can take the place of a Function, if you evaluate a Routine in a Clock, and yield a number, the Routine will be rescheduled, just as in the SystemClock example above.

```
(
r = Routine({
    "foo".postln;
    1.yield; // reschedule after 1 second
    "bar".postln;
    1.yield;
    "foobar".postln;
});
SystemClock.sched(0, r);
)
```

```
// Fermata
s.boot;
(
r = Routine({
    x = Synth(\default, [freq: 76.midicps]);
    1.wait;

    x.release(0.1);
    y = Synth(\default, [freq: 73.midicps]);
    "Waiting...".postln;
    nil.yield;// fermata

    y.release(0.1);
    z = Synth(\default, [freq: 69.midicps]);
    2.wait;
    z.release;
});
)
// do this then wait for the fermata
r.play;
// feel the sweet tonic...
r.play;
```

Figure 3.1
A simple Routine illustrating a musical use of yield.

Figure 3.1 is a (slightly) more musical example that demonstrates a fermata of arbitrary length. This makes use of `wait`, a synonym for `yield`, and of Routine's `play` method, which is a shortcut for scheduling it in a clock. By yielding nil at a certain point, the clock doesn't reschedule, so you'll need to call play again when you want to continue, thus "releasing" the fermata. Functions understand a message called `fork`, which is a commonly used shortcut for creating a Routine and playing it in a Clock.

```
(
{
    "something".postln;
    1.wait;
    "something else".postln;
}.fork;
)
```

Figure 3.2 is a similar example with a simple GUI control. This time we'll use a `Task`, which you may remember from chapter 1. A Task works almost the same way

```
(
t = Task({
    loop({   // loop the whole thing
        3.do({   // do this 3 times
            x.release(0.1);
            x = Synth(\default, [freq: 76.midicps]);
            0.5.wait;
            x.release(0.1);
            x = Synth(\default, [freq: 73.midicps]);
            0.5.wait;
        });
        "I'm waiting for you to press resume".postln;
        nil.yield;// fermata
        x.release(0.1);
        x = Synth(\default, [freq: 69.midicps]);
        1.wait;
        x.release;
    });
});

w = Window.new("Task Example", Rect(400, 400, 200, 30)).front;
w.view.decorator = FlowLayout(w.view.bounds);
Button.new(w, Rect(0, 0, 100, 20)).states_([["Play/Resume", Color.black,
Color.clear]])
    .action_({ t.resume(0);});
Button.new(w, Rect(0, 0, 40, 20)).states_([["Pause", Color.black, Color.clear]])
    .action_({ t.pause;});
Button.new(w, Rect(0, 0, 40, 20)).states_([["Finish", Color.black, Color.clear]])
    .action_({
        t.stop;
        x.release(0.1);
        w.close;
    });
)
```

Figure 3.2
Using Task so you can pause the sequence.

that a Routine does, but is meant to be played only with a Clock. A Task provides some handy advantages, such as the ability to pause. As well, it prevents you from accidentally calling play twice. Try playing with the various buttons and see what happens.[1]

Note that the example above demonstrates both fixed scheduling and waiting for a trigger to continue. The trigger needn't be from a GUI button; it can be almost anything, for instance, audio input. (See chapter 15.)

By combining all of these resources, you can control events in time in pretty complicated ways. You can nest Tasks and Routines or combine fixed scheduling with triggers; in short, anything you like. Figure 3.3 is an example that adds varying tempo to the mix, as well as adding some random events.

You can reset a Task or Routine by sending it the reset message.

```
r.reset;
```

3.2.2   Other Ways of Controlling Time in SC

There are 2 other notable methods of controlling sequences of events in SC: Patterns and the Score object. Patterns provide a high-level abstraction based on Streams of events and values. Since Patterns and Streams are discussed in chapter 6, we will not explore their workings in great detail at this point, but it is worth saying that Patterns often provide a convenient way to produce a Stream of values (or other objects), and that they can be usefully combined with the methods shown above.

Figure 3.4 demonstrates two simple Patterns: Pseq and Pxrand. Pseq specifies an ordered sequence of objects (here numbers used as durations of time between successive events) and a number of repetitions (in this case an infinite number, indicated by the special value inf). Pxrand also has a list (used here as a collection of pitches), but instead of proceeding through it in order, a random element is selected each time. The "x" indicates that no individual value will be selected twice in a row.

Patterns are like templates for producing Streams of values. In order to use a Pattern, it must be converted into a Stream, in this case using the asStream message. Once you have a Stream, you can get values from it by using the next or value messages, just as with a Routine. (In fact, as you may have guessed, a Routine is a type of Stream as well.) Patterns are powerful because they are "reusable," and many Streams can be created from 1 Pattern template. (Chapter 6 will go into more detail regarding this.)

As an aside, and returning to the idea of flexibility, the value message above demonstrates an opportunity for polymorphism, which is a fancy way of saying that different objects understand the same message.[1] Since all objects understand "value" (most simply return themselves), you can substitute any object (a Function, a

```
(
r = Routine({
    c = TempoClock.new; // make a TempoClock
    // start a 'wobbly' loop
    t = Task({
        loop({
            x.release(0.1);
            x = Synth(\default, [freq: 61.midicps, amp: 0.2]);
            0.2.wait;
            x.release(0.1);
            x = Synth(\default, [freq: 67.midicps, amp: 0.2]);
            rrand(0.075, 0.25).wait; // random wait from 0.1 to 0.25 seconds
        });
    }, c); // use the TempoClock to play this Task
    t.start;
    nil.yield;

    // now add some notes
    y = Synth(\default, [freq: 73.midicps, amp: 0.3]);
    nil.yield;
    y.release(0.1);
    y = Synth(\default, [freq: 79.midicps, amp: 0.3]);
    c.tempo = 2; // double time
    nil.yield;
    t.stop; y.release(1); x.release(0.1); // stop the Task and Synths
});
)

r.next; // start loop
r.next; // first note
r.next; // second note; loop goes 'double time'
r.next; // stop loop and fade
```

Figure 3.3
Nesting Tasks inside Routines.

```
(// random notes from lydian b7 scale
p = Pxrand([64, 66, 68, 70, 71, 73, 74, 76], inf).asStream;
// ordered sequence of durations
q = Pseq([1, 2, 0.5], inf).asStream;
t = Task({
    loop({
        x.release(2);
        x = Synth(\default, [freq: p.value.midicps]);
        q.value.wait;
    });
});
t.start;
)
t.stop; x.release(2);
```

Figure 3.4
Using Patterns within a Task.

Routine, a number, etc.) that will return an appropriate value for p or q in the example above. Since p and q are evaluated each time through the loop, it's even possible to do this while the Task is playing. (See figure 3.5.) Taking advantage of polymorphism in ways like this can provide great flexibility, and can be useful for anything from generic compositions to algorithmically variable compositions.

The second method of controlling event sequences is the Score object. Score is essentially an ordered list of times and OSC commands. This takes the form of nested Arrays. That is,

```
[
[time1, [cmd1]],
[time2, [cmd2]],
...
]
```

As you'll recall from chapter 2, OSC stands for Open Sound Control, which is the network protocol SC uses for communicating between language and server. What you probably didn't realize is that it is possible to work with OSC messages directly, rather than through objects such as Synths. This is a rather large topic, so since the OSC messages which the server understands are outlined in the Server Command Reference Help file, we'll just refer you there if you'd like to explore further. In any case, if you find over time that you prefer to work in "messaging style" rather than "object style," you may find Score useful. Figure 3.6 provides a short example. Score also provides some handy functionality for non-real-time synthesis (see chapter 18).

```
(
p = 64; // a constant note
q = Pseq([1, 2, 0.5], inf).asStream; // ordered sequence of durations
t = Task({
    loop({
        x.release(2);
        x = Synth(\default, [freq: p.value.midicps]);
        q.value.wait;
    });
});
t.start;
)
// now change p
p = Pseq([64, 66, 68], inf).asStream; // to a Pattern: do re mi
p = { rrand(64, 76) }; // to a Function: random notes from a
chromatic octave
t.stop; x.release(2);
```

Figure 3.5
Thanks to polymorphism, we can substitute objects that understand the same message.

```
(
SynthDef("ScoreSine",{ arg freq = 440;
Out.ar(0,
    SinOsc.ar(freq, 0, 0.2) * Line.kr(1, 0, 0.5, doneAction: 2)
)
}).add;
x = [
// args for s_new are synthdef, nodeID, addAction, targetID, synth args ...
[0.0, [ \s_new, \ScoreSine, 1000, 0, 0,  \freq, 1413 ]],
[0.5, [ \s_new, \ScoreSine, 1001, 0, 0,  \freq, 712 ]],
[1.0, [ \s_new, \ScoreSine, 1002, 0, 0,  \freq, 417 ]],
[2.0, [\c_set, 0, 0]] // dummy command to mark end of NRT synthesis time
];
z = Score(x);
)
z.play;
```

Figure 3.6
Using "messaging style": Score.

```
(
// here's a synthdef that allows us to play from a buffer, with a fadeout
SynthDef("playbuf", { arg out = 0, buf, gate = 1;
    Out.ar(out,
        PlayBuf.ar(1, buf, BufRateScale.kr(buf), loop: 1.0)
            * Linen.kr(gate, doneAction: 2); // release synth when fade done
    )
}).add;
// load all the paths in the sounds/ folder into buffers
~someSounds = "sounds/*".pathMatch.collect{ |path |  Buffer.read(s, path)};
)
// now here's the score, so to speak
// execute these one line at a time
~nowPlaying = Synth("playbuf", [buf: ~someSounds[0]]);
~nowPlaying.release; ~nowPlaying = Synth("playbuf", [buf: ~someSounds[1]]);
~nowPlaying.release; ~nowPlaying = Synth("playbuf", [buf: ~someSounds[2]]);
~nowPlaying.release;
// free the buffer memory
~someSoundsBuffered.do(_.free);
```

Figure 3.7
Executing one line at a time.

3.2.3   Cue Players

Now let's turn to a more concrete example. Triggering sound files, a common technique when combining live performers with a "tape" part, is easily achieved in SuperCollider. There are many approaches to the construction of cue players. These range from a list of individual lines of code that you evaluate one by one during a performance, to fully fledged GUIs that completely hide the code from the user.

One question you need to ask is whether to play the sounds from RAM or stream them from hard disk. The former is convenient for short files, and the latter for substantial cues that you wouldn't want to keep in RAM. There are several classes (both in the standard distribution of SuperCollider and within extensions by third-party developers) that help with these 2 alternatives. Here's a very simple example which loads 2 files into RAM and plays them:

```
~myBuffer = Buffer.read(s, "sounds/a11wlk01.wav"); //load a sound
~myBuffer.play; // play it and notice it will release the node after
playing
```

Buffer's play method is really just a convenience method, though, and we'll probably want to do something fancier, such as fade in or out. Figure 3.7 presents an

```
(
SynthDef("playbuf", { arg out = 0, buf, gate = 1;
    Out.ar(out,
        PlayBuf.ar(1, buf, BufRateScale.kr(buf), loop: 1.0)
        * Linen.kr(gate, doneAction: 2) * 0.6;
        // with 'doneAction: 2' we release synth when fade is done
) }).add;
~someSounds = "sounds/*".pathMatch.collect{ |path |  Buffer.read(s, path)};
n = 0; // a counter
// here's our GUI code
w = Window.new("Simple CuePlayer", Rect(400, 400, 200, 30)).front;
w.view.decorator = FlowLayout(w.view.bounds);
//this will play each cue in turn
Button.new(w, Rect(0, 0, 80, 20)).states_([["Play Cue", Color.black,
Color.clear]]).action_({
    if(n < ~someSounds.size, {
        if(n != 0, {~nowPlaying.release;});
        ~nowPlaying = Synth("playbuf", [buf: ~someSounds[n]]); n=n+1;
    });
});
//this sets the counter to the first cue
Button.new(w, Rect(0, 0, 80, 20)).states_([["Stop / Reset", Color.black,
Color.clear]]).action_({ n=0; ~nowPlaying.release; });
// free the buffers when the window is closed
w.onClose = { ~someSounds.do(_.free); };
)
```

Figure 3.8
Playing cues with a simple GUI.

example which uses multiple cues in a particular order, played by executing the code one line at a time. It uses the PlayBuf UGen, which you may remember from chapter 1.

The middle 2 lines of the latter section of figure 3.7 consist of 2 statements, and thus do 2 things when you press the enter key to execute. You can of course have lines of many statements, which can all be executed at once. (Lines are separated by carriage returns; statements, by semicolons.)

The "1 line at a time" approach is good when developing something for yourself or an SC-savvy user, but you might instead want something a little more elaborate or user-friendly. Figure 3.8 is a simple example with a GUI.

SC also allows for streaming files in from disk using the DiskIn and VDiskIn UGens (the latter allows for variable-speed streaming). There are also a number of third-party extension classes that do things such as automating the required house-keeping (e.g., Fredrik Olofsson's `RedDiskInSampler`).

The previous examples deal with mono files. For multichannel files (stereo being the most common case) it is simplest to deal with interleaved files.[2] Sometimes, however, you may need to deal with multiple mono cues. Figure 3.9 shows how to sort them based on a folder containing subfolders of mono channels.

3.3   Generating Sound Material

The process of composition deals as much with creating sounds as it does with ordering them. The ability to control sounds and audio processes at a low level can be great for finding your own compositional voice. Again, an exhaustive discussion of all of SuperCollider's sound-generating capabilities would far exceed the scope of this chapter, so we'll look at a few issues related to generating and capturing material in SC and give a concrete example of an approach you might want to adapt for your own purposes. As before, we will work here with sound files for the sake of convenience, but you should keep in mind that what we're discussing could apply to more or less any synthesis or processing technique.

3.3.1   Recording

At some point you're probably going to want to record SC's output for the purpose of capturing a sound for further audio processing or "assembly" on a DAW, for documenting a performance, or for converting an entire piece to a distributable sound file format.

To illustrate this, let's make a sound by creating an effect that responds in an idio-syncratic way to the amplitude of an input file and then record the result. You may not find a commercial plug-in that will do this, but in SC, you should be able to do what you can imagine (more or less!).

The `Server` class provides easy automated recording facilities. Often, this is the simplest way to capture your sounds. (See figure 3.10.)

After executing this, you should have a sound file in SC's recordings folder (see the doc for platform-specific locations) labeled with the date and time SC began record-ing: SC_YYMMDD_HHMMSS.aif. `Server` also provides handy buttons on the Server window (appearance or availability varies by platform) to prepare, stop, and start recording. On OSX it may look like this, or similar (see figure 3.11).

The above example uses the default recording options. Using the methods `prepareForRecord(path)`, `recChannels_`, `recHeaderFormat_`, and `recSampleFormat_`, you can customize the recording process. The latter 3 methods must be called before `prepareForRecord`. A common case is to change the sample format; the default is to

```
// gather all your folder paths
//this will path match each folder in the collection, i.e. we will have a collection
of collections of paths

~groupOfindivCueFolders = "sounds/*".pathMatch.collect{ | item |
(item.asSymbol++"*").pathMatch };

Post << ~groupOfindivCueFolders;  //see them all !

//check how many cues you will have in the end
~groupOfindivCueFolders.size;

//automate the buffering process for all cues:
~bufferedCues = ~groupOfindivCueFolders.collect{|item, i| item.collect{| path |
Buffer.read(s,  path)}}; //now all our cue files are sitting in their buffers !

~bufferedCues[0];  //here is cue 1

// see it in the post window:
Post << ~bufferedCues[0];

// play them all in a Group, using our previous synthdef
// we use bind here to ensure they start simultaneously
(
s.bind({
    ~nowPlaying = Group.new(s); // a group to put all the channel synths in
    ~bufferedCues[0].do({|cue| Synth("playbuf", [buf: cue], ~nowPlaying)})
});
)
// fade them out together by sending a release message to the group
~nowPlaying.release;
```

Figure 3.9
Gathering up files for multichannel cues.

```
s.boot; // make sure the server is running
(   // first evaluate this section
b = Buffer.read(s, "sounds/a11wlk01.wav"); // a source
s.prepareForRecord; // prepare the server to record (you must do this first)
)
(   // simultaneously start the processing and recording
s.bind({
    // here's our funky effect
    x = { var columbia, amp;
        columbia = PlayBuf.ar(1, b, loop: 1);
        amp = Amplitude.ar(columbia, 0.5, 0.5, 4000, 250); // 'sticky' amp follower
        Out.ar(0, Resonz.ar(columbia, amp, 0.02, 3)) // filter; freq follows amp
        }.play;
s.record;
});
)
s.pauseRecording; // pause
s.record // start again
s.stopRecording; // stop recording and close the resulting sound file
```

Figure 3.10
Recording the results of making sounds with SuperCollider.

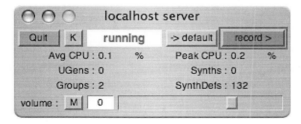

Figure 3.11
A screen shot of a Server window.

record as 32-bit floating-point values. This has the advantage of tremendous dynamic range, which means you don't have to worry about clipping and can normalize later, but it's not compatible with all audio software.

```
s.recSampleFormat_("int16");
```

More elaborate recording can be realized, of course, by using the DiskOut UGen. Server's automatic functionality is in fact based on this. SC also has non-real-time synthesis capabilities, which may be useful for rendering CPU-intensive code. (See chapter 18.)

3.3.2   Thinking in the Abstract

Something that learners often find difficult to do is to stop thinking about exactly what they want to do at the moment, and instead consider whether the problem they're dealing with has a general solution. Generalizing your code can be very powerful. Imagine that we want to make a sound that consists of 3 bands of resonated impulses. We might do something like this:

```
(
{
Resonz.ar(Dust2.ar(5), 300, 0.001, 100) +
Resonz.ar(Dust2.ar(5), 600, 0.001, 100) +
Resonz.ar(Dust2.ar(5), 900, 0.001, 100) * 3.reciprocal; // scale to ensure
no clipping
}.play
)
```

Now, through a bit of careful thinking, we can abstract the problem from this concrete realization and come up with a more general solution:

```
(
f = 300;
n = 3;
{
Mix.fill(n, {|i| Resonz.ar(Dust2.ar(5), f * (i + 1), 0.001, 100)})
* n.reciprocal; // scale to ensure no clipping
}.play
)
```

This version has an equivalent result, but we've expressed it in terms of generalized instructions. It shows you how to construct a Synth consisting of resonated impulses tuned in whole-number ratios rather than as an exact arrangement of objects and connections, as you might do in a visual patching language such as Max/MSP. We've also used variables (f for frequency and n for number of resonators) to make our code easy to change. This is the great power of abstraction: by expressing something as a general solution, you can be much more flexible than if you think in terms of exact implementations. Now it happens that the example above is hardly shorter than the first, but look what we can do with it:

```
(
f = 40;
n = 50;
{
Mix.fill(n, {|i| Resonz.ar(Dust2.ar(5), f * (i + 1), 0.001, 300)})
* n.reciprocal; // scale to ensure no clipping
}.play
)
```

By changing f and n we're able to come up with a much more complex variant. Imagine what the hard-coded version would look like with 50 individual Resonz UGens typed out by hand. In this case, not only is the code more flexible, it's shorter; and because of that, it's much easier to understand. It's like the difference between saying "Make me 50 resonators" and saying "Make me a resonator. Make me a resonator. Make me a resonator. . . ."

This way of thinking has potential applications in almost every aspect of SC, even GUI construction (see figure 3.12).

3.3.3   Gestures

For a long time, electroacoustic and electronic composition has been a rather "manual" process. This may account for the computer's being used today as a virtual analog studio; many sequencer software GUIs attest to this way of thinking. However, as software has become more accessible, programming may in fact be replacing this virtual splicing approach.

One of the main advantages of a computer language is generalization, or abstraction, as we have seen above. In the traditional "tape" music studio approach, the composer does not differentiate gesture from musical content. In fact, traditionally they amount to much the same thing in electronic music. But can a musical gesture exist independently of sound?

In electronic music, gestures are, if you will, the morphology of the sound, a compendium of its behavior. Can we take sound material and examine it under another abstracted morphology? In ordinary musical terms this could mean a minor scale can be played in crescendo or diminuendo and remain a minor scale. In electroacoustic music this can happen, for example, when we modulate 1 sound with the

```
(
f = 300;
n = 30; // number of resonators
t = Array.fill(n, { |i|
{
Resonz.ar(Dust2.ar(5), f * (i + 1), 0.001, 300)
* n.reciprocal; // scale to ensure no clipping
}.play;
});

// now make a GUI
// a scrolling window so we don't run out of space
w = Window.new("Buttons", Rect(50, 100, 290, 250), scroll:true);
w.view.decorator = FlowLayout.new(w.view.bounds); // auto layout the widgets
n.do({|i|
Button.new(w, Rect(0, 0, 130, 30)).states_([
["Freq" + (f * (i + 1)) + "On", Color.black, Color.white],
["Freq" + (f * (i + 1)) + "Off", Color.white, Color.black]
])
.action_({ arg butt;
t[i].run(butt.value == 0);
});
});
w.front;
)
```

Figure 3.12
A variable number of resonators with an automatically created GUI.

spectrum of another. The shape of 1 sound is generalized and applied to another; we are accustomed to hearing this in signal-processing software. In this section we would like to show how SuperCollider can be used to create "empty gestures," gestures that are not linked to any sound in particular. They are, in a sense, gestures waiting for a sound, abstractions of "how to deliver" the musical idea.

First we will look at some snippets of code that we can reuse in different patches, and then we will look at some Routines we can call up as part of a "Routine of Routines" (i.e., a score, so to speak). If you prefer to work in a more traditional way, you can just run the Routines with different sounds each time, record them to hard disk, and then assemble or sample as usual in your preferred audio editing/sequencing software. However, an advantage of doing the larger-scale organization of your piece within SC is that since you are interpreting your code during the actual performance of your piece, you can add elements of variability to what is normally fixed at the time of playback. You can also add elements of chance to your piece without necessarily venturing fully into algorithmic composition. (Naturally, you can always record the output to a sound file if desired.) This, of course, brings us back to issues of design, and exactly what you choose to do will depend on your own needs and inclinations.

3.3.4   Making "Empty" Gestures

Let's start by making a list where all our Buffers will be stored. This will come in handy later on, as it will allow us to call up any file we opened with our file browser during the course of our session. In the following example we open a dialogue box and can select any sound(s) on our hard disk:

```
( //you will be able to add multiple sound files; just shift click when
selecting!
var file, soundPath;
~buffers = List[];
Dialog.getPaths({arg paths;
paths.do({|soundPath|
//post the path to verify that it is the one you expect!
    soundPath.postln;
//adds the recently selected Buffer to your list
    ~buffers.add(Buffer.read(s, soundPath);); })
});
)
```

You can check to see how many Buffers are in your list so far (watch the post window!),

```
~buffers.size;
```

and you can see where each sound is inside your list. For example, here is the very first sound stored in our Buffer list:

```
~buffers[0];
```

Now that we have our sound in a Buffer, let's try some basic manipulations. First, let's just listen to the sound to verify that it is there:

```
~buffers[0].play;
```

Now, let's make a simple SynthDef so we can create Synths which play our Buffer (for example, in any Routine, Task, or other Stream) later on. For the purposes of this demonstration we will use a very simple percussive envelope, making sure we have doneAction: 2 in order to free the synth after the envelope terminates:

```
(
// buffer player with done action and control of envelope and panning
SynthDef(\samplePlayer, {arg out = 0, buf = 0,
rate = 1, at = 0.01, rel = 0.1, pos = 0, pSpeed = 0, lev = 0.5;
var sample, panT, amp, aux;
sample = PlayBuf.ar(1, buf, rate*BufRateScale.kr(buf), 1, 0, 0);
panT= FSinOsc.kr(pSpeed);
amp = EnvGen.ar(Env.perc(at, rel, lev), doneAction: 2);
Out.ar(out, Pan2.ar(sample, panT, amp));
}).add;
)
```

As mentioned in chapter 1, we use the add method here rather than one of the more low-level SynthDef methods such as send. In addition to sending the def to the server, add also stores it within the global SynthDescLib in the client app, so that its arguments can be looked up later by the Patterns and Streams system (see chapter 6). We'll need this below. Let's test the SynthDef:

```
Synth(\samplePlayer,[\out, 0, \bufnum, ~buffers[0], \rel, 0.25]);
```

As you can hear, it plays 0.25 second of the selected sound. Of course, if you have made more than 1 Buffer list, you can play sounds from any list, and also play randomly from that list. For example, from the list we defined earlier we could do this:

```
Synth(\samplePlayer,[\out, 0, \bufnum, ~buffers.choose, \rel, 0.25]);
```

Let's define a Routine that allows us to create a stuttering/rushing gesture in a glitch style. We'll use a new Pattern here, Pgeom, which specifies a geometric series.[3] Note that Patterns can be nested. Figure 3.13 shows a Pseq whose list consists of two Pgeoms.

Remember that you can use a Task or Routine to sequence several such gestures within your piece. You can, of course, modify the Routine to create other accel/decel Patterns by substituting different Patterns. You can also add variability by making some of them perform choices when they generate their values (e.g., using Prand or Pxrand). You can use this, for example, to choose which speaker a sound comes from without repeating speakers:

```
Pxrand([0, 1, 2, 3, 4, 5, 6, 7, 8], inf)
```

The advantage of having assigned your gestures to environment variables (using the tilde shortcut) is that now you are able to experiment in real time with the ordering, simultaneity, and internal behavior of your gestures.

Let's take a quick look at 1 more important Pattern: Pbind. It creates a Stream of Events, which are like a kind of dictionary of named properties and associated values. If you send the message play to a Pbind, it will play the Stream of Events, in

```
(/* a routine for creating a ritardando stutter with panning, you must have
run the code in fig 3.9 so that this routine may find some sounds already loaded
into buffers, you can change the index of ~bufferedCues to test the routine on
different sounds */


~stut = Routine( { var dur, pos;
~stutPatt = Pseq([Pgeom(0.01, 1.1707, 18), Pn(0.1, 1),Pgeom(0.1, 0.94, 200) ]);
~str= ~stutPatt.asStream;
100.do{
    dur = ~str.next;
    dur.postln;     //so we can check values on the post window
    ~sample = Synth("samplePlayer",[\out, 0, \buf,  ~bufferedCues[0], \at, 0.1,
\ rel, 0.05,\pSpeed, 0.5]);
    dur.wait;
}
});
)

//now play it
~stut.play;
// reset before you play again!
~stut.reset;
```

Figure 3.13
Making a stuttering gesture using a geometric Pattern.

a fashion similar to the Clock examples above. Here's a simple example which makes
sound using what's called the "default" SynthDef:

```
// randomly selected frequency, duration 0.1 second
Pbind(\freq, Prand([300, 500, 231.2, 399.2], 30), \dur, 0.1).play;
```

It's also possible to substitute Event Streams as they play. When you call play on
a Pattern, it returns an EventStreamPlayer, which actually creates the individual
Events from the Stream defined by the Pattern. EventStreamPlayer allows its Stream
to be substituted while it is playing.

```
~gest1 = Pbind(\instrument, \samplePlayer, \dur, 2, \rel, 1.9);
~player = ~gest1.play; //make it play
~player.stream = Pbind(\instrument, \samplePlayer, \dur, 1/8, \rate,
Pxrand([1/2, 1, 2/3, 4], inf), \rel, 0.9).asStream; //substitute the
stream
~player.stop;
```

If you have evaluated the expressions above, you will notice that you don't hear the simple default SynthDef, but rather the one we made earlier. Since we added it above, the Pbind is able to look it up in the global library and get the information it needs about the def. Now, the Pbind plays repeatedly at intervals specified by the \dur argument, but it will stop playing as soon as it receives nil for this or any other argument. So we can take advantage of this to make Streams that are not repetitive and thus make single gestures (of course, we can also choose to work in a looping/layering fashion, but more of that later). Here is a Pbind making use of our accelerando Pattern to create a rushing sound:

```
~gest1 = Pbind(\instrument, \samplePlayer, \dur, Pgeom(0.01, 1.1707, 20),
\rel, 1.9);
~gest1.play;
```

When the Stream created from the Pgeom ended, it returned nil and the EventStreamPlayer stopped playing. If you call play on it again, you will notice that it makes the same rushing sound without the need to reset it, as we had to do with the Routine, since it will return a new EventStreamPlayer each time. More complex gestures can be made, of course, by nesting patterns:

```
Pbind(\instrument, \samplePlayer, \dur, Pseq([Pgeom(0.01, 1.1707, 20),
Pgeom(0.01, 0.93, 20)], 1), \rel, 1.9, \pSpeed, 0.5).play;

Pbind(\instrument, \samplePlayer, \dur, Pseq([Pgeom(0.01, 1.1707, 20),
Pgeom(0.01, 0.93, 20)], 1),\rate, Pxrand([1/2, 1, 2/3, 4], inf), \rel,
1.9, \pSpeed, 0.5).play;
```

Similar things can be done with the Pdef class from the JIT library (see chapter 7). Let's designate another environment variable to hold a sequence of values that we can plug in at will and change on the fly. This Pattern holds values that would work well for \dur:

```
~rhythm1 = Pseq([1/4, 1/4, 1/8, 1/12, 1/24, nil]); //the nil is so it will
stop!
```

We can then plug it into a Pdef, which we'll call \a:

```
~gest1 = Pdef(\a, Pbind(\instrument, \samplePlayer, \dur, ~rhythm1, \rel,
1.9, \pSpeed, 0.5) );
~gest1.play
```

If we define another sequence of values we want to try,

```
~rhythm1 = Pseq([1/64, 1/64, 1/64, 1/32, 1/32, 1/32, 1/32, 1/24, 1/16,
1/12, nil]);
```

and then reevaluate the Pdef,

```
~gest1 = Pdef(\a, Pbind(\instrument, \samplePlayer, \dur, ~rhythm1, \rel,
1.9, \pSpeed, 0.5) );
```

we can hear that the new ~rhythm1 has taken the place of the previous one. Notice that it played immediately, without the need for executing ~gest1.play. This is one of the advantages of working with the Pdef class: once the Stream is running, anything that is "poured" into it will come out. In the following example, we assign a Pattern to the rate values and obtain an interesting variation:

```
~gest1 = Pdef( \a , Pbind(\instrument, \samplePlayer, \att, 0.5, \rel, 3,
\lev, {rrand(0.1, 0.2)}, \dur, 0.05, \rate, Pseq([Pbrown(0.8, 1.01, 0.01,
20)])));
```

Experiments like these can be conducted by creating Patterns for any of the arguments that our SynthDef will take. If we have "added" more than 1 SynthDef, we can even modulate the \instrument by getting it to choose among several different options. Once we have a set of gestures we like, we can trigger them in a certain order using a Routine, or we can record them separately and load them as audio files to our audio editor. The latter approach is useful if we want to use a cue player for the final structuring of a piece.

3.4   Conclusions

What next? The best way to compose with SuperCollider is to set yourself a project with a deadline! In this way you will come to grips with specific things you need to know, and you will learn it much better than just by reviewing everything it can do. SuperCollider offers a variety of approaches to electronic music composition. It can be used for sound creation thanks to its rich offering of UGens (see chapter 2), as well as for assembling your piece in flexible ways. We have shown that the assembly of sounds itself can become a form of synthesis, illustrated by our use of Patterns and Streams. Another approach is to review some of the classic techniques used in electroacoustic composition and try to re-create them yourself using SuperCollider. Below we refer you to some interesting texts that may enhance your creative investigations.

Further Reading

Budón, O. 2000. "Composing with Objects, Networks, and Time Scales: An Interview with Horacio Vaggione." *Computer Music Journal*, 24(3): 9–22.

Collins, N. 2010. *Introduction to Computer Music*. Chichester: Wiley.

Dodge, C., and T. A. Jerse. 1997. *Computer Music: Synthesis, Composition, and Performance,* 2nd ed. New York: Schirmer.

Holtzman, S. R. 1981. "Using Generative Grammars for Music Composition." *Computer Music Journal,* 5(1): 51–64.

Loy, G. 1989. "Composing with Computers: A Survey of Some Compositional Formalisms and Music Programming Languages." In M. V. Mathews and J. R. Pierce, eds., *Current Directions in Computer Music Research,* pp. 291–396. Cambridge, MA: MIT Press.

Loy, G., and Abbott, C. 1985. "Programming Languages for Computer Music Synthesis, Performance, and Composition." *ACM Computing Surveys (CSUR),* 17(2): 235–265.

Mathews, M. V. 1963. "The Digital Computer as a Musical Instrument." *Science,* 142(3592): 553–557.

Miranda, E. R. 2001. *Composing Music with Computers.* London: Focal Press.

Roads, C. 2001. *Microsound.* Cambridge, MA: MIT Press.

Roads, C. 1996. *The Computer Music Tutorial.* Cambridge, MA: MIT Press.

Wishart, T. 1994. *Audible Design: A Plain and Easy Introduction to Practical Sound Composition.* York, UK: Orpheus the Pantomime.

Notes

1. You may have noticed that the terms "message" and "method" used somewhat interchangeably. In polymorphism the distinction becomes clear: different objects may respond to the same message with different methods. In other words, the message is the command, and the method is what the object does in response.

2. Scott Wilson's De-Interleaver application for OSX and Jeremy Friesner's cross-platform command line tools audio_combine and audio_split allow for convenient interleaving and deinterleaving of audio files.

3. A geometric series is a series with a constant ratio between successive terms.

4 Ins and Outs: SuperCollider and External Devices

Stefan Kersten, Marije A. J. Baalman, and Till Bovermann

4.1 Introduction

Sometimes SuperCollider alone isn't enough, and you want to have input from external devices or other programs, to use output in other programs, or to control devices from SC. Common examples are interfacing with programs such as Processing[1] (Reas and Fry, 2007), and PureData[2] (Puckette, 2007). Devices can be anything ranging from MIDI keyboards, to game devices, to home-built sensor interfaces. This chapter will provide an overview of the most common ways of getting data in and out of SC. Because of limited space we will not provide a detailed explanation of the devices or protocols themselves, nor in most cases of any associated technical terminology. We suggest that you research these using the Internet and/or standard texts on computer music or computer hardware if you need more information. Where appropriate, however, we will provide references to Help files, Quarks (the name for certain SuperCollider extensions which can be pulled in and updated via commands from the language, see the Quarks Help file), external resources, and other chapters in this book.

SuperCollider provides many ways to work with external data and to send external data. In this chapter we will look into *Open Sound Control*, *MIDI*, *HID*, *Serial-Port*, and analog sensing. Another option to interface with an external program would be by piping data (see the `Pipe` Help file); this topic is touched upon in chapter 12 (Linux).

Let's say you have a device that you want to use as a musical interface to perform your music, or you may have an idea for an interface and be looking for the right way to build it. In either case the questions you will have are the following:

1. How do I get data from the device?
2. How do I send data to the device?
3. How do I create a sensible mapping?

The first 2 questions are mostly of a technical nature and will be described in detail in the next section for different protocols; the last question is quite complicated and is tightly linked to your artistic purposes. We will present some basic approaches to get started in tackling this question. We will not go into the mechanical questions of what sensors to use to capture the parameters that one wants to measure in the real world, as this goes beyond the scope of this chapter. More information on these topics can be found at the SensorWiki[3] and in the proceedings of the NIME conference.[4]

4.2   Getting the Data

4.2.1   Human Interface Devices

Human interface devices (HID) are devices through which the external world can communicate with computers. Most common are the keyboard and the mouse; other examples are gamepads and joysticks. These devices are nowadays usually connected via USB (Universal Serial Bus).

For USB an HID specification has been defined. This ensures that computers running different operating systems can recognize a connected device as an HID and load the appropriate driver for it, so that programs can use its data. Though HIDs are normally used for input, it is also possible to send output to them in some cases. The latter is usually done to give the user feedback, for example, the Caps Lock LED that is found on many keyboards.

Within SuperCollider it is possible to access HIDs through the class `GeneralHID`. This wrapper class provides a cross-platform interface to the platform-dependent implementations. Wacom Tablets and the Nintendo Wii Remote are special cases and will be treated separately in this section.

4.2.1.1   Server-side methods of accessing HID devices

For some input devices there are specific UGens that access their data (for example, the mouse UGens `MouseX`, `MouseY`, and `MouseButton`, and the keyboard UGen `KeyState`, all of which are included in SuperCollider). There are several others available as extensions. The advantage of accessing data server-side is that you do not need to pass on data from the language to the server in order to affect a synthesis process. The disadvantage is less flexibility in the mapping of the data.

```
(
SynthDef(\mouseExample, {
    Out.ar(0,
        Resonz.ar(WhiteNoise.ar,
            MouseX.kr(400, 3000,\exponential), // mouse x is frequency
```

```
                   MouseY.kr(0.01, 2, \exponential) // mouse y is bandwidth
           ) * MouseButton.kr // mouse button is on and off
      );
}).add;
);
```

```
// create an instance:
x = Synth(\mouseExample);
// now move the mouse to different places on the screen and push the left
button. If you keep it pressed and move the mouse, you sweep through the
filter.
```

```
// free the Synth again:
x.free;
```

4.2.1.2   Client GUI methods of accessing HID devices

SuperCollider GUI widgets provide the ability to capture keyboard and mouse events through callback functions such as mouseDownAction and keyDownAction. Since these are discussed in detail in chapters 9 and 10, they will not be explored in any depth here. A simple example is presented below.

```
(
w = Window.new("Key Example", Rect(0,0, 150, 150));
c = UserView(w, Rect( 0, 0, 150, 150)).background_(Color.white);
c.keyDownAction = {arg view, char, modifiers, unicode, keycode;
    [char, modifiers, unicode, keycode].postln;
};
w.front;
)
```

From an interaction design viewpoint, using a GUI widget to capture an HID event should be done only if the interaction makes sense only with that GUI widget (e.g., if the GUI widget provides visual feedback that is essential to the interaction).

4.2.1.3   GeneralHID

Note: HID is currently working natively only on OSX and Linux. On Windows, GeneralHID may be used with the external program hidserver (distributed with the Windows version).

GeneralHID provides a cross-platform interface to access HID devices. The basic approach is the following:

1. Create a list of devices: GeneralHID.buildDeviceList, followed by d = GeneralHID .deviceList
2. Choose the desired device from this list: GeneralHID.postDevices; a = GeneralHID .open(d[3]); or GeneralHID.open(GeneralHID.findBy(vendorID, productID))

3. Get some info about the device: a.info and a.caps (arguments that can be used for the .findBy method) can be retrieved with a.info.findArgs
4. Start the event loop: GeneralHID.startEventLoop;
5. Check whether data come in: a.debug_(true);
6. Define a "spec," a mapping of symbols to device slots, for the device. You can save this spec and load it in future sessions.

The capabilities of the device are translated into different types of slots: typically there are buttons, relative axes, absolute axes, and LEDs. Absolute axes are, for example, joystick x and y positions, where the position is clearly connected to a physical state of the joystick. Relative axes are, for example, mouse coordinates; since the mouse can move over an arbitrary surface, we don't know where on the surface the mouse is, we know only how much it moved left, right, up, or down in a time unit. Within GeneralHID, these "delta" movements are translated to an absolute coordinate that goes up and down. For example, the output of a.caps for an external mouse is the following:

```
GeneralHIDSlot(Button, type: 1, id: 272, value: 0)
GeneralHIDSlot(Button, type: 1, id: 273, value: 0)
GeneralHIDSlot(Button, type: 1, id: 274, value: 0)
GeneralHIDSlot(Button, type: 1, id: 276, value: 0)
GeneralHIDSlot(Button, type: 1, id: 275, value: 0)

GeneralHIDSlot(Relative, type: 2, id: 1, value: 0)
GeneralHIDSlot(Relative, type: 2, id: 0, value: 0)
GeneralHIDSlot(Relative, type: 2, id: 8, value: 0)

GeneralHIDSlot(Syn, type: 0, id: 1, value: 0)
GeneralHIDSlot(Syn, type: 0, id: 0, value: 0)
```

The last 2 lines of this output can be ignored, as they have no real use for us. From the rest we can see that we have 5 buttons (with numbers 272 to 276) and 3 relative axes (0, 1, and 8). For each of these we can now check which feature on the device they represent by turning debugging on and off for the individual slots. For example:

```
a.slots[1][272].debug_(true)
```

Once we have identified what's what, we can assign functionality to the slots. For this there are several methods:

Retrieving the current value of a slot

```
a.slots[1][272].value
```

Assigning an action to be performed when a new value has arrived

```
a.slots[1][272].action_({arg v; "hi, my value is".post; v.value.postln;})
```

Creating a bus for the slot on the server

```
a.slots[1][272].createBus(s);
```

that can later be accessed with

```
a.slots[1][272].bus
```

In the case of LEDs on a device, you can set the value of the slot, which will turn the LED on or off. You can also set an action for the device as a whole, to act upon any incoming data value:

```
a.action = {|type, code, rawvalue, value| [type, code, rawvalue, value].
postln;};
```

You get a simple GUI representation of the device with the following:

```
a.makeGui
```

An example is given in the Web site materials for this chapter in the file *gamepad _example.scd*.

4.2.1.4   Wacom Tablets
Note: Wacom support is currently working only on OSX and Linux.[5]

Wacom[6] Tablets are tablets on which you can draw with a pen that were developed mainly with a target market of graphical designers. Nonetheless, they have gained popularity as musical controllers (Zbyszynski et al., 2007) because they provide many axes of control through an interface with which many people are familiar: the pen.

Within SuperCollider, Wacom Tablets are accessible through either the GUI classes `TabletView` and `TabletSlider2D` (OSX only) or the `GeneralHID` class.

`TabletView` creates a view that receives the extended Wacom data: x and y location within the view in subpixel accuracy, the pressure on the tablet, tilt in x and y directions, the deviceID (which is an indication of whether the tip or the eraser is used), the button number, the click count, absolute z (the wheel on the side of some mice), and rotation in degrees (on the 4D mice). `TabletSlider2D` basically receives the same data but displays x and y positions as a 2D slider.

Example patches for accessing the Wacom Tablet are given in the Web site materials in the files *wacom_example_linux.scd* and *wacom_example_osx.scd*.

4.2.1.5   Wii Remote
Note: `WiiMote` *is currently working only on OSX and Linux.*

The Wii Remote (WiiMote) from Nintendo[7] has become very popular in very little time among sound and media artists because it provides a relatively robust and easy-to-access method to capture acceleration data, as well as more standard controls (buttons, joysticks), wirelessly. It is a BlueTooth device which can be held in one hand, and it has an extension port to which either a "nunchuk" controller or a "classic" controller (a game pad) can be connected.

The basic approach is the following:

1. Start the event loop (`WiiMote.start`)
2. Discover a WiiMote (`WiiMote.discover`)
3. Select a WiiMote (`w = WiiMote.all[0]`)
4. Enable options on the device (the device itself, the expansion, the buttons, the accelerometer, or the IR sensor)
5. Assign actions to capabilities (see table 4.1).

In addition to actions for each capability, you can assign actions to the time when the device connects or disconnects; this can be useful to create an automatic backup solution or alert to reestablish a connection.

With `x = WiiMoteGUI.new(w)`, a simple GUI is created to show the current values of the incoming data, as well as controls to turn on and off the LEDs and rumble (vibration).

Table 4.1
Capabilities of the Wii Remote Devices

WiiMote		
Buttons	11	input
Motion	3 axes	input
IR	up to 4 objects	input
LEDs	4	output
Rumble	1	output
Speaker*	1	output
Memory*	—	—
Nunchuk		
Buttons	2	input
Motion	3 axes	input
Joystick	2 axes	input
Classic		
Buttons	15	input
Analog	2 axes	input
Joystick	2x2 axes	input

*These features had not yet been implemented in SuperCollider at the time of writing.

See also

Help files: GeneralHID, HIDDeviceService, LID, Wacom, WiiMote

Third-party programs: ixi hidserver

In this book: chapter 12.

4.2.2   MIDI

MIDI, which stands for Musical Instrument Digital Interface,[8] is an asynchronous serial protocol that was introduced in 1983. A MIDI message consists of 3 bytes; the first is a status byte containing the message type and channel, and the other 2 are data bytes.

Devices that send or receive MIDI are typically keyboards, (hardware) synthesizers, drum pads, and so on, but there are also several sensor interfaces available which use MIDI.

Within SuperCollider a low-level MIDI implementation is provided by the classes `MIDIClient`, `MIDIIn`, `MIDIOut`, and `MIDIEndPoint`. For higher-level usage, there are MIDI responder classes which allow one to register functions that will be evaluated based on incoming messages. These are similar to `OSCresponder`, which was introduced in chapter 2 (and is discussed further below, in section 4.2.3).

4.2.2.1   MIDI input

As a simple example, we will show how to connect to a MIDI input port, wait for a note on message, and post the result.

```
// connects 1 input to the first available output from a device or program
MIDIIn.connect;
// assigns a function to incoming noteOn messages
MIDIIn.noteOn = {|port, chan, note, vel| [port, chan, note, vel].postln};
```

Now, whenever a note on message is received, the port, channel, note number, and velocity of the note will be posted. This is a simple example, but the function could also do something more complex, for instance, create a Synth that plays a note at the indicated pitch.

The disadvantage of using the method `MIDIIn.noteOn` directly is that you can have only 1 function assigned to it, so all the logic for handling any note on messages received need to be in that function. As an alternative, you can use 1 or more `NoteOnResponder` objects, which will allow you to assign as many functions as you want to note on messages and to individually add or remove responders as desired.

```
// first unassign the noteOn method:
MIDIIn.noteOn = nil;
```

```
// create a NoteOnResponder and assign it to the variable n
n = NoteOnResponder({|src, chan, num, vel| [src, chan, num, vel].postln},
nil, nil, (0..127), (0..127) );
```

This example will do exactly what the previous one did. But suppose that now that we have tested whether data come in, we want to have a responder that listens only to note number 64. We can add an additional NoteOnResponder to do this:

```
// create a NoteOnResponder and assign it to the variable m
m = NoteOnResponder({|src, chan, num, vel| [src, chan, num, vel].
postln},nil, nil,[64], (0..127) );
```

Now, if you hit note 64 on your keyboard, you will get 2 posts, 1 coming from the NoteOnResponder n and 1 coming from m. To remove a responder, execute the following:

```
// remove the NoteOnResponder n:
n.remove;
```

Hit note 64 again, and you'll get only 1 post.

```
// remove the NoteOnResponder m:
m.remove;
```

Now you've removed all the responders. Similar methods are available for other types of MIDI messages. See table 4.2 for a list.

Table 4.2
MIDI Messages and Their Corresponding Implementation in SuperCollider

MIDIn Method	Wait Method	Responder Name	Description
NoteOn	waitNoteOn	NoteOnResponder	note-on
NoteOff	waitNoteOff	NoteOffResponder	note-off
Control	waitControl	CCResponder	control message
Bend	waitBend	BendResponder	pitch bend
Touch	waitTouch	TouchResponder	aftertouch
Polytouch	waitPoly	—	polyphonic aftertouch/pressure
Program	waitProgram	ProgramChangeResponder	program change
Sysex	—	—	system exclusive
Sysrt	—	—	song select, clock, and transport control
Smpte	—	—	MIDI time code

Note: The responder methods are documented in the MidiResponder Help file.

One note about the MIDI note off message: not all programs and/or devices implement this message; many use a MIDI note on message with a velocity of 0 instead.

4.2.2.2   MIDI output

In order to send MIDI output, an instance of MIDIOut needs to be created. MIDIOut takes 2 parameters: the output port number and the device to which it sends output (on Linux this parameter is optional; see chapter 12). Then, from this instance you can send any MIDI message: noteOn, noteOff, polyTouch, control, touch, bend, allNotesOff, smpte, and so on.

Here is an example that sends out MIDI using a Task:

```
MIDIClient.init;
m = MIDIOut(0, MIDIClient.destinations.at(0).uid);
(
t = Task({
    [60, 64, 61, 60, 65, 61].do{|it|
        m.noteOn(16, it, 60);
        1.0.wait;
        m.noteOff(16, it, 60);
    };
    [64, 65, 67].dup(4).flatten.do{|it|
        m.noteOn(16, it, 120);
        0.25.wait;
        m.noteOff(16, it, 120);
    };
    [61, 65, 60, 61, 64, 60].do{|it|
        m.noteOn(16, it, 60);
        1.0.wait;
        m.noteOff(16, it, 60);
    };
    m.noteOn(16, 60, 40); m.noteOn(16, 52, 40);
    2.0.wait;
    m.noteOff(16, 60, 40); m.noteOff(16, 52, 40);
    m.noteOn(16, 57, 40); m.noteOn(16, 52, 40);
    2.0.wait;
    m.noteOff(16, 57, 40); m.noteOff(16, 52, 40);
    m.noteOn(16, 53, 40);
    2.0.wait;
    m.noteOff(16, 53, 40);
    m.noteOn(16, 52, 40);
    4.0.wait;
    m.noteOff(16, 52, 40);
});
);
t.play;
t.stop;
```

See also
Help files: MIDI, UsingMIDI, MIDIIn, MIDIOut, MIDIResponder
Quarks: ddwMIDI
In this book: chapters 12 and 20.

4.2.3   Open Sound Control

Open Sound Control (OSC) is a protocol designed at Berkeley's CNMAT for exchanging control data between audio applications[9] (Wright et al., 2003), but it is general enough to allow for a wide range of possible applications. OSC itself is transport independent (i.e., the underlying transport protocol is—except for the details of opening and closing connections—of little interest to higher application layers. OSC has been used with transports ranging from serial communication to high-speed Ethernet communication, but the most popular protocols are those of the IP family, because of their widespread support in operating systems.

Before we delve into the details of sending and receiving OSC messages in Super-Collider, let's have a short look at the 2 most important IP protocols, User Datagram Protocol (UDP) and Transmission Control Protocol (TCP). Although some details differ, both protocols have a common way of addressing services on a particular machine (which might be the same as the sending one). Computers (hosts) within the same network segment are uniquely identified by their IP address, a 32-bit (in IPv4) or 64-bit (in IPv6) number. IPv4 addresses are usually given in "dot" notation (i.e., by 4 numbers of 8 bits each, separated by dots: 192.168.1.2).

The special address 127.0.0.1 usually denotes the local host address (i.e., the address of the machine the sending or receiving program is running on. Numeric IP addresses are hard to memorize, and in many networks a host providing *Domain Name Service* (DNS) makes it possible to resolve host addresses based on a hierarchical naming scheme (`host.domain.suffix`). Each host is assigned a unique name within the network which can be used instead of the numeric IP address (e.g., `nicola.kgw.tu-berlin.de`. The special host name `localhost` is usually mapped to the IP address 127.0.0.1, and there is a similar mechanism for link-local addresses—used, for example, by Apple in its *Rendezvous* implementation—the domain `.local` (note the missing suffix).

In order to differentiate between different services on the same host, each program allocates a resource (a socket) which is bound to a specific integer port. Usually ports below 1024 are reserved for system services; user applications are free to use any port number above 1024. The default port for *scsynth* is 57110, and the one for *sclang* and *SuperCollider.app* is 57120. The combination of IP address and port makes it possible to address any service on any machine seen by the sending host.

The UDP protocol is message oriented (i.e., communication takes place by sending individual packets of limited size, without any guarantee of correct delivery). It is used in many audio and video applications because of its lower overhead compared with TCP and its ease of use. It is also the default protocol used by *sclang* and *scsynth*. TCP, on the other hand, is connection oriented (i.e., conceptually, communication is an exchange of infinite Streams of unstructured binary data between 2 connected hosts. Since OSC itself is message based, the Stream needs to be "packetized" by prepending a 32-bit byte count to each OSC packet before sending. (Note that the SC objects discussed below will do this for you automatically.)

Among other things, as noted in chapter 3, SuperCollider uses OSC for controlling the synthesis server *scsynth* from the language application, so let's have a look at how the concepts explained above are realized in *sclang*. Hosts and services are represented by objects of the type `NetAddr`.

```
// Create a network address representing sclang itself
~host = NetAddr("localhost," NetAddr.langPort);
```

OSC packets come in 2 varieties: messages and bundles. Messages represent individual commands (e.g., triggering an action in the receiving host). A command is denoted by an ASCII string that is in a hierarchical format similar to Unix file system paths (e.g., "/synth/filter"). Bundles are collections of messages paired with a 64-bit time tag that denotes the intended time of execution in the standardized NTP format. Messages in the same bundle are guaranteed to be executed *atomically* by the receiving host. (That is, either they are all executed at the same logical time or none of them is executed. Logical time represents the scheduled time at which the events are executed and is distinct from physical time, which of course still advances while the execution occurs.) Being able to schedule messages slightly ahead of time is particularly important in audio synthesis, in order to rectify the messaging jitter introduced by system-level process scheduling and network transport.

OSC messages are represented in SuperCollider by Arrays containing the command string and any number of arguments of primitive types (e.g., `String`, `Number`, `Boolean`, `Nil`, etc.) and Arrays encoded as binary "blobs." The method `sendMsg` of `NetAddr` takes a list of arguments and sends them as an OSC message.

```
// Send an OSC message
~host.sendMsg("/testMsg", 42, "string", pi);
```

To send a bundle, we use the `sendBundle` method of `NetAddr`, providing a time tag as an offset from the current time and a list of messages.

```
// Send an OSC bundle and execute its contents
// 200 ms from "now"
```

```
~host.sendBundle(0.2,
    ["/testMsg", 42, "string", pi],
    ["/testMsg", 183]);
```

Until now, we've sent messages to the language without actually reacting to them; in order to have a piece of code executed whenever a particular OSC message is received, we use instances of the OSCresponder class:

```
// Create an OSCresponder
~responder = OSCresponder(
    ~host, "/testMsg",
    {|time, responder, message, address|
        [\responder, time, message, address].postln;
    }
).add;
```

The example above registers an OSCresponder via the add method, so that the function specified will be executed whenever the message "/testMsg" is received from the network address ~host. If a bundle containing multiple "/testMsg" messages is received, the logical time at which the registered function will be executed will be the same for all messages in the bundle.

Sometimes the address of the sending host is unknown, and therefore it's possible to pass nil instead of a NetAddr to OSCresponder; a responder created like this will execute its action whenever a specific command is received from *any* address.

OSCresponder allows only a single action to be registered for a given OSC command. If you need to register multiple actions for the same OSC command, you can use OSCresponderNode, which has the same interface as OSCresponder. (See figure 4.1.)

SuperCollider's implementation of the OSC specification is not complete; for example, wild cards are not matched, and any OSC blobs (blocks of binary data) are always interpreted as an Int8Array.

SuperCollider can also act as a TCP client (i.e., NetAddr can be used to connect to a TCP service and send and receive messages). To demonstrate this, we will need to start a service to connect to. We'll use the Unix utility *netcat*, named *nc* on many systems. Start *netcat* from a terminal window as a TCP server listening on a local port.

```
nc -lp 7878
```

Then use NetAddr to connect to the service.

```
~host = NetAddr("localhost", 7878);
~host.connect;
~host.sendMsg("/tcpTest", "tcp test message");
```

```
Create a network address representing sclang itself
~host = NetAddr("localhost", NetAddr.langPort);
// Create two OSC responders for the same command
~r1 = OSCresponderNode(
    ~host, "/testMsg",
    { | time, responder, message, address |
        [\responder1, time, message, address].postln;
    }
).add;
~r2 = OSCresponderNode(
    ~host, "/testMsg",
    { | time, responder, message, address |
        [\responder2, time, message, address].postln;
    }
).add;

// Send an OSC message
~host.sendMsg("/testMsg", "OSCresponderNode test");

// Remove responders
~r1.remove;
~r2.remove;
```

Figure 4.1
Example of OSCresponderNode.

When you are done with using the service, call the disconnect method of NetAddr:

~host.disconnect;

OSC communication via TCP is still relatively rare in comparison to the ubiquity of the UDP protocol, but some SuperCollider subsystems use TCP (e.g., SwingOSC; see chapter10).

See also
Help files: NetAddr, OSCresponder, OSCresponderNode, OSCpathResponder, Server-Command-Reference.

4.2.4   SerialPort

In SuperCollider, communication with serial devices is by use of the SerialPort class, which encapsulates a connection to a specific device and supplies methods for reading, writing, and error discovery. Note that at the time of writing, SerialPort is available only on POSIX systems (i.e., Linux and OSX).

The `SerialPort.new` method takes a number of (rather technical) arguments that determine which serial port driver to use and how to configure the connection. The `port` argument is either a special device in the `/dev/` directory pointing to a serial communications device, or an index to the default list of devices returned by `SerialPort.devices`. `baudrate` determines the bit rate of the serial communication—possible values are all standard POSIX baud rates, and the default is 9600. `databits` configures the number of actual data bits in each transmitted symbol; 8 is the default for usual applications. `stopbit` is a flag indicating whether to transmit a single stop bit after each symbol for synchronization at the receiving device. `parity` configures the type of parity bit sent after each symbol—the default "none" omits the parity bit, while "even" and "odd" add a parity bit such that each symbol including the parity bit contains an even or odd number of bits, respectively. `crtscts` is a Boolean flag specifying whether to use the *Request to Send* and *Clear to Send* hardware flow control lines. `xonxoff` enables or disables software flow control. Finally, `exclusive` attempts to open the device driver in exclusive mode.

Once a `SerialPort` object is created, data should be written to and read from the device from within a `Routine` (i.e., not from the top-level interpreter), in order not to block execution while performing serial communication.

The `put` method transmits a single byte of data to the device, as determined by `databits` when opening the port. The behavior of `put` is always synchronous (i.e., it blocks the currently running SuperCollider thread until the whole byte can be transmitted). The optional `timeout` parameter specifies the granularity at which write attempts are scheduled. `putAll` is a wrapper around `put` that writes a collection of bytes to the serial device.

For reading from the device there are two different options: `next` returns either a single byte read from the serial device or `nil` (when currently there are no data to be read). `read` performs a blocking read, taking control of the current thread until an entire byte of data can be read.

`SerialPort` makes error detection and recovery entirely the programmer's responsibility. The method `rxErrors` can be of help for this task: it returns the number of data bytes received from the device but not consumed by the SuperCollider application, indicating a communication error of some sort and the need for resynchronization with the sending device.

Since the details of serial communication are highly dependent on the devices and communication protocols involved, more detailed usage examples will be given in the following sections.

4.2.4.1   Ambient Lights example

The Ambient Light[10] project arose out of the need to have 3 or more computer-controllable RGB lights. It was developed at Bielefeld University during a lecture on ambient displays in 2006. It consists of a programmable PIC microcontroller placed on a printed circuit board controlling 3 RGB lights, each consisting of 6 pairwise controllable LEDs (red, green, blue). The PIC here sends 9 PWM signals to the lights, resulting in 3 RGB color values.

It is possible to control the lights by sending 4 characters to its rs232 interface, for example, A255. The first character determines the channel and may be A, B, C, D, E, F, G, H, or I. The next 3 characters are used to define the saturation of the channel. Since the PWM regulator used has a resolution of 8 bits, the range of possible values is between 000 and 255. Using SuperCollider's SerialPort interface, setting the value of 1 (red, green, or blue) light can be achieved by

```
// serialport setup
SerialPort.devicePattern = "/dev/tty.usbserial*"; // osx usb serial
SerialPort.devices; // look if the device is there
(
~serial = SerialPort(
    SerialPort.devices.first,
    baudrate: 115200,
    crtscts: true
);
)

~serial.putAll("A120"); // set red component
~serial.putAll("B255"); // set green component
~serial.putAll("C100"); // set blue component
```

To abstract from the concrete hardware-related implementation, we can define a simple programming interface.

```
// function example with values between 0..1
a = {|char, val, serial|
    serial.putAll(char ++ ((val*255).asInt + 1000).asString[1..3]);
};
```

A change of color now can be forced by evaluating

```
a.value("A", 0.1, ~serial);
```

Further abstraction is achieved by changing the character input to a more usable number between 0 and 2. In addition, we added support for standard SuperCollider Color objects.

```
a = {|which, color, serial|
    // create an empty message
    var msg = "";
```

```
    // is there a color defined in the arguments?
    color = color? Color.black;

    // convert color to an array [r, g, b, a]
    color = color.asArray;

    // convert number of used orb into its corresponding ASCII character
    (determining colors)
    // convert light value [0..1] into a value between [000..255]
    // collect all values in the message
    (65 + #[0, 1, 2] + (which * 3)).collect{|val, i|
        val.asAscii ++ ((color[i]*255).asInt + 1000).asString[1..3]
    }.do{|elem|
        msg = msg ++ elem;
    };

// send it to the serial port
    serial.putAll(msg);
}
```

This function now allows one to set all the lights using 1 collect statement.

```
[Color.red, Color.yellow(0.4), Color.rand].collect{|color, which|
    a.value(which, color, serial)
}
```

Don't forget to close the device after using it.

```
~serial.close
```

4.2.4.2 Arduino

Arduino is one of a number of available physical computing devices which give the artist easy access to a programmable chip for interfacing analog and digital sensors such as ultrasound and infrared devices, accelerometers, custom circuits, and more. Quoting from the Arduino Web site:[11] "Arduino is an open-source electronics proto-typing platform based on flexible, easy-to-use hardware and software. It's intended for artists, designers, hobbyists, and anyone interested in creating interactive objects or environments."

The board connects to a host computer through a serial port, either a hardware RS232 port or a serial device emulated over a USB link. It contains an Atmel AT-mega CPU that can be programmed from the Arduino development environment using a superset of the C/C++ programming language, and features 14 digital (including pulse-width modulation and serial lines) and 6 analog (of 10-bit resolution each) in-/outputs. Code can be written, compiled, and uploaded to the board's flash memory, keeping development turnaround times short and easing experimentation.

Once programmed, the board can run in stand-alone mode, communicating with the outer world via its digital and analog ports, or it can communicate with other applications via its built-in serial port.

In SuperCollider, communication with the Arduino board is encapsulated in the `Arduino` class (available as a Quark). It provides an abstraction of the serial connection and allows for pluggable protocol parsers for reading from and writing to a program running on the board. You can use existing protocol handlers or write one for your own serial protocol by subclassing `Arduino` and `ArduinoParser`.

One prebuilt protocol is the *SimpleMessageSystem* (SMS), an Arduino extension that provides a simple ASCII-based means of data exchange. In order to experiment with SuperCollider and Arduino, first install the Arduino Quark from the central Quarks repository. It contains the SuperCollider classes and some simple Arduino projects. The class `ArduinoSMS` is an abstraction for device communication via SMS and is used just as its base class `Arduino` is. The constructor takes 2 arguments: a serial device identifier `portName` and the serial `baud rate`, which should match the one selected during Arduino's serial device initialization.

Open the project *SimpleMessageSystem_analog_read* in the Arduino development environment and upload the compiled program by pressing the board's *reset* button and the IDE's *upload* button in succession. The *RX/TX* will blink during the upload, and the Arduino IDE prints as message when the upload is done. Now connect to the Arduino board, using the correct serial device for your system and USB serial driver, and register a function to be executed when a message arrives from the board.

```
~arduino = ArduinoSMS("/dev/tty.usbserial-181", 115200);
~arduino.action = {| ... msg |(msg[1]/1024).postln };
```

Arduino's analog inputs allow for sensing real-world data in a resolution sufficient for many control applications, while the configurable digital ports can be used to connect to a wide variety of external hardware, including devices employing Philips's I²C bus.

See Also
Help files: SerialPort
Quarks: Arduino

4.2.5 Analog Audio Sensing

In many cases there's a very viable alternative to dedicated sensor boards and environments: use the unused analog inputs of your multichannel audio interface. The synthesis server *scsynth* provides a plethora of *Unit Generators* for massaging incoming sensor data according to the application's needs. Of particular interest are digital filters such as Median, LPF, HPF, and BPF; signal analysis UGens such as RunningSum and Slope; trigger-oriented UGens such as Trig, Latch, and Gate; and the whole spectrum of machine-listening plug-ins (see chapter 15).

As noted in chapter 2, SendTrig and SendReply are the main means of communicating triggers and signal values to the language, where they can be appropriately acted upon. Below is a small example of how one might process data from the first audio input, extract triggers in the time domain, and send the value to the language—a possible use case is triggering actions via piezoelectrical percussion pickups.

```
{
    var in = RunningSum.rms(SoundIn.ar([0, 1]).sum, 10),
        thresh = MouseX.kr(0, 2),  // variable threshold
        trig = in >thresh;                // define trigger
    SendTrig.ar(trig, 0, in);
}.play;

OSCresponder(s.addr, "/tr", {| ... args| args.postln}).add;
```

4.3   Using the Data

Since the input controls are disconnected from the acoustic output, the connection between them necessarily becomes a part of the compositional process. There are several approaches that can be taken toward this problem, and there is no definite best choice for every case.

Approaches could include the following:

1. Mapping of control parameters to sound synthesis parameters (instrumental or "micro" level) (Chadabe, 2002; Miranda and Wanderley, 2006)
2. Mapping of control parameters to algorithmic parameters (algorithmic or "meso" and "macro" levels) (Doornbusch, 2002)
3. Gesture recognition algorithms (Hunt and Kirk, 2000; Bevilacqua et al., 2007)
4. Dynamical systems
5. Artificial agent algorithms (Downie, 2005)

The exact approach you choose depends on what you try to create: if you are creating an interactive sound installation, you have to create a connection between input and sonic result that is easy to understand for a novice user, as well as engaging, so that it maintains interest even after the initial exploration. If you are creating a performance instrument, you may want to think about what certain gestures mean; gestures themselves may be made up of data arising from several inputs at once. If you are using sensor technology in dance, you may not want to force movement in a certain way to create a certain sound, but rather to let the sound evolve based upon the movements that occur.

You may need to scale your data or map it to a different range. The `ControlSpec` class can be useful for this. Your data may need to be massaged or filtered before they will be useful. We've noted some of the UGens that can be used to do this server-side in the section above on analog audio input. In the language you might try storing incoming data in Arrays and using methods such as `median` to limit the effect of stray values, or `maxItem` to get the highest value. The SenseWorld Quark also provides some useful techniques for massaging and filtering incoming data.

We recommend taking several development cycles, getting feedback from audience members or test users, and practicing with the interface you have created (including the mapping). Based on the results of this, you can more reliably determine what you might want to change. But at some point in a cycle you have to stop changing the instrument and start learning to play it, in order to achieve full control over it (training your muscle memory).

See Also
Help files: ControlSpec, Array, ArrayedCollection, SequenceableCollection
Quarks: SenseWorld

4.4   Conclusions

In this chapter we have reviewed several ways to get data in and out of Super-Collider, using the protocols OSC, serial, HID, and MIDI. We have suggested some directions in which to look for your own way to deal with the data. With all this in mind, the extensive programming capabilities within SuperCollider should enable you to realize your ideas.

Further examples are given in the SETO code on the Web site and in the Sense-World and TUIO Quarks.

References

Bevilacqua, F., F. Guédy, N. Schnell, E. Fléty, and N. Leroy. 2007. "Wireless Sensor Interface and Gesture-Follower for Music Pedagogy." In *Proceedings of the 2007 Conference on New Instruments for Musical Expression* (NIME-07), pp. 124–129. New York: ACM.

Chadabe, J. 2002. "The Limitations of Mapping as a Structural Descriptive in Electronic Musical Instruments." In *Proceedings of the 2002 Conference on New Instruments for Musical Expression* (NIME-02), pp. 1–5. Media Lab Europe, Dublin, Ireland.

Doornbusch, P. 2002. "Composers' Views on Mapping in Algorithmic Composition." *Organised Sound* 7(2): 145–156.

Downie, M. 2005. "Choreographing the Extended Agent: Performance Graphics for Dance Theater." Ph.D. thesis, Massachusetts Institute of Technology, Media Laboratory. Available from <http://hdl.handle.net/1721.1/33875>.

Hunt, A., and R. Kirk. 2000. "Mapping Strategies for Musical Performance." In M. M. Wanderley and M. Battier, eds., *Trends in Gestural Control of Music*. Paris: IRCAM. Available from <http://www.music.mcgill.ca/~mwanderley/Trends/Trends_in_Gestural_Control _of_Music>.

Miranda, E. R., and M. M. Wanderley. 2006. *New Digital Musical Instruments: Control and Interaction Beyond the Keyboard*. Middleton, WI: A-R Editions.

Puckette, M. 2007. *The Theory and Technique of Electronic Music:* Hackensack, NJ: World Scientific Publishing Co., Inc.

Reas, C., and B. Fry. 2007. *Processing: A Programming Handbook for Visual Designers and Artists*. Cambridge, MA: MIT Press.

Wright, M., A. Freed, and A. Momeni. 2003. "OpenSoundControl: State of the Art 2003." In *Proceedings of the 2003 International Conference on New Interfaces for Musical Expression* (NIME-03), pp. 153–159. McGill University, Montreal.

Zbyszynski, M., M. Wright, and A. Momeni. 2007. "Ten Years of Tablet Musical Interfaces." In *Proceedings of the 2007 International Conference on New Interfaces for Musical Expression* (NIME-07), pp. 100–105. New York University.

Notes

1. Processing: <http://processing.org>.

2. Puredata, a real-time graphical programming environment for audio, video, and graphical processing: <http://puredata.info>.

3. Sensorwiki: <http://www.sensorwiki.org>.

4. New Interfaces for Musical Expression (NIME): <http://www.nime.org>.

5. For Linux you may find details on setting up Wacom tablets at <http://linuxwacom .sourceforge.net>.

6. Wacom is a trademark of Wacom: <http://www.wacom.com>.

7. Wii is a trademark of Nintendo: <http://www.nintendo.com>.

8. MIDI: <http://www.midi.org>.

9. OpenSoundControl portal: <http://www.opensoundcontrol.org>.

10. Ambient Lights Web site: <http://LFSaw.de/hardware/ambient_lights.shtml.>

11. Arduino community Web site: <http://www.arduino.cc>.

Advanced Tutorials

5 Programming in SuperCollider

Iannis Zannos

5.1 Introduction

This chapter provides an introduction to the SuperCollider programming language from a more technical viewpoint than David Cottle's beginner's tutorial (chapter 1). Some material presented there and elsewhere in this book is also covered here, but in a more methodical and exhaustive manner. Although I try to convey programming skills without presupposing any previous knowledge of programming languages and compiler technology, some of the more advanced programming concepts in this chapter can take a little getting used to. The explanations provided here aim to be complete within the space allowed, but readers new to object-oriented programming may wish to seek out a good general introductory text to accompany their explorations (<http://en.wikipedia.org/wiki/Object-oriented_programming> isn't bad!). Musicians new to computer music may prefer to start earlier in the book and return here only once they have acquired some basic familiarity with the language; for experienced computer musicians new to SuperCollider, or experienced programmers new to audio, this chapter may be the preferred entry route. For everyone, it should provide a useful reference on the SuperCollider language.

Mechanisms underlying the interpretation and execution of programs and the programming concepts of SuperCollider will be explained. This will serve as a basis for understanding how to write and debug effectively in SuperCollider. We will consider the following questions:

What are the basic concepts underlying the writing and execution of programs?
What are the fundamental program elements in SuperCollider?
What are objects, messages, methods, and classes, and how do they work?
How are classes of objects defined?
What are the characteristic techniques of object-oriented programming, and how are they applied in SuperCollider?

SuperCollider employs syntactic elements from C, C++, Java, Smalltalk, and Matlab, creating a style that is both concise and easy to understand for programmers who know one of these common programming languages. A summary of the SuperCollider language syntax is given in the appendix of this book.

5.2   Fundamental Elements of Programs

5.2.1   Objects and Classes

The language of SuperCollider implements a powerful method for organizing code, data, and programs known as *object-oriented programming* (OOP). SuperCollider is a pure OOP language, which means that all entities inside a program are some kind of object. It also means that the way these entities are defined is uniform, as are the means for communicating with them.

5.2.1.1   Objects
Objects are the basic entities that are manipulated within programs. They bundle together data and methods that can act on that data (a musical scale object might store the pitches in the scale and a method to play back those pitches up and down as a sequence of notes in order). In the simplest case they might look like a single number or letter (a character), but they still respond to a number of methods for acting on themselves (return the negative of the current number, return the ASCII key code for the letter) or to more complex methods combining multiple objects of that type (add this number to another to make a third number, combine this letter with another to make a 2-letter word). In practice, there are 2 main types of objects, categorized according to how their internal contents are organized: objects with a fixed number of internal slots for storing data and objects with a variable number of slots. The generic term for the latter type of object is *collection*. Collections prove useful for handling big sets of data, such as a library of musical tunings or a mass of partial frequency, amplitude, and phase data for additive synthesis.

Some examples of objects include those shown in figure 5.1. You can see various different objects in the code listing, from simple numbers and letters to more abstract types that will be explained in more detail during the course of this chapter.

5.2.1.2   Classes
A *class* describes the attributes and behavior that are common to a group of objects. All objects belonging to a class are called *instances* of that class. For example, all integer numbers (e.g., 0, –1, and 50) are instances of class Integer. All integers are able to perform arithmetic operations on other numbers; therefore the class Integer describes—among other things—how integers perform arithmetic operations. In-

```
1                   // the Integer number 1
1.234               // the floating-point (Float) number 1.234
$a                  // the character (Char) a
"hello"             // a String (an array of characters)
\alpha              // a Symbol (a unique identifier)
'alpha 1'           // another notation for a Symbol
100@150             // a Point defined by coordinates x, y
[1, \A, $b]         // an Array containing 3 elements
(a: 1, b: 0.2)      // an Event
{ 10.rand }         // a Function
String              // the Class String
Meta_String         // the Class of Class String
```

Figure 5.1
Objects.

stances are created as literals (which act as primitives of the language, such as 1, –10, $a, \a; more on this below) with one of the shortcut constructor syntax forms (e.g., {}, (), a@b, a->b) or by sending a special message to a class that demands an instance. The most common message for creating instances is new, which can be omitted for brevity: Rect.new(10, 20, 30, 40) is equivalent to Rect(10, 20, 30, 40), and both create a rectangle with the specified numbers determining its size and position.

A class can inherit properties and behavior from another class, called its *super-class*. A class that inherits properties is a *subclass* of the class from which it inherits. The mechanism of inheritance is central in object-oriented programming for defining a hierarchical family tree of categories that relate to each other. This promotes sharing of common functionality while allowing the specialization of classes for particular tasks. (We'll return to this later.)

5.2.2   Literals

Literals are objects whose value is represented directly in the code (rather than computed as a result of sending a message to an object). Literals in SuperCollider are the following:

Integers (e.g., –10, 0, 123) and floating-point numbers (e.g., –0.1, 0.0, 123.4567), which can be in exponential notation (e.g., 1e4, 1.2e-4); alternative radices up to base 36 (e.g., binary for 13 is 2r1101, and the hexadecimal for 13 is 16rD); or combined with the constant pi (e.g., 2pi, –0.13pi).
Strings, enclosed in double quotes: "a string."
Symbols, enclosed in single quotes ('a symbol') or preceded by \:\a_Symbol.

Literal Arrays: immutable Arrays of literals declared by prepending the number sign #.

Classes: A class is represented by its name. Class names start with a capital letter.

Characters (instances of Char), a single character preceded by the dollar sign $ (e.g., $A, $a); non-printing characters (tab, linefeed, carriage return) and backslash are preceded by a backslash (e.g., $\n, $\t, $\\).

Variables and constants (see also the SuperCollider Help file on Literals and the appendix).

5.2.3 Messages and Methods

To interact with an object, one sends it a *message*. For example, to calculate the square of a number, one sends the message squared:

```
15.squared  // calculate and return the square of 15
```

The object to which a message is sent is called the *receiver*. In response to the message, the receiving object finds and runs the code that is stored in the *method* which has the same name as the message, then returns a result to the calling program, which is called the *return value*. In other words, a method is a function stored under a message name for an object that can be recalled by sending that object the message's name (see figure 5.2).

Instance methods operate on an instance (such as the integer 1), and *class methods* operate on a class. The most commonly used class method is New, which is used to create new instances from a class.

An alternative way of writing a message is in C-style or Java-style function-call form. The above example can also be written as follows:

```
squared(15)  // calculate and return the square of 15
```

SuperCollider often permits one to choose among different writing forms for expressing the same thing. It is up to the programmer to decide which form of an expression to use. Two main criteria that programmers take into account are readability and conciseness.

5.2.3.1 Chaining messages

It is possible to write several messages in a row, separated by dots (.), like the one below:

```
Server.local.boot  // boot the local server
```

Or this:

```
Server.local.quit  // quit the local server
```

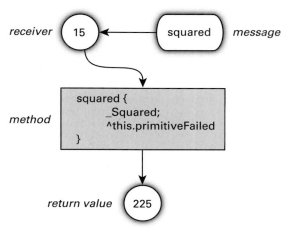

Figure 5.2
Receiver, message, method, return value.

When "chaining" messages, each message is sent to the object returned by the previous message (the previous return value). In the examples above, Server is the class from which all servers are made. Among other things, it holds by default 2 commonly used servers, the *local server* and the *internal server*, which can be obtained by sending it the messages local and internal, respectively. The objects and actions involved are the following:

```
Server // the class Server
// message local sent to Server returns the local server: localhost
Server.local
Server.local.boot     // the message boot is sent to the local server
```

5.2.3.2   Performing messages

In some cases, the message to be sent to an object may change, depending on other conditions. When the message is not known in advance, the messages perform and performList are used, which allow an object to perform a message passed as an argument:

```
Server.local.perform(\boot)          // boot the local server
// boot or quit the local server with 50% probability of either:
Server.local.perform([\boot, \quit].choose)
```

performList permits one to pass additional arguments to the message in Array form. Thus Rect.performList(\new, [0, 10, 200, 20]) is equivalent to Rect.new(0, 10, 200, 20). (See also the example in section 5.4.5.)

5.2.4   Arguments

The operation of a message often requires the interaction of several objects. For example, raising a number to some power involves 2 numbers: the base and the exponent. Such additional objects required by an operation are sent to the receiver as *arguments* accompanying the message. Arguments are enclosed in parentheses after the message:

```
5.pow(8)     // calculate the 8th power of 5
```

If several arguments are involved, they are separated by commas:

```
// construct an Array of 5 elements starting at 10 and incrementing by 10
Array.series(5, 10, 10)
```

The same is true in the "function-call" format:

```
series(Array, 5, 10, 10)
```

If the arguments are provided as 1 collection containing several objects, they can be separated into individual values by prepending the * sign to the collection:

```
Array.rand(*[5, -10, 10])
```

is equivalent to

```
Array.rand(5, -10, 10)
```

This can be useful when one wants to provide arguments as a collection that was created in some other part of the program. The next example shows how to construct an Array of random size between 3 and 10 with elements whose values have a random range with 3 as the lowest, and 10 as the highest, possible value.

```
Array.rand(*Array.rand(3, 3, 10))
```

When the only argument to a message is a function, the parentheses can be omitted:

```
10.do {10.rand.postln}//function as sole argument to a message
```

5.2.4.1   Argument forms for implied messages **at** and **put**

When square brackets are appended to an object, they imply the message at or put (this follows the C or Java syntax for Array indexing). Thus [1, 5, 12][1] is equivalent to [1, 5, 12].at(1), and ()[\a] = pi is equivalent to ().put(\a, pi).

5.2.4.2   Argument keywords

When calling a function, argument values must be provided in the order in which the arguments were defined (see section 5.4.4.1). However, when only a few out of many

```
// Boot the default server first:
Server.default.boot;
// Then select all lines between the outermost parentheses and run:
(
{
    Resonz.ar(GrayNoise.ar,
        XLine.kr(100, 1000, 10, doneAction: 2),
        XLine.kr(0.5, 0.01, [4, 7], doneAction: 0)
    )
}.play
)
// further examples:
{ WhiteNoise.ar(EnvGen.kr(Env.perc, timeScale: 3,
doneAction: 2)) }.play;
{ WhiteNoise.ar(EnvGen.kr(Env.perc, timeScale: 0.3,
doneAction: 2))}.play;
```

Figure 5.3
Keyword arguments.

arguments of a function need to be provided, one can specify those arguments by name in "keyword" form; for instance, if the name of the argument provided is freq, the call is foo.value(freq: 400). And the kr method for XLine takes the arguments start, end, dur, mul, add, and doneAction. To provide values only for start, end, dur, and doneAction, write (for example): XLine.kr(100, 100, 10, doneAction: 2). As a result, start, end, and dur get the values 100, 1000, and 10, respectively; doneAction gets the value 2; and mul and add rely on their default values 1 and 0, respectively. (See figure 5.3.)

5.2.5   Binary Operators

SuperCollider uses signs from mathematics, logic, and other programming languages, such as + (addition), – (subtraction), and & (binary "and"). These are called binary operators because they operate on 2 objects. For example, ++ joins 2 SequenceableCollections: [\a, \b] ++ [1, 2, 3].

Furthermore, any message that requires just 1 argument can be written as a binary operator by adding : to the name of the message. Thus, 5.pow(8) can also be written as 5 pow: 8. With this and other syntax shortcuts included in this chapter, there may seem to be a bewildering variety of alternatives available. SuperCollider supports a few different common programming syntaxes, but in vanilla SC, the 'dot' notation would be most common, and with practice you can pick up additional syntax as you

```
((1 + 2).asString).interpret            // = 3
"1" ++ "2". interpret                   // 12: 2 is translated to string by ++
("1" ++ "2").interpret                  // 12
(1.asString ++ 2.asString).interpret    // 12
"1+2". interpret                        // 3
(1.asString ++ "+2"). interpret         // 3
(1 + 2).interpret                       // error: interpret not understood by
Integer 3
```

Figure 5.4
Grouping and Precedence.

code and gain experience. Further details are available in the Syntax Shortcuts Help file.

5.2.6 Precedence Rules and Grouping

When one combines several operations in 1 expression, the final result may depend on the order in which those operations are executed. Compare, for example, the expression 1 + (2 * 3), whose value is 7, with the expression (1 + 2) * 3, whose value is 9. The order in which operations are executed is determined by the precedence of operators. The precedence rules in SuperCollider are simple but differ somewhat from those used in mathematics:

Binary operators are evaluated in strict left-to-right order. Thus the expression 1 + 2 * 3 is equivalent to (1 + 2) * 3 and not to 1 + (2 * 3).

Message passing, as in receiver.message(arguments) or in collection[index], has precedence over binary operators. Thus, in 10 * (1..3).addAll([0.1, 0.2, 0.3]) the elements of [0.1, 0.2, 0.3] are first appended to [1, 2, 3], and then the resulting new Array is multiplied by 10.

To override the order of precedence, one uses parentheses (). For example:

```
1 + 2 * 3 // Left-to-right order of operator evaluation. Result: 9.
1 + (2 * 3) // Forced the evaluation of * before that of +. Result: 7.
```

Figure 5.4 illustrates the effects of grouping by parentheses and message passing.

5.2.7 Statements

The single-line code examples introduced above normally constitute parts of larger programs that include many lines of code. The smallest stand-alone elements of code

```
(
a = 5;
5 do: { a = a + 10; a.postln };
Post << "The value of variable 'a' is now " << a << "\n";
)
```

Figure 5.5
Statements.

are called *statements*.[1] One creates programs by grouping sequences of statements. When a program contains more than 1 statement, the individual statements are separated by a semicolon. The last statement at the end of a program does not need to have a semicolon, since there are no more statements to separate it from. Figure 5.5 contains 3 statements.

The first statement (a = 5;) assigns the value 5 to variable a. The second statement (5 do: {a = a + 10; a.postln};) repeats a function 5 times that assigns to a its previous value incremented by 10, and posts the new value of a each time. The third statement (Post << "The value of variable 'a' is now "<< a << "\n";) posts the new value of a.

It is important to distinguish between the lines of code text in a Document window as seen by a human programmer, and the part of the code that SuperCollider processes as program when the programmer runs a selected portion of that code. SuperCollider does not run the whole code in the window, but only the code that was selected; or, if no code is selected, the line on which the cursor is currently located. Every time that one runs a piece of code, SuperCollider creates and runs a new program that contains only the selected code. Code that is meant to be run as a whole is usually indicated by enclosing it in parentheses. This is useful because one can select it easily, typically by double clicking to the right of an opening parenthesis.

5.3   Variables

A variable is used to store an object that will be used in other parts of a program. One way to visualize variables is as containers with labels. The name of the variable is the label pointing to the container. (See figure 5.6.)

One creates variables by declaring them with the prefix var. Several variables can be declared in one var statement. Variables may be declared only at the beginning of a function (or a selected block of code, which is essentially the same thing; see section 5.4.3).

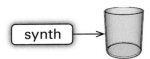

Figure 5.6
Variable as a label pointing to a container.

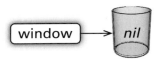

Figure 5.7
`nil` stands for the contents of an empty variable.

```
var window; // create a variable named 'window'
// rest of program follows here
```

When a variable is first created, it is empty, so its value is represented by the object nil, which is the object for no value. (See figure 5.7.)

```
(
var window; // create a variable named 'window'
window.postln;    // post the contents of variable 'window' (nil)
)
```

One cannot run the lines of a program that use a declared variable separately; one must always run the code as a whole. This is because the variables declared in the beginning of a function disappear from memory as soon as the function that declared them finishes, unless other functions within that function also use them. In figure 5.7, running the line `window.postln;` alone produces the error message `Variable 'window' not defined`.

To store an object in a variable, use the assignment sign =. For example, after storing a Window in the variable window, one can send it messages to change its state, as well as use it as an argument to other objects. (See figure 5.8.)

In the above example, the variable window was indispensable to specify which window the button was going to appear in.

5.3.1 Variable Initialization

The assignment sign (=) can be used in a declaration statement to initialize the value of a variable.

```
(
// A window with a button that posts: "hello there!"
var window, button;
// create a GUI window and store it in variable window
window = Window.new("OLA!", Rect(200, 200, 120, 120));
// create a button in the window and store it in variable button
button = Button.new(window, Rect(10, 10, 100, 100));
button.states = [["'ALLO"]];     // set one single label for the button
button.action = { "hello there!".postln }; // set the action of the button
window.front;          // show the window
)
```

Figure 5.8
Variables can store objects that need to be used many times.

```
(
var bounds = Rect(10, 20, 30, 50), x = 100, y = 200;
bounds.width.postln;// post the width of a rectangle
bounds.moveTo(x, y);    // move the rectangle to a new position
)
```

5.3.2   Use of Variables

The object stored in a variable remains there until a new assignment statement replaces it with something else. Variables also are often used as temporary placeholders to operate on a changing choice from a set of objects. Figure 5.9 is an example that makes extensive use of variables to create a chain of upward- and downward-moving runs of short tones.

5.3.3   Instance Variables

An instance variable is a variable that is contained in a single object. Such a variable is accessible only inside instance methods of that object—unless special code is written to make it accessible to other objects. For example, objects of class Point have 2 instance variables, x and y, corresponding to the coordinates of a point in 2-dimensional space. (See figure 5.10.)

```
(
var point = Point(0, pi);
point.x.postln; point.y.postln; point.y == pi;
)
```

```
(
// execute this first to boot the server and load the synth definition
Server.default.waitForBoot({
    SynthDef("ping", { | freq = 440 |
        Out.ar(0,
            SinOsc.ar([freq, freq * (4/3)], 0,
                EnvGen.kr(Env.perc(0.05, 0.3, 0.1, -4), doneAction: 2)
            )
        )
    }).add
});
)


(
// execute this next to create the sounds
var countdown = 100;
var note = 50;
var increment_func, decrement_func;
var action;
increment_func = {
    note = note + [2, 5, 7, 12].choose;
    if (note > 100) { action = decrement_func };
};
decrement_func = {
    note = note - [1, 2, 5, 7, 12].choose;
    if (note < 50) { action = increment_func };
};
action = increment_func;
{
    countdown do: {
        Synth("ping", [\freq, note.midicps]);
        action.value;
        0.1.wait;
    }
}.fork;
)
```

Figure 5.9
Variables can point to different objects during a process.

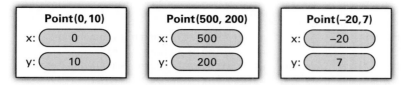

Figure 5.10
Three instances of `Point` with their instance variables.

5.3.4   Class Variables

A class variable is defined once for the class it belongs to and is shared with all its subclasses. It is accessible to class methods and to instance methods of its class and all its subclasses. For example, the class variable `all` of OSCresponder holds all currently active instances of OSCresponder. The instance method add of OSCresponder adds a responder instance to the class variable `all`, and the method remove removes a responder from `all`. In that way the system keeps track of all responders that are active, and checks every OSC message received to see if it matches any of the responders contained in `all`. One can write `OSC.all  do:  _.remove` to remove all currently active OSCresponders.

5.3.5   Environment Variables

Environment variables are preceded by a tilde (~). For example, ~a = pi. These reference the value of a named variable in the current Environment, a special holding place for data. They do not need to be declared, but are instantly added to the Environment when assigned. An Environment is a kind of Dictionary that represents the set of bindings of values to names; that is, the Environment variables. These bindings differ from those created by normal variable declarations in that they have a less limited scope (though not truly "global" variables in the traditional sense, they can sometimes be treated as such), and they can be modified more easily (see section 5.6.7 for more details).

The relationship between Environment variables and the Environment that contains them can be seen by printing the current Environment. (See figure 5.11.)

5.3.6   Variables with Special Uses

The variables described in this section provide access to objects that are useful or indispensable, but either cannot be accessed by conventional programming within the SuperCollider class system or need to be accessed by all objects in the system.

```
// run each line separately:
currentEnvironment; // empty if no environment variables have been set
~alpha = pi;            // set env. variable ~alpha to pi
currentEnvironment; // see current Environment again: ~alpha is set
~freq = 800;            // set another environment variable
Server.local.boot;
{ LFNoise0.ar(~freq, 0.1) }.play; // use an environment variable
// setting an environment variable to nil is equivalent to removing it:
~alpha = nil;
currentEnvironment; // alpha is no longer set
```

Figure 5.11
currentEnvironment.

5.3.6.1 Interpreter variables
The class Interpreter defines 26 instance variables whose names correspond to the lowercase letters a to z. Since all code evaluated at runtime is run by an instance of Interpreter, these variables are accessible within that code without having to be declared. However, this works only when evaluating code from outside of class definitions, that is, with code selected to be run by the Interpreter. The following example can be executed one line at a time (first boot the default server with Server.default .boot).

```
n = {| freq = 400| LFDNoise1.ar(freq, 0.1)}.play; // store a synth in n
n.set(\freq, 1000);   // set the freq parameter of the synth to 1000
n.free;       // free the synth (stop its sound)
```

5.3.6.2 Pseudo variables
Pseudo variables are not declared anywhere in the SuperCollider library but are provided by the compiler. They are the following:

this represents the object that is running the current method. In runtime code this is always the current instance of Interpreter (see also section 5.4.3.1). Thus one can run this.dump to view the contents of the current Interpreter instance, including the variables a–z.
thisProcess is the process that is running the current code. It is always an instance of Main. Although rarely used, some possible applications are to send the current instance of Main messages that affect the entire system, such as thisProcess.stop (stop all sounds), or to access the Interpreter variables from any part of the system (thisProcess.interpreter.a accesses the Interpreter variable a).

thisMethod is the method within which the current statement is running. One can use this in debug messages to print the name of the method where some code is being checked. For example, [this, this.class, thisMethod.name].postln.

thisFunction is the innermost function within which the current statement is running. It is indispensable for recursion in functions (see section 5.4.9).

thisFunctionDef is the definition of the innermost function within which the current statement is running. The function definition contains information about the names and default values of arguments and variables. Section 5.4.10 briefly discusses its uses.

thisThread is the thread running the current code. A thread is a sequence of execution that can run in parallel with other threads and can control the timing of the execution of individual statements in the program. Examples of the use of thisThread are found in the classes Pstep and Pseg, where it is employed to control the timing of the thread.

One special case: The keyword super redirects the message sent to it to look for a method belonging to the superclass of the object in which the method of the current code is running. This is not a variable at all, because one cannot access its value but can only send it a message. super is used to extend a method in a subclass. For example. the class method new of Pseq extends the method new of its superclass ListPattern, which in turn extends the method new of Object. This means Pseq's new calls super.new—thereby calling method new of ListPattern—but adds some statements of its own. In turn, ListPattern also calls super.new—thereby calling method new of Object to create a new instance of ListPattern—but again adds some stuff of its own.

5.3.6.3   Class variables of Object

The following variables are class variables of class Object. Since all objects are instances of some subclass of Object, they have access to these variables, and thus these variables are automatically accessible everywhere.

currentEnvironment is the Environment being used right now by the running program. This can be changed by the programmer.

topEnvironment is the original currentEnvironment of the Interpreter instance that runs programs in the system. It can be accessed independently of currentEnvironment, which changes in response to Environment's use or make methods. (See figure 5.12)

uniqueMethods holds a dictionary that stores unique methods of objects. Unique methods are methods that are defined not in a class but only in a single instance. For example:

```
(
~q = "TOP";                              // store "TOP" in ~a, top environment
(a: "INNER") use: { // run function in environment with ~a = "INNER"
    currentEnvironment.postln; // show the current environment
    topEnvironment.postln;       // show the top environment (different!)
    ~a.postln                    // show ~a's value in current environment
};
~a;                              // show ~a's value in top environment
)
```

Figure 5.12
topEnvironment versus currentEnvironment.

```
(
// create 2 windows and store them in variables p, q
#p, q = [100, 400].collect {|i|
    Window(i.asString, Rect(i, i, 200, 200)).front
}
)
// add a unique method to p only
p.addUniqueMethod(\greet, {|w| w.name = "Hello!"});
p.greet;    // p understands 'greet'
q.greet;    // but q does not understand 'greet'
```

dependantsDictionary holds a dictionary that stores *dependants* of objects. A dependant of an Object o is any object that needs to be notified when o changes in some way. To notify the dependants of an object that the object has changed, one sends the message changed. Details of this technique are explained in section 5.7.7.

5.3.7 Variables versus References

A variable is a container with which one can do only 2 things: store an object and retrieve that object. One cannot store the container itself in another container, so it is not possible to store a variable x *itself* in another variable y. As the following example shows, what is stored is the *content* of variable x. When the content of variable x is changed, the previous content still remains in variable y. (See figures 5.13 and 5.14.)

To store a container in a variable, one uses a reference object.

```
var aref, cvar;
aref = Ref.new; // first create the reference and store it in aref
cvar = aref;  // then store the contents of aref in cvar
```

```
(
var alpha, beta, gamma;
gamma = alpha;   // storing variable alpha in gamma only stores nil
alpha = 10;      // store 10 in alpha ...
gamma.postln;    // but the value of gamma remains unchanged
alpha = beta;    // so one cannot use gamma as 'joker'
beta = 20;       // to switch between variables alpha and beta.
gamma.postln;    // gamma is still nil.
)
```

Figure 5.13
Variables store only values, not other variables.

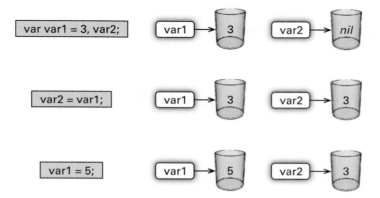

Figure 5.14
Assigning a variable to another variable stores its contents only.

```
aref.value = 10;     // change the value of the reference in aref
cvar.value.postln;   // and retrieve that value from cvar
```

5.4   Functions

A function is an object representing a bit of code that can be evaluated from other code at runtime. In this sense it is like a miniature program. One can "package" a code that does something useful inside a function and then run that function wherever one wants to do that thing, instead of writing out the same code in different places. The code that creates a function is called the *definition* of the function. When a program runs a function, it is said to *call* or *evaluate* that function.

To "package" a code into a function, one encloses it in braces {}.

```
{1 + 1} // a function that adds 1 to 1
```

This creates a function object or, in other words, *defines* a function. To run the function, one sends it the message value:

```
{1 + 1}.value // evaluate {1 + 1}
```

This is called function evaluation.

5.4.1   Return Value versus Side Effect

The use of the term "evaluate" here comes from the idea of requesting a value that is computed and returned by the function for further use. The return value of a function is the value of the last statement that is computed in the function. However, in many cases one calls a function not to obtain a final value but to start a process that will result in some change, such as to create sounds or to show graphics on the screen. For example, {10.rand} provides a random number between 0 and 9 as a return value, and {Window.allWindows do: _.close} closes all GUI windows. It is the effect of the latter, rather than the return value, that matters.

This is also true for methods. In the example presented in section 5.2.3.1, Server .local.boot, the message local is sent to class Server to obtain the object representing the local server as a return value, whereas the message boot is sent to the local server in order to boot it. In the first case (message local) it is the return value of the operation that is of further use, while in the second case (message boot) it is the effect of the boot operation that matters.

5.4.2   Functions as Program Modules

Since functions are objects that can be stored in variables, it is easy to define and store any number of functions (i.e., miniature programs) and run them, whenever required, any number of times. Thus, defining functions and configuring their combinations can be a major part of programming in SuperCollider.

Figure 5.15 illustrates how to call a function that has been stored in a variable in various ways. The function change_freq in the example does 2 things:

It calculates a new frequency for the sound by moving 1 minor tone upward or downward from the previous pitch.
It sets the frequency of the sound to the new pitch.

The code of the function consists of 2 statements:

```
Server.default.boot;          // (boot Server before running example)
(
// Define a function and call it in different contexts
var synth;                    // Synth creating the sound that is changed
var freq = 220;               // frequency of the sound
var change_freq;              // function that changes the frequency of the sound
var window;                   // window holding buttons for changing the sound
var button1, button2, button3; // buttons changing the sound

// Create a synth that plays the sound to be controlled:
synth = { | freq = 220 | LFTri.ar([freq, freq * 2.01], 0, 0.1) }.play;
// Create frequency changing function and store it in variable change_freq
change_freq = {                                      // start of function definition
        freq = freq * [0.9, 0.9.reciprocal].choose; // change freq value
        synth.set(\freq, freq);                      // set synth's frequency to new
value
};                                                   // end of function definition

// Create 3 buttons that call the example function in various ways
window = Window("Buttons Archaic", Rect(400, 400, 340, 120));
// ----------------------- Example 1 -----------------------
button1 = Button(window, Rect(10, 10, 100, 100));
button1.states = [["I"]]; // set the label of button1
// button1 calls the function each time that it is pressed
button1.action = change_freq;    // make button1 change freq once
// ----------------------- Example 2 -----------------------
button2 = Button(window, Rect(120, 10, 100, 100));
button2.states = [["III"]];
// Button2 creates a routine that calls the example function 3 times
button2.action = {            // make button2 change freq 3 times
    { 3 do: { change_freq.value; 0.4.wait } }.fork; // play as routine
};
// ----------------------- Example 3 -----------------------
button3 = Button(window, Rect(230, 10, 100, 100));
button3.states = [["VIII"]];
button3.action = {            // like example 2, but 8 times
    { 8 do: { change_freq.value; 0.1.wait } }.fork; // play as routine
};
// use large size font for all buttons:
[button1, button2, button3] do: _.font_(Font("Times", 32));
// stop the sound when the window closes:
window.onClose = { synth.free };
window.front; // show the window
)
```

Figure 5.15
Multiple use of a function stored in a variable.

```
{
    freq = freq * [0.9, 0.9.reciprocal].choose; // change freq value
    synth.set(\freq, freq);         // set synth's frequency to new value
}
```

This function is stored in the variable change_freq and then called in 2 different ways:

It is stored in the action part of a GUI button so that when that button is pressed, it runs the function.
It is called explicitly by a function inside a Routine that sends it the message value. (As noted in chapter 3, Routine has the ability to time the execution of its statements, and therefore can run the function in question at timed intervals.)

5.4.3   Compilation and Evaluation: The Details

SuperCollider undergoes a 3-step process every time that it executes code entered in a work space window: First, it *compiles* the code of the program and creates a function that can be evaluated. Second, SuperCollider *evaluates* that function. Finally, SuperCollider prints out the result of the evaluation in the *post* window.

Figure 5.16 shows what happens when one runs the code 3 + 5. The equivalent of the entire compilation plus evaluation process can be expressed by the code "3 + 5". interpret.

5.4.3.1   Who does the compiling?
In SuperCollider, even the top-level processes of interaction with the user are defined in terms of objects inside the system. An easy way to see what happens is to cause an error and look at the error message. For example, evaluate: 1.error. The bottom line shows the beginning of the compilation process.

```
Process:interpretPrintCmdLine   14A562F0
    arg this = <instance of Main>
```

Immediately above that is the next method call:

```
Interpreter:interpretPrintCmdLine   15055D00
    arg this = <instance of Interpreter>
```

This shows that the top-level object responsible for compiling and interpreting text input is an instance of class Main, and that it delegates the interpretation to an instance of Interpreter, calling the method interpretPrintCmdLine.

5.4.3.2   Byte code: Looking at the compiled form of a function
The compilation process consists in successively replacing the SuperCollider code of the program with pieces of byte code and data in the computer's memory. The

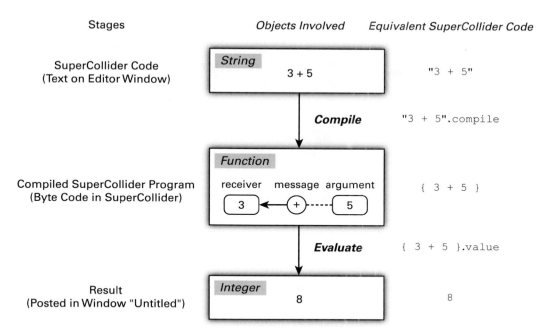

Figure 5.16
Compiling and Evaluating Code.

compiler's task is first to parse (i.e., understand the program structure contained in the code) and then to translate that exact structure—including data and instructions—into byte code. To display the actual byte code of a compiled SuperCollider program, one sends the definition of the function representing the program the message dumpByteCodes. To obtain the definition of the function, one sends it the message def. Thus, to display the byte code of the above example $3 + 5$, evaluate this line:

```
{3 + 5}.def.dumpByteCodes
```

This first sends the message def to the function to obtain its definition, and then the message dumpByteCodes to the definition, to print out the byte code. Figure 5.17 explains the resulting printout.

5.4.4   Functions with Arguments

Functions can have inputs for receiving data from the context that calls them. The inputs, if any, are defined at the beginning of the function, before any variables, and

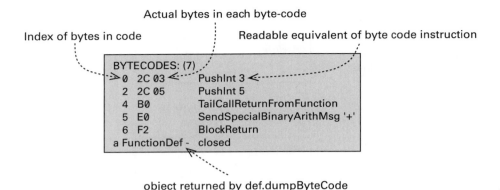

Figure 5.17
Bytecode of Function { 3 + 5 }.

are called *arguments*. Arguments are variables of a function whose values can be set by the program that calls it. When a function needs to be evaluated with different sets of data each time, it defines as many arguments as there are data items required. The program can then give data to a function by appending them as arguments in the value message. Here is how to define and call a function that computes and returns the sum of 2 numbers, a and b:

```
(
var sum2; // define variable to store the function;
// define the function and store it in variable sum2:
sum2 = {arg a, b;      // start of function definition, arguments a, b
    // the body of the function (the program) is here
    a + b     // compute and return the function of a and b
};              // end of function definition
// call the function, giving it the numbers 2 and 3as arguments:
sum2.value(2, 3);      // the returned value is 5
)
```

See the Functions Help file for a depiction of the metaphorical "inputs" and "output" of a function.

5.4.4.1 Defining arguments

In SuperCollider, arguments are defined by prepending the declaration keyword arg or by enclosing them in vertical bars | |. (See figure 5.18.)

Three dots (. . . argName) before the final (or only) argument name in the argument list can be used to collect any number of provided arguments into 1 array passed as a single argument to the function. (See figure 5.19.)

```
(
// a function that calculates the square of the mean of two numbers
var sq_mean;
sq_mean = { arg a, b;   // arguments a, b defined in arg statement form
    (a + b / 2).squared;
};
// calculate the square of the mean of 3 and 1:
sq_mean.value(3, 1);
)
```

Figure 5.18
Simple function with arguments.

```
(
// a function that calculates the square of the mean of any numbers
var sq_mean_all;
sq_mean_all = { | ... numbers | // using ellipsis and | | argument form
    (numbers.sum / numbers.size).squared;
};
// calculate the square of the mean of [1, 3, 5, -7]:
sq_mean_all.(1, 3, 5, -7); // short form: omit message 'value'
)
```

Figure 5.19
Using ... for undefined number of arguments.

5.4.4.2   Default argument values

The default values of arguments can be included in argument definitions, in the same manner as variables. A default value is used only if no value was provided for the argument when the function was called. (See figure 5.20.)

Since functions are objects in SuperCollider—or, more exactly, *"first-class objects"*[2]—their behavior can easily be extended to include other things besides running them with the message value. The following sections describe common ways of using functions.

5.4.5   Customizing the Behavior of Objects with Functions

Several classes of objects that deal with user interface, or with interactive features that should be easily set by the programmer, store functions in variables. Such

```
(
var w_func;
w_func = { arg message = "warning!", bounds = Rect(200, 500, 500, 100);
    var window;
    window = Window("message window", bounds).front;
    TextView(window, window.view.bounds.insetBy(10, 10))
        .string = message;
};
 // provide text, use default bounds
w_func.(String.new.addAll(Array.new.addAll(" Major news! ").pyramid(7)));
)
```

Figure 5.20
Using and overriding default values of arguments.

```
(
var window, button;
window = Window("Server Button", Rect(400, 400, 200, 200));
button = Button(window, Rect(5, 5, 190, 190));
button.states = [["boot!"], ["quit!"]];
button.action = { |me| Server.default perform: [\quit, \boot][me.value] };
window.front;
)
```

Figure 5.21
Performing messages chosen by index.

functions in variables define how an object should react to certain messages. For example, buttons or other GUI widgets use the variable action to store the function that should be called when the user activates the widget by a mouse click.

Example 1. The action of the button chooses between 2 messages to perform on the default Server, depending on the value (state) of the button. (See figure 5.21.) Example 2. The action chooses between 2 functions, depending on the state of the button. (See figure 5.22.)

5.4.6 Functions as Arguments in Messages for Asynchronous Communication

Asynchronous communication happens when a program requests an action from the system but cannot determine when that action will be completed. For example, it

```
(
var window, button;
window = Window("Server Button", Rect(400, 400, 200, 200));
button = Button(window, Rect(5, 5, 190, 190));
button.states = [["boot"], ["quit"]];
button.action = { | me |
    [{ "QUITTING THE DEFAULT SERVER".postln;
        Server.default.quit;
    },{ "BOOTING THE DEFAULT SERVER".postln;
        Server.default.boot;
    }][me.value].value;
};
window.front;
)
```

Figure 5.22
Evaluating functions chosen by index.

may ask for a file to be loaded or to be printed, but the time required for this to finish is unknown. In such a situation, it would be disruptive to pause the execution of the program while waiting for the action to complete. Instead, the program delegates the processing of the answer expected from the action to an independent process—represented by a function—that waits in the background. Two common cases are the following.

5.4.6.1   Asynchronous communication with a Server

The system asks for an action to happen on a server, for example, to load a sound file into a buffer (Buffer.read). Since the time it will take the server to load the file is not known in advance, a function is given to read as argument, which is executed when the server completes loading the buffer. Figure 5.23 demonstrates that the action passed as an argument to the read method is executed *after* the statement following Buffer.read.

5.4.6.2   Dialogue windows

Dialogue windows that demand input from the user employ an action argument to determine what to do when input is provided. This prevents the system from waiting indefinitely for the user. (Boot the server first with Server.default.boot.)

```
(
Buffer.loadDialog(action: {|buffer|
    format("loaded % at: %", buffer, Main.elapsedTime).postln;
```

```
Server.default.boot // boot default server before running example
(
var buffer;
buffer = Buffer.read(path: "sounds/a11wlk01.wav",
    action: { | buffer |
        format("loaded % at: %", buffer, Main.elapsedTime).postln;
    });
format("Reached this after 'Buffer.read' at: %", Main.elapsedTime).postln;
buffer;
)
```

Figure 5.23
Asynchronous communication with the server.

```
});
format("continuing at: %", Main.elapsedTime).postln;
)
```

5.4.7   Iterating Functions

Iteration is the technique of repeating the same function a number of times. It may be run for a prescribed number of times (anInteger.do(aFunction)), an unlimited number of times (loop(aFunction)) while a certain condition is true (while), or over the elements of a Collection (see section 5.6.3).

5.4.7.1   Iterating a specified number of times

```
do: Iterate n number of times, pass the count as argument:
10 do: {|i| [i, i.squared, i.isPrime].postln}
!: Iterate n number of times, pass the count as argument, collect results
in an Array:
{10.rand * 3}!5
for: Iterate between a minimum and a maximum integer value:
30.for(35, {|i| i.postln});
forBy: Iterate between 2 values, using a definable step:
2.0.forBy(10, 1.5, {|i| i.postln})
```

5.4.7.2   Iterating while a condition is true

The message while will repeatedly evaluate a function as long as a test function returns true: {[true, false].choose}.while({"was true".postln;}). It is usually coded like this:

```
Server.default.boot;   // do this first
(                              // then the rest of the program
var window, routine;
window = Window("close me to stop").front;
window.onClose = { routine.stop };
routine = {
    loop {
        (degree: -10 + 30.xrand, dur: 0.05, amp: 0.1.rand).play;
        0.05.rand.wait;
    }
}.fork;
)
```

Figure 5.24
loop.

```
(
var sum = 0;
while {sum = sum + exprand(0.1, 3); sum <10} {sum.postln}
)
```

5.4.7.3   Infinite (indefinite) loop

loop repeats a function until the process that contains the loop statement is stopped. It can be used only within a process that stops or pauses between statements; otherwise, it will hang the system with an infinite loop. (See figure 5.24.)

5.4.8   Partial Application: Shortcut Syntax for Small Functions

It is possible to construct functions that apply arguments to a single message call by using the underscore character _ as a placeholder for an argument. For example, instead of writing {arg x; x.isPrime}, one can write _.isPrime. If more than 1 _ is included, then each _ takes the place of a subsequent argument in the function. Examples are shown in figure 5.25.

5.4.9   Recursion

Recursion is a special form of iteration in which a function calls itself from inside its own code. To do this, the function refers to itself via the pseudo variable thisFunction. (A pseudo variable is a variable that is created and set by the system, and is not declared anywhere in the SuperCollider class library. See section 5.3.6.2.) The value of thisFunction is always the function inside which thisFunction is accessed. Figures

```
_.isPrime ! 10
_.squared ! 10
_@_.(30, 40) // equivalent to: { | a, b | Point(a, b) }.value(30, 40)
Array.rand(12, 0, 1000).clump(4) collect: Rect(*_)
(1..8).collect([\a, \b, _]);
(a: _, b: _, c: _, d: _, e: _).(*Array.rand(5, 0, 100));
```

Figure 5.25
Partial application.

```
(
var iterative_factorial;
iterative_factorial = { | n |
    var factorial = 1;  // initialize factorial as factorial of 1
    // calculate factorial n times, updating its value each time
    n do: { | i | factorial = factorial * (i + 1) };
    factorial;  // return the final value of factorial;
};
iterative_factorial.(10).postln;    // 10 factorial: 3628800
)
```

Figure 5.26
Iterative factorial.

5.26 and 5.27 show the difference in implementing the algorithm for computing the factorial of a number iteratively and using recursion. The recursive algorithm is shorter.

Conciseness is not the only reason for using recursion. There are cases when only a recursive algorithm can be used. Such cases occur when one does not know in advance the structure and size of the data to be explored by the algorithm. An example is shown in figure 5.28.

5.4.10   Inspecting the Structure of a Function

A particular feature of functions is the ability to access a function's parts, which define its structure. An example is the following:

```
var foo;
foo = {|a = 1, b = 2| a.pow(b)};
foo.def.sourceCode.postln; // print sourceCode
```

```
// Define the factorial function and store it in variable f:
f = { | x | if ( x > 1) { x * thisFunction.value(x - 1) } { x } };
 f.value(10);              // 10 factorial: 3628800
```

Figure 5.27
Recursive factorial.

```
(
/* a function that recursively prints all folders and files
   found in a path and its subfolders */
{ | path |
    // store function here for use inside the if's {}:
    var thisFunc = thisFunction;
    format("====== now exploring: %", path).postln;
    // for all items in the path:
    path.pathMatch do: { | p |
        // if the item is a folder, run this function on its contents
        // otherwise print the file found
        if (p.last == $/) { thisFunc.(p ++ "*") }{ p.postln }
    }
}.("*") // run function on home path of SuperCollider
)
```

Figure 5.28
Recursion over a tree of unknown structure.

The source code of a function is stored only if that function is *closed*, that is, if it does not access the variables of an enclosing function. A function's def variable contains a FunctionDef object that also contains the names of the arguments and variables of the function and their default values. These are used by the SynthDef class, for example, to compile a function into a UGen graph and then into a SynthDef that can be used to create synths on the Server.

5.4.11   Scope of Variables in Functions

As mentioned in section 5.3, variables are accessible only within the context (i.e., the function) that defines them. However, if a function *mother_func* creates another function *child_func*, then *child_func* has access to the variables created within *mother_func*. This is useful when several functions want to share data. Thus, in figure 5.15, the variable freq is defined in the (implicit) top-level function, and the function stored in change_freq is a *child_func* that has access to this variable. The function change_freq can therefore both *read* (access) the value of the variable freq and set (*write*) it whenever it is called. The set of variables created by a function *f* and made available to functions created within that function *f* is called a function's *closure.*[3]

It is in fact possible to view a closure as a simple and limited form of an object, where the variables defined in the top-level function of the closure serve as instance variables. This technique has been used in *Pyrite,* an "external object" that provides a programming language inside *Max.* Pyrite was created by James McCartney in 1994 and is one of the direct precursors of SuperCollider. The following 2 examples show how to model the behavior of the Counter class shown in section 5.5 without writing a class definition.

5.4.11.1   Modeling instances through functions that create other functions

Figure 5.29 defines a *mother_func* stored as counter_maker, which in turn creates and returns a *child_func*. Each time that counter_maker is run, it creates a new instance of its *child_func*. It also creates copies of its own variables, in this case the argument variable max_count and the variable current_count, which are accessible only to its own child function.

So from 1 mother function one can create multiple closures, each closure having its own set of variables and functions, and each function in that closure is able to run multiple times. In this way, one can construct programs that make smaller programs that work on their own copies of data. In the present example, the function stored in counter_maker is run once with a max_count argument value of 10 and once with a max_count argument value of 5. Consequently, the first time it creates a function that counts to 10 and the second time, one that counts to 5.

The effect of this technique is similar to defining instance variables, and the child functions that have access to these variables are similar to instances of a class that has access to these variables. Figure 5.30 shows how closures with their own variables are generated from a function.

5.4.11.2   Functions in Events as methods

This section extends the example of section 5.4.3.1 to add a further feature: the ability of each counter to reset itself. It also shows a more flexible technique for creating a graphical user interface: instead of a fixed number of counter items, a function is defined that can generate a GUI for any number of counters, whose maximum counts are given as arguments to the function. Instead of a function, the counter_maker in this example returns an Event. An Event is an object that can hold values associated to named keys. Instead of having a fixed, predefined number of instance variables, an Event can hold any number of key-value associations that function similarly to

```
(
// a function that creates a function that counts to any number
var counter_maker;
var window, button1, button2; // gui for testing the function

// the function that makes the counting function
counter_maker = { | max_count |
    // current_count is used by the function created below
    // to store the number of times that it has run
    var current_count = 0;
    {   // start of definition of the counting function
        if (current_count == max_count) {
            format("finished counting to %", max_count).postln;
            max_count;       // return max count for eventual use
        }{
            current_count = current_count + 1; // increment count
            format("counting % of %", current_count, max_count).postln;
            current_count   // return current count for eventual use
        }
    }   // end of definition of the counting function
};

// ----- Test application for the counter_maker function -----
// window displaying 2 buttons counting to different numbers
window = Window("Counters", Rect(400, 400, 200, 80));
// make a button for triggering the counting:
button1 = Button(window, Rect(10, 10, 180, 20));
button1.states = [["counting to 10"]];    // labels for button1
// make a function that counts to 10 and store it as action in button1
button1.action = counter_maker.(10);
button2 = Button(window, Rect(10, 40, 180, 20));
button2.states = [["counting to 5"]];     // labels for button2
// make a function that counts to 5 and store it as action in button2
button2.action = counter_maker.(5);
window.front;            // show the window
)
```

Figure 5.29
A function that creates functions that count.

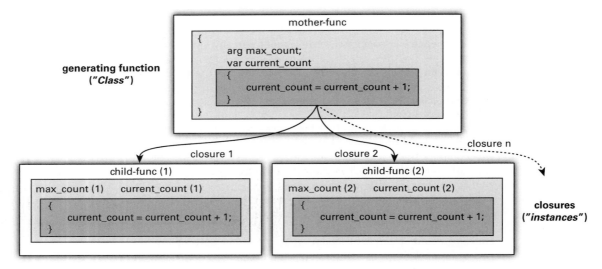

Figure 5.30
Functions created by functions as models of instances.

the named instance variables of an Object. In the current example the Event contains 3 keys—'count1,' 'reset_count,' and 'max_count'—whose values are bound to functions that operate on the variables of the counter_maker closure. These functions assigned as values to keys act the way an instance method would in a normal class definition. Thus, an Event made by counter_maker is the model of an object with 2 variables and 3 methods. The code in the example of figure 5.31 is hardly any bigger than the previous version, despite the addition of 2 features.

The above example can be seen as a rudimentary class definition constructed without employing the regular class definition system of SuperCollider. It is left to the reader to extend the example in one further step, by storing the functions of counter _maker and make_counters_gui in an Event to model a class Counter with 2 class methods.

The syntax for running the functions stored in an Event is the same as that of a method call, (receiver.message), the only difference being that the first argument passed to a function in an Event is the Event itself. There is a catch, however. If one stores a function in an Event under the name of an instance method that is defined in the class Event, then that method will be run instead of the function stored by the user. So, for example, one cannot use a function stored in an Event under reset:

```
(reset: {"this is never called".postln;}).reset;
```

For more information on this approach, see chapter 8.

```
(
var counter_maker;        // creator of counters
var make_counters_gui;   // function making counters + a gui
/* a function that creates an event that counts to any number,
   and resets: */
counter_maker = { | max_count |
    var current_count = 0;
    (    // the counter object is an event with 3 functions:
        count1: // function 1: increment count (stored as count1)
        {    // start of definition of the counting function
            if (current_count == max_count) {
                format("finished counting to %", max_count).postln;
            }{
                current_count = current_count + 1; // increment count
                format("counting % of %", current_count, max_count).postln;
            }
        },   // end of definition of the counting function
        reset_count: { // function 2: reset count (stored as reset_count)
            format("resetting % counter", max_count).postln;
            current_count = 0
        },
        max_count: { max_count } // function 3: return value of max_count
    )
};
// Function that makes several counters and a GUI to control them
make_counters_gui = { | ... counts |
    var window, counter;
    window = Window("Counters",
            Rect(400, 400, 200, 50 * counts.size + 10));
    // enable automatic placement of new items in window:
    window.view.decorator = FlowLayout(window.view.bounds, 5@5, 5@5);
    counts collect: counter_maker.(_) do: { | counter |
        Button(window, Rect(0, 0, 190, 20))
            .states_([["Counting to: " ++ counter.max_count.asString]])
            .action = { counter.count1 };
        Button(window, Rect(0, 0, 190, 20))
            .states_([["Reset"]])
            .action = { counter.reset_count };
    };
    window.front;
};
make_counters_gui.(5, 10, 27); // example use of the GUI test function
)
```

Figure 5.31
Functions stored in events as instance methods.

5.5   Program Flow Control and Design Patterns

Control structures are structures that permit you to choose the evaluation of a function depending on a condition. That is, a function is evaluated only if the value of a test condition is true. There are variants involving 1 or more functions. (For alternative syntax forms, see the Help file Syntax-Shortcuts.)

5.5.1   If Statements

Run a function only if a condition is true:

```
if ([true, false].choose) {"was true".postln}
```

Run a function if a condition is true; otherwise, run another function:

```
if ([true, false].choose) {"was true".postln} {"was false".postln}
```

5.5.2   Case Statements

A case statement is a sequence of function pairs of the form "condition-action." The condition functions are evaluated in sequence until one of them returns true. Then the action function is evaluated and the rest of the pairs are ignored. One can add a single default action function at the end of the pairs sequence, which will be executed if none of the condition functions returns true.

```
(
i = [0, 1, inf].choose;
x = case {i == 0} {\no}
    {i == 1} {\yes}
    {\infinity};
)
```

5.5.3   Switch Statements

A switch statement matches a given value to a series of alternatives by checking for equality. If a match is found, the function corresponding to that match is evaluated. The form of the switch statement is similar to that of the case statement. The difference is that the switch statement uses a fixed test—that of equality with a given value—whereas the case statement uses a series of independent functions as tests.

```
(
switch ([0, 1, inf].choose,
    0, {\no},
```

```
     1, {\yes},
     {\infinity})
)
```

5.5.4   Other Control Techniques: Behavior Patterns

Selecting among alternatives for directing the execution flow of a program is not limited to the statements above. There are many techniques addressing this topic, some of which are also known as *Design Patterns* (Gamma et al. 1994; Beck, 1996). Typically, techniques of this category would fall under the group *Behavior Patterns*. Examples of such patterns are *Chain of Responsibility, Command, Iterator, Mediator, Observer,* and *State*. Beck (1996) classifies Behavior Patterns into 2 major categories. Under "Method" he lists patterns that are based on the organization of an algorithm inside methods. Under "Message" he classifies patterns that use message passing to create algorithms. These patterns can be very small but equally powerful. An example is the *Choosing Message* pattern (Beck, 1996, pp. 45–47). Instead of choosing among a number of alternatives with an if statement or a switch statement, one delegates the choice to the methods of the possible objects involved. For example, consider an object that represents an entry in a list of publications, and that responds to the message responsible by returning some object that represents the name of the person who is responsible for the object. For film publications, the "responsible" is the producer, for edited books it is the editor, for single-author books it is the author. The Choosing Message pattern says that instead of writing

```
responsible {|entry|
    case {entry.isKindOf(Film)} {^entry.producer}
        {entry.isKindOf(EditedBook)} {^entry.editor}
        {^entry.author}     // in all other cases, return the author
}
```

one writes

```
responsible {|entry|^entry.responsible}
```

and then codes the different reactions to responsible in the classes of the objects that are involved:

```
// add method "responsible" in 3 previously defined classes:
+ Publication {responsible {^author}}
+ Film {responsible {^producer}}
+ EditedBook {responsible {^editor}}
```

In this example, Publication is the default class for entries and gives the default method; all other classes for entries are subclasses of Publication. Only those classes which deviate from the default responsible method need to redefine it. (See section 5.2.1.2 for syntax of methods and class extensions.)

The power of this technique is, first, that the number of choices can easily be extended by creating new classes and, second, that the method responsible for each class can be as complex as needed, without resulting in a huge case statement that aggregates all the choices for "responsible" in 1 place. In other words, complexity is reduced—or, rather, broken down into pieces in an elegant way—by delegating responsibility for different parts of the algorithm to different classes. Thus, algorithms are organized by the combination of a number of method calls, which split the algorithm into pieces and delegate the responsibility for different parts of the algorithm to different classes. As a result, methods tend to contain very little code, often just a single line. Although this may seem confusing at the first encounter, it gets clearer as one becomes familiar with the style of code that pervades good object-oriented programming.

5.6   Collections

Collections are objects that hold a variable number of other objects. For example, figure 5.32 shows a program that adds a new number to a sequence each time the user clicks on a button, and then plays the sequence as a "melody."

The above example builds a sequence of notes by adding a new random integer between 0 and 15 each time. Note that adding an element to nil creates an array with the added element (i.e., nil add: 1 results in [1]).

```
Server.default.boot;     // boot the server first;
(
var degrees, window, button;
window = Window("melodies?", Rect(400, 400, 200, 200));
button = Button(window, window.view.bounds.insetBy(10, 10));
button.states = [["click me to add a note"]];
button.action = {
    degrees = degrees add: 0.rrand(15);
    Pbind(\degree, Pseq(degrees), \dur, Prand([0.1, 0.2, 0.4], inf)).play;
};
window.front;
)
```

Figure 5.32
Building an Array with add.

The subclass tree of Collection is extensive (Collection.dumpClassSubtree) and is summarized in the Help file Collections. Collections can be classified into 3 types according to the way in which their elements are accessed:

Collections whose elements are accessed by numeric index. For example, [0, 5, 9]. at(0) accesses the first element of the array [0, 5, 9], and [0, 5, 9].put(1, \hello) puts the symbol \hello into the second position of array [0, 5, 9]. Such collections include Array, List, Interval, Range, Array2D, Signal, Wavetable, and String. Numeric indexes in SuperCollider start at 0; that is, 0 refers to the first element in a collection. Accessing an element at an index past the size of the collection returns nil. Other messages for access exist—wrapAt, clipAt, foldAt—that modify invalid index numbers so they always return some element. There are collections that hold only a specific kind of object, such as Char (String), Symbol (SymbolArray), Float (Signal, Wavetable).

Collections whose elements are accessed by using a symbol, or another object, as index. For example (a: 1, b: 2)[\a] returns 1. Such collections are Dictionary, IdentityDictionary, MultiLevelIdentityDictionary, Library (a global, nested MultiLevelIdentityDictionary that can be accessed by series of objects as indices), Environment, and Event. All such collections are made up of Association objects, which are pairs that associate a key to a value and are written as key->value. Although it is possible to look up such pairs both by key and by value, dictionaries are optimized for lookup by key.

Collections whose elements are accessed by searching for a match to a condition. For example, Set[1, 2, 3, 4, 5] select: (_ > 2). These are Set and Bag.

5.6.1   Creating Collections

The generic rule for creating a collection is to enclose its elements in brackets [], separating each element by a comma. If the class of a collection is other than Array, it is indicated before the brackets:

```
List[1, 2, 3]; LinkedList[1, 2, 3]; Signal[1, 2, 3]; Dictionary[\a->1,
2->pi, \c-> 'alpha']; Set[1, 2, 3]
```

Additionally, there are several alternative techniques for notating and generating specific types of collections:

An arithmetic series can be abbreviated by giving the beginning and end values and, optionally, the step between subsequent values: (1..5); (1, 1.2 .. 5).

An Event can be written as a pair of parentheses enclosing a list of the associations of the Event written as keyword-value pairs: (a: 1, b: 2).

Environments and Events can be created from functions with the message make (see section 5.6.8).

There are several messages for constructing numerical Arrays algorithmically. For example:

```
Array.series(5, 3, 1.5); Array.geom(3, 4, 5); Array.rand(5, -10, 10)
```

Wavetables and Signals are raw Arrays of floating-point numbers that can be created from functions such as sine or Chebyshev polynomials, or window shapes such as Welch.

The class Harmonics constructs Arrays that can be used as wavetables for playing sounds with the UGen Osc and its relatives.

5.6.2 Binary Operators on Collections

Most binary operators on collections can work both between 2 collections of any sizes and between a collection and a non-collection object: (0..6) < (3..0); (0..6) + (3..0); 10 * (1..3); (2..5) + 0.1. One can append an adverb to a binary operator to specify the manner in which the elements of 2 collections are paired for the operation. For example:

```
[10, 20, 30, 40, 50] + [1, 2, 3] // default: shorter array wraps
[10, 20, 30, 40, 50] +.s [1, 2, 3] // s = short. operate on shorter array
[10, 20, 30, 40, 50] +.f [1, 2, 3] // f = fold. Use folded indexing
```

5.6.3 Iterating over Collections

The following messages iterate over each element of a collection with a function:

do(function): Evaluate function over each element, return the receiver. (1..5) do: _.postln

collect(function): Evaluate function over each element, return the collected results of each evaluation. (1..5) collect: _.sqrt.

pairsDo(function): Iterate over adjacent pairs of elements of a collection.

inject(function): Iterate passing the result of each iteration to the next one as an argument:

keysDo, keysValuesDo, associationsDo, pairsDo, keysValuesChange. These work on dictionaries as follows:

```
(a: 10, b: 20) keysDo: {|key, index| [key, index].postln}
(a: 10, b: 20) keysValuesDo: {|k, v, i| [k, v, i].postln}
(a: 10, b: 20) associationsDo: {|assoc, index| [assoc, index].postln}
(a: 10, b: 20) pairsDo: {|k, v, i| [k, v, i].postln}
(a: 10, b: 20) keysValuesChange: {|key, value, index| value + index}
```

5.6.4   Searching in Collections

The following messages search for matches and return either a subset or a single element from a collection:

select(foo): Return those elements for which foo returns true: (1..5) select: (_ > 2).
reject(foo): Return those elements for which foo returns false: (1..5) reject: (_ > 2).
detect(foo): Return the first element for which foo returns true: "asdfg" detect: {|c| c.ascii > 100}.
indexOf(obj): Return the index of the first element that matches obj: "asdfg" indexOf: $f.
includes(obj): Return true if the receiver includes obj in its elements: "asdfg" includes: $f.
matchRegexp(string, start, end): Perform matching of regular expressions on a string.

5.6.5   Restructuring Collections

A full account of the structure-manipulation features of the SuperCollider language would require a chapter of its own. For full details the reader is referred to the Help files of the various Collection classes (and those of their superclasses, such as Collection and SequenceableCollection). Here are a few examples of some of the more commonly used methods:

reverse: Reverse the order of the elements. (1..5).reverse.
flop: Turn rows into columns in a 2-dimensional collection. [[1, 2] [\a, \b]].flop.
scramble: Rearrange the elements in random order. (1..5).scramble.
clump(n): Create subcollections of size n. (1..10).clump(3).
stutter(n): Repeat each element n times. (1..5).stutter(3).
pyramid(n), where $1 <= n <= 10$: Rearrange in quasi-repetitive patterns. (1..5) .pyramid(5).
sort(foo): Sort using foo as sorting function. Default sorts in ascending order: "asdfg".sort. Descending order is specified like this: "asdfg" sort: {|a, b| a > b}

Further powerful restructuring, combinatorial, and search capabilities are discussed in the Help files J Concepts in SC and List Comprehensions.

5.6.6   IdentityDictionary

IdentityDictionary is a dictionary that retrieves its values by looking for a key identical to a given index. "Identical" means that the key should be the same object as the index. For example, the 2 strings "hello" and "hello" are equal but not identical:

```
"hello" == "hello"; // true: the two strings are equal
"hello" === "hello"; // false: the two strings are not identical.
```

By contrast, symbols that are written with the same characters are always stored as 1 object by the compiler, and are therefore identical: \hello === \hello returns true. Thus:

```
a = IdentityDictionary["foo"->1]; // store 1 under the "foo" as key
a["foo"]; // nil!
```

The second "foo" is not identical to the first one.

However:

```
a = IdentityDictionary[\foo->1];
a[\foo]; // Returns 1
```

Searching for a matching object by identity is much faster than searching by equality. Therefore, an IdentityDictionary is optimized for speed. It serves as superclass for Environment, which is the basis for defining Environment variables. Accessing an Environment variable thus means looking it up by identity match. Though this is a fast process, it is still considerably more expensive in computing cycles than accessing a "real" variable!

IdentityDictionary defines 2 instance variables: proto and parent. These are used by the classes Environment and Event to provide a default environment when needed (see section 5.6.8). The parent scheme makes it possible to build hierarchies of parent events in a way similar to that for class hierarchies.

5.6.7   Environment

An Environment is an IdentityDictionary that can evaluate functions which contain environment variables (see section 5.5). To make an Environment from a function, use the message make:

```
Environment make: {~a = 10; ~b = 1 + pi * 7.rand;}
```

This is not just a convenient notation; it also allows one to compute variables that are dependent on the value of variables previously created in the Environment:

```
Environment make: {~a = pi + 10.rand ; ~b = ~a pow: 5}
```

The message use evaluates a function within an Environment.

```
Environment make: {~c = 3} use: {~a = 2 pow: 10.rand; ~c + ~a}
```

Environment.use(f) evaluates f in an empty environment:

```
Environment use: {~a = 10; ~b = 1 + pi * 7.rand; ~c}
```

Additionally, an Environment can supply values from its variables to the arguments of a function that is evaluated in it with the message valueEnvir. Only values for those arguments that are not provided by valueEnvir are supplied:

```
(a: 1, b: 2).use({ ~a + ~b});  // using Environment variables
```

Supplying arguments to a function from the Environment with valueEnvir:

```
(a: 1, b: 2).use({{|a, b|a + b }.valueEnvir(3)})
```

Note that the function must be explicitly evaluated with valueEnvir for this to work. Therefore, the following is not the right way to supply arguments with use:

```
(a: 1, b: 2).use({|a, b| a + b})
```

valueEnvir in normal code text outside of use draws on the currentEnvironment:

```
~a = 3; ~b = 5;
{|a, b| a + b}.valueEnvir
```

Patterns are a specific extension library within SuperCollider that is very useful for musical scheduling, and they rest on the Environment mechanisms to manipulate musical data. (They actually use Event, a subclass of Environment, which we will introduce next.) Patterns exploit the ability to supply values for arguments from an Environment with valueEnvir when playing instruments that are defined as functions.

5.6.8   Event

Event is a subclass of Environment with several additional features. An Event itself is playable:

```
(degree: 2, dur: 3).play
```

Event stores several prototype Events in its class variables that embody default musical event types (a class variable is globally available to the instances of its class and its subclasses). These Events define a complete musical environment, covering aspects such as tuning, scales, legato, chords and chord strumming, MIDI, and playing with different instruments. To play, an Event receives or selects a parent Event as its Environment, and overrides only those items of the parent that deviate from the default settings. For example, the parent Event of (degree: 5) is nil before playing: (degree: 5).parent. To run (degree: 5).play, the Event sets its own parent Event, which can be printed by (degree: 5).play.parent.asCompileString. The parameters of this Environment also compute and set the final parameters that are needed to play the Event. In the present example, these are freq, amp, and sustain, as can be seen in the resulting Event:

```
Server.default.boot;    // boot the server first. Run each following line
separately:
(degree: 5).parent; // the parent before playing is nil
(degree: 5).play.parent.asCompileString; // The parent has been set
(degree: 5).play; // Event, becomes ('degree': 5, 'freq':440,...)
```

5.7   Working with Classes

Classes are the heart of the SuperCollider system because they define the structure and behavior of all objects. All class definitions are contained in the folder SCClassLibrary or in the platform-specific extension folder, in files with the extension .sc. By studying these definitions one can understand the function of any part of the system in depth. By writing one's own classes or modifying existing classes, one can extend the functionality of the system.

5.7.1   Encapsulation, Inheritance, Polymorphism

The 3 defining principles of object-oriented languages are Encapsulation, Inheritance, and Polymorphism. Encapsulation means that data inside an object are accessible only to methods that belong to that object. This protects the data of the object from external changes, thereby aiding in creating consistent and safe programs. In Polymorphism, the same message can correspond to different behaviors according to the class of the object that receives it. In section 5.5.4, an entry of class Film responds differently to the message responsible than an entry of class EditedBook does. Inheritance, on the other hand, entails that any subclass of Publication that does not define its own method responsible will use the method as defined in Publication instead (see also section 5.7.4). Together, these 3 features are responsible for the capabilities of object-oriented languages.

5.7.2   Compiling the SuperCollider Class Library

In contrast to code executed from a window holding SuperCollider code, which can be run at any time, changes made in class definition code take effect only after recompiling the SuperCollider Class Library. (See the Shortcuts Help file for platform-specific info on how to do this.) Compiling the library rebuilds all classes and resets the entire memory of the system.

5.7.3   Defining a Class

The structure of a class is defined by its variables and its methods. Additionally, a class may define class variables, constants, and class methods.

As noted above, class variables are accessible by the class itself as well as by all instances, whereas instance variables are accessible only inside methods of the instance in question. Constants are like class variables, except that their values are set at the definition statement and cannot be changed subsequently. For example, the class Char defines several constants that hold the unprintable characters for new line, form feed, tab, and space as well as the character comma.

Class methods are addressed to the class, and instance methods to instances of that class. For example, in Window.new("test," Rect(500, 500, 100, 100)).front the class method new is addressed to the class Window and returns an appropriate window for the platform on which SuperCollider is running, and the method front is addressed to the instance created by method New.

A class may inherit variables and methods from another class, which is called its *superclass*. Inheritance works upward over a chain of superclasses, and always up to the superclass of all classes: Object. Before explaining the role and syntax of each element in detail, here is an example showing the main parts (figure 5.33).

As seen in figure 5.33, the code that defines a class has 2 major characteristics in common with that of a function: it is enclosed in {}, and it starts with variable declarations followed by program code. The code of a class definition is organized in 2 sections: variable declarations and method definitions. (No program statements may be included in the definition of a class other than those contained in variable declarations and methods.) Class syntax is summarized below.

The name of the class is indicated at the start of the definition. If the class has a superclass other than Object, it is indicated like this:

```
Integer: SimpleNumber {// define Integer as subclass of SimpleNumber
```

In addition to var statements that declare instance variables, there can also be classvar statements that declare class variables and const statements that create constants. For example, class Server has a class variable set that stores all servers known to the system. One can quit these servers with Server.set do: _.quit. Class Char has several const statements declaring special characters.

The special signs < and > prepended to a variable name in a variable declaration statement construct corresponding methods for getting or setting the value of that variable:

```
var <freq; // constructs method: freq {^freq};
var >freq: // constructs method: freq_ {|argFreq| freq = argFreq}
```

For example, the class definition Thing {var <>x;} is equivalent to

```
Thing {var x;
    x {^x}
    x_ {arg z; x = z;}
}
```

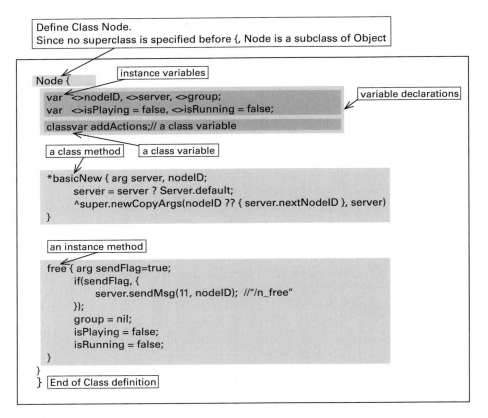

Figure 5.33
Summary of Class Definition Parts (Excerpt from Definition of Class Node).

The declaration of any variables of a class is followed by the definitions of its methods. A method is defined by the name of the method followed by the definition of the function that is executed by that method.

The sign * before a method's name creates a class method.

```
*new {arg x=0, y=0; ^super.newCopyArgs(x, y);} // (from class Point)
```

The default return value of an instance method is the instance that is executing that method (the receiver of the message that triggered the method). To return a different value, one writes the sign ^ before the statement whose value will be returned. The method freq {^freq} returns the value of the variable freq. The sign ^ also has the effect of *returning* from the function of the method, which means any further statements will not be executed. This effect can be useful.

```
count1 {
    if (current_count >= max_count) {^current_count};
    // the next statement is executed only if current_count > max_count:
    ^current_count = current_count + 1;
}
```

Identifiers starting with underscore (_) inside methods call *primitives*, that is, computations that are done by compiled code in the system, and whose code can be seen only in the underlying source code of the SuperCollider application. A primitive returns a value if it can be called successfully. Otherwise, execution continues to the next statement of the method's code.

```
*newCopyArgs {arg ... args; // (from class Object)
    _BasicNewCopyArgsToInstVars
    ^this.primitiveFailed
}
```

Three special keywords can be used in methods: this refers to the object that is running the method (the *receiver*); thisMethod refers to the method that is running; *super* followed by a message looks up and evaluates the method of the message in the superclass of the instance that is running the method.

If the class method *initClass is defined, then it will be run right after the system is compiled. It is used to initialize any data needed. To indicate that a class needs to be initialized *before* the present initClass is run, one includes the following code in the definition of initClass:

```
Class.initClassTree(NameOfClassToBeInitialized).
```

A class is usually defined in 1 file. If the same class name is found in definitions in 2 or more files, then the compiler issues the message duplicate class found, followed by the name of the duplicate class. However, one can extend or modify a class by adding or overwriting methods in a separate file. The syntax for adding methods to an existing class is

```
+Function { // + indicates this extends an existing class
    // the code of any methods comes here
    update { ... args | // method update
        this.valueArray(args);
    }   // other methods can follow here
}
```

5.7.4   Inheritance

A class may inherit the properties of another class. This principle of inheritance helps organize program code by grouping common shared properties of objects in

```
1.class          // the class of Integer 1: Integer
1.class.class    // the Class of the Class of Integer 1: Meta_Integer
// the Class of the Class of the Class of Integer 1:
1.class.class.class                      // Class
// the Class of the Class of the Class of the Class of Integer 1
1.class.class.class.class                // Meta_Class
// the Class of the Class of the Class of the Class of the Class of 1
1.class.class.class.class.class          // Class
Class.class                              // the Class of Class is Meta_Class
Meta_Class.class       // the Class of Meta_Class is Class
```

Figure 5.34
Classes of classes.

one class, and by defining subclasses to differentiate the properties and behaviors of objects that have a more specialized character. For example, the class Integer inherits the properties of the class SimpleNumber. SimpleNumber is called the *superclass* of Integer, and Integer is called a *subclass* of SimpleNumber. Float, the class describing floating-point numbers such as 0.1, is also a subclass of SimpleNumber. Classes are thus organized into a family tree. The following expression prints out the complete SuperCollider class tree: Object.dumpClassSubtree.

5.7.5   Metaclasses

Since all entities in SuperCollider are objects, classes are themselves objects. Each class is the sole instance of its "*metaclass.*" For example, the class of Integer is Meta _Integer, and consequently Integer is the only instance of the class Meta_Integer. All metaclasses are instances of Class. The following examples trace the successive classes of objects starting from the Integer 1 and going up to Class as the class of all Metaclasses.

The cycle Class-Meta_Class-Class in figure 5.34 shows the end of the Class relationship tree. Since the class of Class is Meta_Class and Meta_Class is also a Class, those 2 classes are the only objects that are instances of one another:

Class.class   // the class of Class is Meta_Class
Meta_Class.class   // the class of Meta_Class is Class

Class methods are equivalent to instance methods of the class's Metaclass. For instance, the class method *new of Server is an instance method of Meta_Server. (See figure 5.35.)

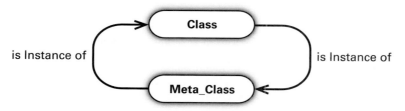

Figure 5.35
`Class` and `Meta_Class` are mutually instances of each other.

5.7.6   The SuperCollider Class Tree

At the top of the class hierarchy of SuperCollider is the class Object. This means all other classes inherit from class Object as its subclasses, and consequently all objects in SuperCollider share the characteristics and behavior defined in class Object. Object defines such global behaviors as how to create an instance, how an object should react to a message that is not understood, how to print the representation of an object as text, and so on. Any subclass can override this default behavior in its own code, as well as extend it by defining new variables and methods. The tree formed by Object and its subclasses thus describes all classes in the SuperCollider system.

5.7.7   Notifying Objects of Changes: Observer and Adapter/Controller Patterns

This section shows how to convert the class model from earlier in the chapter into a *real* class. The Observer design pattern implemented in class Object allows one to attach objects (called dependants) to any object in such a way that they are updated when that object notifies itself with the message changed and an optional list of arguments. This results in the message update (along with the arguments) being sent to each of the dependants. It is the responsibility of the dependants to know how to respond correctly to an update message, and the changing object can remain ignorant of the kind and number of its dependants. Thus it is possible to attach a sound, a GUI element, or any other object or process to another object and make it respond to changes of that object in any manner. Crucially, this can happen without having to modify the class definition of the changing object to deal with the specifics of the objects being notified. This technique is similar to the design pattern known as Model-View-Controller (MVC) (see chapters 9 and 10), and serves as its basis. The goal of this pattern is to separate data or processes (the model) from their display (views) and from the control mechanisms, so as to permit multiple displays across different media and platforms.

```
Counter {
    // variables: maximum count, current count
    var <>max_count, <>current_count = 1;
    // class method for creating a new instance
    *new { | max_count = 10 |
        ^super.new.max_count_(max_count)
    }
    // if maximum count not reached, increment count by 1
    count1 {
        if (current_count >= max_count) {
            this.changed(\max_reached)
        }{
            current_count = current_count + 1;
            this.changed(\count, current_count);
        }
    }
    // reset count
    reset {
        current_count = 1;
        this.changed(\reset);
    }
}
```

Figure 5.36
Counter Class.

The present example adds auditory displays and a GUI display that respond to counter changes. These displays are completely independent from each other and from the counter both in code and in functionality, in the sense that one can attach a display or remove it from any counter at any moment, and that one can attach any number of displays to one counter.

The definition of the Counter class is shown in figure 5.36.

This must be placed in a file Counter.sc in the SCClassLibrary folder and compiled with [command-K]. After that, boot the server and add the SynthDefs for the sounds (see figure 5.37).

Next, create 5 counters and store them in ~counters:

```
~counters = (6, 11 .. 26) collect: Counter.new(_);
```

Now create a sound adapter to follow changes in any counter it is added to (see figure 5.38).

The sound_adapter function receives update messages from a Counter object and translates them to actions according to the further arguments of the message. In this

```
Server.default.boot;
(
SynthDef("ping", { | freq = 440 |
    Out.ar(0,
        SinOsc.ar(freq, 0,
            EnvGen.kr(Env.perc(level: 0.1), doneAction: 2)
    ))
}).add;

SynthDef("wham", {
    Out.ar(0, BrownNoise.ar(
        EnvGen.kr(Env.perc(level: 0.1), doneAction: 2)
    ))
}).add;
)
```

Figure 5.37
SynthDefs for the Counter model example.

```
(
~sound_adapter =  { | counter, what, count |
    switch (what,
        \reset, { Synth("wham"); },
        \max_reached, { counter.reset },
        \count, { Synth("ping",
            [\freq, count.postln * 10 + counter.max_count * 20]
            )
        }
    )
};
)
```

Figure 5.38
A dependant that plays sounds.

sense it is similar to an Adapter pattern. (An Adapter pattern translates between incompatible interfaces.)

This works because class Function defines the method update as a synonym for value, thus conveniently allowing it to work as a dependant in a straightforward manner:

```
update {|obj, what ... args| this.value(obj, what, *args)}
```

Attach the sound adapter to all 5 counters:

```
~counters do: _.addDependant(~sound_adapter);
```

Then start a routine that increments the counters at 0.25-second intervals:

```
~count = {loop {~counters do: _.count1; 0.25.wait}}.fork;
```

The routine can be stopped with ~count.stop. But before doing that, let's add GUI displays for the counters. (See figure 5.39.)

Now one can make displays for any of the counters at any time.

```
~make_display.(~counters[0]);
```

```
(
~make_display = { | counter |
    var window, label, adapter, stagger;
    window = Window(
        "counting to " ++ counter.max_count.asString,
        Rect(stagger = UniqueID.next % 20 * 20 + 400, stagger, 200, 50)
    );
    label = StaticText(window, window.view.bounds.insetBy(10, 10));
    adapter = { | counter, what, count |
            { label.string = counter.current_count.asString }.defer
    };
    counter addDependant: adapter;
    /* remove the adapter when window closes to prevent error in
       updating non-existent views: */
    window.onClose = { counter removeDependant: adapter };
    window.front
};
)
```

Figure 5.39
A dependant that displays the count.

Or all of them at once:

```
~counters do: ~make_display.(_);
```

The Observer pattern is considered so important that it is implemented in class Object and is thus available to all objects.

5.8   Conclusion

The present chapter has attempted to describe the programming language of Super-Collider and its capabilities in as much detail as possible in the given space. It also has presented some techniques of programming that may serve as an introduction to advanced programming. Many other techniques exist. A great many of these are described in print and on the Web in publications that deal with design patterns for programming. Kent Beck's *Smalltalk Best Practice Patterns* (Beck, 1996) is recommended as a basic manual of good style and because the patterns it describes are as powerful as they are small. Gamma et al. (1994) is considered a standard book on patterns. Beck (2000) and Fowler et al. (1999) deal with more advanced techniques of coding.

The SuperCollider class library itself is a good source for learning more about programming techniques. The GUI class implements the Factory pattern. The Lilt library (included on the Web site of this book as supplementary material to the present chapter) makes extensive use of the Observer pattern and defines a class Script that enables one to code algorithms for performance in prototypes that create their own GUIs.

SuperCollider as an open-source project depends on the active participation of members of the community to continue developing as one of the most advanced environments for sound synthesis. Contributions by musicians and programmers, through suggestions and bug reports to the sc-dev mailing list, through Quarks in the quark repository, or through proposals for inclusion in the SCClassLibrary itself, are vital for the further development of this environment. Even though SuperCollider has already gained considerable popularity, there is still much room for growth. One of the most attractive aspects of this environment is that it is equally a tool for music making, experimentation, research, and learning about programming and sound. The features and capabilities of the SuperCollider programming language outlined in the present chapter can serve as a springboard for projects that will further expand its capabilities and user base. It remains to be seen how the trend for coding for performance or composition as a musically creative activity matures in practice. Yet whatever the future may bring, the particular marriage of toolmaking and music making that SuperCollider embodies so successfully will mark it as an exceptional achievement, and hopefully will give birth to further original ideas and amazing sounds.

References

Beck, K. 1996. *Smalltalk Best Practice Patterns*. Upper Saddle River, NJ: Prentice Hall.

Beck, K. 2000. *eXtreme Programming eXplained: Embrace Change*. Reading, MA: Addison-Wesley.

Burstall, R. 2000. "Christopher Strachey—Understanding Programming Languages." *Higher-Order and Symbolic Computation,* 13(1/2): 52.

Fowler, M., K. Beck, J. Brant, W. Opdyke, and D. Roberts. 1999. *Refactoring: Improving the Design of Existing Code*. Addison-Wesley Object Technology series. Reading, MA: Addison-Wesley.

Gamma, E., R. Helm, R. Johnson, and J. Vlissides. 1994. *Design Patterns: Elements of Reusable Object-Oriented Software*. Addison-Wesley Professional Computing series. Boston: Addison-Wesley.

Strachey, C. 2000. "Fundamental Concepts in Programming Languages." *Higher-Order and Symbolic Computation,* 13(1/2): 11–49.

Notes

1. Two relevant definitions of statements are "An elementary instruction in a programming language" (<http://www.thefreedictionary.com/statement>) and "A statement is a block of code that does something. An assignment statement assigns a value to a variable. A for statement performs a loop. In C, C++, and C# Statements can be grouped together as 1 statement using curly brackets" (<http://cplus.about.com/od/glossar1/g/statementdefn.htm>). In Super-Collider, statements enclosed in {} create a function object, which is different from a statement group in C or C++.

2. When a program can construct functions while it is running and store them as objects in variables, it is said that it treats functions as "first class objects" (Burstall, 2000).

3. Wikipedia writes about closures: "In computer science, a closure is a function that is evaluated in an environment containing one or more bound variables. When called, the function can access these variables. The explicit use of closures is associated with functional programming and with languages such as ML and Lisp. Constructs such as objects in other languages can also be modeled with closures."

6 Events and Patterns

Ron Kuivila

6.1 SynthDefs, Events, and Patterns

SuperCollider's `Event` and `Pattern` classes work together to provide both a concise score language and a flexible set of programming tools. This introduction emphasizes their use as a score language for nonprogrammers. As in other programming approaches in SC, the `SynthDef` class defines the actual sound sources and processors that run on the *synthesis server*. The discussion of SynthDefs is limited to those issues directly relevant to Events and Patterns. It is helpful, but not mandatory, to have reviewed the structure of the synthesis server and to have a basic understanding of Functions, arguments, and variables in reading this chapter. For this reason it may be helpful to review the earlier chapters of this book before proceeding. Two appendices to this chapter provide a more detailed technical treatment that requires greater knowledge of the language. Chapter 5, with its in-depth overview, may be useful for filling in any gaps.

6.1.1 SynthDefs

A `SynthDef` assigns a name to a "patch diagram" of *unit generators* and additional names to the patch's control inputs. Figure 6.1 creates a SynthDef named `sine`. The synthesis function's arguments (`gate`, `out`, `freq`, `amp`, `pan`, `ar`, and `dr`) define the patch's *control inputs*. The patch is defined in the body of the function using the `UGen` classes that provide language-side representations of the unit generators available on the server.

The patch diagram specified by a SynthDef must be downloaded to the server to be used. In addition, a description of a SynthDef's control inputs must be maintained within the language so Events can play it correctly. The `store` and `add` methods perform this bookkeeping (creating a corresponding `SynthDesc` object for language side *Synth Description*). The former writes the SynthDef to disk, and the latter does not (they have equivalents in the `load` and `send` methods which don't create SynthDescs,

```
SynthDef(
    "sine",                        // name of SynthDef
    {                              // function begins with a brace
    arg gate = 1, out = 0,         // arguments serve as Control declarations
    freq = 400, amp = 0.4,
    pan = 0, ar = 1, dr = 1;

    var audio;
    audio = SinOsc.ar(freq, 0, amp);        // start with a SinOsc
    audio = audio * Linen.kr(gate, ar, 1, dr, 2); // apply an envelope
    audio = Pan2.ar(audio, pan);            // stereo pan,
    OffsetOut.ar(out,audio);                // to bus out and out+1
    }
).add;              // make and store a SynthDesc and SynthDef
```

Figure 6.1
Example of a SynthDef

though the standard SynthDef method has been add since SuperCollider 3.4). In addition, SynthDefs can be organized into separate libraries rather than simply using the global one. These refinements are discussed in the Help files for the classes SynthDef and SynthDesc.

6.1.2   Events and Key/Value Arrays

In SuperCollider, parameters are often specified as *key/value* pairs. The key is a Symbol,[1] and the value is any object of the language (usually a Number, an Array, a Symbol, or a Function). For example, when a synth is created, the values of its controls are specified as a *key/value array* consisting of keys interleaved with values (e.g., [controlName1, value1, controlName2, value2 . . .]). An Event is a collection of key/value pairs that defines a specific action to be taken in response to the message play. By default, Events specify notes to be played on the server.

An Array can be written with a pair square brackets enclosing its comma-separated elements; an Event is enclosed with parentheses.[2] Within an Event definition, key/value pairs are written by appending a colon as a suffix to the key; Arrays accept this syntax as well. Figure 6.2 creates a key/value array and an event, assigning them to the interpreter variables a and e, respectively.

When a note event is sent a play message, it looks up the description (the SynthDesc) of the SynthDef identified by the value of the key \instrument. It uses that description to determine the names of the SynthDef's controls and uses those *control*

```
a = [
     type:            \note,
     instrument:      'sine',
     freq:            400,
     amp:             0.1,
     pan:             0,
     ar:              2,
     dr:              4,
     sustain:         2
];

e = (
     type:            \note,
     instrument:      'sine',
     freq:            400,
     amp:             0.1,
     pan:             0,
     ar:              2,
     dr:              4,
     sustain:         2
);
e.play;                        // play the note
```

Figure 6.2
Example of a key/value `Array` and a note `Event`

keys to generate the OSC commands needed to create and release a synth that plays the SynthDef. It then schedules those commands to be sent to the server at the appropriate times. An array of those OSC commands and their time offsets can be created by sending the event an `asOSC` message, as shown in figure 6.3.

Events also specify a time increment that is returned in response to the message `delta`. The increment returned is normally determined by taking the product of the values of the keys `\dur` and `\stretch`. This timing value is used to determine the rhythm of events specified by *Event patterns*.[3]

6.1.3   Sequences of Values and Events

`Patterns` specify sequences of values. For example, the class `Pseq(array, repeats, offset)` is used to define a pattern that specifies a sequence created by repeatedly iterating over the entirety of `array` beginning at `offset`. More concretely, the pattern `Pseq([0,1,2,3,4,5,6,7], 3, 1)` specifies the sequence `[1,2,3,4,5,6,7, 0,1,2,3,4,5,6,7,0,1,2,3,4,5,6,7,0]`.

```
e.asOSC.do{ | osc | osc.postcs };

// the result that would be posted:
// [ 0.0, ['s_new', 'sine', 1000, 0, 1, 'out', 0, 'freq', 400.0,
'amp', 0.1, 'pan', 0, 'ar', 2, 'dr', 4] ]
// [ 2.0, [ 'n_set', 1000, 'gate', 0 ] ]
```

Figure 6.3
The OSC commands created by the note event

```
1. Pbind( *[
    dur:    0.2,
    freq:   Pseq([100, 200, 300, 400, 500, 600, 700, 800])
] );

2. Pbind(
    \dur, 0.2,
    \freq,  Pseq([100, 200, 300, 400, 500, 600, 700, 800])
);
```

Figure 6.4
Two ways of writing the same event pattern

Patterns that specify sequences of events are called *Event patterns*, and they can specify complete musical sequences. The class Pbind(key, pattern, key2, pattern2...) defines event patterns by *binding* different *value patterns* to different event keys. Each event in the sequence specified begins as a copy of a *prototype event*. Then the next value of each value pattern[4] is taken and assigned to its corresponding key to produce the next element in the Pbind's sequence. That sequence ends when any of its constituent value patterns end.

When defining a Pbind object, the key/pattern pairs can be written as a key/value array[5] or as symbols interleaved with patterns; both are illustrated in figure 6.4, which defines a pattern that will produce the first 8 overtones of 100 Hz in an arpeggio and then stop.

In figure 6.5, an event pattern is assigned to the Interpreter variable p; it specifies a repeated sequence of the first 11 notes of the overtone series with a 4-event accent pattern, a 7-event duration pattern, and a 5-event sustain pattern. The pattern is then rendered as a sound file with a render message[6] and played in real time with a play message.

```
p = Pbind(*[
    instrument: \default,
    detune:     [0,1,3],
    freq:       Pseq( (1..11) * 100,  4 * 5 * 7),
    db:         Pseq([-20, -40, -30, -40], inf),
    pan:        Pseq([-1,0,1,0], inf),
    dur:        Pseq([0.2,0.2,0.2,0.2, 0.4,0.4,0.8], inf),
    legato:     Pseq([2,0.5,0.75,0.5,0.25], inf)
] );
// render 40 seconds of the pattern in the file named "sf.aif"
p.render("sounds/sf.aif", 40)
// now play the pattern in real-time
p.play;
```

Figure 6.5
A more elaborate event pattern

We detail below how patterns can be defined as combinations of other patterns. Programmers familiar with Routines can use the class Pspawner(routineFunction) to dynamically create sequential and parallel combinations of event patterns.

6.2 The Default Event

Event and its parent classes Environment and IdentityDictionary have a particularly wide range of application within SuperCollider (detailed in chapters 5 and 20). Here we focus on the structure of Event's default mechanism as it is used in conjunction with the patterns library. This default mechanism is implemented as a prototype Event with an extensive collection of predefined keys.

6.2.1 Event Types

The default Event contains an extensible collection of *event types* that specify different actions to be taken in response to play. Using an event involves setting the correct type and overriding the value of any keys whose default values are inappropriate. By default, the Event type is \note, which plays a note. The remainder of this section may be skipped on first reading, as our primary focus will be on the note event type discussed in section 6.2.2.

Table 6.1 is a reference list of default event types and their corresponding OSC commands.[7] Most event types provide a direct interface to an OSC command and can be understood by consulting the Server-Command-Reference Help file.

Table 6.1
Event Types of the Default Event

Type	OSC	Relevant Keys	Action
note	s_new	see below	create a synth with release
on	s_new	server, group, addAction, id	create a synth without release
set	n_set	server, id, args	set values of controls named by args
off	n_set	server, id, hasGate	release a node by setting gate to 0
	n_free		if there is no gate control, free it
group	g_new	server, group, addAction, id	create a group
kill	n_free	server, id	free a node (usually a group)
bus	c_setn	server, id, array	send array to consecutive control buses, starting at id
alloc	b_alloc	server, bufnum	allocate buffer
free	b_free	server, bufnum	free buffer
gen	b_gen	server, bufnum, gencmd, genflags, genarray	generate values in buffer
load	b_allocRead	server, bufnum, frame, filename, numframes	allocate and load file to buffer
read	B_read	server, bufnum, frame, filename, numframes, bufpos, leaveOpen	read file into preallocated buffer
rest	—	delta	defines a rest

Table 6.2 lists the keys that determine event timing; table 6.3 lists the keys that control the transmission of OSC commands;[8] and table 6.4 lists the keys that specify the creation of groups and synths on the server.

In figure 6.6, a group event creates a group with nodeID 2, a note event plays a note within that group, then all the notes in the group are released, and the group itself is freed.

6.2.2   Keys for Note Events

The note event types (\note, \on, \set, \off, \kill) play and release synths on the server. By convention, SynthDefs reserve the control names amp, pan, sustain, and freq to set the volume, position (usually in a stereo field), duration, and pitch of the note to be played, respectively. For each of these control keys, the default event provides a more abstract interface. For example, note amplitude can be set by assigning a multiplier between 0 and 1 to the key \amp or a decibel value between –100 and 0 to the key \db. Similarly, note sustain can be set directly through \sustain, or implicitly as the product of \dur and \legato.

Table 6.2
Event Timing Keys

dur	time until next note, defaults to 1.0
stretch	expansion/contraction of durations, defaults to 1.0
tempo	tempo of the TempoClock, defaults to nil, leaving current tempo
timingOffset	a delay imposed before the event is played, in beats
lag	A delay imposed before the event is played, in seconds
delta	delay until the next event in the sequence, usually ~dur * ~stretch

Table 6.3
Command Transmission Keys

server	defaults to nil, in which case Server.default is used
schedBundle	sends bundle to server or accumulates into a score
schedBundleArray	same as schedBundle, but the commands are in an array
schedStrummedNote	implements strumming, using schedBundle

Table 6.4
Node-Related Keys

id	nodeID of the synth or group, often left nil for dynamic allocation
group	The nodeID of the synth's placement target (group or synth) default value is 1; the nodeID of the "default group"
addAction	The placement of the synth in the node tree on the server, defaults to 0. It can be specified using integers or symbols, as listed below, and defined by the class Node
	\addToHead \h 0
	\addToTail \t 1
	\addBefore 2
	\addAfter 3
	\addReplace 4
instrument	the name of the SynthDef to be played, defaults to \default
out	output bus for the synth, defaults to 0

```
(
(type:  \group,
id: 2
).play;                                    // create a group with nodeID 2

    (   type:      \note,       // play note
        sustain:   100,         // lasting 100 seconds
        group:     2            // in group 2

    ).play;

)
(
    (type:  \off,   id: 2).play;           // release all notes in the group
    (type:  \kill, id: 2,  lag: 3).play;   // and free the group  3 seconds later
)
```

Figure 6.6
Using event types

Table 6.5
Amplitude-Related Keys

amp	amplitude as a multiplier
db	amplitude expressed in decibels (0 dB is the maximum level)
pan	pan position: −1 is left, 0 is center, 1 is right

Tables 6.5 through 6.7 enumerate keys that specify the amplitude, articulation, and pitch of notes. These keys create additional layers of abstraction that allow note properties to be specified in different ways.

These layers of specification are implemented with functions. Each function computes its value in terms of the next higher level of representation. For example, the value of the key \amp is a function that converts the value of the key \db into an amplitude multiplier. Assigning a value directly to \amp eliminates the function, overriding the \db specification. This is true in general: assigning a value to a key overrides any related higher-level specifications.

The pitch specification is elaborately layered, and pitch can be determined as

- a degree within a scale
- a note in a gamut of stepsPerOctave equal tempered steps
- a midinote in a 12-tone pitch set, or
- directly as a frequency, using the key freq.

Table 6.6
Note Articulation-Related Keys

sustain	time until note is released
legato	ratio that determines sustain in relation to dur * stretch
dur	time until next note in the pattern
gate	if it is a control of instrument, it is set to 0 to release the note
trig	used to trigger and release an envelope without releasing the note

Table 6.7
Frequency-Related Keys

stepsPerOctave	defines the equal tempered gamut (normally 12)
scale	array of intervals within the equal tempered gamut
root	fractional transposition within the equal tempered gamut
degree	pitch as a scale degree within the scale scale
mtranspose	modal transposition of degree within a scale
note	position within the equal tempered gamut
gtranspose	fractional transposition within the equal tempered gamut
octave	default transposition of note within 12-tone chromatic scale
midinote	fractional MIDI key# (69 -> 440, 69.5 is a quarter tone sharp)
ctranspose	fractional transposition within the 12-tone scale
freq	pitch directly as a frequency in Hertz
harmonic	is multiplied by the frequency determined by midinote
detune	usually 0 or an array of values to "fatten" the sound
detunedFreq	the function that determines the value of freq used to create the note; by default this is {~freq * ~harmonic + ~detune}

Each layer has an associated transposition value.

- root transposes scale.
- mtranspose transposes degree within scale.
- gtranspose and octave transpose note within the gamut defined by stepsPerOctave.
- ctranspose transposes midinote within equal temperament.
- harmonic transposes freq.

Assigning a value to a pitch key overrides both the higher-level pitch keys and their associated transpositions. Assigning a Symbol to a pitch key that has not been overridden specifies a rest.

As long as the SynthDef has a properly stored SynthDesc, note events will automatically send a synth all of its controls, whatever their names. Nevertheless, it is best to reserve default keys for their predefined purposes. There is little utility in

```
// 2nd inversion - e loudest
( degree: [-3,0,2],     sustain: 2,          db: [-20, -20, -10] ).play
// 2nd inversion - c loudest
( degree: [-3,0,2],     sustain: 2,          db: [-20, -10, -20] ).play
// note "fattened" by three detuned copies
( degree: 0,            sustain: 2,          detune: [0,3, 5] ).play
// each detune is assigned to a different pitch, fat free.
( degree: [-3,2,4],     sustain: 2,          detune: [0,3, 5] ).play
// detune rotates through each note in the chord
( degree: [-3,2,4],     sustain: 2,          detune: [0,0,0,3,3,3,5,5,5] ).play
```

Figure 6.7
Chord events

using the keys freq, amp, pan, out, in, and trig for anything other than their default purposes; changing the significance of server, group, addAction, or instrument will break the default mechanism altogether.

6.2.3   Note Events and Chords

Assigning an array to a control key (i.e., a key that actually names a control in the SynthDef identified by instrument) produces a chord. If several keys are assigned arrays, the event plays as many notes as the largest array. For each note in the chord, key values are obtained by iterating through whatever values were assigned. This is implemented by sending the key/value array generated by the event a flop message.[9] For example, here is a key/value array with arrays as values:

```
[
    freq: [100, 200, 300, 400], amp: [0.1, 0.2], pan: [-1, 0, 1]
]
```

After receiving a flop message, it becomes

```
[
    [freq: 100, amp: 0.1, pan: -1],
    [freq: 200, amp: 0.2, pan: 0],
    [freq: 300, amp: 0.1, pan: 1],
    [freq: 400, amp: 0.2, pan: -1]
]
```

Figure 6.7 provides examples of Events using this feature.

Table 6.8
Numerical Pattern Classes

`Pwhite(lo, hi, repeats)`	uniform random values between lo and hi
`Pbrown(lo, hi, step, repeats)`	"Brownian motion"; step is the maximum jump
`Pseg(array, dur, curves, repeats)`	break-point envelope; array must be numerical

Table 6.9
Event Pattern Classes

`Pbind(key, pat, key2, pat2...)`	bind patterns to keys
`Ppar(eventPatternArray, repeats)`	play the event patterns in list in parallel
`Pchain(pat1, pat2, ...)`	compose multiple patterns
`Pmono(name, key, pat...)`	start a single synth and control it

6.3   Patterns

6.3.1   An Overview of Patterns and Streams

Patterns are analogous to musical notation; they are abstract representations of sequences independent of any specific performance. Any object in the language can be viewed as a pattern, but most patterns specify a sequence whose values are simply the object itself. We will refer to these as *trivial patterns*, in contrast to *nontrivial patterns* that specify sequences with changing values. Numbers and Symbols are examples of trivial patterns, whereas classes such as `Pseq` are used to define nontrivial patterns.

To play a pattern, it is sent an `asStream` message. This returns a `Stream` object that will generate the sequence the pattern specifies. It does so 1 element at a time in response to the message `next`. Streams created by event patterns are called `event streams`. When patterns are treated as a score language, these details can be largely ignored. (We will return to them later, in the context of real-time performance.)

Tables 6.8, 6.9, and 6.10 list representative pattern classes, grouped according to the values of the sequences that instances of those classes will specify. An initial source of confusion is that many Pattern classes create patterns of patterns. For example, `Pseq` sequences produce whatever is in their array, which could be numbers, event patterns, or any other objects in the language. The important point is that such *pattern patterns* can be used to specify sequences of values assigned to a key within a `Pbind` or sequences of entire event patterns defined with `Pbind`.

Table 6.10
Pattern Pattern Classes

`Pseq(array, repeats, offset)`	iterate entire array repeat times, starting at offset
`Prand(array, repeats)`	randomly choose from array repeat times
`Pstutter(pattern, repeat)`	repeat each value of the pattern repeat times
`Pstep(array, dur, repeats)`	iterate the array, holding each value for dur seconds
`Pfunc(function, resetFunction)`	the entire function defines sequence elements
`Prout(function)`	Uses `embedInStream` to embed individual values or entire subsequences into the stream

6.3.2   Combining Patterns

Patterns can be used recursively in the definition of other patterns. For example, the arguments `lo` and `hi` of the random-value pattern `Pwhite` could be patterns defined with `Pseq` or `Pstep` or `Pseg`.

In addition, numerical patterns can be arithmetically combined to define new patterns. Combinations can be made using any of the unary and binary messages defined by `AbstractFunction`:

```
a = Pseq([1, 2, 3], 1);          // iterate 1, 2, 3 once
b = Pseq([a, 3, 2, 1], 2);       // pattern defined with another pattern
a + b;                           // sum of patterns
a * b * 33;                      // product of patterns
midiratio(b);                    // modified by unary message midiratio
a round: 4                       // modified by binary message round
```

Event patterns cannot be combined arithmetically. Instead, sequential and parallel combinations are made using the patterns `Pseq` and `Ppar`.

```
a = Pbind(*[dur: Pseq([0.4], 5)]);
b = Pbind(*[degree: Pseq([10, 6], inf), dur: Pseq([0.5], 4)]);

Pseq([a, b], 2).play;
Ppar([a, b], 4).play;
```

6.3.3   Time-Based Pattern Classes

Most patterns define sequences of values that are independent of time; the patterns `Pstep` and `Pseg` specify sequences that are sampled as functions of time. They are useful for attributes, such as dynamics and chord progressions, that are most easily described independent of the specific rhythmic sequences that articulate them. In

```
Pbind(*[
    stretch:        Pseg([0,0.1,0.2,1],8).linexp(0,1, 1,0.125),
    midinote:       100.cpsmidi,
    harmonic:       Pwhite(1, 16),
    legato:         Pkey(\stretch) * Pkey(\harmonic)/2 ,
    db:             -10 - Pkey(\harmonic),
    detune:         Pwhite(0.0,3.0),
    dur:            0.2,
]).play
```

Figure 6.8
Interdependent key values in a pattern

conjunction with the patterns Ppar and Pchain (discussed below) they can be used to specify attributes shared by different patterns running concurrently.

6.3.4 Interdependent Key Values in Event Patterns

Pbind allows completely independent patterns to specify key values, but it is often more natural to use a single sequence that determines several key values at once. For example, a melodic phrase may be better represented as a sequence of note/duration pairs than as 2 independent sequences. To do this, a pattern can be bound to an array of keys rather than a single key. In this case, the pattern specifies a sequence of arrays. The elements of each value array are assigned to the corresponding keys in the key array.

```
Pbind(*[
    #[degree, dur],     Pseq([[0, 1], [3, 1/2], [6, 1/3], [8, 1/4], [7, 1]]
                        ),
    db:                 -20
] ).play
```

When a Pbind is played, each pattern bound to a key (more precisely, the stream generated by that pattern) is advanced in turn. This makes it possible for a value pattern to determine the values of any keys bound earlier in the key/pattern array. The pattern Pkey(key) is a pattern that reads those values.[10] Figure 6.8 shows an event pattern whose pitches are the first 16 overtones of 100 Hz. The duration of each note is directly proportional to its harmonic number, and its volume is inversely proportional. The whole texture is stretched with a Pseg scaled to range from 1 to 0.125, effectively octupling the tempo.

The pattern Pchain(pat1, pat2, ..) allows the events of 1 pattern to be defined as a combination of values generated by others. In this context, the time-based

```
a = Pbind(*[
    scale:  Pn( Pstep([[0,2,4,5,7,9,11], [0,1,3,5,6,8,11] ], 5 ) ),
    db: Pn(Pseg([-20, -30, -25, -30], 0.4))
]);
b = Pbind(*[
    degree: Pbrown(0, 6, 1),
    mtranspose: Prand([\rest, Pseq([0], 5.rand)],inf),
    dur: 0.2,
    octave: 6
]);
c = Pbind(*[
    degree: [0,2,4],
    mtranspose: Pbrown(0, 6, 1),
    dur: 0.4,
    db: -35
]);
d = Pchain(Ppar([b, c]),a);
d.play;
```

Figure 6.9
Chaining event patterns

patterns can be used to define attributes shared by patterns running in parallel. In figure 6.9, pattern a specifies a changing scale, and patterns b and c define notes and chords within a scale. Pattern d chains a to the parallel combination of b and c so both share the same scale.

Events in a Pchain are computed from right to left. The event returned by the rightmost pattern is used as the protoype event for the pattern to its left, the result of that pattern is applied to the pattern to its left, and so forth. Patterns to the left can override any values received from patterns to the right. There is 1 exception; Ppar calculates the delta of its subpatterns in order to schedule them. Thus it is not possible to alter the \dur key of an event coming from a Ppar. Any such changes must be done by patterns to the right of the Ppar in the Pchain.

6.3.5   Defining Patterns with Pfunc and Prout

Pfunc and Prout make it possible to define patterns with a function. Within a Pfunc the function receives the event as an argument and returns a value. For example, here is a Pfunc that duplicates the functionality of Pkey: Pfunc({|ev|ev[\aKey]}).

Within a Prout the function returns values by sending them an embedInStream message. Trivial patterns respond to embedInStream by embedding themselves as a

```
Prout({| ev |
    var pat, refPat;

    refPat = Pbind(*[dur: 0.2, note: Pseq([0,0, 0, 7,0, 7])]);

    loop {
        ev = refPat.embedInStream(ev);

        pat = Pbind(*[
            dur: [0.2, 0.4].choose,
            note: Pseq(Array.fill(5, { 10.rand }), 3.rand )
        ]);
        ev = pat.embedInStream(ev);
    }

}).play
```

Figure 6.10
Using a Prout to define and play patterns on the fly

single-valued sequence; nontrivial patterns embed the entire sequence they specify. Thus, a Prout can select or even define new patterns on the fly and embed them in the current sequence.

In the following example, the function defines its own events and embeds them in the event stream. The first event in the stream appears as the argument of the function, and subsequent events appear as the return value embedInStream. The function stops at each embedInStream message and resumes immediately after, so the sequence of expressions in the function directly determines the sequence of events in the pattern.

```
Prout({|ev|              // modifies protoEvents
    ev = (freq: 400).embedInStream(ev.copy);
    ev = (freq: 500).embedInStream(ev.copy);
    ev = (freq: 600).embedInStream(ev.copy);
    ev = (freq: 700).embedInStream(ev.copy);
    ev = (freq: 800).embedInStream(ev.copy);
}).play;
```

Figure 6.10 shows a more elaborate example in which the Prout creates a reference pattern that it alternates with new patterns created on the fly in the midst of performance.

In figure 6.11, ~patA creates an array of notes and alters a randomly selected note in the array each time the array has been played. In ~patB, an event pattern is se-

```
~patA = Pbind(*[
    dur:    0.2,
    degree: Prout({ | ev |
        var noteArray  = (0..5);
        loop {
            ev = Pseq(noteArray ).embedInStream(ev);
            noteArray[6.rand] = 7.rand;
        }
    })
]);


~patB = Prout({ | ev |
    var pat, pats= [
        Pbind(*[ degree: Pseq([  0, 7]), dur: 0.2   ]),
        Pbind(*[ degree: Pseq([11, 7]), dur: 0.2 ]),
        Pbind(*[ degree: Pseq([16, 7]), dur: 0.2 ]).
        (type: \rest, delta: 1)
    ];

    loop {
        pat = pats.choose;
        ev = pat.embedInStream(ev);
    }
});

Pchain(
    Pbind(*[
        db:       Pn(Pstep([-15, -25,-25, -20, -30, -25], 0.2) )
            + Pseg([-30, -5,-10, -40], 12)
    ]),
    Ptpar([
        0, ~patA,
        0,  ~patA,
        12,  ~patB
    ])
).play;
```

Figure 6.11
Using Prout to define value and event patterns

```
~pattern = Pbind(*[
    instrument: "default",
    freq:   Pseq([100, 200, 300, 400, 500, 600, 700, 800, 900, 1000, 1100], 5),
    db:     Pseq([-10, -30, -20, -30], inf),
    dur:    Pseq([0.2,0.2,0.2,0.2, 0.4,0.4,0.8],inf),
    legato: Pseq([2,0.5,0.75,0.5,0.25], inf)
] );

~score = ~pattern.asScore(24 * 11/7);
~score.render("recordings/test.aif");
SoundFile("recordings/test.aif").play;
```

Figure 6.12
Rendering and playing a pattern

lected at random to be embedded. These patterns are combined with Ptpar, which schedules the entrance of 2 copies of ~patA and 1 copy of ~patB. This parallel combination is faded in and out, using Pchain.

6.3.6   Rendering Event Patterns

An event pattern can be rendered into a sound file either by sending it a render message directly or by creating a Score object with the asScore message and rendering that score with asScore. The latter approach allows an alternative protoEvent to be used and for the score to be offset in time for subsequent manipulation. Here are those methods and their arguments.

```
render(path, maxTime, sampleRate, headerFormat,
        sampleFormat, options, inputFilePath)
    path is the path name for the resultant audio file.
    headerFormat is "AIFF" by default; could be "WAV" or "SD2"
    sampleFormat is "int16" by default, could be "int24", "int32", or
    "float"

    asScore(duration, timeOffset, protoEvent)
    duration and timeOffset are self-explanatory.
    protoEvent defines the prototype event used by the pattern
```

Figure 6.12 defines a pattern, turns it into a score, renders the score, and then plays that file.

6.4   Timing Considerations

6.4.1   Timing and Articulation

Music is filled with examples of events and actions that, though conceived as simultaneous, actually occur at different times. Notes may be played before or after a beat, chords can be broken or strummed, signals can be given a beat ahead, and so forth. The \lag and \timingOffset keys set delay times between the time an event receives its play message and the time the resultant OSC commands are sent to the server. Lag is expressed in seconds; timingOffset is in time units altered by the value of tempo.

For file rendering, notes that occur off the beat can be specified simply by assigning a positive or negative value to \lag or \timingOffset, and the key \strum sets a delay time between notes in a chord.

```
(lag: 0, strum: 0.1, note: [12, 16, 19], sustain: 1).play;
```

A negative strum value will cause the notes in the chord to precede the beat. If the key \strumEndsTogether is set to true, individual notes will be lengthened or shortened to end the chord at the time specified by \sustain.

Real-time performance requires special measures described in section 6.5.2.

6.4.2   Audio Rate, Control Rate, and Sample Accurate Scheduling

As noted in chapter 2, Supercollider, like most software synthesis systems, computes audio in blocks of samples. This introduces a distinction between *audio rate*, the sample rate of audio samples, and *control rate*, the rate at which sample blocks are computed. A 44.1 kHz sampling rate with a block size of 64 will yield approximately a 690 Hz control rate and 0.00145-second control period. The server responds to OSC commands at control rate.

Starting synths at sample block boundaries can create objectionable artifacts in the sound. The UGen OffsetOut provides sample accurate scheduling by using the time stamp of the synth's creation command to determine how many samples to provide to its first sample block. This places the beginning of the synth's audio at the correct time.

A related issue is that synths can respond to control changes only at control rate. Attempts to gate an envelope with a duration less than the control period will have undefined results (the note may not occur or may sustain indefinitely). With very tightly articulated sounds, it is best to use fixed-duration envelopes running at audio rate that are time scaled by the sustain value of the event. In this case, the event type \on can be used with the key \id set to −1 (which indicates to the server that the language will not attempt to communicate with the synth). Granular synthesis is an example of an approach in which these timing issues are extremely important. Figure 6.13 granulates a sound file, steadily increasing grain size from 0.01 second to 2 seconds with an overlap of 4 grains.

Chapter 16 provides a detailed exploration of granular synthesis and related techniques in SC.

6.4.3   Freeing Synths

The single most common mistake made when first working with patterns is to write a SynthDef that does not free created synths when they are done. Though not strictly a timing issue, the main impact of this mistake is to overload the server and destroy the integrity of the audio output. The following example illustrates the problem and its solution; the Help file UGen-doneActions provides further details.

```
SynthDef("eternal", {|out, freq, amp, pan, gate|
        var audio, env;
        audio = SinOsc.ar(freq, 0, amp);
        env = Linen.kr(gate);                    // mistake: does not
                                                 delete synth
//      env = Linen.kr(gate, doneAction: 2);     // doneAction of 2 is
                                                 needed
        audio = audio * env;
        audio = Pan2.ar(audio, pan);
        Out.ar(out,audio);
    });
```

6.5   Real-Time Performance and Interactive Control of Patterns

6.5.1   TempoClocks and Quantization

Here is Pattern's play method with its associated arguments:

```
play(clock, protoEvent, quant)
    clock is a TempoClock, and its default value is TempoClock.default
    protoEvent is an Event used to set default values for the pattern
    quant is a quantization value that constrains when the pattern will
    begin playing
```

The method returns an EventStreamPlayer object, which provides interactive control through the messages play, pause, resume, and stop. The EventStreamPlayer creates a stream out of the pattern and then plays it, using the specified clock to determine event timing and the specified protoEvent (or the default Event) as the starting point for each event the stream produces.

```
SynthDef("playbuf", { | out=0, bufnum = 0, rate = 1,
                           startPos = 0, amp = 0.1, sustain = 1,
                           pan = 0, gate = 1|
    var audio, env;
    rate = rate * BufRateScale.kr(bufnum);
    startPos = startPos * BufFrames.kr(bufnum);
    env = EnvGen.ar(Env.sine, 1, timeScale: sustain, doneAction: 2);
    audio = PlayBuf.ar(1, bufnum, rate, 1, startPos, 0);
    audio = env * audio;
    audio = Pan2.ar(audio, pan, amp);
    OffsetOut.ar(out, audio);
}).add;

    Pseq([
        (   type:         \load,
            filename:     "sounds/a11wlk01.wav",
            bufnum:       1,
            delta:        0
        ),

        Pbind(*[
            instrument: "playbuf",
            type:         \on,
            id:           -1,
            dur:          Pseg([0,1],21).linexp(0,1,0.01,2),
            legato:       4,
            startPos:     Pn(Pseg([0,1], 10)),
            bufnum:       1,
        ]),
        (   type:         \free,
            bufnum:       1
        )
    ]).play(quant: 0)
```

Figure 6.13
Sound file granulation with a pattern

As noted in chapter 3, a TempoClock has a controllable tempo, so its logical time is expressed in *beats* rather than seconds. Event Patterns can set the clock tempo through the key \tempo. Any other patterns that share the same clock will experience the same tempo change. In contrast, the \stretch key affects only the pattern it is defined within.

The specific time at which the pattern begins playback depends on the value of quant. If quant is 0, performance begins as soon as the message is sent. Otherwise, the pattern begins at the beat that is the earliest integer multiple of quant.

Sometimes simple quantization is not enough. The quant argument can also be a 2-value array that specifies quant and phase. Phase is an offset relative to quant. For example, if quant is 1 and phase is 0.75, the pattern will commence playing 1/4 beat before the basic beat time.

A pattern may need to play at a timingOffset as well. This sets a delay time between the computation of an event and the transmission of the OSC commands it generated, providing some leeway for notes that play ahead of the beat. Such notes can be scheduled by setting the \timingOffset key to the sum of its current value and the desired (negative) delay. As long as this sum remains nonnegative, correct timing will be maintained.

As a 3-value array, the quant argument specifies quant, phase, and offset. This provides the specified timingOffset to the entire EventStream while guaranteeing that its first note sounds at the time specified by quant and phase. As a convenience, it is also possible to specify the timingOffset in the prototype event used by the EventStreamPlayer.

6.5.2 Compensating for Delays Between the Language and the Server

In SuperCollider the language is decoupled from synthesis in order to prevent timing problems from creating "glitches" in audio output. This creates a need for additional layers of timing specification that enable the language to specify different trade-offs between timing accuracy and fast execution.

In the real-time context, synchronization between the language and the server is maintained by a network time base. Commands sent by the language have *time stamps* that indicate when they should be performed. Because network connections can have delays that vary from message to message, a *latency* is usually added to these time stamps. If the latency is larger than the longest network delay, relative timing will be accurately maintained. This value is kept in the latency instance variable of the Server object. By default the latency is 0.2 seconds.

If the Server and language do not share a network time base, time stamps cannot be used and the Server object's latency should be set to nil. This exposes an additional nuance in the actual timing of audio generation. Audio interfaces are often configured to maintain sample buffers much larger than typical sample block sizes. In this case, the server must compute enough sample blocks to fill the buffer. Time stamps enable the server to respond to commands at the correct time, in spite of the timing variations these large buffers create, but those variations will be exposed when using an unsynchronized server. Reducing the hardware buffer size to the block size will correct this.

6.5.3   Conduction with PatternConductor

When an EventStreamPlayer is paused or stopped, it may have notes sustaining. These notes can be left at their intended durations, released immediately, or, in the case of a pause, sustained until the EventStreamPlayer is resumed. Note releases are scheduled by the EventStreamPlayer's clock, so all of these possibilities can be realized by adjusting its tempo. `PatternConductor` is a variant of EventStreamPlayer that creates its own TempoClock and provides a tempo argument for its pause and stop methods.

6.5.4   Conductor and CV

Interactive control naturally includes issues concerning graphical user interface, external control devices, and the structure of the objects that are to be controlled interactively.

The `CV` and `Conductor` classes provide a framework that can be used to quickly create a GUI to control a pattern or set of patterns and to link it to external control sources provided by MIDI or HID. These classes are available as a Quark named Conductor.

6.6   Appendix 1: How Patterns Are Performed by Streams

6.6.1   Defining Streams with Patterns and Routines

Sending a pattern an `asStream` message creates a `Stream` object that generates an instance of the sequence the pattern specifies. The sequence is generated 1 element at a time in response to a sequence of next messages. Trivial patterns simply return themselves in response to both `asStream` and next. Thus a trivial Pattern is also a trivial Stream.

Here we define a `Pseq`, create a stream from it, and assemble the stream's values into an array.

```
r = Routine{
    Pseq([1,2,3]).yield;
    Pseq([1,2,3]).embedInStream;
    123445.embedInStream;
    123445.embedInStream;
};

[next(r), next(r), next(r), next(r), next(r), next(r)];
// the result: [ a Pseq, 1, 2, 3, 123445, 123445, nil]
```

Figure 6.14
yield versus embedInStream

```
a = Pseq([1, 2, 3]).asStream;
[a.next, a.next, a.next, a.next];
// [1, 2, 3, nil] // the result
```

Once a stream runs out of values, it returns nil in response to next. Since the pattern specified a 3-element sequence, the fourth element of the array is nil.

The class Routine is used by patterns to create their associated streams. As noted in chapter 3, a Routine is a Function that can return from any point in its definition and, when called again with a next message, resume where it left off. The messages yield and embedInStream define the exit and entry points, respectively, within the function used to define the routine. For trivial patterns (and streams) embedInStream is identical to yield; it yields the object once and returns. For a nontrivial pattern, it performs asStream and *embeds* the resultant stream in the routine. The stream maintains control until it has yielded all of the values in its sequence in response to next messages sent to the routine. Figure 6.14 illustrates the difference between yield and embedInStream, and figure 6.15 presents the definition of the Routine used by Pseq(array, offset, repeats) to create its associated streams.

As the stream plays, each element in the array is sent the embedInStream message. Thus each element of the array can be a trivial pattern, a nontrivial pattern, or even a stream. This makes it possible to define patterns within patterns to arbitrarily deep levels of nesting without explicitly invoking any methods. To a large degree, this accounts for the remarkable concision of patterns definitions.

6.6.2 EventStream and ScoreStream Players

An Event Pattern is performed by an EventStreamPlayer. The player sends the pattern an asStream message that creates the EventStream that actually generates the

```
Routine({
    repeats.value.do({
        list.size.do({ arg i;
            item = list.wrapAt(i + offsetValue);
            inval = item.embedInStream(inval);
        });
    });
});
```

Figure 6.15
The definition of the stream created by Pseq.

pattern's event sequence. The player obtains these events by sending the stream a next(protoEvent) message, which returns the protoEvent as altered by the event stream. It plays the event and then sends the EventStream a delta message to determine the delay until its next event. It uses this time increment to reschedule itself within the time base of its TempoClock.

Scores and rendered files are created with a ScoreStreamPlayer. This object simulates the role of both a Server (for id allocation) and a TempoClock (for tempo control), and alters the \schedBundle and \schedBundleArray keys of the protoEvent to collect OSC commands and their time stamps rather than sending them to a server.

6.7   Appendix 2: Event and its Superclasses

6.7.1   The Class Derivation of Event

Event is derived from the classes Dictionary, IdentityDictionary, and Environment. Dictionary defines the methods at(key) and put(key, value), which allow the values of existing keys to be examined and altered and new key/value pairs to be added.

IdentityDictionary implements a faster lookup mechanism in which equivalent keys must be *identical objects*. Because of this, Symbols are generally used as keys. IdentityDictionary also defines the instance variables parent and proto. The method at attempts to retrieve a key's value first from the dictionary, then from its protodictionary, and finally from its parent dictionary, returning the first non-nil value it finds. This provides the basis for Event's default mechanism.

Environment implements features akin to "name spaces" in other languages. When the language starts, it creates and stores an Environment in topEnvironment and currentEnvironment (class variables of Object, which are globally accessible). The topEnvironment variable is generally left unchanged, so it can provide a globally accessible name space. In contrast, currentEnvironment is often altered to provide access to different local name spaces. The compiler provides a shortcut syntax in which ~ substitutes for currentEnvironment, making the following expressions equivalent.

```
// "getter" messages that retrieve a value from a key within
currentEnvironment
    ~key;
    currentEnvironment[\key];
    currentEnvironment.at(\key);
    // "setter" messages that set the value of a key within
    currentEnvironment
    ~key = 888;
    currentEnvironment[\key] = 888;
    currentEnvironment.put(\key, 888);
```

The messages make(theFunction) and use(theFunction) allow theFunction to be evaluated within the name space defined by the receiving Environment. The message make returns the Event, and the message use returns the return value of the function. In the following example, an event is made that defines ~freq in terms of ~note and ~octave. That event is then used to compute the frequency when ~note is 0.

```
a = Event.make {
    ~octave = 5;
    ~freq = {(~note + (~octave * 12)).midicps};
}
a.use {~note = 0; ~freq.value};
```

This is the basic approach used by Event's default mechanism. In that context, one could bind patterns to \note and \octave or directly to \freq. To allow this kind of overriding of the default mechanism, a new copy of the protoEvent must be used to generate each event in the sequence.

6.7.2   The Default Parent Event and Event Types

Event's default mechanism is implemented through a default parent event stored in the class variable defaultParentEvent. This event defines the play functions of different event types and provides values for all of the keys they use. Figure 6.16 provides the definition of Event's play method, and figure 6.17 provides the default definition of the key \play that method uses.

Thus the defaultParentEvent is used unless the event specifies otherwise, and the function stored at \play defines the event's response to play. The final line of that function implements event types.

An event type is simply a play function that receives server as an argument. All event types are held in an Event stored in defaultParentEvent[\eventTypes]. New

```
play {
    if (parent.isNil) { parent = defaultParentEvent };
    this.use { ~play.value };
}
```

Figure 6.16
The definition of the play method in Event.

```
{
    var tempo, server;

    ~finish.value;                              // user callback
    server = ~server ?? { Server.default };
    tempo = ~tempo;                    // assigning to a variable
                                       // saves repeated look ups
    if (tempo.notNil) {                // if not nil, change tempo of
        thisThread.clock.tempo = tempo;    // the clock playing the pattern
    };
    ~eventTypes[~type].value(server);    // select play function from ~type
}
```

Figure 6.17
Definition of the key \play in the default event

```
{ |server|
    var lag, array;
    lag = ~lag + server.latency;
    array = ~array.asArray;
    server.sendBundle(lag,
        [\c_setn, ~out.asUGenInput, array.size] ++ array);
}
```

Figure 6.18
Implementation of the event type \bus.

event types can be added using the class method *addEventType(key, function).
Figure 6.18 presents the definition of the event type bus as an example.

Notes

1. As noted in chapter 5, Symbols are objects that uniquely represent a sequence of alphanumeric characters. The language ensures that there is one, and only one, Symbol for any given sequence of characters. Symbols are written enclosed within single quotes or preceded by a backslash (e.g., 'a Symbol with spaces' or \aSymbol).

2. A possible source of confusion is the convention that blocks of code in examples are also enclosed in parentheses. Such parentheses make it possible to select the text of the example with a double click and are usually not included in the block of text evaluated by the Interpreter.

3. The value returned by delta can be set directly by assigning a value to the key \delta. This option is used by patterns that run several subpatterns in parallel. It enables them to schedule those subpatterns without altering their internal rhythmic specification (i.e., \dur and \stretch).

4. Strictly speaking, the value pattern specifies a sequence, and it is that sequence that determines the value of the key to which the pattern is bound.

5. The asterisk causes Pbind to treat the elements of the key/value array as individual arguments.

6. There is no direct way to determine the duration of the sounds specified by a pattern. For example, the last event could play a synth with an arbitrarily long decay envelope. Consequently, render requires the duration of the sound file to be specified.

7. The pattern Pproto and the class EventTypesWithCleanup are recent additions to the language that simplify the allocation, deallocation, and use of buffers and buses in patterns. These classes provide a supplemental collection of buffer-related eventTypes (table, sine1, sine2, sine3, cheby, cue, and allocRead) that perform standard initialization tasks. Consult Pproto's Help file for details.

8. The server-related keys are altered when a pattern is used to generate a score or render an audio file.

9. A similar mechanism provides *multichannel expansion* in SynthDefs.

10. When an event pattern defined by Pbind is sent asStream, it creates a key/stream array corresponding to the key/value array that defines it. It relays next(protoEvent) messages to those streams in order, setting each bound key in the protoEvent to the value returned by its stream.

7 Just-in-Time Programming

Julian Rohrhuber and Alberto de Campo

It is impossible to write a program while it runs. A program describes and determines a process, so changing the description implies a new outset, a new process. Yet it is possible to structure a program in such a way that parts of it can be interchanged dynamically, and its textual form can be arranged to allow rewriting those parts while the whole process continues. Thus, instead of first designing an application that has fixed interaction points (*parameters*), the program text itself becomes the main interface. Instead of planning ahead and providing a large number of parameters, we may modify the program at any point. Although in many fields the program is of interest only for the desired application, here the program is a reflection of thinking and an integral part of the reasoning process.

This paradigm is relevant for improvised music and performance art, since in live coding, artists write algorithmic compositions in the concert and use code as a conversational medium.[1] Also, programming is an integral part of concept formation both in scientific research and in the experimental prototyping of algorithms, so that often a new idea emerges from minor details or misconceptions that, not unlike the fringe of an atoll, turn out to be the eventual solutions.

Sound programming is at the same time a difficult and a captivating activity because of the way abstract expressions and listening experiences relate to each other—the static text structure of code on the one side, the unfolding of sound in time on the other. Programming is not merely the construction of a calculating mechanism to receive the answer to a question, but rather a way to find the right question. Thus, conversational and interactive programming have been undercurrents in computer science and experimental mathematics since the 1960s (Klerer and Reinfelds, 1968), developing further in the form of live coding, operating system design, and scientific experimental programming (e.g., Vogt et al., 2007). Here, we will discuss a class library within SuperCollider (*Just-in-Time Programming Library*) that provides such an experimental and improvisational environment.

One interacts with SuperCollider in a manner similar to Smalltalk or Lisp: although conversational approaches, like terminal applications, work more or less on

```
(
Task {
    x = 4; y = 13;
    loop {
        x = (x * y) % 5;
        (note: x.postln, dur: 0.125).play;
        0.125.wait;
    }
}.play
);        // creates a loop of values

// change x and y
x = 5;  // new initial value
y = 4;  // new multiplication factor
```

Figure 7.1
A modulo algorithm that operates over states of variables.

a line-by-line basis, here, appropriate *parts* of the program text are selected and evaluated while the rest of the system is active.

Whether considering programming as a dialogue or as symbiosis with the "thinking machine" (Licklider, 1960), a process of external reasoning (Suchman, 2007; Clark and Chalmers, 1998; Iverson, 1979), an "exploratory object" (Guardans 2010), or the formation of an "epistemic thing" (Rheinberger, 1997), the relation between program text and running program is not trivial; analysis and experiment are interdependent. Thus, in order to be able to change one's mind while changing one's program, one has little choice but to include the programming activity itself in the program's operation.

7.1 Changing State

After showing the basic issues of just-in-time programming by simple examples, we demonstrate how programs can be written as they run. Figure 7.1 shows a small algorithm that multiplies 2 values of the (interpreter) variables x and y, determines the remainder after division by 5, and changes x to the result (so, e.g., 4 * 13 mod: 5 results in 2).

After x and y are assigned initial values, the algorithm runs within a task that waits a little after each of these steps. The variables x and y represent a momentary *state* of the program, one that is partly changed by the program at runtime. As a consequence, the expression x = 4; y = 13; which initialized this state, does not directly stand for these 2 values at runtime: the code represents only the *initial moment*.

```
(
{
    x = SinOsc.kr(4);
    y = SinOsc.kr(13);
    SinOsc.ar(x * y % 0.4 * 500 + 600) * 0.2
}.play;
)


// change x and y?
x = SinOsc.kr(4); // no effect.
y = SinOsc.kr(4); // no effect either.
```

Figure 7.2
Synthesis graph.

Because interpreter and task run concurrently, we may now use the line of code
x = 5 and change either x or y to a different value *while* it is being operated on. (This
change will always fall between 2 operations while the task is waiting. The series of
resulting numbers proceeds from this new state.

Thus, as long as we have access to a state that is read repeatedly over time, such
as the number in this example, modifying code at runtime is simple; once we are
concerned with more abstract descriptions of changing or shared state, this is not as
trivial: figure 7.2, though similar, uses variables assigned to unit generators. Here
sine oscillators, each with its own frequency, are multiplied by each other. The remainder after division by 0.4 is then used, with some scaling, as the frequency input
of another sine oscillator. A slightly "creaky" tone results.

In figure 7.2, any attempt to change the value of x or y fails. One can only stop the
whole program, change it, and then rerun it. This is because the variable does not
stand for a changing state here but for a unit generator, an *abstract description of a
whole process* rather than of an initial condition. In other words, this description
holds for the entire time the process will run, not just at a single moment. As a consequence, it is not trivial to say what it would mean to change this description at a
given moment.

To briefly foreshadow a solution, figure 7.3 shows a specific kind of environment,
a ProxySpace. In this code, each line can be evaluated in any order—there is no
longer any difference between the code used for initializing and the code used in
rewriting. Furthermore, there is no difference between changing a number, an
operator, or a unit generator, since any change in the text is reflected in a change to
the running system.

To understand the principle behind this type of solution, we give an introduction
to a common form of abstract description of processes in SuperCollider.

```
p = ProxySpace.push;
~x = { SinOsc.kr(4) };
~y = { SinOsc.kr(13) };
~z = { SinOsc.ar(~x * ~y % 0.4 * 500 + 600) * 0.2 };
~z.play;


// now ~x and ~y can be replaced
~x = { SinOsc.kr(0.4) };
~y = { SinOsc.kr(1.3) };

p.clear(2).pop; // release environment (2 sec fadeout)
```

Figure 7.3
Dynamic synthesis graph.

7.2   Abstraction and Proxies

Many objects in SuperCollider are *abstract* in the sense that when operating with them, we do not get a completed value, but an algorithm that produces values only when applied. The simple comparison: x = [1910, 1911, 1912]; y = x + 96.rand; results in an array of numbers for y. On the other hand, an expression such as y = x + {96.rand} results in a BinaryOpFunction, an object that describes this addition without yet performing it. Unlike the previous example, this function returns a new value not only once, but *each time* it is evaluated—the function represents the operation of adding a new random number to x (the result is calculated each time y.value is called). Thus we have *composed* a new calculation rather than directly calculating a result once; we have described a description.[2]

In SuperCollider, this type of behavior is common—all subclasses of Abstract-Function, such as UGen, Stream, and Pattern, behave analogously. This is an important feature for working with sound: rather than specify each moment in time directly, we can calculate with sound generators on a more abstract level (figure 7.2 shows such a case), combining them into complex graphs of calculation. In fact, even this combination of UGens and patterns is commonly represented as a program. For instance, the expression

```
{var x = 1.0; 5.do {x = x * SinOsc.ar(1911.0.rand)}; x}.play
```

specifies a chain of multiplied oscillators which, when instantiated, processes a value "continually" (i.e., for each sample at audio rate). Inside a SynthDef, this chain can be used to define further processing. The SynthDef itself can be used to define any number of synth nodes, which is where the process actually happens.

In other words, abstraction permits the interpretation of math operations and other messages as *potential operations* or "operations on the future," combinations of possibly multiple future processes. Since these processes are not precalculated, their behavior may depend on external changes such as audio input or some other interaction.

The structures of operations and interconnections may be changed not only via their parameters but also at runtime (figure 7.3). In SuperCollider, *proxies* allow for such structural changes. Here, a proxy is a placeholder for potential redefinitions. It forms a link between the domain of stateless, functional language and the imperative domain, the action of rewriting (Rohrhuber et al., 2005; or, for comparison with a much earlier approach, Mathews 1969). Using different types of placeholders, program code can be refactored at runtime or even created as an empty skeleton of "roles" to be filled later (this is essentially a type of *late binding*).

To be compatible with the different processes, a proxy has to behave differently, depending on whether it refers to a *server node*, a *task*, a *pattern*, or an *object* in general (the latter is touched upon in chapter 23). The proxies we will discuss here form a bridge between abstract stateless descriptions of processes such as UGen graphs or patterns, and interactive stateful processes unfolding in time. Somewhat similar to free variables, proxies provide *schemes of access* (in order to reach a description from multiple places) and *schemes of replacement* (in order to change a description and affect multiple processes).

Usually, free variables have to be bound to some object before they can be used in a process. To allow a proxy to be used in multiple places before its object is known, the proxy schema abstracts from this order of assignment. Creating a proxy and changing its object (its *source*) may be done explicitly; alternatively, the implicit *def syntax* or a special environment such as *LazyEnvir* or *ProxySpace* allows a syntactical unification of instance creation, reference, and assignment for each type of proxy (e.g., `Ndef(\x)` for reference and `Ndef(\x, { WhiteNoise.ar})` for assignment). As a consequence, the same code that created the placeholder instance can be modified and evaluated at any time after the process is first running.

7.3   ProxySpace, Ndef, and NodeProxy

The SuperCollider server allows interconnecting synth processes and exchange nodes at runtime. For efficiency reasons, there is a strict conceptual difference between the graph of units *inside* 1 synth process, and the graph *between* synth processes which depend on each other. While it is all still SuperCollider language, code that describes synth definitions has a semantics different from the code that is used to interconnect them. For example, Synth objects are kept meticulously outside of SynthDefs, and there is no place for changes to the UGen graph within Synth objects. *ProxySpace* is an Environment (a set of things that can be accessed by name; see the Environment

```
p = ProxySpace.push;    // if needed

~a = { Lag.ar(LFClipNoise.ar(2 ! 2, 0.5, 0.5), 0.2) };
(
~b = {
        var c, d;
        c = Dust.ar(20 ! 2);
        d = Decay2.ar(c, 0.01, 0.02, SinOsc.ar(11300));
        d + BPF.ar(c * 5, ~a.ar * 3000 + 1000, 0.1)
}
);

~b.play;

// the refactored code from above

(
~a = {
        var a;
        a = Lag.ar(LFClipNoise.ar(2 ! 2, 0.5, 0.5), 0.2);
        BPF.ar(~c.ar * 5, a * 3000 + 1000, 0.1)
}
);
~c = { Dust.ar(20 ! 2) };
~d = { Decay2.ar(~c.ar, 0.01, 0.02, SinOsc.ar(11300)) };
~b = ~a + ~d;

~b.play;
```

Figure 7.4
Refactoring a synthesis graph at runtime.

Help file for more details) that brings these 2 sides into a more direct relation: hiding some functionality, it makes it easier to rewrite parts of a UGen graph as a synth graph and to combine a synth graph into a single UGen graph.

Figure 7.4 shows refactoring code at runtime: in the upper part, there are 2 UGen graphs (one in ~a and one in ~b) which have been rewritten into the equivalent node graph (now with ~a, ~b, ~c, and ~d). Figure 7.5 visualizes such operations.

On the whole, a ProxySpace behaves like any other environment: externally, it can be accessed via messages such as put and at; from within, the tilde (~) can instead be written. Although environments normally represent objects on the client side, ProxySpace represents descriptions and running instances of synthesis processes on the server.

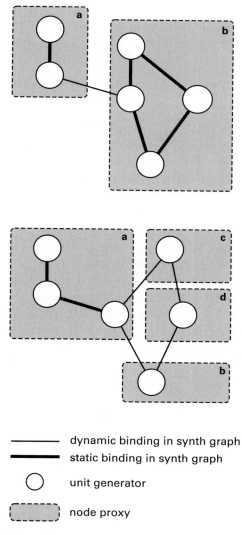

dynamic binding in synth graph

static binding in synth graph

unit generator

node proxy

Figure 7.5
Dynamic synthesis graph.

```
// self reference (~x) constructs a loop at control rate

~out.play;
~x = 0.2; ~a = 1.1; ~c = 0.13;
~x = (~a * ~x) + ~c % 1.0;   // leaving out the .kr message assumes a control rate
ugen.

~out = { Pan2.ar(SinOsc.ar(~x * 4000 + 200) * 0.1, ~x) };
```

Figure 7.6
A dynamic graph of a chaotic linear congruence. Self reference (~x) constructs a loop at control rate.

Whenever it is accessed, ProxySpace returns a placeholder for a server node —instances of NodeProxy. Thus, assigning a value to the environment (e.g., ~x = [1, 2]) results not only in keeping this value but also in its conversion into a UGen graph, and a corresponding synthesis process on the server which the NodeProxy takes care of. Without any reference to bus numbers or execution order, each node is addressed only by name—thus one may reason about synthesis from a symbolic point of view.[3] Each symbol represents a place for a synth process that can be accessed from any other synth process on the same server (even from within itself: ~x = ~x + ~y % 11 is a recursive and slightly chaotic function; see also figure 7.6).

When using a placeholder inside a UGen graph, it can be employed empty (returning silence) and may be filled later (e.g., ~x.play; ~x = ~y * ~z). By abstracting away execution order, it is now easy to use a piece of program text not only as a single block but also in parts that can be evaluated either together or apart, thus accessing and changing a sound aspect by aspect. By itself, the synthesis graph has no privileged observer position. A node becomes audible only when explicitly playing it through an out channel (~x.play), so that any audio rate proxy can be listened to equally, perhaps shifting the center of attention from one to the next. On multichannel systems, the playN variant allows a further method of monitoring a NodeProxy: mapping multiple outputs to multiple channels (see the *playN Help* file).

So far, we have used ProxySpace "from within" for simplicity, employing p = ProxySpace.push to temporarily replace the current environment with this specific environment. To return to the usual mode, p.pop is evaluated; we may of course also create a proxy space without pushing it (p = ProxySpace.new). So if one prefers to use the default environment instead of variables, it is as valid to write ~x = ... as it is to write p[\x] = ... Furthermore, ~x.ar is equivalent to p[\x].ar. As an overview, figures 7.7–7.9 show the same sound expressed in different ways—inside other

```
n = NodeProxy.new;
x = { SinOsc.ar(n.kr * 200 + 300) * 0.1 }.play;
n.source = { LFPulse.kr([1.3, 2.1, 3.2]).sum };
n.clear; x.free;
```

Figure 7.7
Creating a proxy object explicitly and changing its source.

```
Ndef(\out, { SinOsc.ar(Ndef.kr(\x) * 200 + 300) * 0.1 }).play;
Ndef(\x, { LFPulse.kr([1.3, 2.1, 3.2]).sum });
Ndef.clear;
```

Figure 7.8
Unified creation and access syntax with Ndef.

```
p = ProxySpace.push; // if needed
~out = { SinOsc.ar(~x.kr * 200 + 300) * 0.1 }
~out.play;
~x = { LFPulse.kr([1.3, 2.1, 3.2]).sum };
p.clear.pop;
```

Figure 7.9
Unified creation and access syntax within an environment.

classes it is usually better to create an object instance, whereas for the development of a network of interconnected nodes, either Ndef or ProxySpace may be more appropriate. The same scheme applies to the other proxies, which we will discuss further below, such as PatternProxy (Pdefn, Pdef) and TaskProxy (Tdef), and to LazyEnvir, which has a function similar to ProxySpace.

Because UGen graphs always have a fixed *rate* and number of *channels*, a node proxy, unlike other proxies, has to be initialized to this format. This can be done either explicitly, before it is "filled" with something, or implicitly, derived from what is assigned to it first; monitoring a neutral proxy (x.play) will normally initialize it to 2 audio channels (see figure 7.10; for more details, see *the_lazy_proxy.help*). If required, the message clear neutralizes the proxy again, so that it is free for reassignment. When a fadeTime is specified, a slow transition maintains perceptual continuity (see also section 7.7); interesting timbral shifts can be achieved with different

```
p.clear; // neutralize space, free all buses and synths
p.push; // if needed
~a.ar(3); // 3 channels, audio rate
~b.kr(8); // 8 channels, control rate
~c.play; // playing an uninitialized proxy assumes (per default) 2
channels, audio rate
~d = { LFNoise0.kr([1, 1, 1, 1]) }; // 4 channels, control rate
```

Figure 7.10
Initialisation of node proxies in a proxy space.

```
~out.play; ~out.fadeTime = 3;
(
// name with a_ represents audio rate argument
~out = { |freq=440, mod=0.4, detune=0.1, a_in = #[1,1]|
    freq = freq * ([0, detune] + 1);
    LFTri.ar(LFTri.ar(mod * freq).range(freq * mod, freq)) * a_in * 0.2
}
);

(
~mod2 = { LFNoise1.kr(1).range(0, 1) };
~mod1 =  { LFPulse.kr(~mod2.kr * 30 + 1, 0, 0.3) };
~freq1 = { ~mod1.kr * 13100 + 100 };
~freq2 = { LFTri.kr(30) * 200 + 300 };
~audio1 = { BrownNoise.ar(LFClipNoise.kr(10.dup), 1) };
~audio2 = { SinOsc.ar(LFNoise2.kr(1.dup).exprange(4, 1000)) };
);

~out.map(\freq, ~freq2, \mod, ~mod1);
~out.set(\detune, 0.01);
~out.map(\freq, ~freq1, \mod, ~mod1);
~out.xmap(\freq, ~freq1, \mod, ~mod2); // xmap crossfades over fade time to new
value.
~out.xmap(\freq, ~freq2, \mod, ~mod1, \a_in, ~audio2);
~out.map(\a_in, ~audio1);
```

Figure 7.11
Parameter mapping and setting.

```
// this synthdef is used in the subsequent figures
(
SynthDef(\wave, { |out, freq=440, amp=0.1, sustain=0.1, mod=0.2|
    OffsetOut.ar(out,
        EnvGen.ar(Env.perc(ExpRand(0.001, 0.05), sustain, amp), doneAction: 2)
        *
        SinOsc.ar(freq, SinOsc.ar(sustain.reciprocal * 8, [0, Rand(0, pi)], mod))
    )
}).add
);
(
Tdef(\x, {
    x = 4; y = 13;
    loop {
        x = (x * y) % 11;
        (instrument: \wave, note: x.postln, sustain: 0.5, octave: 6).play;
        0.125.wait;
    }
}).play
);
```

Figure 7.12
Rewriting a synth definition and a task definition while running.

times for different proxies. At control rate this is a linear, and at audio rate an equal power transition.

In SuperCollider, running synth nodes may have controls representing their parameters which can be mapped to control rate buses (e.g., x = Synth(\default); x.set(\freq, 210)). A node proxy provides access to these controls in a very similar way, but it can be set before any synth is present. As soon as a source is given, a synth's parameters are set or mapped accordingly (e.g., ~x.set(\freq, 210)). Through this, networks of control or audio rate proxies can be changed more efficiently than by reassigning the source (figure 7.11). The additional messages xset and xmap allow for cross-fading parameter transitions.

7.4   Structured Waiting and Rewriting: TaskProxy, Tdef

In sound programming, one typically experiments by evaluating small pieces of code. Once they are understood properly, they can be incorporated into an automatic sequence which replaces the programmer's actions in time and in turn becomes the basis for further modification. On the most basic level, *tasks* are a way to structure sequences of such actions—in essence, they are time streams of structured

```
(

Tdef(\a, { 10.do { (instrument: \wave, freq: 50.rand + 1500).play;
0.03.wait } });
Tdef(\b, { [1, 5, 1, 2, 8, 4, 12].do { |x| (instrument: \wave, note:
x + 8).play; 0.1.wait } });
Tdef(\c, { "c is just a waiting message".postln; 2.wait; });


Tdef(\x, {
    loop {
            Tdef(\a).embed; // play in sequence
            1.wait;
            Tdef(\b).embed;
            2.wait;
            Tdef(\a).fork; // play in parallel
            Tdef(\b).fork;
            Tdef(\c).embed;
    }
}).play
);

// rewrite with infinite loop
Tdef(\a, { inf.do { (instrument: \wave, freq: 50.rand + 500).play;
0.1.wait } });
// rewrite with finite loop
Tdef(\a, { 10.do { (instrument: \wave, freq: 50.rand + 500).play;
0.1.wait } });
```

Figure 7.13
Combining different task proxies: embed and fork.

waiting. *Task proxies* provide an interface that makes such tasks easily accessible and rewritable, and wherever combinable subtasks are needed, they provide the necessary abstraction. For instance, in order to change code in the running algorithm shown in figure 7.12, one can arbitrarily modify either the SynthDef or the Tdef at runtime. This allows for variables local to the process, in contrast to the very first example, enabling any part of the code to be altered without prior reorganization.

Like other proxies, a Tdef may be implicitly created and played without any content (e.g., Tdef(\x).play), or be accessed like any other object (x = TaskProxy.new; x.play) with no change of functionality (analogous to figures 7.7–7.9). Using the embed and fork messages, several Tdefs can be combined: while any waiting done in the *embedded* task will cause the outer task to wait, the Tdef does not wait for a

```
(
Tdef(\a, { |in|
    in.at(\n).do { |i|
        in = (instrument: \wave, detune: 5.rand2).putAll(in);
        in.postln.play;
        in.delta.wait;
    }
})
);


(
Tdef(\x, { |inevent|
    loop {
        Tdef(\a).embed((note: [15, 17], dur: 0.01, n: 13));
        1.wait;
        Tdef(\a).embed((note: 9, dur: 0.4, n: 4));
        1.wait;
    }
}).play;
)
```

Figure 7.14
Passing an environment into a task proxy when embedding it.

forked task to finish and will play in parallel. Figure 7.13 shows how to branch 2 tasks into parallel streams. In both cases, changes in the Tdef itself are threaded into each running process, so that infinite sequences remain responsive to modification. Environments may be passed to the forked and embedded tasks to influence each of their behaviors (figure 7.14).

7.5   Empty Patterns

Like unit generators, patterns are stateless descriptions of how processes work. However, unlike unit generators, networks of patterns specify streams of objects in general, or streams of events, that run within an instance of a clock on sclang (the client). Because patterns are only descriptions of processes, the same pattern can be the source of a variety of derivations: other patterns are derived, each of which may serve as a description for any number of streams. These patterns should be entirely independent of generated streams so that their code can be guaranteed to express the process they describe. Thus no stream should modify its pattern, nor should the pattern know about any of its streams.

```
Pdefn(\x, Pseq([0, 2, 0, 7, 6, 5, 4, 3], inf));
(
Task {
    var stream = Pdefn(\x).asStream;
    var val;
    loop {
        val = stream.next;
        (instrument: \wave, note: val).play;
        0.2.wait
    }
}.play
);

Pdefn(\x, Pseq([0, 2, 0, 8, 6, 5, 2, 3, 4, 5], inf)); // rewrite the
definition at runtime.
Pdefn(\x, Pseq([0, 2, 0, 7, 6, 5, 4, 3].scramble + 4, inf));
```

Figure 7.15
A pattern proxy as an entry point into a stream.

This clear abstraction demands careful implementation of a just-in-time approach. We want to be able to define a neutral placeholder not for a stream (which would be simple), but for such an abstract description. A suitable implementation has a number of requirements: first, a *patternproxy* should be usable before its content is known, as shown in the empty Tdef above. Second, the proxy's description should be amenable to rewriting at any point. And third, changes caused by any such rewriting should affect all processes specified by the pattern proxy. To achieve this, the subclasses of PatternProxy insert points of interaction into the abstract layer so that a change of its description is threaded into the system at runtime without creating any dependencies. For *object streams* such as numerical patterns (e.g., Pseq([0, 2, 3])), PatternProxy and Pdefn provide such an interface; for *event streams* (e.g., Pbind(\note, 4)), EventPatternProxy and Pdef are interaction points in a network of streams.

Figure 7.15 shows an instance of an object stream in which an instance of Pdefn is used directly as the source of a stream of numerical values. Figure 7.16 uses the same definitions to create a stream of arrays from variations of this definition. Using math operations on the placeholder, we are able to derive new patterns that represent independent yet rewritable calculations with processes that will happen in the future. This type of *late binding* is a typical feature of patterns and streams. An *empty* Pdefn (or, equivalently, PatternProxy) embeds a series of integer 1 into the stream, a value that, though it is as generic as 0, is safer for use in time streams (an

```
Pdefn(\y, Pdefn(\x) + 2); // derive a transposition
Pdefn(\z, Pdefn(\x) + Pseq([0, 5, 0, 7, 2], inf)); // derive a variation
Pdefn(\a, Ptuple([Pdefn(\y), Pdefn(\z)])); // combine them in a stream of arrays
(
Task {
    var stream = Pdefn(\a).asStream;
    var val;
    loop {
        val = stream.next.postln;
        (instrument: \wave, note: val, sustain: rrand(0.5, 0.9)).play;
        0.2.wait
    }
}.play
);

// rewriting the definitions causes all derivations to vary
Pdefn(\x, Pseq([0, 11], inf));
Pdefn(\x, Pseq([0, 2, 0, 7, 6, 5, 4, 3].scramble + 5, inf));
Pdefn(\z, Pdefn(\x) + Pseq([1, 5, 1, 11, 1], inf)); // change a variation

Pdefn(\a, 5); // a number as a source
Pdefn.clear; // clearing all - the empty pattern returns a series of 1.
```

Figure 7.16
Deriving variations from nonexisting streams by math operations.

endless stream of wait times of 0 second is a guaranteed program lockup). Any object or pattern that returns objects can fill the source of a pattern proxy, so that one may calculate with streams of functions just as well as with streams of numbers; a single value will be streamed out indefinitely (e.g., Pdefn(\x, [5, 3, 2]); Pdefn(\x) .asStream.next), until it is replaced by something else.

Event streams behave analogously to object streams shown above, but with the following differences: an event stream may create synth or group nodes on the server, set their controls, and even embed filtering synths into each other. For this slightly different kind of stream the third pair of proxies discussed here forms an abstract placeholder: EventPatternProxy and its named equivalent Pdef. Calculating with events, however, is a different matter from doing so using the numerical mathematics on object streams shown above. Since events of some specification are always required, an empty proxy returns a silent event (Event.silent) until further modified, and when a given definition is rewritten, the stream takes care of releasing any synths within it. Pchain and Pbindf are used to combine the event patterns, and their use also enables the composition of sequences of parallel or subsequent patterns (for a

```
Pdef(\a).play; // play silence in sequence
Pdef(\a, Pbind(\instrument, \wave)); // insert a sequence of notes
Pdef(\a, Pbind(\instrument, \wave, \dur, Pseq([1, 3, 2, 3], inf) /
6)); // add some rhythm
Pdef(\a).pause;
Pdef(\a).resume;
Pdef(\a).stop;
```

Figure 7.17
Pdef as a player: play, pause and resume.

Pbind-like but incremental pattern definition, see the Pbindef Help file, which takes arbitrary pairs of keys and values and implicitly converts them into pattern proxies).

In addition to their placeholder functionality, event stream proxies, like task proxies, provide the option to play one stream internally. As shown in figure 7.17, we can implicitly create a pattern proxy and play, stop, pause, and resume it via the def interface, just as we can with Tdef. Generally, a Pdef may take the place of any event or event pattern, so that just like synth graphs with node proxies, networks of patterns can be refactored at runtime (figure 7.18). Further below, we will show how to combine these two worlds.

7.6   Symbol Streams and Recursive Patterns

A structure with a large number of pattern placeholders can look more complex than necessary, in particular the combination of parallel and serial streams. A simple pair of classes is useful here: Psym (for event streams) and Pnsym (for object or number streams). Every Pdef (or Pdefn, respectively) can be reached by a pattern of symbols passed into this pattern. Thus, the sequence Pseq([Pdef(\x), Pdef(\y), Pdef(\z)]) becomes Psym(Pseq([\x, \y, \z])), and the partly parallel sequence Pseq([Pdef(\x), Ppar([Pdef(\y), Pdef(\z)])]) can be simplified as Psym(Pseq([\x, [\y, \z]])) (see figure 7.19).

It is much easier to restructure musical material in such a way, bringing serial and parallel approaches syntactically closer to each other. Furthermore, when using a Pdefn for the sequence of symbols, the composition of the whole piece may be rearranged hierarchically (see figure 7.20).

With the Pnsym pattern, the numerical stream variant works analogously, except that instead of expanding in the form of a Ppar, it does so in the form of a Ptuple, returning arrays of numbers or objects.[4] Note that as an alternative, Psym and Pnsym can be given a dictionary with patterns that they use as a lookup, so that they can be used independently of Pdef and Pdefn.

```
(
(
Pdef(\x,
    Pbind(
        \instrument, \wave,
        \mod, Pseq([1, 0, 1, 0], inf),
        \dur, Pn(1/2, 8),
        \note, 7
    )
)
);

(
Pdef(\y,
    Pbindf(
        Pdef(\x),
        \amp, 0.2,
        \note, Pshuf([0, 2, 3, 5], 2) + Prand([0, 5, [0, 4]], inf),
        \dur, Pseq([1, 3, 2, 3], inf) / 6
    )
)
);

(
Pdef(\z, Pbindf(Pdef(\y), \dur, 1/4))
);

// the combination of all placeholders into a new placeholder
(
Pdef(\a,
    Pmul(\dur, Pwhite(-0.02, 0.02) + 1,
        Pseq([
            Ppar([Pdef(\x), Pdef(\y)]),
            Pdef(\x),
            Pdef(\y),
            Pdef(\z),
            Ppar([Pdef(\x), Pbindf(Pdef(\y), \ctranspose, 2)])
        ], inf)
    )
);
))
```

Figure 7.18
A larger combination of Pdefs.

```
Pdef(\a).play; // play it

// go into a looping vamp
(
Pdef(\x,
    Pbind(
        \instrument, \wave,
        \dur, Pseq([1, 3, 2, Prand([3, 2])], inf) / 6,
        \octave, [6, 4]
    )
)
);

// release a break
(
Pdef(\x,
    Pbind(
        \instrument, \wave,
        \dur, Pseq([1, 3, 2, Prand([3, 2])], 1) / 6,
        \octave, [6, 4]
    )
)
);

Pdef(\a).stop; // stop the player
```

Figure 7.18
(continued)

```
// the combination of all placeholders into a new placeholder
(
Pdef(\b, Pbindf(Pdef(\y), \ctranspose, 2));
Pdef(\a,
    Pmul(\dur, Pwhite(-0.02, 0.02) + 1,
        Psym(Pseq([[\x, \y], \x, \y, \z, [\x, \b]], inf).trace) //
trace it to post which
    )
).play;
)
```

Figure 7.19
Simplifying the code in Figure 7.18 with Psym.

```
(
Pdefn(\sequence, Pseq([[\x, \y], \x, \y, \z, [\x, \b]], inf));
Pdef(\a,
    Pmul(\dur, Pwhite(-0.02, 0.02) + 1,
        Psym(Pdefn(\sequence).trace)
    )
).play;
)

// rewrite the sequence
Pdefn(\sequence, Pseq([\x], inf));
Pdefn(\sequence, Pseq([\x, \y, \x, [\x, \y]], inf));

Pdef(\a).stop; // stop playing
```

Figure 7.20
Using a Pdefn for the sequence of symbols itself.

A second type of parallelism, resembling the branching of a tree rather than the lanes of the highway next to it, is implemented in a specific *event type*, named *phrase*. When such an event is played, instead of sending a single sound event to the server, the event retrieves a Pdef matching its instrument key (alternatively, from a repository given in the event itself). The event then plays a phrase—a stream of events—from this template, applying the event's sustain value as a temporal limit. Consequently, (instrument: \x, type: \phrase, sustain: 3).play will play 1 phrase (given that Pdef(\x) has been defined in one of the above examples), and Pbind(\type, \phrase, \instrument, \x, \legato, 1.5).play will play an overlapping sequence of these phrases (for an alternative, see Pspawn and Pspawner Help file). Taking advantage of the syntactical similarity of Pdef and SynthDef, a Pdef may be written, and thought of, as a parameterized phrase generator (figures 7.21–7.22). Here, in common with a synth definition, the arguments supplied by the function specify the sound generation, but in the case of Pdef, on a phrase-by-phrase basis. As a result, as each event from the outer pattern is passed in, its values may be used for further processing and even for creating other phrase patterns in turn. Multiple channels branch out into their respective subphrases.

The event type *phrase* has a number of parameters that may be used to extend this behavior and to compose recursive phrases: if a numerical recursionLevel is provided, the branching of a subpattern does not stop at the first level of replacement but continues recursively to the depth specified. In this way, what was earlier a simple pattern of sound clusters changes to something in which every grain of each cloud becomes a (usually faster) copy of this very cluster. Moreover, depending on

```
(instrument: \x, type: \phrase).play; // a single phrase from Pdef(\x)

// a pattern of overlapping phrases
(
Pbind(
    \type, \phrase,
    \instrument, \x,
    \legato, 2.5,
    \note, Pseq([0, 5, 7], inf)
).play
);
```

Figure 7.21
Event type 'phrase'.

the number specified in the recursion level, each cluster passes on its parameter variations to a new subcluster until the last level is reached. Also here, we may change the definition while it is being used (for efficiency reasons, a phrase will finish before the change is picked up), but one should keep in mind that recursion can easily become too complex for real-time synthesis.

Passing a function into a PatternProxy (Pdefn) instead of the EventPatternProxy (Pdef) works analogously, with the difference that not all the arguments are passed to the function in a PatternProxy; instead, the event itself is passed in directly as an argument. Pdefn behaves essentially like Tdef here: we may receive parameters from the embedding outer process and use them for each subprocess. A phrase structure makes no sense in this case, because object streams do not generally represent a timed sound algorithm. In the next section we discuss behaviors common to the proxies thus far introduced.

7.7   Perceptual Continuity and Context

Within programming experiments and live coding sessions, changes that interfere with the algorithmic processes and restructure their rules are part of one and the same musical stream. A rupture introduced as part of the algorithm and one that stems from a rewriting of the algorithm may sometimes be clearly distinguishable, while in other cases, minor modifications remain subliminal. Sonic research is a field in which the relation between an algorithm and a sound can be likened to a measuring instrument. Here, just as in learning sound synthesis, *differential hearing* becomes an essential method: in order to understand what a program does, minor changes to the code are superimposed upon the changes in the result. The perceptual continuity

```
(
Pdef(\x, { |note=0, n=6, step=3, modulo=15, sustain=1|
    Pbind(
        \instrument, \wave,
        \note, note.value + (Pseries(1, step, n) % modulo) + 7,
        \dur, sustain.value / n
    )
})
);

(
Pdef(\a,
    Pbind(
        \type, \phrase,
        \instrument, \x,
        \note, Pseq([0, 5, 4, 8, 0], inf),
        \n, 5,
        \modulo, Pseq([3, [4, 3, 5], [13, 15]], inf),
        \dur, Pseq([1, 2, 0.5, 1.5], inf)
    )
).play
);

(
Pdef(\a,
    Pbind(
        \type, \phrase,
        \instrument, \x,
        \note, Pseq([0, 5, 4, 8, 0], inf),
        \n, 5,
        \modulo, Prand([3, [4, 3, 5], [13, 15]], inf),
        \recursionLevel, 1,
        \dur, Pseq([1, 2, 0.5, 1.5], inf) * 2
    )
).play
);
```

Figure 7.22
Recursive phrasing.

required may be achieved by a context of processes that remain unchanged. The persistence of parameter settings, and cross-fading or interpolation between old and new versions, contribute to this continuity. Finally, the exact timing of the modification may also be important, for instance, when rewriting trigger algorithms.

In the last part of section 7.3, we showed how to set parameters for a NodeProxy that are applied to each new synth created within it. Using the equivalent Ndef syntax, we can write, for instance, Ndef(\x).set(\freq, 367). When we add a synthesis function to this code (e.g., Ndef(\x, {|freq| SinOsc.ar(freq) * 0.1 })), the frequency of the sine osciallator is adapted to this context. A different function may interpret this context entirely differently.

Earlier we also noted that setting a quantization (quant) value (Ndef(\x).quant = ...) allows changes to be scheduled sample accurately to a clock's beat, and that by supplying a fadeTime, a continuous transition is achieved. All pattern proxies (i.e., Tdef, Pdefn, Pdef, and their respective base classes) support both a similar syntax for setting the context of a process and an extensible scheme of exactly *when* a replacement becomes effective.

Pattern proxies have an optional variable for a context, an environment that is implicitly created if need be. This environment keeps variables across changes of the proxy source and is reachable from within the latter. Using the set message, the pair of key and value in this environment can be set or may be directly accessed by the envir getter. In the case of Pdefn and Tdef, this environment is passed as an argument to any function provided there (see also figure 7.14), whereas with Pdef, the environment is chained into the event stream. A Pdef may also be given a fade time which then cross-fades between old and new streams.

To specify when the fadeTime transition should happen, a number of parameters come into play. First, a quant value that works as elsewhere in SC: a number specifies the quantization and an array specifies the triple of quant, phase, and timingOffset (see Quant Help file). Furthermore, pattern proxies understand a fourth value, the onset, which, when given, helps to modify longer sequences interactively without reset. Second, a condition function can be provided, which acts to defer any change until the current stream value fulfills it; thus, for instance, specific insertion points into a melody may be defined.

Although just-in-time programming is very convenient for the composition of algorithms and for keeping code present in mind, it is less ideal for tasks such as mixing or setting parameters. To overcome this problem, a number of loosely coupled GUI classes accompany the different proxies (figures 7.23 and 7.24): PdefEditor, TdefEditor, NodeProxyEditor. In particular, they provide an alternative way of accessing and overseeing playing state, involving parameters such as node settings, mappings, and stream environment variables. Drawing on experience with live coding performance situations, use of these GUIs combines typical tasks such as volume

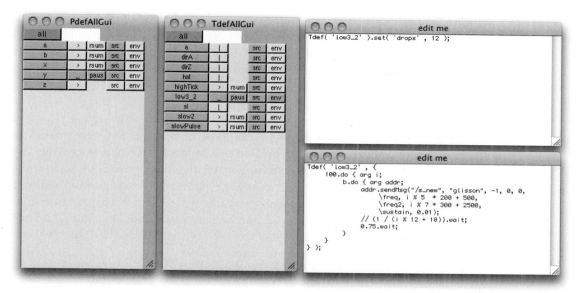

Figure 7.23
Throw-away GUIs for `Tdef` and `Pdef`.

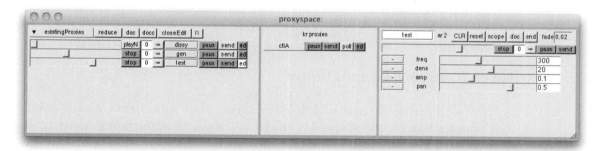

Figure 7.24
`ProxyMixer`, for accessing processes in a `ProxySpace`.

adjustment and quick editing of source code, and are designed to be completely independent from the rest of the system (*throwaway GUIs*). These can be used in custom GUIs, and the classes PdefAllGui, TdefAllGui, NdefMixer, and ProxyMixer provide an overview of all currently used proxies.

7.8   Combinatorics

To finally combine all those different types of processes, one may use proxies as adapters. Many kinds of objects can be used as a source for a NodeProxy—they are converted internally so that their synths play on the appropriate bus and group. While a pattern proxy may be used to rewrite patterns that are used in multiple places, a NodeProxy can host an event stream, represented by a pattern (or, of course, a pattern proxy, which is just another pattern). Thus, in figure 7.25 the stream plays in ~x and is filtered by ~y and ~z (as usual, Ndef(\x), Ndef(\y), and Ndef(\z) would behave equivalently; see figure 7.26).

The output of a control rate node proxy may also be mapped to values in a running stream—in the second part of this code example, the modulator proxy (containing an LFNoise process) is mapped to a number of the synths spawned by ~x.

Another typical practice is to use Tdefs to spawn synth processes. This can be done as shown in section 7.4, but Tdefs may also interact with other proxies. Setting a NodeProxy source at a high speed is efficient only when using precompiled synthdefs (see *jitlib_efficiency.help*), but by using the send message, the proxy can become a placeholder for multiple synths from a single definition, as shown in figure 7.27.

7.9   Networked Live Coding and Recursive History

After devoting much space to detailed examination of proxy behaviors, we end this chapter with a broader discussion involving 2 areas. First, the proxy system can be seen as an interaction point not only for a synthesis process but also between persons. Second, interaction leaves a trace, a history of changes that can mirror future possibilities.

The easiest way of achieving *networked live coding* is perhaps through the use of Tdefs, which send messages to different servers. In figures 7.1 and 7.12–7.22, we could easily add a remote server to the event (e.g., (note: x, dur: 0.125, server: x).play or Pdef(\x).set(\server, x)), and even use a BroadcastServer to select an address algorithmically by index. Furthermore, a NodeProxy or a ProxySpace can play just as well on a remote server as on a local one.[5]

Nevertheless, this is only half of what networked live coding is about: we are just as interested in the program text that gives rise to the sound as in the sound itself.

```
(
SynthDef(\train, { |out, xfreq=15, sustain=1.0, amp=0.1, pan|
    Line.ar(1, 1, sustain, doneAction:2);
    OffsetOut.ar(out, Pan2.ar(Impulse.ar(xfreq), pan, amp));
}).add
);


p = ProxySpace.push;
~z.play;

// A pattern in an audio rate node proxy ...
(
~x = Pbind(
    \instrument, \train,
    \xfreq, Pseq([50, Pwhite(30, 800, 1), 5, 14, 19], inf), // only non-standard
keys, i.e. xfreq
    \sustain, Pseq([Pwhite(0.01, 0.1, 1), 0.1, 1, 0.5, 0.5], inf),
    \pan, Prand([-1, 1], inf) * 0.1
)
);
~y = { Ringz.ar(~x.ar, 5000 * [1, 1.2], 0.01) }; // resonant filter on the impulses
from ~x
~mod = { LFNoise1.kr(0.1).exprange(200, 5000) }; // a modulator
~z = { ~y.ar * (SinOsc.ar(~mod.kr) + 1) }; // ring modulation with frequency ~mod

// ... and a control rate node proxy in a pattern.
// To pass on modulation like this, the standard event parameters like freq cannot
be used.
// Here, we use xfreq instead.

(
~x = Pbind(
    \instrument, \train,
    \xfreq, Pseq([50, ~mod, 5, ~mod, 19], inf), // read from the ~mod proxy bus.
    \sustain, Pseq([Pwhite(0.01, 0.1, 1), 0.1, 1, 0.5, 0.5], inf),
    \pan, Prand([-1, 1], inf) * 0.1
)
);
```

Figure 7.25
Combinations between patterns and ugen graphs, using a ProxySpace.

```
(
SynthDef(\train, { |out, xfreq=15, sustain=1.0, amp=0.1, pan|
    Line.ar(1, 1, sustain, doneAction:2);
    OffsetOut.ar(out, Pan2.ar(Impulse.ar(xfreq), pan, amp));
}).add
);


Ndef(\z).play;

// a pattern in an audio rate node proxy ...
(
Ndef(\x, Pbind(
    \instrument, \train,
    \xfreq, Pseq([50, Pwhite(30, 800, 1), 5, 14, 19], inf),
    \sustain, Pseq([Pwhite(0.01, 0.1, 1), 0.1, 1, 0.5, 0.5], inf),
    \pan, Prand([-1, 1], inf) * 0.1
))
);
Ndef(\y, { Ringz.ar(Ndef(\x).ar, 5000 * [1, 1.2], 0.01) });
Ndef(\mod, { LFNoise1.kr(0.1).exprange(200, 5000) });
Ndef(\z, { Ndef(\y).ar * (SinOsc.ar(Ndef(\mod).kr) + 1) }); // ring
modulation with Ndef(\mod)

// ... and a control rate node proxy in a pattern

(
Ndef(\x, Pbind(
    \instrument, \train,
    \xfreq, Pseq([50, Ndef(\mod), 5, Ndef(\mod), 19], inf), // read
from the Ndef(\mod) proxy bus
    \sustain, Pseq([Pwhite(0.01, 0.1, 1), 0.1, 1, 0.5, 0.5], inf),
    \pan, Prand([-1, 1], inf) * 0.1
))
);
```

Figure 7.26
Combinations between patterns and ugen graphs, using Ndef.

```
Ndef(\x).play; // here an Ndef is used, the same can be done within a ProxySpace
Ndef(\x, { |freq=5, detune=0| Impulse.ar(freq * [detune, 1 - detune]) * 0.2 });
(
Tdef(\c, {
    loop {
        Ndef(\x).fadeTime = rrand(0.1, 3.5);
        Ndef(\x).send([\freq, exprand(2, 400), \detune, [0.0, 1.0].choose.rand]);
        2.wait;
    }
}).play
);
```

Figure 7.27
Using a Tdef to create textures of overlapping synths within a node proxy.

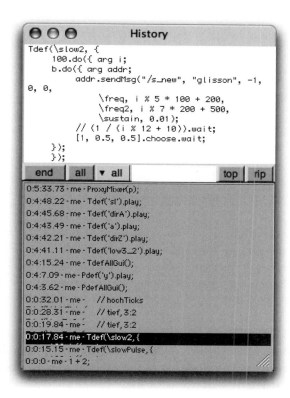

Figure 7.28
Distributed live coding with the History class.

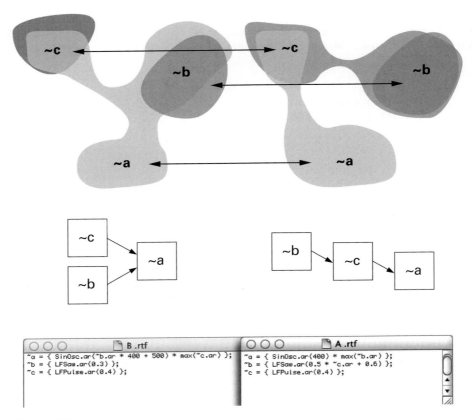

Figure 7.29
Shared variables between remote proxy spaces.

An elegant way to share this source code is provided by the class History. Through adding a hook to the codeDump variable of Interpreter, we are able to use History to distribute all evaluated code to all participants; furthermore, its GUI offers text filters for easy searching (see chapter 8), so that new algorithmic sounds not only may become delocalized in the room, but their source code may be appropriated by others on the fly. (See figure 7.28.)

For a more radical interlocking of performances, any LazyEnvir, such as ProxySpace, can be supplied with a dispatch function, which is called when objects are put in. As a result, an environment variable such as ~x may be shared between participants, so that the modifications of some of the network affect a number of proxies within the group. Where this is the case, the variable's identity becomes delocalized, and the refactoring that happens between synth and node graph (see section 7.3) is extended to different locations and persons (the class Public is such a dispatch). As a result, one and the same variable may be used differently by each participant, so that local changes result in a whole family of related, but not necessarily identical, changes in the entire ensemble.

By modifying code at runtime, we include the programming activity in the flow of the program itself; changing our minds, we fold the representation onto the process. This can become a fairly linear development in itself—never going back, always changing what is present as code. As a concluding example, available on the book Web site, *eternal return* shows how we can voyage back to past states. Here, past becomes future, as we may edit past states that affect future placeholders. In time, we not only fold programming back onto the program, but eventually the memory of its alterations as well.

References

Clark, A., and D. Chalmers. 1998. "The Extended Mind." *Analysis,* 58(1): 10–23.

Collins, N., A. McLean, J. Rohrhuber, and A. Ward. 2003. "Live Coding Techniques for Laptop Performance." *Organised Sound,* 8(3): 321–330.

Guardans, R. 2010. "A Brief Note on the anwaa' Texts of the Late Tenth Century." In S. Zielinski and E. Fürlus, eds., *Variantology 4—On Deep Time Relations of Arts, Sciences and Technologies In the Arabic–Islamic World and Beyond.* Köln: Verlag der Buchhandlung Walther König.

Matthews, H. F. 1968. "Venus: A Small Interactive Nonprocedural Language." In M. Klerer and J. Reinfelds, eds., *Proceedings of the ACM SIGPLAN Symposium on Interactive Systems for Experimental Applied Mathematics,* pp. 97–105. New York: Academic Press.

Iverson, K. 1980. "Notation as a Tool of Thought" (The 1979 Turing Award Lecture). *Communications of the ACM* 23(8): 444–465.

Klerer, M., and J. Reinfelds, eds. 1968. *Proceedings of the ACM SIGPLAN Symposium on Interactive Systems for Experimental Applied Mathematics.* New York: Academic Press.

Licklider, J. C. R. 1960. "Man–Computer Symbiosis." *IRE Transactions on Human Factors in Electronics,* HFE-1: 4–11.

Mathews, M. V. 1969. *The Technology of Computer Music.* Cambridge, MA: MIT Press.

Rheinberger, H.-J. 1997. *Toward a History of Epistemic Things: Synthesizing Proteins in the Test Tube.* Stanford, CA: Stanford University Press.

Rohrhuber, J. 2008. "Network Music." In N. Collins and J. d'Escriván, eds., *The Cambridge Companion to Electronic Music.* Cambridge: Cambridge University Press.

Rohrhuber, J., and A. de Campo. 2004. "Waiting and Uncertainty in Computer Music Networks." In *Proceedings of the 2004 International Computer Music Conference.*

Rohrhuber, J., A. de Campo, and R. Wieser. 2005. "Algorithms Today—Notes on Language Design for Just-in-Time Programming." In *Proceedings of the 2005 International Computer Music Conference,* Barcelona, pp. 455–458.

Rohrhuber, J., A. de Campo, R. Wieser, J.-K. van Kampen, E. Ho, and H. Hölzl. 2007. "Purloined Letters and Distributed Persons." In *Proceedings of the Conference Music in the Global Village, 2007.* Available online at <http://wertlos.org/articles/Purloined_letters.pdf>.

Suchman, L. 2007. *Human–Machine Reconfigurations: Plans and Situated Actions,* 2nd ed. Cambridge: Cambridge University Press.

Vogt, K., W. Plessas, A. de Campo, C. Frauenberger, and G. Eckel. 2007. "Sonification of Spin Models: Listening to the Phase Transitions in the Ising and Potts Model." In *Proceedings of the 13th International Conference on Auditory Display.* Montreal: Schulich School of Music, McGill University.

Notes

1. For more on live coding, see the references and the papers referenced at TOPLAP (<http://toplap.org>).

2. This procedure is typical for functional languages such as Haskell, in which all operations (such as currying) are essentially compositions of functions. In computer science and mathematics, such a function whose domain consists of other functions is called an *operator*.

3. The actual order of nodes matters in cases where external audio input is processed. In such cases, one can reorder the nodes while playing orderNodes(~x, ~y, ~z).

4. We leave as an open question whether it makes sense as a next step to map such streams that return symbols as an input to other streams that return symbols.

5. Note that one should not forget either to synchronize the system clocks of two computers or to set the server's latency to nil.

8 Object Modeling

Alberto de Campo, Julian Rohrhuber, and Till Bovermann

Programming can be thought of as expressing concepts in code for other human beings to understand. Especially in artistic work, but also in scientific contexts, concepts usually are initially "underspecified" if not "ill-defined," and one refines ideas iteratively. SuperCollider provides elegant ways to model objects by designing their behavior in a continuous flow while one is not yet completely sure of where the current exploration of ideas is leading.

In fully dynamic programming languages such as Smalltalk, a programmer may change a class while using the very same class for writing an e-mail or for editing an image. In SuperCollider this is not supported for runtime efficiency reasons; rather, classes and object models play different practical roles: class methods can be looked up very rapidly, and classes are very useful for capturing ideas that have mostly settled. Object modeling can be applied when working in a more dynamic live system is desired.

In this chapter we provide some general background on object orientation from the perspective of object modeling (i.e., a way of simulating objects without creating full-fledged classes. We present examples written in this efficient and enjoyable development style and, discussing the flow of design decisions, we show how to convert object models into classes and methods if desired. We end with larger examples realized with object modeling.

8.1 Object Orientation, Behavior, and Polymorphism

The way in which a program works shows the labyrinth of consequences that follow the automatic, ignorant observance of rules implied by a concept. Thus, programming does not simply *express* preexisting concepts in code; often, concepts are also *formed* in the process of developing programs. To support such a coevolution of concepts and programs that embody them, programming languages have to provide very open and generic concepts. One of them is the *object*, or the paradigm of *object orientation*, which is a central idea in SuperCollider. Are objects the right metaphor for a programming language designed for sound synthesis research? At first glance, sound and objects may almost seem to be ontological opposites.

One of the original ideas of object orientation was a paradigm shift: whereas in procedural programming the *subject* of a program (the operations/the operator) decided how to operate on the *object* of the program (the data), in object orientation, this is turned inside out. Here, it is the object which is responsible for the operations, and the closest thing to a subject is the other objects from which it receives messages. This shift made it possible to transpose the idea of a network of cooperating computers into a concept for programs themselves, in which every part is a miniature version of the whole; all that happens is that a large number of isolated entities (composed of further entities) communicate with each other. Here it becomes more obvious why objects may be a good metaphor for sound: it is all about conversation, exchange, resonance, call, and response.

Object orientation is often explained in terms of things that have properties and that belong to classes because they share properties: all cars, as a class, have wheels, and all bank accounts have a balance. If we know the class of an object, we know what messages it understands. But there is a different side to this, perhaps best described by Brian Cantwell Smith: "an object is something on which one can have a perspective" (1996, 117). Historically, the novelty of object orientation was not that it implements a taxonomy of things—computers have always been good at categorizations—but rather that it was a step in a new direction, in which data and operations were seen as inseparably linked. In his description of how this paradigm emerged in the late 1960s, Alan Kay noted how indexing into an array (the 'at' operation in a = [1, 0, 0, 1, 1, 2, 0, 1]; a.at(5);) was better *not* seen as an operation (*at*) on data (*the array*); but it was the array that *behaved* in a certain way in response to the message '*at*.' In 1993, Kay wrote: "It took me a remarkably long time to see this, partly I think because one has to invert the traditional notion of operators and functions, etc., to see that objects need to privately own all of their behaviors: *that objects are a kind of mapping whose values are its behaviors.*" (1993, 8) In consequence, we are not confined to thinking of an object only in terms of its descent, its parent classes, but also can think of it purely in terms of what it responds to. The fact that different objects may respond to the same message differently is called *polymorphism*, and, as we will see, that makes it easy to extend and modify a system. Only behavior matters—this notion is sometimes called "duck typing": *If it looks like a duck, swims like a duck, and quacks like a duck, then it's probably a duck.*

Looking at what kinds of objects respond to a given message in SuperCollider, we find many examples that do not share any common class (apart from the mother of all objects, the class Object). The most heterogeneous entities may respond to the same message. Take, for example, the message squared. Any object that responds to it can be used in an expression such as x.squared. So if all that really matters about an object is how it behaves, then the same expression can be used in many different contexts without changing anything: we may square integers and floats, and also unit generators, streams, and patterns. We can square not only arrays of integers but also arrays of arrays of integers and arrays of arrays of unit generators. This system is extendable for new concepts with minimal effort: by defining a new kind of object that responds to *squared*, we may square not only that object but also arrays of it.

The statement "everything is an object" can be complemented with "everything behaves." This is even true when an object does *not* understand a given message—how it then responds is specified (in SC3) in its doesNotUnderstand method definition. Normally this is useful for error information (see, e.g., the error created by {SinOsc.ar}.pay). This also means that if we want to define new behavior of an object dynamically without recompiling, we can override doesNotUnderstand in a subclass to forward the selector (the message name that was not understood) and the argument (*args*) to any functionality we like. As discussed in chapter 5, the class IdentityDictionary, and its subclasses Environment and Event, do this: when its instance variable know is true (so that it always "knows"), the dictionary will check whether it contains a value defined for the key that was the message name it did not understand. Consequently, object prototyping can be done without losing the old state of the system; one simply adds or removes a function in the Event (or instance of an equivalent class) and, by doing so, changes its behavior. Such an object can be passed around in the system and used for calculation, just like any other object. This is how object modeling begins.

8.2   Common Compromises in Programming Languages

Every programming language is based on compromises, and there is no advantage without disadvantage; languages are designed with different tasks in mind, and so an idea can be very simple to realize in one language and very tricky in another. In computer science, these design aims are very thoroughly (and sometimes heatedly) discussed.

Some design aims for programming languages are *conceptual purity*, which many functional languages aim for; *elegance*, which can be rather elusive (see, e.g., Chaitin, 1998); *"naturalness" of use*—among other things, Smalltalk was designed for children to learn programming easily; *extensibility* (i.e., being able to add features to the language as needed); *runtime efficiency*, which many lower-level languages such as C are designed for; *programming time efficiency*, being able to realize complex systems within reasonable amounts of time; *scalability*, being able to extend architectures up to very big and complex systems; *real-time performance*, which is critical for music systems for live use; *generality*, covering a wide range of domains;

domain-specific features, such as doing audio DSP efficiently; and (maybe most important), *support of different programming styles*.

Existing languages influence programming styles, just as programming styles influence new language design. SC3 has absorbed and adapted many concepts and styles from other languages, such as object orientation from Smalltalk, syntax from C++, functional notation from Lisp, concepts for multidimensional arrays from the J language, and list comprehensions from functional languages; for details see the Language Reference section on the main Help page.

Naturally, no language can achieve all the above objectives fully, so every language is essentially a set of trade-offs. By comparison, SuperCollider tends to be oriented toward efficient real-time performance, flexibility to express concepts in very many different ways, and programming time efficiency, which is why it makes sense to keep a distinction between a static class library, on the one hand, and dynamic object modeling, on the other.

8.3   Keeping Things Around

For one to be able to work fluently on groups of objects, they must persist long enough. The simplest option is to keep objects as interpreter variables (which are global for runtime code), using the lowercase letters a–z. However, there are only 25 letters (s is not counted, because by convention it is the server), so one runs out of names quickly, and it can be hard to remember which letter was which object.

A second option is keeping things in the current environment, as in ~melA = [0, 2, 3], which allows for more descriptive names. For bigger projects, it is still inconvenient that this is 1 flat space of names. Furthermore, when one uses special environments such as ProxySpace (see chapter 7), one replaces the currentEnvironment; switching between different environments can be confusing.

A third option is keeping environments (or events) as global variables and storing things in them by name:

```
q = ( );
q[\melA] = [0, 2, 3];
```

Equivalently, put and at operations can be written like getter and setter messages:

```
q.melA_([0, 2, 3]);
```

or as

```
q.melA = [0, 2, 3];
q.melA + 7;
```

One can also organize repositories of objects hierarchically:

```
q.mels = ();
q.mels.melA = [0, 2, 3];
```

The message-like syntax allows for a different perspective: we can say that the event q has acquired new behavior for new message names. Since the event does not understand the setter-like method melodies_, this method call is redirected to put the object assigned to it, [0, 2, 3], into the event under the key melodies. Calling q.melodies does the inverse; since the method is not understood, it is redirected to look up what the event currently contains at that key, and returns that object. Looking at this as behavior becomes clearer when one considers how functions are treated: when they are accessed, they are evaluated with the event itself as the first argument.

```
q.playMel = {|ev| Pbind(\note, Pseq(ev.melA), \dur, 0.2).play};
q.playMel;
```

8.4   Classes and Events as Object Models

SC3 allows for very efficient implementations of objects and their behavior as classes. Figure 8.1 shows an example of a simple object called Puppet, written as a class, and some tests of its methods.

```
Puppet {
    var <>myfreq; // an instance variable with a getter and a setter method

        // a method for creating a new object of this kind
    *new { |myfreq=50| ^super.new.myfreq_(myfreq) }

        // a simple method that uses 'myfreq' for something audible.
    blip { { Blip.ar(myfreq, 11) * XLine.kr(1, 0.01, 0.6, doneAction: 2) }.play; }
}

    // tests for the behavior implemented so far:
m = Puppet.new(50);// make an instance of Puppet, pass in myfreq

m.dump;         // test that myfreq is set correctly
m.myfreq;       // test accessing myfreq
m.blip;         // should sound
m.myfreq_(100); // test setting myfreq
m.blip;         // should sound differently
```

Figure 8.1
A Puppet class and tests for it.

```
m = ();              // make an empty event
m.myfreq_(50);  // put something in it with a setter method: a pseudo-instance
variable
m.myfreq;            // look it up with a getter method
                     // put a function into it with a setter:
                     // this becomes a pseudo-method
m.blip_({ |ev| { Blip.ar(ev.myfreq, 11) * XLine.kr(1, 0.01, 0.6, doneAction: 2)
}.play; });
m.blip;        // execute the function with a pseudo-method call (same name)
```

Figure 8.2
A puppet modeled as an event.

```
(
m.numHarms_(20);    // a new instvar
m.decay_(0.3);   // and another
                       // update the blip method to use them:
m.blip_({ |ev|
    { Blip.ar(ev.myfreq, ev.numHarms)
    * XLine.kr(1, 0.01, ev.decay, doneAction: 2) }.play;
});
)
m.blip; // test
```

Figure 8.3
Add more instance variables; change the blip method.

When working with objects as classes, making a single change or addition to an object's behavior requires (1) changing the source file (e.g., *Puppet.sc*) and saving it, (2) recompiling the language, and (3 rebuilding the state of things needed for testing the new behavior. In other words, one needs to make and maintain a script to get back to where one was in order to continue working. Here, the rebuilding script is m = Puppet.new(50); often, it is much longer.

The same design steps can be taken with an Event to model the new object (see figure 8.2).

Now, changing or adding more variables and methods to m is extremely simple (see figure 8.3).

Note the use of the argument |ev| in the function that becomes the pseudo method: this makes the event itself (the modeled object) accessible inside the pseudo method, in the way an object is accessible inside one of its methods through the pseudo variable `this`.

There are caveats here. When using a pseudo method name that already exists as a legal method name, the event (i.e., the object model) will call the "real" method, not the pseudo method! Since this can create quite obscure bugs, one gets warned (e.g., executing `m.size_(12)` posts a warning). Accessing the variable with `m.size` returns 5 (if the event `m` currently contains 5 objects), whereas `m[\size]` returns 12, the value previously stored. This can be remarkably confusing. A second potential problem is that misspelled messages do not throw errors: after having set `q.puppet = ()`, the message `q.pupet` (spelled incorrectly) does not complain, as a misspelled "real" method would, but just returns `nil`.

A related idea, prototype-based modeling, is explored in more detail in chapter 20. The rest of this chapter goes through larger examples in ascending complexity; whereas in the first example, every design decision is discussed thoroughly, the later examples are viewed more generally, considering issues from a larger distance. The focus is on the working style and the flow of decisions; both could be shown equally well with many other examples.

8.5   Example 1: Shout Window

8.5.1   Background

Two of the authors perform in the ensemble Powerbooks UnPlugged.[1] In this band, both code and sound are shared among all players; whenever 1 player executes a "codelet," this codelet is sent to all others by network and becomes available in the History window. (`History` keeps a log of all the code executions and can display them for later access, such as for rewriting; see also the History Help file.)

In performance, discussing flow and structural decisions (such as "move to next section?," "come down to end?") goes through the same mechanism, which causes problems: while one is reading or rewriting code, one easily misses calls for discussion or attention messages; because the band members like to sit distributed in the audience, eye contact also is unreliable.

Thus, we needed a mechanism for writing messages to all players that get displayed very prominently and that is simple to use, with minimal extra effort. Tom Hall's SC3 extension `honk`, which uses the freeware tool *BigHonkingText*, provided a clear idea of how to display messages so they are very difficult to miss. After seeing them displayed in this fashion (as a large, top-level, floating window), Alberto de Campo and Hannes Hölzl designed a similar utility in SC3 in a joint session, using

```
z = z ? ();     // make an empty event as a pseudo-object
z.win = Window("Shout", Rect(0, 900,1200, 100)).front;
z.txtView = TextView(z.win, Rect(0, 0,1200, 100));
z.txtView.string_("Shout this!");
z.txtView.font_(Font("Monaco", 32));

    // tune appearances
z.win.alpha_(0.7);       // make the window slightly transparent
z.win.view.background_(Color.clear);     // make the window's top view,
z.txtView.background_(Color.clear);      // and textview fully transparent
z.win.alwaysOnTop_(true);    // make sure it is always on top .

z.win.close;    // close when done
```

Figure 8.4
A minimal Shout window sketch.

the object-modeling approach described; here, we go through a reconstruction of the
design steps, showing the concepts at work.

8.5.2   As an Object Model

First, we make an empty event and create two variables, a window and a text view;
then we tune their appearance (see figure 8.4).

On OSX, full transparency luckily allows typing through the transparent window.
When the model is good enough, it is pulled into a single pseudo method and tested
(see figure 8.5).

Next, we add more methods to our object model and test them. setMessage sets
only the message displayed, whereas shout is meant to be the top-level interface: create a window, if needed, and display the message (see figure 8.6).

When only the text changes on an existing window, that still might be ignored
under performance conditions. So we flash the text in several colors (figure 8.7).
Figure 8.8 shows the window as sketched so far.

How best to use this in performance? Typing something like z.shout("OK, take
it to the bridge!") seemed rather clumsy; in discussion, we came up with writing
Shout messages as comment with a special prefix:

//!! this is a comment line with a 'shout tag' prefix.

Executing this line of comment does nothing, but it should be recognized as a message to be shouted, and forwarded to the Shout window automatically. The code-

```
(
z.makeWin = { |z, message="Shout this!"|
    z.win = Window("Shout", Rect(0, 900,1200, 100)).front;
    z.win.alpha_(0.7);
    z.win.view.background_(Color.clear);
    z.win.alwaysOnTop_(true);

    z.txtView = TextView(z.win, Rect(0, 0,1200, 100));
    z.txtView.string_(message);
    z.txtView.font_(GUI.font.new("Monaco", 32));
    z.txtView.background_(Color.clear);
};
)
z.makeWin("Try showing that.");
```

Figure 8.5
Add a pseudo-method.

```
z.setMessage = { |z, str| z.txtView.string_(str) };

z.setMessage("Does this update?");  // test
(
z.shout = { |z, str|
    if (z.win.isNil or: { z.win.isClosed }) { z.makeWin };
    z.setMessage(str);
};
)
z.shout("Do we get this?"); // test

z.win.close;
z.shout("Do we get this too?"); // also when window has closed?
```

Figure 8.6
More pseudo-methods.

```
z.txtView.stringColor_(Color.red);  // try a single color
(
z.animate = { |z, dt=0.2, n = 6|
    var colors = [Color.red, Color.green, Color.black];
    Task {
        n.do { |i|
            dt.wait;
            z.txtView.stringColor_(colors.wrapAt(i))
        }
    }.play(AppClock)
};
)
z.animate;              // test with default values
z.animate(0.1, 24);     // and test with arguments given
```

Figure 8.7
Text color animation.

Figure 8.8
A Shout window in use (screen shot).

forwarding mechanism in the networking setup for Powerbooks UnPlugged uses the interpreter variable codeDump. By default, codeDump is nil; putting a function here allows additional reactions to the string after it has been interpreted (see figure 8.9).

Playing around with shout messages of different lengths revealed 1 more wish: the font size should adjust to the message, such that the message is displayed as large as possible but always in full length. Intuitively, longer messages should use smaller fonts, so roughly, fontsize = constant * width/messageSize. Some experimentation led to a constant of 1.64 for Monaco, which has equal character spacing. (Though line wrapping and elastic resizing of the text view may be nice options, we decided not to spend time on them.) To use font resizing in z.makeWin as well, we rewrite it to use z.setMessage (see figure 8.10).

```
this.codeDump = { |str, result, func| [str, result, func].printAll };

a = 1 + 2;   // code appears in post window

z.shoutTag = "//!!";
this.codeDump = { |str| if (str.beginsWith(z.shoutTag)) {
z.shout(str.drop(z.shoutTag.size)) } };

//!! a comment with a 'shout tag' now gets shouted!
```

Figure 8.9
Using codeDump to shout.

```
(
z.setMessage = { |z, str|
    var messSize = str.size;
    var fontsize = (1.64 * z.txtView.bounds.width) / max(messSize, 32);
    z.txtView.font_(GUI.font.new("Monaco", fontsize));
    z.txtView.string_(str);
    z.animate;
};
)
//!! a long comment gets scaled down to a rather smaller font size, minimally
fontsize 32!

//!! short is big!
(
z.makeWin = { |q, message="Shout this!"|
    z.win = Window("Shout", Rect(0, 900,1200, 100)).front;
    z.win.alpha_(0.7);
    z.win.view.background_(Color.clear);
    z.win.alwaysOnTop_(true);

    z.txtView = TextView(z.win, Rect(0, 0,1200, 100));
    z.txtView.background_(Color.clear);
    z.setMessage(message);
};
)
z.makeWin("shout.");
```

Figure 8.10
Updated setMessage flashes text.

```
// begin of file - Shout.sc
Shout {
    classvar <>tag="//!!";
    var <win, <txtView;

    *new { ^super.new }
}
// end of file - Shout.sc

// tests:
Shout.tag;
Shout.tag_("//SHOUT");

a = Shout.new;
a.win;
a.txtView;
```

Figure 8.11
A Shout class.

8.5.3   Conversion to a Class

When a design has sufficiently converged, it is often useful to convert it into a class. Converting an object model to a class is simple: All pseudo variables become class or instance variables, and all pseudo methods become class or instance methods.

Moving the variables in z into a new class Shout is straightforward: z.win, z.txtView, and z.shoutTag become instance variables win, txtView, tag = "//!!" and codeDumpFunc, the function that will redirect shout messages. Note that win and txtView can be accessed but not set, whereas tag and codeDumpFunc can be changed.

The following code is also available on the book Web site as a file called *Shout.sc*, which can be put in SuperCollider's user extensions folder or system extension folder; their paths can be looked up with Platform.userExtensionDir or Platform .systemExtensionDir. (See figure 8.11.)

Added here are the class variables width (window width) and defaultCodeDump-Func, a default for the redirecting function. If desired, one also could consider deriving width from Window.screenBounds. The defaultCodeDumpFunc is initialized in *initClass, which is always called on compilation. (See figure 8.12.)

Next, z.makeWin becomes an instance method in Shout, called from the *new method. As z.makeWin calls z.setMessage, a simple method setMessage is also implemented (see figure 8.13).

```
// begin of file - Shout.sc
Shout {
    classvar <>tag="//!!", <>width=1250, <>defaultCodeDumpFunc;
    var <win, <txtView;

    *initClass {
        defaultCodeDumpFunc = { |str| if (str.beginsWith(tag)) {
Shout(str.drop(tag.size)) } };
    }
    *new { ^super.new }
}
// end of Shout.sc

Shout.width;
Shout.defaultCodeDumpFunc;
```

Figure 8.12
More class variables and an `initClass` method.

`z.shout` is needed next, which raises a question: the notion that there should be only a single Shout window at any time is quite atypical. It calls for the *Singleton* design pattern: keeping a single Shout window as a class variable which can be re-used if available, making a new one only when needed. Calling the method `Shout.shout` seems clumsy, but `Shout.top("message")` would work for expressing the idea. A subtle variant is redefining `*new` to do what `*top` does, so that writing `Shout("something")` gets shouted in the top window as default. This requires renaming the current `*new` method `*basicNew`, for example, so one can still create a new shout instance. For symmetry, `*close` tries to close the top window (see figure 8.14).

If one wants to use `"message".shout`, one can add an extension method `shout` to the `String` class very simply (see *extStringShout.sc*):

```
+ String {
    shout {^Shout.new(this)}
}
```

`z.animate` also transfers easily (see figure 8.15).

Now `setMessage` can be refined with font scaling and calling `animate`. (See figure 8.16.)

Some usability wishes came up here. It would be nice to turn shouting on and off easily; and when shouting is on, the current text document should stay in front, so one can continue typing. (On OSX, a new GUI window always jumps to the front.)

```
z.makeWin = { |message="Shout this!"|
    z.win = GUI.window.new("Shout", Rect(0, 900,1200, 100)).front;
    z.win.alpha_(0.7);
    z.win.view.background_(Color.clear);
    z.win.alwaysOnTop_(true);

    z.txtView = GUI.textView.new(z.win, Rect(0, 0,1200, 100));
    z.txtView.background_(Color.clear);
    z.setMessage(message);
};


Shout {
    ...
    *new { |message| ^super.new.makeWin(message); }

    makeWin { |message="Shout this!"|

        win = Window("Shout'er", Rect(20, 800, width, 80)).front;
        win.alpha_(0.7);
        win.view.background_(Color.clear);
        win.alwaysOnTop_(true);

        txtView = TextView(win, win.bounds.moveTo(0,0));
        txtView.background_(Color.clear);
        txtView.font_(Font.new("Monaco", 32));
        this.setMessage(message);
    }

    setMessage { |message|
        txtView.string_(message.asString)
    }
}

// tests:
Shout.new;
a = Shout.new("Blabla");
a.setMessage("Otto");
```

Figure 8.13
Converting makeWin.

```
z.shout = { |z, str|
    if (z.win.isNil or: { z.win.isClosed }) { z.makeWin };
    z.setMessage(str);
};

Shout {
    classvar <top;
    ...
    *new { |message="¡Shout'er!"|

        if (top.isNil or: { top.win.isClosed }) {
            top = this.basicNew(message);
        } {
            top.setMessage(message);
        };
    }
        // the method formerly known as *new
    *basicNew { |message="Shout this!"| ^super.new.makeWin(message) }

    *close { try { top.win.close } }

    ...
}

// tests:
Shout("Test 1, 2");
Shout("Test 1, 2, 3, 4");     // same window
Shout.close;

Shout("Test 1, 2");           // new window
```

Figure 8.14
Converting shout to Shout.new.

First, turning Shout on and off; the safe and polite way to use codeDump is to assume that others may have added functions to it. First we try direct usage, then add 2 class methods. (See figure 8.17.)

For distributing messages to networked performers, one could modify codeDump-Func to broadcast Shout messages, for instance, by sending messages to the local network's broadcast address, with an OSCresponder listening for them and doing the shouting when a message comes in. Such an example would go into a Help file for Shout (see *Shout.html*). Finally, let us consider how to keep the current document in front. (See figure 8.18.)

```
z.animate = { |z, dt=0.2, n = 6|
    var colors = [Color.red, Color.green, Color.black];
    Task {
        n.do { |i|
            dt.wait;
            z.txtView.stringColor_(colors.wrapAt(i))
        }
    }.play(AppClock)
};

Shout {
    ...
    animate { |dt=0.2, n=6|
        var colors = [Color.red, Color.green, Color.black];
        Task {
            n.do { |i|
                txtView.stringColor_(colors.wrapAt(i));
                dt.wait
            };
            txtView.stringColor_(Color.black); // make sure we end black
        }.play(AppClock);
    }
    ...
}

// tests:
a = Shout("Test 1, 2");
Shout.top.animate;
```

Figure 8.15
Converting animate to a class method.

Versions of Shout have been used in several concerts, and they have improved and simplified communication within the band considerably.

8.6 Example 2: Aspects in QCD Sonification

The techniques described above are often sufficient for rapid prototyping of classes in SC3, but sometimes the development process of a desired application is more complex. Though some parts settle sufficiently to warrant making them a class, others need to remain open for longer experimentation, especially when implementing both data preparation (complex routines for getting and preprocessing data) and complex data usage (which must be flexible for experiments). For the scientific con-

```
z.setMessage = { |z, str|
    var messSize = str.size;
    var fontsize = (1.64 * z.txtView.bounds.width) / max(messSize, 32);
    z.txtView.font_(Font.new("Monaco", fontsize));
    z.txtView.string_(str);
    z.animate;
};

Shout {
    ...
    setMessage { |message|
        var messSize, fontSize;
        messSize = message.size;
        fontSize = (1.64 * width) / max(messSize, 32);

        defer {
            txtView.font_(Font("Monaco", fontSize))
                .string_(message.asString);
        };
        this.animate;
    }
    ...
}

Shout("Test 1, 2");
Shout("Test" + (1..16));
```

Figure 8.16
Converting `setMessage`.

text shown here, it was desirable to keep some options open even longer; we wanted to allow users to explore further ideas for data usage, allowing them to test new hypotheses at runtime.

The Quantum chromodynamics (QCD) sonification environment was developed within the *SonEnvir* project in 2006, with Katharina Vogt as the main physics researcher, Till Bovermann as the SC3 specialist, and Philipp Huber preparing QCD lattice data.[2] We created a system that both uses classes and has the possibility to modify the functionality of its parts at runtime.

QCD is the theory of the strong interaction between quarks and gluons. Partner researchers of the SonEnvir project computed several kinds of QCD model data. Each data item is an element of a high-dimensional vector space ($\mathbb{R}^{16\times16\times16\times32}$) and

```
this.codeDump.postcs;    // anything there yet? by default, this is nil.
this.codeDump = this.codeDump.addFunc(Shout.defaultCodeDumpFunc); // add Shout
this.codeDump.postcs     // should be there now
//!! test whether Shout works now
this.codeDump = this.codeDump.removeFunc(Shout.defaultCodeDumpFunc);
this.codeDump.postcs     // should be gone now

//!! should be off again

Shout {
    ...
    *add { var interp = thisProcess.interpreter;
        interp.codeDump = interp.codeDump
            .removeFunc(defaultCodeDumpFunc) // remove it first so it will
                                             // only be in the list once
            .addFunc(defaultCodeDumpFunc);
    }
    *remove { var interp = thisProcess.interpreter;
        interp.codeDump = interp.codeDump.removeFunc(defaultCodeDumpFunc);
    }
    ...
}

// tests
Shout.add;
//!! test whether Shout works now - it should!
Shout.remove;
//!! test whether Shout works now - should be off.
```

Figure 8.17
codeDump tests and usage in Shout.

was provided to us split into 4 csv text files of 2.6MB each. Each file holds either the raw data or 1 of 3 so-called *smearing steps*, as precomputed by our colleagues.

Reading in the data text files (with CSVFileReader) allowed the first audible experiments by serializing the numerical values and playing the resulting time series like an audification (see chapter 13). But reading in all 4 files of 1 data item took quite long, so we wrote a converter from csv to aiff files; this was fast enough for interactive comparison between different data items and smearing steps.

Discussion revealed that the audification used in the first pass produced artifacts due to the arbitrary way the high-dimensional data were put into a sequence. We concluded that for experimentation, we required runtime choice between sequencing

```
Shout.close;
Shout("blabla");      // now typing is impossible, because the new window is in front.

Shout("blabla blabla"); // now one can type, because Shout window was already there.
Shout.close;

    // this does not work, because the shout window gets put in front later:
d = Document.current; Shout(\bla); d.front;


    // This can be wrapped around the call to this.makeWin in Shout:new:
Shout {
    ...
    *new { |message="¡Shout'er!"|
        var currDoc;

        if (win.isNil or: { win.isClosed }) {
            currDoc = Document.current;
            top = this.basicNew(message);
                // wait a little before restoring front window
            defer ({ currDoc.front }, 0.1);
        } {
            top.setMessage(message);
        };
    }
    ...
}
```

Figure 8.18
Keeping Shout out of the way.

algorithms and runtime selection of a region of interest in the data item under exploration. One should be able to navigate a region through the data set, selecting its
position and radius by mouse over, mouse click, or keyboard events, or by hardware
interfaces. Furthermore, both sequencing algorithm and sonification strategy should
be modifiable at runtime.

    While prototyping these features we found that half the code for an example was
data preparation and visualization setup. Therefore we moved all the data preparation and setup into a class while providing code interfaces to user-adjustable
functionality, leaving possibilities to add and modify them at runtime. For each
user-changeable algorithm we created a dictionary in the QCD class, filled with at

```
serialize {|index, pos, extent = 8|
    var ranges, slice;

    // get ranges
    ranges = pos.collect{|pos, i|
        ((pos-(extent*0.5))..(pos+(extent*0.5)-1)) % this.shape[i]
    };
    // get sub-slice
    slice = this.slice(index, *ranges);
    // trivial serialization of multidim. slice
    ^slice.flat
}
```

Figure 8.19
A fixed serialization method.

```
serialize {|index, pos, extent = 8, how = \hilbert|
    // [...]
    slice = this.slice(index, *ranges);
    // call function in serTypes dictionary
    ^serTypes[how].(slice.asArray, extent)
}
```

Figure 8.20
Flexible serialization by lookup.

least 1 (trivial) algorithm written as a function with a fixed interface. Thus, instead of calling a fixed sequencing algorithm, such as flat (see figure 8.19), we called the function in a dictionary at a specific key (see figure 8.20).

Now, one can provide several methods to choose from within initClass and add more choices later, while experimenting. (See figure 8.21.)

Figure 8.22 shows the working environment for QCD.

This mixed approach of classes and object-modeling technique combines the efficiency of classes (also in hiding settled functionality) with the flexibility to try new ideas at runtime—in the case of the serialization by adding functions to the serTypes dictionary. Applying the same strategy for sonification variants proved helpful in understanding which representations seemed more expressive of data properties.

```
*initClass {|numDims = 4|
        ...
        // slice here is a 4d hypercube of extent <extent>
        serTypes = (
            hilbert: {|slice, extent|
                extent.isPowerOfTwo.not.if({
                    "QCD:serialize: extent has to be a power of two".error
                });
                HilbertIndices.serialize(slice)
            },
            torus: {|slice, extent|
                slice.flat;
            },
            scramble: {|slice|
                slice.flat.scramble;
            }
        );
    }

    // add a new serialization type at runtime
QCD.serTypes.put(\star, {|slice|
    var starSize = slice.size div:2;
    var numDims = 4;
    var starShape;

    starShape = neighbours1.collect({ |nb|
        (0..starSize).collect(_ * nb)
    }).flatten(1).collect {|indexN|
        indexN + (starSize.div(2)+1).dup(numDims)
    };

    starShape.collect{|iA| slice.slice(*iA)}
});
```

Figure 8.21
Some initial serialization methods, and adding an alternative.

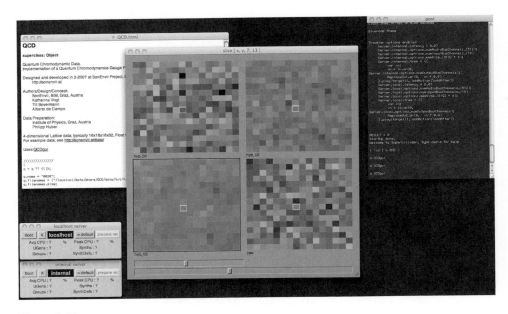

Figure 8.22
The QCD sonification working environment.

8.7   Example 3: A Miniature CloudGenerator

As the final example, we demonstrate a slightly larger project written in object modeling and just-in-time style (see chapter 7). *CloudGenMini* is reimplementation of a classic granular synthesis program by Curtis Roads and John Alexander, *CloudGenerator*, which creates clouds of sound particles based on statistical distributions. Though the discussion here focuses on coding style, the synthesis technique and aesthetic aspects are also discussed in chapter 16.

CloudGenMini combines several components: a selection of SynthDefs to generate single granular sounds; a task that generates a cloud of sound particles; functions to create random ranges for the control parameters and to store them; functions to cross-fade between stored settings; and, finally, a lightweight GUI to play the instrument. CloudGenMini can be run entirely from the file *ObjMod2_CloudGenMini .scd* (on the book Web site).

Figure 8.23 shows 2 of the SynthDefs. It is recommended practice to write tests which verify that all parameters in a SynthDef work as expected, and one can also find good parameter ranges this way.

Figure 8.24 creates an event q and stores globally needed names for parameter ranges, as well as specs for grain parameters. A named TaskProxy is created with

```
(
    // a gabor (approx. gaussian-shaped) grain
SynthDef(\gab1st, { |out, amp=0.1, freq=440, sustain=0.01, pan|
    var snd = FSinOsc.ar(freq);
    var env = EnvGen.ar(Env.sine(sustain, amp * AmpComp.ir(freq) *
0.5), doneAction: 2);
    OffsetOut.ar(out, Pan2.ar(snd * env, pan));
}, \ir ! 5).add;


            // a simple percussive envelope
SynthDef(\percSin, { |out, amp=0.1, freq=440, sustain=0.01, pan|
    var snd = FSinOsc.ar(freq);
    var env = EnvGen.ar(
        Env.perc(0.1, 0.9, amp * AmpComp.ir(freq) * 0.5),
            timeScale: sustain, doneAction: 2
        );
    OffsetOut.ar(out, Pan2.ar(snd * env, pan));
}, \ir ! 5).add;


/*
    // tests for the synthdefs:
Synth(\gab1st);
Synth(\percSin);
Synth(\percSin, [\amp, 0.2, \sustain, 0.1]);
Synth(\gab1st, [\out, 0, \amp, 0.2, \freq, 2000, \sustain, 0.05,
\pan, 0.5] );
*/
);
```

Figure 8.23
Two granular synthdefs and tests for them.

Tdef(\cloud0) (see the Tdef help file), and its internal environment is created with a default SynthDef name to use; also created is an event called current, which contains default settings for all the parameter ranges. This design already makes the necessary preparations for using multiple settings (i.e., presets).

The Tdef function itself is very simple: in a loop, it creates values for the next grain by random choice within the ranges for each parameter stored in the current settings. Using s.sendBundle is low-level but very efficient messaging, which is useful for high-density granular clouds. The tests given exercise all the behaviors created so far: playing and stopping the cloud; putting new ranges for densRange, freqRange,

```
(
q = q ? ();

    // some globals
q.paramRNames = [\freqRange, \durRange, \densRange, \ampRange, \panRange];
q.paramNames = [\freq, \grDur, \dens, \amp, \pan];
q.syndefNames = [\gab1st, \gabWide, \percSin, \percSinRev, \percNoise];

    // specs for some parameters
Spec.add(\xfadeTime, [0.001, 1000, \exp]);
Spec.add(\ring, [0.03, 30, \exp]);
Spec.add(\grDur, [0.0001, 1, \exp]);
Spec.add(\dens, [1, 1000, \exp]);

    // make an empty tdef that plays it,
    // and put the cloud parameter ranges in the tdef's environment
Tdef(\cloud0)
    .set(
    \synName, \gab1st,
    \vol, 0.25,
    \current, (
        freqRange: [200, 2000],
        ampRange: [0.1, 1],
        durRange: [0.001, 0.01],
        densRange: [1, 1000],
        panRange: [-1.0, 1.0]
    )
);

        // make the tdef that plays the cloud of sound particles here,
        // based on parameter range settings.
Tdef(\cloud0, { |e|

    loop {
        s.sendBundle(s.latency, [
            "/s_new", e.synName ? \gab1st,
            -1, 0, 0,
            \freq,   exprand(e.current.freqRange[0], e.current.freqRange[1]),
            \amp,    exprand(e.current.ampRange[0], e.current.ampRange[1]) * e.vol,
            \sustain,  exprand(e.current.durRange[0], e.current.durRange[1]),
            \pan,   rrand(e.current.panRange[0], e.current.panRange[1])
        ]);
        exprand(e.current.densRange[0].reciprocal,
e.current.densRange[1].reciprocal).wait;
    }
}).quant_(0);
);
```

Figure 8.24
Global setup and a player Tdef for the cloud.

```
Tdef(\cloud0).play;

    // try changing various things from outside the loop.
    // change its playing settings

Tdef(\cloud0).envir.current.put('densRange', [ 50, 200 ]); // dense, async
Tdef(\cloud0).envir.current.put('densRange', [ 1, 10 ]);  // sparse, async
Tdef(\cloud0).envir.current.put('densRange', [ 30, 30 ]); // synchronous

    // for faster access, call the tdef's envir d
d = Tdef(\cloud0).envir;
d.current.put('freqRange', [ 800, 1200 ]);
d.current.put('durRange', [ 0.02, 0.02 ]);

d.current.put('ampRange', [ 0.1, 0.1 ]);

d.current.put('panRange', [ 1.0, 1.0 ]);
d.current.put('panRange', [ -1.0, 1.0 ]);

d.current.put('densRange', [ 30, 60 ]);
d.synName = \percSin;
d.synName = \gab1st;
d.current.put('durRange', [ 0.001, 0.08 ]);
```

Figure 8.25
Tests for the cloud.

and so on into the current settings; verifying that they change the running cloud; and changing the grain SynthDef used. (See figure 8.25.)

A common heuristic for exploring the possibilities of a synthesis process is to employ random ranges, which may reveal more interesting areas than one might encounter by making changes manually. Figure 8.26 shows a method for creating random ranges for all parameters, based on the global maximum settings defined in figure 8.24. This method is then employed for creating 8 random settings, so that one can try switching between different cloud parameter states. The concept of presets and interpolation goes back to SC2 classes written by Ron Kuivila. He noted that he was inspired to implement this multidimensional interpolation by David Tudor, who would play a mixer polyphonically with 5 fingers at a time. The current version of his approach is available in the Conductor quark.

The original CloudGenerator program creates clouds by specification: one sets values for cloud duration, grain duration, density, and amplitude, and for high and low band limits (i.e., minimum and maximum grain frequencies); setting start and end values allows one to define a *tendency mask* for grain frequency. In

```
(
    // make the Tdef's envir a global variable for easier experimenting
d = Tdef(\cloud0).envir;
    // a pseudo-method to make random settings, kept in the Tdef's environment
        // randomize could also do limited variation on existing setting.
d.randSet = { |d|
    var randSet = ();
    q.paramRNames.do { |pName, i|
        randSet.put(pName,
            q.paramNames[i].asSpec.map([1.0.rand, 1.0.rand].sort)
        );
    };
    randSet;
};

/*  test randSet:
d.current = d.randSet;
*/

// make 8 sets of parameter range settings:
d.setNames = (1..8).collect { |i| ("set" ++ i).asSymbol };
d.setNames.do { |key| d[key] = d.randSet; }

/*  test switching to the random presets
d.current = d.set1.copy;     // copy to avoid writing into a stored setting when it
is current.
d.current = d.set3.copy;
d.current = d.set8.copy;
*/
);
```

Figure 8.26
Making random settings, and 8 random presets to switch between.

CloudGenMini, this is generalized to setting ranges for all parameters and being able
to cross-fade between range settings for every parameter. (To make a parameter deterministic, one simply sets its minimum and maximum to the same value.) The new
functions in figure 8.27 allow creating defined-length clouds based on tendency
masks: a flag d.stopAfterFade is used for the optional ending when a parameter
cross-fade has ended; d.xfadeTime sets cross-fade time. A TaskProxy (see chapter 7),
d.morphtask, is used to create the intermediate values of the ranges between the setting d.current and the setting d.target. Using a TaskProxy (rather than a plain
task) has the benefit that restarting it while playing stops the previous cross-fade
task, and begins again seamlessly from the current interpolated setting. Finally, the

```
(
    // and some parameters for controlling the fade
d.stopAfterFade = false;
d.xfadeTime = 5;

d.morphtask = TaskProxy({
    var startSet = d[\current], endSet = d[\target];
    var stepsPerSec = 20;
    var numSteps = d.xfadeTime * stepsPerSec;
    var blendVal, morphSettings;

    if (d.target.notNil) {
        (numSteps).do { |i|
        //  ["numSteps", i].postln;
            blendVal = (i + 1) / numSteps;
            morphSettings = endSet.collect({ |val, key|
                (startSet[key] ? val).blend(val, blendVal)
            });
            d.current_(morphSettings);
            (1/stepsPerSec).wait;
        };
        d.current_(d.target.copy);
        "morph done.".postln;
        if (d.stopAfterFade) { Tdef(\cloud0).stop; };
    };
}).quant_(0);        // no quantization so the task starts immediately

/* test morphing
(
Tdef(\cloud0).play;
d.target = d.set6.copy;
d.morphtask.play;
)
Tdef(\cloud0).stop;

    // playing a finite cloud with tendency mask:
(
Tdef(\cloud0).play;       // begin playing
d.stopAfterFade = true;   // end cloud when crossfade ends
d.xfadeTime = 10;         // set fade time
d.target = d.set8.copy;   // and target
d.morphtask.play;         // and start crossfade.
```

Figure 8.27
Crossfading between different settings with a TaskProxy.

```
)
*/

    // put fading into its own method, with optional stop.
d.fadeTo = { |d, start, end, time, autoStop|
    d.current = d[start] ? d.current;
    d.target = d[end];
    d.xfadeTime = time ? d.xfadeTime;
    if (autoStop.notNil) { d.stopAfterFade = autoStop };
    d.morphtask.stop.play;
};

/*  // tests fadeTo:
Tdef(\cloud0).play;
d.fadeTo(\current, \set2, 20);
d.fadeTo(\current, \set6, 10);
d.fadeTo(\current, \set5, 3, true);

Tdef(\cloud0).play;
d.fadeTo(\current, \set1, 3, false);
*/
);
```

Figure 8.27
(continued)

method d.fadeTo allows for fading from any stored setting to any other, with arguments for fadetime and autostop. This completes the functions necessary for creating a cloud that evolves based on specifications.

The final addition to this example is a GUI. Developing this was incremental, as before; however, rather than maintaining intermediate steps of a GUI, it is much easier to put the GUI creation into 1 function, add more elements, and run the function again when more details have been added. For just-in-time programming, we have created the notion of "throwaway GUIs." Creating and removing such a GUI should never influence the state of what it displays, so it can be opened and closed at any time (e.g., to save CPU); it should require little writing effort and should spend little effort on displaying what it displays. For throwaway GUIs, slow update rates are fine, so that, for instance, replaying fast recorded control changes does not cause CPU spikes when they are being displayed. Seeing changes at, say, every 0.2 second is often fully sufficient, so a Model-View-Controller scheme is not useful here.

In figure 8.29, passing the Tdef and a screen position as arguments would allow creating GUIs for multiple CloudGenMinis (though the code above would need modifications for that). To display the parameter ranges, the EZRanger class is used.

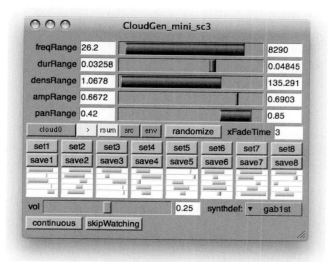

Figure 8.28
CloudGenMini graphical user interface (screen shot).

Tdefs have a GUI class, TdefEditor,, that can be put into a window like a single view. A TdefEditor shows a number of aspects of its Tdef: name, playing state, and whether the Tdef has a source and an environment. Clicking on the src and env buttons opens text windows for editing their code.

A "randomize" button cross-fades from the current setting to a new random setting in the cross-fade time displayed in the number box next to it.

Slow display updating is handled by a SkipJack: every 0.5 second, while the window exists, it displays the parameter ranges in d.current in the appropriate EZ-Rangers, and it updates the xfadeTime box if the fade time has changed. This could be optimized by caching previous states (as done, e.g., in TaskProxyGui), but it was not deemed necessary here.

The next section in q.makeCloudGui creates 3 elements for each stored setting: a button to cross-fade to that setting; a button to store the current setting at that location; and miniature visual reminders of the setting stored in each location.

Though it is not ideal that these mini displays are updated only when settings are stored with the buttons, it was considered acceptable for a sketch; experimenting with other features was more interesting.

The bottom line of GUI elements provides volume control, switching between SynthDefs, and toggling stopAfterFade mode. Finally, there is a button for turning the SkipJack off, so one can write into the number boxes. (Currently, the SkipJack always writes the current values back into the GUI without checking whether one

```
(
q.makeCloudGui = { |q, tdef, posPoint|
    var w, ezRangers, fdBox;
    var setMinis, skipjack;

    posPoint = posPoint ? 400@400;   // where to put the gui window

    w = Window.new("CloudGen_mini_sc3",
        Rect.fromPoints(posPoint, (posPoint + (400@320))), false).front;
    w.view.decorator_(FlowLayout(w.bounds.copy.moveTo(0, 0)));

    w.view.decorator.nextLine;
        // the range sliders display the current values
    ezRangers = ();

    q.paramRNames.do { |name, i|
        ezRangers.put(name,
        EZRanger(w, 400@20, name, q.paramNames[i],
            { |sl| tdef.envir.current[name] = sl.value; },
            tdef.envir.current[name], labelWidth: 70, numberWidth: 50, unitWidth:
10)
            .round_([0.1, 0.00001, 0.0001, 0.0001, 0.01][i])
        );
    };
        // a just in time - gui for the Tdef
    TdefGui(tdef, parent: w);

    w.view.decorator.nextLine;

    Button.new(w, 80@20).states_([[\randomize]])
        .action_({
            tdef.envir.target_(d.randSet);
            tdef.envir.morphtask.stop.play;
        });

    fdBox = EZNumber.new(w, 110@20, \xFadeTime, [0, 100, \amp],
        { |nbx| tdef.envir.xfadeTime = nbx.value },
         tdef.envir.xfadeTime, false, 65);

            // skipjack is a task that survives cmd-period:
            // used here for lazy-updating the control views.
    skipjack = SkipJack({
```

Figure 8.29
A lightweight graphical user interface for CloudGenMini (code).

```
        q.paramRNames.do { |name| ezRangers[name].value_(tdef.envir.current[name])
};

        fdBox.value_(tdef.envir.xfadeTime);

        // mark last settings that were used by color?
        // a separate color when changed?

    }, 0.5, { w.isClosed }, name: tdef.key);

    w.view.decorator.nextLine;

    // make a new layoutView for the 8 presets;
    // put button to switch to that preset,
    // a button to save current settings to that place,
    // and a miniview of the settings as a visual reminder in it.

        // make 8 setButtons
    tdef.envir.setNames.do { |setname, i|
        var minisliders, setMinis;
        var zone = CompositeView.new(w, Rect(0,0,45, 84));
        zone.decorator = FlowLayout(zone.bounds, 0@0, 5@0);
        zone.background_(Color.white);

        Button.new(zone, Rect(0,0,45,20)).states_([[setname]])
            .action_({
                // just switch: // tdef.envir.current.putAll(d[setname] ? ())
                tdef.envir.target = tdef.envir[setname];
                tdef.envir.morphtask.stop.play;
            });

        Button.new(zone, Rect(0,0,45,20))
            .states_([["save" ++ (i + 1)]])
            .action_({
                d[setname] = tdef.envir.current.copy;
                setMinis.value;
            });

        minisliders = q.paramRNames.collect { |paramRname|
            RangeSlider.new(zone, 45@8).enabled_(false);
        };
        setMinis = {
            q.paramRNames.do { |paramRname, i|
```

Figure 8.29
(continued)

```
                    var paramName = q.paramNames[i];
                    var myrange = d[setname][paramRname];
                    var unmapped = paramName.asSpec.unmap(myrange);
                    minisliders[i].lo_(unmapped[0]).hi_(unmapped[1]);
                }
            };
            setMinis.value;
        };

    /*  Some extras:
        a volume slider for simple mixing,
        a popup menu for switching syndefnames;
        a button to stop/start the skipjack for refreshing,
        so one can use numberboxes to enter values.
    */
        EZSlider(w, 245@20, "vol", \amp, { |sl|tdef.set(\vol, sl.value) },
            0.25, false, 20, 36);

        StaticText.new(w, 55@20).string_("synthdef:").align_(\right);
        PopUpMenu.new(w, Rect(0,0,80,20))
            .items_([\gab1st, \gabWide, \percSin, \percSinRev, \percNoise])
            .action_({ |pop| tdef.envir.synName = pop.items[pop.value] });

        Button.new(w, 80@20).states_([[\continuous], [\fadeStops]])
            .value_(tdef.envir.stopAfterFade.binaryValue)
            .action_({ |btn|
                tdef.set(\stopAfterFade, btn.value == 1)
            });

        Button.new(w, 80@20).states_([[\skipWatching], [\skipWaiting]])
            .action_({ |btn|
                [ { skipjack.play }, { skipjack.stop }][btn.value].value
            });

    };
    q.makeCloudGui(Tdef(\cloud0))
);
```

Figure 8.29
(continued)

is typing. Though checking is possible, coding it is more effort than turning the SkipJack on and off when needed.)

8.8   Conclusion

Objects and object models are wonderful means to experiment with concepts, and SuperCollider supports elegant ways of developing ideas fluidly. As the Smalltalk tradition maintains, exploring ideas interactively by writing code is a great way to find out what one actually wants to achieve. By experimenting with different working approaches and coding styles such as those described here, one can study the art of maintaining a flow of evolving ideas, making things efficient where necessary, and keeping things flexible wherever possible.

References

Alpert, S. R., K. Brown, and B. Woolf. 1998. *The Design Patterns Smalltalk Companion.* Reading, MA: Addison-Wesley.

Beck, K. 1996. *Smalltalk Best Practice Patterns.* Upper Saddle River, NJ: Prentice Hall.

Chaitin, G. 1998. *The Limits of Mathematics.* Singapore: Springer.

Dannenberg, R., D. Rubine, and Neuendorffer, T. 1991. "The Resource-Instance Model of Music Representation." In *Proceedings of ICMC 1991*, Montreal, Canada: International Computer Music Association, pp. 428–432.

Gamma, E., R. Helm, R. Johnson, and J. Vlissides. 1994. *Design Patterns: Elements of Reusable Object-Oriented Software.* Reading, MA: Addison-Wesley.

Hofstadter, D. 1995. *Fluid Concepts and Creative Analogies.* New York: Basic Books.

Iverson, K. E. (1979) 1980. "Notation as a Tool of Thought" (ACM Turing Award Lecture). *Communications of the ACM*, 23(8): 444–465.

Kay, A. C. 1993. "The Early History of Smalltalk." 1993. In *Proceedings of the 2nd ACM SIGPLAN Conference on the History of Programming Languages*, pp. 69–95. New York: ACM.

McCartney, J. 2002. "Rethinking the Computer Music Language: Super Collider." *Computer Music Journal*, 26(4): 61–68.

Smith, B. C. 1996. *On the Origin of Objects.* Cambridge, MA: MIT Press.

Notes

1. See <http://pbup.goto10.org>.

2. See <http://sonenvir.at/data/lattice>.

Platforms and GUI

9 Mac OSX GUI

Jan Trützschler von Falkenstein

In addition to the document-based text interface, SuperCollider has the ability to provide a graphical user interface (GUI). It can help to interact with code more intuitively, visualize data, and give applications the look and feel of commercial programs. In the following we will have a look at how to create such GUIs, how to establish communication between them and other code, and how to expand and tweak them. The final part of this chapter focuses on the manipulation and functional expansion of documents themselves (i.e., the text windows in which SC is programmed and their associated files). Most classes mentioned in this chapter have a Help file in the distribution which provides additional information. For all examples that include audio processing, it is presumed that the default server has been booted and is running. An image providing a visual overview of all GUI elements—hereafter referred to as "views"—can be found at the end of the chapter.

Much of the information in this chapter is applicable to all platforms; but details and code will refer specifically to the Mac OSX version of the software. The native OSX GUI implementation is interchangeably referred to as CocoaGUI or OSX GUI. Users on other operating systems can check the GUI Classes Help file in Super-Collider to see the various cross-platform equivalents for all the standard GUI classes and the cross-platform way to call them. (For example using the generic `Window` class. See section 9.6 for more detail.) On Windows and Linux, these cross-platform classes usually direct calls to the cross-platform GUI implementation SwingOSC, which is the subject of chapter 10. Since users may be interested in only one of these implementations, this chapter will necessarily duplicate some of the information found there. Most examples from this chapter are available in both CocoaGUI and cross-platform forms on the book Web site. Note that in most cases, the cross-platform form is used for GUI examples elsewhere in this book.

Probably the simplest way to create a GUI is by selecting New SCWindow in the UI menu of the application's main menu bar. This opens up a little construction kit, with an empty window and a palette window containing all views, which can be placed on the window by drag and drop. The main purpose of this construction kit

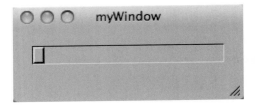

Figure 9.1
A simple GUI with an SCSlider on an SCWindow.

is to place widgets at the right position, allowing a simple and interactive approach to GUI design. But in order to understand GUI integration, we need to approach this subject from the side of code. In this chapter we are going to have a look at several simple graphical interfaces and formulate principles which can be applied in almost any other situation.

9.1 Creating Windows and Views

To begin with, let's have a look at a simple example of a small GUI. The code below creates a window with a slider, as shown in figure 9.1.

```
(
var window, slider;
window = SCWindow("myWindow", Rect(100, 100, 240, 80));
slider = SCSlider(window, Rect(20, 20, 200, 20));
window.front;
)
```

In the code above, we instantiate an SCWindow, which is SC's class for a standard OSX window. We provide a name for the window, which will be shown in the window's title bar, and a rectangle, which sets size and position. The rectangle is defined using the Rect class with the following argument scheme: Rect(left of window, bottom of window, width of window, height of window), which refer to location and size in pixels. Note that the origin of the coordinate system (i.e., 0, 0) is at the lower left corner of the screen.

In the next line we place a slider, called SCSlider, on the window. The size and position of the slider are again defined on the basis of a Rect, with the exception that inside the window the coordinate (0, 0) is in the upper left corner, and the Rect can be interpreted as (left, top, width, height). This same convention is used for all the views you place within a window; a y coordinate that increases as you go down the screen is a standard in computing. SCSlider, like all OSX views, is a subclass of SCView and inherits many methods from it that enable us to change the view's look and behavior. For instance, the Rect, which specifies the size and position of the view, is stored in the variable bounds. We will see more of this later, including an overview of all settings (table 9.2).

After instantiating an object of SCWindow and placing the slider, we tell the window to display and place itself on the foremost layer of the screen by calling its method front. The window can be closed either with the mouse or programmatically, by using its method close. In both cases the SC object remains active, which can lead to errors when trying to interact with a window or a view which has already been closed. The reason for this is that the GUI classes are wrappers for code and data on a lower level, for which data pointers are stored in SC. If the window has been closed, the pointers lose their data and point to empty chunks of memory. This implementation means that a closed window cannot be opened anymore. The following is a typical error resulting from an unsuccessful attempt to interact with a closed view.

```
ERROR: Primitive '_SCView_SetProperty' failed.
Failed.
RECEIVER:
Instance of SCButton {(011BEC10, gc = E4, fmt = 00, flg = 00, set = 05)
    instance variables [18]
        dataptr : nil
...
```

The first instance variable, dataptr, is nil, meaning that there is no visible instance of a button anymore. As many changes to a view's appearance or behavior are dispatched to the low-level implementation via a setProperty message, it is common to see a failure of that primitive.

It is possible to check, however, if a view or window is open by calling the method isClosed. We can also receive a notification of a closing action by assigning a function to a view's or a window's onClose variable. We will see the use of this action in more detail later.

9.1.1 Getting and Setting Values

The current state of most views is stored in a variable called value, and the usual setter and getter methods can be used to access it. Values of most continuous tools, such as sliders, range from 0.0 to 1.0, with the minimum being on the left side for horizontal views and at the bottom for vertical ones. A function, which can be set in the view's action variable, is evaluated whenever the user interacts with the view. The view itself is passed as the first argument to this function, allowing us to access its state there.

Table 9.1
Scaling Methods Defined in SimpleNumber

Scaling Methods	
`linlin(inMin, inMax, outMin, outMax, clip)`	linear-to-linear mapping
`linexp(inMin, inMax, outMin, outMax, clip)`	linear-to-exponential mapping
`explin(inMin, inMax, outMin, outMax, clip)`	exponential-to-linear mapping
`expexp(inMin, inMax, outMin, outMax, clip)`	exponential-to-exponential mapping
`bilin(inCenter, inMin, inMax, outCenter, outMin, outMax, clip)`	triangular linear mapping
`biexp(inCenter, inMin, inMax, outCenter, outMin, outMax, clip)`	triangular exponential mapping

In the following example the slider's value (set initially to 0.7) is posted to the post window when it is changed through user interaction. In all examples of this chapter, the setter methods are being called in sequence after the constructor to save space.

```
(
var window, slider;
window = SCWindow("myWindow", Rect(100, 100, 220, 40));
slider = SCSlider(window, Rect(8, 4, 200, 20))
    .value_(0.7)
    .action_({|view| view.value.postln});
window.front;
)
```

If we want to change the view's value from another point in our code, we can use the setter method `value_`, which does not call the action, or `valueAction_`, which does call the action after having set the new value.

9.1.2   Mapping Values

The slider's range from 0 to 1 is often impractical when controlling parameters of synths and the like. The view's value can be scaled either directly, by using scaling methods defined by `SimpleNumber`, or by using a `ControlSpec`, a special class for the purpose of mapping a range between 0 and 1. Methods for scaling a number directly can be found in table 9.1.

Figure 9.2 shows an example in which a slider's value is exponentially scaled from 20 to 20,000 and then used to set the frequency of a synth. Upon closing the window, we release the synth. (For cleanup purposes we also register a function with the

```
(
var window, slider, mySynth;
mySynth = Synth(\default);
window = SCWindow("myWindow", Rect(100, 100, 220, 40));
slider = SCSlider(window, Rect(8, 4, 200, 20))
        .value_(440.explin(20,20000,0,1))
        .action_({|view|
            mySynth.set(\freq,
                view.value.linexp(0,1,20,20000).postln
            )
        })
        .onClose_({mySynth.release;});
window.front;
CmdPeriod.doOnce({window.close});
)
```

Figure 9.2
Scaling the values of an SCSlider.

CmdPeriod class, which will close the window if the user frees the synth by pressing Cmd-.)

The ControlSpec class is a bit more sophisticated. It allows us to convert a value between a normalized range of 0 and 1 and another range back and forth by means of a certain curve, for instance, a linear or exponential one. It provides the option to set a default value, a description of the units being used, and an increment step quantization. Besides the normal construction with ControlSpec(minval, maxval, warp, step, default, units), there are a number of presets which can be conveniently accessed by calling asSpec on an associated key, which will be an instance of Symbol. The exponentially mapped frequency range from the last example would, for instance, look like ControlSpec(20, 20000, \exp, 0, 440, "Hz"). However, because that range is used quite often, it can be found in the ControlSpec class's dictionary of presets, which is stored in the class variable specs. It can be accessed as ControlSpec.specs[\freq], or even more concisely as \freq.asSpec. We can of course store our own mappings there, and thus benefit from the same shortcuts. Figure 9.3 shows the earlier example reworked to use a ControlSpec.

9.1.3   Model-View-Controller

Now that we have seen how to use a GUI to set the parameters of an audio process, we take a step back again for a closer look at the design of the function that does the

```
(
var window, slider, mySynth, spec;
mySynth = Synth(\default);
spec = \freq.asSpec;
window = SCWindow("myWindow", Rect(100, 100, 220, 40));
slider = SCSlider(window, Rect(8, 4, 200, 20))
        .value_(spec.unmap(440))
        .action_({|view|
            mySynth.set(\freq,
                spec.map(view.value).postln
            )
        })
        .onClose_({mySynth.release;});
window.front;
CmdPeriod.doOnce({window.close});
)
```

Figure 9.3
Scaling the values of an SCSlider using ControlSpec.

work. In the examples above, our whole little program is encapsulated and driven by the GUI. This is simple, but sometimes not very practical; for instance, when dealing with more complicated GUIs which provide multiple representations of the same thing.

When defining a view's action, we have to be careful not to give too much specific information to that particular function; otherwise, we may lose flexibility later: it will be harder to add new features and more difficult to find errors and bugs. In general, it is good practice to code in such a way that the data that are changed by a GUI are also accessible outside of the GUI and can be manipulated without it. This separates the data from the interface used to control them and from their visual representation. The view then acts solely as a representation, leaving everything else to other objects.

There are different strategies, or "design patterns," which describe the relationship between a user interface and the object(s) it affects. A widely used one is called Model-View-Controller (MVC), which was touched upon in chapter 5. MVC can be a complicated subject, and there are numerous subtle variants of it, but we'll discuss its simplest form here. In MVC, *Model* refers to the data or object whose state is being changed by user input. This might be a single value, an Array, a synth parameter, or something more complex, such as a custom object. It is called a model because the data are being used to model something; for example, a float can be used

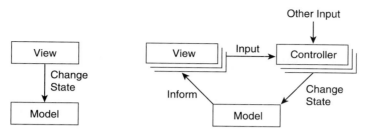

Figure 9.4
A simple action function vs. MVC

to represent a frequency. *View* in MVC refers to the GUI object which represents the model to the user. The *controller* refers to an object which processes user input (for instance, scaling and offseting, using a ControlSpec) and tells the model to change. Note that there can be multiple views and controllers attached to a single model.

The crucial bit is in how the communication takes place: classic MVC is in fact an extension of the Observer pattern discussed in chapter 5. Through the latter's implementation in SC, views can register as dependants of models and thus be informed when a model calls changed on itself, so that they can redraw themselves appropriately through their individual update methods. Figure 9.4 contrasts the the MVC approach with the simple action function approach discussed above.

To make this clearer, let's go through the steps in each case. In the simple action function example, the user interacts with a view through the keyboard or a mouse. This causes the view to redraw and fires the action function, which gets the current state of the view and updates the state of the model accordingly. This is simple to implement, and in simple cases (i.e., where interacting with the view is the *only* way to change the model) it can be sufficient.

In the MVC case things are a little more complicated, but also much more flexible. To start things off, the user provides some input. This can be from one of the views (which may or may not accept user input), but it also can be from another source, for example, directly from the keyboard or from another hardware device such as a joystick. This input is connected to the controller object, which contains any logic (for instance) necessary to interpret the input data (e.g., through a ControlSpec) and determine any changes which need to be made to the model as a result. The controller then tells the model object to change its state. As a side effect of this change, the model notifies the view(s) and any other dependants that it has changed, so that they can update themselves accordingly.

The most important thing to note about this is the flexibility it provides. Any number of views and controllers can be connected to a single model, and they will all be updated when a change occurs! Views and controllers can be added and removed as desired. Since the views' state is always derived from the model itself, there is never any issue with synchronization. As in the Observer pattern, the model doesn't need to know anything about its dependants; it just lets the views know that it's changed, and it is up to them to determine how to represent that change. This separation of roles is highly adaptable and conceptually clear.

In simple cases in SC, an MVC approach is not necessary, since most views redraw in response to user interaction anyway. Nevertheless, MVC demonstrates some important design principles and can be useful in some common cases, for instance, linking a slider and a number box.

Figure 9.5 uses a variation of MVC in which 1 or more controller objects act in a bidirectional fashion, taking responsibility for both changing the model and updating the views. (This is sometimes called Model-View-Presenter.) For the view updating, we'll make use of a Function which we'll call *updater*. As noted in chapter 5, Function implements update as a synonym for value, which allows it to act here as an intermediary between model and dependants, intercepting and delegating changed messages and allowing one to add customized dependancy behavior without having to code a custom object such as a view subclass. In practical terms this means that it becomes simple to use generic views to represent specific models. The updater function contains the knowledge of how the views should draw in response to the state of the model, so the views don't have to.

In the example our model is an Event, which holds only 1 item at the key myValue. In order to prevent writing the same function for the views' actions twice, we set a function to the variable setValueFunction. This function expects a number as argument and sets the value stored in the model; thus the Event. In this way it functions as the input portion of the controller. Then it invokes the method changed on the model with the key \value and the value itself. This will notify the updater function so that it can update the views. In the lines that follow, we create a simple GUI with an SCNumberBox, an SCSlider, and an SCLevelIndicator, all representing the same data. When closing the window, we remove the updater function from the model's list of dependants. The updater needs to be removed in order to prevent errors that may result from trying to modify closed views. The function itself is set up and added as a dependant in the final part of this code snippet. The last line demonstrates that the function setValueFunction changes the data as well as their representations in the views.

There are a number of other design patterns which can be used in object-oriented GUI programming, but the description of such design principles is not the main focus here. For a more detailed discussion of basic patterns, you might consult other sources [Gamma et al., 1994, Noble, 1997].

```
// simple MVC example
(
var window, slider, level, updater, model, numberbox, setValueFunction;

//model
model = (myValue: 1);
setValueFunction = {|value|
            model [\myValue] = value;
            model.changed(\value, value);
};

//view
window = SCWindow("myWindow", Rect(100, 100, 288, 80));
numberbox = SCNumberBox(window, Rect(20, 20, 44, 20))
            .value_(model[\myValue])
            .action_({|view| setValueFunction.value(view.value)});
slider = SCSlider(window, Rect(68, 20, 200, 20))
            .value_(model[\myValue])
            .action_({|view| setValueFunction.value(view.value)});

level = SCLevelIndicator(window, Rect(272, 20, 5, 20))
            .warning_(0.8)
            .critical_(1.0);

window.front;
window.onClose_({model.removeDependant(updater);});

//updater
updater = {|theChanger, what, val|
                  if(what == \value, {
                      numberbox.value_(val);
                      slider.value_(val);
                      level.value_(val);
                  });
              };
model.addDependant(updater);

setValueFunction.value(0.4);
)
```

Figure 9.5
An MVC implementation.

```
(
var window;
window = SCWindow("AppClock").front;
Task({
    100.do{|i|
        window.view.background_(Color.grey(i/100));
        0.04.wait;
    }
}).play(AppClock);
)
```

Figure 9.6
Controlling views using AppClock.

9.1.4 Manipulating Views from Other Processes

As noted in chapter 3, if we want to manipulate views from other processes, we have to make sure that those processes either run on the application clock called AppClock or are deferred to that clock. The latter can be done by using the method defer on a function. Attempts to invoke methods from another clock throw the following error:

```
ERROR: Primitive '_SCView_SetProperty' failed.
operation cannot be called from this Process.
...
```

Figure 9.6 demonstrates a Task which runs on the application clock. AppClock is set as an argument to the play method.

In figure 9.7, we display values from a synth which are sent via OSC. We set up an OSCresponder, which sets the value of a slider. Since the responder is running in another thread, we have to defer the GUI operation. We are using the MVC code from above but enclose the code that updates the views in a deferred function.

9.1.5 Complex Views

Until now we have only placed views directly onto a window, but sometimes it is advantageous to group views that are associated with related bits of data. Such grouping can be done with the aid of an SCCompositeView. Such a composite view can hold any number of views, which it stores in an Array called children. (The composite view is the parent of the views it contains.) A composite view can be placed onto a window or another composite view. In fact, SCWindow also uses a

```
(
var window, slider, updater, model, level, numberbox, setValueFunction,
oscresponder;

//model
model = (myValue: 1);
setValueFunction = {|value|
            model [\myValue] = value;
            model.changed(\value, value);
};

//view
window = SCWindow("myWindow", Rect(100,100, 288, 80));
numberbox = SCNumberBox(window, Rect(20, 20, 44,20))
            .value_(model[\myValue])
            .action_({|view| setValueFunction.value(view.value)});
slider = SCSlider(window, Rect(68,20, 200, 20))
            .value_(model[\myValue])
            .action_({|view| setValueFunction.value(view.value)});
level = SCLevelIndicator(window, Rect(272, 20, 5, 20))
            .warning_(0.8)
            .critical_(1.0);

window.front;
window.onClose_({model.removeDependant(updater); oscresponder.remove;});

//updater
updater = {|theChanger, what, val|
                    {
                    if(what == \value, {
                        numberbox.value_(val);
                        slider.value_(val);
                        level.value_(val);
                    });
                    }.defer;
            };
model.addDependant(updater);

// play a Synth on the server
SynthDef("send_trig",{
    SendTrig.kr(Dust.kr(2.0), 0, LFNoise1.kr(1, 0.5, 0.5));
}).play(s);
```

Figure 9.7
Controlling a view via Open Sound Control.

```
// register to receive the message from the Synth above and let it set the model
oscresponder = OSCresponderNode(s.addr, '/tr', { arg time, responder, msg;
    setValueFunction.value(msg[3]);
}).add;

)
```

Figure 9.7
(continued)

subclass of SCCompositeView, called SCTopView, to hold its views. The use of composite views can make it easier to create dynamic GUIs. It can also help to identify certain parts of an interface by setting a background color. Finally, it encourages a modular approach toward interface building and facilitates reusability of code.

The example in figure 9.8 shows how to use a button in order to show and hide some part of a GUI which is grouped using an SCCompositeView. Note that the coordinates of views added to a composite view are relative to the upper left corner of the composite view rather than to the upper left corner of the window. This is especially important for making GUI code reusable.

There are a number of other composite views. In some cases it may be useful to have a scolling view, which is capable of containing a larger area than its visible bounds. For this there is SCScrollView. (One can also make a window with a scrollable area by setting the scroll argument of SCWindow::new to true.) There are 2 composite views which automate the layouts of their child views: SCHLayoutView and SCVLayoutView. These views place their children in a horizontal or a vertical row, respectively. The spacing between the views can be accessed and modified through the getter/setter methods spacing and spacing_.

Besides these 2 layout views, a composite view can also use a decorator, which takes care of laying out child views. When using such a decorator, the position of the view is set internally. We can therefore ignore the left and top of the supplied rectangle (Rect), which in this case are irrelevant, and simply use a Point to set a view's dimensions (e.g., Point(width, height) or use the shortcut width@height). Currently, the only decorator which comes with the distribution is FlowLayout, which adds child views one after the other in a row and starts a new row automatically when the right boundary of the window has been reached or when the method nextRow has been invoked. Spacing between the items is defined by the layout's variable gap, and the spacing of the layout in relation to the view to which it is applied is defined by the variable margin. Both variables require a Point, which describes the horizontal and vertical spacing. The default for both is 4@4.

```
(
var window, button, composite, slider, numberbox;
window = SCWindow("myWindow", Rect(100,100, 288, 80));
button = SCButton(window, Rect(4,4, 100, 20))
            .states_([["hide"], ["show"]])
            .action_({|v|
                if(v.value==0){
                    composite.visible_(true)
                }{
                    composite.visible_(false)
                }
            });

composite = SCCompositeView(window, Rect(0, 40, 268, 28))
            .background_(Color.blue);
numberbox = SCNumberBox(composite, Rect(4, 4, 40,20));
slider = SCSlider(composite, Rect(48,4, 200, 20));

window.front;
)
```

Figure 9.8
Show and hide parts of a view.

It would be possible to implement other custom decorators. Such custom classes would need to provide a place(view) method similar to that defined in FlowLayout, which is responsible for the positioning of the views. A decorator can be attached to any composite view, including the SCTopView of a window.

The decorator in the example below demonstrates this. The top view is accessible via the window's variable view. All composite views have the option to set a decorator, which is held in a variable with the same name.

```
(
var window, sliders;
window = SCWindow("myWindow", Rect(100, 100, 208, 94));
window.view.decorator_(FlowLayout(window.view.bounds));
sliders = 3.collect{SCSlider(window, Point(200, 20))};
window.front;
)
```

Since this is a very common operation, SCWindow and all composite views implement a shortcut method: addFlowLayout(margin, gap).

Figure 9.9
Resizing behavior of views before and after resizing.

For all views, including composite views, a behavior can be defined to specify how to handle resizing after the window's size has been changed. Figure 9.9 shows the 9 different options.

9.2   Further User Interaction

9.2.1   Keyboard and Mouse Actions

Besides the action, which is executed whenever the state of a view is changed by the user, there are a few other ways to interact with GUIs which are not directly connected to its state. On most views one can receive various keyboard and mouse events, which are handled by dedicated functions, similar to the standard action. Whenever an event is received, a function is called with information about the event passed to it as arguments.

In order to handle keyboard interaction there are keyDownAction and keyUpAction functions, which are executed when a key is being pressed or released, respectively. The arguments which are passed to both functions are the view itself, the character, modifiers, the unicode representation, and the keycode. A simple keyDownAction would look like the following:

```
keyDownAction_{|view, char, modifiers, unicode, keycode| ...};
```

Through the first argument one has access to all the settings and variables of the particular GUI object, and through the others one can sort out which key or combination of key and modifiers is being pressed. The second argument (char) is an object of the type Char, which in SC is written with a $ identifier. Modifiers, such as the command key, control key, and option key, are passed in as integers and can be sorted out using the bitwise OR; for instance: 0x00010000|0x00020000.

The last 2 arguments are the unicode representation, which is identical to the character, and the key code, which represents the physical location of the key on the keyboard (which may vary depending on different national keyboard layouts).

Each view has a defaultKeyDownAction, which is called whenever there is no other action set. If the custom action returns nil, then the KeyDown event is passed on to the action of its superview. This way, key actions can be set which are valid for multiple views. Returning nil is also the way to decide whether a key event is consumed by the view or passed on to its parent. Key events can be handled globally by using globalKeyDownAction and globalKeyUpAction, which are thus evaluated by all windows. The currently pressed key is stored in the variable keyTyped.

An easy solution for mapping key commands is to use a KeyCodeResponder or a UnicodeResponder; both of them are part of the crucial library extension. (In SC 3.4 they are included in main distribution, but in future versions they may be moved to a Quark.) With these classes one can register functions for keys and modifiers without the need to set up a long case or several if statements. It can also help to keep the key command modular and to look clearer. These classes can generate a small GUI which posts the right key code or unicode values in response to user input. In order to use this GUI, we can evaluate KeyCodeResponder.tester; or UnicodeResponder.tester;

In order to receive a message when only the modifiers have changed, we can set up a keyModifiersChangedAction, which passes only the view and the modifier into the function. Changes in modifiers alone are not pushed into a view's keyDownAction or keyUpAction.

Mouse events are handled in a similar manner. A view's mouseDownAction is called when a mouse button is pressed with the pointer over the view; a mouseMovedAction, when the mouse is moved while the button is still pressed; and a mouseUpAction, when the button is released. One can also receive mouse-over events through the mouseOverAction. In order to enable this last action, one has to set acceptsMouseOver_ in the associated window to true. (This saves CPU in most cases, since tracking mouse-over movement is relatively expensive.) Functions for the actions look like this:

```
mouseDownAction_{|view, x, y, modifiers, buttonNumber, clickCount| ...};
mouseMovedAction_{|view, x, y, modifiers| ...};
mouseUpAction_{|view, x, y, modifiers, buttonNumber, clickCount| ...};
mouseOverAction_{|view, x, y, modifiers| ...};
```

In the example in figure 9.10 we use a mouse-down event to filter out a double click on a certain item. Upon a double click we open another window with a text field which can modify the selected item. This code shows again how an MVC approach achieves a clear overview.

9.2.2   Drag and Drop

One can drag and drop from 1 view to another, from a view to a document, or vice versa. Dragging from views is usually enabled by holding down the [cmd] key while dragging the mouse from a view.

Each view has a default drag item that can be changed by setting a `beginDrag-Action`, which returns the desired object for dragging. When something is dropped on a view, the view determines whether to accept that item by using the function `canReceiveDragHandler`, which returns a Boolean value. If it does accept the dragged type, it calls a `receiveDragHandler` function. The drag object itself is stored in the class variable `SCView.currentDrag`, which means that if we want to get information about the dragged item, we use that class variable. In the example in figure 9.11, 2 instances of `SCListView` are set up in a way that they accept Symbols and Strings from a mouse drop and deliver a drag of the selected item. The canReceiveDragHandler returns `true` for Symbols and Strings. The receiveDragHandler first checks whether the dropped item already exists in the model, and if it does, it selects it; otherwise, it adds the item to the model. We define the beginDragAction for the SCListView such that it returns the currently selected item rather than the index, which would be the default for this view. Figure 12 shows what the resulting GUI looks like.

9.3   Other View Settings

In order to set the value of a view with the mouse or keyboard, the view needs to be enabled. One can disable the view by setting the variable `enabled` to false. Selecting an enabled view with the mouse will focus it and enable it to receive all keyboard actions, as described earlier. We can also use the [tab] key to focus the next view or use the method focus with the argument `true` to focus an arbitrary view. We can tell a view not to receive any focus by setting a Boolean flag for the variable `canFocus`.

The background color of a view can be changed by setting an object of the class `Color` to the variable called `background`. A Color can be constructed with red, green, blue, and alpha values between 0 and 1. For instance, `Color(1, 0, 0, 1)` would be 100% red. There are a few convenience methods available to get various colors. The Color Help file provides more information.

Views which display text have the option to define a font type by setting the variable `font` to an object of the class `Font`. A font can be instantiated with its name as

```
(
var window, listView, updater, changeItemGui, model;

model = [\item1, \item2, \item3];

window = SCWindow("double click example", Rect(200,200,180, 320)).front;
listView = SCListView(window, Rect(4,4,172, 310))
                .items_(model)
                .mouseDownAction_({|view, x, y, modifiers, buttonNumber, clickCount|
                    if(clickCount == 2){
                        changeItemGui.value(view)
                    }
                })
                .onClose_({model.removeDependant(updater)});

changeItemGui = {|view|
    var win;
    win = SCWindow("chnage item", Rect(200,250, 150, 30)).front;
    SCTextField(win, Rect(4,4, 142, 20))
        .string_(view.item.asString)
        .action_({|v|
            model[view.value] = v.string.asSymbol;
            model.changed(\value);
            win.close;
        })
        .focus;
};

updater = {|theChanger, what, moreArgs|
    listView.items_(theChanger)
};
model.addDependant(updater);

)
```

Figure 9.10
Handling mouse actions and double click.

```
(
    var window, listViews, model, updater;

    model = (   left: [ "SinOsc", "Saw", "LFSaw", "WhiteNoise", "PinkNoise",
"BrownNoise", "Osc" ],
                right: []);

    window = SCWindow("list view drag & drop", Rect(200,200, 255, 100)).front;
    window.view.decorator_(FlowLayout(window.view.bounds));

    listViews = [\left, \right].collect{|it|
        SCListView(window, Rect(10,10,120,70))
            .items_(model[it])
            .canReceiveDragHandler_{ SCView.currentDrag.isKindOf(Symbol) or:
SCView.currentDrag.isKindOf(String)}
            .receiveDragHandler_{|v|
                var index;
                index = model[it].indexOfEqual(SCView.currentDrag);
                if(index.notNil){
                    v.value_(index);
                }{
                    model[it] = model[it].add(SCView.currentDrag);
                    model.changed(it);
                    v.value_(v.items.size-1);
                }
            }
            .beginDragAction_{|v| v.item}
            .action_({|view|
                [view.value, view.item].postln;
            })
            .onClose_({model.removeDependant(updater)});
    };

    updater = {|theChanger, what, moreArgs|
            switch(what,
                \left, {listViews[0].items_(model[\left])},
                \right, {listViews[1].items_(model[\right])}
            )
            };
    model.addDependant(updater);
)
```

Figure 9.11
Implementation of custom drag and drop behavior.

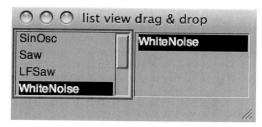

Figure 9.12
The resulting GUI from the example in figure 9.11.

a String and its size in points. For example, Font("Helvetica", 12) would represent 12-point Helvetica. A list of installed font types can be obtained by calling Font .availableFonts. There are a few more attributes which can be set for various views, but to cover all of them goes beyond the capacities of this chapter.

9.4   SCUserView

If we want to create a custom view, we can use an SCUserView, which enables us to implement custom drawing. While the drawing is handled in the view's function called drawFunc, the user interaction can be implemented with the above-described mouse actions. The drawFunc expects a sequence of SCPen methods, which represent a vector-graphic model. SCPen is not a class in the common sense, in which one makes an object and invokes methods; it is, rather, a service which manipulates the graphic context of a view. All its methods are used directly on the SCPen class. Most basic shapes, such as rectangles, circles, and ovals, can be drawn in a straightforward manner with SCPen, using methods such as addRect and addOval. For more complex forms we can describe a path. All forms can be either filled or stroked with a specified color. In addition, text using a String can be plotted.

The drawing has to be set up in a specific order. First we set the fill color or stroke color. Then we can use the simple shapes or start a path by moving the SCPen to a specific point. From there we can set a line to another point, which can be the origin for another line. When we are finished with the path, we can stroke or fill it with the color defined earlier. It is good practice to put each group of objects into a function to be passed as the argument to the use method for SCPen. This way we make sure that the graphic state is set to the default after the function has been executed. It is beyond this tutorial to describe all SCPen methods in detail. For more detailed information and examples, consult the Help file.

Figure 9.13 is an example of using an SCUserView straight, without creating a subclass, and figure 9.14 shows the same code encapsulated in a class. Both create a

```
(
var window, userView, value=false;
window = SCWindow("toggle view", Rect(200,200, 166, 66)).front;
userView = SCUserView(window, Rect(10,10, 40,40))
                .drawFunc_({|v|
                    var width, height, offset=2;
                    width =  v.bounds.width;
                    height = v.bounds.height;
                    SCPen.use{
                        //draw outline and background
                        SCPen.strokeRect(Rect(offset, offset, width-
(offset*2), height-(offset*2)));
                        SCPen.fillColor_(Color.white);
                        SCPen.fillRect(Rect(offset, offset, width-
(offset*2), height-(offset*2)));

                        if(value){
                            //draw the toggle cross
                            SCPen.line(Point(offset, height-offset),
Point(width-offset, offset));
                            SCPen.line(Point(offset, offset),
Point(width-offset, height-offset));
                            SCPen.stroke;

                        };
                    }
                })
                //switch states on mouse-down
                .mouseDownAction_({|view|
                    value = value.not;
                    view.refresh;
                });
~win = window;
)
```

Figure 9.13
Using SCUserView directly.

```
TToggle : SCUserView{
    var <> value=false;

    init{ arg argParent, argBounds;
        super.init(argParent, argBounds);
        background = Color.white
    }

    *viewClass{
        ^SCUserView
    }

    draw{
        var width, height, offset=2;
        width =  this.bounds.width;
        height = this.bounds.height;
        SCPen.use{
            //draw outline and background
            SCPen.strokeRect(Rect(offset, offset, width-(offset*2),
height-(offset*2)));
            SCPen.fillColor_(Color.white);
            SCPen.fillRect(Rect(offset, offset, width-(offset*2),
height-(offset*2)));

            if(value){
                //draw the toggle cross
                SCPen.line(Point(offset, height-offset), Point(width-
offset, offset));
                SCPen.line(Point(offset, offset), Point(width-offset,
height-offset));
                SCPen.stroke;

            };
        }
    }

    //override
    mouseDown{arg x, y, modifiers, buttonNumber, clickCount;
        value = value.not;
        this.refresh;
        mouseDownAction.value(this, x, y, modifiers, buttonNumber,
clickCount);
    }
}
```

Figure 9.14
Subclassing SCUserView to create view as shown in figure 9.15.

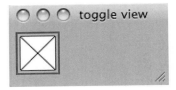

Figure 9.15
A toggle view resulting from the code in figure 9.13.

toggle view (figure 9.15) similar to those in other popular sound synthesis programs. In 9.13 we set the draw and mouse functions, whereas in 9.14 we override the methods directly. Note that as in composite views, drawing coordinates are relative to the upper left corner of the UserView, rather than to the window.

To clarify, if we want to write a custom view, we can subclass SCUserView and override its draw method to implement the visualization, and set its mouseDownAction to handle interaction. An important detail is that when any view is subclassed, it must implement a class method named viewClass, which returns the actual class name of the view we are extending. This is due to the internal design of views in SC. (See figure 9.14.)

9.5   Dynamic Views

Because of SC's object-oriented design, it is possible to create GUIs dynamically from previously unknown content. We can, for instance, design an interface for controlling a synth object without advance knowledge of its parameters. We have to be consistent with the design of SynthDefs and their arguments, though. Figure 9.16 shows 1 solution of an implementation of a prototype for playing and controlling synths. This makes use of information which is available from the global SynthDescLib, which, you will recall from chapter 6, is a library that collects basic information such as control names from SynthDefs created using add.

For the synth we have started, we register an OSCpathResponder, which notifies the Play Button when the synth has ended. In this way we can keep the button in sync with the state on the server. The sliders to control the synth are collected from the control names, which were provided by the SynthDescLib. Mappings for the controls are not provided by the library. In the example we presume that each control name corresponds to a mapping in the ControlSpec's dictionary and that we can access it with the appropriate key. If there is no spec available, we set a default range from 0 to 1. We use an EZSlider, a convenience class that combines a descriptive label, a number box, and a slider, including a ControlSpec to map its value. (Note that there are a number of other "EZ" views, which are outlined in the EZGui Help file.) (See figures 9.16 and 9.17.)

```
(
var createGUIFor, synthDefName, eventForSynthDef;
synthDefName = \default;
SynthDescLib.global.read;

//create a custom ControlSpec if necessary:
ControlSpec.specs.put(\out, ControlSpec(0, 128, \lin, 1, 0));

//model

eventForSynthDef = {|synthDefName|
    var event, node;
    event = (
            instrument: synthDefName,
            play: {
                var args = event.select{|it| it.isKindOf(Number)}.asKeyValuePairs;
                node = Synth(~instrument, args);
                    OSCpathResponder(Server.default.addr, ["/n_end", node.nodeID],
                        {|time, resp, msg|
                            node = nil;
                            event.changed(\play, 0);
                            resp.remove;
                        }
                    ).add;
                event.changed(\play, 1);

            },
            stopPlaying:{
                if( SynthDescLib.global[synthDefName].hasGate) {
                    node.release;
                }{
                    node.free;
                };
                node = nil;
                event.changed(\play, 0);

            },
            setArg: {|inevent, argName, value|
                inevent.use{
                    if(node.notNil){
                        node.set(argName, value);
```

Figure 9.16
Code for a GUI to control Synths without knowing their arguments.

```
                            };
                            inevent.put(argName.asSymbol, value);
                            inevent.changed(argName.asSymbol);


                    }
                }
        );
        SynthDescLib.global[synthDefName.asSymbol].controls.do{|it|
            event.put(it.name.asSymbol, it.defaultValue);
        };
        event
};

createGUIFor = {|event, window|
    var controlNames, playButton, height, updater, funcDict;

    //GUI

    controlNames = SynthDescLib.global[event[\instrument]].controls;

    height = controlNames.size * 24 +40;

    window = SCWindow("myWindow", Rect(100,100, 328, height));
    window.view.decorator_(FlowLayout(window.view.bounds));

    SCStaticText(window, 80@20).string_(event[\instrument].asString);

    playButton = SCButton(window, 120@20)
            .states_([["play"],["stop"]])
            .action_({|view|
                if(view.value==1){
                    event.play;
                }{
                    event.stopPlaying;
                }
            });

    funcDict = IdentityDictionary.new;

    //register button in funcDict
    funcDict.put(\play, {|value| {playButton.value_(value)}.defer});
```

Figure 9.16
(continued)

```
        window.view.decorator.nextLine;

        //create sliders

        controlNames.do{|control, i|
            var spec, name, action, initValue, slider;
            name = control.name;
            spec = name.asSymbol.asSpec ? [0,1].asSpec;
            action = {|view| event.setArg(name, view.value)};
            initValue = control.defaultValue;
            slider = EZSlider(window, 300@20, name, spec, action, initValue);
            window.view.decorator.nextLine;

            //register slider at controller

            funcDict.put(control.asSymbol, {|value|
                {
                    slider.value_(spec.unmap(value));
                }.defer
            })
        };

        // updater
        updater = {|theChanger, what, value|
            funcDict[what].value(value);
        };
        event.addDependant(updater);

        window.front;
        window.onClose_{event.stopPlaying; event.removeDependant(updater)};


};

//evaluate the GUI function

createGUIFor.value(eventForSynthDef.(synthDefName));
)
```

Figure 9.16
(continued)

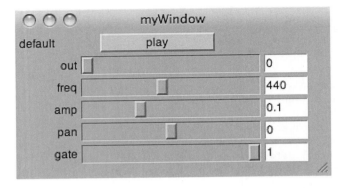

Figure 9.17
The GUI resulting from the code in figure 9.16.

9.6   Static (Singleton) Views

For some tasks it might be convenient to have only a single graphical representation of an object or some functionality, in order to prevent duplication. Such an object is called a *singleton*. Figure 9.18 shows an example in which not more than 1 instance of the window titled "singleton" can be created. In order to achieve this behavior, the window is stored in the variable called singletonWindow, which can be checked for nil. As long as the window is open, it is set to front, but when the window is being closed and the variable holding it is set to nil, a new window is created.

9.7   Cross-Platform GUI

In this chapter we have until now dealt only with the native OSX view classes provided by SuperCollider. Since their use is limited to the Macintosh operating system, a factory class called GUI and a set of redirecting classes have been developed, which enables us to create graphical interfaces in a platform-independent manner. In this factory class we can currently switch between the GUI kits Cocoa and Swing, where Cocoa refers to the classes described here and Swing to the ones in SwingOsc (see chapter 10). Both kits provide more or less the same functionality and are to a large extent interchangeable, albeit with a few important differences or omissions. The main difference in utilizing the redirecting classes is that the code looks slightly different. This is usually quite straightforward: For example, instead of `SCWindow.new.front`, we would write `Window.new.front`. A list of all redirect counterparts to the native classes can be found in the GUI-Classes Help file.

```
(
var window, button, createSingletonFunc, singletonWindow;

createSingletonFunc = {|view|
    if(singletonWindow.isNil){
        singletonWindow = SCWindow("singleton").front
            .onClose_({singletonWindow = nil});
    }{
        singletonWindow.front;
    }
};

window = SCWindow("open Singleton", Rect(300,300, 200, 40)).front;
button = SCButton(window, Rect(4,4,192, 30))
            .states_([["singleton"]])
            .action_(createSingletonFunc);
)
```

Figure 9.18
A simple implementation of a singleton.

Figure 9.19 gives an overview of all widgets available on OSX, and table 9.2 presents an overview of the most common getters and setters that alter the look or behavior of a view.

9.8   Document

Every text file which is opened in the SuperCollider application is an object of the class CocoaDocument, which for cross-platform compatibility can be accessed through the Document class. We can also create documents programmatically, providing a title (which appears on the window bar) and some text which displays in the text field. There is also the option to make the document a listener in order to receive the interpreter's output (i.e., replace the 'post' window). In SC there can be only 1 listener active at any 1 time. The following line of code demonstrates creating a document programmatically:

```
Document("my new document", "{SinOsc.ar(220)}.play");
```

We can also open any type of text file that SC can handle (e.g., rtf, doc, html, plain text), using the class method open and providing a path to an existing file. For instance:

```
Document.open("Help/Help.html");
```

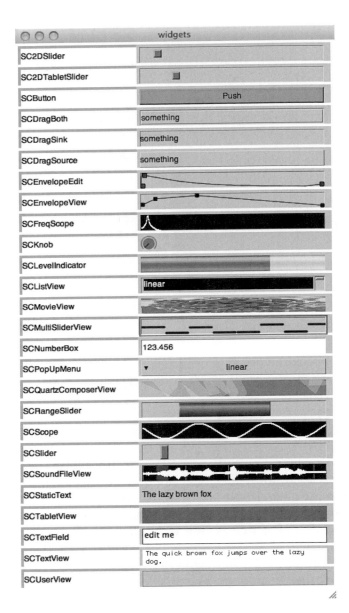

Figure 9.19
Overview of all widgets available on OS X; not shown are all EZView convenience classes.

Table 9.2
The Most Common Variables to Alter the Look of SCViews

Method or Variable Name	Object of Class	Description
bounds bounds_(rect)	Rect	bounds of the view relative to its parent
visible visible_(bool)	Boolean	set to false to hide the view
focusColor focusColor_(color)	Color	used to mark a view as focused
background background_(color)	Color	background color
font font_(font)	Font	font for views which display a string
stringColor stringColor_(color)	Color	color of the font for views which display a string
knobColor knobColor_(color)	Color	color of the knob of SCSlider

Table 9.3
Methods and Variables to Change CocoaDocument Properties

Method or Variable Name	Object of Class	Description
background background_(color)	Color	background color
bounds bounds_(rect)	Rect	defines size and position
fontColor fontColor_(color)	Color	sets the font color
syntaxColorize	–	colorizes the syntax
font font_(font, start, size)	Font start: Number size: Number	sets font of the document if start == –1, then the whole document is modified
defaultFont defaultFont_(font)	Font	sets the default font for each new document or class file

Table 9.4
Methods to Handle CocoaDocument Content

Method or Variable Name	Object of Class	Description
selectionStart	Number	returns the start of the current selection as a character count
selectionSize	Number	returns the size of the current selection as a character count
string(rangestart, rangesize) string_(string, rangeStart, rangeSize)	String rangestart: Number rangesize: Number	gets/sets the string of a defined range; if no rangestart is set, the content of the whole document is returned as a string
selectedString selectedString_(string)	String	gets/sets the currently selected string

```
(
var k;
k= KeyCodeResponder.new;
//  shift control p
k.register(  35  ,   true, false, false, true, {
    CocoaDialog.getPaths({|paths|
        Document.current.selectedString_(paths[0].asCompileString);
    });
});
Document.globalKeyDownAction_(k)
)
```

Figure 9.20
A shortcut to insert a path into a Document.

We can find any document in the class variable allDocuments, which is an Array of all open documents. The document which is currently focused on can be accessed through the class variable current. Whenever a document is opened, a function is called which is set in Document's class variable initAction. The action enables us to attach a certain look or behavior to the document.

There are a number of possibilities to modify the look and the behavior of a document programmatically as well as creating and opening it. Many methods are similar or the same as those of SCWindow and SCView described above.

Table 9.3 gives an overview of all attributes which change the appearance of a document, and table 9.4 shows methods which help to interact with the content of the document.

The method `front` brings the document to the first layer of the screen and focuses it, and `unfocusedFront` brings it to the front without placing the cursor on it. We can set the variable `alwaysOnTop` to true, to create a floating window which stays on top. The method `close` forces the document to be closed without any warning if changes should be saved. We can interact with the content of the document by getting or setting a certain range of text, expressed as an offset in characters from the start of the document and a selection length.

The document class provides almost the same functions to customize mouse and keyboard interaction as SCView: mouseDownAction, mouseUpAction, keyUpAction.

Figure 9.20 shows a convenient way of inserting a path while programming: we register a keyboard shortcut for all documents, which opens a file dialogue and inserts the path upon selecting "open" at the current cursor location.

You can also drag and drop files to a document to insert their paths as text. If you hold down the [alt] key while dropping, the path will be relative to that of the receiving document, providing it has been saved. This can be useful for creating portable folders of related files.

9.9   Other Approaches

This chapter has examined most of the basic concepts that are needed to create GUIs from scratch. However, there are a few libraries around, such as *Crucial* by Chris Sattinger and *Preset* by Ron Kuivila, which provide shortcuts to create certain interfaces even faster. Have a look at these and study the Help files and source code. There is also an increasing number of custom widgets around, which can be found in Quarks and other third-party libraries.

References

Collins, D. 1994. *Redesigning Object-Oriented User Interfaces*. Redwood City, CA: Benjamin Cummings.

Gamma, E., R. Helm, R. Johnson, and J. Vlissides. 1994. *Design Patterns: Elements of Reusable Object-Oriented Software*. Reading, MA: Addison-Wesley.

Noble, J. 1997. "GOF Patterns for GUI Design." In *Proceedings of the Second European Conference on Pattern Languages of Program Design* (EuroPLoP 97). Munich: Siemens.

Tidwell, J. 2005. *Designing Interfaces*. Sebastopol, CA: O'Reilly Media.

10 SwingOSC

Hanns Holger Rutz

10.1 Introduction

SwingOSC is the name of a separately running application (the "server") and of a class library for SuperCollider: both work hand in hand just as SuperCollider's synthesis server (*scsynth*) works hand in hand with the server abstraction objects of the class library (Server, Synth, Group, Bus, Buffer, etc.). In fact, the SwingOSC server was designed in the *style* of scsynth. Instead of managing nodes, buffers, and buses, SwingOSC manages objects in the Java programming language.

The class library that comes with SwingOSC mainly provides a tool kit for graphical user interfaces (GUIs), but also facilitates dynamic scripting of the Java language and thus provides a useful tool to combine the SuperCollider language with Java. This potentially allows the use of a vast number of general Java classes, not just GUI-related functionality. As discussed below, SwingOSC was designed for purposes of compatibility with CocoaGUI, the native OSX GUI system implemented in the OSC SuperCollider app. (SwingOSC runs on Windows and Linux, as well as OSX.) CocoaGUI is discussed in detail in chapter 9, as are the GUI factory class and redirect classes which make it possible to write cross-platform GUI code. Since readers may not be interested in both SwingOSC and CocoaGUI, there is some duplication here of information presented in chapter 9. Note that most of the GUI examples in this book are written in cross-platform style, but the examples in this chapter use the SwingOSC classes directly.

In this chapter, an initial example is taken and elaborated through the sections by step-by-step modifications. Both inline code and the longer code sections in the referenced figures are supposed to be executed *sequentially*.

10.2 Installation

The starting point will be a simple GUI: a window containing a button that can trigger an action inside SuperCollider. But before we can take on this, the SwingOSC software needs to be installed properly. It can be found on the book Web site or downloaded from <http://www.sciss.de/swingOSC>. Once it is extracted, the following important items will be found:

- *build/SwingOSC.jar* contains the server application itself. It can be copied into any preferred application folder.
- *SuperCollider/SCClassLibrary* and *SuperCollider/Help* contain the SwingOSC folders with all the necessary class and Help files, respectively. As explained in the *Using-Extensions Help* file in SuperCollider and the *SuperCollider/readme.html* file included with SwingOSC, they will work right away if you copy both to an operating-system-specific SuperCollider extensions directory and recompile the library.

The SwingOSC server is run on a Java virtual machine (JVM); therefore, a prerequisite is the installation of a Java Standard Edition (SE) runtime environment (JRE), version 1.4 or higher. This environment is preinstalled on Mac OSX systems, but you may need to install Java on a Windows- or Linux-based system. It is provided by Oracle/Sun from their Web site <http://java.sun.com>. The main *readme.html* file in SwingOSC contains further information regarding Java installation.

As a next step, SuperCollider needs to be configured a little bit. This can be done in the user configuration file, as described in the Help text *Using-the-Startup-File*. For SuperCollider 3.4, this file is

- On Mac OSX: *~/Library/Application Support/SuperCollider/startup.rtf*
- On Linux: *~/.sclang.sc*
- On Windows: *startup.sc* (in the same directory as SuperCollider).

This file can be edited with any text editor or directly from within SuperCollider. If it does not exist on a computer, a new empty file with that name must be created. The following lines should be added:

```
SwingOSC.program = "<installPath>/SwingOSC.jar";
g = SwingOSC.default;
```

The first line indicates where the *SwingOSC.jar* file was put, so *<installPath>* is to be replaced accordingly. The path can be absolute or relative to the current working directory. Here are two possible locations for Mac OSX and Linux:

```
SwingOSC.program = "/Applications/SwingOSC/build/SwingOSC.jar";
SwingOSC.program = "/usr/local/SwingOSC/build/SwingOSC.jar";
```

On Linux, alternative Java virtual machines such as GCJ are available. As of this writing, one should only use OpenJDK (<http://openjdk.java.net>) or the Oracle/Sun implementation (<http://java.sun.com>). In order to use a specific JVM with SwingOSC, an explicit path to the *java* program should be specified:

```
SwingOSC.java = "<javaPath>/java";
```

For example:

```
SwingOSC.java = "/usr/lib/jvm/java - .5.0-sun/jre/bin/java";
```

The second line of the startup file modification, g = SwingOSC.default, puts the default server instance into the interpreter variable g, which is a very convenient analogy to storing the default *scsynth* server in the interpreter variable s. The SwingOSC and Server classes have many things in common; for example, both can be launched using the boot method:

```
s.boot;  // boot the sound synthesis server (scsynth)
g.boot;  // boot the GUI server (SwingOSC)
```

10.3   A Simple GUI Example

After saving the startup file, SuperCollider is opened (or the class library is recompiled), and g.boot is executed to start a SwingOSC server. A text like the following will be printed out in the post window:

```
a SwingOSC
booting java <options> - jar SwingOSC.jar - t 57111 - L - i ...
SwingOSC v<version>. receiving TCP at address 127.0.0.1:57111
SwingOSC: server connected.
```

The starting point for every GUI is a window:

```
~win = JSCWindow.new;
~win.front;
```

The first line instantiates the Window class. The initial letters JSC indicate that this is a basic SwingOSC class. The second line calls the method front on the new window. Although JSCWindow.new *created* the window, it needs to be *opened* explicitly through the front method.

The next step is to populate the window with views such as buttons, sliders, text labels, number boxes, and so on. A list of available view classes can be retrieved from the *SwingGUI* Help file. Here we will create a 2-state button which will later be used to switch a Synth on and off:

```
(
~playButton = JSCButton(~win, Rect(4, 4, 40, 56));
~playButton.states = [["Play", Color.white, Color.green(0.4)], ["Stop",
Color.white, Color.red]];
~playButton.action = {arg view; "New value is %\n".postf(view.value)};
)
```

Like any other subclass of JSCView, JSCButton follows a pattern in which the 2 constructor arguments are the parent view and the view's bounding box. Here the parent view is the window itself (or, more precisely, ~win.asView, that is, the window's so-called top view). The bounding box is a Rect object with arguments left, top, width, and height, which are measured in pixels relative to the left top corner of the inner part of the window (excluding its border and title bar). The states_ setter method configures the button's appearance. Its argument is an array of "states," in which each state is again an Array of 3 elements: the label text, the text foreground Color, and the button background Color. If the button is clicked, the state toggles between a green "Play" label and a red "Stop" label.

How can clicking the button be coupled to a particular behavior? JSCView defines a number of fields to which *callback* functions can be assigned. The generic callback function for user input feedback is the action function which is registered using the action_ setter method. The function gets invoked with the view as the first argument. This allows the inspection of the current (modified) state of the view: for example, the value method of JSCButton returns the 0-based index of the currently visible state. The action function can thus be overwritten with a new one that creates or destroys a Synth, depending on the button's value, as shown in figure 10.1.

Next, 2 more environment variables, ~amp and ~speed, are added; they are controlled by horizontal sliders. SwingOSC's Slider class is JSCSlider. As with JSCButton, an action function can be assigned that gets notified when the slider is dragged, and the current slider position (which is in the interval [0,1]) can be queried by calling the value method, as depicted in figure 10.2. In the case of the speed parameter, a ControlSpec is used to convert the value from and to the normalized interval of [0,1].

Text labels are useful to explain the purpose of other views. SwingOSC's Text Label class is JSCStaticText. The string_ setter method sets the actual label string, and the align_ setter method specifies the horizontal layout of the text within the view's bounding box. Since setter methods return not a particular value but instead the view itself, the calls can be cascaded in a very compact way. A more verbose version would be

```
// this is an alternative variant that should not be executed:
~label = JSCStaticText(~win, Rect(56, 4, 40, 25 ));
~label.align = \right;
~label.string = "Amp:";
```

10.4   Using the Model-View-Controller Pattern

People coming from a "visual" programming environment background such as Max or Pure Data often find it hard to abstract their concepts from the visual presentation

```
// boot the sound synthesis server and prepare a SynthDef for buffer playback
(
s.waitForBoot({
    SynthDef( \bufPlay, { arg buf, amp = 1.0, speed = 1.0;
        Out.ar( 0, Pan2.ar(
            PlayBuf.ar( 1, buf, speed * BufRateScale.kr( buf ), loop: 1 ) * amp )
            );
    }).add;
    ~buf = Buffer.read( s, "sounds/a11wlk01.wav" );
});
)


// now replace the action function
(
~playButton.action = { arg view;
    if( view.value == 1, {
        ~node = Synth( \bufPlay, [ \buf, ~buf ]);
    }, {
        ~node.free; ~node = nil;
    })
};
)
```

Figure 10.1
Assigning an action function to play a buffer.

(where a parameter is considered a "number box," the starting and stopping of a sound is a "toggle button," a volume modification is a "signal fader," etc.).

The learning curve for SuperCollider is obviously steeper since GUI elements need to be created separately and connected to synthesis processes. However, the benefit is often greater: a clean decoupling of musical/sound synthesis processes and the graphical interface improves the maintainability and scalability of the code. The GUI can be exchanged, modified, or even removed at a later point in time without the need to touch or rewrite the actual processes.

Though not specific to SwingOSC, a common pattern called *Model-View-Controller* (MVC) can be used to design GUIs. MVC was conceived in the late 1970s but still forms the core of many contemporary GUI tool kits, including Java's Swing framework. Figure 10.3 illustrates this pattern and contrasts it with the simple action-function approach demonstrated above.

The term "view" must be seen here as something more general than a particular GUI view. In a general sense a view is a representation of an underlying data structure (or "model"). The key concept is that the model has no knowledge of the views,

```
~amp   = 0.5;  // initial amplitude
~speed = 1.0;  // initial speed (1.0 is normal, 0.5 is half-speed, etc.)
(
~playButton.action = { arg view;
    if( view.value == 1, {
        ~node = Synth( \bufPlay, [ \buf, ~buf, \amp, ~amp, \speed, ~speed ]);
    }, {
        ~node.free; ~node = nil;
    })};
)
~win.setInnerExtent( 370, 72 );  // more suitable dimensions for the window
~win.resizable = false;
JSCStaticText( ~win, Rect( 56, 4, 50, 25 )).align_( \right ).string_( "Amp:" );
(
~ampSlider = JSCSlider( ~win, Rect( 110, 4, 200, 25 ))
    .value_( ~amp ) // initial slider position
    .action_({ arg view;
        ~amp = view.value;
        ~node.set( \amp, ~amp );
    });
)
JSCStaticText( ~win, Rect( 56, 32, 50, 25 )).align_( \right ).string_( "Speed:" );
~speedSpec = ControlSpec( 1/8, 8, \exp );
(
~speedSlider = JSCSlider( ~win, Rect( 110, 32, 200, 25 ))
    .value_( ~speedSpec.unmap( ~speed )) // initial slider position
    .action_({ arg view;
        ~speed = ~speedSpec.map( view.value );
        ~node.set( \speed, ~speed );
    });
)
```

Figure 10.2
Adding sliders to control the synth.

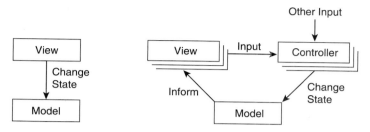

Figure 10.3
Action Function vs. Model-View-Controller.

and thus views can be dynamically added, modified, and removed without affecting the model. MVC is an extension of the *Observer pattern* which is provided by SuperCollider via the addDependant/removeDependant/update/changed methods in the Object class: when changed is called on an object, this object traverses the list of views (called "dependants" in SuperCollider) that have been registered through the addDependant method, and the update method is called on each dependant.

The initial GUI example is now modified to incorporate the Observer pattern: an Event instance can serve as a model (this is also explained in chapter 8). SwingOSC's UpdateListener class takes a model, a dependant Function (so we do not need to write a special class that overrides the update method), and an optional filter Symbol, and therefore simplifies the dependant registration, as depicted in figure 10.4.

The model parameters amp (amplitude) and speed (playback speed) are modified by calling the adjust function. For brevity, the starting and stopping of the Synth is not implemented in a full MVC way. The adjust function updates the corresponding fields of the model but also fires a notification through the changed method. The sliders now merely adjust the model but are ignorant of the audio synthesis control. Instead, 2 UpdateListener objects for amp and speed are created that track changes of the observed values and forward them to the Synth, using node.set(...). In this sense the Synth is like an "audible view."

Figure 10.5 moves closer to a traditional MVC arrangement, adding views to display the slider values, and figure 10.6 shows the corresponding screen shot.

As before, the slider value views are updated using the Observer pattern. The benefit of this style is apparent: more views can now be added without affecting the previous code.

Finally, an algorithmic controller can be defined that is independent of the slider's mouse controllers:

```
(
~ctrlFunc = {60.do({
```

```
~node.free; ~node = nil;


(
~model           = Event.new;
~model.amp       = ~amp;
~model.speed     = ~speed;
~model.node      = ~node;
~model.buf       = ~buf;
~model.adjust = { arg mod, key, value, source;
    mod.put( key, value );
    mod.changed( key, value, source )};

UpdateListener.newFor( ~model, { arg upd, mod, value;
    mod.node.set( \amp, value )}, \amp );
UpdateListener.newFor( ~model, { arg upd, mod, value;
    mod.node.set( \speed, value )}, \speed );

~playButton.action = { arg view;
    if( view.value == 1, {
        ~model.node = Synth( \bufPlay, [
            \buf, ~model.buf, \amp, ~model.amp, \speed, ~model.speed ]);
    }, {
        ~model.node.free; ~model.node = nil;
    })};
~ampSlider.action   = { arg view;
    ~model.adjust( \amp, view.value, view )};
~speedSlider.action = { arg view;
    ~model.adjust( \speed, ~speedSpec.map( view.value ), view )};
)
```

Figure 10.4
Using an Event to create a model.

```
        ~model.adjust(\speed, exprand(1/8, 8), thisFunction);
        0.1.wait})};
)
~ctrlFunc.fork;  //run as a Routine
```

Since the slider label ~speedText is a dependant of the model, it redraws automatically. The slider itself, however, is not moving. This flaw can be easily solved with additional dependants, as shown in figure 10.7.

The GUI-related dependants should be removed when their associated GUI views are closed.

```
(
~ampText = JSCStaticText( ~win, Rect( ~ampSlider.bounds.right + 2, 4, 50, 25 ));
~ampTextUpd = UpdateListener.newFor( ~model, { arg upd, mod, value;
    ~ampText.string = "% dB".format( value.ampdb.round( 0.1 ))}, \amp );
~speedText = JSCStaticText( ~win, Rect( ~speedSlider.bounds.right + 2, 32, 50, 25
));
~speedTextUpd = UpdateListener.newFor( ~model, { arg upd, mod, value;
    ~speedText.string = "%\\%".format( (value * 100).round( 0.1 ))}, \speed );
)
// note: the sliders must be initially dragged to cause view updates!
```

Figure 10.5
Adding labels to reflect the slider values.

Figure 10.6
The current GUI, using Aqua (Mac OSX) look-and-feel.

```
(
~ampSliderUpd = UpdateListener.newFor( ~model, { arg upd, mod, value, source;
    if( source !== ~ampSlider, {
        ~ampSlider.value = value;
    })}, \amp );
~speedSliderUpd = UpdateListener.newFor( ~model, { arg upd, mod, value, source;
    if( source !== ~speedSlider, {
        ~speedSlider.value = ~speedSpec.unmap( value );
    })}, \speed );
)
```

Figure 10.7
Registering the sliders with the model.

```
~ampSlider.onClose = {~ampSliderUpd.remove};
~speedSlider.onClose = {~speedSliderUpd.remove};
~ampText.onClose = {~ampTextUpd.remove};
~speedText.onClose = {~speedTextUpd.remove};
```

Now the MVC implementation is complete.

```
~ctrlFunc.fork;
```

You may have noticed the third argument to the model's `adjust` function, named `source`. It helps to avoid *feedback* problems; the `~ampSlider`'s action-function calls `~model.adjust`, and at the same time listens for changes via `~ampSliderUpd`. When one is dragging the slider, the model value will be sent back to the slider (with a little delay due to OSC transmission), causing the slider to become "sticky." The feedback is intercepted by the conditional `if( source !== ~ampSlider,... )`. The complete control flow is depicted in figure 10.8.

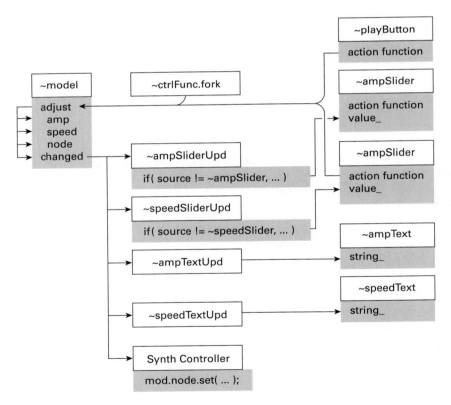

Figure 10.8
Connections between the model, views and controllers.

Another, somewhat more detailed discussion of MVC can be found in chapter 9.

10.5   Under the Hood: The Inner Workings of SwingOSC

Although the SuperCollider classes can be used perfectly without knowing the internals, such knowledge will help to improve the performance of GUI design and to detect and locate mistakes, and it forms the basis for developing custom views.

SwingOSC's name is composed of two parts: *Swing* and *OSC*. Swing is the name of a versatile GUI package in the Java language. As discussed in chapter 4, OSC is the acronym of *Open Sound Control*, the communication protocol used to connect the server with the client (SuperCollider). OSC is also used for communication to scsynth, which is why the SwingOSC server has many similarities to scsynth, and the SwingOSC class is modeled closely after the Server class.

Most SuperCollider GUI classes, such as JSCWindow and JSCButton, are proxies for corresponding Java classes that are instantiated on the server side. They communicate using OSC via the *SwingOSC.sc/SwingOSC.java* classes, as illustrated in figure 10.9.

The OSC traffic can be revealed by calling g.dumpOSC(*<code>*, *<reply>*), where *<code>* determines the printout of outgoing messages (client to server), and *<reply>* refers to incoming messages (server to client). Possible values are

• 0: no printout
• 1: text printout
• 3: text and hexdump printout.

Using g.dumpOSC(1), the initial example translates into the outgoing OSC messages as shown in figure 10.10. (The ["query", "status"] messages are not shown; they are suppressed by calling g.stopAliveThread. The depicted OSC messages refer to SwingOSC version 0.62 and may differ slightly in other versions.)

If the bracket strings "[" and "]" in the messages are understood as parentheses in the Lisp or Scheme language (i.e., expressions that have side effects and may return a value), reading this becomes very easy. Message arguments are processed by the server in a left-to-right order, where any argument can be another OSC command due to the insertion of a "[" ... "]" block, and are evaluated in depth-first order. For example, the SuperCollider statement JSCWindow.new results in 4 OSC messages: the first creates the actual window by using the "/new" OSC command to instantiate the class de.sciss.swingosc.Frame with 3 arguments: the window's title ("panel"), its bounding box on the screen, and flags (in this case 0):

```
"[", "/new", "de.sciss.swingosc.Frame", "panel",..., 0, "]"
```

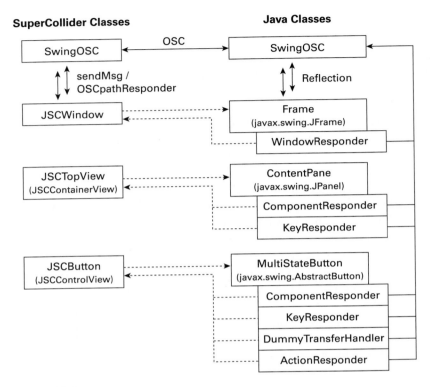

Figure 10.9
OSC communication diagram. Solid arrows indicate direct communication; dashed arrows indicate mediated communication. Superclasses are listed in parentheses.

Since the bounding box is not a primitive value (a number or a string), a *nested* OSC command must be used here to instantiate a `java.awt.Rectangle` with 4 arguments for the position and size of the rectangle:

```
"[", "/new", "java.awt.Rectangle", 128, 64, 400, 400, "]"
```

Finally, the result of the `"[", "/new", "de.sciss.swingosc.Frame",..., "]"` command—the new frame instance—is used as the second argument to the `"/local"` OSC command, which stores the Java object in a server variable named 1000.

```
"[", "/local", 1000, ..., "]"
```

Variable names can be either strings or numbers. This way the variable name, also called *object-ID*, has the same meaning as the *node-ID* on *scsynth*. `"/local"` implies that the variable is visible only to the client (SuperCollider) that created it, so a single

```
// ~win = JSCWindow.new;
    [ "/local", 1000, "[", "/new", "de.sciss.swingosc.Frame", "panel", "[", "/new",
    "java.awt.Rectangle", 128, 64, 400, 400, "]", 0, "]" ]
    [ "/local", "ac1000", "[", "/new", "de.sciss.swingosc.WindowResponder", 1000,
    "]", 1001, "[", "/method", 1000, "getContentPane", "]" ]]
    [ "/local", "key1001", "[", "/new", "de.sciss.swingosc.KeyResponder", 1001,"]" ]
    [ "/local", "cmp1001", "[", "/new", "de.sciss.swingosc.ComponentResponder",
    1001, "]" ]]

// ~win.front;
    [ "/set", 1000, "visible", 1 ]
    [ "/method", 1000, "toFront" ]]

// ~playButton = JSCButton( ~win, Rect( 4, 4, 40, 56 ));
    [ "/local", 1002, "[", "/new", "de.sciss.gui.MultiStateButton", "]", "ac1002",
    "[", "/new", "de.sciss.swingosc.ActionResponder", 1002, "[","/array",
    "selectedIndex", "lastModifiers", "]", "]" ]
    [ "/set", 1002, "bounds", "[", "/new", "java.awt.Rectangle", 1, 1, 46, 62, "]",
    "font", "[", "/ref", "font", "]" ]
    [ "/local", "dnd1002", "[", "/new", "de.sciss.swingosc.DummyTransferHandler",
    1002, 2, "]" ]
    [ "/local", "key1002", "[", "/new", "de.sciss.swingosc.KeyResponder", 1002,"]" ]
    [ "/local", "cmp1002", "[", "/new", "de.sciss.swingosc.ComponentResponder",
    1002, "]" ]]
    [ "/method", 1001, "add", "[", "/ref", 1002, "]" ]
    [ "/method", 1001, "revalidate" ],
    [ "/method", 1001, "repaint" ]]

// ~playButton.states = [[ "Play", Color.white, Color.green( 0.4 )],
//                       [ "Stop", Color.white, Color.red ]];
    [ "/method", 1002, "removeAllItems" ]
    [ "/method", 1002, "addItem", "Play", "[", "/new", "java.awt.Color", 1.0, 1.0,
    1.0, 1.0, "]", "[", "/new", "java.awt.Color", 0.0, 0.4, 0.0, 1.0,"]" ]
    [ "/method", 1002, "addItem", "Stop", "[", "/new", "java.awt.Color", 1.0, 1.0,
    1.0, 1.0, "]", "[", "/new", "java.awt.Color", 1.0, 0.0, 0.0, 1.0,"]" ]]
```

Figure 10.10
OSC messages used to create the window and button.

GUI server may be safely connected to several clients without causing naming conflicts.

Most views are created with a plain constructor that has no extra arguments. The view's properties, such as its bounds, are then set with an additional "/set" message that takes a list of property key and value pairs. In the case of the button:

```
["/set", 1002, "bounds", "[", "/new", "java.awt.Rectangle", 1, 1, 46, 62,
"]", "font", "[", "/ref", "font", "]"]
```

The "/set" OSC command is a convenient shortcut for the more general "/method" command that invokes *any* public Java method on an object. "/set" is restricted to methods whose signature follows the Java Beans pattern, implying that the property bounds is translated into the setter method setBounds(*<bounds>*), and that the property font is translated into the setter method setFont(*<font>*). Thus each property name is capitalized and prefixed by "set," and the method signature is supposed to have exactly 1 argument. When using "/method", 2 messages would be required instead.

- ["/method", 1002, "setBounds", "[", "/new", "java.awt.Rectangle", 1, 1, 46, 62,"]"]
- ["/method", 1002, "setFont", "[", "/ref", "font", "]"]

10.6 Responders and Asynchronicity

The other 3 messages generated by JSCWindow.new create *responders*, objects that communicate back to the client when the view state changes. The WindowResponder reports position and dimension changes, the gain and loss of focus of the window. The KeyResponder forwards keyboard input to the client, and the ComponentResponder handles bounds, focus, and visibility of views (here, the ContentPane that corresponds with JSCTopView on the client side). Although the views themselves, such as the Frame class, do not know about SwingOSC—they just get "scripted"—the responders *are* aware of SwingOSC and generate specialized OSC reply messages. Those messages can be printed out by executing g.dumpOSC(0, 1). When the window is moved, focused, or unfocused, messages similar to those shown in figure 10.11 are generated.

The only reply messages defined by SwingOSC itself are "/set" and "/info", but the responders add their own commands: "/component" comes from a Component-Responder, and "/window" from a WindowResponder.

Section 10.8 shows how to utilize the responder classes that come with Swing-OSC. The important thing to learn about them is that, with OSC being transported over a network protocol (TCP or UDP), the communication is inherently asynchro-

```
[ "/component", 1001, "resized", 0, 0, 400, 400 ]
[ "/window", 1000, "opened" ]
[ "/window", 1000, "activated" ]
[ "/window", 1000, "gainedFocus" ]
[ "/window", 1000, "resized", 128, 414, 400, 421 ]
[ "/component", 1001, "resized", 0, 0, 400, 399 ]
[ "/window", 1000, "moved", 128, 414, 400, 421 ]
[ "/window", 1000, "lostFocus" ]
[ "/window", 1000, "deactivated" ]
```

Figure 10.11
OSC messages sent by the responders when window state changes.

nous: it takes a short moment—in the magnitude of 100 microseconds—for a command to be sent from client to server and a short moment for a reply to arrive at the client. In SuperCollider, however, for code to be able to *wait* for a reply, it needs to run inside a Routine (the Routine class is explained in chapters 3 and 5).

```
2.wait; "hello".postln;                    // not allowed!
fork {2.wait; "hello".postln}; // ok!
```

SwingOSC was designed to mimic the application programming interface (API) of the previously existing CocoaGUI—the native Mac OSX GUI library—which works synchronously and single-threaded, so all queries must be satisfied *instantaneously.* The solution is to *mirror* that part of the GUI state on the client side that can be queried through the API. For example, the text field view is realized on the client side as the JSCTextField class, and on the server side as the de.sciss.swingosc .TextField class. If the current text content is queried using the string getter method, an instantaneous result needs to be provided—a DocumentResponder is responsible for sending all text changes to the client, which then constructs a *copy* of the text, as indicated in the lower part of figure 10.12.

When writing custom views, the responder pattern with the data structure mirrored on the client side should be used. During the discussion of the JavaObject class it will be shown that one can nevertheless query values ad hoc from the server by placing code inside a Routine (cf. upper part of figure 10.12).

10.7   Extending the GUI Repertoire Using JSCUserView

Sometimes the ready-made views that come with SwingOSC do not cover a specific GUI demand. JSCUserView represents a convenient way of extending the body of views by providing a kind of empty "canvas" that can be filled with arbitrary graphics

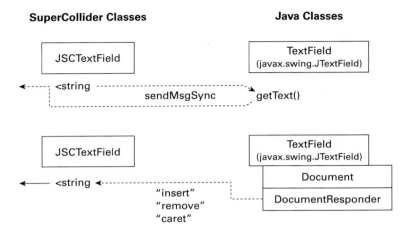

Figure 10.12
Two possible forms of data query from client to server. Upper part: placing the <string call inside a Routine and waiting for the ad hoc delivery of data from the server. Lower part: the model that is actually implemented in SwingOSC; the server automatically updates the client-side data mirror through the DocumentResponder, allowing <string to deliver the text instantaneously.

and can be configured to use arbitrary interaction—all in plain SuperCollider code. As a demonstration, the speed slider will be replaced with a custom slider whose knob sits on an arbitrary curve constructed from line segments. The old slider is removed using the remove method:

```
~speedSlider.remove;
```

To develop the view "just in time," in figure 10.13 an Event is again used as a class replacement.

~mySlider.view now holds an instance of JSCUserView. Its appearance is defined in a Function that is assigned to the view using the drawFunc_ setter method. Inside this function, drawing commands provided as class methods in JPen can be used. The appearance defined in figure 10.13 is that of 2 diagonal lines drawn across the view's bounding box. Each call to JPen.line adds a line to the stack of drawing commands. JPen.stroke executes the drawing commands by stroking the outline of the previously defined shape.

The other entries of ~mySlider become important as soon as the final drawing function is introduced: pos stores the current slider position in the interval [0,1], and pressed indicates whether the mouse is being pressed, resulting in special visual feedback (a thicker knob outline). ~mySlider.adjustPos sets pos to a new value but also executes an assignable action function. Since the visual appearance will indicate

```
(
~mySlider              = Event.new;
~mySlider.view         = JSCUserView( ~win, Rect( 110, 32, 200, 145 )).focusVisible_(
false );
~mySlider.pos          = ~speedSpec.unmap( ~model.speed );
// these will be used in the final draw func:
~mySlider.pressed      = false;
~mySlider.project      = false;
// this will update the slider position and refresh the view:
~mySlider.adjustPos    = { arg slid, pos;
    slid.pos           = pos;
    slid.view.action.value( slid );
    slid.view.refresh };
// these will set the slider track curve and refresh the view:
~mySlider.adjustCurve= { arg slid, curve;
    slid.curve         = curve;
    slid.lines         = curve.slide( 2, 1 ).clump( 2 );
    slid.lineLens      = slid.lines.collect({ arg pair; pair[ 0 ].dist( pair[ 1
])}).normalizeSum;
    slid.projections = nil;
    slid.view.refresh };
// a primary draw function just to indicate the view's bounds:
~mySlider.view.drawFunc = { arg view; var b = view.bounds;
    JPen.line( 0 @ 0, b.width @ b.height );
    JPen.line( 0 @ b.height, b.width @ 0 );
    JPen.stroke };
// make the window a little bigger:
~win.setInnerExtent( 370, 180 );
)
```

Figure 10.13
Adding a quasi-class for a custom view using Event. The user view itself is stored in
~mySlider.view.

the slider's knob position, slid.view.refresh needs to be called here to evaluate
the drawing function anew. adjustCurve sets the slider track curve. Its argument
is an Array of Point objects with coordinates being normalized to [0,1]. lines and
lineLens are helper entries in ~mySlider to simplify the drawing function. This final
drawing function is shown in figure 10.14.

In the drawing's coordinate system, (0@0) refers to the left top corner of the user
view. Thus, the curve's breakpoints, being in the interval [0,1], simply need to be
multiplied by a scale factor, using the view's width and height. The curve is then
constructed with an initial JPen.moveTo and successive JPen.lineTo statements.

```
(
~mySlider.adjustCurve([ 0 @ 0, 0.25 @ 1, 0.5 @ 0, 1.0 @ 0.5 ]);
~mySlider.view.drawFunc = { arg view;
    var b, scale, lnP1, lnP2, linePos, proj, inner, sum = 0;
    b      = view.bounds;
    // scaling factor for coordinates normalized to 0...1
    scale = b.width @ b.height;
    // set the initial curve coordinate
    JPen.moveTo( ~mySlider.curve[ 0 ] * scale );
    (1..(~mySlider.curve.size-1)).do({ arg i;
        // create the curve by adding successive line segments
        JPen.lineTo( ~mySlider.curve[ i ] * scale );
    });
    // stroke the curve with a 2-pixel wide black pen
    JPen.width = 2;
    JPen.color = Color.black;
    JPen.stroke;
    // draw the knob: iterate over the line segments until
    // the one is found inside which the knob (read from ~mySlider.pos)
    // is located.
    block { arg break;
        ~mySlider.lineLens.do({ arg len, i;
            // if we have found the line segment...
            if( sum + len >= ~mySlider.pos, {
                // calucate the point inside this segment
                // (proj) and draw a filled circle around it
                #lnP1, lnP2    = ~mySlider.lines[ i ];
                linePos        = (~mySlider.pos - sum) / len;
                proj           = lnP1 + ((lnP2 - lnP1) * linePos);
                JPen.fillOval( Rect.aboutPoint( proj * scale, 8, 8 ));
                // if this view is focused, use blue color, otherwise grey
                JPen.fillColor = Color.hsv( 0.7, view.hasFocus.if( 0.7, 0.0 ), 1.0
);
                // if the mouse is pressed, the outline should be thicker
                inner          = if( ~mySlider.pressed, 5, 7 );
                JPen.fillOval( Rect.aboutPoint( proj * scale, inner, inner ));
                break.value;
            });
            sum = sum + len;
        });
    };
```

Figure 10.14
The user view's drawing function that strokes the track using a segmented curve and fills the knob using ovals.

```
    // a debugging utility to visualize the point projections
    // of the mouse dragging
    if( ~mySlider.project, {
        ~mySlider.projections.do({ arg pt;
            pt = pt * scale;
            JPen.line( pt + (-5 @ -5), pt + (5 @  5) );
            JPen.line( pt + (-5 @  5), pt + (5 @ -5) );
        });
        JPen.width = 1; JPen.stroke;
    });
};
)
```

Figure 10.14
(continued)

Next, the curve's outline is stroked with a call to JPen.stroke (we could fill it instead by using JPen.fill). The knob is painted using 2 JPen.fillOval calls.

As a refinement, the knob color changes from gray to blue if the view gets focused. The corresponding statement is Color.hsv(0.7, view.hasFocus.if(0.7, 0.0), 1.0), which queries the view's focus state and sets the knob color's saturation to 0 for unfocused state and 70% for focused state. This works because the view is automatically refreshed (and the drawFunc is reevaluated!) when its focus state changes. Note that Color.hsv creates a Color instance from the *Hue-Saturation-Value* model, so the hue is a constant 0.7 (some blue), the value (or brightness) is a constant 1.0, and the saturation depends on the focus.

However, the knob cannot be dragged yet, since the mouse interaction still needs to be implemented. Four callback functions can be assigned using the setter methods:

- mouseDownAction_: an action to be performed when the mouse button is *pressed*
- mouseUpAction_: when the button is *released*
- mouseMoveAction_: when the mouse is *dragged* with depressed button
- mouseOverAction_: when the mouse is *moved* without depressed button.

These functions are executed with the mouse coordinates and keyboard modifier keys passed in (such as a flag to indicate that the [SHIFT] key is pressed). The custom mouse control is shown in figure 10.15.

The behaviors of mouseDownAction and mouseMoveAction are not differentiated here, so the same function, mouseFunc, is assigned to both. In mouseFunc, the normalized mouse position (nx, ny) is calculated from the coordinates (x, y), which are—like

```
(
var mouseFunc = { arg view, x, y, modifiers, buttonNumber, clickCount;
    var b, nx, ny, dx, dy, lnP1, lnP2, linePos, lineLenSq,
        proj, dist, sum = 0, minDist = inf, newValue;

    b   = view.bounds;
    nx  = x / b.width;
    ny  = y / b.height;
    ~mySlider.projections = Array( ~mySlider.lines.size );
    // look up the line segment which is closest to the mouse
    ~mySlider.lines.do({ arg pair, i;
        #lnP1, lnP2 = pair;
        dx              = lnP2.x - lnP1.x;
        dy              = lnP2.y - lnP1.y;
        lineLenSq       = (dx*dx) + (dy*dy);
        dist            = (((nx - lnP1.x) * dx) + ((ny - lnP1.y) * dy)) / lineLenSq;
        proj            = (lnP1.x + (dist * dx)) @ (lnP1.y + (dist * dy));
        if( lnP1.x != lnP2.x, {
            linePos = (proj.x - lnP1.x) / dx;
        }, {
            linePos = (proj.y - lnP1.y) / dy;
        });
        if( linePos < 0, {
            proj = lnP1;
        }, { if( linePos > 1, {
            proj = lnP2;
        })});
        ~mySlider.projections.add( proj );
        dist = proj.dist( nx @ ny );
        if( dist < minDist, {
            newValue = sum + (linePos.clip( 0, 1 ) * ~mySlider.lineLens[i]);
            minDist  = dist;
        });
        sum = sum + ~mySlider.lineLens[ i ];
    });
    ~mySlider.pressed = true;
    ~mySlider.adjustPos( newValue );
};
~mySlider.view.mouseDownAction = mouseFunc;
~mySlider.view.mouseMoveAction = mouseFunc;
~mySlider.view.mouseUpAction   = { arg view; ~mySlider.pressed = false; view.refresh
};
~mySlider.view.action          = { arg view;
    ~model.adjust( \speed, ~speedSpec.map( ~mySlider.pos ), ~mySlider )};
)
```

Figure 10.15
Adding interactive mouse control.

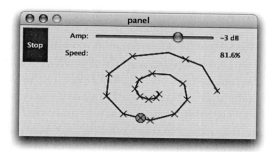

Figure 10.16
The GUI now showing the custom slider, using GTK+ (Linux) look-and-feel.

the pen drawing commands—relative to the view's left top corner. Dividing by the view's dimensions produces x and y coordinates in the interval [0,1]. The division is necessary because the slider track curve is also specified in 0 to 1 coordinates. We iterate over all line segments, project (nx, ny) onto each segment,[1] and determine the shortest distance to these projections (using Point's `dist` method). The new slider value is thus calculated as the running sum of iterated line segments and the relative position `linePos` of the projection on the closest segment. The projections are stored for debugging purposes and can be made visible:

```
~mySlider.project = true; ~mySlider.view.refresh;
```

Finally, a more elaborate curve for the slider is set up (the resulting screen shot is shown in figure 10.16).

```
(
~mySlider.adjustCurve(Array.fill(20, {arg i;
    Polar((i + 1)/40, i/19 * 4pi).asPoint + (0.5 @ 0.5)}));
)
```

An extra flavor of keyboard control using [Cursor-Left] and [Cursor-Right] strokes can be added by assigning the `keyDownAction` callback function:

```
(
~mySlider.view.keyDownAction = {arg view, char, modifiers, unicode,
keycode;
    switch(keycode, 37, {// decrease slider-value with cursor-left
        ~mySlider.adjustPos((~mySlider.pos - 0.05).max(0.0))},
    39, {// increase slider-value with cursor-right
        ~mySlider.adjustPos((~mySlider.pos + 0.05).min(1.0))})};
)
```

10.8   Generic Java Scripting

It was stated earlier that SwingOSC allows "dynamic scripting of the Java language," and it was shown in section 10.6 how OSC commands such as "/new" and "/method" in fact instantiate and manipulate Java objects. If we stick to the Swing framework, the body of views can be extended with a custom subclass of javax.swing.JComponent (the base class for views in the Swing framework). A proxy class JavaObject exists on the SuperCollider side that makes manipulation of any java.lang.Object fairly easy. To see the underlying OSC messages, the dumping of incoming and outgoing messages is activated:

```
g.dumpOSC(1, 1);
```

Swing's Window class is javax.swing.JFrame. The following lines show how to instantiate and operate on it:

```
~frame = JavaObject("javax.swing.JFrame", nil, "Test");
~frame.setSize(400, 400);
~frame.setVisible(true);
```

The resulting OSC messages are the following:

- ["/local", 1000, "[", "/new", "javax.swing.JFrame", "Test", "]"]
- ["/method", 1000, "setSize", 400, 400]
- ["/method", 1000, "setVisible", 1]

The JavaObject constructor instantiates on the server side the class whose name is given as the first argument. The second argument specifies the SwingOSC server, where nil (as in the above example) is replaced by SwingOSC.default. All remaining arguments are passed into the Java constructor, so "Test"—the frame's title—is the first argument to the constructor of javax.swing.JFrame. The first OSC message reveals that 2 commands are executed on the server: "/new" instantiates the class, and "/local" stores its result (the reference to the new JFrame) in the variable or object-ID 1000. Note that the actual ID can vary, as it is taken dynamically from SwingOSC:nextNodeID. This object-ID is known on the client side and can be read using ~frame.id. Calls to setSize and setVisible work because JavaObject *catches* unknown methods in the doesNotUnderstand method and *translates* them to ["/method" <object-ID>,...] OSC messages, passing along all arguments. Manipulating Java objects this way can become very intuitive—even the conversion of the Boolean argument in setVisible to an OSC integer (since SuperCollider supports only the type tags i for Integer, s for String, and f for Float) and back to a Java boolean on the server side happens automatically.

The following code snippet will populate the frame with a JFileChooser, which is a view to browse the hard disk for files:

```
~cp = ~frame.getContentPane__;
~fileChooser = JavaObject("javax.swing.JFileChooser");
~cp.add(~fileChooser);
~cp.revalidate;
```

The resulting OSC messages are the following:

- ["/local", 1001, "[", "/method", 1000, "getContentPane", "]"]
- ["/local", 1002, "[", "/new", "javax.swing.JFileChooser", "]"]
- ["/method", 1001, "add", "[", "/ref", 1002, "]"]
- ["/method", 1001, "revalidate"]

The JFileChooser is added to the so-called content pane of the JFrame which is stored in the variable ~cp. The final call ~cp.revalidate is necessary to refresh the content pane after the view has been added, so that it gets laid out properly.

Of notable interest is the first statement: adding 2 underscore _ characters at the end of the method name will wrap the "/method" call inside a "/local" command, and on the SuperCollider side a new JavaObject referring to this method's result is created (assigned to ~cp here). Why must this behavior be explicitly asked for? If *any* method call from JavaObject would create and return a new JavaObject (mirrored by an object on the server side), the server's symbol table would be unnecessarily polluted, particularly for calls with void results (~frame.setSize(...), ~frame .setVisible(...), etc.).

On the other hand, we might sometimes want to transfer objects from the server back to the client. For primitive data types this can be achieved by adding a *single* underscore character _ to the method call, which is not to be confused with the underscore used for setter methods (such as an instance field var <>test resulting in a setter method test_!):

```
fork {~title = ~frame.getTitle_; ~title.postln};
```

The call needs to be run inside a Routine (fork { ... } is a convenient shortcut) because instead of creating another JavaObject proxy, the actual primitive value is returned by the server with an OSC reply message, and ~title will hold a Symbol. The communication here is

```
r: ["/query", 1006, "[", "/method", 1000, "getTitle", "]"] // client-to-
server
s: ["/info", 1006, "Test"] // server-to-client
```

. . . so the server replies to a ["/query", <query-ID>,...] OSC message with an ["/info", <query-ID>,...] message. To be able to wait for the reply, the code must be run inside a Routine.

```
(
~action = { arg fileName; "Selected file is '%'\n".postf( fileName
)};
~sResp  = JavaObject( "de.sciss.swingosc.ActionResponder", nil,
~fileChooser.id );
~cResp  = OSCpathResponder( g.addr, [ '/action', ~fileChooser.id ], {
    fork { var file, fileName;
        file     = ~fileChooser.getSelectedFile__;
        fileName = file.getAbsolutePath_;
        file.destroy;
        ~action.value( fileName.asString );
    };
}).add;
)
```

Figure 10.17
Listening to view state changes with ActionResponder on the server side and OSCpathResponder on the client side.

Finally, it is necessary to recognize when the user clicks on the "Open" or "OK" button and then retrieve the file name selected in the JFileChooser. If a file has been selected, its path can be read like this:

```
(
fork {~file = ~fileChooser.getSelectedFile__;
    ~fileName = ~file.getAbsolutePath_; ~file.destroy; ~fileName.postln};
)
```

Note that getSelectedFile returns a java.io.File, and since only primitive types can be transmitted, ~file = ~fileChooser.getSelectedFile_ would not work. Thus the double underscore (~fileChooser.getSelectedFile__) is used to create a proxy. getAbsolutePath returns a java.lang.String, though, and we can use the single underscore syntax here. ~file.destroy does not delete the file; it simply removes the object-ID from the server's symbol table. Whenever a JavaObject is not in use anymore, calling destroy makes the server-side object available to garbage collection.

To be notified about button clicks, a combination of a server-side ActionResponder and a client-side OSCpathResponder can be used. ActionResponder implements the java.awt.event.ActionListener interface and can register with any object that provides the methods addActionListener and removeActionListener. JFileChooser notifies the responder when the "Cancel" or "Open" button is clicked. The complete procedure is shown in figure 10.17.

```
(
~cp.remove( ~fileChooser );
~frame.dispose;
~cp.destroy; ~frame.destroy;
~win.setInnerExtent( 760, 340 );    // again a bit bigger
~plug = JSCPlugView( ~win, Rect( 370, 2, 386, 336 ), ~fileChooser );
~action = { arg fileName; var sf, oldBuf;
    // try to open as a sound file. returns nil if it could not be opened
    if( (sf = SoundFile.openRead( fileName )).notNil, {
        sf.close;  // the header info was read, we can close the file
        if( sf.numChannels == 1, {  // allow mono files only
            oldBuf = ~model.buf;
            if( ~model.node.notNil, {  // free old buffer when synth is freed
                UpdateListener.newFor( ~model.node, { arg upd;
                    upd.remove; oldBuf.free }, \n_end );
                ~model.node.register;
            }, {
                oldBuf.free;
            });
            ~model.buf = Buffer.read( s, fileName );  // replace buffer
        }, {
            "Sound file must be mono".error;
        });
    });
};
)
```

Figure 10.18
Moving the file chooser into the buffer player GUI.

10.9 Embedding Arbitrary Swing Views in a JSCWindow

It is desirable to mix the existing views based on JSCWindow and JSCView with additional views, such as the JFileChooser, presented in the previous section. In order to use the JFileChooser inside a JSCWindow, it needs to support a few methods of JSCView. A helper class JSCPlugView comes into play: it wraps the essential functionality of JSCView around an arbitrary Swing view. The code in figure 10.18 shows how the JFileChooser is removed from the JFrame and added to our initial window ~win, using JSCPlugView.

Note that the ActionResponder is still active, so we simply replace the ~action function here. It will verify whether the selected file is a mono sound file; if it is, ~model.buf is replaced to hold the new sound file. This new buffer will be heard once the "Play" button is clicked again.

10.10   Using Custom Java Classes

The `JFileChooser` class is sufficient for some applications, but often it needs tweaking. For example, one might want to use a custom "Open" button, remove the "Cancel" button, and filter the file list so it contains only sound files. When a sound file is selected, additional information, such as the number of channels or duration, can be displayed. The `JSCPlugView` is useful for trying out things, but eventually one will want to cast the view into a real subclass of `JSCView`.

The 2 steps of writing subclasses of `javax.swing.JFileChooser` and `JSCView` will be performed. The Swing class will be called `SoundFileChooser`, and the source code is shown in figure 10.19.

You can open this file from the SuperCollider book Web site code. To edit it, several options exist. Integrated Development Environments (IDEs) include Eclipse SDK and NetBeans IDE, and on Mac OSX there is Xcode. Otherwise, any text editor such as jEdit can be used and the code can be compiled from the terminal. You will need at least a Java 1.4 SE JDK (development kit)—the JRE (Runtime Environment) is not sufficient because it does not include the *javac* compiler.

Assuming that the source code is saved in a file named *SoundFileChooser.java*, the terminal commands for compilation should look like this:

```
$ cd <javaSourceCodePath>
$ javac - source 1.4 - cp <installPath>/SwingOSC.jar SoundFileChooser.java
$ jar cfM SoundFileChooser.jar SoundFileChooser*.class
```

The `$` character symbolizes the terminal prompt and is not to be entered. On Unix systems, launching the terminal application may open the Bourne Again Shell (*bash*), and on Windows systems the command line interpreter is created by executing *cmd. exe* from the Start menu. *cmd.exe* uses the > character as prompt.

Replace `<javaSourceCodePath>` with the folder in which *SoundFileChooser.java* was saved, and `<installPath>` as described in section 10.2. The inclusion of *SwingOSC.jar* in the class path is essential to make the `AudioFile` and `AudioFile-Descr` classes available. The *javac* command compiles the source code into class files (*SoundFileChooser.class* and an inner, anonymous class *SoundFileChooser$1.class*, representing the `FileFilter`). The *jar* command packages them together in an archive.

`SoundFileChooser` subclasses `JFileChooser` to apply slight modifications and additions. First of all, a `FileFilter` class is created that accepts only directories and sound files for inclusion in the chooser's list. `AudioFile.retrieveType( ... )` tries to identify the sound file type according to a list of values defined in `AudioFileDescr` (`TYPE_UNKNOWN` means the file type is not known). This `FileFilter` is then added to the list of selectable filters and is made the default filter. The default control buttons

```
import java.io.File;
import javax.swing.filechooser.FileFilter;
import javax.swing.event.ChangeEvent;
import javax.swing.event.ChangeListener;

public class SoundFileChooser extends javax.swing.JFileChooser
implements java.beans.PropertyChangeListener
{
    private final java.util.List listeners = new java.util.ArrayList();

    public SoundFileChooser() {
        super();
        final FileFilter filter = new FileFilter() {
            public boolean accept( File f ) {
                if( f.isDirectory() ) return true;
                try {
                    return( de.sciss.io.AudioFile.retrieveType( f ) !=
                            de.sciss.io.AudioFileDescr.TYPE_UNKNOWN );
                }
                catch( java.io.IOException e ) { return false; }
            }

            public String getDescription() { return "Audio Files"; }
        };
        addChoosableFileFilter( filter );
        setFileFilter( filter );
        setControlButtonsAreShown( false );
        addPropertyChangeListener( SELECTED_FILE_CHANGED_PROPERTY, this );
        addPropertyChangeListener( DIRECTORY_CHANGED_PROPERTY, this );
    }

    public String getSelectedPath() {
        final File f = getSelectedFile();
        return f == null ? "" : f.getAbsolutePath();
    }

    public void setSelectedPath( String path ) {
        setSelectedFile( new File( path ));
    }

    public String getCurrentDirectoryPath() {
        return getCurrentDirectory().getAbsolutePath();
```

Figure 10.19
SoundFileChooser.java: the server class.

```
    }

    public void setCurrentDirectoryPath( String path ) {
        setCurrentDirectory( new File( path ));
    }

    public void addChangeListener( ChangeListener l ) { listeners.add( l ); }
    public void removeChangeListener( ChangeListener l ) { listeners.remove( l ); }

    public void propertyChange( java.beans.PropertyChangeEvent pce ) {
        final ChangeEvent ce = new ChangeEvent( this );
        for( int i = 0; i < listeners.size(); i++ ) {
            ((ChangeListener) listeners.get( i )).stateChanged( ce );
        }
    }
}
```

Figure 10.19
(continued)

"Open" and "Cancel" are hidden so that custom JSCButton views can be used instead. The PropertyChangeListener interface is implemented and registered. Whenever the user selects a file or switches the current directory, the propertyChange method is invoked, which in turn will notify registered ChangeListeners. This way, the ChangeResponder class that comes with SwingOSC can be used (see further below). To ease the transfer of the view's state from and to SuperCollider, extra getter and setter methods for the selected file and current directory are defined that use java.lang.String instead of java.io.File, since a string can be sent directly over OSC.

On the SuperCollider side the small class JSCSoundFileChooser is created. The source code is shown in figure 10.20.

The most important methods to implement are prInitView, invoked in the instantiation process, and prClose, invoked when the view is removed or its window is closed. The superclass JSCView is taking responsibility for many aspects, such as mouse and keyboard tracking. prInitView is the place to instantiate the server view and register custom responders to track the view's interactivity. This is accomplished by passing an Array of OSC messages to this.prSCViewNew. Here a ChangeResponder is created. Its constructor takes as its first argument the object-ID of the view to track (this.id), and the second argument is either a single property or an Array of properties to report upon user interaction. The responder is asked to report the

```
JSCSoundFileChooser : JSCView {
    var <path;          // String : current file selection (or nil)
    var <directory;     // String : currently visible directory
    var chResp;         // OSCpathResponder for ChangeResponder

    path_ { arg value;
        path = value;
        server.sendMsg( '/set', this.id, \selectedPath, value );
    }

    directory_ { arg value;
        directory = value;
        server.sendMsg( '/set', this.id, \currentDirectoryPath, value );
    }

    prSCViewNew {
        chResp = OSCpathResponder( server.addr, [ '/change', this.id ], {
            arg time, resp, msg; var oldPath = path;
            path      = if( msg[ 4 ] !== '', { msg[ 4 ].asString });
            directory = msg[ 6 ].asString;
            if( oldPath != path, {{ this.doAction }.defer });
        }).add;
        ^super.prSCViewNew([[ '/local', this.id, '[', '/new', "SoundFileChooser",
']', "ch" ++ this.id, '[', '/new', "de.sciss.swingosc.ChangeResponder",
this.id, '[', '/array', \selectedPath, \currentDirectoryPath, ']', ']' ]]);
    }

    prClose {
        chResp.remove;
        ^super.prClose([[ '/method', "ch" ++ this.id, \remove ],
                        [ '/free', "ch" ++ this.id ]]);
    }
}
```

Figure 10.20
JSCSoundFileChooser.sc: the client class.

selectedPath and currentDirectoryPath properties (equal to invoking the methods getSelectedPath and getCurrentDirectoryPath on the SoundFileChooser Java object), so an Array is required here. To pass an Array argument in an OSC message, the nested command ["/array", <element1>,..., <elementN>] is used. The ChangeResponder is stored under the object-ID "ch<viewID>" in order to be able to remove it when the view is closed. The messages that are sent back to SuperCollider are in the form

```
["/change", <viewID>, "performed", "selectedPath", <newSelectedFilePath>,
"currentDirectoryPath", <newCurrentDirectory>]
```

They are identified by a matching OSCpathResponder which stores the new current directory and the selected file's path in the view's fields and evaluates the view's action function. The latter is done inside a { ...}.defer block to make it better match CocoaGUI, which requires view accessing code to run in the AppClock thread.

The prClose method removes the OSCpathResponder and creates additional OSC messages passed to the superclass that take care of removing the ChangeResponder and deleting its object-ID.

The setter methods for path (the selected file) and directory (the displayed folder) generate appropriate "/set" OSC messages and store the new values in the view's fields.

To use this new JSCSoundFileChooser class, it needs to be placed in a valid class library folder (either SCClassLibrary or the SuperCollider Extensions folder, as explained in the *Using-Extensions* Help file), and the class library must be recompiled. Furthermore, the *SoundFileChooser.jar* file must be made known to the JVM. The easiest way is to use SwingOSC's addClasses method after the server has been booted.

```
g.addClasses("file://<javaSourceCodePath>/SoundFileChooser.jar")
```

... where <javaSourceCodePath> should be replaced accordingly. Note that the argument must be formatted as a URL. Here is an example URL on the local hard disk:

```
g.addClasses("file:///Users/myUserName/Desktop/SoundFileChooser.jar" );
```

Alternatively, the custom class can be registered by integrating it into *SwingOSC .jar*, by adding *SoundFileChooser.jar* to the class path of the *java* command that launches SwingOSC, or by moving *SoundFileChooser.jar* into a system wide class path (e.g., */Library/Java/Extensions* on Mac OSX).

If all the code of this chapter is re-executed after the class library recompilation, it is possible to replace the JSCPlugView with the new JSCSoundFileChooser class (figure 10.21).

```
(
~plug.remove;    // this implicitly calls ~fileChooser.destroy!
~soundChooser        = JSCSoundFileChooser( ~win, Rect( 370, 2, 386, 306 ));
~soundChooser.path   = "sounds/a11wlk01.wav".absolutePath;
~loadButton          = JSCButton( ~win, Rect( 370, 312, 60, 24 )).states_([[ "Load"
]]).enabled_( false );
~infoText            = JSCStaticText( ~win, Rect( 438, 312, 318, 24 ));
~soundChooser.action = { arg view; var enabled = false, info = "", sf;
    if( view.path.notNil and: { (sf = SoundFile.openRead( view.path )).notNil }, {
        sf.close;
        enabled      = sf.numChannels == 1;
        info         = "% audio, %-chan. % % kHz, %".format( sf.headerFormat,
    sf.numChannels, sf.sampleFormat, sf.sampleRate/1000,
    (sf.numFrames/sf.sampleRate).asTimeString );
    });
    ~loadButton.enabled = enabled;
    ~infoText.string    = info;
};
~loadButton.action   = { ~action.value( ~soundChooser.path )};
)
```

Figure 10.21
Integrating the custom file chooser class.

~soundChooser.action is evaluated whenever the file selection changes. If a file is selected (view.path.notNil) and it is a valid sound file, the sound file's header information is displayed in a JSCStaticText. The custom JSCButton to "Load" a new sound buffer is enabled if the selected file is monophonic.

As a last refinement, the window will be made resizable again, using ~win .resizable_(true), and the views are taught to grow along with the window. This is achieved with different values for the resize property of the views, as shown in figure 10.22. Figure 10.23 illustrates the directions in which the bounding boxes will grow when the window is resized (a resize value of 1 is default).

Further Reading

Now that you have gained insight into the basic setup of a GUI, the internals of SwingOSC's Open Sound Control communication, and the integration of custom Java Swing views, there are three paths to follow.

To learn about the ready-made views and their configuration, the SwingGUI Help file provides a list of views with links to their Help files. In particular, the Help files

```
(
~ampSlider.resize      = 2;
~mySlider.view.resize  = 5;
~ampText.resize        = 3;
~speedText.resize      = 3;
~soundChooser.resize   = 6;
~loadButton.resize     = 9;
~infoText.resize       = 9;
~win.resizable         = true;
)
```

Figure 10.22
Configuring the views to resize their window.

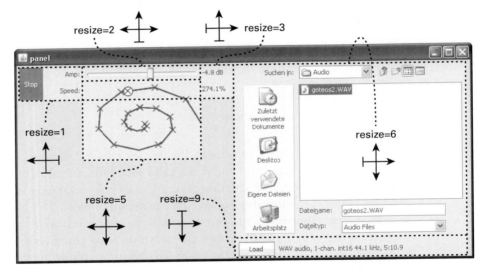

Figure 10.23
Effect of the resize values: final GUI using Windows look-and-feel.

for JSCView and JSCWindow should be consulted. JSCCompositeView provides a means to nest views inside containers. The Help files for user views are JSCUserView and JPen.

To learn more about general GUI concepts, see chapters 9 and 21. As noted above, the possibility to write cross-platform GUI code that can potentially use the native Mac OSX CocoaGUI library is covered by chapter 9; since the SwingOSC GUI is very similar to CocoaGUI, this provides valuable information.

To continue the trail of Java Swing view development, the Swing overview on <http://java.sun.com/products/jfc/tsc/articles/architecture> and the tutorial on <http://java.sun.com/docs/books/tutorial/uiswing> form a good starting point. To look up constructor and method signatures of Java classes, use the online API reference at <http://java.sun.com/reference/api/index.html>. For the development of SuperCollider proxy view classes, refer to the files *SuperCollider/DeveloperInfo .html* and *OSC-Command-Reference.html* that come with SwingOSC.

Note

1. Using an algorithm described at <http://mathworld.wolfram.com/Point-LineDistance2-Dimensional.html>.

SuperCollider on Windows

Christopher Frauenberger

Although SuperCollider was originally developed for the Apple Mac platform, it has been ported to other platforms, such as Linux and Windows, and versions of Super-Collider on other platforms can provide almost identical functionality. Thanks to the more cross-platform-friendly architecture of SuperCollider 3, SuperCollider provides a highly efficient and versatile sound synthesis system for the Windows operating system. This chapter covers using the Windows SuperCollider available from the sourceforge Web site. This is the version that was originally called *PsyCollider*—it's the standard Windows port of SuperCollider. At the time of writing, it is the most commonly used port, but readers may also be interested to explore the Java-based Eclipse plug-ins for SuperCollider (<http://jsce.sourceforge.net>).

The historical name PsyCollider was given to the port by Benjamin Golinvaux, who started the project in late 2004. He used the Python language to replace the Mac-specific user interface for Windows; hence the name (almost!). Because the Python programming language itself is cross-platform, PsyCollider can be run on many platforms. However, although it has indeed been ported back to the Mac operating system, the focus of the project remains serving Windows users. Because we now refer to the current descendant of PsyCollider just as SuperCollider, the remainder of this chapter refers to SuperCollider in the majority of cases.

Having SuperCollider available on the Windows platform has had a great impact on the user base of the application. Though most of the initial community that grew around SuperCollider used Apple computers, an increasing demand for a Windows version became apparent as its user base grew bigger. Especially when SuperCollider became used in schools, university courses, and other areas predominantly fitted with Windows computers, the need for a cross-platform solution was apparent.

A fully functional and freely available version of SuperCollider on Windows also addresses the responsibility of reaching people in all countries. Though Linux is becoming increasingly widespread and easier to use, it is still the Windows operating system that is the most accessible system on affordable hardware. The composer Julio d'Escriván[1] has experienced these difficulties while teaching in Latin

America; in the workshops and lectures he has given in Venezuela and Mexico, he has used SuperCollider to introduce young people to electroacoustic music. Neither the schools involved nor many of the participants could afford to invest in expensive Apple hardware, and too few were familiar with Linux. SuperCollider for Windows makes one of the most powerful sound synthesis applications generally available.

This chapter aims to provide a natural entry point for people running Microsoft Windows who would like to use SuperCollider. It will show how SuperCollider is installed on Windows and what comes with the package. The following sections provide information about basic operation, how to evaluate code, use the Help system, and other essentials. Throughout, the example code (also available on the Web site accompanying the book) will make it easy to follow the explanations and immediately experience the power of sound creation with SuperCollider. One section is devoted to the hardware that is supported and how users can use their sound cards or MIDI controllers with SuperCollider. A subsequent section will highlight the differences between the Windows port and other versions of SuperCollider and provide guidance to make your code work across platforms. Although there have been efforts to make SuperCollider on Windows behave as similarly as possible to the original Mac implementation, some features are either not yet available or not available due to fundamental differences between the platforms. The last 2 sections in this chapter will go deeper into the internal mechanics of Windows SuperCollider, providing background information about its workings and architecture, and explore the topic of how to extend it. A discussion of future plans for development and a summary will conclude the chapter.

11.1   Getting Started

11.1   Installing SuperCollider for Windows

SuperCollider comes as a Windows Installer file (.msi). Alongside it, a bootstrapper application (*startup.exe*) is provided for older platforms that do not support msi files directly. Once the installation is started (either directly by double clicking the msi file or by the bootstrapper application), the Windows Installer guides the user through the installation process. The only decision to be made is where SuperCollider should be installed. The default location is within the usual Programs folder, but it can be customized at will. The installer will also install all of the system libraries (dynamic-link libraries) needed for SuperCollider to operate correctly. You will need to have certain permissions on the computer on which you are installing SuperCollider (write permission for the system's registry) in order to complete the installation.

Once it is installed, you will find the Application file *SuperCollider.exe* in the installation folder. Double click this file, and SuperCollider will start. Alternatively, SuperCollider will also be added to Programs available from the Start menu.

The SuperCollider installation comes with the following standard components: the SuperCollider server, the standard extensions (or plug-ins), the Help system, examples, and the class library—providing all the classes that can be used as part of the SuperCollider language. It also includes SwingOSC, a Java-based package that allows one to create graphical user interfaces (GUIs) from within the SuperCollider code (see chapter 10 for a detailed description of this package).

11.2   Working in SuperCollider on Windows

When SuperCollider is started, a lot of information will be displayed in the SC post window. This window is special and is the place to look for all feedback from Super-Collider and the synthesis server. Messages about how SuperCollider starts the language, parses the class library, and performs other startup tasks will be displayed here. Closing this window will shut down the server and quit the application.

The *startup.sc* file in the installation directory plays a decisive role when the application is launched. It contains regular SuperCollider code that is executed immediately after initializing the language. The default *startup.sc* will start the SwingOSC server to make GUI elements available. Subsequently, it will show a window for the synthesis server that provides controls for booting the server and changing the main volume, and displays other useful information (number of UGens running, CPU, etc.). The synthesis server can also be booted from within SC or *startup.sc* by evaluating the command s.boot. Figure 11.1 shows a screen shot of the post window and the server window after startup.

When starting the synthesis server by pressing *Boot* in the server window, your device options will be posted to the post window and the server will be booted using the first audio device available in the list (selecting different audio devices is discussed in section 11.2.1). If you are successful, the status message in the server window will change to *running*, and a message will appear in the post window:

```
SuperCollider server ready...
    notification on
```

A good starting point is to test the new installation. The installation directory contains a file called *Win32Tests.sc* with some simple code to test if everything was installed properly and all hardware was recognized correctly. When the file is opened from the File menu, a code window will open up which displays the colorized code indicating class names and other special keywords. Besides the colorization, the code window allows for folding and unfolding blocks of code, a convenient way of hiding

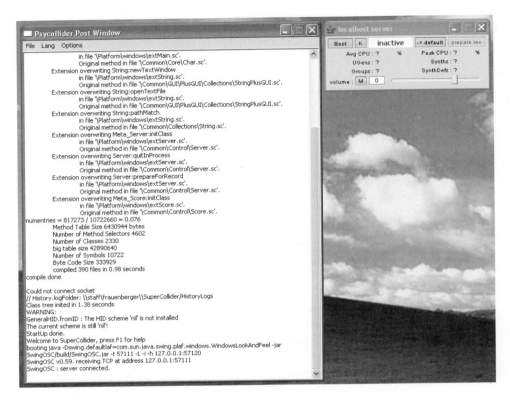

Figure 11.1
Screen shot of the post window and the server window after launching SuperCollider for Windows.

code within a function or between braces. Matching braces are also highlighted for better readability. Figure 11.2 shows a screen shot of the *Win32Tests.sc* file opened in a code window.

There are two basic ways to evaluate code:

- By selecting text blocks and pressing [Ctrl+Enter]
- By pressing [Ctrl+Enter] to evaluate only the line in which the cursor is positioned.

If the cursor is moved into the following line near the top of *Win32Tests.sc*,

```
{SinOsc.ar(LFNoise0.kr([8, 12], 200, [300, 400]),0, 0.1)}.play;
```

and is evaluated by hitting [Ctrl+Enter], a modulated sine wave sound can be heard—the installation is working correctly; to stop all sound, press [Alt+.]. For convenience, selecting a code block can be achieved by double clicking one of a pair

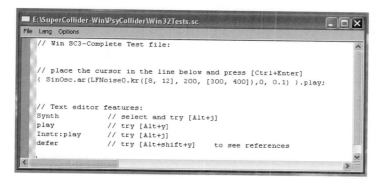

Figure 11.2
A code window in SuperCollider for Windows (*SCWin32Tests.sc*).

of round brackets that encloses a certain code block that is meant to be evaluated as a whole.

There are various other useful commands that can be evoked from within a code window; the most important is the Help system. By pressing F1, the main Help window will open. These Help windows differ from normal code windows because they are formatted in HTML and cannot be edited. However, code can still be selected within these windows and evaluated as usual. It can be copied into code windows, or a whole Help window can be converted into a code window by a command from the File menu. This will strip the Help file of HTML formatting and will then allow the user to alter the code and save the file separately. If help on specific classes or functions is required, the Help system will jump directly into a specific Help file once the name is selected and the Help system is invoked by F1. Other useful keyboard commands include [Alt+J], and a class name is selected for displaying the implementation of the class in question. [Alt+Y] with a method name selected opens a new window listing all the classes that implement this method. Similarly, [Alt+Shif+Y] shows all references to a specific method. Table 11.1 summarizes the most important shortcuts available in a code window.

The following code snippets show examples of some basic concepts in Super-Collider and are fully cross-platform, that is, they produce the same sound as on the Mac version. The first snippet, in figure 11.3, uses a Task to create Synths on the server with randomized base frequency. The definition of the sound (the SynthDef) that is stored on the server uses a dynamic filter bank with pink noise as input and a simple envelope. The envelope removes the Synth from the server when it is finished (doneAction: 2). (For more on Tasks and Routines, see chapter 3.)

The second example, in figure 11.4, uses patterns. The sound is again defined as a SynthDef and stored on the server before the pattern is played. A low-pass filtered

Table 11.1
Shortcuts Available in SuperCollider for Windows

Shortcut	Function
[Ctrl+Enter]	evaluate a line or a selected block of code
[Alt+.]	stop all sound processing on the server
F1	open the Help file for a specific class, if selected, or the main Help
[Alt+J]	show the implementation of a class or a method
[Alt+Y]	show all classes that implement the method selected
[Alt+Shift+Y]	show all references to a method selected

```
// Tasks
(
SynthDef("task", { arg out=0, freq=2000;
    var env = EnvGen.kr(Env.perc, 1.0, 0.2, doneAction:2);
    var source = DynKlank.ar('[ [0.5, 0.8, 1, 1.2, 2, 4]*freq, nil,
nil ], PinkNoise.ar(0.007));
    Out.ar(out, source * env ! 2);
}).add;

t = Task({
    var freq;
    loop {
        freq = ((1..10)*220).choose;
        Synth("task", [\freq, freq]);
        0.3.wait;
    }
})
)

t.start;
t.stop;
```

Figure 11.3
A Task example.

```
// Patterns
(
SynthDef("pattern", { arg out=0, freq=220, pan=0, gate=1;
    var ctl = RLPF.ar(Saw.ar(5, 1.0, 2), 25, 0.03);
    var source = SinOsc.ar(ctl * freq) * 0.1;
    var env = EnvGen.kr(Env.adsr, gate, doneAction: 2);
    Out.ar(out, Pan2.ar(source * env, pan));
}).add;

e = Pbind(
    \midinote, Pxrand(#[60, 61, 63, 65, 72], 20),
    \dur, 0.4,
    \pan, Pwhite(-1.0, 1.0, 20),
    \instrument, \pattern
);
)

e.play;
```

Figure 11.4
A Pbind example.

Saw is used to modulate a sinusoid; the result is multiplied with a sustaining envelope and panned in the azimuth plane. The pattern (Pbind) plays the sound with a
sequence of randomized frequencies given as MIDI notes and also pans the output
randomly between left and right. The duration in the pattern controls the gate argument of the envelope and determines the length of a single sound event. (For more
on patterns, see chapter 6.)

Another powerful concept available in SuperCollider is a ProxySpace. A ProxySpace
makes defining and handling Synths very convenient and allows replacing sounds
and controlling Synths on the fly, that is, in real time (just-in-time programming).
The code in figure 11.5 should be evaluated line by line: the NodeProxy ~out creates
a simple sound by modulating the frequency of a ringing filter; ~ctl is a NodeProxy
with control rate and is subsequently mapped onto the frequency parameter of ~out.
Note that this NodeProxy can be replaced seamlessly without stopping the sound.
The ProxyMixer is a very convenient way of controlling all NodeProxies in the
ProxySpace through a graphical interface. It provides a volume slider for each audio
NodeProxy per default and allows for altering any other parameter defined. (For
more on ProxySpaces and just-in-time programming, refer to chapter 7.)

The examples above are intended to illustrate only a few of the many techniques
in SuperCollider that work seamlessly in the Windows version. The next section will

```
// ProxySpace
p = p ?? ProxySpace.push(s);

~ctl = { SinOsc.kr(1) * 110 + 440 };
~out = { arg freq=220, amp=0.5; Ringz.ar(Dust.ar(2, 0.4), freq, 0.8) ! 2 };

~out.play;

~out.map(\freq, ~ctl);

~ctl = { SinOsc.kr(LFSaw.kr(5, add: 2.0) * 10) * 220 + 440 };

ProxyMixer(p);

~out.stop;
~out.clear;
```

Figure 11.5
A `ProxySpace` example.

show how to use hardware such as sound cards and MIDI controllers with Windows SuperCollider. Section 11.3 highlights the differences between the Windows and the Mac versions of SuperCollider.

11.2   Your Hardware

11.2.1   Audio Interfaces

SuperCollider on Windows uses the PortAudio package to access any audio hardware. The package is actively developed and maintained, and supports the majority of external and internal sound cards available. For a complete list of which hardware is supported, check the project Web page (<http://www.portaudio.org>).

Without specific parameters, SuperCollider uses the default sound device on your computer. While booting, however, the server lists all devices detected. When the server is started, a message like the one in figure 11.6 will be printed in the post window.

A different sound card can be selected from within SuperCollider by altering the server options. The following command prints the available options and their current settings.

```
s.options.dump;
```

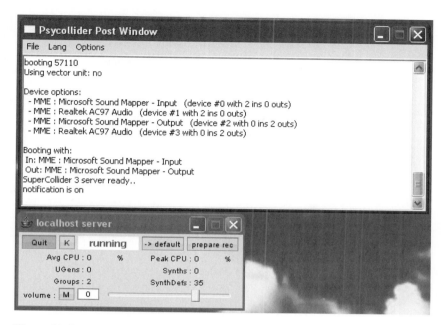

Figure 11.6
The server printing available device options into the post window at startup.

The device option determines which sound card is used when the server is booted. The list of devices shown while booting provides the names for all input and output channels available. The device option must be the common substring of the input and an output channels for a given device to be recognized correctly (e.g. "MME : Microsoft Soundmapper" rather than "MME : Microsoft Soundmapper—Input"); mixing devices (i.e., using a different device for input and output) is not yet supported. The following lines show some examples.

```
s.options.device_("ASIO : ASIO4ALL v2");
s.options.device_("MME : Microsoft Soundmapper");
s.options.device_("MME : Realtek AC97 Audio");
```

Which other options can be used depends on the specific hardware. If a specific option is set but is not supported by the hardware, the option either will not have an effect or default values will be used. After all settings have been specified, the server can be rebooted by evaluating:

```
s.reboot;
```

If a specific sound card should be used by default when SuperCollider is started, the options should be set in the *startup.sc* file, which is in the same location as

```
// MIDI Example
(
SynthDef(\midi, { arg out=0, midinote=60, dur=0.1;
    var source = Blip.ar(midinote.midicps, 4, 0.2);
    var env = EnvGen.kr(Env.perc(0.1, dur), 1.0, doneAction: 2);
    Out.ar(out, (source * env) ! 2);
}).add;

c = NoteOnResponder( { |src, chan, num, vel|
    [num, vel].postln;
    Synth.new(\midi, [\midinote, num, \dur, vel/512]);
});
)
c.remove;
```

Figure 11.7
A MIDI example.

SuperCollider.exe. The file provides examples that can be used as a starting point for customization.

11.2.2   Controllers

SuperCollider can communicate with MIDI controllers and any device that provides or understands OSC (Open Sound Control; see chapter 4) messages over a network connection. As with audio hardware, SuperCollider employs a widely used package to implement the MIDI interface (PortMIDI, which is part of PortAudio). Refer to the Web site for a complete list of devices supported (<http://www.portaudio.org>). Figure 11.7 shows how to use the MIDIResponder classes to control sound from a MIDI device.

Though MIDI support is built in directly, all other devices must be interfaced through an OSC connection. For sending information to a device, a NetAddr object can be used, since receiving an OSCresponder object provides easy access to the data (figure 11.8).

SuperCollider supports UDP and TCP connections, and the default port for incoming messages for OSCresponder is 57120. A similar concept is implemented in the HIDServer package (<http://www.ixi-software.net>). The Python-based server sends out OSC messages for any event received from Human Interface Devices (HIDs), such as joysticks and game pads.

```
// NetAddr and OSCresponder example
n = NetAddr("localhost", 57120);
r = OSCresponder(n, '/good/news', { arg time, resp, msg; [time,
msg].postln }).add;

n.sendMsg("/good/news", "you", "not you");

r.remove;
n.disconnect;
```

Figure 11.8
OSC messaging in SuperCollider for Windows.

11.3   Is It Different?

Although most of the functionality of SuperCollider is similar to that of the Mac version, some differences exist. They are mostly caused by the availability or unavailability of certain features on the different operating systems. The following paragraphs highlight the most important differences for the user to consider when cross-platform code is of importance.

11.3.1   The Server

Although the Mac and Linux versions provide 2 default synthesis servers to choose from ("local" and "internal"), Windows SuperCollider implements only one. It is automatically assigned to the variable s and usually is booted from the server window or from within the *startup.sc* file when SuperCollider is launched. The server does not run in the same address space as the language application (i.e., it is like the localhost server in the Mac version) and hence cannot be used for the SharedIn/Out classes that take advantage of the common memory space.

11.3.2   Graphical User Interfaces

All graphical elements in the original Mac version of SuperCollider were implemented using Apple's native Cocoa framework. Although Windows SuperCollider is built around Python and the widget package wxPython to create the working environment, it uses the SwingOSC package to create any GUIs from within SuperCollider code.

SwingOSC is preinstalled in the package and can be used out of the box. Fortunately, the interface is almost identical with the original Cocoa system, and

SuperCollider language provides a number of redirect classes for GUI objects which delegate to the appropriate GUI kit via the GUI factory class. This makes the usage of different kits transparent. The *startup.sc* file starts the SwingOSC server and specifies that the GUI factory class should use SwingOSC.

```
SwingOSC.program = "SwingOSC/build/SwingOSC.jar";
g = SwingOSC.default;
g.boot;

GUI.swing;
```

After the last line, code can access GUI classes through the redirects and is truly cross-platform, usable on the Windows, Linux, and Mac versions of SuperCollider. Figure 11.9 shows an example.

The so-called Plus GUI methods are methods added to classes such as Server, Buffer, and String and provide some GUI functionality within these classes. Thanks to

```
// GUI Example
(
    SynthDef(\gui, { arg out=0, freq=8, decay=0.11;
        var in = Formlet.ar(Impulse.ar(freq, 0, 0.4), 800, 0.01, decay);
        Out.ar(out, in ! 2);
    }).add;
)
(
    a = Synth.newPaused(\gui);
    w = Window.new( "A GUI window", Rect( 128, 64, 340, 250 ));
    w.view.decorator = FlowLayout( w.view.bounds );

    b = Button.new( w, Rect( 50, 20, 75, 24 ));
    b.states = [[ "Start"],[ "Stop"]];
    b.action_({ arg butt;
        if (butt.value == 1, { a.run }, { a.run(false) });
    });

    c = Slider2D.new( w, Rect(50, 120, 330, 200));
    c.x_(0.5).y_(0.5).action_({|sl|
            a.setn(\freq, [sl.x * 10 + 3, sl.y / 5 + 0.01]);
    });
    w.front;
)
```

Figure 11.9
A cross-platform GUI example.

the abstract GUI factory class, these methods are cross-platform and hence can be used seamlessly in Windows SuperCollider. The following code demonstrates these methods.

```
Server.inspect;                              // inspect a class

UGen.browse;                                 // ClassBrowser
SynthDescLib(\myLib).read.browse;

s.makeWindow;                                // a server control window

Env.perc.test.plot;                          // plotting

{SinOsc.ar(LFSaw.kr(1, 0, 220, 440)) *0.1}.scope // scope
```

A more detailed discussion of SwingOSC can be found in chapter 10. Chapter 9 covers the CocoaGUI implementation and also contains some information relevant to cross-platform use.

11.3.3   Document

Because the SuperCollider Windows port uses the wxPython library to create code windows, the powerful Document class needs to be reimplemented. As of Super-Collider 3.4, this has not been achieved but is on the wish list for later versions. A workaround for opening new code windows from within SuperCollider is provided through the String class.

```
"This is a new code window".newTextWindow;
```

11.3.4   Extensions and Paths

There are 2 locations where SuperCollider will look for extensions. If an extension should be available to all users of the computer, it must be placed within the appropriate installation directory (*SCClassLibrary, Help,* or *plugins,* depending on type). For personalized extensions, users can create a SuperCollider folder within their home directory (usually found in *Documents and Settings\username*). Any extensions present in *SuperCollider\Extensions* will be made available whenever the server is booted. This extension folder can hold class files, Help files, and plug-ins without the need to organize them in special folders. SuperCollider recognizes the type by the file extension.

There is also the possibility to create user-specific startup files. SuperCollider will look for a file called *startup.sc* in the *SuperCollider* directory of the home directory and evaluate the code after the systemwide *startup.sc* in the program folder.

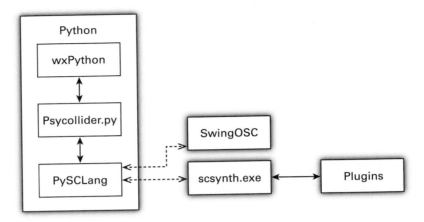

Figure 11.10
The internal structure of SuperCollider for Windows.

11.4   How the Windows SuperCollider Port Works

This section aims to show how the Windows SuperCollider port works internally. Though it is not essential for a user to be fully aware of these structures, it provides a starting point for all who want to get involved in the development of SuperCollider for Windows. Figure 11.10 illustrates the components of SuperCollider and shows how they interact.

Central to the system is the PsyCollider Python script. It implements the user interface, code windows, and menus by using standard widgets provided by the wxPython package. It also interfaces with the PySCLang module. PySCLang is a Python module (a shared object like a DLL) written in C that incorporates the whole SuperCollider language. It provides a simple interface for the PsyCollider script to compile the SC library and evaluate code. It also allows the script to assign any object that can handle text streams as a sink for log messages from the language—SuperCollider creates the post window for this purpose.

Like the SuperCollider application on the Mac, the PySCLang module uses network sockets to connect to the server. The server application is launched during startup, loads all available plug-ins, and communicates with PySCLang through OSC messages (see also the server command reference in the SuperCollider Help system). The module communicates in the same way with any other OSC peer, such as SwingOSC or HIDServer.

Finally, the downloadable package uses the py2exe extension to create a Windows executable that includes all components and the Python environment, so that end users do not need to install any other packages to be able to run SuperCollider.

11.4.1 PySCLang: A Generic Python Bridge

The PySCLang module can be used as a generic Python bridge to create specific stand-alone applications or to integrate SuperCollider into other projects. When the module is installed (in the site-packages directory of the Python installation), it can be used directly from the Python prompt.

```
C:\python.exe
>>> import PySCLang, os
>>> os.chdir("C:\Program Files\SuperCollider")
>>> PySCLang.start()
>>> PySCLang.setCmdLine("s = Server.local; s.boot;")
>>> PySCLang.sendMain('interpretPrintCmdLine')
>>> PySCLang.setCmdLine("s.initTree; s.serverRunning = true")
>>> PySCLang.sendMain('interpretPrintCmdLine')
>>> PySCLang.setCmdLine("{Ringz.ar(Impulse.ar(6, 0, 0.3), 2000,
    XLine.kr(0.04, 4, 8))}.play")
>>> PySCLang.sendMain('interpretPrintCmdLine')
```

The first step is to import the module and change into a directory in which *scsynth.exe* and the SCClassLibrary are present. After starting the module, text can be evaluated by setting the command line, then sending it to the module to be processed using sendMain, as shown above.

11.4.2 Windows SuperCollider Back on the Mac

Because Python is available on multiple platforms, the Windows SuperCollider port itself is cross-platform. The project has been ported back to the Mac OSX operating system but is not widely used or maintained. The major value, however, is to have a generic bridge between the Python programming language, which is part of every Mac OSX installation, and SuperCollider. This makes SuperCollider scriptable from a powerful programming language and enables developers to create new applications.

11.5 The Future of SuperCollider on Windows

Windows SuperCollider takes advantage of the largely common code base with the Mac version of SuperCollider. Every change, bug fix, and introduction of a new feature is incorporated because it is based on the same code. To streamline the process of aligning the features and the behavior of the Windows version with the Mac version, there are plans to address some fundamental issues in a future version.

As of version 3.4, the required development environment is Microsoft Visual Studio. In the spirit of making not only the application itself, but also the development process, as accessible as possible, the compilation environment will be changed to a GNU-based system. The Cygwin project provides the GNU compiler gcc and a ported version of the GNU standard C library for the Windows operating system. This will provide a number of advantages:

- Accessible open-source environment engaging the community of developers
- Further unification of the code base using the POSIX standard
- Decreasing external dependencies
- Seamless porting of new extensions or features.

11.6   Conclusions

SuperCollider is a fully featured, powerful sound synthesis application for the Windows operating system. It takes advantage of many years of experience on the Mac OSX platform and brings all these features to the most widely used operating system in the world.

Note

1. Julio d'Escriván is a composer, sound designer, and music producer who obtained his doctorate in electroacoustic composition from City University, London, in 1991.

12 "Collision with the Penguin": SuperCollider on Linux

Stefan Kersten and Marije A. J. Baalman

12.1 Introduction

Shortly after SuperCollider 3 was released under the GPL, the application was ported to the Linux operating system, which is known for its moderate use of resources and availability on a great number of different platforms. This chapter describes the idiosyncrasies of working with SuperCollider on Linux and describes interfaces to important subsystems of the Linux audio toolbox.

The first part of the chapter gives an overview of the compilation options and requirements on Linux. The command-line application is explained in detail, along with special modes such as script invocation, unsupervised daemon operation, and pipe-driven usage. After a short introduction to the Linux audio platform, Super-Collider's interoperation with prominent Linux audio subsystems, such as the JACK audio connection daemon, the ALSA sequencer architecture, and the Linux input device layer is covered along with concrete usage examples.

The last part of the chapter is dedicated to the Emacs IDE *scel* (SuperCollider Emacs Lisp), which allows tight 2-way integration between the Emacs text editor and the *sclang* terminal application. After explaining installation and configuration options, important work flows such as code editing, automatic indentation, symbol completion, introspection, and programatic Emacs-Lisp integration are shown by example.

Alternative editor interfaces will be discussed briefly in order to give a complete picture of working with SuperCollider on Linux.

Although most of the functionality of SuperCollider on Linux is the same as on OSX, there are a few differences. The purpose of this chapter is to give an overview of these differences and to introduce the features that are not available on Mac OSX.

The main differences are the following:

1. Installation: There is no single binary distribution of SuperCollider, so either manual compilation or the installation of a packaged version from a Linux distribution is necessary.

2. The editor: On Mac OSX there is a special editor for SuperCollider. On Linux there are several options for editing: *scel* (an Emacs extension), *sced* (a Python-based gedit extension), *scvim* (a vim extension), *qcollider* (Qt-based), and *scfront* (Tcl/Tk based).

3. The GUI: Mac OSX's graphical interface is based upon Cocoa, which is not available on Linux. This affects all the GUI items and the Document interface. Alternatives for the GUI are SwingOSC (see chapter 10) and the user interface widgets available within Emacs.

12.2   Installing

There are a few Linux distributions which provide a packaged version of Super-Collider, such as *pure:dyne*, *Debian*, *Ubuntu*, and *PlanetCCRMA*. Just look for the package with your system's package manager and install just as you would install other packages. If you've done this and it meets your needs, feel free to skip ahead. Move on to section 12.2.2 if you need to know about configuring SC on Linux, and go on to section 12.4 if you need to know about interfacing with JACK or ALSA. If you're fine with all this and just want to get going with scel (the most common Linux editor), turn to section 12.5.

In some cases—for example, when the version packaged with your distribution is a bit outdated and you want to use the newest features of SuperCollider—you will need to build SuperCollider yourself. To do so, you can download the source code of the latest stable release from the SourceForge Web site, or if you want to be really "cutting edge," you can download the sources from the Subversion repository. For this you need to install the software "subversion," which is available in your packaging system, and type from the command line:

```
svn co https://supercollider.svn.sourceforge.net/svnroot/supercollider/
trunk SuperCollider3
```

This will create a directory called *SuperCollider3* and download all the sources to it. To compile, you will need a number of other programs, as shown in table 12.1. All of them are quite common, so you should be able to find them in your Linux distribution as a package. Some distributions make a distinction for libraries that you need to compile software yourself and libraries that are needed only for running a program. If this distinction is made, you can see in the package manager that there is a version for developers; this is the version you need.

There are several options for the editor to edit SuperCollider source code: *scel*, *sced*, *scvim*, *qcollider*, and *scfront*. The first is based on Emacs and is the one maintained by the SuperCollider developers. sced and scvim are also distributed with the source code. Later in this chapter there is a survey of the various editors.

Table 12.1
Programs Needed on Linux to Download, Install, and Build SuperCollider

Name	Type	Description
Subversion	program	for downloading the sources from the repository
JACK	program and library	audio back end
Libsndfile	library	deals with sound files
fftw3f	library	fast Fourier transfrom
ALSA	drivers and library	for MIDI (optional)
Scons	program	Python-based build software
Cwiid	library	Wii-Mote (optional)
Emacs	program	editor (optional)
emacs-w3m	program plug-in	HTML viewer for Emacs (optional)
Gedit	program	editor (optional)
Vim	program	editor (optional)

ALSA and *cwiid* are only needed when the added functionality is desired. The editors (and plugins for these) are only needed if SuperCollider is to be used with that editor.

Before you start building, make sure that the C and C++ compiler is installed (usually gcc) and has the right version (3 or higher): gcc -v and g++ -v will print the version numbers.

Now change to the SuperCollider 3 directory and execute:

```
scons
scons install
```

The second command needs to be executed with root rights (e.g., with "sudo"). By default *scsynth*, *sclang*, and the libraries will be installed to */usr/local*. On most Linux systems this is the default location where packages that do not come from the package manager are installed, so it is recommended that you do not change this location. *scons* will look for the necessary libraries and output a summary of the ones it has found and the options with which it will compile SuperCollider.

scons has several build options; a complete list can be retrieved by executing scons -h, and a summary of generic options supported by *scons* can be retrieved with scons -H. Of main interest are the options SCEL, LID, PREFIX, SCED, and SCVIM. The first is for running SuperCollider with Emacs (default is on; *scel* stands for SuperCollider Emacs Lisp); the second is for Linux Input Device support (default is off); the third changes the install directory. So to turn *scel* off, and *LID* on, and set the installation prefix to */var/opt/*, you would execute

```
scons SCEL = no LID = yes PREFIX = /var/opt/
scons install
```

Once you set an option, it is remembered for the next time you execute *scons*, so if you want to change an option later, you will need to set it explicitly. Note that the rest of this chapter assumes the default install directory, so change */usr/local/* to your prefix where appropriate if you are using another install directory.

Now you will be able to run SuperCollider3. Depending on your system setup, though, you may run into 2 problems which have to do with the Linux operating system. When *scsynth* and *sclang* are run, they need to link to libraries installed dynamically at runtime. For this the system needs to know where these libraries are. The locations the system looks into are defined in the file */etc/ld.so.conf* or by the environment variable *LD_LIBRARY_PATH*. If *sclang* or *scsynth* complains on startup about not being able to link to the installed libraries, refer to the manpages ldconfig(8) and ld.so(8) for the correct settings.

You will also want to run SuperCollider with real-time permissions, which means that the operating system will give the program priority over other programs, so that audio samples are calculated in time for the sound card to output a steady stream of audio. There are various ways to accomplish this, and they are evolving as the Linux kernel is being further developed. One way is to run a modified kernel that is configured specially for audio, and another option is to give programs that belong to a certain group—and that are executed by users belonging to that group—higher priority than other programs. On your Linux distribution's mailing list, or on the Linux Audio mailing lists and Web sites (see htttp://www.linuxaudio.org), you may find advice on the latest options for real-time operation for audio programs.

12.2.1 Deinstalling and Updating

If you installed SuperCollider as a package from your distribution, it is recommended to uninstall it before you start building it yourself with the procedure described above. This will avoid conflicts during runtime.

If you built and installed from source and want to make an update of SuperCollider, you can type svn update while in the directory *SuperCollider3* to update the source files. You can then execute the scons commands again, and it will build the changed sources and install the changed files.

When there have been major changes to the source, it may be necessary to uninstall SuperCollider before reinstalling it. This is done with the command scons install -c. In certain cases it may be necessary to manually remove old class files with rm -r /usr/local/share/SuperCollider/.

12.2.2 Startup File

You can put SuperCollider code that will be executed each time you start up the language in the startup file. The file is called *.sclang.sc* and should be put in your home directory. Common settings to put in there are the location of the server program Server.program = "/usr/local/bin/scsynth"; and the default number of inputs and outputs the server should use.

It can also be used to load another file, for example, when you are creating a sound installation and you want SuperCollider to automatically start the installation.

12.2.3   The Class Library, Its Extensions, and Its Quarks

The SuperCollider language uses class files. The default library is included in the distribution and is installed to *usr/local/share/SuperCollider/SCClassLibrary*. The class library can be extended with more specific classes by using extensions to the default library. These extensions are class files, written by you or someone else, which are distributed separately from the default distribution. To use these extensions, you need to put the class files into directories where SuperCollider can find them. On Linux the default location for systemwide (i.e., all users on the same computer will be able to use them) extensions is */usr/local/share/SuperCollider/Extensions*; the user location is *$HOME/share/SuperColllider/Extensions*. Within these directories, all subdirectories are parsed (so you can organize your extensions), except when they are called: *CVS, .svn, _darcs, test, Help, windows,* or *osx*. The first 3 are directories created by the version control systems CVS, Subversion, and Darcs, respectively; the last 2 are platform-specific directories (directories called *linux* will be ignored on other platforms, so these should contain Linux-specific classes).

If you want more detailed control over the class library locations, you can use a special configuration file, *.sclang.cfg*, which must be located in your home directory. In this file you can specify the paths which sclang will search for class files and also exclude specific paths; you can even mark specific class files. Here is an example:

```
# linux extensions
+/usr/local/share/SuperCollider/Extensions
# but not using scvim
-/usr/local/share/SuperCollider/Extensions/scvim
# default class library
+/usr/local/share/SuperCollider/SCClassLibrary/Common
+/usr/local/share/SuperCollider/SCClassLibrary/DefaultLibrary
+/usr/local/share/SuperCollider/SCClassLibrary/backwards_compatibility
```

A # indicates a comment; +, a path that should be included; and –, a path that should be excluded.

The Quarks class provides a system within SuperCollider to dynamically install and uninstall extensions called Quarks. On Linux they are placed in the folder *$HOME/share/SuperCollider/quarks*. Symbolic links to its subdirectories are made when a Quark is installed.

12.2.4   Installing External Plug-ins

The server application uses UGen plug-ins from which it builds up Synths. These plug-ins are dynamically loaded libraries and are by default installed to */usr/local/lib/ SuperCollider/plugins*.

If you want to install other plug-ins—for example, if you have written one your-self (see chapter 25) or have downloaded one from the *sc3-plugins* project—you will normally have to build the plug-in first, using *scons*. The plug-in should come with an SConstruct file (or another method to build it).

In order to build the plug-in, you need to have built SuperCollider with the option DEVELOPMENT = yes, so that the appropriate headers will be available.

After you have built the plug-in, you can install it to *$HOME/share/SuperCollider/ Extensions* or to the path above. Its corresponding class files must be installed to one of the extension directories, as mentioned above.

12.3   *sclang* on Linux

On Linux *sclang* is built as a command-line application with the possibility of con-trolling the interpreter by sending SuperCollider expressions through a Unix pipe. This design allows the editing component to be provided by a stand-alone, third-party editor, with all the advantages (and disadvantages) of modern programming editors and integrated development environments.

12.3.1   Command-Line Operation

When starting *sclang* without any options, the SuperCollider class library is com-piled and the interpreter starts reading commands from standard input (the exact protocol is further described in section 12.3.4) and printing output from Super-Collider expressions to standard output. Table 12.2 lists the various command-line options that modify the default behavior.

In addition to the above switches, *sclang* can read a file with SuperCollider expres-sions upon startup and execute its contents after initialization. After processing ar-guments and the optional code file, *sclang* enters its command loop.

12.3.2   Noninteractive Use

With the -D command-line option, *sclang* can operate in *daemon* mode (i.e., it does not attempt to open standard input for reading). Daemon mode is useful mostly when running *sclang* without input from a terminal (e.g., in sound installations or as a Web service). Of course, *sclang* retains its ability to communicate with other pro-grams or devices via network communication or other means of external interfacing

Table 12.2
sclang Command-Line Options

Option and Argument	Description
-d <path>	set runtime directory
-D	enter daemon mode (no standard input)
-g <memory-growth>[km]	set heap growth (default 256 kB)
-h	display command-line options and exit
-l <path>	set library configuration file
-m <memory-space>[km]	set initial heap size in bytes, kilobytes (k), or megabytes (m) (default 2 MB)
-r	call Main.run on startup
-s	call Main.stop on shutdown
-u <network-port-number>	set UDP listening port (default 57120)

(see chapter 4), and output from SuperCollider code is printed on standard output for debugging purposes.

12.3.3   Scripting

The Linux command-line application is able to access the process's argument vector as passed by the operating system. thisProcess.argv returns the command-line arguments as an Array of Strings, not including the switches and arguments processed by *sclang* itself.

Scripts can be passed to *sclang* on the command line explicitly (as the command file argument) or can make use of the Unix *shebang* syntax, consisting of the string #! followed by an interpreter path and optional arguments. The script file is then passed to the *sclang* executable automatically. Since *sclang* enters either its command loop or the daemon loop, depending on the arguments passed, scripts have to exit the interpreter explicitly by calling the exit method of class Integer, which returns the specified exit code to the calling process. Figure 12.1 shows a simple example of how to write a script in *sclang*; it prints its arguments to standard output along with the index and exits with an exit code of 0, unless no argument was given on the command line. In order to execute the script, make it executable with chmod a + x chapter12script.scd and run it from the terminal by entering ./chapter12script .csd <arguments>.

12.3.4   Interfacing

When built with *scons*, the *sclang* application by default reads commands from standard input (unless inhibited with the -D switch). This simple interface is used for

```
#!/usr/local/bin/sclang
if (thisProcess.argv.isEmpty) {
    "Missing arguments!".postln;
    exit(1);
};
thisProcess.argv.do { | argu, i |
    "% : %\n".postf(i, argu);
};
exit(0);
```

Figure 12.1
Example of SuperCollider script.

scel, the integrated development environment based on Emacs (see section 12.5), and for interoperation with other editors and languages.

Commands consist of SuperCollider expressions delimited by ASCII characters that determine how the preceding expression is to be processed by the interpreter. ASCII *0x1b* (in hex notation) executes the currently accumulated SuperCollider statement, and ASCII character *0x0c* executes the statement and prints the resulting value to standard output. *scel* makes use of both features extensively for interacting with the interpreter and inspecting the SuperCollider runtime environment.

12.4 Interoperability: Talking to the Linux Subsystems

12.4.1 JACK

The JACK audio connection kit[1] allows flexible patching of audio between applications on Linux. It has been developed since 2001 by Paul Davis and several others, and has established itself as a standard for professional audio programs on Linux. For SuperCollider on Linux, JACK is the audio back end, that is, SuperCollider gets its audio input from and sends its audio output to JACK. With JACK the audio can then be patched to the sound card or to another program. Thus, it is easy to process sounds from other audio programs with SuperCollider or to process SuperCollider's output further. JACK itself can take an ALSA sound device as the sound card or a Firewire audio device (with the FreeBoB drivers or the newer FFADO drivers[2]).

You can configure which inputs and outputs SuperCollider will connect to automatically by setting the environment variables SC_JACK_DEFAULT_INPUTS and SC_JACK_DEFAULT_OUTPUTS. For example, you could put the following into your startup file:

```
"SC_JACK_DEFAULT_INPUTS".setenv(
    "alsa_pcm:capture_1",
    "alsa_pcm:capture_2"
)

"SC_JACK_DEFAULT_OUTPUTS".setenv(
    "alsa_pcm:playback_1",
    "alsa_pcm:playback_2"
)
```

so that each time you start the Server from the language, scsynth will automatically connect to the first 2 inputs of the audio card and to the first 2 outputs. The order in the list corresponds to the input and output channels of SuperCollider. So if you need to do more complicated routing, this can be set in the environment variables by changing the order in which the outputs are set. For example,

```
"SC_JACK_DEFAULT_OUTPUTS".setenv(
    "alsa_pcm:playback_2",
    "alsa_pcm:playback_1"
)
```

would connect output channel 0 of SuperCollider to output channel 2 on the sound card, and SuperCollider's channel 1 to output channel 1.

You can, of course, also make the connections with the common JACK tools, such as jack_connect and jack_disconnect, on the command line or the graphical tool *QJackCtl*.[3]

There is a Quark available, JACK, which provides classes to handle JACK connections from SuperCollider, as well as to start the JACK meter bridge, a tool to view JACK inputs and outputs in a VU meter, DPM, or scope view.

12.4.2   ALSA

ALSA, the Advanced Linux Sound Architecture,[4] is used by SuperCollider for MIDI access (the sound card is accessed via JACK, which again talks to ALSA). To use it during compilation of SuperCollider, the headers of *libasound* must be installed on your computer (or the package of your distribution must have been built with a dependency on *libasound*). At runtime the kernel modules related to the ALSA sequencer, *snd_seq*, must be loaded. You can check this by executing the command lsmod (if it does not execute as a normal user, you have to execute it as root). The output should contain lines that look like this:

```
snd_seq_dummy              3844           0
snd_seq_oss           28768 0
snd_seq_midi           8192           0
```

```
snd_rawmidi              22560 1     snd_seq_midi
snd_seq_midi_event       7008        2          snd_seq_oss,snd_seq_midi
snd_seq                        45680 6
     snd_seq_dummy,snd_seq_oss,snd_seq_midi,snd_seq_midi_event
snd_seq_device                 7820             5
     snd_seq_dummy,snd_seq_oss,snd_seq_midi,snd_rawmidi,snd_seq
```

Since a general overview on using MIDI within SuperCollider is presented in chapter 4, we will say only a few words here on how SuperCollider interacts with the ALSA sequencer. Just as JACK allows you to patch the audio input and output between different programs and devices, the ALSA sequencer allows you to patch MIDI input and output between different programs and devices.

As an example, imagine we have 2 other programs running which do something with MIDI: a virtual MIDI keyboard, which can give us MIDI note input, and a MIDI monitor, which checks which MIDI messages are sent out by the port it is connected to.

If we execute the code `MIDIClient.init(2, 2)`, we create 2 MIDI inputs and 2 outputs for SuperCollider, and a list is built of the available MIDI end points and is output to the post window as

```
Sources: [System-Timer : System-Timer, System-Announce : System-Announce,
Midi Through-Midi Through Port-0 : Midi Through-Midi Through Port-0,
SuperCollider-out0 : SuperCollider-out0, SuperCollider-out1 :
SuperCollider-out1, Virtual Keyboard-Virtual Keyboard : Virtual Keyboard-
Virtual Keyboard]
Destinations: [Midi Through-Midi Through Port-0 : Midi Through-Midi
Through Port-0, SuperCollider-in0 : SuperCollider-in0, SuperCollider-in1 :
SuperCollider-in1, KMidimon-input : KMidimon-input]]
```

Now, suppose we want to connect the first input of SuperCollider to the virtual keyboard. We can execute

```
MIDIIn.connect(0, 5);
```

connecting the first input of SuperCollider to the sixth item in the list of sources. Then we can connect the second MIDI output of SuperCollider to the MIDI monitor with

```
MIDIOut.connect(1, 3);
```

In *QJackCtl* these connections can now be seen in the MIDI tab, as shown in figure 12.2.

The connections can be undone with corresponding `disconnect` methods. Naturally, you can also use *QJackCtl*, or any other external tool, directly to make connections to MIDI inputs and outputs of SuperCollider.

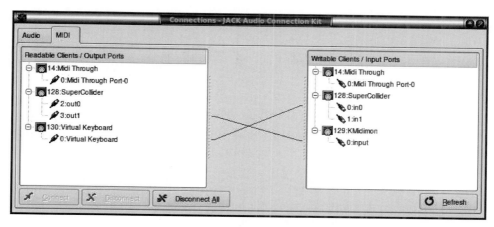

Figure 12.2
The MIDI connections as created by the example code, viewed in the MIDI tab of *QjackCtl*.

To send MIDI out of SuperCollider, you must create an instance of MIDIOut. It has as its arguments the port number and a uid, which is a unique identifier. This uid is a parameter of a destination port and can be retrieved, for example, by MIDIClient .destinations.at(2).uid, so we can do, for example:

```
m = MIDIOut(0, MIDIClient.destinations.at(2).uid);
```

Then, each message sent out by m is sent to that destination only. If we leave the parameter out and do

```
m = MIDIOut(0);
```

instead, each message is sent to any port connected to SuperCollider's first MIDI output. A connection can be made through

```
m.connect(2);
```

Note that by connecting in this way, you can connect more than 1 destination to the MIDI output.

12.4.3   The Event Interface

The event interface is a way to access human input devices (HIDs) connected to the computer, such as the mouse, keyboard, and joystick. SuperCollider can access and use these devices for input and output, as long as it has been set up to do so with the scons option LID. At compilation, it needs to be able to find the Linux kernel header file *input.h*, normally installed under */usr/include/linux/*.

To use the input device support, you need to make sure that the device can be read by sclang. On modern Linux systems (since kernel version 2.6.12), "udev" is used for hotplugging devices. The settings for the devices are found in the file */etc/udev/udev.rules* (at least on Debian-based systems). If you open this file, you will find a line like this:

```
KERNEL == "event[0-9]*", NAME = "input/%k"
```

If you are a member of the group "audio" on your system, then you can change the line to

```
KERNEL == "event[0-9]*", NAME = "input/%k", GROUP = "audio"
```

so that any program that belongs to the group "audio," and is run by a user of that group, can access the device.

If SuperCollider has been succesfully compiled with LID support, the devices can be accessed using the LID class. Using HID devices from SuperCollider is covered in more detail in chapter 4, where a cross-platform class, GeneralHID, which uses LID underneath, is introduced. It is recommended to use that class.

12.5   *scel*: The Emacs Interface

Emacs[5] is a powerful programmer's editor customizable through a Lisp-like language called Emacs Lisp (*Elisp*). *scel* is an interface to the SuperCollider programming language on Linux and other platforms. Its goal is to integrate SuperCollider as seamlessly as possible while retaining Emacs's advanced features for common (and not so common) editing tasks.

scel is installed by default when building SuperCollider with scons, so in most cases the only thing that needs to be done is loading the Emacs package by putting (require 'sclang) into the Emacs startup file, *.emacs,* located in your home directory. In some cases it may be necessary to add the install location (*/usr/local/share/emacs* by default) to the Emacs variable load-path. Consult the Help text for this variable (see below) for further information.

12.5.1   First Steps in Emacs

For users new to Emacs, extensive online help is available. Invoking *Emacs Tutorial* from the Help menu or browsing the info manual is a good way to start learning Emacs. In order to follow the examples in this section, only a basic understanding of how to invoke Emacs commands is necessary.

Emacs commands are invoked either from the menu, through keystrokes, or by entering them in the minibuffer (the 1-line buffer at the bottom of each Emacs window).

Key bindings associate commands with keystroke sequences. Common modifiers are M (*Meta*), C (*Control*), and S (*Shift*). In the following, keys that should be pressed simultaneously are connected by a hyphen -; an entire key sequence can contain any number of simultaneous key presses. The *Meta* key is bound to the [Alt] key on many PC keyboards.

Typing [C-h f describe-key] invokes the Elisp function `describe-function` to display the documentation for the function `describe-key`, which includes associated key bindings and programmatic uses. You can hide the buffer at the bottom that contains the function documentation again by typing [C-x 1].

[C-h k] invokes the function `describe-key`, which can be used to find out which command a key sequence is bound to.

Entering commands interactively is done by pressing [M-x] and then typing the command name into the minibuffer. Incomplete commands can be completed against all known commands by pressing [Tab]; pressing [Space] completes the input up to the next hyphen. Try it yourself: [M-x emacs-version].

There is a Help file called EmacsEditor with useful shortcuts for Emacs and some customization tips.

12.5.2 Customization

All relevant customization options are accessible through Emacs's graphical customization interface (see *Customization* in the Emacs info manual). When setting a customization option from the graphical interface, a corresponding Lisp statement is appended to the file specified by the variable `custom-file`. Type [C-h v custom-file] for more information about how to use this variable.

Scel's top-level customization group is *sclang*, which is directly accessible by executing [M-x sclan-customize] in the minibuffer. Let's have a look at the customization group hierarchy:

sclang
sclang-mode   editing SuperCollider code
sclang-interface   sclang process interface
sclang-programs   paths to helper programs
sclang-options   command-line options for sclang

In a vanilla installation, none of the customization options need to be edited, but they can be used to fine-tune *scel*'s and SuperCollider's behavior.

12.5.3   Interpreter Interaction

All of the important commands for interacting with the *sclang* subprocess are accessible from the *SCLang* menu in any *sclang-mode* buffer. Commands bound to keyboard shortcuts are shown in parentheses after the menu entry.

(Re-)Start Interpreter [C-c C-l] (re)starts the sclang subprocess and compiles the library in one go. *Stop Interpreter* attempts to exit the subprocess cleanly if possible, and *Kill Interpreter* kills a nonresponsive subprocess abruptly. In order to follow the examples below, start the interpreter now by typing [C-c C-l]. Alternatively, *scel* and the SuperCollider interpreter can be started automatically by passing the *-sclang* command line option to Emacs upon invocation.

The following two commands allow for general interpreter control. *Run Main* [C-c C-r] and *Stop Main* [C-c C-s] invoke the methods Main.run and Main.stop, respectively. The default implementation of Main.run is empty and can be overwritten in a class extension to do anything that's needed. Main.stop by default frees all nodes on all servers, stops all clocks, and runs notifications registered with CmdPeriod. This is *scel*'s panic button.

The *post buffer* is a special Emacs buffer named **SCLang:PostBuffer** where command execution results are printed (or *posted*). Evaluating a command or invoking *Show Post Buffer* [C-c >] from the *SCLang* menu splits the current window and makes the post buffer visible in the lower half. Output to the post buffer is appended at the bottom and made visible automatically if the cursor is positioned at the end of the buffer. A prefix argument to *sclang-show-post-buffer* (specified by pressing [C-u] before executing the command) shows the buffer and positions the cursor at the end. The post buffer can be cleared of any previously output messages by invoking *Clear Post Buffer* [C-c <].

One of the most frequent tasks in *scel* is executing pieces of SuperCollider code, and there are several different means of piping expressions to the interpreter. SuperCollider expressions can be evaluated from *sclang-mode* buffers, Help buffers, and the post buffer. *Evaluate Region* [C-c C-d] executes the currently active region. Regions of text can be selected by pressing [C-Space] and moving the cursor with the mouse or by double clicking an open parenthesis.

Evaluate Line [C-c C-c] executes the line with the current cursor position (figure 12.3). It is recommended to activate *transient-mark-mode* (e.g., interactively by typing [M-x customize-variable Enter transient-mark-mode]). When *transient-mark-mode* is activated, [C-c C-c] selectively evaluates the current line or the region if it is active. Additionally, in *transient-mark-mode*, the active region is highlighted visually (see figure 12.4).

If the value of *sclang-eval-line-forward* is not nil, *sclang-eval-line* moves to the next line after evaluating the current line, mimicking the behavior of

```
// select the following lines and type C-c C-d
// stop synthesis with C-c C-s
{
    var trem = LFTri.kr(3).range(-12.dbamp, 0.dbamp);
    SinOsc.ar(
        { rrand(60, 80).midicps } ! 6,
        mul: -10.dbamp * trem
    ).clump(2).sumP

}.play
```

Figure 12.3
Example for executing a region in *scel*.

```
// evaluate the following lines by double-clicking on the
// first paranthesis when 'transient-mark-mode' is enabled
// and pressing C-c C-c
(
x = {
    Saw.ar(
        XLine.kr(20, [400,403,407], 20),
mul: 0.7
    ).clump(2).sum
}.play; "scel";
)
// evaluate this line by pressing C-c C-c
x.free; "rocks";
```

Figure 12.4
Example for executing regions and lines in *scel*.

the SuperCollider editor on OSX. This variable can be customized (see section 12.5.2).

Evaluate Defun [C-M-x] evaluates an expression enclosed in parentheses—positioned at the beginning of separate lines—when the cursor is positioned inside the expression. This is quite a handy feature when dealing with SuperCollider interactively, since expressions no longer need to be selected explicitly.

```
// position the cursor anywhere between the parentheses
// and press C-M-x
```

```
(
    "line 1".postln;
    "line 2".postln;
    "last line";
)
```

Note that expressions cannot be nested in this mode of evaluation (i.e., there should be only one pair of parantheses enclosing the expression to be evaluated). *Evaluate Expression* [C-c C-e] finally prompts for code to be executed in the mini-buffer (the single-line buffer at the bottom of each Emacs window). Pressing [Enter] evaluates the code entered.

12.5.4   Help File Access

SuperCollider comes with extensive online help in HTML format that can be accessed from within any *sclang-mode* or Help buffer.

Find Help ... [C-c C-h] prompts for a Help topic to be displayed in the mini-buffer. Completion of Help topics is available, which means that you can complete partial entries against known Help entries by pressing [Tab]. If the cursor is positioned within a documented identifier, a default based on the current word is shown in parentheses and can be invoked by pressing [Enter]. Invoking a Help topic opens a browser containing the rendered content of the HTML Help file. Links to other Help topics, such as class or method names, can be conveniently navigated with the cursor keys. For an exhaustive overview of key bindings of type [C-h m] in a Help buffer.

```
// position the cursor on the line below and type C-c C-h Enter
// you can kill the Help buffer by typing C-x k Enter

Object
```

Help buffers cannot be edited in place because Emacs lacks a *WYSIWYG* HTML editor. Pressing [E] in a Help buffer, however, turns the Help browser into an editable version of the original Help file, whose contents can be changed deliberately without fear of modifying the file stored on disk. This feature is essential for trying out modified versions of the extensive code examples in SuperCollider's library help. Pressing [C-M-h] returns to the HTML Help browser.

In case you want to have a look at or even edit the machine-generated HTML code, press [C-c C-v] in a view-only or editable Help buffer.

Upon first access of the Help system, *scel* caches Help topics for fast lookup. The menu entry *Index Help Topics* rebuilds the Help topic cache (e.g., when additional Help files are added to the Help directory).

12.5.5   Introspection

When writing SuperCollider code, the ability to look up method and class implementations, as well as symbol references, interactively is an invaluable aid. *Find Definitions* . . . [C-c :] prompts for a symbol (a method or class name), and displays its definition in the corresponding source file. If the symbol is defined in more than 1 source file, either because class extensions define additional methods for a class, or because several classes implement the same method, a browser window is displayed that allows the interactive selection of a particular definition. Pressing [C-c : Object Enter] shows a buffer similar to the following:

```
Definitions of 'Object'

Object.sc            Object
ObjectPlusGUI.sc   + Object
asScore.sc         + Object
asDefName.sc       + Object
asSize.sc          + Object
storeLispOn.sc     + Object
```

Object's main definition is in *Object.sc,* and several class extensions provide additional methods in different source files. Browser links can be navigated with [Tab] and [Shift-Tab], and pressing [Enter] or the middle mouse button on a link brings up the corresponding definition. The browser can be closed without following any link simply by pressing q. Pressing [C-c : play Enter] might show the following:

```
Definitions of 'play'

Environment.sc     Event-play
Stream.sc          EventStreamPlayer-play
asDefName.sc       Function-play
Clock.sc           Meta_Clock-play
Score.sc           Meta_Score-play
Clock.sc           Meta_TempoClock-play
Nil.sc             Nil-play
Patterns.sc        Pattern-play
Stream.sc          PauseStream-play
SCUMObject.sc      SCUMObject-play
GUIScreen.sc       SCWindow-play
Clock.sc           Scheduler-play
Score.sc           Score-play
Stream.sc          Stream-play
SynthDef.sc        SynthDef-play
Clock.sc           TempoClock-play
```

Find References . . . [C-c ;] allows you to browse references to a class or method in method implementations. Browsing works exactly as in the case of browsing a definition. *Pop Mark* [C-c }] pops back to the buffer position where *sclang-find-definitions* or *sclang-find-references* were last invoked, eventually leading back to the originating buffer position. *Dump Full Interface* [C-c {] prints the complete (including inherited) interface of a class in the post buffer. *Dump Interface* [C-c []] prints only the class's own interface.

If the variable *sclang-use-symbol-table* is non-nil—it can be customized through the customization interface—symbol completion for the introspection commands is available in the minibuffer, again a convenient feature for daily work. It is also possible to complete partial symbols against defined symbols by pressing [M-Tab] or [C-c C-n] after an incomplete symbol in any *sclang-mode* buffer, similar to symbol completion in other Emacs programming modes.

```
// place the cursor at the end of the line below,
// press M-Tab and select 1 of the possible completions
F
```

It is often hard to memorize all the method arguments and their names, especially for UGen constructors. *scel* makes life a little easier by providing a means of displaying method arguments and their default arguments. Currently this works only for the pattern of a class name directly followed by a constructor call (e.g., SinOsc.ar). Typing [C-c C-m] displays information for the innermost constructor call followed by an open paranthesis. You can try it by placing the cursor at different positions in the following example. If it is positioned after the first parenthesis, but before the second, the arguments of SinOsc.ar are displayed; otherwise, those of LFNoise0.kr are.

```
SinOsc.ar(      // Try placing the cursor here ...
   LFNoise0.kr( // ... or here.
```

12.5.6   Work Spaces

The *work space* is a scratch buffer for evaluating SuperCollider expressions. It will not be saved when Emacs exits and thus should not be used for code that needs to survive across editing sessions. *Switch To Workspace* [C-c C-w] switches to the work space buffer; it can be hidden by typing [C-c}].

12.5.7   Executing Elisp Code

The foundation of the *scel* Emacs interface is a 2-way communication between *sclang* and Emacs through a pipe. Emacs sends SuperCollider expressions and handles the received results. This pipe-based interface also makes it possible to execute expressions in Elisp, the Lisp dialect used by Emacs, and to control the editor programmatically from SuperCollider code. The class method `Emacs.evalLispExpression` sends a Lisp expression to Emacs and optionally executes the function argument `handler` with the returned result. A Lisp expression can be either a `String` or a list of expressions (in SuperCollider, an instance of `Array`). For example, you could display a message in Emacs's minibuffer by calling `evalLispExpression`

```
// evaluate Lisp expression (message "Hello from SuperCollider!")
Emacs.evalLispExpression(
    "(message \"Hello from SuperCollider!\")"
);
```

or the predefined method `Emacs.message`. If you want to use the result returned by Emacs, you have to pass a handler function.

```
// initialize argument variable
~argm = 17;
// evaluate Lisp expression (+ 12 ~arg) => (+ 12 17)
// and show the result
Emacs.evalLispExpression(
    ['+', 12, ~argm],
    {|result| result.postln}
);
```

Due to the asynchronicy of *scel*'s communication with Emacs, results are not returned to the interpreter directly but are passed to a handler function that is executed at a point later in time. This functionality is used extensively in `EmacsBuffer` and `EmacsDocument`.

12.5.8   ScelDocument and EmacsDocument

`ScelDocument` provides an interface compatible with `Document`. It interacts with `EmacsDocument`, which in turn implements communication with Emacs to access to Emacs's internal representation of the buffer contents. This means that certain methods are asynchronous (i.e., that data requested are not returned directly, but rather are put into a class variable which can be accessed later).

12.5.9   Emacs UI

The Emacs interface also provides functions to create user interfaces. It allows you to create number boxes, text fields, buttons, and so on in an Emacs buffer.

```
// create a buffer:
p = EmacsBuffer.new;
```

```
// create a key action for the buffer:
p.defineKey("hello", {"hey there".postln;});

// type hello on the window and look at the postbuffer
p.front;

// create a close button:
p.closeButton;
// clicking it will close the buffer!

// make a new line:
p.newline;

p.editableField("write something here", "like this?", {|v|v.postln;});

// making a number box
n = EmacsNumber.new(p, "number box", [0,5].asSpec, {|v|v.postln;}); //
args: buffer, tag/label, spec, action
p.newline;

t = EmacsText(p, "hello", 30); // args: buffer, string, size, align

p.newline;
e = EmacsEditableField(p, "edit field", "edit me").action_({|v|
v.postln;});
p.newline;

b = EmacsPushButton(p, "hello").action_({"do it".postln;});

p.front;
```

The Help file for Emacs widgets is called EmacsGUI.

12.6   Other Interfaces

The Emacs editor interface was the first to be distributed with SuperCollider; now scvim (a plug-in for vim) and sced (a plug-in for gedit) are distributed with the source code as well. In addition, several alternative editors have been created. An overview is now given of these editors. In the Shortcuts Help file, shortcuts in the various editors are compared.

12.6.1   Editors

12.6.1.1   *scfront*: The Tcl/Tk interface
scfront[6] was developed by August Black in 2003 and 2004 and is a simple editor interface implemented in Tcl/Tk. It provides basic editor functionality and the possibility to send code to sclang. It is possible to work with this interface, although it

lacks several options, such as integrated Help file access (its implementation is incomplete) and undo functions for editing. Development of the project has been discontinued by Black, but the interface can still be useful because it is quite a small editor which uses few resources. This interface has also been included in some packages for SuperCollider in several Linux distributions.

12.6.1.2   *scvim*: The Vim interface

scvim[7] has been in development since April 2005 by Alex Norman and is a SuperCollider plug-in for the popular editor *vim* or *gvim*. It features syntax colorization, code execution, and integrated Help file access.

12.6.1.3   *sced*: The gedit interface

sced[8] is a plug-in for the editor *gedit*, originally written in Python. It extends *gedit* with sclang interaction and provides syntax colorization. Help support has not yet been integrated.

12.6.1.4   *qcollider*: The Qt interface

qcollider[9] is a Qt-based editor. It aims to be a cross-platform editor for SuperCollider and is (at the time of writing) in its early stages of development.

12.6.1.5   *squeak*

Another way to use SuperCollider is via the Environment *squeak*, a Smalltalk environment which gives a graphical interface for executing code blocks. This extension for SuperCollider has been created by Cesare Marilungo and is available from <http://www.cesaremarilungo.com>.

12.6.2   Graphical Interfaces

There are many different possibilities for building graphical user interfaces for SuperCollider, some ad hoc and some tightly integrated with the SuperCollider language. The ubiquitous *OpenSoundControl* (OSC) protocol (see chapter 4) allows any application capable of sending OSC to control the SuperCollider language by means of a graphical user interface. Examples of applications that have been used to build graphical interfaces for SuperCollider include synthesis environments such as *Pure Data*, *Max/MSP* and *Reaktor,* as well as general-purpose GUI tool kits such as *GTK+*, Qt, Swing (Java), and Cocoa (OSX).

SwingOSC is a general-purpose, cross-platform graphical interface which has been tightly coupled to SuperCollider and thus is a good option for creating a graphical interface on Linux (figure 12.5). In chapter 10 this interface is presented elaborately, so here only some instructions on installing it under Linux are given.

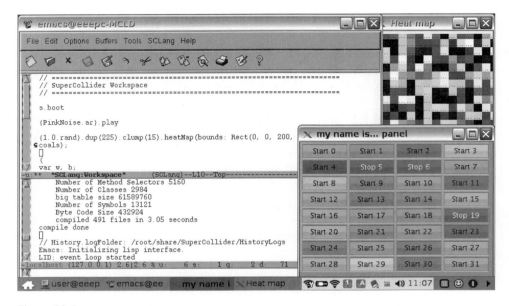

Figure 12.5
Screen shot of the *scel* Emacs IDE and *SwingOSC*.

SwingOSC is written in *Java* and requires *Java runtime environment* (JRE) version 1.4 or better. This has to be the official version of Java from Sun. On Linux platforms, other runtime environments for *Java* may be available, such as the *GNU libgcj*, but *SwingOSC* is incompatible with that version. So the first task when setting up *SwingOSC* (besides downloading it) is to make sure that you have a Sun Java runtime environment installed and check where it is located on your computer.

Next, in order to use *SwingOSC* with SuperCollider, the associated class files must be in an extension path. These should be copied (or linked) to either */usr/local/share/ SuperCollider/Extensions* for systemwide use of *SwingOSC* or *$HOME/share/ SuperColllider/Extensions* for your own use only. In the latter case, it is recommended that you make a link to the path where you downloaded and unpacked *SwingOSC*, so that after an update, you do not need to delete and copy files each time (provided, of course, that you unpack an updated version in the same path).

You should then add a few lines to your startup file, to ensure that SwingOSC is the standard GUI.

```
// set SwingOSC as default GUI
GUI.swing;
```

```
// set the path to the SwingOSC program:
SwingOSC.java = "/usr/lib/jvm/java-1.5.0-sun/jre/bin/java";
SwingOSC.program = "/path/to/SwingOSC/build/SwingOSC.jar";

// boot SwingOSC, and assign it to the variable "g"
g = SwingOSC.default.boot;
```

In the line containing SwingOSC.java, the complete path to Sun's Java is given, and in SwingOSC.program, the complete path to where SwingOSC.jar is located. You should adjust these paths to the ones applicable to your system.

12.7   Concluding Remarks

Although we have attempted to give a comprehensive overview of installation instructions, details may vary according to your Linux distribution, and also over time as both the operating system SuperCollider and the programs it cooperates with evolve. It is therefore recommended that you read the installation instructions that come with downloads and online documentation.

Notes

1. <http://www.jackaudio.org>.

2. <http://www.ffado.org>.

3. <http://qjackctl.sourceforge.net>.

4. <http://www.alsa-project.org>.

5. Emacs is an extensible, customizable, self-documenting real-time display editor (<http://www.gnu.org/software/emacs>).

6. <http://aug.ment.org/scfront/index.php>.

7. <http://www.x37v.info/scvim> and <http://www.neisis.net/alex/scvim>.

8. <http://artfwo.googlepages.com/sced>.

9. <http://tapas.affenbande.org/qcollider>.

Practical Applications

13 Sonification and Auditory Display in SuperCollider

Alberto de Campo, Julian Rohrhuber, Till Bovermann, and Christopher Frauenberger

13.1 Introduction

Sonification, the perceptualization of data by sound, is a fascinating activity from many perspectives: modern societies deal with large amounts of data, especially in science, but also in politics and economics. Human-Computer Interaction (HCI) researchers are becoming more aware of the potential strengths of auditory perception as a communication channel, and many avant-garde musicians and media artists have taken up sonification as an interdisciplinary art/science venture.

For musicians, sonification is particularly interesting: Data and their context provide extra-musical "content" for experimental music and sound-related art projects. Sonification also addresses a central problem in experimental computer music in an interesting way; while it is easy to design new synthesis variants, creating control data that structure them in artistically satisfying ways is not trivial. Sonification inverts this problem: one is given data that may contain latent structures and patterns; inventing audible translations that make these patterns perceptible as emerging sound objects becomes a challenging task.

This chapter covers general background and basic concepts of sonification and provides some smaller examples in detail, as well as a few extended examples of sonification and auditory display applications realized in SuperCollider. Drawing on experience in *SonEnvir*, an interdisciplinary research project on sonification for different scientific contexts, we show how the interactive nature of the SC3 environment offers flexible ways to manipulate static data, run scientific models in real time, and design alternative translations into sound.

13.2 A Short History of Sonification

13.2.1 Precursors

The prehistory and early history of sonification are covered authoritatively in Kramer (1994a). Employing auditory perception for scientific research was not always as unusual as it is in today's visually dominated scientific cultures; in fact, sonification has had a number of precursors: in medicine, auscultation (listening to the body's internal sounds for diagnostic purposes) seems to have been present in Hippocrates' time (McKusick et al., 1957), long before the invention of the stethoscope in 1819. In engineering, some mechanics excel at listening to machines; for example, expert car mechanics can often tell where problems originate just by listening to a running engine.

Galileo Galilei may have employed listening for scientific purposes: he seems to have verified the quadratic law of falling bodies by running strings across an inclined plane at distances increasing according to the quadratic law (1, 4, 9, 16, etc.), so the ball running down the plane would ring bells attached to the strings in a regular rhythm (Drake, 1980). Riess et al. (2005) reconstructed the experiment and found that the water clocks used for time measurement in the 17th century were too imprecise, so listening for rhythmic accuracy provided the more plausible procedure.

The Geiger-Müller counter renders an environment variable that is normally imperceptible to humans: incidence of radioactive decay particles on a detector causes audible clicks, and the density of the sequence of clicks informs users about changes in radiation intensity.

Sonar is an interesting case: passive sonar, listening to underwater sound to determine distances and directions of ships, apparently was experimented with by Leonardo da Vinci (Urick, 1967; cited in Kramer, 1994a); in active sonar, sound pulses are projected in order to penetrate visually opaque volumes of water. Listening to reflections allows the analysis of local topography as well as the detection of moving objects such as vessels, whales, or fish swarms.

In seismology, Speeth (1961) had subjects try to differentiate between seismograms of natural earthquakes and artificial explosions by listening to speeded-up recordings. Although subjects could classify the data very successfully and rapidly, little use was made of this until Hayward (1994) and Dombois (2001) revived the discussion.

Pereverzev et al. (1997) reported auditory proof of a long-standing hypothesis: in the early 1960s, Josephson and Feynman had predicted quantum oscillations between weakly coupled reservoirs of superfluid helium; 30 years later, the effect was verified by listening to an amplified vibration sensor signal of these mass-current oscillations.

13.2.2   Sonification as a Discipline

The official history of sonification research began with the first International Conference on Auditory Display (ICAD)[1] in 1992, which brought many researchers working on related topics into one research community. The book based on the conference proceedings (Kramer, 1994b) is still the main reference on this topic, and ICAD conferences are central events for sonification researchers.

Since then, many interesting applications of sonification have been made. For example, Fitch and Kramer (1994) showed that an auditory display of medical patients' life signs can be superior to visual displays; Gaver et al. (1991) found that monitoring a simulated factory by acoustic means works remarkably well.

The connection between neural signals and audition has its own history, from neurophysiologists listening to nerve signals by telephone (Wedensky, 1883) to current EEG sonifications (Baier et al., 2007; Hermann et al., 2006; Hinterberger and Baier, 2005), as well as musicians' fascination with brain waves, beginning with Alvin Lucier's "Music for Solo Performer" (1965).

13.2.3   Sonification and SuperCollider

A number of sonification projects have been realized in SuperCollider: Mark Ballora's heart rate variability sonification in SC2 (Ballora, 2000) and Julian Rohrhuber's ProteinBioSynthesis (in SC2 first, now an SC3 Quark), to name just two. In the last few years, the *SonEnvir* project[2] at IEM Graz has realized sonification designs for various scientific contexts and has implemented a framework for them; and the Neuro-Informatics group at the University of Bielefeld[3] has done a wide range of research on sonification, human-computer interaction, and cognitive interaction with SuperCollider.

13.3   Some Sonification Theory

13.3.1   Terminology

The entities to be perceptualized can be either well-known information or data potentially containing unknown patterns. For information, establishing easy-to-grasp analogies is central, and for data, it is enabling the perceptual emergence of latent phenomena of unforeseeable types. Some common terms in auditory display and sonification research can be defined accordingly.

Auditory display is the rendering of data and/or information into sound designed for human listening. This is the most general, all-encompassing term.

There are two subspecies:

Auditory information display is the rendering of well-understood information into sound designed for communication to human beings. This can include speech messages, as in airports; auditory feedback sounds on computers; and alarms and warning systems.

Sonification is the rendering of (typically scientific) data into (typically nonspeech) sound designed for human auditory perception. The informational value of the rendering is often unknown beforehand, particularly in data exploration.

13.3.2   Sonification Strategies

Sonification methods are often classified as audification and parameter mapping (Kramer, 1994b) and model-based sonification (Hermann, 2002); however, one can differentiate more sharply.

Continuous data representation treats data as if they were sampled continuous signals, relying on 2 preconditions: equal distances along at least 1 dimension, typically time or space; and sufficient sampling rate. Treating data directly as time-domain audio waveforms is called *audification*, frequency domain treatment being rare; of course, data-driven signals can also be used for the modulation of synthesis parameters.

Discrete point data representation creates individual sonic events for each data point, often with several dimensions of a data point being *mapped* to parameters of the sound event. Here, one can easily arrange the data in different orders (e.g., choose subsets by certain criteria or by navigation input).

Model-based data representation employs more complex mediation between data and sound rendering by introducing a model whose properties are informed by the data. Such models can capture domain knowledge, and they transfer well to different application domains.

13.3.3   A Theory of Sonification

The *Sonification Design Space Map* (de Campo, 2007, 2009) puts all these notions in 1 context and suggests various sonification strategies to experiment with, based on general data properties (number of data points, number of data dimensions), current working hypotheses (which data subset sizes are expected to contain patterns), and perceptual considerations (most important, sonifying data subsets within time frames suitable for human working memory). Within this conceptual framework, the map supports reasoning about the next experimental design steps. Successive design choices can often be likened to movements on the map.

13.4   Basic Sonification Concepts

The 2 central decisions in designing a sonification are *mapping* (which data properties should control which aspects of the sounds created) and *time scaling* (how many data points should be rendered within a time frame that allows for perception as 1 auditory gestalt, ca. 2–3 secs.).

13.4.1   Mapping

Mapping data onto perceptible aspects of sounds requires familiarity with auditory sensations and their physical correlates. We consider a few prominent cases here.

Pitch—frequency: The human ear resolves pitch very well; in the middle range, one can discern frequency modulations of less than 0.5%, and for individual tones, about 1% (or 1/6 of a semitone) can be distinguished. Such a threshold is called the just-noticeable difference (JND). Extrapolated to a range of 100–6000 Hz, this allows for about 400 distinguishable steps.
Loudness—amplitude: For amplitude, the JND is between 0.5 and 1 dB for most sounds, so given a usable dynamic range of 50 dB, this is roughly 50–100 resolvable steps. Listeners always adjust to drifting dynamics, so amplitude is not a good choice for rendering high-resolution data. However, one can use amplitude in parallel renderings to portray importance as weighting: softer sounds will draw less attention in a complex sound scene, which may express their background role correctly.
Localization—spatial position: Although humans can detect changes in direction of a physical sound source on the order of a few degrees, panning as implemented on most audio systems relies on phantom sources created by energy distribution across speakers; outside the sweet spot, however, this often fails. Thus, relying on fine panning resolution is not recommended. However, for distinguishing parallel auditory streams, panning is very efficient, especially if multiple loudspeakers are used.
Timbre: Although there is no general definition of timbre, most other properties are subsumed under it, and some can be used in sonification. For instance, brightness works as a perceptual concept for most listeners, whereas auditory resolution will depend on the particular synthesis algorithm. One can always programmatically generate examples for the range intended to be used and try to verify good ranges of variation.

Many dimensions interact; for example, amplitude and frequency: sine tones below 200 Hz and above about 10 kHz will appear progressively softer, while sine tones between 2 and 4 kHz will appear louder. These curves, first measured by Fletcher and Munson (1933), have been the basis for many standards for equal loudness measurement In SC3, the `AmpComp` and `AmpCompA` classes provide compensation for this dependency.

Understanding meaning in sonifications depends crucially on the metaphors implied. Consider rendering measured temperature: higher temperature may be mapped to higher pitch, higher event density, higher volume, brighter sound quality, and so on; both polarity and scaling of the numerical ranges, as well as choices for other mapped parameters, will influence how easily a sonification design is understood by its intended listeners.

13.4.2   Time Scaling

To find patterns in data, one needs a working hypothesis on which data subset sizes may contain patterns. Patterns may occur at different scales, such as near-repetitions of groups of 10 data points or slow trends over millions of data points. A single sonification design is unlikely to render both as easily perceptible gestalts, but designs with flexible time scaling may well work adaptively for a wide range of data subset sizes and ordering choices.

13.4.3   A Small Example

Our first example is based on experiments with sonifying social data in 1998 (de Campo and Egger de Campo, 1999); it shows sonification variants with a simple data set. The data are social statistics,[4] namely, the number of death penalties carried out in the United States since reinstatement of the death penalty in 1977 up to 2007, split into 4 regions: the Northeast, West, Midwest, and South; we include data for the entire United States and for the state of Texas.

To prepare, we load the data into memory (see figure 13.1).

Then we play the data as discrete events. This design maps data values of 0 to 76 to MIDI notes between 36 and 112, into a total time of 5 seconds (see figure 13.2).

Next, we try continuous sonification. This design maps data values of 0–76 to frequencies from 200 to 4000 Hz. Note that data value interpolation does not seem very suitable here (see figure 13.3).

In the original discussions on sonifying these data, we reached agreement that a value of, for example, 5 should be represented by 5 countable sound events, and a value of 0 by silence. This also suggests providing a ticking sound to indicate the beginning of each year. Third, panning the sound to 4 speakers should be possible for playing multiple regions in parallel. The final design scales 1 year to 2 seconds, resulting in a total presentation time of 1 minute, and maps data values to pulses per period (see figure 13.4). The 4 regions sequentially are in figure 13.5. The 4 regions in parallel are in figure 13.6.

13.5   Tour d'Horizon of Sonifications

Many works of code art can also be considered sonifications; for instance, Fredrik Olofsson's *redWorm*, *redSnail*, and *redSnake* (see the Examples folder included with

```
(
q = q ? ();
q.execdata = ();
q.execdata.years = (1977 .. 2008);
    // data is: [total for each region, 1977 ... 2007];
q.execdata.regions = (
    Total: [1099,1,0,2,0,1,2,5,21,18,18,25,11,16,23,14,31,38,31,
            56,45,74,68,98,85,66,71,65,59,60,53,42,37],
    Northeast: [4,0,0,0,0,0,0,0,0,0,0,0,0,0,0,0,0,0,0,0,2,0,0,0,1,0,0,
                0,0,0,1,0,0,0],
    Midwest: [129,0,0,0,0,1,0,0,0,1,0,0,0,1,5,1,1,4,3,11,9,10,5,12,5,
              10,9,7,7,14,6,5,2],
    South: [933,0,0,1,0,0,2,5,21,16,18,24,10,13,17,13,26,30,26,41,29,
            60,55,74,76,50,61,57,50,43,44,36,35],
    West: [67,1,0,1,0,0,0,0,0,1,0,1,1,2,1,0,4,4,2,2,7,4,8,11,4,4,1,0,
           2,2,3,1,0],
    Texas: [423,0,0,0,0,0,1,0,3,6,10,6,3,4,4,5,12,17,14,19,3,37,20,
            35,40,17,33,24,23,19,24,26,18]
);
q.getReg = { |q, regName| q.execdata.regions[regName].drop(1) };
)
```

Figure 13.1
Loading the data.

```
(
Pbindef(\exec,
    \note, Pseq(q.getReg(\Midwest)),
    \octave, 3,
    \dur, 5 / q.execdata.years.size
).play;
)
    // the different regions
Pbindef(\exec, \note, Pseq(q.getReg(\Northeast)));
Pbindef(\exec, \note, Pseq(q.getReg(\West)));
Pbindef(\exec, \note, Pseq(q.getReg(\South)));
```

Figure 13.2
Mapping the data to pitch in discrete events.

```
b = Buffer.sendCollection(s, q.getReg(\Northeast), 1);
(
Ndef(\exec, { |dur = 5, scale=50, offset=200|
    var vals = PlayBuf.ar(1, b, dur / SampleRate.ir );
    Pan2.ar(
        SinOsc.ar(vals  * scale + offset), 0,
        EnvGen.kr(Env.linen(0.01, dur, 0.01, 0.2), doneAction: 2)
    );
}).play;
)
    // load other regions into buffer
b.sendCollection(q.getReg(\Midwest));    Ndef(\exec).send;
b.sendCollection(q.getReg(\West));      Ndef(\exec).send;
b.sendCollection(q.getReg(\South));      Ndef(\exec).send;
```

Figure 13.3
Continuous data sonification.

```
(
SynthDef( "noisepulses", { arg out = 0, sustain=1.0, numPulses = 0,
pan = 0.0, amp = 0.2;
    Out.ar(out,
        PanAz.ar(4,
            PinkNoise.ar
            * Decay2.ar(Impulse.ar(numPulses / sustain, 0,
numPulses.sign), 0.001, 0.2),
            pan,
            EnvGen.kr( Env.linen(0.0, 0.995, 0.0), levelScale: amp,
timeScale: sustain, doneAction: 2)
        )
    );
}).add;
SynthDef(\tick, { |out, amp=0.2, pan|
    OffsetOut.ar(out, Pan2.ar(Impulse.ar(0) * Line.kr(amp, amp,
0.001, doneAction: 2), pan))
}).add;
)
(instrument: \noisepulses, numPulses: 10, legato: 1, dur: 2).play;
(instrument: \tick).play
```

Figure 13.4
Sound design with noise pulses.

```
(
Tdef(\execs, {
    var yearDur = 2;     // one year is 2 seconds
    var region, numExecs, numyears = q.execdata.years.size;
    [\Northeast, \Midwest, \West, \South].do { |regName, i|

        region = q.execdata.regions[regName].postln;
        q.execdata.years.do { |year, i|
            numExecs = region[i + 1];
            [regName, year, numExecs].postln;
            (instrument: \tick).play;
            if (numExecs > 0) {
                (instrument: \noisepulses, legato: 1,
                    numPulses: numExecs, dur: yearDur).play;
            };
            yearDur.wait;
        };
        yearDur.wait;
    };
}).play;
```

Figure 13.5
Four regions in sequence.

SC) pick an open text document and walk along its characters, playing sounds dependent on the characters they find (see also chapter 23).

The same piece of code can often be seen in different ways. For instance,

```
{SinOsc.ar([MouseX.kr(200, 3000, 1), MouseY.kr(200, 3000, 1)]) * 0.01 }.
play;
```

can be considered a minimalist duophonic instrument. But when it is surreptitiously sent to play on other musicians' computers in a networked live coding performance,[5] it becomes a virus softly sonifying their mouse movements.

Chaos UGens such as QuadN, HenonL, GbManC, and many others employ iterative functions and differential equations with chaotic behavior for generating sound. These could be considered audifications of the data sequence that is generated by these functions:

```
{HenonC.ar(2000, LFNoise2.kr([1, 1], 0.2, 1.4), 0.14) * 0.2 }.play(s);
```

The sonification of Emil Post's *Tag Systems*[6] applies sonification in experimental mathematics. Symbolic systems can show intractable behavior for some initial

```
(
// four channels playing, ordered by total number.
// On stereo systems, only the first 2 channels play.
Tdef(\execs, {
    var yearDur = 2;      // one year is 2 seconds
    q.execdata.years.do { |year, i|
    var region, numExecs, numyears = q.execdata.years.size;
        // ordered by total number, on stereo, only first 2 play.
    [\South, \Midwest,  \West, \Northeast ].do { |regName, j|

        region = q.execdata.regions[regName].postln;
            numExecs = region[i + 1];
            [regName, year, numExecs].postln;
            (instrument: \tick).play;
            if (numExecs > 0) {
                (instrument: \noisepulses, legato: 1,
                    dur: yearDur,
                    numPulses: numExecs,
                    pan: j * 0.5 - 0.25    // to 4 channels
                ).play;
            };
        };
        yearDur.wait;
    };
}).play;
)
```

Figure 13.6
Four regions in parallel.

conditions—in the case of universal machines these conditions may be inherently undecidable (De Mol, 2007); since the human ear is very sensitive to subtle varieties of repetition, a sonification of such algorithms reveals characteristic patterns very quickly (see figure 13.7).

Sturmian sequences show interesting formal properties and have been used for ventures between mathematics and musical composition by, for instance, Tom Johnson and Jean-Paul Allouch; the piece "Sturmian Constellations" by J. Rohrhuber is available on the book Web site. These are applications where sonification lets us explore complex consequences of simple formal rules, and where the object of measurement is not external to the device being measured in the strict sense.

To finish this necessarily incomplete tour, we visit 3 applications realized within SonEnvir[7] and then move on to longer examples.

```
(
// compare two axioms on left and right channels
// ? = 4 (size of alphabet)
// v (deletion number) varies [1..6] with horizontal cursor position
{
    var tag, rules, val;
    rules = [[0, 1, 1], [1, 3, 2, 0], [1, 2], [3, 1, 1]]; // same rule for both
    v = MouseX.kr(1, 6);
    val = dup {
        var axiom = Array.fill(14, { #[0, 1, 2, 3].choose }); axiom.join.postln;
        Duty.ar(1 / SampleRate.ir, 0,  Dtag(7e5, v, axiom, rules), doneAction:2);
    } * 0.1
}.play;
)
```

Figure 13.7
Sonification of tag systems.

In neurology, we designed sonifications for 2 clinical usage scenarios (de Campo et al., 2007). With patients who may have neurological disorders, one often makes long-term EEG recordings, up to 36 hours. Screening these is time-consuming and demanding; the EEGScreener provides acoustical screening as a complementary option.

EEG recordings in clinics are supervised by watching the patient on a video screen and looking at EEG data being recorded; this is difficult to concentrate on for several hours. The EEGRealtimePlayer (see figure 13.8) provides continuous sonification of the live EEG signals; personnel can quickly habituate to the typical soundscape created but notice any sudden changes, and thus can intervene when necessary.

In physics, the Ising and Potts models are commonly used to study the behavior of complex dynamical systems. For these, we implemented both the running models themselves (see figure 13.9) and different audification and sonification strategies in SC3 (Vogt et al., 2007).

In sociology and other fields, data are often geographically distributed. The *Wahlgesänge* (in German, "whale songs" and "election songs" sound identical) sonification is intended to explore such data (see de Campo et al., 2006). The idea is adapted from a model-based sonification concept called data sonogram (Hermann, 2002), and the implementation is based on an example implementation by Till Bovermann. The data are laid out on a 2D map, and by clicking somewhere on the map, a shock wave expands from this center (see figure 13.10); as the wave hits data points, sound is produced based on the points' data values. Thus the spatial distribution of 1 data

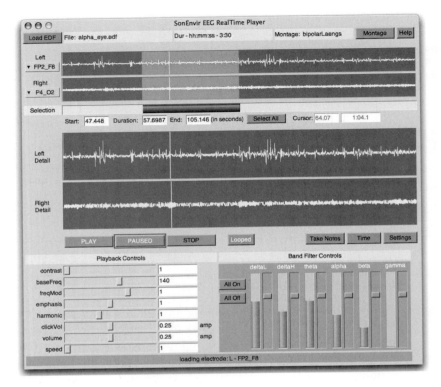

Figure 13.8
The `EEGRealtimePlayer` graphical user interface.

dimension (here, election results) is sonified, and one can explore it interactively by clicking in different regions.

13.6 Auditory Displays in Human-Computer Interaction

The current practice of designing the interaction between humans and technology is dominated by visual means. Devices make little use of hearing to convey information (e.g., the Apple iPod has a single auditory cue as part of its user interface: the virtual click of the wheel. This makes the device almost inaccessible without looking at the screen).

Alternative interaction modalities will play an increasingly important role in HCI in the future: First, the emerging interaction paradigms in fields such as mobile and pervasive computing demand nonvisual interfaces to fit the constraints imposed by the user's mobility or the environment (e.g., changing the music on an iPod while bike riding is still hazardous). Second, the miniaturization of devices restricts the

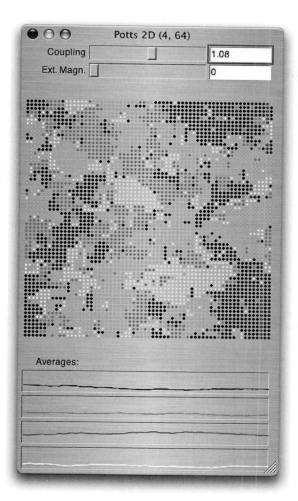

Figure 13.9
The user interface for the running Potts model.

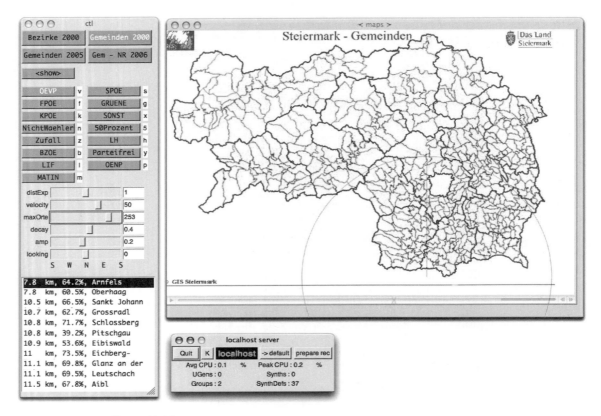

Figure 13.10
The interface for the *Wahlgesänge* sonification.

space available for visual screens (e.g., mobile phones integrated in wearable items
such as watches). And finally, visually dominated interaction with technology prevents equal access for users with visual impairments.

Auditory display is a promising candidate to address these issues. A key requirement for auditory display research is the availability of efficient and flexible means
to create sound that can be designed for interaction with users. SuperCollider is increasingly recognized by the community as a powerful system to facilitate such research prototypes. We discuss an auditory menu navigation system implemented in
SC3 as 1 example.

A prototype was developed to provide audio-only access to a complex menu structure such as is found in many desktop applications, such as e-mail clients and Internet browsers. To organize the menu items, it implemented a spatial metaphor in a
virtual audio environment: the user was positioned in front of a big horizontal dial

which could be rotated, with the menu items located on its edge. Menu items were represented by synthesized speech, and users used a game pad to rotate the dial to bring the desired menu item to the front and then select it. Several nonspeech sounds supported the metaphor, such as a rolling sound for rotation and a swishing sound for entering submenus. A recording is provided on the book Web site (*Auditory _Menu_demo.mp3*; see also Frauenberger and Stockman, 2006).

SuperCollider was a very suitable environment for realizing this prototype. The HRTF rendering package AmbIEM (available now as a quark) allowed construction of convincing virtual environments with several sound sources and real-world room simulation, as well as support for HID devices, made designing the interaction straightforward. Because of its server-client architecture SuperCollider lends itself to being embedded in other systems, and sound synthesis servers like SC may become a standard component of operating systems, in order to create a more complete and efficient user experience when interacting with technology.

13.7 Juggling Sounds

Juggling is a complex activity; throwing and catching several objects in aesthetically satisfying ways is quite difficult. As with any art involving physical skill, jugglers need to develop automatisms for movements, allowing them to spend less effort on monitoring single throws and to focus instead on the flow of performed patterns and transitions. Progressing toward technical perfection literally creates headroom for reflection on the artistic statement. That said, the training situation benefits from close monitoring of the juggling movements for improving skills-related aspects such as precision and hand-to-hand symmetry (see figure 13.11).

JugglingSounds was developed by Till Bovermann with Jonas Groten (Bovermann et al., 2007) within SonEnvir in 2006. It represents the motions of juggling clubs in real time, using spatialized sounds surrounding the artist. This provides monitoring for the juggler *(How precise is the timing of my movements right now?)* and supports deeper understanding of juggling-specific dynamics in a kinesiological context. It may heighten awareness of motion details for both jugglers and audiences, and may possibly serve as a juggling display for visually impaired people. Finally, juggling to juggling-controlled sound is enriching and enjoyable for both audience and performer.

For flexible experimentation, JugglingSounds combines direct mappings of low-level feature streams with detected events for controlling sound synthesis. The feature streams are based on real-time position and orientation of the juggling clubs (acquired with a Vicon motion-tracking system running at 120 Hz). We derived rotation velocity, absolute position in the room (xyz coordinates), and position and distance relative to the juggler's head from these streams. Discrete triggers were

Figure 13.11
Jonas Groten juggling with tracking markers applied.

generated when a club crossed 1 of 6 specified horizontal planes, as well as the lateral (left/right) and the coronal plane (behind/in front) of the juggler's head. (For details on interfacing and data handling, see chapter 4).

We focused on sonifying 3-club juggling (roughly, throwing clubs into the air in different patterns and catching them) and 2-club swinging (holding a club in each hand and rotating them in different patterns), as these approaches differ both in the clubs' motions and the artist's need for information.

We created 5 different sonification designs (all using ProxySpace, see chapter 7, and requiring tracking data to be present), each focusing on different aspects of the juggling performance (see figure 3.12).

Although the rotation speed of each club controls the triggering rate of a grain stream, each individual grain's pitch is directly coupled to the height of its club. As rotation speeds and heights become more consistent, the grain streams become more similar (see figure 13.13).

Every full rotation cycle of a club triggers a sound with a resonant pitch determined by its current height. Since the sound is triggered when the club's rotational axis is at a specific angle (e.g., horizontal), the timing pattern of identical angles for

```
(
~rotater = {|amp = 1|
    var rotVel = ~rotVel.kr;     // rotVel and height from tracking
data proxies
    BPF.ar(
        Impulse.ar((rotVel > 0.5) * rotVel * 5).lag(0.0001),
        (~height.kr * 120 + 36 + [[0, 7], [0, 12], [0, 16]]).midicps,
        0.2
    ).collect({ |pair| (pair * [1, 0.125]).sum }).          * 6 * amp
};
)
```

Figure 13.12
Rotational Grain Train.

```
(
~planeTicker = {|saw2sin = 1, filterFreq = 2000, fSpread = 0.4, amp = 0.1|

    var freq = 3000 * fSpread * (~height.kr * 4 - 1).range(0.5, 2);

    var src = SelectX.ar(
        saw2sin,
        [LFSaw.ar(freq) , SinOsc.ar(freq)]
    )
    * Decay2.ar(
        Trig1.ar(~zeroCrossing.ar, 0.001) * 0.1,
        0.001,
        0.3
    );

    LPF.ar(src, filterFreq, mul: amp * 0.1)
};
)
```

Figure 13.13
Rotation Trigger.

```
(
~backCross = {|amp = 1|
    var     numObj = 3;
    var     in = ~isLeft.kr(numObj);
    var     height = ~height.kr(numObj),
            front = ~isFront.kr(numObj);
    var aEnv, fEnv, aEnvNoise;

    var trig = Trig1.ar((in - Delay1.kr(in)).abs - 1, 0.00001) > 0.5;
    // only trigger if behind the body and near ground
    trig = trig * (front < 0) * (height < 0.26);
    aEnv = EnvGen.kr(Env.perc(0.05, 2), gate: trig);
    aEnvNoise = EnvGen.kr(Env.perc(0.01, 0.1), gate: trig);
    fEnv = EnvGen.kr(
        Env.perc(0.01, 0.1), gate: trig,
        levelScale: 900, levelBias: 50
    );

    aEnv * ((0.2 * WhiteNoise.ar * aEnvNoise) +
    SinOsc.ar(fEnv * (height * 8).squared * 0.4, 0, 1.5).softclip) *
    amp
};
)
```

Figure 13.14
Distances to the head.

the different clubs becomes audible. The juggler can hear the throwing accuracy attained in both time and height (see figure 13.14).

This sonification captures and mediates much of the inherent dynamics of juggling. Each juggling pattern creates its own characteristic sound pattern (see figure 13.15).

Each crossing of a club through the lateral plane triggers a sound whose pitch corresponds to the club's height, with different sounds for in front of and behind the head (see figure 13.16).

We designed a discrete level indicator by placing several virtual horizontal planes in the air at equidistant heights, each linked to a differently pitched resonator. Each crossing of a club triggers a sound grain with different sound characteristics for up or down movement.

These sonification designs are best understood by seeing the juggling performance and hearing the sonifications together, as provided in the example videos on the book Web site.

```
(
~distances = {|amp = 0.2795|
    LFSaw.ar(min((~dist.kr * 2.5 * 90 + 20).midicps, 44100)) * amp
};
)
```

Figure 13.15
Left-right trigger.

```
(

~clackUp = { |amp = 0.1|
    Formlet.ar(
        ~trigsUp.ar.lag(0.0004),
        (~height.kr).exprange(25, 2500),
        0.002,
        0.05
    )
    * (~height.kr * 4 ** 2)
    * amp
};
)
```

Figure 13.16
Rain on bells.

13.8   Two Sonification Concert Pieces

The following 2 pieces were created for the ICAD 2006 concert "Global Sound—The World by Ear."[8] The concert call invited sonifications of social data of 190 nations, with 48 data dimensions ranging from such basic statistics as state population and area, to GDP (gross domestic product) per capita, to the percentage of good access to water and sanitation for each population.

13.8.1   "Navegar É Preciso, Viver Não É Preciso"

For "Navegar" (de Campo and Dayé, 2006) we combined the given geographical data with a time/space coordinates data set of historical significance: the route of Magellan's expedition to the Moluccan Islands (1519–1522), the first circumnavigation of the globe.

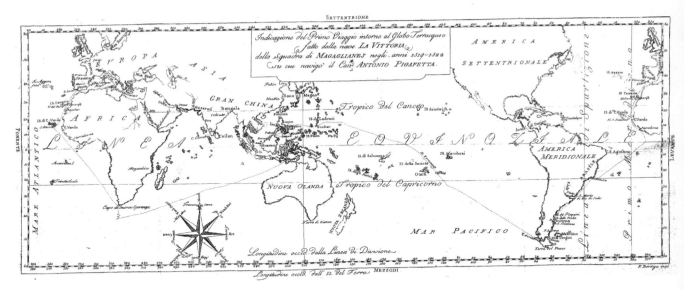

Figure 13.17
The map of Magellan's travel route given in Pigafetta (1530). This image is courtesy of the University Library Graz, Austria.

Navigation has exerted a major influence on world history; drastic changes began with expeditions by Díaz, Columbus, and da Gama.[9] Magellan's voyage was reported by Antonio Pigafetta (1530, 1525), and novelists (e.g., Zweig, 1938) and historians have recounted the story.

In August 1519, Magellan departed for the Spice Islands with 5 ships and a crew of 270. They looked for a passage to the Pacific near today's Argentina, where winter storms forced them to wait for 6 months. One ship sank, another deserted; 3 ships found the passage in October 1520 and headed across the Pacific, toward the Philippines. They landed on several islands there, and on Mactan, Magellan was killed by natives.

The crew (now down to 115 people) and 2 ships continued. They reached the Spice Islands in November 1521. Only the *Victoria* sailed across the Indian Ocean in December 1521, and rounded southern Africa with only rice for food. In September 1522, the *Victoria* reached Spain with a crew of 18 and 26 tons of spices, including cloves and cinnamon. One is reminded of Caetano Veloso, who, pondering the mentality and fate of the Argonauts, wrote in a song: "Navegar é preciso, viver não é preciso" (Seafaring is necessary, living is not). (See figure 13.17.)

Table 13.1
Mappings of Data to Sonification Parameters in "Navegar"

Data Dimension	Sonification Parameter
GDP per capita of country	Central frequency of the resonator group
Ratio of top 20% to bottom 20%	Pitches of the inner 2 satellite resonators
Ratio of top 10% to bottom 10%	Pitches of the outer 2 satellite resonators (missing values for these become dense clusters)
Water access	Decay time of resonators (short tones mean dry)
Distance from ship	Volume and attack time (far away is "blurred")
Direction relative to ship	Spatial direction of the stream in the loudspeakers (direction north is constant)
Ship speed, direction, winds	Direction, timbre, and volume of windlike noise

13.8.1.1   Which dimensions to sonify?

We felt that conquistadores today would want to know about a country's economic power and natural resources. For economic power, GDP is a myopic measure, as income is never evenly distributed. The *Gini index* measures this inequality: 0 means equal income for everyone, and 100 is all income for 1 person. So we kept GDP and added the ratios of incomes of the top 10% and bottom 10%, and the top 20% and bottom 20%, as dimensions to sonify. (In Denmark, with the lowest Gini index of 124 nations listed, the top 10% earn 4.5 times more than the bottom 10%; in Namibia, at last rank, the ratio is 128.8:1.)

The ICAD06 Concert data also provided a percentage of population with adequate access to drinking water. Unfortunately, this United Nations indicator has many missing values, so we excluded countries not touched by Magellan's route and substituted data values of neighboring countries for the missing values. (e.g., in France, it is very likely that nearly 100% of the population has good access to drinking water.)

13.8.1.2   Mapping choices

We deliberately chose higher display complexity; though it demands more listener concentration and attention, a more complex piece hopefully invites repeated listening. Every country is represented by a sound stream composed of 5 resonators; all parameters of this sound stream are determined by data properties of the associated country and the navigation process (the ship's distance and direction toward a given country). At any time, the 15 countries nearest to the route are heard, which provides display clarity and reduces CPU load (see table 13.1).

Figure 13.18 shows the sound design: the 10% and 20% ratios are converted to satellite frequencies symmetrically above and below the root; the exciter signal is

```
(
~single = { |rootFreq = 220, outProp = 4.5, inProp = 2.2, attack=0.00, decay = 1.0,
    dens = 2, amp=0.2, x=1, y = 0, step=0.33333|

    var numChans = 4;

    var freqs = rootFreq * [ 1/outProp, 1/inProp, 1, inProp, outProp];

    var exciter = (Dust2.ar(dens * [ 1,2,4,2,1] * 0.07)   // five individual rd
triggers for
                                          // each component, weighted for center
        + Dust2.ar(dens * 0.3))           // + some common attacks
            .clip2(0.5)
            .lag(0.0003)                  // slightly filtered
            * (dens ** -0.5)              // amplitude comp for dust density
        + PinkNoise.ar(0.002)             // some fused background noise
        * (decay ** -0.5);                // amplitude comp. for decay

    var resonator = Formlet.ar( exciter, freqs,
        Ramp.kr(attack, step), decay,
        AmpComp.kr(freqs.max(50))
    ).softclip.sum;

    var pos = atan2(Ramp.kr(y, step), Ramp.kr(x, step)) * (pi.reciprocal) + 1; //
look west.

    PanAz.ar(numChans, LeakDC.ar(resonator, 0.95), pos, Ramp.kr(amp, step));
};
~single.play;
)
```

Figure 13.18
"Navegar": sound design for a single country.

composed of individual random triggers for each resonator, some common pulses, and a noise halo to help perceptual fusion of this aggregate. The resonators use Formlet Ugens so their attack can be softened, which is used to suggest sound source distance.

The code example *PlaySingleCountries.rtf* (on the book Web site) allows direct comparison between countries by switching to the parameters for 1 country at a time. The full piece itself as code and a headphone-rendered audio file are also provided.

13.8.2   "Terra Nullius"

13.8.2.1   Missing data

Social data are measured in many different ways; their numerous dimensions (such as population density, life expectancy, illiteracy) may reveal interesting correlations and give insight into human life on this planet. However, a single parameter may not always mean the same thing, and typically, not every factor is measured equally everywhere. When experimenting with the ICAD 2006 world social data at the Science by Ear workshop,[10] we wrote an event-based system for experiments with combinations of data dimensions. To give the events temporal order, we sorted them by 1 given dimension and along this axis sonified the magnitudes of a number of other dimensions (for instance, sorting by GDP and then interpreting access to drinking water as a frequency value).

But what to do with data sets that lack the measurement we want to sort them by? How to sonify absence? We can leave out that data point, but this affects comparability of the rest of the parameters; we may interpolate missing data, but from which neighbors? There is no general law for correct substitution of missing data. The piece "Terra Nullius" takes this fundamental problem as a starting point (Rohrhuber, 2006).

13.8.2.2   Model and mapping

Imagine a set of countries (or their capitals) within a zone parallel to the equator, starting with latitudes near England (see figure 13.19). Instead of sonifying the existing data values, the missing dimensions of each country are sonified: A broadband noise source is filtered into 48 bands, each representing 1 data dimension. When the country currently being sonified has a missing value in a dimension, the corresponding noise band becomes audible.

We spin the imaginary globe and move eastward: all countries inside the zone are sonified one at a time, ordered by longitude. The noise spectrum pans according to longitude around the ring of speakers. With every round the latitude slice becomes wider and wider, until all countries are included in 1 round.

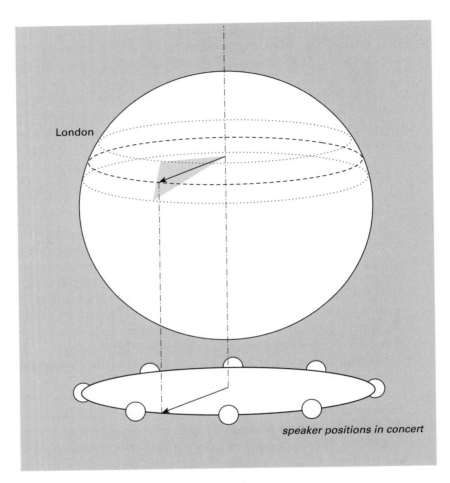

Figure 13.19
"Terra Nullius": moving latitude zone on the globe.

Then the zone narrows again, this time sonified with smaller filter bandwidth, so the dimensions progressively separate more. We end with the latitude and longitude of London. Over time, a background noise on all speakers has slowly faded in and remains as the ending.

Technically, a NodeProxy (see chapter 7) plays the noise bands, and the amplitudes of each spectral band, pan position, and background noise level are set from a task that iterates over the data. Some sorting and task functions are defined: q.makeSelection(10, 40) selects countries by latitude band (here, within 10 degrees of 40 degrees north). q.makeOrder(9) sorts by population density; q.makeCycle(0.04) .play creates a routine with a delta time of 0.04 and plays once around the globe. In the code file (in the Web site materials), these functions can be used to experiment with the sonification. Tdef(\x) plays the entire piece.

Finally, "Terra Nullius" can be regarded as a meditation on the status of missing points in a generalized geometry, as Bernhard Riemann proposed in 1854. Riemann suggested abandoning the conventional idea of a point, and by relying only on quantitative and qualitative *Bestimmungsweisen* (translated as modes of determination), he redefined the concept of dimensionality. The former can be mutually ordered (e.g., different degrees of temperature), but the latter can't (such as temperature with speed). Now missing data is *quantitative* in the sense that it is a possible measurement; if we forget to measure temperature, we still forget to measure *temperature*; by consequence, it should be sortable. But on the other hand, since it is missing, it has no measure and nothing to specify an order, just like any *qualitative* dimension. There is no solution to this dilemma. We can only desist and come back to the only available complete data—a consequence of the very act of measuring—geographical location. To characterize this *terra nullius* by different shades of filtered noise is perhaps the only compromise between quality and quantity: the missing dimension itself is represented by its position in the spectrum, and the absence of the data is represented by the presence of noise; we are left with only the sonification of the act of measuring and its incompleteness.

13.9 Conclusion

Shifts in scientific worldview have always been accompanied by changes in representations, just as inventions of representation have caused paradigm shifts, such as Riemann's generalization of geometry, which became a foundation for Einstein's space-time. In a sense, sonification opens a different perspective on things: listening. For the sciences, this may imply reconsidering underlying premises and rethinking what it is one is looking for; it also may lead to novel ways of didactic representation. For the sonic arts, sonification brings about curiosity toward the origins of sounds and toward a broader cultural and social context. Perhaps sonification is for sound art what documentary is for film. Certainly it is an area open for explorations, full of inspiration and potential insights for sciences and the arts. SuperCollider has become one of the main platforms for sonification research, providing a system in which an equally joyful and rigorous transdisciplinary cooperation is possible—and necessary.

References

Baier, G., T. Hermann, and U. Stephani. 2007. "Event-Based Sonification of EEG Rhythms in Real Time." *Clinical Neurophysiology*, 118(6): 1377–1386.

Ballora, M. 2000. "Data Analysis Through Auditory Display: Applications in Heart Rate Variability." Ph.D. thesis, McGill University.

Barrass, S. 1997. "Auditory Information Design." Ph.D. thesis, Australian National University.

Bovermann, T., J. Groten, A. de Campo, and G. Eckel. 2007. "Juggling Sounds." In *Proceedings of the 2nd International Workshop on Interactive Sonification.*

Conner, C. D. 2005. *A People's History of Science: Miners, Midwives and "Low Mechanicks."* New York: Nation Books.

de Campo, A. 2009. "Science by Ear: An Interdisciplinary Approach to Sonifying Scientific Data." Ph.D. thesis, University for Music and Dramatic Arts, Graz, Austria.

de Campo, A. 2007. "Toward a Data Sonification Design Space Map." In *Proceedings of the 13th International Conference on Auditory Display (ICAD)*, pp. 342–347. Montreal: Schulich School of Music, McGill University.

de Campo, A., and C. Dayé. 2006. "Navegar É Preciso, Viver Não É Preciso." In *Proceedings of the 12th International Conference on Auditory Display* (ICAD). London: Department of Computer Science, Queen Mary University.

de Campo, A., and M. Egger de Campo. 1999. "Sonification of Social Data." In *Proceedings of the 1999 International Computer Music Conference* (ICMC).

de Campo, A., C. Frauenberger, K. Vogt, A. Wallisch, and C. Dayé. 2006. "Sonification as an Interdisciplinary Working Process." In *Proceedings of the 12th International Conference on Auditory Display* (ICAD), pp. 28–35. London: Department of Computer Science, Queen Mary University.

de Campo, A., A. Wallisch, R. Hoeldrich, and G. Eckel. (2007). "New Sonification Tools for EEG Data Screening and Monitoring." In *Proceedings of the International Conference on Auditory Display (ICAD)*, Montreal, Canada.

De Mol, L. 2007. "Tracing Unsolvability: A Mathematical, Historical and Philosophical Analysis with a Special Focus on Tag Systems." Ph.D. thesis, University of Ghent, Belgium.

Dombois, F. 2001. "Using Audification in Planetary Seismology." In *Proceedings of the 7th International Conference on Auditory Display* (ICAD).

Drake, S. 1980. *Galileo.* New York: Oxford University Press.

Fitch, W. T., and G. Kramer. 1994. "Sonifying the Body Electric: Superiority of an Auditory over a Visual Display in a Complex Multivariate System." In *Auditory Display*, G. Kramer, ed., pp. 307–326. Reading, MA: Addison-Wesley.

Fletcher, H., and W. A. Munson. 1933. "Loudness, Its Definition, Measurement, and Calculation." *Journal of the Acoustical Society of America*, 5:82–108.

Frauenberger, C., and T. Stockman. 2006. "Patterns in Auditory Menu Design." In *Proceedings of the 12th International Conference on Auditory Display* (ICAD). London: Department of Computer Science, Queen Mary University.

Gaver, W. W., Smith, R. B., and O'Shea, T. 1991. "Effective Sounds in Complex Systems: The ARKola Simulation." In *Proceedings of CHI '91*, pp. 85–90. New York: ACM Press.

Hayward, C. 1994. "Listening to the Earth Sing." In *Auditory Display*, G. Kramer, ed., pp. 369–404. Reading, MA: Addison-Wesley.

Hermann, T. 2002. "Sonification for Exploratory Data Analysis." Ph.D. thesis, Bielefeld University, Germany.

Hermann, T., G. Baier, U. Stephani, and H. Ritter. 2006. "Vocal Sonification of Pathologic EEG Features." In *Proceedings of the 12th International Conference on Auditory Display* (ICAD), pp. 158–163. London: Department of Computer Science, Queen Mary University.

Hinterberger, T., and G. Baier. 2005. "POSER: Parametric Orchestral Sonification of EEG in Real-Time for the Self-Regulation of Brain States." *IEEE Multimedia*, special issue on sonification, 12(2):70–79.

Kramer, G. 1994a. "An Introduction to Auditory Display." In *Auditory Display: Sonification, Audification, and Auditory Interfaces*, G. Kramer, ed. Reading, MA: Addison-Wesley.

Kramer, G., ed. 1994b. *Auditory Display: Sonification, Audification, and Auditory Interfaces*. Reading, MA: Addison-Wesley.

McKusick, V. A., W. D. Sharpe, and A. O. Warner. 1957. "Harvey Tercentenary: An Exhibition on the History of Cardiovascular Sound Including the Evolution of the Stethoscope." *Bulletin of the History of Medicine*, 31: 463–487.

Pereverzev, S. V., A. Loshak, S. Backhaus, J. C. Davies, and R. E. Packard. 1997. "Quantum Oscillations Between Two Weakly Coupled Reservoirs of Superfluid 3 He." *Nature*, 388(449): 449–451.

Pigafetta, A. 1530. *Primo viaggio intorno al globo terracqueo*. Milan: Giuseppe Galeazzi.

Pigafetta, A. 2001. *Mit Magellan um die Erde*. Lenningen, Germany: Edition Erdmann. (1st ed., Paris, 1525.)

Riemann, B. [1854] 1867. "Über die Hypothesen, welche der Geometrie zugrunde liegen." *Abhandlungen der Königlichen Gesellschaft der Wissenschaften zu Göttingen*, 13.

Riess, F., and Heering, P. 2005. "Reconstructing Galileo's Inclined Plane Experiments for Teaching Purposes." In *Proceedings of the 8th Conference on International Philosophy, Sociology and Science Teaching*.

Rohrhuber, J. 2006. "Terra Nullius." In *Proceedings of the 12th International Conference on Auditory Display*. London: Department of Computer Science, Queen Mary University.

Speeth, S. D. 1961. "Seismometer sounds." *Journal of the Acoustical Society of America*, 33: 909– 916.

Urick, R. J. 1967. *Principles of Underwater Sound*. New York: McGraw-Hill.

Vogt, K., W. Plessas, A. de Campo, C. Frauenberger, and G. Eckel. 2007. "Sonification of Spin Models: Listening to Phase Transitions in the Ising and Potts model." In *Proceedings of the 13th International Conference on Auditory Display* (ICAD), pp. 258–265. Schulich School of Music, McGill University.

Wedensky, N. 1883. "Die telefonische Wirkungen des erregten Nerven" (The Telephonic Effects of the Excited Nerve). Centralblatt für medizinische Wissenschaften, XXI(26): 465–468.

Zweig, S. (1938). *Magellan—Der Mann und seine Tat.* Frankfurt am Main, 1983. First ed. Vienna, 1938.

Notes

1. See <http://www.icad.org>.

2. See <http://sonenvir.at>.

3. See <http://www.sonification.de> and <http://www.techfak.uni-bielefeld.de/ags/ni>.

4. The data are taken from the file *exest.csv*, downloaded from <http://www.ojp.usdoj.gov/bjs/cp.htm> December 29, 2007.

5. This is an example written for the networked ensemble powerbooks_unplugged; see <http://pbup.goto10.org>.

6. Available from <http://sourceforge.net/projects/sc3-plugins>.

7. These are all documented in the SonEnvir data collection at <http://sonenvir.at/data>, and the code can be obtained from the sonenvir svn repository.

8. See the ICAD 2006 concert call at <http://www.dcs.qmul.ac.uk/research/imc/icad2006/concert.php>. See also the Web site for the papers and audio files of the pieces.

9. Both the art of navigation outside Europe, especially in Polynesia, and the history of knowledge acquisition about navigation, maps, and mapmaking, are covered by Conner (2005).

10. See <http://sonenvir.at/workshop> for documentation.

14   Spatialization with SuperCollider

Marije A. J. Baalman and Scott Wilson

14.1   Spatial Sound

The notion of spatial sound is a tautology, as sound is a spatial phenomenon in itself. Sound is a wave phenomenon, which means that it is not in 1 specific location but fills the medium, although its strength at certain points may vary. Sound can be caused by movement of an object and can be transported in a solid, gas, or fluid.

If there is a sound source at a certain position in space, the acoustic wave will propagate outward in all directions. Only when there are changes in the medium (such as an obstacle, wind, or, more generally, a transition to another medium) will the propagation direction change. At the borders between media, part of the energy of the wave will be transmitted into the other medium, and part of it will be reflected. An example of transmitted energy would be a discotheque whose windows are vibrating as a result of loud music. What you hear coming through the windows has been transmitted. Reflections create what is usually referred to as room acoustics.

Within room acoustics, reflections are distinguished in 3 zones within the impulse response: very early reflections (also referred to as pseudo-direct sound), up to circa 5 ms after the direct sound; early reflections, up to 80–100 ms; and reverb, everything above 80–100 ms. For the very early and early reflections we can distinguish, or at least have a sense of, the direction from which the reflection is coming; this is the information which helps us get an idea of the location of the sound (especially the distance) and also the size of the sounding object. The reverb gives us an overall sense of the acoustics of the room and a feeling of envelopment. The ratio between the level of the direct sound and the reverb gives us a sense of presence of the sounding object. For reverb we can distinguish around 8 directions (Sonke and De Vries, 1997).

14.2   Spatial Perception

Our spatial perception has its biological roots as a warning system: we need to know where a sound comes from, so we can direct our visual attention to it and determine whether the sound is coming from something we can eat or from something that wants to eat us (or to warn us of any other danger). We can distinguish spatial properties of sound because we have 2 ears, so we can compare the 2 different signals. Generally, we can compare the time difference (called the interaural time difference or ITD) and the level difference (interaural level difference or ILD) of the signals that reach our ears; the first is a result of the difference in the path length a sound has traveled to each ear, and the second is a result of both the difference in path length and the masking effect of our head. Our spatial perception can be quite accurate in the horizontal plane, down to 1 or 2 degrees right in front of the head and varying somewhat, depending on the type of sound. In the vertical plane the accuracy is bit more crude, circa 3 to 5 degrees. It is generally understood that the perception in the horizontal plane is based on the ITD and the ILD, whereas in the vertical plane, the shape of our ears plays a role, as it filters the sound in a specific way (Blauert, 1997). Furthermore, head movements help us while locating a sound.

Apparent source width is often related to the interaural cross correlation coefficient (IACC) (Ando, 1985), which is a measure of how closely the 2 ear signals are correlated with one another.

Reflections help us determine the location of a sound; they also give us a feeling of the presence of and envelopment by the sound.

Finally, different locations of sounds help us distinguish between different streams of sound. This is one aspect of what is generally known as the "cocktail party effect." That is, even when everyone around us is talking, we can focus our attention on our conversation partner and choose to listen to what he or she says. This effect can be used similarly in composition: different melodies played from different locations will be perceived as separate melodies, whereas if they come from the same location, they may be perceived as a single, more complex melody. Put another way, spatial location helps us to segregate audio into separate streams of information.

14.3   Standard Spatial Techniques in SuperCollider

Before creating multichannel sound with SuperCollider, you must configure the server to output an appropriate number of channels to your sound card:

```
s = Server.local;
// if you have 16 channels to output:
s.options.numOutputBusChannels = 16;
s.boot; // must configure this before booting
```

14.3.1   Multichannel Signals in SuperCollider

Multichannel signals in SuperCollider are represented as Arrays. Although a detailed discussion of Arrays in SC (and, indeed, of SC's extensive Collections support in general) is beyond the scope of this chapter, the reader is encouraged to become familiar with this aspect of SC, as it is very useful for the manipulation (i.e., mixing, routing, etc.) of multiple channels. Multichannel expansion (see chapter 1 and the *MultiChannel* Help file) provides an elegant way to create multichannel signals.

14.3.2 Monophony

The simplest way to place a sound somewhere spatially is to let it come from a specific loudspeaker. When you have several speakers, this is called multiple mono. It is a method which will always result in a perceptually correct spatialization, as the loudspeaker functions as a point source. Multiple mono can be used for serial compositional techniques in which the location of the sound is serialized. Another use can be stream segregation as described above (see figure 14.1).

14.3.3 Pairwise Panning (Stereophony) and Its Extensions

Stereophony is a way to simulate a spatial field by sending 2 different signals to 2 speakers. The optimal listening position should subtend an angle of 60 degrees between the speakers, or +/–30 degrees from the median plane, as shown in figure 14.2. It is possible to simulate the positioning of a sound between these 2 speakers through *panning* techniques. Many popular "surround" sound techniques have been derived from stereophony, and they extend the pairwise panning paradigm to larger arrays of loudspeakers. Examples include quadraphony (usually where 1 speaker is placed in each corner of a square, but sometimes in other configurations), octophony (most often adjacent speakers at 45 degree angles from each other), Dolby Surround (left, right, center, and a mono "surround" channel, originally matrixed onto 2 channels for use with film), and 5.1 (a normal stereo pair with an additional center speaker, a subwoofer which plays an optional "low frequency effects" channel, and 2 rear surround channels, usually at approximately +/–110 degrees from the median plane).

The normal technique for panning a signal between 2 speakers is as follows. If a sound is to appear to come from in between 2 speakers, each speaker gets a proportion in level of that signal, thus simulating an appropriate ILD. This can be done either with equal power between the 2 channels or with equal amplitude (linear) between them. (The former is perceptually smooth, whereas the latter has an audible dip of –3dB in amplitude when a mono signal is panned to the center.)

Although effective under controlled circumstances, pairwise panning has some important limitations. While a detailed discussion of them is beyond the scope of this chapter (see Rumsey, 2001, for a discussion of this and of spatial audio in general), one is of particular importance: the Precedence Effect, or the Law of the First

```
(
/// basic setup
s = Server.local.boot;

s.doWhenBooted({
    SynthDef( \nicepoc, { |out=0,freq=440,amp=0.1,dur=0.3|
        Out.ar( out, SinOsc.ar( freq, mul: amp )*EnvGen.kr(
Env.perc(0.05,1), timeScale: dur, doneAction:2 ) )
    }).add;
});
)

// mono, 1 channel:
(
p = Pbind(
    \degree, Pseq([0, 3, 5, 6, 7],5),
    \dur, 0.2,
    \instrument, \nicepoc
).play;
)

p.stop;

// multiple mono:
// the melody gets played on both channels, the second note in the
pattern differs,
// so when listening to it, the space "spreads" out
(
p = Pbind(
    \degree, Pseq([0 ,[3,4], 5, 6, 7],5),
    \out, [0,1],
    \dur, 0.2,
    \instrument, \nicepoc
).play;
)

p.stop;
```

Figure 14.1
Mono and multiple mono.

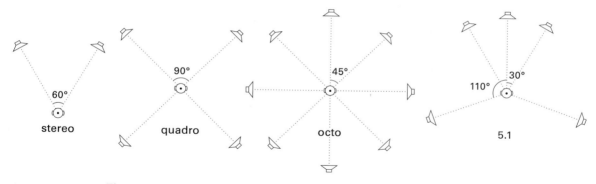

Figure 14.2
Stereophonic configurations, from left to right: stereo, quadro, octophonic, and 5.1.

Wave Front. Pairwise panning assumes that the listener is equidistant from each of the 2 loudspeakers. If the ITD resulting from not being equidistant is greater than about 1 ms, the panning illusion will collapse and the listener will tend to locate the sound in the closer speaker. This has strong implications for multichannel setups, particularly in concert situations where the position of some listeners may be less than ideal. In general, the closer the 2 speakers are to one another, and the farther they are from the listener, the less likely this is to be a problem. Similarly, many multichannel implementations attempt to use pairwise panning between distant and closer speakers, or to pan "through the middle" of a ring of speakers (i.e., the audience area). Though this may achieve a general effect of movement, attempts to simulate locations in between the speakers in such cases are unlikely to be thoroughly convincing.

In SuperCollider there are a number of pairwise panning UGens. Figure 14.3 shows these UGens and their arguments. The 2 basic channel panners are Pan2 and LinPan2 (the "reverse" versions of these are XFade2 and LinXFade2, to mix 2 inputs to 1 channel). With the UGen Balance2 you can correct the balance of a stereo signal. Rotate2 rotates a sound field by taking 2 inputs and rotating them with angle pos; this UGen is actually meant for Ambisonics but also gives interesting effects on a stereo signal.

Pan4 is a quadraphonic panner which pans between left-right and front-back.

PanAz is a multichannel panner with an arbitrary number of channels. It is assumed that the speakers are laid out in a circle at equally spaced angles. The first argument is the number of channels, and the second argument is the input signal. The third is the position in the circle. Channels are evenly spaced over a cyclic period of 2.0 with 0.0 equal to the position directly in front; 2.0/numChans is a clockwise

```
// 2 channel panners:
    Pan2.ar( in, pos, level );
    LinPan2.ar( in, pos, level );
    Balance2.ar( left, right, pos, level );
    Rotate2.ar( x, y, pos );

// 4-channel panner:
    Pan4.ar( in, xpos, ypos, level );

// N-channel panner:
    PanAz.ar( numChans, in, pos, level, width, orientation );

// spread M channels over a stereo field:
    Splay.ar( inArray, spread, level, center, levelComp );

// spread M channels over N channels:
    SplayAz.ar( numChans, inArray, spread, level, width, center,
orientation, levelComp );
```

Figure 14.3
Overview of the different panners in SuperCollider with their argument names.

shift 1/numChans of the way around the ring (–2.0/numChans is a counterclockwise shift by 1 speaker); 4.0/numChans is equal to a shift of 2/numChans; and so on. The width (the fifth argument) is the width of the panning envelope. Normally this is 2.0, which pans between adjacent pairs of speakers. If it is greater than 2.0, the pan will be spread over more speakers, and if it is smaller than 1.0, it will leave gaps between the speakers. The orientation should be 0 when the first speaker is directly in front and 0.5 when the front is halfway between 2 speakers; thus the position directly in front may or may not correspond to a speaker, depending on the setting of this argument. (See also figure 14.4.)

Splay spreads an Array of channels across a stereo field. The first argument is an Array with input channels, and the second argument determines the spread of the channels, where 0 is no spread and 1 is complete spread. The center argument determines the central point around which the channels are spread. levelComp is a Boolean where true means equal power and false means linear. SplayAz does the same thing for a circular setup of equally spaced loudspeakers, like that assumed in the case of PanAz. SelectX and SelectXFocus can be seen as the reverse versions of these panners, selecting a channel from an array of channels.

Some examples using pairwise panner UGens are provided in the Web site materials.

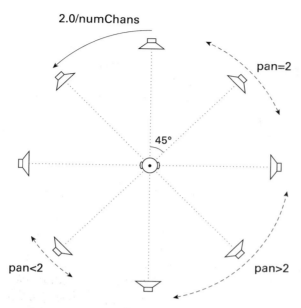

Figure 14.4
Visualisation of the arguments of PanAz.

14.3.4   Delay

With delay lines you can create single echoes of sound or more complex patterns of early reflections. There are a number of delays available in SuperCollider (see also figure 14.5): `Delay`, `Allpass`, `Comb`, `Tap`, and `PingPong`. The first 3 are also available in versions that use a Buffer for their internal memory: `BufDelay`, `BufAllpass` and `BufComb`. Most delays are available with a choice of interpolation scheme: cubic (postfix: `C`, so `DelayC`, etc.), linear (postfix: `L`), and no interpolation (postfix: `N`). Interpolation makes a smoother sound when changing the delay time but is computationally more expensive.

   In the non-buffer versions, the argument `maxdelaytime` is the maximum delay time that can be used. It has to be set when the UGen is created and cannot be changed afterward. In the buffer versions, the size of the buffer determines the maximum delay time. When you want to use long delay times, it is better to use the buffer versions, since the allocation of a large buffer in real time (i.e., upon instantiation of a Synth using a delay) is a bad idea; you can also run out of real-time allocatable memory (you can set the amount *scsynth* may use with `s.options.memSize`).

   An `Allpass` filter has no effect on a steady-state sound; you will hear the effect only when you add it to the unfiltered version. A `Comb` filter, on the other hand, can

```
// single tap delay lines
DelayN.ar(in, maxdelaytime, delaytime, mul, add)
DelayL.ar(in, maxdelaytime, delaytime, mul, add)
DelayC.ar(in, maxdelaytime, delaytime, mul, add)

// allpass filters:
AllpassN.ar(in, maxdelaytime, delaytime, decaytime, mul, add)
AllpassL.ar(in, maxdelaytime, delaytime, decaytime, mul, add)
AllpassC.ar(in, maxdelaytime, delaytime, decaytime, mul, add)

// comb filters (delaylines with feedback):
CombN.ar(in, maxdelaytime, delaytime, decaytime, mul, add)
CombL.ar(in, maxdelaytime, delaytime, decaytime, mul, add)
CombC.ar(in, maxdelaytime, delaytime, decaytime, mul, add)

// buffer versions:

BufDelayN.ar(buf, in, delaytime, mul, add)
BufDelayL.ar(buf, in, delaytime, mul, add)
BufDelayC.ar(buf, in, delaytime, mul, add)

BufAllpassN.ar(buf, in, delaytime, decaytime, mul, add)
BufAllpassL.ar(buf, in, delaytime, decaytime, mul, add)
BufAllpassC.ar(buf, in, delaytime, decaytime, mul, add)

BufCombN.ar(buf, in, delaytime, decaytime, mul, add)
BufCombL.ar(buf, in, delaytime, decaytime, mul, add)
BufCombC.ar(buf, in, delaytime, decaytime, mul, add)


// special delay lines utilising PlayBuf:
Tap.ar(bufnum, numChannels, delaytime)
PingPong.ar(bufnum, inputArray, delayTime, feedback, rotate)
```

Figure 14.5
Delay lines and their arguments.

be used as a resonator. Both can be used to create echoes from an input sound. Examples of these can be found in the Help files.

Tap is a delay line implemented using PlayBuf; you can create several outputs from it, and generate a kind of impulse response with it. This is useful to simulate early reflections. (See figure 14.6.)

PingPong bounces a signal between channels by doing the following. The input channels are recorded to a buffer; the buffer is played back with a delayTime; that output is rotated with rotate channels (so all the channels shift position); this is then multiplied by the feedback factor and in turn is added to the input to the recording buffer. The output that you hear is summation of the input with the delayed signal after the rotation and the feedback multiplication.

14.3.5   Convolution

If you have a lot of delay taps, it is more efficient to use a Convolution UGen. In SuperCollider there are several UGens available to do convolution. Convolution allows you to convolve 2 running signals with one another; this can be useful for creating complex spectra of 2 different sounds. For spatialization the Convolution2 UGens (Convolution2, Convolution2L, and StereoConvolution2L) are more useful, since they use a buffer for the impulse response with which an input signal is convolved. Convolution3 implements a time-based calculation of convolution; since this is a highly inefficient way of calculating a convolution, it is not recommended to use it at audio rate. The other Convolution UGens calculate the convolution in the frequency domain, that is, they calculate a Fourier transform of the input signal and of the kernel (either the other input signal or the impulse response buffer), then multiply the coefficients before the output is transformed back into the time domain. This is computationally efficient but leads to significant latency with large impulse responses. PartConv implements real-time partitioned convolution, which addresses this problem by breaking the impulse response into smaller chunks. (See figure 14.7.)

14.3.6   Reverb

For reverberation you can use the Comb and AllPass UGens as shown above, or you can use a recorded impulse response and one of the Convolution UGens. Other options are using resonating filters or UGens such as Decay.

There are 3 UGens (see figure 14.8) designed specifically for reverb: FreeVerb, FreeVerb2, and GVerb. FreeVerb takes as parameters the dry/wet balance (called mix), a measure for the room size, and the amount of damping of the high frequencies; each of these parameters has to be in the range 0–1. FreeVerb2 is a 2-channel

```
// Create a buffer.
b=Buffer.alloc(s, s.sampleRate, 1); //enough space for one second of mono audio

// Write to the Buffer with BufWr, read using several taps and mix them together:
(
SynthDef(\helpTap, {|bufnum|
    var source, capture;
    source= Impulse.ar(1);
    capture= BufWr.ar(source, bufnum, Phasor.ar(0,1, 0, BufFrames.ir(bufnum),1));
        Out.ar(0, Mix.new([1,0.95,0.94,0.93,0.8,0.4,0.4]*Tap.ar(bufnum, 1, [0.04,
0.1,0.22,0.88,0.9,0.91,0.93])));
}).add;
)

x=Synth(\helpTap,[\bufnum, b.bufnum]);
x.free;

( // alternate source; use headphones to avoid feedback
SynthDef(\helpTap2, {|bufnum|
    var source, capture;
    source= SoundIn.ar(0);
    capture= BufWr.ar(source, bufnum, Phasor.ar(0,1, 0, BufFrames.ir(bufnum),1));
        Out.ar(0, Mix.new([1,0.95,0.94,0.93,0.8,0.4,0.4]*Tap.ar(bufnum, 1, [0.04,
0.1,0.22,0.88,0.9,0.91,0.93])));
}).add;
)

x=Synth(\helpTap2,[\bufnum, b.bufnum]);
x.free;

// free buffer:
b.free;
```

Figure 14.6
Tap example.

```
// convolving two signals with each other:
Convolution.ar( in, kernel, framesize, mul, add )

// convolving one signal with a buffer:
Convolution2.ar( in, kernel, trigger, framesize, mul, add )
// as above with linear interpolation:
Convolution2L.ar( in, kernel, trigger, framesize, crossfade, mul, add
)
// as above, with two buffers:
StereoConvolution2L.ar( in, kernelL, kernelR, trigger, framesize,
crossfade, mul, add )

// time based convolution (highly inefficient for audio rate)
Convolution3.ar( in, kernel, trigger, framesize, mul, add )
Convolution3.kr( in, kernel, trigger, framesize, mul, add )

// partitioned convolution
PartConv.ar(in, fftsize, irbufnum, mul, add)
```

Figure 14.7
The Convolution UGens and their arguments.

```
// one channel input:
FreeVerb.ar(in, mix, room, damp, mul, add)
// 2 channel input and output:
FreeVerb2.ar(in, in2, mix, room, damp, mul, add)

// stereo reverb
#left, right = GVerb.ar(in, roomsize, revtime, damping, inputbw,
 spread, drylevel, earlyreflevel, taillevel, maxroomsize, mul, add)
```

Figure 14.8
The Reverb UGens with their input arguments.

version that has 2 inputs and 2 outputs. GVerb gives a stereo output and has several more parameters to tune the reverb: room size (in meters), reverberation time (in seconds), damping (high-frequency roll-off, range: 0–1), input bandwidth (high-frequency roll-off on the input signal), amount of stereo spread and diffusion, the dry level, the amount of early reflections, the tail level, and the maximum room size.

Using different directions for reverb will enhance the feeling of envelopment; this is what GVerb does with 2 channels. For more channels, you can achieve this effect by using reverbs from several directions with slightly different settings for each direction.

14.3.7   Arbitrary Spatialization

Depending on the project you are working on, you may want to use a different kind of spatialization, considering the setup of the speakers that you have and the content of your work. As an example, we have included in the Web site materials a class created for spatialization of the sound of the dance theater piece "Schwelle" (Baalman, Moody-Grigsby, and Salter, 2007). For this piece a setup was used which had an inner space and an outer space. The inner space was created by 4 speakers (2 stereo pairs) surrounding the stage; the outer space, by speakers behind and above the audience. Various sound movements were defined within this space.

This example demonstrates one approach for creating a spatialization for a piece and how one might set up a framework for dealing with it. Similarly, in your own work you can assign any algorithm to determine which speaker a sound is routed to and at what amplitude; this is your compositional freedom.

14.4   3D Audio

3D audio encompasses all methods which try to recreate a 3-dimensional wave field in one way or another. This can be done either with headphone-based methods such as binaural audio or through loudspeaker methods, such as ambisonics and wave field synthesis. We will discuss each of these methods and how they can be used within SuperCollider.

In all of these methods there is a shift from a track- or channel-based approach to an object-oriented way of working. That is, instead of thinking about which sound should come from which channel, you think about the virtual position that the sound should have and feed the sound into the 3D audio system, along with the desired spatial coordinates and other spatial properties. From this metadata, the 3D audio system then calculates the appropriate signals for each channel, which will be fed to either headphones or loudspeakers.

14.4.1 Binaural Audio

Binaural methods attempt to present audio signals at each ear that correspond to the 3D audio field of an auralized scene. This is done by measuring the head-related transfer function (HRTF) for each ear, for all desired directions from which a sound source may come.[1] These HRTFs can be stored in a database as impulse responses. If we want to auralize a sound coming from a direction with an elevation of 30 degrees and an azimuth of 10 degrees, the corresponding HRTF (1 impulse response for each ear) can be looked up and the audio can be convolved with these impulse responses. The problem is actually a bit more complicated, as we can move our heads, and thus we need to change the HRTF not only when the source moves to another position but also when we turn our heads. For this we need to have a device that measures our head position, called a head tracker.

When the auralized source is to appear to be in a room, HRTFs need to be created (measured or calculated) that include the acoustics of the room. This means that head and source position must be treated separately and that an HRTF needs to be available for the following:

- each sound source position,
- each listener position, and
- with each possible head position.

It can be seen that the amount of data easily becomes very large and is organized across several dimensions. The impulse response data will not fit into RAM of a normal computer anymore, and a clever algorithm needs to be created which dynamically loads HRTFs from disk and caches them in RAM, so that they are quickly available when needed. (An example of how to deal with this problem is discussed in chapter 19.) The amount of data can be reduced by adapting the resolution: we can take an HRTF at coarser intervals and at fewer listening positions. This is of course a trade-off between data size and the accuracy of the binaural reproduction. Another limitation will be the number of sources we can auralize simultaneously. For each source we need to do 2 convolutions with the appropriate impulse response (and maybe even more, if we want to ensure that we can switch to another HRTF quickly), so our CPU power and the performance of the convolution algorithm will determine this limit.

The general structure of a binaural audio engine is shown in figure 14.9. The SynthDef for one binaural source is the following:

```
(
SynthDef(\binauralconvolver, {|out = 0, in = 0, bufL = 0, bufR = 1, t_trig
= 0, amp = 1|
```

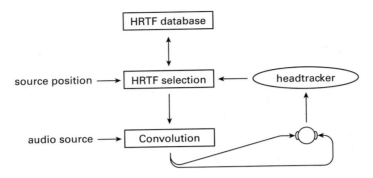

Figure 14.9
Binaural audio engine.

```
    Out.ar(out,
        StereoConvolution2L.ar(In.ar(in, 1), bufL, bufR, t_trig, 2048, 1,
        amp)
        // 2048 is the FIR size, 1 means that we crossfade over 1 block
        between buffers
    );
}).add;
)
```

We can set the input bus with the argument in and the HRTF buffers with bufL and bufR. The HRTF buffers need to be chosen based on the head orientation and the source position. Suppose we have a database with just angular positions relative to the head (azimuth and elevation); then we can create a matrix (~HRTF) which maps the azimuth and elevation angles to pairs of HRTF buffers.

Suppose we have a head tracker attached to the headphones of the listener and data from it is streaming into SuperCollider. We have assigned the instance of the class dealing with the device to the variable ~headtracker. Then we need to define an action to be performed when data change (we assume that the class has a method action for this and that it takes the arguments azimuth and elevation). The source is represented in a class which contains the source position in the variables azimuth and elevation and is instantiated as ~source; it also has an action that can be set to be done when the source position changes.

```
x = Synth.new(\binauralconvolver, [\bufL, ~HRTF.at(~sourceazi).
at(~sourcelev )[0], \bufR, ~HRTF.at(~sourceazi).at(~sourcelev)[1]]);

~headtracker.action_({|azim,elev| x.setn(\bufL, ~HRTF.at(~source.azimuth
- azim ).at( ~source.elevation - elev ));});
```

```
// 5.1 array (subwoofer must be treated separately)
VBAPSpeakerArray.new(2, [ -30, 30, 0, -110, 110 ]);

// 16 channel partial dome
VBAPSpeakerArray.new(3, [[-22.5, 14.97], [22.5, 14.97], [-67.5,
14.97], [67.5, 14.97], [-112.5, 14.97], [112.5, 14.97], [-157.5,
14.97], [157.5, 14.97], [-45, 0], [45, 0], [-90, 0], [90, 0], [-135,
0], [135, 0], [0, 0], [180, 0]]);
```

Figure 14.10
2D and 3D VBAP speaker arrays.

```
~source.action_({|azim,elev| x.setn(\bufL, ~HRTF.at(~azim - ~headtracker.
azimuth).at( ~elev - ~headtracker.elevation)});
```

See Also
In this book: Chapter 19
External: IEM UGens

14.4.2   Vector Base Amplitude Panning (VBAP)

Finnish researcher Ville Pulkki has developed an extension of pairwise panning techniques called Vector Base Amplitude Panning (Pulkki, 2001), which was ported to SC by Scott Wilson (Wilson, 2007). VBAP can be applied between pairs of loudspeakers (2D VBAP) or triplets (3D VBAP). As in basic stereophony, VBAP assumes that speakers are equidistant from the listener, so in the 3D case this means a complete or partial dome or sphere.[2]

A useful innovation in VBAP is that (in contrast to PanAz) the speakers do not have to be evenly spaced around the ring or dome. VBAP abstracts panning control from speaker configuration and allows for accurate pairwise or triplet panning with arbitrary spacings, so that it is easy, for instance, to move from an octophonic ring to a 5.1 setup. An algorithm determines the optimal pairs or triplets for a given setup. Panning position is indicated using 2 parameters expressed in degrees: azimuth, or horizontal pan, with 0 degrees directly to the front, and elevation (for 3D VBAP), expressed in degrees above or below the azimuth plane. Speaker positions are specified with the same parameters, which are used as input to the VBAPSpeakerArray object. Figure 14.10 presents examples of these.

The VBAP UGen does the actual panning. In addition to the azimuth and elevation parameters, it also has a *spread* parameter. When spread is equal to 0, a panned signal will be output from a single speaker if the pan azimuth and elevation exactly

```
a = VBAPSpeakerArray.new(3, [[-22.5, 14.97], [22.5, 14.97], [-67.5,
14.97], [67.5, 14.97], [-112.5, 14.97], [112.5, 14.97], [-157.5,
14.97], [157.5, 14.97], [-45, 0], [45, 0], [-90, 0], [90, 0], [-135,
0], [135, 0], [0, 0], [180, 0]]); // zig zag partial dome

b = a.loadToBuffer; // send speaker config to the server

(
// pan around the circle up and down
x = { |azi = 0, ele = 0, spr = 10|
var source;
source = PinkNoise.ar(0.2);
VBAP.ar(16, source, b, LFSaw.kr(0.5, 0).range(-180, 180) * -1,
SinOsc.kr(3, 0).range(0, 14.97), spr);
}.play;
)
```

Figure 14.11
3D VBAP example.

match that of a speaker's location. Spread values greater than 0 (expressed as a percentage, with 100 indicating the entire array) ensure that this never happens by always having the signal played over at least 2 speakers. This can prevent signals from suddenly sounding "in the box" as they pan to an exact speaker position, by smoothing out the changes in "localization blur" that occur when panning between speakers (Pulkki, 1999). Values in the range of 10–20 have been found to be useful in informal testing.

Figure 14.11 gives an example of some 3D VBAP panning. A more elaborate example involving GUI control can be found in the VBAP Help file, which is included in the Web site materials.

14.4.3   Ambisonics

The ambisonic sound system (Malham and Myatt, 1995) is a 2-part technological solution to the problem of encoding sound directions and amplitudes, and reproducing them over practical loudspeaker systems, so that listeners can perceive sounds located in a 3-dimensional space. This can occur only over a 360 degree horizontal sound stage (pantophonic system) or over the full sphere (periphonic system). The system encodes the signals in so-called *B-format*; the first-order version of this encodes the signal in 3 channels for pantophonic systems and a further channel for the periphonic (i.e., "with height" reproduction).

Essentially the system gives an approximation of a wave field by a plane wave decomposition of the sound field at the listener's position. This approximation gets more precise when the order of ambisonics is increased, which also means that more channels are needed for encoding and that more speakers are needed for decoding.

Thus there are 2 stages: encoding the signal to the B-format, and then decoding it for the actual speaker layout. An encoded signal can also be manipulated before it is decoded, allowing you to rotate the sound field around different axes.

Within the main distribution of SuperCollider there are several UGens available to encode and decode ambisonics; more are available in the sc3-plug-ins.[3] Figure 14.12 gives an overview of these UGens and their arguments.

See Also
External: IEM UGens

14.4.4   Wave Field Synthesis

Wave field synthesis (WFS) was introduced in 1988 (Berkhout, 1988) and is an approach to spatial sound field reproduction based on the Huygens Principle. With WFS it is possible to create a physical reproduction of a wave field; this has an advantage over other techniques in that there is no *sweet spot* (i.e., there is no point in the listening area where the reproduction is remarkably better than at other places); rather, there is a *sweet area* that is quite large.

In comparison with ambisonic techniques, wave field synthesis is better at reproducing spatial depth, though the vertical dimension which can be used in ambisonics is lacking in most WFS implementations. For very high orders, ambisonics can be equated to wave field synthesis (Daniel et al., 2003).

A disadvantage is that you need a lot of loudspeakers to get the desired effect, as well as appropriate multichannel sound cards, and the necessary CPU power.

The Huygens Principle states that when you have a wave front, you can synthesize the next wave front by imagining on the wave front an infinite number of small sound sources whose waves together will form the next wave front (Huygens, 1690) (figure 14.13a). A listener will then not be able to determine the difference between a situation in which the wave front is real and one in which it is synthesized.

This principle can be translated to mathematical formulae using theories of Kirchhoff and Rayleigh and can then be applied for use with a linear array of loudspeakers (see, e.g., Baalman, 2008). By sending the correct signals to each loudspeaker—sending to the loudspeaker the signal that would be measured at the location of the speaker if the sound source would really have a given location—sound sources can be placed at any virtual place in a horizontal plane behind, or even in front of, the speakers (figure 14.13b). The actual derivation of the WFS operator is

```
// 3D encoding:
PanB.ar(in, azimuth, elevation, gain)
// 2D encoding:
PanB2.kr(in, azimuth, gain)
// 2D encoding of a stereo signal:
BiPanB2.kr(inA, inB, azimuth, gain)

// decoding (2D):
DecodeB2.kr(numChans, w, x, y, orientation)

// rotating (in the horizontal plane):
Rotate2.kr(x, y, pos)


/** From AmbisonicUGens in sc3-plugins: **/

// encoding (3D):
BFEncode1.ar(in, azimuth, elevation, rho, gain, wComp)
BFEncode2.ar(in, point_x, point_y, elevation, gain, wComp)

// encoding of a stereo signal (3D)
BFEncodeSter.ar(l, r, azimuth, width, elevation, rho, gain, wComp)

// decoding (3D):
BFDecode1.ar(w, x, y, z, azimuth, elevation, wComp, mul, add)

// manipulating (3D):
BFManipulate.ar(w, x, y, z, rotate, tilt, tumble)
// rotate is rotation around the z-axis, tilt around the x-axis, and
tumble around the y-axis
```

Figure 14.12
The Ambisonic UGens in SuperCollider.

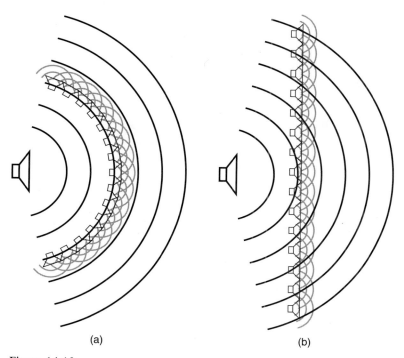

(a)   (b)

Figure 14.13
From the Huygens Principle (a) to Wave Field Synthesis (b).

beyond the scope of this chapter, but the resulting driver function $Q(x, \omega)$ is (in the frequency domain)

$$Q(x,\omega) = S(\omega)\sqrt{\frac{jk}{2\pi}}\sqrt{\frac{\Delta r_0}{\Delta r_0 + r_0}}\cos(\phi_0)\frac{e^{-jkr_0}}{\sqrt{r_0}},$$

where x is the coordinate of the speaker at the speaker array, $S(\omega)$ is the source signal, Δr_0 is the distance from the speaker array to a reference line, r_0 is the distance of the (virtual) source from the loudspeaker, ϕ_0 is the angle the vector source-loudspeaker makes with the normal on the loudspeaker, and $k = \omega/c$ is the wave number (see also figure 14.14).

So what does this mean? If we look at the driver function carefully, we see that it can be divided into an amplitude factor $\sqrt{\frac{\Delta r_0}{\Delta r_0 + r_0}}\frac{\cos(\phi_0)}{\sqrt{r_0}}$, a delay factor r_0/c (from e^{-jkr_0}), and a filter $\sqrt{\frac{jk}{2\pi}}$ that is not dependent on the source position.

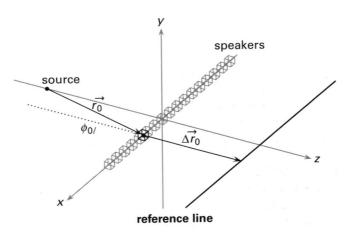

Figure 14.14
Parameters in the WFS operator.

In the Netherlands, the *Game of Life* Foundation sponsored the creation of a WFS system (see figure 14.15) implemented in SuperCollider and created by Wouter Snoei, Raviv Ganchrow, and Jan Trützschler. We will look at how the WFS calculations are implemented there to give an idea of how to do WFS in SuperCollider (figure 14.16).

The tricky part comes as the WFS array gets larger, since at some point 1 computer cannot manage all the calculations, and you need a technique for synchronizing several machines. A solution was created for the *Game of Life* system, but nonetheless it may be preferable to control an external WFS system; for example, a system controlled by the open-source software *sWONDER* (Baalman et al., 2007).

14.5   Techniques for Spatial Diffusion (Decorrelation)

There are various spatial techniques that do not attempt to locate a sound precisely, but rather to make it more spatially diffuse (i.e., less localized), to broaden its sonic image, to increase its sense of physical volume, and so on. These usually work by taking a source signal and making decorrelated versions of it, which are distributed to 2 or more loudspeakers. As used here, the term "decorrelation" can be understood as the process of creating related yet dissimilar versions of a signal; that is, signals with different wave forms that nevertheless sound very similar (Kendall, 1995). These effects have the advantage of being relatively stable across a wider variety of listening positions (i.e., a very large "sweet spot"), but all of them introduce artifacts of 1 sort or another.

Figure 14.15
WFS speakers for the the Game of Life system (August 2007).

It is possible to compare 2 signals in terms of their correlation and determine a correlation measure, which will be 1 for completely correlated signals and 0 for completely uncorrelated signals.[4] Consider the following 2 examples:

```
{Array.fill(2, WhiteNoise.ar(0.1))}.play; // sounds like it comes from the
center
```

```
{Array.fill(2, {WhiteNoise.ar(0.1)})}.play; // sounds wide
```

The difference between the 2 examples is that in the first, the 2 channels play the same noise signal (so the correlation measure is 1), whereas in the second example they play 2 different noise signals (so the correlation measure is close to 0). This effect is very obvious when you listen to the white noise directly, but it will still be apparent if you filter the sound afterward. For example:

```
{LPF.ar(Array.fill(2, WhiteNoise.ar(0.8)), 300, 0.2)}.play;
```

```
{LPF.ar(Array.fill(2, {WhiteNoise.ar(0.8)}), 300, 0.2)}.play;
```

```
// no interpolation
*arBufN { arg sound = 0, bufnum, location, speakerSpec, speedOfSound = 334, ampType
= 'ws';
    var numChannels, distArray;

// WFSPoint is a 3D representation of a point in cartesian space

    speakerSpec = speakerSpec ? [WFSPoint.new(-2.7, 1.8, 0), WFSPoint.new(2.7,1.8,
0)]; //default 2 speakers

    if( speakerSpec.class == WFSConfiguration )
        { speakerSpec = speakerSpec.allSpeakers; };

    numChannels = speakerSpec.size; // speakerSpec = Array of WFSPoint objects

    location = location ? WFSPoint.new(0,0,0); // the location of the sound source

    distArray = Array.fill(numChannels, { |i| speakerSpec.at(i).dist(location)});
// distance of the sound source to each speaker (r_0)

    cosPhiArray = Array.fill(numChannels, { |i|
speakerSpec.at(i).cosphi(location)}); // cosine phi_0 of the sound source to each
speaker (cos phi_0)
    ^BufDelayN.ar(bufnum, sound,
        distArray / speedOfSound, // delay
        WFSPan.wfsAmp(distArray,cosPhiArray));
    }

*wfsAmp{ arg inDist, inCosPhi, refDist=4.0, minDist = 0.1;
    // refDist is the reference line distance
    // minDist is the minimal distance to the speaker array (to avoid explosion at
/0)

    // avoid explosion:
    inDist = inDist.max( minDist );

    ^(ampFactor * ((refDist/(refDist + inDist)).sqrt)*(inCosPhi/(inDist.sqrt)))
}
```

Figure 14.16
Example for WFS calculation from the WFS-lib by Wouter Snoei; from the WFSPan class.

```
s.boot;
(
b = Buffer.alloc(s,2048,1);
c = Buffer.read(s,"sounds/a11wlk01.wav");
d = Buffer.alloc(s,2048,1);
)


(
//make stereo from mono
// MouseX controls decorrelation
x = SynthDef("PV_DecorrelateStereo", { arg out=0, bufnum=0, bufnum2, soundBufnum=2;
    var in, chain, chain2;
    in = PlayBuf.ar(1, soundBufnum, BufRateScale.kr(soundBufnum), loop: 1);
    chain = FFT(bufnum, in);
    chain2 = PV_Copy(chain, bufnum2);
    chain = PV_Decorrelate([chain, chain2], 1,  MouseX.kr);
    Out.ar(out, 0.5 * IFFT(chain));
}).play(s,[\out, 0, \bufnum, b, \bufnum2, d, \soundBufnum, c]);
)

x.free; [b, c, d].do(_.free);
```

Figure 14.17
An example of the use of PV_Decorrelate.

14.5.1   Phase Spectrum Decorrelation

The noise examples above work because the 2 noise sources are *statistically* (and sonically) essentially the same, but decorrelated. When using general signals you can create decorrelated variants by altering the phase spectrum of a signal, using techniques such as those described by Kendall (1995). This involves applying a random phase offset to each bin of an FFT analysis. The standard distribution of Super-Collider contains the PV_Diffuser UGen, and as part of the BEASTmulch project at the University of Birmingham, Scott Wilson has developed a variant of this called PV_Decorrelate (Wilson, 2007). PV_Decorrelate has an additional scaling factor applied to the random offsets, effectively allowing for the maximum offset to be limited. Setting this argument to 0 will result in completely correlated signals (no phase randomization), and setting it to 1 should result in maximum phase randomization (and a correlation measure close to 0). Controlling this is desirable in some cases, since the phase offsets can introduce audible artifacts such as transient smearing. Figure 14.17 demonstrates the use of PV_Decorrelate. Moving the mouse to the right increases the amount of decorrelation, creating a more spatially diffuse stereo effect but also adding phasing artifacts.

14.5.2   Granular Techniques

Granulation refers to a group of related techniques which involve breaking a sound into a small number of very short, usually overlapping, pieces. This has applications for time stretching, pitch shifting, brassage, and so on. A detailed discussion of this rather extensive topic is beyond the scope of this chapter, but for general information on granulation see Roads (2001) and Truax (1990). For information on granulation in SC, see chapter 16.

It is possible to create diffusion effects by granulating over a number of channels. Individual grains can either be panned between channels or hard assigned.[5] SC contains a number of UGens for granulating sound, such as TGrains, GrainBuf, and GrainIn; all of them support multichannel output. Figure 14.18 presents an example of a *client-side* approach for smooth spatial granulation. Granulation procedures are not without audible artifacts (increasing the number of grains can help to smooth this out at the cost of increased CPU load), but they are nevertheless capable of producing a number of interesting effects, spatial and otherwise.

14.5.3   Spectral Diffusion

It is possible to spatially distribute the spectral content of a sound across a number of loudspeakers. Such techniques arguably have their roots in the analog "spectral splitting" effects of loudspeaker orchestras such as the Gmebaphone/Cybernéphone of the Institut International de Musique Electroacoustique de Bourges (IMEB), the Acousmonium of the Groupe de Recherches Musicales (GRM), and Birmingham ElectroAcoustic Sound Theatre (BEAST). These systems either intentionally or implicitly use filtering and nonhomogeneous loudspeaker arrays in order to increase the diffuseness of sounds through spectral distribution in space.[6]

Similar effects can be created digitally through FFT-based analysis/resynthesis techniques. These approaches can be divided roughly according to the resynthesis technique used: Overlap-Add versus Oscillator Bank. The former are more straightforward in real time and generally less computationally expensive. The latter are generally more robust, however, and result in fewer artifacts when subjected to transformation.

These effects work best when done over larger numbers of channels (i.e., preferably more than stereo). The effect can be subtle, depending on the material, but can be very effective at creating an impression of envelopment, sometimes rendering sounds impossible to localize.

```
(
b = Buffer.read(s, "sounds/a11wlk01.wav");
SynthDef("grain",{ arg i_out=0, i_sampbufnum, dur = 0.05,
    pointer, offset = 0.005, amp = 1.0, loop = 1;
    var thisStart, thisDur, grain;
    thisStart = pointer + IRand(0, offset); // adds random time offset
    grain = EnvGen.ar(Env.sine, 1.0, amp, 0.0, dur, 2)
        * PlayBuf.ar(1,i_sampbufnum, BufRateScale.ir(i_sampbufnum),
            1, thisStart,loop);
    OffsetOut.ar(i_out,grain); // use OffsetOut for precise sub-block timing
}).add;
)


(
x = {
var numGrains = 32; // approximate number of simultaneous grains
var numChannels = 2; // adjust for your setup
var dur = 0.05, durRand = 0.05, thisDur;
var start, now;
var numGrainsRecip;
numGrainsRecip = numGrains.reciprocal; // save some divides by converting to
reciprocal

start = Main.elapsedTime;
loop({
    now = Main.elapsedTime - start;
    thisDur = dur + durRand.rand;
    s.bind({Synth("grain", [i_out: numChannels.rand, i_sampbufnum: b, dur: thisDur,
        pointer: now * b.sampleRate, amp: numGrainsRecip]);
    }); // send as a bundle for precise sub-block timing
    (thisDur * numGrainsRecip).wait;
})
}.fork;
)

x.stop; b.free;
```

Figure 14.18
Spatial diffusion through granulation.

```
Server.default = s = Server.internal;
s.boot;
(
n = 512; // number of bins
b = Buffer.alloc(s, n, 1);
c = Buffer.alloc(s, n, 1);

// create arrays of magnitude scalars and load them to buffers
d = Array.fill(n, {1.0.linrand});
e = 1.0 - d;
d = Buffer.loadCollection(s, d);
e = Buffer.loadCollection(s, e);

f = Buffer.read(s,"sounds/a11wlk01.wav");
)


(
x = SynthDef("spectral diffusion", { arg out=0, analBuf, analBufCopy, scalBuf1,
scalBuf2, soundBuf;
    var chain1, chain2;
    chain1 = FFT(analBuf, PlayBuf.ar(1, soundBuf, BufRateScale.kr(soundBuf),
loop: 1));
    chain2 = PV_Copy(chain1, analBufCopy); // copy the initial analysis
    chain1 = PV_MagMul(chain1, scalBuf1);
    chain2 = PV_MagMul(chain2, scalBuf2);
    Out.ar(out,  0.5 * IFFT([chain1, chain2]));
}).play(s,[out: 0, analBuf: b, analBufCopy: c, scalBuf1: d, scalBuf2: e, soundBuf:
f]);
s.scope; // compare the two channels
)

// execute this multiple times to change the distribution
(
g = Array.fill(n, {1.0.linrand});
h = 1 - g;
d.loadCollection(g);
e.loadCollection(h);
)

x.free; [b, c, d, e, f].do(_.free);
```

Figure 14.19
Simple spectral diffusion example.

Figure 14.19 presents an example of an Overlap-Add approach. As in the phase decorrelation examples discussed above, this approach creates decorrelated variants of a signal, in this case by dividing the energy in the magnitude spectrum between copies.

Techniques which use Oscillator Bank resynthesis generally require that the analysis be done in advance and thus are not suitable for use with real-time input. Two such approaches have SC-based implementations: Juan Pampin's ATS Pampin (1999; SC port by Joshua Parmenter) and Kelly Fitz and Lippold Hakken's Loris (Fitz et al., 2002; SC port by Scott Wilson, 2007). Both of these provide the user with a list of partials, each of which can be individually spatialized when resynthesized using any of the techniques described in this chapter. An example of spectral diffusion using Loris can be found in the Web site materials.

14.6   Conclusion

As you have (hopefully) seen from the above examples, considering the aspect of space in your work with SuperCollider can add richness, depth, and realism. Some of the approaches presented in this chapter work best on large numbers of speakers, but even in stereo on a laptop you can do a lot. Why not take some of the other examples in this book and alter or adapt them using some of the techniques we have discussed? As we noted at the start, in the real world, sounds always have a spatial aspect; there is no reason why your SC sounds should not as well, regardless of how synthetic their origins might be.

References

Ando, Y. 1985. *Concert Hall Acoustics*. Springer Series in Electrophysics 17. Berlin: Springer.

Baalman, M. A. J. 2008. "On Wave Field Synthesis and Electro-Acoustic Music, with a Particular Focus on the Reproduction of Arbitrarily Shaped Sound Sources." PhD thesis, Technical University of Berlin.

Baalman, M. A. J., T. Hohn, S. Schampijer, and T. Koch. 2007. "Renewed Architecture of the sWONDER Software for Wave Field Synthesis on Large-Scale Systems." In *Proceedings of the 5th Linux Audio Conference 2007*, Berlin: Technical Universität, pp. 76–83.

Baalman, M. A. J., D. Moody-Grigsby, and C. Salter. 2007. "Schwelle: Sensor Augmented, Adaptive Sound Design for Live Theater Performance." In *Proceedings of the 7th International Conference on New Interfaces for Musical Expression,* New York: New York University, pp. 178–184.

Berkhout, A. J. 1988. "A Holographic Approach to Acoustic Control." *Journal of the Audio Engineering Society*, 36(12): 977–995.

Blauert, J. 1997. *Spatial Hearing*, rev. ed. Cambridge, MA: MIT Press.

Clozier, C. 2001. "The Gmebaphone Concept and the Cybernéphone Instrument." *Computer Music Journal*, 25(4): 81–90.

Daniel, J., R. Nicol, and S. Moreau. 2003. "Further Investigations of High Order Ambisonics and Wavefield Synthesis for Holophonic Sound Imaging." In *Proceedings of the 114th Convention of the Audio Engineering Society.* Convention preprint 5825.

Fitz, K., L. Haken, S. Lefvert, and M. O'Donnell. 2002. "Sound Morphing Using Loris and the Reassigned Bandwdith-Enhanced Additive Sound Model: Practice and Applications." In *Proceedings of the 2002 International Computer Music Conference.* Ann Arbor: Scholarly Publishing Office, University of Michigan Library.

Harrison, J. 1998. "Sound, Space, Sculpture: Some Thoughts on the 'What,' 'How' and 'Why' of Sound Diffusion." *Organised Sound*, 3(2): 117–127.

Huygens, C. 1690. *Traité de la lumière; Ou sont expliquées les causes de ce qui luy arrive dans la réflexion et dans la réfraction et particulièrement dans l'étrange refraction du cristal d'Islande; avec un discours de la cause de la pesanteur.* Leiden: P. van der Aa.

Kendall, G. 1995. "The Decorrelation of Audio Signals and Its Impact on Spatial Imagery." *Computer Music Journal*, 19(4): 71–87.

Malham, D. G., and A. Myatt. 1995. "3-D Sound Spatialization Using Ambisonic Techniques." *Computer Music Journal*, 19(4): 58–70.

Pampin, J. 1999. "ATS: A Lisp Environment for Spectral Modeling." In *Proceedings of the 1999 International Computer Music Conference.* Ann Arbor: Scholarly Publishing Office, University of Michigan Library.

Pulkki, V. 2001. *Spatial Sound Generation and Perception by Amplitude Panning Techniques.* Technical Report 62. Laboratory of Acoustics and Audio Signal Processing, Helsinki University of Technology.

Pulkki, V. 1999. "Uniform Spreading of Amplitude Panned Virtual Sources." In *Proceedings of the 1999 IEEE Workshop on Applications of Signal Processing to Audio and Acoustics,* pp. 187–190.

Roads, C. 2002. *Microsound.* Cambridge, MA: MIT Press.

Rumsey, F. 2001. *Spatial Audio.* Oxford: Focal Press.

Sonke, J.-J., and D. de Vries. 1997. "Generation of Diffuse Reverberation by Plane Wave Synthesis." Preprint 4455. In *Proceedings of the 102nd AES Convention,* Munich: AES.

Truax, B. 1990. "Time Shifting of Sampled Sound with a Real-Time Granulation Technique." In *Proceedings of the 1990 International Computer Music Conference,* San Francisco, CA: ICMA.

Tutschku, H. n.d. "On the Interpretation of Multi-channel Electroacoustic Works on Loudspeaker-Orchestras: Some Thoughts on the grm-acousmonium and BEAST." Translated by George Goodman, <http://www.tutschku.com/content/interpretation.en.php>.

Wilson, S. 2007. BEASTmulch, <http://www.beast.bham.ac.uk/research/mulch.shtml>.

Notes

1. As noted above, the filtering effects resulting from reflections off the ridges of the ears—as well as other parts of the body, such as the shoulders and chest—play a crucial role in spatial hearing. Head-related transfer functions model this mathematically and allow one to simulate this effect for a given position.

2. One can compensate for other shapes, such as cylinders, by applying appropriate delays to the closer speakers so that the precedence effect does not come into play.

3. <http://sourceforge.net/projects/sc3-plugins>.

4. The technical term for this process is the cross-correlation function. See Kendall (1995) for a discussion of this.

5. In informal testing the author (Wilson) has found that the perceptual differences between panned and hard assigned grains are very small when using a reasonable number of short concurrent grains over more than 2 channels.

6. See Clozier (2001), Harrison (1999), and Tutschku (n.d.) for further discussion.

15 Machine Listening in SuperCollider

Nick Collins

15.1 Background and First Steps

15.1.1 What Is Machine Listening?

Machine listening is the capability of machines to simulate human auditory and musical abilities. Why would we want to forge that talent in machines? Well, imagine being the poor musician who has to play along with a prerecorded tape part or click track. Wouldn't it be more natural to play with an accompanist who can adapt in the event of a mistake or a change of plan? What if you wished to engage in improvisational dialogue, sparring with an artificial musician, or to interact with a sound installation via your voice? Computers can provide remarkable generative and processing powers, but are integrated so much more naturally if supportive of human mechanisms of interaction. Machine listening gives a way to equip the computer for those social musical and sonic circumstances which we take for granted when resting on our own cultural training and biological heritage.

Nevertheless, millions of years of evolutionary fitness testing in sounding environments and the frantic pace of cultural memetics are a tall order to match with a computer program. It is best to confess at the outset that the state of the art in machine listening falls short of human auditory acuity, particularly in tracking multiple simultaneous objects in an auditory scene or extracting high-level culturally contingent musical information. In many cases, the proof that a certain ability is possible rests with human beings alone and has not been successfully matched by machine. Nevertheless, I hope this chapter will demonstrate that we can engineer useful aural and musical abilities, and indeed do so within our SuperCollider patches. As the subject of intensive research efforts, many enhancements will be released in the years to come, but the reader will no doubt be eager to see what can be done right now.

Machine listening in SuperCollider operates causally in real time, allowing the recognition of auditory objects and the tracking of features such as fundamental frequency, loudness, and timbre and event onset, as well as musical constructs such

```
(
x={
    var in, amp, freq, hasFreq, out;
    in = SoundIn.ar(0);
    amp = Amplitude.ar(in);
    # freq, hasFreq = Pitch.kr(in);
    LFTri.ar(freq*[1,2]) * amp;
}.play
)

x.free;
```

Figure 15.1
Immediate machine listening example using `Pitch` and `Amplitude` UGens. The original detected pitch appears in your left ear and an octave up in the right.

as beat, key, and phrase. In this chapter I will describe the various UGens and classes in SuperCollider that support such abilities, in turn enabling real-time interactive music systems. The chapter will gradually progress according to the complexity of the tools, ending with a discussion of interactive music systems themselves that potentially combine many machine-listening UGens with higher-level compositional decisions.

15.1.2   A Practical Example

The SuperCollider patch in figure 15.1 combines the `Pitch` and `Amplitude` UGens to let you control a triangle waveform with your voice; you might want to try it with headphones on in case of any feedback. The Pitch UGen is continuously extracting an estimate of the fundamental frequency, and Amplitude is continually tracking the amplitude level of your voice. These parameters are then used to drive a triangle oscillator, though they could very well be controlling a massed bank of oscillators, playback of someone else's prerecorded voice, or an arbitrarily strange network of UGens. Both UGens operate in the time domain, and we'll explore both time and frequency domain processes in this chapter. You won't often need to worry about this distinction, since UGens will be doing the hard work for you, but you need to be aware that for frequency domain processes we might use the FFT UGens as a first step in real-time analysis; examples below will make this clear.

The Amplitude UGen tracks the amplitude of a signal—typically in the range −1.0 to 1.0 for floating-point audio, where 0 is silence and 1.0 is the absolute maximum output level of the sound card—smoothed over a short time period. The amount of smoothing is determined by the attack and release time parameters, as further discussed in the Help file.

The Pitch UGen is more complicated and has quite a few arguments, which you'll see if you check the code or Help file:

```
Pitch.kr(in = 0.0, initFreq = 440.0, minFreq = 60.0, maxFreq = 4000.0,
execFreq = 100.0, maxBinsPerOctave = 16, median = 1, ampThreshold = 0.01,
peakThreshold = 0.5, downSample = 1)
```

In practice, you can often accept the defaults, and that goes for many of the UGens described in this chapter. As you become more expert, you'll naturally end up tweaking things; no machine-listening UGen is perfect for all circumstances, and it's great to have a wide selection of analyzers and feature extractors to choose from.

The reader may be concerned by the 2 outputs from the Pitch UGen, which are (1) the current fundamental frequency estimate in Hertz, and (2) a measure of whether a pitch was detected in the signal, as a simple flag of 1 for yes and 0 otherwise. The #freq, hasFreq construction in the code deals with assigning the 2 outputs to 2 separate variables for ease of reuse; the output would otherwise be an array of 2 elements. We'll see multiple outputs many times in the following.

How does the Pitch UGen work? Though we're not going to dwell on every detail of the mechanisms of the machine-listening UGens in this chapter (there isn't space, and the average user probably doesn't need to know), I'll try to drop a few hints to get the curious reader started. Pitch extracts fundamental frequency, often written as f0 in technical literature; f0 denotes the base partial of a harmonic series, though the phenomenon of the missing fundamental in psychoacoustics means that this partial does not have to be physically present in order for that pitch to be heard. The UGen implements a time-domain autocorrelation-based f0 follower, which means that it measures at what spacing in time a shifted version of the waveform best lines up with itself. It tries a number of possible shift sizes, called lags, which essentially reveal the period of the waveform. Unfortunately, there are a few ambiguities; the waveform will also line up well at double the period, causing a potential error of an octave. Indeed, a host of different pitch extraction algorithms have been devised, all with various possible confounds. But to get you started, the Pitch UGen in Super-Collider is a good f0 tracker for most circumstances. If you're curious about the theory, I heartily recommend Alain de Cheveigné's exposition (de Cheveigné, 2006).

15.1.3   The Information Which Machine-Listening Plug-ins Provide

Let's pause at this stage to consider 2 practical questions that may be preying on the reader's mind in the context of the last section:

1. What if I need discrete musical notes rather than continuous frequency information?

2. How do I get the outputs from a Pitch UGen back to the language so I can make compositional decisions based on them?

Though I've written both questions as they pertain to the pitch-following UGen we just used, these are actually more general questions that may occur for any feature extraction process.

Answering these points in turn, the first draws our attention to the status of different time scales of activity; certain structures are convenient for describing the auditory information at each level of granularity. The lowest level is the smallest grain of individual samples, effectively continuous for frequencies below the Nyquist frequency. Multiple consecutive samples can be combined in a short-term window (also called a frame), perhaps of around 1–100 milliseconds, and a particular single value, a feature, obtained as a descriptor of some meaningful property (such as pitch or amplitude) of the audio within that window. A compression of data and of sampling rate is necessarily effected. Such a process typically operates at the level of multiple blocks; a standard window size is that of an FFT frame, such as 1024 samples (16 sample blocks of 64 each, around 23 milliseconds for a 44.1 kHz sampling rate). A higher level combines frames, describing longer-scale sound objects that are intuitively sonic events, "clangs" (Tenney, 2006), or musical notes; features might transfer to this level by taking a statistic over the object in question, such as a peak power, a median pitch, or the mean of some other feature value such as the spectral centroid. The combination or apportioning of these to phrases, measures, sections, or indeed whole works, proceeds in turn.

Segmentation is a process which partitions an audio stream into more discrete musical objects, though again we may identify such salient events at a number of time scales (Roads, 2001). Although Trevor Wishart (Wishart, 1985), among others, has decried "lattice" thinking and the dominance of notation over pure experiential gesture, a categorization giving a small set of permissible "objects" for ease of use is a standard tactic in human endeavor and a necessity in many algorithms; we acknowledge, however, the multiple time scales and representations of objects over which audio analysis can operate.

In the familiar MIDI representation, the note objects have already been identified (though their "offs" may have been separated from their "ons," but that's another story). MIDI is an example of a clearly symbolic paradigm, and though this granularity of information can be helpful to us, it has also dropped certain fine-scale information on temporal variation. In considering interactive music systems at the end of this chapter, I'll return to MIDI and discuss an example of an interactive music system which is inherently symbolic and entirely language-side in its decision making.

The second of our questions is a practical matter of getting information from the synthesis server, where the machine-listening UGens are running, back to the language. There are a number of ways to do this, and different UGens may promote different methods. The possibilities are polling control buses (including shared buses on the internal server) or buffers on the server from the language, and UGens (such as SendTrig and SendReply), which send OSC messages from the server back to the language. The code examples accompanying this chapter demonstrate these approaches.

Briefly, the server is the location for low-level signal processing, starting from an audio signal. The language is a better location for higher-level musical decisions, that is, *symbolic* processing. When making design decisions on your code, you might want to ponder how electronic music composition lets you make compositional decisions at a number of scales. Further illustrations of these issues will occur in later examples.

15.2   Features and Segmentation

15.2.1   Feature Extraction

So, we've already seen 2 UGens which, respectively, extract fundamental frequency and amplitude. What other features might we extract? Well, audio signal-processing engineers have discovered many interesting features which can be obtained from signals, all of them potentially useful for artistic purposes. Though those features that are most analogous to the capabilities of our own hearing systems are often more powerful, any abstract feature obtained from a signal might prove valuable in art. However, the bias of this chapter is toward machine listening, which is close to human listening.

There is some distinction between relatively low-level features and higher-level features. The progression of this chapter is to gradually move upstream. The convention is to associate *higher = more discrete = summarizing larger time scales* and *lower = more continuous = closer to an audio signal itself*.

Table 15.1 lists a selection of features which may be extracted and the corresponding SuperCollider UGens. Many are in the core of SuperCollider, but there are also some third-party UGens and classes; their author and project name are revealed as necessary. No doubt this list will change by the time this book is published, and certainly after it; but I hope this chapter will still provide a useful starting point to the reader in exploring these possibilities. As is normal for third-party UGens, you will need to add the binaries, class, and Help files to your platform-specific Super-Collider *Extension* folder; instructions on completing this process are available in

Table 15.1
Overview of Machine-Listening Resources for SuperCollider

Category	UGen	Description	Availability (core unless otherwise stated)
Amplitude	Amplitude		
	RunningSum	RMS amplitude	
	Loudness	perceptual loudness	
Pitch	ZeroCrossing	simplistic pitch detection; also as a timbral feature	
	Pitch	autocorrelation in time domain	
	Tartini	adaptation from Phil McLeod's Tartini program	Nick Collins (NC)
	Qitch	constant Q transform pitch detector after Judith Brown and Miller Puckette	NC
Timbre	SpecCentroid	spectral features correlating, respectively, with perceived brightness, noisiness, and roll-off point	
	SpecFlatness		
	SpecPcile		
	MFCC	Mel Frequency Cepstral Coefficients	
Onset detection	PV_HainsworthFoote		
	PV_JensenAndersen		
	Onsets	Dan Stowell's onset detector encapsulates his research work including many different functions	
Event Extraction	AnalyzeEvents2		NC
Beat tracking	BeatTrack	Autocorrelation beat tracker	
	BeatTrack2	Crosscorrelation beat tracker	
	DrumTrack	Drum pattern template detector	NC
Key extraction	KeyTrack		
Psychoacoustics	Dissonance classes	Language-side classes for sensory dissonance analysis	Juan Sebastián Lach

```
b = Buffer.alloc(s,1024,1);    //for sampling rates 44100 and 48000
//b = Buffer.alloc(s,2048,1); //for sampling rates 88200 and 96000

( //analyse loudness and poll result
x={
    var in, fft, loudness;

    in = SoundIn.ar(0);

    fft = FFT(b.bufnum, in);

    loudness = Loudness.kr(fft);

    loudness.poll(20); //poll for testing 20 times per second

    Out.ar(0,Pan2.ar(in));
}.play
)

x.free;
b.free;
```

Figure 15.2
Loudness.

other chapters in this book, in the *Using Extensions* Help file, and in the README files that come with such downloads.

As an example, we will next consider extracting 2 psychoacoustically motivated features.

The first is a measure of perceptual loudness (Moore, 2004; Zwicker and Fastl, 1993) which utilizes a simple auditory model, making use of equal loudness contours and spectral and temporal masking. The output of the Loudness UGen, in the psychoacoustic unit of sones, is a better measure of the human cognition of volume than the Amplitude UGen, which treats only a physical (as opposed to perceptual) definition of signal level. Figure 15.2 demonstrates the extraction of perceptual loudness, using the Loudness UGen on an audio input.

One important factor to note concerning some machine-listening UGens is that they are highly sample-rate-dependent. The Loudness UGen supports 4 sample rates: 44,100 and 48,000, using a 1024-point FFT; and 88,200 and 96,000, using a 2048-point FFT. Such issues are noted in the associated Help files, and readers should take care when running patches that they are aware of the server sample rate (s.sampleRate) which will match that of their assigned sound card.

The second psychoacoustic feature is actually a set of features rather than a single quantity. The Mel Frequency Cepstral Coefficients (Logan, 2000) are often used to measure timbre in speech recognition and music information retrieval. In this case, we can choose how many coefficients to extract, getting 1 output channel (feature stream) for each coefficient. In technical terms, the coefficients are the result of matching a cosine basis to a frequency-warped spectrum. The MFCC UGen uses the Mel scale, a common psychoacoustic scale modeling auditory sensitivity on the basilar membrane (other work might use critical bands in Barks or ERBs). The cosine transform which takes us from a spectrum to a Mel Cepstrum is really just an approximation to principal component analysis that allows a dimensionality reduction, that is, finding the most important summary features for the spectral content of the signal. A side effect of MFCC analysis is to separate the excitation from the body filter of an instrument, thus further confirming the measurement of timbre.

Figure 15.3 demonstrates obtaining 13 MFCCs with the MFCC UGen and observing those values from the language.

15.2.2   Onset Detection

An important step between continuous and discrete auditory representation is the extraction of sound objects (typically 100–500 ms long; you might like to imagine them as "notes" or "events"), a process often dubbed *onset detection* or *segmentation*. We have to be careful about the kind of audio signal we consider here: polyphonic audio, with many simultaneous parts, or complex auditory scenes such as cocktail parties, require additional treatment in grouping information both vertically in frequency and horizontally across time. It is much easier to consider the case of monophonic audio with a solo instrument or speaker. Indeed, true polyphonic extraction in real time is beyond the cutting edge of audio processing, and in many cases is not a well defined operation, so I make no apologies for avoiding it here.

There are various UGens in the SuperCollider core which can be used for onset detection, some specialized and some which can be adapted and combined into detectors. Starting from the observation that new events often begin with a transient burst of energy, it is instructive to try to build onset detectors using the combination of some simple UGens, such as Amplitude, <, and Trig (consider Trig1.kr(Amplitude .kr(input) > 0.5), for example). The reader who tries this may quickly discover that it is not necessarily as simple a process as it might intuitively appear; not all note boundaries show up as changes in signal amplitude, and even if energy detection is appropriate, the right threshold and time scale to employ are tricky questions. In general, the better onset detectors are specialist UGens devised by researchers (PV_HainsworthFoote and PV_JensenAndersen are 2 examples).

```
b = Buffer.alloc(s,1024,1); //for sampling rates 44100 and 48000
//b = Buffer.alloc(s,2048,1); //for sampling rates 88200 and 96000

//d=Buffer.read(s,"sounds/a11wlk01.wav");


(
x= {
    var in, fft, array;

    //in= PlayBuf.ar(1,d.bufnum,BufRateScale.kr(d.bufnum),1,0,1);

    in = SoundIn.ar(0);

    fft = FFT(b.bufnum, in);

    array = MFCC.kr(fft);

    array.size.postln;

    Out.kr(0,array);

    Out.ar(0,Pan2.ar(in));
}.play
)


c= Bus.new('control', 0, 13);

//poll coefficients
c.getn(13,{arg val; {val.plot;}.defer});


//Continuous graphical display of MFCC values; free routine before
closing window

(
var ms;

w = Window("Thirteen MFCC coefficients", Rect(200,400,300,300));

ms = MultiSliderView(w, Rect(10,10,260,280));
```

Figure 15.3
MFCC.

```
ms.value_(Array.fill(13,0.0));
ms.valueThumbSize_(20.0);
ms.indexThumbSize_(20.0);
ms.gap_(0);

w.front;

r = {

    inf.do{

        c.getn(13,{arg val; {ms.value_(val*0.9)}.defer});

        0.04.wait; //25 frames per second
    };

}.fork;

)


//tidy up
(
r.stop;
b.free;
c.free;
x.free;
w.close;
)
```

Figure 15.3
(continued)

Dan Stowell has released an easy-to-use collection of onset detectors as a by-product of his research into real-time vocal processing (Stowell and Plumbley, 2007). These are now encapsulated in the Onsets UGen in the standard distribution. Figure 15.4 gives an example of using the UGen with a particular choice of *detection function* from among various options available. The code shows how the SendTrig UGen can be used to send a message back to the language when an onset is detected.

Essentially, onset detection is most effective for percussive signals. Soft onsets, such as slow attacks and subtle changes marked in pitch, vibrato, or multiple feature combinations, are more troublesome; you will need to try out different solutions

```
// Prepare the buffer
b = Buffer.alloc(s, 512);

(
x = {
    var sig, chain, onsets, pips, trigger;

    sig = SoundIn.ar(0);

    chain = FFT(b, sig);

    // - move the mouse left/right to change the threshold:
    onsets = Onsets.kr(chain, MouseX.kr(0,1), \complex);

    trigger= SendTrig.kr(onsets);

    pips = SinOsc.ar(880, 0, EnvGen.kr(Env.perc(0.001, 0.1, 0.2),
onsets));

    Out.ar(0, ((sig * 0.1) + pips).dup);
}.play;
)

(
// register to receive message
a= OSCresponder(s.addr,'/tr',{ arg time,responder,msg;
    [time,responder,msg].postln;
}).add;
)

a.remove; //Free the OSCresponder
x.free; // Free the synth
b.free; // Free the buffer
```

Figure 15.4
Onsets.

(UGens and their arguments, particularly thresholds and FFT settings) to find the best-performing detectors for the singing voice or nonpercussive instruments, in negotiation with particular microphones and acoustics.

15.3   Higher-Level Musical Constructs

We proceed now to a higher-level viewpoint and consider the extraction of what are more definite musical parameters, from the perspective of conventional Western music theories. While we keep an ear to the wider currents of music in the world, the musical structures we now seek to extract are related to common-practice notions of meter and key, and they assume particular theories on the perception and structuring of rhythm and of 12-note equal temperament with major and minor modes.

15.3.1   Beat Tracking

Computational beat tracking is the use of a computer to "extract" the metrical structure of music (actually a culturally consensual and cognitive construction). In certain musicologically unambiguous situations, this can correspond to the location of beats where average listeners would clap their hands or tap their feet along to a musical signal. In more complicated settings, the extraction of meter is accomplished by identifying multiple metrical levels, any duple/triple hierarchical structure, or even other metrical frameworks outside the canon of conventional Western music theory; phase and period (as well as further marking events or patterns) must be determined in more difficult cases. For instance, beat tracking of Balkan dance music (*aksak*) or Norwegian Hardanger fiddle music would require the resolution of higher-level patterns than any simple isochronous beat, and generalized meter tracking would precede any notion of beat subdivision.

Methods for computational beat tracking are varied (Gouyon and Dixon, 2005; Collins, 2006), from rule-based systems for symbolic data to correlation and oscillator methodologies for audio feature data. In engineering practice, the beat-tracking model that infers the current metrical state may be distinct from an observation front end that collates evidence from the audio stream.

That's enough theory. Figure 15.5 presents a practical beat tracker for you to try.

There are weaknesses in tracking that should be acknowledged, some of them particular to the BeatTrack UGen and some also in common with the current state of the art. BeatTrack uses a window of 6 seconds to obtain a stable estimate of the current tempo and beat phase, but this assumes that the tempo and metrical state do not change during that time. You will find that if you stick to a particular reasonable midtempo periodic pattern, BeatTrack will synchronize, but that you can easily lose

```
b = Buffer.alloc(s,1024,1); //for sampling rates 44100 and 48000
//b = Buffer.alloc(s,2048,1); //for sampling rates 88200 and 96000

//track audio in (try clapping a beat or beatboxing, but allow up to 6 seconds for
tracking to begin); events will be spawned at quarter, eighth and sixteenth note
rates
(
SynthDef(\beattrack,{
    var trackb,trackh,trackq,tempo;
    var source;
    var bsound,hsound,qsound;

    source = SoundIn.ar(0);

    #trackb,trackh,trackq,tempo = BeatTrack.kr(FFT(b.bufnum, source));

    bsound = Pan2.ar(LPF.ar(WhiteNoise.ar*(Decay.kr(trackb,0.05)),1000),0.0);

    hsound = Pan2.ar(BPF.ar(WhiteNoise.ar*(Decay.kr(trackh,0.05)),3000,0.66),-0.5);

    qsound = Pan2.ar(HPF.ar(WhiteNoise.ar*(Decay.kr(trackq,0.05)),5000),0.5);

    Out.ar(0, bsound+hsound+qsound);
}).add;
)

x = Synth(\beattrack); // Go!

x.free;
b.free; // Free the buffer
```

Figure 15.5
BeatTrack.

the beat tracker by sudden shifts of tempo and continuous slowing or speeding up. The trade-off of stability of estimate and reactivity to change is fundamental in such work.

The BeatTrack2 UGen in the standard distribution provides an alternative algorithm in which the trade-off of reactivity and stability of estimate can be directly controlled by choosing the size of the temporal window, among other arguments. BeatTrack2 makes a majority decision on the winning period and phase hypothesis by analyzing a number of user-specifiable feature stream inputs in parallel. (The Help file gives more details and examples.)

The reader might be curious whether the beat so extracted can drive algorithmically composed parts. An example of how this can be done server-side is implicit in the beat-tracking example, but setting up synchronization via the language is harder. This is the research motive behind my BBCut2 extensions to SuperCollider. I won't go into them here but refer the curious reader to that code library and associated doctoral thesis (Collins, 2006). The reader might also explore examples of synchronization by Florian Paul Schmidt (OSCClocks, available as a Quark), Fredrik Olofsson (sync by successive tempo adjustments), and James Harkins (MIDISyncClock), among others. But as a first step, modifying the example above, the quarter-note level beat can be passed to the language by using SendTrig to drive the scheduling of actions language-side.

Beat tracking raises an interesting point about machine listening; many of the processes we explore are based around "as fast as possible" reaction to a signal. This is not how a human musician works: humming along to a previously unknown melody at a latency of less than 20 ms is impossible for a human but plausible for a computer. Instead, expectation and anticipation are key to human music making, and we are adept at synchronizing ourselves within a performance context, such that the actions we schedule in advance will synchronize as long as our predictions are not astray.

15.3.2   Key Tracking

As a further demonstration of higher-level machine listening, an audio signal can be analyzed for the current key signature (Gómez, 2006). This process assumes that 12-tone equal temperament and major/minor tonality make sense within the musical context being examined, and the particular UGen here described, KeyTrack, also assumes concert A = 440 Hz tuning. To give a short rather than a long explanation, analysis proceeds by matching certain harmonic templates to the spectrum and taking the best-fitting one as indicating the key. Figure 15.6 gives example code.

KeyTrack can be thrown by transient-rich signals—where the audio files to be tracked contain a lot of percussive nonpitched instruments, tracking is less reliable—but the process is designed to operate on polyphonic audio to start with, so don't be afraid to test it on Blondie or Beethoven.

15.3.3   Event Transcription

It is possible to combine pitch detection and onset detection to attempt to transcribe a melodic line over time. We can analyze a sequence of musical events, storing the individually extracted "notes" in a database for algorithmic reuse.

```
//straight forward test file with few transients; training set in e
minor from MIREX2006
//You will need to substitute your own soundfile to load here
d=Buffer.read(s,"/Users/nickcollins/Desktop/ML/training_wav/78.wav")

b = Buffer.alloc(s,4096,1); //for sampling rates 44100 and 48000
//b = Buffer.alloc(s,8192,1); //for sampling rates 88200 and 96000

(
x= {
    var in, fft;
    var key;

    in = PlayBuf.ar(1,d.bufnum,BufRateScale.kr(d.bufnum),1,0,1);

    fft = FFT(b.bufnum, in);

    key = KeyTrack.kr(fft, 2.0, 0.5);

    key.poll; //write out detected key

    Out.ar(0,Pan2.ar(in));
}.play
)

x.free;
b.free;
```

Figure 15.6
KeyTrack.

Figure 15.7 is a relatively minimal example to demonstrate this process, combining the Pitch and Onsets UGens and storing the last n notes (n = 10 by default). The quality of transcription is at the mercy of the onset detection; new onsets are the cue to resolve the previous note event and add it to the database. Why does this process resolve the previous note event rather than the current one? Because a new onset notification is at the start of a note, and pitch will not necessarily have settled yet in the transient region to allow an accurate reading. The code shows how to record a succession of frequency values language-side and take the median for a stable pitch estimate. The code again demonstrates that machine listening must often operate at a delay.

For a more sophisticated version of this process, the reader might investigate the AnalyzeEvents UGens accompanying my thesis work on interactive music systems.

```
//Example uses internal server to demonstrate shared busses

(
s=Server.internal;
Server.default=s;

s.doWhenBooted({

b = Buffer.alloc(s, 512);

//this SynthDef will make no sound, just analyses input
SynthDef(\pitchandonsets,
{
    var in, amp, freqdata, chain, onsets, trigger;

    in = SoundIn.ar(0);
    amp = RunningSum.rms(in, 64); //get rms amplitude value per control block
    freqdata = Pitch.kr(in);

    //allow synchronous polling, Internal Server only
    SharedOut.kr(0,freqdata);
    SharedOut.kr(2,amp);

    chain = FFT(b, in);

    // - move the mouse left/right to change the threshold:
    onsets = Onsets.kr(chain, MouseX.kr(0,1), \complex);

    trigger = SendTrig.kr(onsets);

}).send(s);
});

)


(
var freqlist=List(), amplist=List();
var notelist= List(), numnotes=10; //will hold the last 10 notes
var lasttime, started=false;
var maxlength=0.5, maxkperiods, waittime;
```

Figure 15.7
Simple melodic transcription.

```
maxkperiods = ((maxlength*(s.sampleRate))/(s.options.blockSize)).asInteger;
waittime = (s.options.blockSize)/(s.sampleRate);


// register to receive message
a= OSCresponder(s.addr,'/tr',{ arg time,responder,msg;
    var newnote;

    if(started,{

    //finalise previous note as [starttime, ioi= inter onset interval, dur,
medianpitch, maxamp]
    newnote =    [lasttime, time-lasttime, (time-lasttime).min(maxlength),
if(freqlist.notEmpty, {freqlist.median.cpsmidi},{nil}),amplist.maxItem.ampdb];

    newnote.postln;

    notelist.addFirst(newnote);

    //remove oldest note if over size
    if(notelist.size>numnotes,{notelist.pop});

    },{started = true;});

    //reset lists for collection
    freqlist = List();
    amplist = List();
    lasttime = time;

}).add;

x= Synth(\pitchandonsets);

//poll values
{

    inf.do{
        var freq, hasfreq, rmsamp;

        freq = s.getSharedControl(0);
        hasfreq = s.getSharedControl(1);
```

Figure 15.7
(continued)

```
        rmsamp = s.getSharedControl(2);

        //don't allow notes of longer than 500 control periods or so
        if((hasfreq>0.5) and: (amplist.size<maxkperiods), {freqlist.add(freq)});

        if(amplist.size<maxkperiods, {amplist.add(rmsamp)});

        //poll every control period, intensive
        (waittime).wait;
    };

}.fork;

)




(
a.remove; //Free the OSCresponder
x.free; // Free the synth
b.free; // Free the buffer
)
```

Figure 15.7
(continued)

15.4 Interactive Music Systems

15.4.1 Example Systems

The term *interactive music system*, following the title of Robert Rowe's first book (Rowe, 1993), generally covers a panoply of startling, fascinating, and musically provocative creations (Collins, 2007). These typically involve some independence of computer action in response to human input, emulating musical dialogue, though there are many variations of this task.

It's hard to go through a survey of interactive music systems without mentioning George Lewis and *Voyager*. Lewis's contributions to the field include a great vigor with which he has defended, and indeed promoted, the cause of improvisation as the quintessential musical paradigm; in this vein, some have considered interactive improvisation the most challenging of test cases for virtual musicianship. Voyager itself is an intentionally chaotic and quixotic system, an openly personal set of rules, a reputed million lines of Forth code now converted to a monster Max/MSP patch. It sounds ... well, chaotic and quixotic. It sends out a barrage of MIDI messages—usually, these days, to control the refined acoustic sound source of a Disklavier piano (perhaps what Lewis spent his MacArthur Genius Fund grant on)—though the now out-of-print 1992 CD involves a General MIDI set of voices. The input can be any monophonic instrument which works with a standard pitch to MIDI converter; Lewis enjoys a little extra noise on the line, so perfect conversion isn't the name of the game. This is indeed a pragmatic strategy with the technology. It's all great fun and very inspiring, but not so well documented even in Lewis's academic papers. Although hardly the most high-tech or flexible of solutions, it is extensively gig-tested.

To give a second example, this time of a SuperCollider-based system (originally developed for SuperCollider 2), Joel Ryan has combined an Eventide Harmonizer and additional SuperCollider-based audio processing. He has explored many collaborations with improvising musicians, including the virtuoso of circular breathing, perpetually-in-motion saxophonist Evan Parker; Ryan is actively involved in the control loop here, and the system is not intended to be autonomous during a concert but a conduit for human musical action.

There is no space to delve further into the rich history and musical activity of these systems, but for audio-based work the UGens we have been describing in this chapter are essential props to effective interactive concert work.

15.4.2 A Language-Side Symbolic System Using MIDI

An interactive music system does not have necessarily require an audio signal. Robert Rowe's books (Rowe, 1993, 2001) predominantly treat the case of (complex) MIDI processing systems; and the MIDI representation, though weak in some ways, is a familiar discrete event representation that works especially well for keyboard instruments. In order to illustrate this case, avoiding any audio-based listening process, the code for this chapter includes the `OnlineMIDI` class and associated Help file. OnlineMIDI is a demonstration that should give an insight into how to extract features from symbolic information on the language side. It can be productive to consider purely MIDI-based systems in order to focus on compositional logic and artificial intelligence rather than deal with tricky issues of real-time audio signal processing. Figure 15.8 gives some simple client code for controlling this class, with the specification of a particular response function that utilizes the feature data extracted.

Whereas the objective in audio signal machine listening is to move toward discrete objects more easily treated in SuperCollider language code, MIDI can be a useful tool for prototyping ideas for interaction.

```
//do this first:
MIDIIn.connect;       // init for one port midi interface

//now:
m = OnlineMIDI();

m.analyse(3,1.0); //3 seconds window, step size of 1.0 seconds

m.data //poll current data

m.status = true; //prints analysis data as it goes
m.status= false;

//use analysis data to formulate responses

(
SynthDef(\beep2,{arg freq=440,amp=0.1, pan=0.0, dur=0.1;
var source;

source= SinOsc.ar(freq*[1,1.007],0,amp*0.5);

Out.ar(0,Pan2.ar(Mix(source)*Line.kr(1,0,dur, doneAction:2),pan))}).add;
)

//to echo each note you play on a MIDI keyboard with a sound; your SynthDef must
have freq and amp arguments, and deal with duration and freeing the Synth itself.
(
m.playinput= true;
m.inputsynthdef= \beep2;
)

//set a function that gets called after each window is analysed, to schedule events
over the next second
(
m.response = {|analysis|
    var number;
    number= analysis.density;
    //number= max(0,(10-(analysis.density))); //inverting number of notes playing

    if(analysis.iois.notEmpty, {
        {
```

Figure 15.8
OnlineMIDI.

```
        number.do{

        Synth(\beep2, [\freq, analysis.pitches.choose.midicps, \amp,
0.2*(rrand(analysis.volumemin, analysis.volumemax))]);

        analysis.iois.choose.wait; //could last longer than the next second, but
still fun!

        };

        }.fork;
    });

};
)


m.response= nil; //stop
```

Figure 15.8
(continued)

15.4.3 Audio-Based Systems

There are continua on multiple dimensions from *intelligent signal processing*, such as exhibited by the code in figure 15.1, to more complicated *virtual musicians* who extract multiple layers of information from an audio signal as well as deliberate complex responses based on musical modeling and artificial intelligence. Within the scope of this chapter it is possible only to allude to the existence of larger-scale interactive music systems.

Various examples of audio-based systems for SuperCollider are available, ranging from work by Herve Provini, Dan Stowell, and Julio d'Escriván, to the aforementioned interactive music systems available alongside my doctoral thesis, whose full code is free under the GNU GPL. To briefly mention 2 of the 5, *DrumTrack* involves a duel between a human and a machine drummer where the degree of contest and synchronicity varies over time, utilizing BBCut2; the *Ornamaton* operates in the domain of baroque music, adding improvised embellishments to the playing of a harpsichordist and baroque recorder player via specialized onset detection, event analysis, and key tracking.

15.5   Conclusions

There are wider debates surrounding the technical topics in this chapter, concerning the musical and philosophical status of interactive music systems. To give a taste, we might ask at what point reaction becomes interaction. Evaluation is also a tricky matter, and might be independently couched from the perspectives of technologist, audience, and performer, concerning engineering and musicological and human-computer interaction criteria. Our systems operate on various continua ranging from intelligent signal processing as a fancy effect to the autonomous behavior of software agents exhibiting independent musicianship.

In practice, there are no general easy solutions; readers are advised to try out different machine-listening plug-ins and select those that match their application needs. Concerts are not the only avenue of usage, for machine listening might drive live visuals or provide useful sensor information for installations. Although real-time applications have been emphasized in this chapter, it is often productive to consider their use in non-real-time mode or in the prototyping and preparation of material ahead of a concert. I hope that this chapter has given the reader a taste for the potential and excitement of these technologies.

Readers desiring to pursue their own implementations of machine-listening processes will need either to work language-side, with MIDI processing, say, implementing symbolic algorithms (Rowe, 2001) or, for audio-based work, will need to try plugging together and exploring arguments to existing UGens or to write their own UGen plug-ins (see chapter 25). There is a diverse computer music literature to refer to on these topics. For audio systems, there are a number of other open-source code projects which it may be productive to explore, of which a modest list of current options at the time of writing might include *Tartini, Praat, Sonic Visualiser, aubio, libxtract, CLAM,* and MIR systems such as *marsyas.*

The tools are there at your disposal and will reward your efforts, so you can attempt to create the fantastical virtual musician you have always dreamed of playing with! There is no danger of making human beings obsolete; instead, you will contribute to a grand discourse in experimental art which dates to the automata of antiquity.

References

de Cheveigné, A. 2006. "Multiple F0 Estimation." In D. Wang and G. J. Brown, eds., *Computational Auditory Scene Analysis: Principles, Algorithms, and Applications.* Hoboken, NJ: Wiley/IEEE Press.

Collins, N. 2007. "Musical Robots and Listening Machines." In N. Collins and J. d'Escriván, eds., *The Cambridge Companion to Electronic Music.* Cambridge: Cambridge University Press.

Collins, N. 2006. "Towards Autonomous Agents for Live Computer Music: Realtime Machine Listening and Interactive Music Systems." PhD thesis, University of Cambridge.

Gómez, E. 2006. "Tonal Description of Music Audio Signals." PhD thesis, Universitat Pompeu Fabra, Barcelona.

Gouyon, F., and S. Dixon. 2005. "A Review of Automatic Rhythm Description Systems." *Computer Music Journal*, 29(1): 34–54.

Logan, B. 2000. "Mel Frequency Cepstral Coefficients for Music Modeling." In *Proceedings of the 2000 International Symposium on Music Information Retrieval* (ISMIR). Amherst: University of Massachusetts at Amherst.

Moore, B. C. J. 2004. *An Introduction to the Psychology of Hearing,* 5th ed. London: Academic Press.

Roads, C. 2001. *Microsound.* Cambridge, MA: MIT Press.

Roads, C. 1996. *The Computer Music Tutorial.* Cambridge, MA: MIT Press.

Rowe, R. 2001. *Machine Musicianship.* Cambridge, MA: MIT Press.

Rowe, R. 1993. *Interactive Music Systems.* Cambridge, MA: MIT Press.

Stowell, D., and M. Plumbley. 2007. "Adaptive Whitening for Improved Real-Time Onset Detection." In *Proceedings of the 2007 International Computer Music Conference,* Copenhagen.

Tenney, J. 2006. *Meta-Hodos and META Meta-Hodos.* Oakland, CA: Frog Peak.

Wishart, T. 1985. *On Sonic Art.* York, UK: Imagineering Press.

Zwicker, E., and H. Fastl. 1993. *Psychoacoustics: Facts and Models,* 2nd ed. Berlin: Springer.

16 Microsound

Alberto de Campo

Since the pioneering work of Dennis Gabor and Iannis Xenakis, the idea of composing music and sound from minute particles has been an interesting domain for both scientific and artistic research. The most comprehensive book on the topic, *Microsound* (Roads, 2001a), covers historical, aesthetic, and technical considerations, and provides an extensive taxonomy of variants of particle-based sound synthesis and transformation. Though implementations of these variants are scattered across platforms, many of them were realized in earlier incarnations of SuperCollider.

This chapter provides a collection of detailed example implementations of many fundamental concepts of particle-based synthesis which may serve as starting points for adaptations, extensions, and further explorations by readers.

Human ears perceive sounds at different time scales quite differently; therefore, examples are provided which allow perceptual experiments with sound materials at the micro time scale.

16.1   Points of Departure

Imagine a sine wave that began before the big bang and will continue until past the end of time. If that is difficult, imagine a pulse of infinite amplitude but also infinitely short, so its integral is precisely 1.

In 1947 Dennis Gabor answered the question "What do we hear?" in an unusual way (Gabor, 1947): instead of illustrating quantum wave mechanics with acoustical phenomena, he did the opposite—applying a formalism from quantum physics to auditory perception, he obtained an *uncertainty relation* for sound. By treating signal representation (which is ignorant of frequency) and Fourier representation (which knows nothing about time) as the extreme cases of a general particle-based view on acoustics, he introduced acoustic quanta of information that represent the entity of maximum attainable certainty (or minimum uncertainty). He posited that sound can be decomposed into elementary particles which are vibrations with stationary frequencies modulated by a probability pulse; in essence, this is an envelope shaped like a Gaussian distribution function. This view influenced Iannis Xenakis by 1960 (Xenakis, 1992) to consider sounds as masses of particles he called "grains" that can be shaped by mathematical means.

Sounds at the micro time scale (below, say, 100 milliseconds) became accessible for creative experiments following the general availability of computers. While much computer music models electronic devices (such as oscillators, filters, or envelope generators), a number of pioneers have created programs to generate sound involving decisions at the sample time scale. These include Herbert Brün's SAWDUST (1976), G. M. Koenig's SSP (early 1970s), and Iannis Xenakis's Stochastic Synthesis (described first in Xenakis (1971) and realized as the GENDYN program in 1991; see also Hoffmann (2000), Luque (2006), and N. Collins's Gendy UGens for SuperCollider).

Following concepts by Xenakis, Curtis Roads began experimenting with granular synthesis on mainframe computers in 1974; Barry Truax implemented the earliest real-time granular synthesis engine on special hardware beginning in 1986, and realized the pieces *Riverrun* and *Wings of Nike* with this system (Truax, 1988).

Trevor Wishart has called for a change of metaphor for music composition based on his experience of making electronic music (Wishart, 1994): rather than architecture (of pitch/time/parameter constructions), chemistry or alchemy can provide models for the infinite malleability of sound materials in computer music. This extends to the micro time scale, where it is technically possible to obtain a nearly infinite differentiation in creating synthetic grains, though this is constrained by limitations of differentiation in human hearing.

Horacio Vaggione has explored the implications of musical objects at different time scales both in publications (Vaggione, 1996, 2001) and in fascinating pieces (*Agon*, *Nodal*, and others).

Many physical sounds can be described as granular structures: dolphins communicate by clicking sounds; many insects produce micro sounds (e.g., crickets make friction sounds with a rasping action (stridulation) filtered by mechanical resonance of parts of their exoskeletons; bats echolocate obstacles and possible prey by emitting short ultrasound bursts and listening to the returning sound reflections.

Many sounds that involve a multitude of similar objects interacting will induce global percepts with statistical properties: rustling leaves produce myriad single short sounds, as do pebbles when waves recede from the shore; the film sound staple of steps on gravel can be perceived in these terms, as can bubbles in liquids, whether in a brook or in a frying pan.

Some musical instruments can be described and modeled as granular impact sounds passed through filters and resonators: guiro, rainstick, rattles, maracas, fast tone repetitions on many instruments, fluttertongue effects on wind instruments, and any instrument that can be played with drum rolls.

The microsound perspective also can be applied fruitfully in sound analysis, as initiated by Gabor. Wavelet analysis can decompose signals into elementary waveforms (Kronland-Martinet, 1988), and more recently Matching Pursuit Wavelet Analysis has been employed to create granular representations of sound which offer new possibilities for sound visualization and transformation (Sturm et al., 2006, 2008).

16.2   Perception at the Micro Time Scale

As human listeners perceive sound events quite differently; depending on the different time scales at which they occur, it is quite informative to experiment with the particularities of perception at the micro time scale. While there is a rich and interesting literature on psychoacoustics (Moore, 2004; Buser and Imbert, 1992), it tends to focus on a rather limited repertoire of sounds. For exploring new sound material, making one's own experiments (informed by psychoacoustics) can provide invaluable listening experience.

Pulses repeating at less than about 16 Hz will appear to most listeners as individual pulses, while pulses at 30 Hz fuse into continuous tones. A perceptual transition happens in between:

```
{Impulse.ar (XLine.kr(12, 48, 6, doneAction: 2)) * 0.1!2}.play; // up
{Impulse.ar (XLine.kr(48, 12, 6, doneAction: 2)) * 0.1!2}.play; // down
{Impulse.ar (MouseX.kr(12, 48, 1)) * 0.1 ! 2}.play; // mouse-controlled
```

We are quite sensitive to periodicities at different time scales; periodic pulses are perceived as pitches if they repeat often enough, but how often is enough? With very short-duration tones (on the order of 10 waveform repetitions) one can study how a pitched tone becomes more like a click with different timbre shadings (see figure 16.1).

Very short grains seem softer than longer ones, because loudness impression is formed over longer time windows (in psychoacoustics, this is called temporal integration). One can try comparing 2 alternating grains and adjusting their amplitudes until they seem equal.

```
Pbindef(\grain,
    \instrument, \gabor1, \freq, 1000, \dur, 1,
    \sustain, Pseq([0.001, 0.1], inf),
    \amp, Pseq([0.1, 0.1], inf)
).play;
        // short grain 2x louder
Pbindef(\grain, \sustain, Pseq([0.001, 0.1], inf),\amp, Pseq([0.2, 0.1],
inf) );
        // short grain 4x louder
```

```
(    // a gabor grain, gaussian-shaped envelope
SynthDef(\gabor, { |out, freq = 440, sustain = 1, pan, amp = 0.1, width = 0.25 |
    var env = LFGauss.ar(sustain, width, loop: 0, doneAction: 2);
    var son = FSinOsc.ar(freq, 0.5pi, env);
    OffsetOut.ar(out, Pan2.ar(son, pan, amp));

}, \ir ! 6).add;

    // or an approximation with a sine-shaped envelope
SynthDef(\gabor1, { |out, amp=0.1, freq=440, sustain=0.01, pan|
    var snd = FSinOsc.ar(freq);
    var env = EnvGen.ar(Env.sine(sustain, amp), doneAction: 2);
    OffsetOut.ar(out, Pan2.ar(snd * env, pan));
}, \ir ! 5).add;
)


(
Pbindef(\grain,
    \instrument, \gabor, \freq, 1000,
    \dur, 0.5, \sustain, 20/1000, \amp, 0.2
).play;
)
Pbindef(\grain, \sustain, 10/Pkey(\freq));
Pbindef(\grain, \sustain, 5/Pkey(\freq));
Pbindef(\grain, \sustain, 3/Pkey(\freq));
Pbindef(\grain, \sustain, 2/Pkey(\freq));
Pbindef(\grain, \sustain, 1/Pkey(\freq));

    // successively shorter, end
Pbindef(\grain, \sustain, Pseq((10..1)) / Pkey(\freq)).play;

    // random drift of grain duration
Pbindef(\grain, \sustain, Pbrown(1, 10, 3) / Pkey(\freq), \dur, 0.1).play
```

Figure 16.1
Short grain durations, pitch to colored click.

```
(
p = ProxySpace.push;

~source = { SinOsc.ar * 0.1 };
~silence = { |silDur=0.01|
    EnvGen.ar(
        Env([0, 1, 1, 0, 0, 1, 1, 0], [0.01, 2, 0.001, silDur, 0.001,
2, 0.01]),
        doneAction: 2) ! 2
};
~listen = ~source * ~silence;
~listen.play;
)

~silence.spawn([\silDur, 0.001]); // sounds like an added pulse
~silence.spawn([\silDur, 0.003]);
~silence.spawn([\silDur, 0.01]);
~silence.spawn([\silDur, 0.03]);        // a pause in the sound

    // try the same examples with noise:
~source = { WhiteNoise.ar * 0.1 };

p.pop
```

Figure 16.2
Perception of short silences.

```
Pbindef(\grain, \sustain, Pseq([0.001, 0.1], inf),\amp, Pseq([0.4, 0.1],
inf) );
```

With nearly rectangular envelope grains, the effect is even stronger (see example on the book Web site).

Short silences imposed on continuous sounds have different effects dependent on the sound: on steady tones, short pauses seem like dark pulses; only longer ones seem like silences; and short interruptions on noisier signals may be inaudible (see figure 16.2).

When granular sounds are played almost simultaneously, the order in which they occur can be difficult to discern. Figure 16.3 plays 2 sounds with an adjustable lag between them. Lags above around 0.03 second are easily audible; shorter ones become more difficult.

In fast sequences of granular sounds, order is hard to discern, as the grains fuse into 1 sound object. But when the order changes, the new composite does sound different (see figure 16.4).

```
(
          // a simple percussive envelope
SynthDef(\percSin, { |out, amp=0.1, freq=440, sustain=0.01, pan|
    var snd = FSinOsc.ar(freq);
    var env = EnvGen.ar(
        Env.perc(0.1, 0.9, amp), timeScale: sustain, doneAction: 2);
    OffsetOut.ar(out, Pan2.ar(snd * env, pan));
}, \ir ! 5).add;
)
(
Pbindef(\lo,
    \instrument, \percSin, \sustain, 0.05,
    \freq, 250, \amp, 0.2, \dur, 0.5, \lag, 0
).play;
Pbindef(\hi,
    \instrument, \percSin, \sustain, 0.05,
    \freq, 875, \amp, 0.1, \dur, 0.5, \lag, 0
).play;
)
    // try different lag times between them
Pbindef(\hi, \lag, 0.1);
Pbindef(\hi, \lag, 0.03);
Pbindef(\hi, \lag, 0.01);
Pbindef(\hi, \lag, 0.003);

    // hi too early or too late by a fixed time - which one is first?
Pbindef(\hi, \lag, ([-1, 1].choose * 0.01).postln).play;
Pbindef(\hi, \lag, ([-1, 1].choose * 0.02).postln);

    // is it easier to hear when the sounds are panned apart?
Pbindef(\hi, \pan, 0.5); Pbindef(\lo, \pan, -0.5);
Pbindef(\hi, \pan, 0);   Pbindef(\lo, \pan, 0);
```

Figure 16.3
Order confusion with sounds in fast succession.

```
(
Pbindef(\grain4,
    \instrument, \percSin, \sustain, 0.03, \amp, 0.2,
    \freq, Pshuf([1000, 600, 350, 250]), // random every each time
    \dur, 0.005
).play;
                    // repeat grain cluster
Tdef(\grain, { loop { Pbindef(\grain4).play; 1.wait } }).play;
)
    // fixed order
Pbindef(\grain4, \freq, Pseq([1000, 600, 350, 250].scramble));

    // different order every time
Pbindef(\grain4, \freq, Pshuf([1000, 600, 350, 250]));
```

Figure 16.4
Multiple grains fuse into one composite.

16.3   Grains and Clouds

Any sound particle shorter than about 100 ms (this is not a hard limit, only an order of magnitude) can be considered a grain, and can be used for creating groups of sound particles. Such groups may be called streams or trains, if they comprise regular sequences, or clouds, if they are more varied. We will first look at the details of single grains, and then at the properties that arise as groups of them form streams or clouds.

16.3.1   Grain Anatomy

A grain is a short sound event consisting of a waveform and an envelope. The waveform can be generated synthetically, taken from a fixed waveform, or selected from recorded material, and possibly processed. The envelope is an amplitude shape imposed on the waveform and can strongly influence the grain's sound character. We restrict our initial examples to simple synthetic waveforms and experiment with the effects of different envelopes, waveforms, and durations on single grains. We can create an envelope and a waveform signal as arrays; in order to impose the envelope shape on the waveform, they are multiplied, and the 3 signals are plotted, as shown in figure 16.5.

```
e = Env.sine.asSignal(400).as(Array);
w = Array.fill(400, {|i| (i * 2pi/40).sin});
```

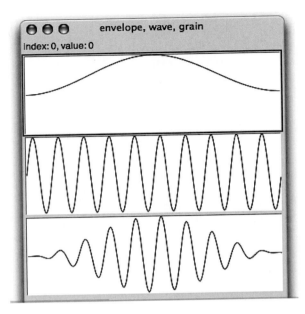

Figure 16.5
Envelope, waveform, grain.

```
g = e * w;
[e, w, g].flop.flat.plot2("envelope, wave, grain", Rect(0, 0, 408, 600),
numChannels: 3);
```

`Env.sine` is close to a Gaussian envelope, providing reasonable approximations of sound quanta as postulated by Gabor. The LFGauss UGen can be used as a higher-precision Gaussian envelope for grains, see { `LFGauss.ar(0.01, 0.26)` }.plot2 or the LFGauss help file.

Assembling these elements in a `SynthDef` allows creating many variants of 1 kind of grain by varying waveform, frequency, grain duration, amplitude, and spatial position:

```
(
SynthDef(\gabor0, {|out, freq = 440, sustain = 0.02, amp = 0.2, pan|
    var env = EnvGen.ar(Env.sine(sustain, amp), doneAction: 2);
    var sound = SinOsc.ar(freq) * env;
    OffsetOut.ar(out, Pan2.ar(sound, pan))
}, \ir.dup(5)).add;
)
Synth(\gabor0);      // test with synth
Synth(\gabor0, [\freq, 1000, \sustain, 0.005, \amp, 0.1, \pan, 0.5]);
```

```
Env.sine.plot2;       // approx. gaussian
Env([0, 1, 1, 0], [0.25, 0.5, 0.25] * 0.1, \sin).test.plot2; // quasi-gaussian
Env([0, 1, 1, 0], [0.25, 0.5, 0.25] * 0.1, \lin).test.plot2; // 3 stage line
segments.
Env([0, 1, 1, 0], [0.25, 0.5, 0.25] * 0.1, \welch).test.plot2; // welch curve
interpolation
Env([1, 0.001], [0.1], \exp).test.plot2;    // expoDec (exponential decay);
Env([0.001, 1], [0.1], \exp).test.plot2;    // revExpoDec (reverse exponential decay);
Env.perc(0.01, 0.09).test.plot2;

(   // a sinc function envelope
q = q ? ();
q.makeSinc = { |q, num=1, size=400|
    dup({ |x| x = x.linlin(0, size-1, -pi, pi) * num; sin(x) / x }, size);
};
a = q.makeSinc(6);
a.plot(bounds: Rect(0,0,409,200), minval: -1, maxval: 1);
)
```

Figure 16.6
Making different envelope shapes.

```
(instrument: \gabor0).play; // test with event
(instrument: \gabor0, sustain: 0.001, freq: 2500, amp: 0.05, pan: -0.5).
play;
Synth.grain(\gabor0, [\freq, 2000, \sustain, 0.003]) // higher efficiency,
as no NodeID is kept

s.sendMsg("s_new", \gabor0, -1, 0, 0, \freq, 2000, \sustain, 0.003); //
even more efficient, as no Synth object is created.
```

This example demonstrates recommended practices for granular synthesis. As grains may have extremely short durations, audio-rate envelopes are preferred. Timing between grains should be as accurate as possible, as the ear is very sensitive to microrhythmic variations; thus one uses OffsetOut to start the grain's synthesis process with single-sample accuracy. Since grain synthesis parameters typically do not change while the grain plays, efficiency can be optimized with \ir arguments. The 2 final lines show possible trade-offs of CPU load versus programming effort. Synth.grain creates nodes without nodeIDs (reducing overhead), and s.sendMsg constructs the same even more efficiently with nodeID –1: it does not create any language side Synth object, but directly messages the Server. Finally, adding synthdefs also makes them available for use in patterns. The tests shown play single grains both as synths and as events, using every parameter at least once to verify that they work correctly.

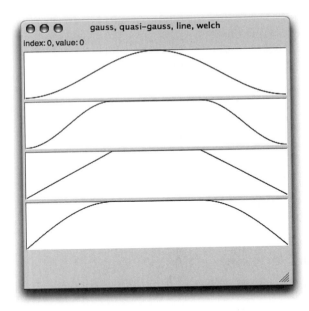

Figure 16.7
Envelopes: Gaussian, quasi-Gaussian, linear, welch.

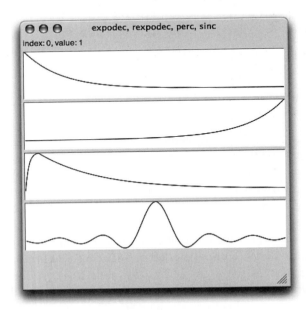

Figure 16.8
Envelopes: expodec, rexpodec, percussive, sinc-function.

```
(    // a gabor (approx. gaussian-shaped) grain
SynthDef(\gabor1, { |out, amp=0.1, freq=440, sustain=0.01, pan|
    var snd = FSinOsc.ar(freq);
    var amp2 = amp * AmpComp.ir(freq.max(50)) * 0.5;
    var env = EnvGen.ar(Env.sine(sustain, amp2), doneAction: 2);
    OffsetOut.ar(out, Pan2.ar(snd * env, pan));
}, \ir ! 5).add;

            // wider, quasi-gaussian envelope, with a hold time in the middle.
SynthDef(\gabWide, { |out, amp=0.1, freq=440, sustain=0.01, pan, width=0.5|
    var holdT = sustain * width;
    var fadeT = 1 - width * sustain * 0.5;
    var snd = FSinOsc.ar(freq);
    var amp2 = amp * AmpComp.ir(freq.max(50)) * 0.5;
    var env = EnvGen.ar(Env([0, 1, 1, 0], [fadeT, holdT, fadeT], \sin),
        levelScale: amp2,
        doneAction: 2);
    OffsetOut.ar(out, Pan2.ar(snd * env, pan));
}, \ir ! 5).add;

            // a simple percussive envelope
SynthDef(\percSin, { |out, amp=0.1, freq=440, sustain=0.01, pan|
    var snd = FSinOsc.ar(freq);
    var amp2 = amp * AmpComp.ir(freq.max(50)) * 0.5;
    var env = EnvGen.ar(
        Env.perc(0.1, 0.9, amp2),
            timeScale: sustain,
            doneAction: 2);
    OffsetOut.ar(out, Pan2.ar(snd * env, pan));
}, \ir ! 5).add;

            // a reversed  percussive envelope
SynthDef(\percSinRev, { |out, amp=0.1, freq=440, sustain=0.01, pan|
    var snd = FSinOsc.ar(freq);
    var amp2 = amp * AmpComp.ir(freq.max(50)) * 0.5;
    var env = EnvGen.ar(
        Env.perc(0.9, 0.1, amp2),
            timeScale: sustain,
            doneAction: 2
        );
    OffsetOut.ar(out, Pan2.ar(snd * env, pan));
}, \ir ! 5).add;
```

Figure 16.9
SynthDefs with different envelopes.

```
                  // an exponential decay envelope
SynthDef(\expodec, { |out, amp=0.1, freq=440, sustain=0.01, pan|
    var snd = FSinOsc.ar(freq);
    var amp2 = AmpComp.ir(freq.max(50)) * 0.5 * amp;
    var env = XLine.ar(amp2, amp2 * 0.001, sustain, doneAction: 2);
    OffsetOut.ar(out, Pan2.ar(snd * env, pan));
}, \ir ! 5).add;

                  // a reversed exponential decay envelope
SynthDef(\rexpodec, { |out, amp=0.1, freq=440, sustain=0.01, pan|
    var snd = FSinOsc.ar(freq);
    var amp2 = amp * AmpComp.ir(freq.max(50)) * 0.5;
    var env = XLine.ar(amp2 * 0.001, amp2, sustain, doneAction: 2)
        * (AmpComp.ir(freq) * 0.5);
    OffsetOut.ar(out, Pan2.ar(snd * env, pan));
}, \ir ! 5).add;
)
```

Figure 16.9
(continued)

SC3 allows for quick testing of envelope variants; below, we create a number of common envelopes which can have quite different effects on the sound character of the grain: *Gaussian* envelopes minimize the spectral side effects of the envelope, leaving much of the waveform character intact; *quasi-Gaussian* envelopes increase grain energy by holding full amplitude in the middle of its duration (*welch* interpolation is similar); *exponential decay* creates grains which can sound like they come from a physical source because physical resonators decay exponentially; *reverse exponential decay* can be an intriguing special case of "unnaturalness"; and *percussive* envelopes with controllable attack time can articulate different attack characteristics. More complex envelopes (e.g., the *sinc* function) can be created with sampled mathematical functions or taken from recorded material and played with buffers. (See figures 16.6–16.8.)

With synthdefs using these envelopes (see figure 16.9), we can experiment with the fundamental grain parameters: waveform frequency, envelope shape, and grain duration.

In order to access all parameters of the granular stream while it is playing, figure 16.10 uses the Pbindef class (see its Help file).

Parameter changes can have side effects of interest. For example, the \rexpodec synthdef's (reverse exponential decay) envelope ends with a very fast cutoff—when the waveform amplitude is high at that moment, it creates a click transient. A (for-

```
     // figure 16.10 - changing grain duration, frequency, envelope
(
Pbindef(\grain0,
    \instrument, \gabor1, \freq, 500,
    \sustain, 0.01, \dur, 0.2
).play;
)
     // change grain durations
Pbindef(\grain0, \sustain, 0.1);
Pbindef(\grain0, \sustain, 0.03);
Pbindef(\grain0, \sustain, 0.01);
Pbindef(\grain0, \sustain, 0.003);
Pbindef(\grain0, \sustain, 0.001);
Pbindef(\grain0, \sustain, Pn(Pgeom(0.1, 0.9, 60)));
Pbindef(\grain0, \sustain, Pfunc({ exprand(0.0003, 0.03) }));
Pbindef(\grain0, \sustain, 0.03);

     // change grain waveform (sine) frequency
Pbindef(\grain0, \freq, 300);
Pbindef(\grain0, \freq, 1000);
Pbindef(\grain0, \freq, 3000);
Pbindef(\grain0, \freq, Pn(Pgeom(300, 1.125, 32)));
Pbindef(\grain0, \freq, Pfunc({ exprand(300, 3000) }));
Pbindef(\grain0, \freq, 1000);

     // change synthdef for different envelopes
Pbindef(\grain0, \instrument, \gabor1);
Pbindef(\grain0, \instrument, \gabWide);
Pbindef(\grain0, \instrument, \percSin);
Pbindef(\grain0, \instrument, \percSinRev);
Pbindef(\grain0, \instrument, \expodec);
Pbindef(\grain0, \instrument, \rexpodec);
Pbindef(\grain0, \instrument, Prand([\gabWide, \percSin, \percSinRev], inf));
```

Figure 16.10
Changing grain duration, frequency, envelope.

```
(    // synchronous - regular time intervals
Pbindef(\grain0).clear;
Pbindef(\grain0).play;
Pbindef(\grain0,
    \instrument, \expodec,
    \freq, Pn(Penv([200, 1200], [10], \exp), inf),
    \dur, 0.1, \sustain, 0.06
);
)
    // different fixed values
Pbindef(\grain0, \dur, 0.06)    // rhythm
Pbindef(\grain0, \dur, 0.035)
Pbindef(\grain0, \dur, 0.02)    // fundamental frequency 50 Hz

    // time-changing values: accelerando/ritardando
Pbindef(\grain0, \dur, Pn(Penv([0.1, 0.02], [4], \exp), inf));
Pbindef(\grain0, \dur, Pn(Penv([0.1, 0.02, 0.06, 0.01].scramble, [3,
2, 1], \exp), inf));

    // repeating values: rhythms or tones
Pbindef(\grain0, \dur, Pstutter(Pwhite(2, 15), Pfunc({ exprand(0.01,
0.3) })));

    // introducing irregularity - quasi-synchronous
Pbindef(\grain0, \dur, 0.03 * Pwhite(0.8, 1.2))
Pbindef(\grain0, \dur, 0.03 * Pbrown(0.6, 1.4, 0.1)) // slower drift
Pbindef(\grain0, \dur, 0.03 * Pwhite(0.2, 1.8))

    // average density constant, vary degree of irregularity
Pbindef(\grain0, \dur, 0.02 * Pfunc({ (0.1.linrand * 3) + 0.9 }));
Pbindef(\grain0, \dur, 0.02 * Pfunc({ (0.3.linrand * 3) + 0.3 }));
Pbindef(\grain0, \dur, 0.02 * Pfunc({ (1.0.linrand * 3) + 0.0 }));
Pbindef(\grain0, \dur, 0.02 * Pfunc({ 2.45.linrand.squared })); //
very irregular


(    // coupling - duration depends on freq parameter
Pbindef(\grain0,
    \freq, Pn(Penv([200, 1200], [10], \exp), inf),
    \dur, Pfunc({ |ev| 20 / ev.freq  })
);
)
```

Figure 16.11
Different control strategies applied to density.

```
    // different freq movement, different timing
Pbindef(\grain0, \freq, Pbrown(48.0, 96.0, 12.0).midicps);

(   // duration depends on freq, with some variation - tendency mask
Pbindef(\grain0,
    \freq, Pn(Penv([200, 1200], [10], \exp), inf),
    \dur, Pfunc({ |ev| 20 / ev.freq * rrand(0.5, 1.5)  })
);
)
```

Figure 16.11
(continued)

ward) \expodec may employ this transient for attack shaping: by adjusting the oscillator's initial phase, different attack colors can be articulated (see, e.g., the book Web site).

16.3.2 Textures, Masses, Clouds

When shifting attention from individual sound particles to textures composed of larger numbers of microsound events, relations between aspects of the individual events in time create a number of emerging perceptual properties. Different terms have been used for these streams: regular sequences are often called trains; texture is a rather flexible term used by, among others, Trevor Wishart (Wishart, 1994); Edgard Varèse often spoke of masses and *volumina* of sound; the cloud metaphor suggests interesting vocabulary for imagining clouds of sound particles, inspired by the rich morphologies of clouds in Earth's atmosphere or in interstellar space, and their evolution in time.

In *synchronous* granular synthesis, the particles occur at regular intervals and form either a regular rhythm at low densities or an emerging fundamental frequency at higher densities. *Quasi-synchronous* streams introduce more local deviations, while in *asynchronous* streams the timing between events is highly irregular; in the latter case, density really becomes a statistical description of the average number of sounding particles per time unit. Figure 16.11 demonstrates some general strategies for controlling cloud parameters, here applied to cloud density:

Fixed values, which create a synchronous stream
Time-varying values, specified by an envelope pattern, creating accelerando and ritardando

Random variation within ranges, with density, which creates a transition to asynchronous streams
Tendency masks, which combine time-varying values with random ranges, such that the range limits change over time
Parameter-dependent values, a cloud parameter derived from another cloud parameter. (The generalization of this approach is called Grainlet Synthesis; see Roads, 2001: 125–129).

These strategies can be applied to any control parameter. Figure 16.12 shows different combinations of control strategies and grain and cloud parameters described so far.

16.3.3   CloudGenMini

CloudGenMini is a reimplementation of *CloudGenerator,* a classic microsound program written by Curtis Roads and John Alexander, which creates clouds of sound particles based on user specifications. Here, the discussion focuses on the synthesis control techniques and the aesthetic aspects; coding style aspects are covered in chapter 5. (For the code, see *CloudGenMiniFull.scd* on the book Web site.) *CloudGenMini* provides a collection of synthdefs for different sound particle flavors, a `Tdef` that creates the grain cloud based on current parameter settings, crossfading between stored settings, and a GUI for playing it. This allows creating clouds based on tendency masks, which was a central feature of *CloudGenerator.*

The `Tdef(\cloud0)` plays a loop which creates values for each next grain by random choice within the ranges for each parameter given in the `current` settings. Especially for high-density clouds, using `s.sendBundle` is more efficient than using `Event.play` or patterns.

Synthesis processes with multiple control parameters have large possibility spaces. When exploring these by making manual changes, one may spend much time in relatively uninteresting areas. One common heuristic that addresses this is to create random ranges which may assist in finding more interesting zones. *CloudGenMini* can create random ranges for all synthesis and cloud parameters, within global maximum settings, and can switch or interpolate between 8 stored range settings.

CloudGenerator allowed specifying a total cloud duration, start and end values for high and low *band limit* (the minimum and maximum frequencies of the grain waveform); and grain duration, density, and amplitude to define a cloud's evolution in time. *CloudGenMini* generalizes this approach: by providing ranges for all parameters, and by crossfading between them, every parameter can mutate from deterministic to random variation within a range (i.e., with a tendency mask. For example, a `densityRange` fading from [10, 10] to [1, 100] creates a synchronous cloud that

```
(
Pbindef(\grain0).clear;
Pbindef(\grain0,
    \instrument, \expodec,
    \freq, 200,
    \sustain, 0.05, \dur, 0.07
).play;
)
    // time-varying freq with envelope pattern
Pbindef(\grain0, \freq, Pn(Penv([200, 1200], [10], \exp), inf));
    // random freq
Pbindef(\grain0, \freq, 400 * Pwhite(-24.0, 24).midiratio);
    // timechanging with random variation
Pbindef(\grain0, \freq, Pn(Penv([400, 2400], [10], \exp), inf) * Pwhite(-24.0, 24).
midiratio);

    // panning
Pbindef(\grain0, \pan, Pwhite(-0.8, 0.8));  // random
Pbindef(\grain0, \pan, Pn(Penv([-1, 1], [2]), inf)); // tendency
Pbindef(\grain0, \pan, Pfunc({ |ev| ev.freq.explin(50, 5000, -1, 1) })); // coupled
to freq

    // time scattering variants
Pbindef(\grain0, \dur, 0.1 * Pwhite(0.5, 1.5));    // random range
Pbindef(\grain0, \dur, 0.05 * Prand([0, 1, 1, 2, 4], inf)); // rhythmic random

    // amplitude - randomized
Pbindef(\grain0, \amp, Pwhite(0.01, 0.2)); // linear
Pbindef(\grain0, \amp, Pwhite(-50, -14).dbamp); // exponential - more depth
Pbindef(\grain0, \dur, 0.025 * Prand([0, 1, 1, 2, 4], inf)); // could be denser now

    // random amplitude envelopes with Pseg
(
Pbindef(\grain0,
    \amp, Pseg(
        Pxrand([-50, -20, -30, -40] + 10, inf), // level pattern
        Pxrand([0.5, 1, 2, 3], inf),            // time pattern
        Prand([\step, \lin], inf)               // curve pattern
    ).dbamp
);
)
    // grain sustain time coupled to freq
Pbindef(\grain0, \sustain, Pkey(\freq).reciprocal * 20).play;
```

Figure 16.12
Control strategies applied to different parameters.

evolves to asynchronicity over its duration. (CloudGenerator also offered sound file granulation; CloudGenMini leaves this as an exercise for the reader.)

16.4   Granular Synthesis on the Server

The examples so far have created every sound particle as 1 synthesis process. However, SC3 also has a selection of UGens that implement granular synthesis entirely on the sound server. Though one can obtain similar sounds using either approach, it is interesting to experimentally learn how parameter control by UGens suggests different solutions and thus leads to different ideas.

The first granular synthesis UGen in SC was TGrains, which granulates sound files (more on this below); with SC version 3.1 the UGens GrainSin, GrainFM, GrainBuf, GrainIn, and Warp1 became part of the SC3 distribution. Third-party UGen libraries (as in sc3-plugins) and Quarks are worth checking for more granular synthesis variants and options.

GrainSin creates a stream of grains with a sine waveform and a Hanning-shaped envelope; grains are triggered by a control signal's transition from negative to positive. Below is a simple conversion of the GrainSin Help file example to JIT style (see chapter 7). Briefly, a ProxySpace is an environment for NodeProxies (placeholders for synthesis processes). NodeProxies can be changed and reconfigured very flexibly while running, making them ideally suited for fluid exploration of synthesis variants.

```
p = ProxySpace.push;
(
~grain.play;
~grain = {arg envbuf = -1, density = 10, graindur = 0.1, amp = 0.2;
    var pan, env, freqdev;
    var trig = Impulse.kr(density);
    pan = MouseX.kr(-1, 1);        // use mouse-x for panning
    // use WhiteNoise and mouse Y to control deviation from center
    freqdev = WhiteNoise.kr(MouseY.kr(400, 0));
    GrainSin.ar(2, trig, graindur, 440 + freqdev, pan, envbuf) * amp
};
)
```

GrainSin allows for custom grain envelopes, which must be uploaded as buffers on the server. In the next example, an envelope is converted to a Signal and is sent to a buffer, and the ~grain proxy is set to use that buffer number. A bufnum of -1 sets it to the default envelope.

```
q = q ? ();     // make a dictionary to keep things around
q.envs = ();     // space for some envelopes
q.bufs = ();     // and some buffers
```

```
                       // make an envelope and send it to a buffer
q.envs.perc1 = Env([0, 1, 0], [0.1, 0.9], -4);
q.bufs.perc1 = Buffer.sendCollection(s, q.envs.perc1.discretize, 1);
~grain.set(\envbuf, -1); // switch to built-in envelope
~grain.set(\envbuf, q.bufs.perc1.bufnum); // or customized
```

Besides changing the parameter controls of the proxy to fixed values, one can also map control proxies to them:

```
~grain.set(\density, 20);
~grain.set(\graindur, 0.03);
    // map a control proxy to a parameter
~grdur = 0.1; ~grain.map(\graindur, ~grdur);
~grdur = {LFNoise1.kr(1).range(0.01, 0.1) }; // random graindur
~grdur = {SinOsc.kr(0.3).range(0.01, 0.1)}; // periodic
~grdur = 0.01; // fixed value
    // create random densities from 2 to 2 ** 6, exponentially distributed
~grdensity = {2 ** LFNoise0.kr(1).range(0, 6)};
    // map to density control
~grain.map(\density, ~grdensity);
```

At this point, exploration becomes more enjoyable with a NodeProxyEditor on the proxy and adding Specs for its parameters with Spec.add (see the NodeProxyEditor Help file).

The GrainFM UGen introduces a variant: as the name implies, a pair of sine oscillators create frequency-modulated waveforms within each grain. Below is the GrainFM Help file example rewritten as a nodeproxy, with MouseY controlling modulation range; such rewrites are useful for learning how different controls affect the sound.

```
~grain = {arg envbuf = -1, density = 10, graindur = 0.1, modfreq = 200;
    var pan = WhiteNoise.kr;
    var trig = Impulse.kr(density);
    var freqdev = WhiteNoise.kr(MouseY.kr(0, 400));
    var modrange = MouseX.kr(1, 10);
    var moddepth = LFNoise1.kr.range(1, modrange);
    GrainFM.ar(2, trig, graindur, 440 + freqdev, modfreq, moddepth, pan,
    envbuf) * 0.2
};
```

For more flexibility in experimentation, one can convert controls of interest to proxies and access them in the main proxy, in this case, ~grain. Controls can then be changed individually, and old and new control synthesis functions can be crossfaded. Figure 16.13 is such a rewrite, where all parameters can be changed freely between fixed values and synthesis functions, line by line, in any order.

```
    // figure 16.13    - GrainFM with individual control proxies
p = ProxySpace.push;


(
~trig = { |dens=10| Impulse.kr(dens) };
~freq = { MouseX.kr(100, 2000, 1) * LFNoise1.kr(1).range(0.25, 1.75)
};
~moddepth = { LFNoise1.kr(20).range(1, 10) };
~modfreq = 200;
~graindur = 0.1;

~grain = { arg envbuf = -1;
    GrainFM.ar(2, ~trig.kr, ~graindur.kr,
        ~freq.kr, ~modfreq.kr, ~moddepth.kr,
        pan: WhiteNoise.kr, envbufnum: envbuf) * 0.2
};
~grain.play;
)
    // change control ugens:
~modfreq = { ~freq.kr * LFNoise2.kr(1).range(0.5, 2.0) }; // modfreq
roughly follows freq
~trig = { |dens=10| Dust.kr(dens)}; // random triggering, same
density
~freq = { LFNoise0.kr(0.3).range(200, 800) };
~moddepth = 3;   // fixed depth
~graindur = { LFNoise0.kr.range(0.01, 0.1) };
```

Figure 16.13
GrainFM with individual control proxies.

Finally, we look at the GrainBuf UGen, which takes its waveform from a buffer on the server. Typically used for sound file granulation, it can potentially produce variety and movement in the sound stream by constantly moving the file read position (i.e., where in the sound file to take the next grain waveform from) and by varying the playback rate. Even simply moving the file read position along the time axis can create interesting articulation of the granular stream. Figure 16.14 rewrites a GrainBuf Help file example with separate control proxies and explores a number of different combinations of controls.

TGrains is very similar to GrainBuf, but only with a fixed envelope shape. GrainIn is also similar, but it granulates an input signal and can use different buffer envelopes. With the built-in multichannel panning (PanAz-like) common to this UGen family, GrainIn can be used elegantly for spatially scattering (e.g., continually processing) live input.

```
b = Buffer.read(s, "sounds/a11wlk01-44_1.aiff");
(
~grain.set(\wavebuf, b.bufnum);
~trig = { |dens=10| Impulse.kr(dens) };
~graindur = 0.1;
~filepos = {LFNoise2.kr(0.2).range(0, 1) };
~rate = { LFNoise1.kr.range(0.5, 1.5) };

~grain = { arg envbuf = -1, wavebuf = 0;
    GrainBuf.ar(2, ~trig.kr, ~graindur.kr, wavebuf,
    ~rate.kr, ~filepos.kr, 2, WhiteNoise.kr, envbuf) * 0.2
};
~grain.play;
)


    // experiment with control proxies
~trig = { |dens=20| Impulse.kr(dens) };
~rate = { LFNoise1.kr.range(0.99, 1.01) };
~filepos = { MouseX.kr + LFNoise0.kr(100, 0.03) };
~graindur = 0.05;
~trig = { |dens=50| Dust.kr(dens) };

c = Buffer.sendCollection(s, Env.perc(0.01, 0.99).discretize, 1);
~grain.set(\envbuf, c.bufnum);
~grain.set(\envbuf, -1);

~trig = { |dens=50| Impulse.kr(dens) }; ~graindur = 0.05;
```

Figure 16.14
GrainBuf with control proxies.

When comparing UGen-based and individual-grain particle syntheses, experimenting with UGens as controls allows for very interesting behavior—even much patternlike behavior can be realized with Demand UGens (see *Demand*.Help file). On the other hand, one cannot write one's own special grain flavors with server-side granular synthesis. Unless one is fluent enough in C++ to implement new UGens (see chapter 25), one is limited to the synthesis processes provided as UGens.

16.5   Exploring Granular Synthesis Flavors

The most flexible starting point for creating one's own microsound flavors is considering that grains can contain any waveform. Reviewing the synthdefs given in figure 16.9, all one needs to change is the sound source itself. As an exercise, we could replicate GrainFM and GrainBuf as synthdefs; \grainFM0 adds 3 parameters and changes the sound source to an FM pair, while \grainFM1 uses a buffer envelope with Osc1, a pseudo-UGen class written for this chapter and available on the book Web site.

```
SynthDef(\grainFM1, {|out, envbuf, carfreq = 440, modfreq = 200, moddepth
= 1,
    sustain = 0.02, amp = 0.2, pan|
    var env = Osc1.ar(envbuf, sustain, doneAction: 2);
    var sound = SinOsc.ar(carfreq, SinOsc.ar(modfreq) * moddepth) * env;
    OffsetOut.ar(out, Pan2.ar(sound, pan, amp))
}, \ir.dup(8)).add;
```

GrainBuf can be re-created with PlayBuf. Both synthdefs can be played with patterns or tasks from sclang (examples are on the book Web site).

```
SynthDef(\grainBuf1, {|out, envbuf, wavebuf, filepos, rate = 1, sustain =
0.02, amp = 0.2, pan|
    var env = Osc1.ar(envbuf, sustain, doneAction: 2);
    var sound = PlayBuf.ar(1, wavebuf,
        rate * BufRateScale.ir(wavebuf), 1,
        startPos: BufFrames.ir(wavebuf) * filepos)
        * env;
    OffsetOut.ar(out, Pan2.ar(sound, pan, amp))
}, \ir.dup(8)).add;
```

Glisson synthesis is based on Iannis Xenakis's use of glissandi (instead of fixed-pitch notes) as building blocks for some of his instrumental music. Introducing a linear sweep from freq to freq2 is sufficient for a minimal demonstration of the concept. Of course, one can experiment freely with different periodic waveforms and envelopes (see figure 16.15).

One possibility for organizing glissando structures is magnetization patterns (Roads, 2001: 121–125). See the example on the book Web site.

Pulsar Synthesis is named after pulsars, spinning neutron stars discovered in 1967 that emit electromagnetic pulses in the range of 0.25 Hz to 642 Hz. This range of frequencies crosses the time scale from rhythm to pitch, a central aspect of Pulsar Synthesis. It also connects back to the history of creating electronic sounds with analog impulse generators and filter responses.

The pulse waveform is determined by a fixed waveform, the *pulsaret*, and an envelope waveform, both of which are scaled to the pulse's duration. Pulsar synthesis was designed by Curtis Roads in conjunction with a special control model: a set of tables which can be edited by drawing is used for designing both waveforms (for pulsaret and envelope) and a group of control functions for synthesis parameters

```
(
b = Buffer.read(s, "sounds/a11wlk01-44_1.aiff");

SynthDef("glisson",
    { arg out = 0, envbuf, freq=800, freq2=1200, sustain=0.001,
amp=0.2, pan = 0.0;
        var env = Osc1.ar(envbuf, sustain, 2);
        var freqenv = XLine.ar(freq, freq2, sustain);
        OffsetOut.ar(out,
            Pan2.ar(SinOsc.ar(freqenv) * env, pan, amp)
        )
}, \ir!7).add;
)


(
Tdef(\gliss0, { |e|
    100.do({ arg i;
        s.sendBundle(s.latency, ["/s_new", "glisson", -1, 0, 0,
            \freq, i % 10 * 100 + 1000,
            \freq2, i % 13 * -100 + 3000,
             \sustain, 0.05,
             \amp, 0.1,
             \envbuf, b.bufnum
        ]);
        (3 / (i + 10)).wait;
    });
}).play;
)
```

Figure 16.15
Glisson synthesis.

over a given time; this concept has been expanded in the *PulsarGenerator* program
(written in SC2 by the author and Curtis Roads).

The 2 main control parameters in *Pulsar Synthesis* are fundamental frequency
(fundfreq), the rate at which pulses are emitted, and formant frequency (formfreq),
which determines how fast the pulsaret and envelope are played back—effectively
like a formant control. For example, at a fundfreq of 20 Hz, 20 pulses are emitted per
second; at a formfreq of 100 Hz, every pulse is scaled to 0.01 second duration, so
within 0.05 second of 1 pulsar period, the *duty cycle* where signal is present is only
0.01 second. Each pulsar train also has controls for amplitude and spatial trajectory.
Figure 16.16 shows the creation of a set of tables that are then sent to buffers.

```
     // figure 16.16 - Pulsar basics - make a set of waveform and control tables
(
q = ();
q.curr = ();      // make a dict for the set of tables
q.curr.tab = ();
                  // random tables for pulsaret  and envelope waveforms:
q.curr.tab.env = Env.perc.discretize;
q.curr.tab.pulsaret = Signal.sineFill(1024, { 1.0.rand }.dup(7));

          // random tables for the control parameters:
q.curr.tab.fund = 200 ** Env({1.0.rand}!8, {1.0.rand}!7, \sin).discretize.as(Array);
q.curr.tab.form = 500 ** ( 0.5 + Env({rrand(0.0, 1.0)}!8, {1.0.rand}!7,
\sin).discretize.as(Array));
q.curr.tab.amp = 0.2.dup(1024);
q.curr.tab.pan = Signal.sineFill(1024, { 1.0.rand }.dup(7));

          // make buffers from all of them:
q.bufs = q.curr.tab.collect({ |val, key| Buffer.sendCollection(s, val, 1) });
)
        // plot one of them
q.bufs.pulsaret.plot2("a pulsaret");
```

Figure 16.16
Pulsar basics: a set of waveform and control tables.

Figure 16.17 realizes 1 pulsar train with a GrainBuf, initially with fixed parameter values. Changing the parameters 1 at a time and crossfading between them demonstrates the effect of movements of formfreq and fundfreq. Finally, replacing the controls with looping tables completes a minimal pulsar synthesis program.

Figure 16.18 shows the sending of different tables to the buffers. One can make graphical drawing interfaces for the tables and send any changes in the tables to the associated buffers.

PulsarGenerator realized several aspects of advanced pulsar synthesis: 3 parallel pulsar trains (sharing fundfreq but with independent formfreq, amp, and pan controls) are being driven from separate control tables. One can switch or crossfade between sets of tables. Both table sets and banks of table sets can be saved to disk.

Pulsar masking was implemented in 2 forms: *burst ratio* specified how many pulses to play and how many to mute; (e.g., 3:2 would play this sequence of pulses: 1, 1, 1, 0, 0, 1, 1, 1, 0, 0). This allowed generating subharmonics of the fundamental frequency. Alternatively, stochastic pulse masking was controlled from a table with values between 1.0 (play every pulse) and 0.0 (mute every pulse); 0.5 meant playing each pulse with a 50% chance, which could create interesting intermittency. In SC3,

```
(
p = ProxySpace.push;

        // fund, form, amp, pan
~controls = [ 16, 100, 0.5, 0];
~pulsar1.set(\wavebuf, q.bufs.pulsaret.bufnum);
~pulsar1.set(\envbuf, q.bufs.env.bufnum);

~pulsar1 = { |wavebuf, envbuf = -1|
    var ctls = ~controls.kr;
    var trig = Impulse.ar(ctls[0]);
    var grdur = ctls[1].reciprocal;
    var rate = ctls[1] * BufDur.kr(wavebuf);

    GrainBuf.ar(2, trig, grdur, wavebuf, rate, 0, 4, ctls[3], envbuf);
};
~pulsar1.play;
)

    // crossfade between control settings
~controls.fadeTime = 3;
~controls = [ 16, 500, 0.5, 0];        // change formfreq
~controls = [ 50, 500, 0.5, 0];        // change fundfreq
~controls = [ 16, 100, 0.5, 0];        // change both
~controls = [ rrand(12, 100), rrand(100, 1000)];

(    // control parameters from looping tables
~controls = { |looptime = 10|
    var rate = BufDur.kr(q.bufs.pulsaret.bufnum) / looptime;
    A2K.kr(PlayBuf.ar(1, [\fund, \form, \amp, \pan].collect(q.bufs[_]),
        rate: rate, loop: 1));
};
)
```

Figure 16.17
Pulsars as nodeproxies using GrainBuf.

```
q.bufs.pulsaret.sendCollection(Array.linrand(1024, -1.0, 1.0)); // noise burst
q.bufs.pulsaret.read("sounds/a11wlk01.wav", 44100 * 1.5);       // sample
q.bufs.pulsaret.sendCollection(Pbrown(-1.0, 1.0, 0.2).asStream.nextN(1024));

    // make a new random fundfreq table, and send it
q.curr.tab.fund = 200 ** Env({1.0.rand}!8, {1.0.rand}!7, \sin).discretize.as(Array);
q.bufs.fund.sendCollection(q.curr.tab.fund);

    // and a new random formfreq table
q.curr.tab.form = 500 ** ( 0.5 + Env({rrand(0.0, 1.0)}!8, {1.0.rand}!7,
\sin).discretize.as(Array));
q.bufs.form.sendCollection(q.curr.tab.form);
```

Figure 16.18
Making new tables and sending them to buffers.

burst ratio could be reimplemented by multiplying the trigger signal with demand UGens to provide a sequence, and random masking with CoinGate.

Pulsar synthesis can also be implemented with client-side control, where one can choose to control parameters from patterns such as envelope segment players or from tables (see the examples on the book Web site). This provides elegant control of finer aspects of pulsar synthesis, such as handling pulsar width modulation (what to do when pulses overlap), extensions to parallel pulse trains, and variants of pulse masking.

Among others, Curtis Roads and Florian Hecker realized a number of pieces with material generated by pulsar synthesis. Pulsars can be used particularly well as exciter signals for filters or as input material for convolution processes (Roads, 2001: 147–154). Tommi Keränen has implemented an SC3 version of PulsarGenerator with a slightly different feature set, which however, has not yet been officially released.

16.6 Sound Files and Microsound

Sound files are a great source for waveform material in microsound synthesis, as they provide a lot of variety almost for free, simply by accessing different segments within their duration. Pitch shifting and time scaling are 2 classic uses of granular synthesis in this context. However, both writing more complex Synthdefs for granulating sound files (e.g., with filtering) and analyzing sound file waveforms to use them as a source for microstructure provide further areas to explore. Below we present examples for both: constant-Q granulation and wave sets.

16.6.1   Granular Pitch Shifting and Time Scaling

The idea of being able to manipulate time and pitch separately in a recorded sound is quite old; in the 1940s Dennis Gabor (who won the Nobel Prize for physics in 1971 for the invention of holography) built a "Kinematical Frequency Convertor," a machine for experimenting with pitch/time manipulations. The principle has remained the same: grains read from a recording are overlapped to create a seamless stream; depending on where in the recording the grain read begins and how fast the signal is read, time and pitch of the original can be changed.

Figure 16.19 provides a setup for experimenting. `pitchRatio` determines how much faster or slower the waveform in each grain is played, `pitchRd` adds randomization to it. `grainRate` is the number of grains per second, and `overlap` sets how many grains will overlap at any time. `posSpeed` determines whether time is stretched or compressed by changing the speed of the read position in the file, and `posRd` adds randomization to it. The `NodeProxyEditor` interface allows tweaking the parameters, so, for example, to time stretch a file by 4, one would set `posSpeed` to 0.25 and adjust `pitchRd` and `posRd` for a compromise between metallic artifacts (common with no randomizing) and scattering artifacts (too much randomness). The `PitchShift` UGen works similarly on input signals.

Tuning pitch-time changes to sound lifelike can be difficult, and many commercial applications spend much effort on it. Bringing forward details in recordings in non-naturalistic ways may be a more rewarding use for writing one's own pitch-time manipulating instruments.

16.6.2   Constant-Q Granulation

Constant-Q granulation is just one of many possible extensions of the file *Granulation*. In it, each grain is bandpass filtered, letting the filter ring while it decays. Figure 16.20 shows the Synthdef for it: a grain is read around a center position within the file, ring time and amplitude compensation are estimated for the given frequency and resonance, and a cutoff envelope ends synthesis after ring time is over.

Parameter tests (on the book Web site) demonstrate accessing different file regions and varying exciter grain duration; high `rq` values color the grain only a little, and low `rq` values create ringing pitches. Because the resonance factor q is constant, lower frequencies will ring longer.

Figure 16.21 demonstrates creating a stream of constant-Q grains with a `Pbindef` pattern, which allows for changing all parameter patterns while playing.

With this synthesis flavor, one can balance how much of the sound file material shines through and how strongly structures in grain timing and resonating pitches

```
p = ProxySpace.push(s.boot);
b = Buffer.read(s, "sounds/a11wlk01-44_1.aiff");
(
~timepitch = {arg sndbuf, pitchRatio=1, pitchRd=0.01, grainRate=10, overlap=2,
    posSpeed=1, posRd=0.01;

    var graindur = overlap / grainRate;
    var pitchrate = pitchRatio + LFNoise0.kr(grainRate, pitchRd);
    var position = LFSaw.kr(posSpeed / BufDur.kr(sndbuf)).range(0, 1)
        + LFNoise0.kr(grainRate, posRd);

    GrainBuf.ar(2, Impulse.kr(grainRate), graindur, sndbuf, pitchrate,
            position, 4, 0, -1)
};
~timepitch.set(\sndbuf, b.bufnum);
~timepitch.play;
);

Spec.add(\pitchRatio, [0.25, 4, \exp]);
Spec.add(\pitchRd, [0, 0.5, \amp]);
Spec.add(\grainRate, [1, 100, \exp]);
Spec.add(\overlap, [0.25, 16, \exp]);
Spec.add(\posSpeed, [-2, 2]);
Spec.add(\posRd, [0, 0.5, \amp]);
NodeProxyEditor(~timepitch, 10);

    // reconstruct original
~timepitch.set(\pitchRatio, 1, \pitchRd, 0, \grainRate, 20, \overlap, 4, \posSpeed,
1, \posRd, 0);

    // four times as long: tweak pitchRd and posJitter to reduce artifacts
~timepitch.set(\pitchRatio, 1, \pitchRd, 0, \grainRate, 20, \overlap, 4, \posSpeed,
0.25, \posRd, 0);

    // random read position, random pitch
~timepitch.set(\pitchRatio, 1, \pitchRd, 0.5, \grainRate, 20, \overlap, 4,
\posSpeed, 0.25, \posRd, 0.5);
```

Figure 16.19
A nodeproxy for time-pitch changing.

```
b = Buffer.read(s, "sounds/a11wlk01-44_1.aiff");
(
SynthDef(\constQ, { |out, bufnum=0, amp=0.5, pan, centerPos=0.5, sustain=0.1,
    rate=1, freq=400, rq=0.3|

    var ringtime = (2.4 / (freq * rq) * 0.66).min(0.5); // estimated
    var ampcomp = (rq ** -1) * (400 / freq ** 0.5);
    var envSig = EnvGen.ar(Env([0, amp, 0], [0.5, 0.5] * sustain, \welch));
    var cutoffEnv = EnvGen.kr(Env([1, 1, 0], [sustain+ringtime,0.01]), doneAction:
2);
    var grain = PlayBuf.ar(1, bufnum, rate, 0,
        centerPos - (sustain * rate * 0.5) * BufSampleRate.ir(bufnum),
        1) * envSig;
    var filtered = BPF.ar( grain, freq, rq, ampcomp );

    OffsetOut.ar(out, Pan2.ar(filtered, pan, cutoffEnv))
}, \ir.dup(8)).add;
)

Synth(\constQ, [\bufnum, b, \freq, exprand(100, 10000), \rq, exprand(0.01, 0.1),
\sustain, 0.01]);
```

Figure 16.20
A constant-Q Synthdef.

shape the sounds created. Many other transformation processes can be applied to each grain, with individual parameters creating finely articulated textures.

16.6.3   Wave Sets

Trevor Wishart introduced the *wave set* concept in *Audible Design* (1994), implemented it in the CDP framework as transformation tools, and employed it in several compositions (e.g., *Tongues of Fire*, 1994). Though Wishart treats wave sets mainly as units for transforming sound material, they can in fact also be used to turn a sound file into a large repository of waveform segments to be employed for a variety of synthesis concepts.

A wave set is defined as the waveform segment from 1 zero-crossing of a signal to the third, so in a sine wave, it corresponds to the sine wave's period. In aperiodic signals (such as sound files) the length and shape of waveform segments vary widely. The Wavesets class analyzes a sound file into wave sets, maintaining zero-crossings, lengths, amplitudes, and other values of each wave set (see the *Wavesets* Help file).

```
(
Pbindef(\gr1Q,
    \instrument, \constQ, \bufnum, b.bufnum,
    \sustain, 0.01, \amp, 0.2,
    \centerPos, Pn(Penv([1, 2.0], [10], \lin)),
    \dur, Pn(Penv([0.01, 0.09, 0.03].scramble, [0.38, 0.62] * 10, \exp)),
    \rate, Pwhite(0.95, 1.05),
    \freq, Pbrown(64.0, 120, 8.0).midicps,
    \pan, Pwhite(-1, 1, inf),
    \rq, 0.03
).play;
)
    // changing parameters while playing
Pbindef(\gr1Q, \rq, 0.1);
Pbindef(\gr1Q, \rq, 0.01);
Pbindef(\gr1Q, \sustain, 0.03, \amp, 0.08);
Pbindef(\gr1Q, \freq, Pbrown(80, 120, 18.0).midicps);

Pbindef(\gr1Q, \rq, 0.03);

Pbindef(\gr1Q, \rate, Pn(Penv([1, 2.0], [6], \lin)));

    // variable duration
Pbindef(\gr1Q, \dur, Pwhite(0.01, 0.02));

    // a rhythm that ends
Pbindef(\gr1Q, \dur, Pgeom(0.01, 1.1, 40));
```

Figure 16.21
A stream of constant-Q grains.

Table 16.1 lists most of Wishart's wave set transforms with short descriptions. Some of these transformations can be demonstrated with just the Wavesets class, a single SynthDef, and a Pbindef pattern. Figure 16.22 creates a wave set from a sound file and shows accessing its internal data. It also displays accessing and plotting individual wave sets or groups of wave sets. Figures 16.23 and 16.24 show a single wave set and a wave set group, respectively.

Figure 16.25 shows accessing the buffer that a wave set automatically creates, as well as a synthdef to play wave sets with: buf is the buffer that corresponds to the wave set, start and length are the start frame and length (in frames) of the wave set to be played, and sustain is the duration for which to loop over the buffer segment. Since the envelope cuts off instantly, one should calculate the precise sustain time and pass it in, as shown in the last section, by using the frameFor or eventFor method.

Table 16.1
Overview of Wave Set Transforms

Transposition	e.g., take every second wave set, play back at half speed
Reversal	play every wave set or group time reversed
Inversion	Turn every half wave set inside out
Omission	play silence for every *m* out of *n* wave sets (or randomly by percentage)
Shuffling	switch every 2 adjacent wave sets or groups
Distortion	multiply waveform by a power factor (i.e., exponentiate with constant peak)
Substitution	replace wave set with any other waveform (e.g., sine, square, other wave set)
Harmonic distortion	add double-speed and triple-speed wave sets to every wave set; weight and sum them
Averaging	scale adjacent wave sets to average length and average their waveforms
Enveloping	impose an amplitude envelope on a wave set or group
Wave set transfer	combine wave set timing from 1 source with wave set forms from another
Interleaving	take alternating wave sets or groups from 2 sources
Time stretching	repeat every wave set or group n times (creates "pitch beads")
Interpolated time stretching	interpolate between waveforms and durations of adjacent wave sets over n crossfading repetitions
Time shrinking	keep every nth wave set or group

In order to show Wishart's transforms, we use a `Pbindef`, so we can replace patterns or fixed values in it while it is running. It reconstructs part of the sound file wave set by wave set (see figure 16.26.)

Now we can introduce wave set transposition, reversal, time stretching, omission, and shuffling in 1-line examples. (See figure 16.27.)

Wave set harmonic distortion can be realized by playing a chord for each wave set at integer multiples of the rate and appropriate amplitudes. *Wave set interleaving* would also be an easy exercise, as it only requires alternating between 2 wave set objects as sources.

Wave set substitution requires more effort, as one needs to scale the substitute waveform into the time of the original waveform. Substituting a sine wave lets the time structure of the wave sets emerge, especially when each wave set is repeated. Figure 16.28 also considers the amplitudes for each wave set: since the substitute signal is full volume, scaling it to the original wave set's volume keeps the dynamic contour intact. Finally, different substitute waveforms can have quite different effects.

```
w = Wavesets.from("sounds/a11wlk01.wav");

w.xings;          // all integer indices of the zero crossings found
w.numXings;       // the total number of zero crossings
w.lengths;        // lengths of all wavesets
w.amps;           // peak amplitude of every waveset
w.maxima;         // index of positive maximum value in every waveset
w.minima;         // index of negative minimum value in every waveset

w.fracXings;      // fractional zerocrossing points
w.fracLengths;    // and lengths: allows more precise looping.

w.lengths.plot;   // show distribution of lengths
w.amps.plot;

    // get data for a single waveset: frameIndex, length (in frames), dur
w.frameFor(140, 1);
w.ampFor(140, 1);         // peak amplitude of that waveset or group

    // extract waveset by hand
w.signal.copyRange(w.xings[150], w.xings[151]).plot("waveset 150");
w.plot(140, 1); // convenience plotting
w.plot(1510, 1);

    // plot a group of 5 adjacent wavesets
w.plot(1510, 5)
```

Figure 16.22
A Wavesets object.

Wave set averaging can be realized by adapting this example to play *n* wave sets simultaneously at a time, all scaled to the same average wave set duration, looped *n* times, and divided by *n* for average amplitude.

Wave set inversion, distortion, enveloping, and *time stretching with interpolation* all require writing special Synthdefs. Of these, interpolation is sonically most interesting. Although one can imagine multiple ways of interpolating between wave sets, in the example on the book Web site the 2 wave sets are synchronized: the sound begins with *wave set1* at original speed and *wave set2* scaled to the same loop duration, but silent. As the amplitude crossfades from *wave set1* to *waveset 2*, so does the loop speed, so that the interpolation ends with only *waveset 2* at its original speed. The example can be extended to plays a seamless stream of parameterizable interpolations.

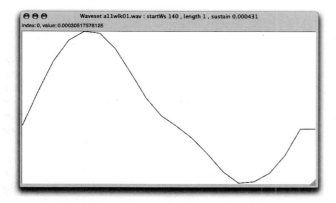

Figure 16.23
A single waveset plotted.

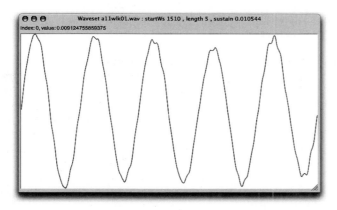

Figure 16.24
A waveset group of size 5.

```
(
    // A wavesets loads the file into a buffer by default.
        b = w.buffer;
    // Wavesets.prepareSynthDefs loads this synthdef:
        SynthDef(\wvst0, { arg out = 0, buf = 0, start = 0, length =
441, playRate = 1, sustain = 1, amp=0.2, pan;
            var phasor = Phasor.ar(0, BufRateScale.ir(buf) *
playRate, 0, length) + start;
            var env = EnvGen.ar(Env([amp, amp, 0], [sustain, 0]),
doneAction: 2);
            var snd = BufRd.ar(1, buf, phasor) * env;

            OffsetOut.ar(out, Pan2.ar(snd, pan));
        }, \ir.dup(8)).add;
)

// play from frame 0 to 440, looped for 0.1 secs, so ca 10 repeats.
(instrument: \wvst0, bufnum: b.bufnum, start: 0, length: 440, amp: 1,
sustain: 0.1).play;

    // get data from waveset
(
var start, length, sustain, repeats = 20;
#start, length, sustain = w.frameFor(150, 5);

(   instrument: \wvst0, bufnum: b.bufnum, amp: 1,
    start: start, length: length, sustain: sustain * repeats
).play;
)

    // or even simpler:
w.eventFor(startWs: 150, numWs: 5, repeats: 20, playRate:
1).put(\amp, 0.5).play;
```

Figure 16.25
Playing Wavesets from buffers.

```
     // by default, this pattern reconstructs a soundfile segment as is.
(
Pbindef(\ws1).clear;
Pbindef(\ws1,
    \instrument, \wvst0,
    \startWs, Pn(Pseries(0, 1, 3000), 1),
    \numWs, 1,
    \playRate, 1,
    \bufnum, b.bufnum,
    \repeats, 1,
    \amp, 0.4,
    [\start, \length, \sustain], Pfunc({ |ev|
        var start, length, wsDur;

        #start, length, wsDur = w.frameFor(ev[\startWs], ev[\numWs]);
        [start, length, wsDur * ev[\repeats] / ev[\playRate].abs]
    }),
    \dur, Pkey(\sustain)
).play;
)
```

Figure 16.26
A pattern to play Wavesets.

Why stick to using wave sets for recognizable sound file transformations? One can also start over with a task that plays a single wave set as a granular stream and extend that gradually. Figure 16.29 begins with a fixed grain repeat rate and starting wave set, later replaced with different values and streams for generating values.

In figure 16.29, wait time is derived from the wave set's duration, and a time gap between wave sets is added. All parameters are called with .next, so they can be directly replaced with infinite streams.

A wide range of possibilities opens here: one can create special orders of the wave sets based, for example, on their lengths or amplitudes; one can filter all wave set indices by some criterion (e.g., keep only very soft ones (see figure 6.30)).

For just 1 example for modifying parameters based on wave set information, see figure 16.31. When we read the wave set lengths as a pitch contour of the file, we can pull all wave set lengths closer to a pitch center, or even invert their lengths around the center to make long wave sets short and vice versa. The pitchContour variable determines how drastically this transformation is applied. Wave set omission is also shown.

```
    // waveset transposition: every second waveset, half speed
Pbindef(\ws1, \playRate, 0.5, \startWs, Pn(Pseries(0, 2, 500), 1)).play;

    // reverse every single waveset
Pbindef(\ws1, \playRate, -1, \startWs, Pn(Pseries(0, 1, 1000), 1)).play;
    // reverse every 2 wavesets
Pbindef(\ws1, \numWs, 2, \playRate, -1, \startWs, Pn(Pseries(0, 2, 1000), 1)).play;
    // reverse every 20 wavesets
Pbindef(\ws1, \numWs, 20, \playRate, -1, \startWs, Pn(Pseries(0, 20, 1000),
1)).play;
    // restore
Pbindef(\ws1, \numWs, 1, \playRate, 1, \startWs, Pn(Pseries(0, 1, 1000), 1)).play;

    // time stretching
Pbindef(\ws1, \playRate, 1, \repeats, 2).play;
Pbindef(\ws1, \playRate, 1, \repeats, 4).play;
Pbindef(\ws1, \playRate, 1, \repeats, 6).play;
Pbindef(\ws1, \repeats, 1).play;    // restore

    // waveset omission: drop every second
Pbindef(\ws1, \numWs, 1, \freq, Pseq([1, \], inf) ).play;
Pbindef(\ws1, \numWs, 1, \freq, Pseq([1,1, \, \], inf) ).play;
Pbindef(\ws1, \numWs, 1, \freq, Pfunc({ if (0.25.coin, 1, \) }) ).play; // drop
randomly
Pbindef(\ws1, \numWs, 1, \freq, 1, \startWs, Pn(Pseries(0, 1, 1000)) ).play; //
restore

    // waveset shuffling (randomize waveset order +- 5, 25, 125)
Pbindef(\ws1, \startWs, Pn(Pseries(0, 1, 1000), 1) + Pfunc({ 5.rand2 })).play;
Pbindef(\ws1, \startWs, Pn(Pseries(0, 1, 1000), 1) + Pfunc({ 25.rand2 })).play;
Pbindef(\ws1, \startWs, Pn(Pseries(0, 1, 1000), 1) + Pfunc({ 125.rand2 })).play;
```

Figure 16.27
Some of Trevor Wishart's transforms.

```
    // the waveform to substitute
c = Buffer.alloc(s, 512); c.sendCollection(Signal.sineFill(512, [1]));
(
Pbindef(\ws1).clear;
Pbindef(\ws1,
    \instrument, \wvst0,
    \startWs, Pn(Pseries(0, 1, 1000), 5),
    \numWs, 1, \playRate, 1,
    \buf, c.bufnum, // sine wave
    \repeats, 1,
    \amp, 1,
    [\start, \length, \sustain], Pfunc({ |ev|
        var start, length, wsDur, origRate;
        origRate = ev[\playRate];

            // get orig waveset specs
        #start, length, wsDur = w.frameFor(ev[\startWs], ev[\numWs]);

            // adjust playrate for different length of substituted wave
        ev[\playRate] = origRate * (512 / length);

            // get amplitude from waveset, to scale full volume sine wave
        ev[\amp] = ev[\amp] * w.ampFor(ev[\startWs], ev[\numWs]);

        [0, 512, wsDur * ev[\repeats] / origRate.abs]
    }),
    \dur, Pkey(\sustain)
).play;
)
    // clearer sinewave-ish segments
Pbindef(\ws1, \playRate, 1, \repeats, 2).play;
Pbindef(\ws1, \playRate, 1, \repeats, 6).play;
Pbindef(\ws1).stop;

    // different waveforms
c.sendCollection(Signal.sineFill(512, 1/(1..4).squared.scramble));
c.sendCollection(Signal.rand(512, -1.0, 1.0));
c.sendCollection(Signal.sineFill(512, [1]));

c.plot;
```

Figure 16.28
Waveset substitution.

```
        // very simple first pass, fixed repeat time
(
Tdef(\ws1).set(\startWs, 400);
Tdef(\ws1).set(\numWs, 5);
Tdef(\ws1).set(\repeats, 5);

Tdef(\ws1, { |ev|
    var startFrame, length, wsSustain;

    loop {
        #startFrame, length, wsSustain = w.frameFor(ev.startWs.next,
ev.numWs);

        (instrument: \wvst0, bufnum: b.bufnum, amp: 1,
            start: startFrame, length:  length,
            sustain: wsSustain * ev.repeats;
        ).play;

        0.1.wait;
    }
}).play;
)

Tdef(\ws1).set(\startWs, 420);
Tdef(\ws1).set(\repeats, 3);
Tdef(\ws1).set(\numWs, 2);

        // drop in a pattern for starting waveset
Tdef(\ws1).set(\startWs, Pn(Pseries(0, 5, 400) + 500, inf).asStream);
```

Figure 16.29
Wavesets played with a Tdef.

16.7   Conclusions

The possibilities of microsound as a resource for both sound material and structural ideas are nowhere near being exhausted. One can easily find personal, idiosyncratic ways to create music by exploring recombinations and juxtapositions of synthesis approaches and methods for structuring larger assemblages of microsound events. Due to its generality, SuperCollider supports many different working methods and allows changing directions quite flexibly. To give just 1 example, the pattern library offers many ways to create intricately detailed structures that may lead to fascinating microsound textures. Independent of one's aesthetic preferences, and of pre-

```
(
Tdef(\ws1).set(\gap, 3);
Tdef(\ws1, { |ev|
    var startFrame, length, wsSustain, reps;

    loop {
        reps = ev.repeats.next;

        #startFrame, length, wsSustain =
            w.frameFor(ev.startWs.next, ev.numWs.next);


        (instrument: \wvst0, bufnum: b.bufnum, amp: 1,
            start: startFrame, length:  length,
            sustain: wsSustain * reps,
            pan: 1.0.rand2
        ).play;

            // derive waittime from waveset sustain time
            // add gap based on waveset sustain time
        (wsSustain * (reps + ev.gap.next)).wait;
    }
}).play;
)
    // experiment with dropping in patterns:
    // very irregular gaps
Tdef(\ws1).set(\gap, { exprand(0.1, 20) });
    // sometimes continuous, sometimes gaps
Tdef(\ws1).set(\gap, Pbrown(-10.0, 20, 2.0).max(0).asStream);

    // random repeats
Tdef(\ws1).set(\repeats, { exprand(1, 20).round });
    // randomize number of wavesets per group
Tdef(\ws1).set(\numWs, { exprand(3, 20).round });
Tdef(\ws1).set(\numWs, 3, \repeats, { rrand(2, 5) });

Tdef(\ws1).stop;
```

Figure 16.30
Waittime derived from waveset duration with a gap added.

```
(
Tdef(\ws1).set(\startWs, Pn(Pseries(0, 5, 400) + 500, inf).asStream);

Tdef(\ws1).set(\gap, 0);
Tdef(\ws1).set(\pitchContour, 0);
Tdef(\ws1).set(\keepCoin, 1.0);
Tdef( 'ws1' ).set( 'repeats' , 5 );
Tdef( 'ws1' ).set( 'numWs' , 3 );

Tdef(\ws1, { |ev|
    var startFrame, length, wsSustain, reps, numWs, len2Avg;
    var squeezer, playRate;
    loop {
        reps = ev.repeats.next;
        numWs = ev.numWs.next;

        #startFrame, length, wsSustain =
            w.frameFor(ev.startWs.next, numWs);

        len2Avg = length / numWs / w.avgLength;
        squeezer = len2Avg ** ev.pitchContour.next;
        wsSustain = wsSustain / squeezer;
        playRate = 1 * squeezer;

        if (ev.keepCoin.next.coin) {
            (instrument: \wvst0, bufnum: b.bufnum, amp: 1,
                start: startFrame, length:  length,
                sustain: wsSustain * reps,
                playRate: playRate,
                pan: 1.0.rand2
            ).play;
        };

        (wsSustain * (reps + ev.gap.next)).wait;
    }
}).play;
)

    // try different pitch Contours:
Tdef(\ws1).set(\pitchContour, 0);   // original pitch

Tdef(\ws1).set(\pitchContour, 0.5); // flattened contour
```

Figure 16.31
Wavesets with pitch contour and dropout rate.

```
        // waveset overtone singing - all equal length
Tdef(\ws1).set(\pitchContour, 1.0);

        // inversion of contour
Tdef(\ws1).set(\pitchContour, 1.5);
Tdef(\ws1).set(\pitchContour, 2);
Tdef(\ws1).set(\repeats, 3);

    // waveset omission
Tdef(\ws1).set(\keepCoin, 0.75);
Tdef(\ws1).set(\keepCoin, 1);

    // fade out by omission over 13 secs, pause 2 secs
Tdef(\ws1).set(\keepCoin, Pn(Penv([1, 0, 0], [13,
2])).asStream).play;

    // add a pitch contour envelope
Tdef(\ws1).set(\pitchContour, Pn(Penv([0, 2, 0], [21,
13])).asStream);
```

Figure 16.31
(continued)

ferred methodologies for creating music, there are plenty of possibilities for further exploration.

References

Buser, P., and M. Imbert. 1992. *Audition*. Cambridge, MA: MIT Press.

Gabor, D. 1947. "Acoustical Quanta and the Theory of Hearing." *Nature,* 159(4044): 591–594.

Hoffmann, P. 2000. "The New GENDYN Program." *Computer Music Journal,* 24(2): 31–38.

Kronland-Martinet, R. 1988. "The Wavelet Transform for Analysis, Synthesis, and Processing of Speech and Music Sounds." *Computer Music Journal,* 12(4): 11–20.

Luque, S. 2006. "Stochastic Synthesis: Origins and Extensions." Master's thesis, Institute of Sonology, Royal Conservatory, The Hague, Netherlands.

Moore, B. C. J. 2004. *An Introduction to the Psychology of Hearing,* 5th ed. London: Academic Press.

Roads, C. 2001a. *Microsound.* Cambridge, MA: MIT Press.

Roads, C. 2001b. "Sound Composition with Pulsars." *Journal of the Audio Engineering Society,* 49(3): 134–147.

Rocha Iturbide, M. "Les techniques granulaires dans la synthèse sonore." Doctoral thesis, Université de Paris-VIII-Saint-Denis.

Sturm, B. L., and J. D. Gibson. 2006. "Matching Pursuit Decompositions of Non-noisy Speech Signals Using Several Dictionaries." In *Proceedings of ICASSP 2006*, Toulouse, vol. 3, pp. 456–459.

Sturm, B. L., J. J. Shynk, L. Daudet, and C. Roads. 2008. "Dark Energy in Sparse Atomic Estimations." *IEEE Transactions on Audio, Speech & Language Processing*, 16(3): 671–676.

Truax, B. 1988. "Real-Time Granular Synthesis with a Digital Signal Processor." *Computer Music Journal*, 12(2): 14–26.

Vaggione, H. 2001. "Some Ontological Remarks About Musical Composition Processes." *Computer Music Journal*, 25(1): 54–61.

Vaggione, H. 1996. "Articulating Micro-Time." *Computer Music Journal*, 20(2): 33–38.

Wishart, T. 1994. *Audible Design*. London: Orpheus the Pantomime.

Xenakis, I. [1971] 1992. *Formalized Music: Thought and Mathematics in Music*, rev. and enl. ed. Hillsdale, NY: Pendragon Press.

17 Alternative Tunings with SuperCollider

Fabrice Mogini

The notions of pitch and tuning are essential to the organization of sound. Our understanding and perception of tuning systems is closely related to the musical instruments that are being used. An audio programming language transforms the composition, performance, and appreciation of alternative systems of pitch because it can transcend the limitations set by acoustic instruments and human players. SuperCollider is a powerful tool that gives the opportunity to create and play alternative tuning systems easily in any possible way, and therefore extend compositional scope.

This chapter will demonstrate the ease with which a variety of tuning systems can be explored within the SuperCollider environment. Since tuning is an area of complex and varied experimentation, this chapter will describe several approaches to writing code for alternative tunings with SuperCollider rather than catalog existing systems. The user can then apply these tools to any specific tuning.

17.1 Standard Tuning: 12-Note Equal Temperament

17.1.1 Tuning

A tuning is a set of frequency relationships. We can quantify these relationships with intervals. A fixed frame is needed to help discriminate these intervals. The frame commonly used in most music is the octave. The octave is fundamental for many cultures, both ancient and modern (Burns, 1999). A common discussion point for musicians, composers, and scientists has been how to divide the octave. A set of intervals spanning the octave leads to a particular choice of tuning system.

17.1.2 Oscillators and Frequency

We will use oscillators to generate sound and listen to the tunings that we create. Most oscillators in SuperColider require a frequency in hertz (cycles per second).

```
{SinOsc.ar(523.2511306012, 0, 0.5)}.play;
```

Although we can specify frequencies directly in hertz, it is often easier to deal with notes that point at a position in the temperament or scale used.

17.1.3   MIDI Notes

MIDI notes are based on the standard 12-note equal-tempered tuning system, in which each octave is split into 12 equal steps. The message midicps in SuperCollider converts MIDI notes to cycles per second. Using the message midicps is an easy way to access different degrees from the 12-note equal temperament without having to know what frequency it corresponds to.

```
60.midicps   // frequency in hertz for the first note, middle C
61.midicps   // C sharp above middle C
72.midicps   // C in the next higher octave
```

Rather than having to know the exact frequency, we can just choose the MIDI note number and use midicps to return the corresponding frequency in hertz.

```
{SinOsc.ar(72.midicps, 0, 0.5)}.play;
```

17.1.4   Midiratio

Some unit generators in SuperColider require a ratio value; for instance, a rise of an octave is represented by the number 2 (to create a frequency twice as fast). This is the case with sample playback using PlayBuf, which has a rate argument representing the speed at which a sample is played relative to a baseline of its original pitch. Speed being related to pitch, we can use this rate argument to modify the sample's pitch. (See figure 17.1.) Here we use midiratio, which converts an interval in semitones to a ratio.

```
//      first note
0.midiratio
//      second note
1.midiratio
//      first note, one octave up
12.midiratio
```

Multiplying the ratio by a constant root, we obtain the frequencies for each degree.

```
(0.midiratio)*440
(1.midiratio)*440
(12.midiratio)*440

{SinOsc.ar((0.midiratio)*440, 0, 0.5)}.play;
{SinOsc.ar((7.midiratio)*440, 0, 0.5)}.play;
```

```
(
// read a whole sound into memory
s = Server.local;
b = Buffer.read(s,"sounds/a11wlk01.wav"); // remember to free the
buffer later.
)
(
SynthDef("help_PlayBuf", { arg out=0,bufnum=0, rate=1;
Out.ar(out,
Pan2.ar(
PlayBuf.ar(1, bufnum, BufRateScale.kr(bufnum)*rate, loop: 1),
0)
)
}).add;
)
p=Synth(\help_PlayBuf, [\rate, 0.midiratio,\out, 0, \bufnum, b.
bufnum]); // original pitch
p.set(\rate, 12.midiratio); // one octave up
p.set(\rate, 7.midiratio);  // seven semitones up (fifth interval)

p.free;
p=nil;
b.free;
b=nil;
```

Figure 17.1
Example of PlayBuf with midiratio.

```
//   third note of the chromatic scale plus a quarter tone
{SinOsc.ar((2.5.midiratio)*440, 0, 0.5)}.play;
```

We can also write this in a different way, using a function.

All the following examples run sequentially. Stop the sound before playing the next example.

```
f = {|degree, root = 440|
(degree.midiratio)*root;
};
```

```
{SinOsc.ar(f.(0), 0, 0.5)}.play;
{SinOsc.ar(f.(7), 0, 0.5)}.play;
{SinOsc.ar(f.(2.5), 0, 0.5)}.play;
```

We can change the root if necessary.

```
{SinOsc.ar(f.(0, 261.5), 0, 0.5)}.play;
{SinOsc.ar(f.(7, 261.5), 0, 0.5)}.play;
{SinOsc.ar(f.(2.5, 261.5), 0, 0.5)}.play;
```

The root can be given as a MIDI note.

```
f = {|degree, root = 60|
(degree.midiratio)*root.midicps;
};
f.(0, 65);
f.(1, 65);
f.(12, 65);
```

17.1.5   Cents

Cents is a measure often used for fine-tuning intervals. Though it might seem that SuperCollider does not support cents directly, MIDI values can describe cents because midicps accepts decimals. We can obtain frequencies between 2 semitones:

```
60.midicps;   // middle C
60.5.midicps; // middle C and a quarter tone
61.midicps; // C#
```

One octave is divided into 1200 cents, and a semitone equals 100 cents. There are 100 cents between 60.midicps and 61.midicps.

```
60.1.midicps // middle C plus 1 cent
60.5.midicps // middle C plus 50 cents or a quarter tone
60.99.midicps;      // just 1 cent below C#
61.midicps;         //C#
// C on the left and D# plus a quarter tone on the right
{SinOsc.ar([60, 63.5].midicps, 0, 0.5)}.play;
```

17.1.6   Pbind and the Pitch Model

There are several ways to access different notes in the 12-note equal temperament using Pbind: modal scale degrees, equal-division note values, MIDI note values, or frequencies in hertz (see also the Help files *Streams-Patterns-Events5, Event,* or *PG_07_Value_Conversions*).

\midinote is similar to midicps but is used exclusively by the Pitch model of an Event. (See figure 17.2.)

You can alter the pitch of \midinote in cents:

62.5 is equivalent to 62 + 50 cents.
62.25 is equivalent to 62 + 25 cents. (See figure 17.3.)

```
(
Pbind(
\midinote, Pseq([0, 2, 3, 5, 7]+60, inf),
\dur, 0.3
).play
)
/////////////////////////////////////////////////
```

Figure 17.2
Example of Pbind with \midinote.

```
(
Pbind(
\midinote, Pseq([0, 2, 3, 5.25, 7.5]+60, inf),
\dur, 0.3
).play
)
/////////////////////////////////////////////////
```

Figure 17.3
Example of Pbind with \midinote and cents.

\note seems quite similar to \midinote, but its octave range is selected by the \octave argument. (See figure 17.4.)

The argument \degree points at a particular position in a scale. In figure 17.5, the scale argument is not specified and is, by default [0, 2, 4, 5, 7, 9, 11], which corresponds to a major scale in 12-note equal temperament.

Note that the \scale argument can also be changed. If the scale was set as the chromatic scale, we could use degree to access all the notes of the standard temperament, though since \note already does this, it is much more typical to exploit unequal scales from major to Hungarian minor and beyond. (See figure 17.6.)

We can alter the pitch of these degrees in cents:

2.1 is equivalent to 3, the next degree, or 2 + 100cents.
2.05 is equivalent to 2 + 50cents.

Note that this is different from the way we altered cents earlier when using \midinote. Figure 17.7 gives an example using degree and cents.

```
(
Pbind(
\note, Pseq([0,2,4,5,7,9,11,12], inf),
\dur, 0.3,
\octave, 5
).play
)
////////////////////////////////////////////////
```

Figure 17.4
Example of Pbind with \note.

```
(
Pbind(
\degree, Pseq([0,1,2,3,4,5,6,7], inf),
\dur, 0.3,
\octave, 5
).play
)
////////////////////////////////////////////////
```

Figure 17.5
Example of Pbind with \degree.

```
(
Pbind(
\degree, Pseq([0,1,2,3,4,5,6,7], inf),
\dur, 0.3,
\octave, 5,
\scale, (0..11)
).play
)
////////////////////////////////////////////////
```

Figure 17.6
Example of Pbind with \degree and \scale (chromatic scale).

```
(
Pbind(
\degree, Pseq([0, 2, 2.1, 2.05], inf),
\dur, 0.3,
\scale, (0..11),
\octave, 5
).play
)
/////////////////////////////////////////////////////
```

Figure 17.7
Example of Pbind with \degree and \scale and cents.

```
(
Pbind(
\note, Pwhite(-6,9),
\dur, 0.3,
\sustain, 1.1,
\stepsPerOctave, 7
).play
)
/////////////////////////////////////////////////////
```

Figure 17.8
Example of Pbind with \stepsPerOctave.

17.2   Other Equal Temperaments

17.2.1   \stepsPerOctave

The Pitch model uses \stepsPerOctave, which is 12 by default, meaning we are in a 12-equal-note system. Just specify a new number of steps per octave and start exploring. . . . Let us start by playing 7 equal notes per octave. We will be using Pwhite to randomize the selection of notes from that tuning and \sustain to create polyphonic layers. (See figure 17.8.)

17.2.2   \scale

When using a large number of notes per octave, it is a good idea to create a mode using \scale. (See figures 17.9 and 17.10.)

```
(
e=Pbind(
\degree, Pwhite(-3, 7),
\dur, 0.25,
\stepsPerOctave, 21,
\sustain, 1.1,
\scale, [0, 4, 8, 11, 14, 17]
).play;
)
//////////////////////////////////////////////////
```

Figure 17.9
Example of Pbind with \stepsPerOctave and \scale.

```
(
// previous example should still be running
e.stream=Pbind(
\degree, Pwhite(-3, 7),
\dur, 0.25,
\stepsPerOctave, 21,
\sustain, 1.1,
\scale, [0, 3, 5, 8, 10, 13]
).asStream;
)
//////////////////////////////////////////////////
```

Figure 17.10
Example of changing mode using \scale.

17.2.3   Calculation of Equal Temperaments

When we don't use existing functionality from midicps to Pbind, it is helpful to know how to calculate equal temperaments for more flexibility. We can start by dividing a value that represents the octave into equal parts. When we divide 1, the space that represents 1 octave, by the number of steps per octave, we obtain the smallest interval in linear terms, 1/12. To get the third note, we multiply this interval by 3: 3*(1/12). The third note also can be divided by steps per octave: 3/12.

However, because frequencies grow exponentially, the space in hertz between each note of the tuning is in fact getting larger and larger, so we need to use the power of 2.

```
2.pow(degree/stepsPerOctave);
//     third note of the 12-equal-note tuning system
2.pow(3/12)
```

Figure 17.11 gives an example of calculating intermediate step ratios automatically based on the octave ratio 2. Pseudo octaves are derived by substituting values other than 2: 3.pow(degree/13) would give the Bohlen-Pierce scale based on 13 equally spaced notes over a tritave (octave and a fifth) basic ratio; more examples will follow later.

17.2.4   Using degreeToKey

degreeToKey has a stepsPerOctave argument but is designed for modal control. As we saw earlier with \scale and Pbind, a mode is a set of notes from the current tuning system. All the notes from the tuning can be accessed by specifying a chromatic scale that contains all degrees within the octave.

```
0.degreeToKey((0..13), 14)
1.degreeToKey((0..13), 14)
15.degreeToKey((0..13), 14)
```

We can limit the scale to a mode:

```
0.degreeToKey([0, 3, 5, 9], 14)
1.degreeToKey([0, 3, 5, 9], 14)
15.degreeToKey([0, 3, 5, 9], 14)
```

Note that degreeToKey only indicates the degree in the tuning according to the scale, but it doesn't actually calculate the frequency for us.

```
//      getting the degree
a = 0.degreeToKey([0, 3, 5, 6], 12)
//      calculating the frequency
2.pow(a/12)*440
```

```
//      another degree in the scale
b = 4.degreeToKey([0, 3, 5, 6], 12)
//      calculating the frequency
2.pow(b/12)*440
```

DegreeToKey is a UGen that converts a signal to modal pitch. It is different from the message degeeToKey that was discussed earlier. Even though we won't cover it in this chapter, it is a useful tool which supports any equal temperament and therefore is worth mentioning.

```
(
var stepsperoctave=3;
Array.fill(stepsperoctave, {arg i; 2.pow(i/stepsperoctave)});
)

//Using a function to calculate the value at a chosen degree
(
f = {|degree, steps|
2.pow(degree/steps)
};
)
//  degree 0
f.(0, 3);
//  degree 1
f.(1, 3);
//  degree 2
f.(2, 3);

//The function is modified to multiply the value by a root frequency in Hertz
(
f = {|degree, steps, root=440|
2.pow(degree/steps)*root
};
)
//  12 notes per octave, degrees 0,1 and 12
f.(0,12)
f.(1, 12)
f.(12, 12)

//  14 notes per octave, degrees 0,1, 12 and 14
f.(0,14)
f.(1, 14)
f.(12, 14)
f.(14,14)
///////////////////////////////////////////////////////
```

Figure 17.11
Example of a simple tuning of three equal notes per octave.

17.3   Unequal Divisions of the Octave

We will now work with frequency ratios more directly.

17.3.1   Custom Unequal Division of the Octave

Any array in SuperCollider can be filled with values between 1 and 2; this array represents the space across one octave.

```
a = [1, 1.030303030303, 1.0606060606061, 1.1212121212121, 1.2121212121212,
1.3636363636364, 1.6060606060606]
```

To obtain frequencies, we can multiply the array by a constant root: `A = a*220`.

With `Pbind` we need to use `\freq` because we have calculated the frequencies ourselves. (See figure 17.12.)

The `linlin` message is a useful method for mapping values to a different range and for adapting your own series to the system you are working with: `this.linlin(inMin, inMax, outMin, outMax, clip)`.

```
a = [1, 2, 3, 5, 8, 13, 21]
```

We can map this array to values between 1 and 2 (the octave) with similar proportions:

```
b = a.linlin(1, 34, 1, 2);
```

We obtain the unequal tuning that was calculated in the earlier example with Pbind.

```
a = [1, 1.030303030303, 1.0606060606061, 1.1212121212121, 1.2121212121212,
1.3636363636364, 1.6060606060606, 2]
```

17.3.2   Ratios

The octave (2/1) is the standard space that can be deconstructed into various proportions. This is different from the equal temperament system, where we had steps of the same size.

SuperCollider will calculate any fraction directly: evaluating 5/4 returns 1.25.

We can also simplify the terms of a fraction with `asFraction`. `(10/8).asFraction` returns [5, 4].

17.3.3   Just Tuning

This ratio-based system is founded on the premise that dissonance is associated with more complex ratios (such ratios tend to beat more). The simpler the ratios, the

```
(
SynthDef("tone2", { arg freq = 440, amp=0.5, gate=1, envdur=1.5;
var sound, env;
env = EnvGen.kr(Env.perc(0.01, envdur), doneAction:2);
sound = Pan2.ar(SinOsc.ar(freq, 0, amp)*env, 0);
Out.ar(0, sound);
}).add;
)
(
a=[ 1, 1.030303030303, 1.0606060606061, 1.1212121212121,
1.3636363636364, 1.6060606060606, 2 ]*220;

// Play the all the notes of the tuning
e=Pbind(
\freq, Pseq( a, inf),
\dur, 0.2,
\amp, 0.5,
\sustain, 0.6,
\instrument, \tone2
).play
)
// Choose the notes randomly
(
e.stream=Pbind(
\freq, Pn(Prand( a, 1)),
\dur, 0.2,
\amp, 0.5,
\sustain, 0.6,
\instrument, \tone2
).asStream
)
/////////////////////////////////////////////////////
```

Figure 17.12
Example of Pbind with unequal octave divisions for \freq.

```
(
~rationames=[1/1, 8/7, 7/6, 6/5, 5/4, 4/3, 7/5, 10/7, 3/2, 8/5, 5/3,
12/7, 7/4];
~scale=[0,3,5,8,10,12];
e = Pbind(
\freq, Pseq([
Pfunc({
(~rationames.wrapAt(~scale).[~scale.size.rand])*440
})
],inf),
\dur, 0.25,
\amp, 0.5,
\instrument, \tone2
).play; // returns an EventStream
)
// set a new scale
~scale=[0,2,5,7,9,11];
~scale=[0,1,3,5,6,8,9];
~scale=[0,3,5,8,10,12];
/////////////////////////////////////////////////////
```

Figure 17.13
Example of Using Odd-Limit ratios with sound.

more consonant the intervals in terms of purity of sound. Consonance is a priority in just intonation, even though this can limit modulatory freedom in changing key (different keys have very different characters, whereas in 12-note equal temperament, all keys have the same character).

A collection of low whole-number ratio intervals forming a diatonic just scale is a = [1/1, 9/8, 5/4, 4/3, 3/2, 5/3, 15/8, 2/1]. We can use this array by multiplying it by a constant root frequency: a = [1/1, 9/8, 5/4, 4/3, 3/2, 5/3, 15/8, 2/1]*440.

17.3.4   Odd Limit

The odd limit is the set of ratios in which odd number factors are inferior or equal to the chosen number (the limit).

The 3-limit tonality is a set of ratios in which the odd numbers are inferior or equal to 3: 1/1, 4/3, 3/2.
The 5-limit tonality is similar to just tuning: 1/1, 6/5, 5/4, 4/3, 3/2, 8/5, 5/3.
The 7-limit tonality is 1/1, 8/7, 7/6, 6/5, 5/4, 4/3, 7/5, 10/7, 3/2, 8/5, 5/3, 12/7, 7/4.
(A musical example appears in figure 17.13.)

```
(
var n, buts, synths, ratios, rationames;
w = Window("tonality diamond", Rect(200,500,420,150));
w.view.decorator = FlowLayout(w.view.bounds);

rationames=[
"7/4", "3/2","5/4","1/1",
"7/5","6/5","1/1","8/5",
"7/6","1/1","5/3","4/3",
"1/1","12/7","10/7","8/7"
];

n=rationames.size;

n.do({ |i|
Button(w, Rect(20,20+(i*30),100,30))
.states_([[rationames[i], Color.black,
if((rationames[i])=="1/1", {Color.red},{Color.yellow})
]
])
.action_({ arg butt;
Synth(\tone2, [\freq, ((rationames[i]).interpret)*440]);

})
});
w.front;
)
/////////////////////////////////////////////////////////
```

Figure 17.14
Code for a Tonality diamond with SuperCollider GUI.

17.3.5   Tonality Diamond

This is a way of ordering ratios belonging to an n-limit tonality set. Harry Partch (1974) experimented with these low-integer rational ratios and built a system in which both simple and complex ratios coexist. One of them is his famous 43-note ratio tuning. (See figure 17.14.)

Note that the arrangement helps in understanding how neighboring ratios are related. 7/4 and 12/7 are close but dissonant when played together. However, 7/4 is harmonious with its adjacent ratio 3/2, and 12/7 is harmonious with 10/7. (See figure 17.15.)

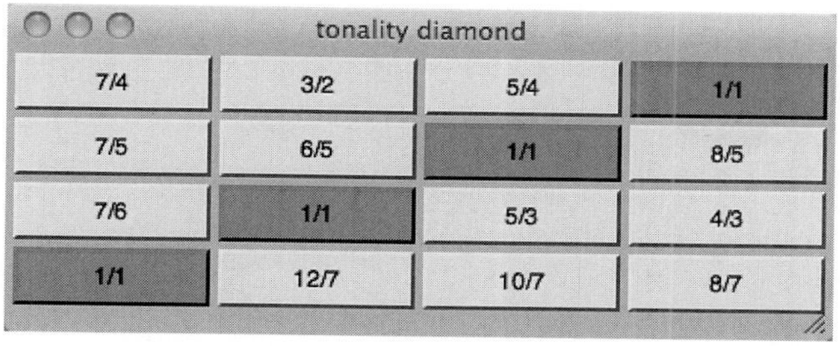

Figure 17.15
Picture of a Tonality diamond with SuperCollider GUI.

17.4   Polytunings (Mixed Tunings)

17.4.1   Simple Mixing

It is possible to mix different tunings in SuperCollider. The process is straightforward. (See figure 17.16.)

Polytunings (Mogini, 2000) is a system that uses different tunings simultaneously. Common frequencies are used as pivots to connect these tunings. In order to choose the best pivot frequencies, we select pairs of frequencies that are close enough to one another. This system can connect 2 or more tunings. Because so many sounds are now available within an octave, we have found a way of accessing and ordering what I call the "total pitch field."

17.4.2   Organizing Pitch

It is important at this stage to create ways of ordering the choice of notes so as to control the level of consonance/dissonance. Finding nodes common to both tunings can be done by comparing the 2 scales linearly.

```
// 2 different equal tunings expressed linearly
a = Array.fill(12, {|i| (1/12)*(i)});
b = Array.fill(14, {|i| (1/14)*(i)});
a.sect(b);
```

The roots, 0 and 0.5, are common to both tunings. We can give priority to these common nodes.

Find in which position the value 0.5 is in each array.

```
a.do({|item, index| if(item = 0.5, {index.postln})});
// returns 6
```

```
(
a=Pbind(
\degree, Pwhite(0, 12),
\dur, 0.5,
\octave, 5,
\amp, 0.4,
\stepsPerOctave, 12,
\instrument, \tone2
);
b=Pbind(
\degree, Pwhite(0, 14),
\dur, 0.25,
\octave, 4,
\amp, 0.4,
\stepsPerOctave, 14,
\instrument, \tone2
);
Ppar([a, b]).play;
)
/////////////////////////////////////////////////////
```

Figure 17.16
Example of 12 and 14-equal note per octave mixed together.

```
b.do({|item, index| if(item = 0.5, {index.postln})});
// returns 7
```

Figure 17.17 gives a musical example.

17.4.3   Tolerance Threshold

In a musical context it is possible to imagine fast passing notes that are dissonant. However, in the slow and regular parts of the music, the sense of dissonance would be increased. The notion of "in tune" can be alternated with "out of tune" if done at the right time and place. One could change the tolerance threshold (limits of the accepted dissonance) according to the compositional context (Mogini, 2000). This system, originally developed by the author, was ported to a GUI by Nick Collins in 2000 in order to have fast control over the tolerance threshold in real time. Below is the author's way of calculating near tones and tolerance threshold in order to define which notes are considered common to both tunings. (See figure 17.18.)

```
(
a=Pbind(
\degree, Pfunc({
[
[0, 6, 12].choose, 12.rand
].choose;
}),
\dur, 0.5,
\octave, 4,
\amp, 0.4,
\stepsPerOctave, 12,
\instrument, \tone2
);
b=Pbind(
\degree, Pfunc({
[
[0, 7, 14].choose, 14.rand
].choose;
}),
\dur, 0.25,
\octave, 5,
\amp, 0.3,
\stepsPerOctave, 14,
\instrument, \tone2
);
Ppar([a, b]).play;
)
/////////////////////////////////////////////////////
```

Figure 17.17
Example of two tunings organized by their most common notes.

This simple function has enabled us to define an area in which 2 notes from different tunings are *in tune*. This notion of what is *in tune* is subjective and can be changed by the user. This example has been simplified for a greater understanding. It would be easy to rewrite the function so that we can change the \degree argument directly or even control the \scale argument in real time. (See figure 17.19.)

Note that we are using results from figure 17.18 to choose the degrees.

17.5   Beyond the Octave Division

Intervals other than the octave can be equally divided and then represent a tuning system.

```
(
~tolerance={|a, b, t, max|
var c, d;
c=[];
d=[];
a.do({ |aitem, aindex|
b.do({ |bitem, bindex|
var x;
x = (aitem-bitem).abs;
if( (x > t) && (x < max),
{
c=c.add(aindex);
d=d.add(bindex);
//[aitem, bitem].post; " out of tune ".post; [aindex, bindex].postln;
//" ".postln;
})
})
});
[(0..a.size).difference(c), (0..b.size).difference(d)];
};
)


(
// use the function function with two tunings
var minthreshold, maxthreshold, int;

// two different equal tunings expressed linearly
a=Array.fill(12, { |i| (1/12)*(i) });
b=Array.fill(21, { |i| (1/21)*(i) });

int=1/21;                    // smallest interval
minthreshold=int*0.15;
maxthreshold=int*0.85;
/*
intervals inferior to minthreshold are in tune
intervals between minthreshold and maxthreshold are out of tune
intervals superior to maxthreshold are in tune
*/

// print a list of notes from the two tunings which form a dissonant
interval
~tolerance.value(a, b, minthreshold, maxthreshold);
)
/////////////////////////////////////////////////////
```

Figure 17.18
Example of calculating near tones, setting a tolerance threshold.

```
(
a=Pbind(
\degree, Pfunc({
// notes which clash with the other tuning have been removed
[0,4,8,12].choose
}),
\dur, 0.5,
\octave, 5,
\amp, 0.4,
\sustain, 0.85,
\stepsPerOctave, 12,
\instrument, \tone2
).play;
b=Pbind(
// notes which clash with the other tuning have been removed
\degree, Pfunc({
[0,7,14,21].choose
}),
\dur, 0.25,
\octave, 4,
\amp, 0.35,
\sustain, 0.85,
\stepsPerOctave, 21,
\instrument, \tone2
).play;
)

(
a.stream=Pbind(
// introducing more notes from that tuning after having changed the
threshold
\degree, Pfunc({
[ 0, 1, 4, 7, 8, 9, 9, 12 ].choose
}),
\dur, 0.75,
\octave, 5,
\amp, 0.4,
\sustain, 0.85,
\stepsPerOctave, 12,
\instrument, \tone2
).asStream;
)
/////////////////////////////////////////////////////////
```

Figure 17.19
Example changing the number of common notes in real-time.

```
(
f = {|steps| Array.fill(steps, { |i| 2.pow(i/steps) }) };
//  Calculation of the twelve equal-note temperament
x =  f.(12);
//  mapping the tuning to a new range beyond an octave
y = x.linlin(1, 2, 1, 2.25);
//  multiplying by a root frequency
a=y*440;

Pbind(
\freq, Pfunc({ a.choose }),
\dur, 0.25,
\octave, 5,
\amp, 0.5,
\sustain, 1.1,
\instrument, \tone2
).play
)
/////////////////////////////////////////////////////////
```

Figure 17.20
Example of 12 equal-note division beyond the octave.

17.5.1   Dividing Any Interval into Equal Notes

We are now going to construct an array of equal values within a range that stretches from 1 to a value greater than 2. We could of course also design an array that has a different range. In fact, any range and number of steps can be used. We already know how to divide an interval of 1 (from 1 to 2) into 12 equal parts mapped to represent an exponential progression.

```
//        Function to generate equal-note temperaments
f = {|steps| Array.fill(steps, {|i| 2.pow(i/steps)})};
//        Calculation of the 12-equal-note temperament
x = f.(12);
```

As we have seen in section 17.3, we can use linlin to map an array to a different range while keeping the same proportions between each item. For instance, we can map the tuning to a new range beyond an octave:

```
y = x.linlin(1, 2, 1, 2.25);
```

We have a new array of 12 equal steps and similar proportions with a new range from 1 to 2.25. We can now multiply our array by a constant root frequency: a = y*220;. (See figure 17.20.)

Table 17.1
Tunings by W. Carlos

Tuning Name	Steps per Octave	Cents per Interval
Alpha	15.385	78
Beta	18.809	63.8
Gamma	34.188	35.1

```
(
Pbind(
\degree, Pwhite(0, 18),
\dur, 0.3,
\sustain, 1.0,
\amp, 0.5,
\sustain, 1.1,
\instrument, \tone2,
\stepsPerOctave,  18.809
).play;
)
/////////////////////////////////////////////////
```

Figure 17.21
Example of Tunings by W. Carlos with SuperCollider.

We can also modify the number of steps per octave to obtain similar results. (See table 17.1 and figure 17.21.)

17.5.2 Dividing Any Interval into Unequal Notes

As we have done earlier with unequal division of 1 octave, we will assume that the space between each item in the arrays presented in the following examples is already calibrated to an exponential progression to work when directly multiplied by a constant frequency.

Any array in SuperCollider can be filled with values between 1 and a value other than 2 to define the range of our tuning.

```
a = [1, 1.09375, 1.1875, 1.28125, 1.375, 1.46875, 1.5625, 1.65625]
```

To obtain frequencies, we multiply the array or each item by a constant root: `B = a*220`. (See figure 17.22.)

```
(
a=[ 1, 1.09375, 1.1875, 1.28125, 1.375, 1.46875, 1.5625, 1.65625];
b=a*440;
e=Pbind(
\freq, Pseq( b, inf),
\dur, 0.2,
\amp, 0.5,
\instrument, \tone2,
\sustain, 0.6
).play
)
// play in a different order
(
e.stream=Pbind(
\freq, Pn(Pshuf( b, 1)),
\dur, 0.2,
\amp, 0.5,
\instrument, \tone2,
\sustain, 0.6
).asStream
)
//////////////////////////////////////////////////////
```

Figure 17.22
Example of Pbind with unequal divisions below an octave.

Further accessing the degrees, we can also extend the range. Simply multiply our array by the maximum value of its range to obtain the next series. Again, we could have used linlin to calculate the next array.

```
a = [1, 1.25, 1.5, 1.75, 2, 2.25];
// 2.5 is the next value, the range is really [1, 2.5] rather than [1, 2]
// next series starts from 2.5
b = a*2.5; // returns:
[2.5, 3.125, 3.75, 4.375, 5, 5.625]
```

17.5.3   Pattern-Based Tunings

These tunings consist of unequal notes and no octave. However, because the proportions between these notes are repeated, a sense of tuning is created. For Burns (1999) a tuning system does not operate independent from other compositional factors.

```
(
// F. Mogini pattern-based Tuning - 2000.
x=880;

Pbind(
\freq, Pn(
Plazy({
if(x<=150, {x=x*2});
if(x>=2000, {x=x/2});
x=[

x*[1.1428,  1.36, 1.26].choose,
x/[1.1428,  1.36, 1.26].choose

].choose
})
),
\dur, 0.14,
\sustain, 0.8,
\cutoff, Pfunc({ 1.0.rand})
).play;
)
///////////////////////////////////////////////////
```

Figure 17.23
Example of a pattern-based tuning.

Melodies are perceived in gestalts or patterns rather than as a succession of intervals. To incorporate this idea, I worked on a tuning system based on melodic permutations. The intervals do not fit in the frame of an octave, but the way they go beyond the octave limit is dictated by melodic permutations.

For the next example, I have used a limited set of intervals of different sizes that are not multiples of each other. I would not classify these intervals among ratios, since ratios are still deduced from the octave.

These intervals have different sizes, but each frequency available in the tuning is not fixed because it is not based on a frame, instead being calculated from the last note. To decide on these intervals I have used unequal parts: [1.1428, 1.36, 1.26]. Each new frequency in the pattern yields a node from which the melodic development takes place. (See figure 17.23.)

```
a=(1..16)*100
(
e=Pbind(
\freq, Pseq( a, inf),
\dur, 0.2
).play
)

// a beautiful tuning system can be created from the harmonic series.
(
e.stream=Pbind(
\freq, Pn(Pshuf( a, 1)),
\dur, 0.2,
\sustain, 0.8
).asStream
)
/////////////////////////////////////////////////////
```

Figure 17.24
Calculation of the first 16 harmonics for a root note of 440 Hertz.

17.6   Tuning Systems and Harmonics

17.6.1   Harmonic Series

Pure sounds with a simple, singular sound wave are rare in nature. Most musical sounds contain partials that are multiples of the fundamental frequency. As the partials fuse for pitch perception, we tend to hear only this single fundamental frequency, but with a particular timbre which is the result of the harmonic complex. (See figure 17.24.)

It is possible to keep dividing some of the notes by 2 so as to rearrange all of the notes inside 1 octave. (See figure 17.25.)

Different arrangements are possible. For instance, you can keep certain notes in the first octave and others, the more dissonant, in the second octave. (See figure 17.26.)

We could invert the process and get a slightly different tuning in which the most dissonant harmonics are in the bass and the most consonant ones are in the highest range.

17.6.2   Creating Artificial Partials for Alternative Equal Temperaments

Inspired by natural harmonics, we can create harmonics specially designed for the tuning we want to use. Of course these aren't real harmonics, but this technique can

```
a=(1..11);
(
a.size.do({ |i|
var x=a[i];
while({x>2},{x=x/2});
a.put(i, x)
});
)

b=a.asSet.asArray.sort;
(
e=Pbind(
\freq, Pn(Pshuf( b*440, 1)),
\dur, 0.2,
\sustain, 0.8
).play
)
//////////////////////////////////////////////////////
```

Figure 17.25
Rearranging the first 16 harmonics within one octave.

bring a new dimension, timbre, to our exploration of alternative tunings (see also Sethares, 2005). Each complex tone will be the result of all these frequencies played together with different amplitudes, a technique similar to wave table synthesis. This simple example is just a starting point. More interesting sounds could result, for instance, from using louder amplitudes for even multiples of the root frequency.

The function can further be rewritten to place the most dissonant notes in the highest range. (See figure 17.27.)

17.7   Tools for Performing and Composing with Alternative Tunings

17.7.1   GUIs

Special tunings deserve interfaces that make them easier to understand and play with. Luckily, SuperCollider has a GUI system that gives much freedom for the design of such user interfaces. As seen earlier with the tonality diamond, buttons can be created to represent the notes from a tuning, not only to trigger them but also to gain a clearer understanding of complex relationships. (See figures 17.28 and 17.29.)

GUIS can also help to visualize a mode or anything you think is useful for investigating these tunings. I recommend the ixiViews library (Thor Magnusson, 2006), which can be useful for this type of work.

```
a=(1..8);
b=(9..16);
(
a.size.do({ |i|
var x=a[i];
var y=b[i];
// harmonics below 8 remain in the first octave
while({x>2},{x=x/2});
// harmonics above 9 remain in the second octave
while({y>4},{y=y/2});
a.put(i, x);
b.put(i, y);
});
)
a;
b;
c=(a++b).asSet.asArray.sort;
c;

(
e=Pbind(
\freq, Pn(Pshuf( c*200, 1)),
\dur, 0.2,
\sustain, 1.1
).play
)
//////////////////////////////////////////////////
```

Figure 17.26
Different arrangements for the first 16 harmonics.

17.7.2   MIDI

SuperCollider supports MIDI, so it is possible to trigger a MIDI note from a MIDI controller and map it to a special tuning in SuperCollider. Of course, we need to keep track of where the notes are on the keyboard, since we might use more than 12 notes per octave. The computer keyboard can be used to trigger tunings or modes.

17.7.3   Scale and Tuning Classes

The examples in this chapter are just a starting point. Two very useful classes are now in the core of SuperCollider and provide easy access for the exploration of the

```
(
//   a function to expand the tuning from one octave to four octaves
~harmsfunc={arg stepsperoctave=7;
var harms;
// calculate each note from the tuning
harms=Array.fill(stepsperoctave, {arg i; 2.pow(i/stepsperoctave)});
harms.size.do({ |i|
if( 0.6.coin, {
// multiply some of the notes to create higher harmonics
harms.put(i, (harms[i])*[1,2,4,8].choose )
})
});
harms.sort;
};
)


//   create an array of virtual harmonics, seven equal-note temperament
~harms=~harmsfunc.value(7);


(
// send a synth definition with some partials and the current value of ~harms

SynthDef(\cfstring1, { arg out=0, freq = 360, gate = 1, pan, amp=0.8;
var sound, eg, fc, osc, a, b, w;
var harms, amps;

// use the harmonics previously calculated
harms=~harms;
//  create new amplitudes for each harmonic
amps=Array.fill(harms.size,{1.0.rand}).normalizeSum*0.1;

osc = Array.fill(harms.size, { |i|
SinOsc.ar(freq * harms[i], 0, amps[i] );
})++[SinOsc.ar(freq , 0, amp*(0.5.rand+0.2) ), SinOsc.ar(freq*2 , 0,
amp*(0.5.rand+0.15) )];

eg = EnvGen.kr(Env.asr(0.02,1,1), gate, doneAction:2);

sound = Pan2.ar(eg * Mix.ar(osc), pan);
Out.ar(0, sound);
}).add;
)
```

Figure 17.27
Creating virtual partials for a seven equal-note tuning.

```
(
e=Pbind(
\instrument, \cfstring1,
// frequencies are rpeated so we can notice the effect of harmonics
\degree, Pseq([0,1,2,3,4,5,6,7],inf),
\dur, 0.25,
\stepsPerOctave, 7,
\octave, 4,
\pan, Pfunc({0.5.rand2 })
).play;
)

Send the SynthDef function again to obtain new amplitudes for each harmonic
(
// send a synth definition with some partials and the current value of ~harms

SynthDef(\cfstring1, { arg out=0, freq = 360, gate = 1, pan, amp=0.8;
var sound, eg, fc, osc, a, b, w;
var harms, amps;

// use the harmonics previously calculated
harms=~harms;
//  create new amplitudes for each harmonic
amps=Array.fill(harms.size,{1.0.rand}).normalizeSum*0.1;

osc = Array.fill(harms.size, { |i|
SinOsc.ar(freq * harms[i], 0, amps[i] );
})++[SinOsc.ar(freq , 0, amp*(0.5.rand+0.2) ), SinOsc.ar(freq*2 , 0,
amp*(0.5.rand+0.15) )];

eg = EnvGen.kr(Env.asr(0.02,1,1), gate, doneAction:2);

sound = Pan2.ar(eg * Mix.ar(osc), pan);
Out.ar(0, sound);
}).add;
)

// re-evalute the function to create new harmonics (update the SynthDef afterwards)
~harms=~harmsfunc.value(7);
//Send the SynthDef function again, as we have done earlier to obtain new amplitudes
for each harmonic
```

Figure 17.27
(continued)

```
// finally playing a random melody to make it less repetitive
(
e.stream=Pbind(
\instrument, \cfstring1,
// frequencies are repeated so we can notice the effect of harmonics
\degree,  Pwhite(0, 7),
\dur, 0.25,
\stepsPerOctave, 7,
\octave, 4,
\pan, Pfunc({0.5.rand2 })
).asStream;
)
// we could develop further and re-write the SynthDef with a partial argument
// and also change the partials directly from Pbind

//////////////////////////////////////////////////////
```

Figure 17.27
(continued)

many varied and fascinating pitch resources associated with the musics of the world. A Tuning object holds a particular tuning system, such as 12-note equal temperament or Partch's 43-note system. A scale is a particular subset of the tuning, such as a major or minor scale. The same scale can be played back with different tunings, or different scales applied to different tunings.

```
a = Scale.major       //represents the major scale [0, 2, 4, 5, 7, 9, 11]
t = Tuning.just;      //just intonation tuning chromatic scale
a.tuning_(t)          //set major scale to use this just tuning
a.semitones           //get (fractional) MIDI note values
a.ratios              //get frequency ratios
```

The Tuning and Scale classes are very well documented and will be useful to anyone wanting to experiment with alternative systems of pitch, whether they create their own system or want to use a preexisting one.

```
Tuning.directory      // interesting and famous tunings already listed
Scale.directory       // interesting and famous scales already listed
```

Creating custom tunings and scales is easy with these classes. Take into account the number of notes that exist in your tuning when creating scales.

```
(
var w, keys, steps, octaves;

w = Window.new.name="Custom keyboard: 7 steps per octave";
steps = 7;
octaves= 2;
// seven steps per octave;
a=Array.fill(7, { |i| (1/7)*(i) })+1;
b= a++(a*2);

c=Synth(\default, [\amp, 0]);

keys=Array.fill(steps*octaves,{ |i|

Button(w, Rect(20+(i*22),20,20,50))
.states_([
if(i.mod(steps)==0,{
[i.asString, Color.black, Color.red]},{
[i.asString, Color.black, Color.yellow]});

])
.action_({ arg butt;
c.set(\freq,b[i]*220, \amp, 0.25)
});
});

w.front;
)
/////////////////////////////////////////////////////
```

Figure 17.28
Code for a simple GUI keyboard to trigger the seven equal-note temperament.

```
// custom tuning with 6 unequal values per octave
t = Tuning.new(#[0, 1.3, 2.8, 3.7, 5.2, 8.6], name: \mynewtuning);
// custom scale using all 6 notes from the tuning
b = Scale.new([0, 1, 2, 3, 4, 5], 6, tuning: t);
// play it in ascending pitch order
// note: the seventh degree is an octave higher than degree 0.
Pbind(\scale, b, \degree, Pseq([0,1, 2, 3, 4, 5, 6, 7],inf), \dur, 0.25).
play;
// play a new scale using only some of the notes from the same tuning
c = Scale.new([0, 2, 3, 5], 6, tuning: t);
Pbind(\scale, c, \degree, Pseq([0, 1, 2, 3, 4],inf), \dur, 0.25).play;
```

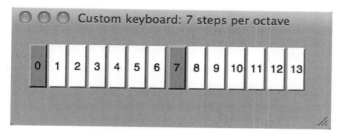

Figure 17.29
Picture of a simple GUI keyboard to trigger the seven equal-note temperament.

17.8   Conclusion

If we consider that Western composers of the past were able to compose such different music with 12 notes, we can deduce that there should be more to alternative tunings than a few calculations made in the hope of obtaining a sonic piece; a single tuning can already be used in so many different ways. . . . Tuning is a rich area of study. A good starting point would be to get familiar with historical and experimental tunings. With the help of this chapter, you should be then able to write these tunings in SuperCollider code and spend some time listening to them. Because Super-Collider is a wonderful environment for experimentation, you can easily modify code and eventually create your own tunings. One warning for those who grew up under its dominant sway: it can take time for perception to really be free from years of listening to 12-equal-note temperament. As a result, it is important to spend enough time listening to these new tunings in order to appreciate them, recognize what is truly liked, and, eventually, choose what you want to create. There is an infinite space between 1 and 2 within an octave, and thanks to SuperCollider, we can explore more deeply than ever the riches from that territory.

References

Burns, E. M. 1999. "Intervals, Scales, and Tuning." In *The Psychology of Music*, 2nd ed. D. Deutsch, ed., pp. 215–264. San Diego: Academic Press.

Carlos, W. 1987. "Tuning: At the Crossroads." *Computer Music Journal*, 11(1): 29–43.

McCartney, J. 1996. "SuperCollider Programming Software for the MacIntosh," <http://www.audiosynth.com>.

Mogini, F. 2000. "Alternative Tuning Systems." Master's thesis, Lansdown Centre for Electronic Arts, Middlesex University, London.

Partch, H. 1974. *Genesis of a Music,* enlarged ed. New York: Da Capo Press.

Sethares, W. A. 2005. *Tuning, Timbre, Spectrum, Scale,* 2nd ed. Berlin: Springer.

Further Third-Party Work

Some SC code and libraries for alternative tunings by the SC community are listed here.

Collins, Nick. 2003. Canonic Hill Loss. Microtonal Tempo Canon Generator System after Nancarrow and Jaffe. For SuperCollider 2.

Harkins, James. "EqualTemperament." Available in the Quarks.

Magnusson, Thor. "ixiViews," <http://www.ixi-software.net>.

Mogini, Fabrice. <http://www.fabricemogini.com>.

18 Non-Real-Time Synthesis and Object-Oriented Composition

Brian Willkie and Joshua Parmenter

18.1 Introduction

SuperCollider provides the means for rendering sound works in non-real-time (NRT). SuperCollider's notoriety for real-time performance often overshadows this aspect of the language, but its object-oriented basis, coupled with the extremely powerful signal-processing tools, makes this dimension important to SuperCollider users. Since the sound is rendered off-line, the real-time considerations of processor performance are not as crucial (though through good coding practices and the efficient use of UGens, you can still benefit from faster render times). In this chapter we look at object-oriented models that provide elaborate control, allowing the user to create musically expressive code and explore new approaches to sound construction.

18.2 SuperCollider NRT Basics

18.2.1 OSC Commands, Score, and the NRT Server

Before discussing advanced techniques involved with SuperCollider's NRT capabilities and more general compositional tools, a brief description of what SuperCollider needs in order to render a non-real-time sound file is necessary, as well as a brief discussion of problems that arise from using the SuperCollider language beyond its more heavily developed real-time capabilities. SuperCollider's NRT mode relies on binary "scores" of OSC command bundles.[1] Inside this binary file, only chronologically ordered OSC bundles are allowed. An OSC bundle (in SuperCollider's specialized treatment of OSC messaging) is an array consisting of a time stamp in seconds, and 1 or more arrays containing OSC commands. For example, [0.0, [\g_new, 1000, 0, 1]] is a bundle. Any approach to NRT in SuperCollider needs to format and store the binary OSC messages that the synthesis server (scsynth) requires. Figure 18.1 shows the basic steps to save binary OSC messages for later use off-line.

```
/*
This example is adapted and extracted from the Non-Realtime Synthesis
helpfile itself, accessible from the Main SuperCollider help page.
*/
(
var f, c, d;
// open a file for writing raw OSC data to
f = File("~/test.osc".standardizePath,"w");
// start a sine oscillator at 0.2 seconds.
c = [ 0.2, [\s_new, \default, 1001, 0, 0]];
// convert the bundle to raw OSC
d = c.asRawOSC;
f.write(d.size); // each bundle is preceded by a 32 bit size.
f.write(d); // write the bundle data.
f.close;
)
```

Figure 18.1
Basic steps to save binary OSC messages for later use offline.

Since most users of the language control events through the server abstraction classes (e.g., Synth, Group, Buffer, and Bus), the first hurdle that you may confront in the above example is the OSC bundle itself. Working with SuperCollider's NRT capabilities at this level requires an understanding of the OSC communication that occurs between the SuperCollider language and scsynth. Though working directly with raw binary OSC messages can be avoided, if you want to create your own system or classes for use with SuperCollider in NRT, an intimate familiarity with the OSC command reference is necessary. A glance at the source code for the server abstraction classes can also give you some important insight into how the underlying OSC is handled.

A Score object gives you a way of managing OSC bundles, provides a basic interface for saving work, and can be used for playing in real time or rendering an event listing off-line. Score handles the conversion of OSC bundles into raw OSC and also has the ability to sort events chronologically. The Score object, and more specifically its instance variable, score, holds an array of bundles. The last time stamp in a Score corresponds to the duration of the output sound file. You can add additional events to a Score, and we recommend that you sort before you save, play, or render a Score, to ensure it orders the time stamps correctly. Figure 18.2 shows the basic usage of Score through a small example event listing.

```
s = Server.local;
s.boot;

// a sample SynthDef
SynthDef(\NRT_beep, {arg freq, dur, amp = 0.1;
    var half;
    half = dur * 0.5;
    Out.ar(0, SinOsc.ar(freq, 0,
        EnvGen.kr(Env.new([0, amp, 0], [half, half], [4, -4])))));
}).load(s);


(
var score;

// A Score, created from a note-list of time-stamped events.
score = Score.new([
    [0.0,
        [\g_new, 1000],
        [\s_new, \NRT_beep, 1001, 0, 1000, \freq, 75.midicps, \dur, 0.2]
    ],
    [0.2,
        [\n_free, 1001],
        [\s_new, \NRT_beep, 1001, 0, 1000, \freq, 75.midicps, \dur, 0.2]
    ],
    [0.4,
        [\n_free, 1001],
        [\s_new, \NRT_beep, 1001, 0, 1000, \freq, 75.midicps, \dur, 0.2]
    ],
    [0.6,
        [\n_free, 1001],
        [\s_new, \NRT_beep, 1001, 0, 1000, \freq, 75.midicps, \dur, 0.2]
    ],
    [0.8,
        [\n_free, 1001],
        [\s_new, \NRT_beep, 1001, 0, 1000, \freq, 71.midicps, \dur, 0.2]
    ],
    [1.0,
        [\n_free, 1001],
        [\s_new, \NRT_beep, 1001, 0, 1000, \freq, 71.midicps, \dur, 0.2]
    ],
    [1.2,
        [\n_free, 1001],
        [\s_new, \NRT_beep, 1001, 0, 1000, \freq, 82.midicps, \dur, 0.2]
```

Figure 18.2
Example Score usage.

```
    ],
    [1.4,
        [\n_free, 1001],
        [\s_new, \NRT_beep, 1001, 0, 1000, \freq, 82.midicps, \dur, 0.2]
    ],
    [1.6,
        [\n_free, 1001],
        [\s_new, \NRT_beep, 1001, 0, 1000, \freq, 82.midicps, \dur, 0.2]
    ],
    [1.8,
        [\n_free, 1001],
        [\s_new, \NRT_beep, 1001, 0, 1000, \freq, 82.midicps, \dur, 0.2]
    ],
    [2.0,
        [\n_free, 1001, 1000]
    ],
    [2.00001, [0]]
]);

score.play(s); // play the Score in real-time...

// ... or render in Non-Real-Time
score.recordNRT("/tmp/trashme", "~/test.aiff".standardizePath,
    options: ServerOptions.new.numOutputBusChannels_(1));
)
```

Figure 18.2
(continued)

18.2.2   Tips for Score Use

One thing to notice in figure 18.2 is that all of the values are hard-coded (i.e., we've used specific numbers to represent values such as \freq and \dur). One of the important life lessons of computer programming is "Never hard-code anything!" Suppose we want all of the notes to overlap. Not only do we have to change the duration of every event, but we have to adjust the node IDs as well. Suppose we want to transpose everything up by a half step. Now suppose our score is 1000 events long. Ugh!

We can make large-scale changes easier by storing values in variables and building relationships between them. (See figure 18.3.)

Now, since we have specified the relationships and substituted variables for specific values, when we highlight and evaluate the code, SuperCollider interprets the variables, substituting 622.2539 for every occurrence of firstPitch. If we want to

```
(
//In this example, we use the higher-level server abstraction classes, Group and
Synth to handle the
// node IDs. At least as important though is the use of variables. Now that the
relationships are
// specified rather than the specific values, we can change the gesture dramatically
by changing
// just one or two variables. To transpose everything, we only need to change the
value of
// ~baseNote. To adjust the duration, we only need to change the ~dur variable, and
this is now
// independent of the deltaOn (i.e. independent of the amount of time between the
start of one
// note and the start of the next note).
var score;
var deltaOn = 0.2;   //amount of time between the start of one note and the start of
the next note
var dur = 0.4;        //try changing dur to 0.3, 1.4, 3.4, or whatever you like
var baseNote = 75;   //transpose the entire fragment up or down
var firstPitch  = (baseNote + 0).midicps;   //alter the relationship between any of
the pitches
var secondPitch = (baseNote - 4).midicps;   // without effecting the others
var thirdPitch  = (baseNote + 7).midicps;

score = Score.new([
    [t =  0.0,
        (g = Group.basicNew(s)).newMsg,
        //we use environment variables here (identified by the preceding ~)
        // since we might add or remove events; hence we don't know ahead of
        // time how many events we have, and therefore how many variables we'll need
        (~s01 = Synth.basicNew(\NRT_beep, s))
            .newMsg(g, [\freq, firstPitch, \dur, dur], \addToHead)
    ],
    [t + dur,
        ~s01.freeMsg
    ],
    [t = t + deltaOn,
        (~s02 = Synth.basicNew(\NRT_beep, s))
            .newMsg(g, [\freq, firstPitch, \dur, dur], \addToHead)
    ],
    [t + dur,
        ~s02.freeMsg
```

Figure 18.3
Build relationships with variables and functions rather than hard-coding specific values.

```
        ],
        [t = t + deltaOn,
            (~s03 = Synth.basicNew(\NRT_beep, s))
                .newMsg(g, [\freq, firstPitch, \dur, dur], \addToHead)
        ],
        [t + dur,
            ~s03.freeMsg
        ],
        [t = t + deltaOn,
            (~s04 = Synth.basicNew(\NRT_beep, s))
                .newMsg(g, [\freq, firstPitch, \dur, dur], \addToHead)
        ],
        [t + dur,
            ~s04.freeMsg
        ],
        [t = t + deltaOn,
            (~s05 = Synth.basicNew(\NRT_beep, s))
                .newMsg(g, [\freq, secondPitch, \dur, dur], \addToHead)
        ],
        [t + dur,
            ~s05.freeMsg
        ],
        [t = t + deltaOn,
            (~s06 = Synth.basicNew(\NRT_beep, s))
                .newMsg(g, [\freq, secondPitch, \dur, dur], \addToHead)
        ],
        [t + dur,
            ~s06.freeMsg
        ],
        [t = t + deltaOn,
            (~s07 = Synth.basicNew(\NRT_beep, s))
                .newMsg(g, [\freq, thirdPitch, \dur, dur], \addToHead)
        ],
        [t + dur,
            ~s07.freeMsg
        ],
        [t = t + deltaOn,
            (~s08 = Synth.basicNew(\NRT_beep, s))
                .newMsg(g, [\freq, thirdPitch, \dur, dur], \addToHead)
        ],
        [t + dur,
            ~s08.freeMsg
```

Figure 18.3
(continued)

```
        ],
        [t = t + deltaOn,
            (~s09 = Synth.basicNew(\NRT_beep, s))
                .newMsg(g, [\freq, thirdPitch, \dur, dur], \addToHead)
        ],
        [t + dur,
            ~s09.freeMsg
        ],
        [t = t + deltaOn,
            (~s10 = Synth.basicNew(\NRT_beep, s))
                .newMsg(g, [\freq, thirdPitch, \dur, dur], \addToHead)
        ],
        [t + dur,
            ~s10.freeMsg,
            g.freeMsg
        ],
    ]
);

score.sort;
score.play(s);
)
```

Figure 18.3
(continued)

transpose the sequence up a fourth, we need to change only the value of baseNote. If we want to change the pitch of only the last 4 notes, we need to change only the value of the variable thirdPitch.

In figure 18.3 we also build a temporal relationship with the little bit of code,

```
t = t + d,
```

that states, "This event starts at the time of the previous event plus some constant offset." As long as all of our events have this relationship, we can substitute that little bit of code for the time stamp of each event (except the first, since it doesn't have a previous event). What's more, we can insert or remove events manually without having to manually adjust the time stamps of all of the subsequent events in our score.

Notice, too, that we used server abstraction classes (Group, Synth, etc.) to handle the node IDs for us. These classes can provide OSC messages for use with the Score class. Synth's basicNew method creates a new Synth object without sending any data to the server itself. The newMsg method returns an OSC message suitable for use

```
(
var score, graingest;

// seed the randomness
thisThread.randSeed_(123);

// a sample SynthDef
SynthDef(\NRT_grain, {arg freq, dur, amp, pan;
    OffsetOut.ar(0, Pan2.ar(
        SinOsc.ar(freq, 0,
            EnvGen.ar(Env.sine(dur, amp), doneAction: 2)),
        pan)
        );
    }).load(s);

score = Score.new;

// envelope times are scaled to 1.
graingest = {arg score, starttime, duration, windur, overlaps, freqenv, ampenv,
panenv;
    var ratio, curfreq, curamp, curpan, notestart, now = 0.0, note;
    while({
        ratio = now / duration;
        curfreq = freqenv[ratio];
        curamp = ampenv[ratio];
        curpan = panenv[ratio];
        notestart = now + starttime;
        note = Synth.basicNew(\NRT_grain);
        score.add([notestart,
            note.newMsg(1, [\freq, curfreq,\amp, curamp, \dur, windur, \pan,
curpan], \addToHead)]
            );
        // check the current event's endtime against the global endtime
        now = now + (windur / overlaps);
        now < duration;
        });
    };

// call the above function to populate the Score

graingest.value(score, 1.0, 10.0, 100.reciprocal, 1, Env([440, 550], [1]),
    Env([0, 0.2, 0], [0.3, 0.7], [4, -4]), Env([0, 0], [1]));
```

Figure 18.4
Algorithmically fill a Score.

```
graingest.value(score, 3.0, 3.0, 130.reciprocal, 2, Env([700, 400], [1]),
    Env([0, 0.2, 0], [0.1, 0.9], [4, -1]), Env([-0.7, 0.7], [1]));

// create a number of short gestures
10.do({arg i;
    graingest.value(score, 5.0.rrand(10.0), 3.0.rrand(5.0), (100 * i).reciprocal,
[1, 2, 4].choose,
        Env([1000, 800], [1]), Env([0, 0.2, 0], [0.5, 0.5]), Env([0.5.rand2,
0.5.rand2], [1]));
    });

// save the endtime to the Score to tell NRT when to stop rendering. The above
gestures won't be more than 16 seconds

score.add([16, [0]]);

// sort the score to ensure events are in the correct order

score.sort;

// render the Score to the users home folder

score.recordNRT("/tmp/trashme", "~/test.aiff".standardizePath,
    options: ServerOptions.new.numOutputBusChannels_(1));

// also save the Score to a file
score.saveToFile("~/test.sc".standardizePath);
)
```

Figure 18.4
(continued)

with Score. These methods allow us to use the server abstraction classes for NRT composition. Though a number of these methods are listed in the Help files, we again suggest that you look through the class definitions for the complete implementation.

If manually adding events to a Score seems too labor intensive, then take a look at figure 18.4, which shows the power of algorithmically creating large Scores from within the SuperCollider language itself.

While the above examples demonstrate how using variables to define relationships helps us make large-scale changes more easily, they also demonstrate a peculiar feature of Score: internally it stores all of its events as bundles. It doesn't know how to evaluate the variables or the relationships between them that we so carefully created. Thus, every time we make a change, we have to re-create the Score before it can reflect our changes. This approach loses the flexible real-time usage, requiring that we populate a Score first, then perform it using the play method. Finally, another approach commonly used in the SuperCollider language for NRT composition is the Pattern class's render and asScore methods. This retains some of the flexibility of real-time composing that Pattern supplies, and handles the Score production for you. (See chapter 6 for examples.)

18.2.3   Score and Memory Allocation

Special consideration for memory allocation of sound files and buffers (used by UGens such as BufDelayC or FFT) for off-line as well as online rendering of a Score is needed. For NRT rendering, you must provide messages for all buffers in the Score, and we recommend that you place these OSC messages at the beginning with a time stamp of 0.0. This ensures that any synthesis processes can access the memory when needed. While it is good practice to add OSC bundles at the end of your Score to free memory buffers after the NRT process finishes, in reality scsynth takes care of this for you when it exits. However, if you want to use a Score's play method, we suggest that you NOT include the buffers in the Score, due to the asynchronous nature of buffer allocation. Figures 18.5 and 18.6 show examples for allocating memory within Score. In figure 18.5, we place memory allocations in the Score because they will take place in NRT and are freed at the end. Figure 18.6 shows the memory allocated in real time. Once the allocation finishes, it is safe to call the play method on the Score. When the Score's performance is complete, the memory is released to free up system resources.

18.2.4   Challenges for NRT Users

Although these approaches offer basic support for NRT work, there are a number of limitations on creating and editing a Score or Pattern. A number of existing extension libraries help overcome these limitations. In addition, the flexibility of SuperCollider's class library lets you add functionality through the addition of custom class definitions, giving you the ability to expand the possibilities of the language to suit your compositional style and needs.[2] The approach to Score creation shown in figures 18.1 and 18.2 reveals some basic problems. Editing compositional details is difficult, and shaping large-scale gestures is even more problematic. The SynthDef's function, with its user-defined parameter list, allows for the creation of flexible and modular code. However, since a Score stores the OSC commands that set those parameters as specific values, there is no easy way to make large-scale changes to those

```
(
var score, sndbuf, starttime, synth, options;

SynthDef(\NRT_playback, {arg buffer, dur, startPos, amp;
    OffsetOut.ar(0, PlayBuf.ar(1, buffer, BufRateScale.kr(buffer),
            startPos: startPos * BufSampleRate.kr(buffer)) *
        EnvGen.ar(
            Env.sine(dur, amp),
            doneAction: 2))
    }).load(s);

score = Score.new;

// create a Buffer object for adding to the Score
sndbuf = Buffer.new;

// for NRT rendering, the buffer messages must be added to the Score
score.add([0, sndbuf.allocReadMsg("sounds/a11wlk01-44_1.aiff")]);

starttime = 0.0;

// a small function to create a series of small notes based on the Buffer
while({
    synth = Synth.basicNew(\NRT_playback);
    score.add([starttime,
        synth.newMsg(s, [\buffer, sndbuf, \dur, 0.1, \startPos, 0.0.rrand(1.0),
\amp, 0.1])]);
    starttime = starttime + 0.05;
    starttime < 10.0;
    });

// the dummy command. The soundfile will be 11 seconds long
score.add([11, 0]);

score.sort;

// the ServerOptions for rendering the soundfile
options = ServerOptions.new.numOutputBusChannels_(1);

// write the soundfile out to disk
score.recordNRT("/tmp/trashme", "~/test.aiff".standardizePath, options: options);
)
```

Figure 18.5
Memory allocation within Score for NRT.

```
(
var score, sndbuf, starttime, synth, options, cond;

SynthDef(\NRT_playback, {arg buffer, dur, startPos, amp;
    OffsetOut.ar(0, PlayBuf.ar(1, buffer, BufRateScale.kr(buffer),
            startPos: startPos * BufSampleRate.kr(buffer)) *
        EnvGen.ar(
            Env.sine(dur, amp),
            doneAction: 2))
    }).load(s);

score = Score.new;

// set up a Condition to check for when asynchronous events are finished.

cond = Condition.new;

// wrap the code that will run in real-time in a Routine, to allow for the Server to
sync
Routine.run({
    // load the buffer
    sndbuf = Buffer.read(s, "sounds/a11wlk01-44_1.aiff");

    // pause while the buffer is loaded
    s.sync(cond);

    // fill the Score with notes

    starttime = 0.0;

    while({
        synth = Synth.basicNew(\NRT_playback);
        score.add([starttime,
            synth.newMsg(s, [\buffer, sndbuf, \dur, 0.1, \startPos, 0.0.rrand(1.0),
\amp, 0.1])]);
        starttime = starttime + 0.05;
        starttime < 10.0;
        });

    // the last command is NOT needed, since no soundfile is being rendered
//  score.add([11, 0]);
```

Figure 18.6
Memory allocation outside of Score for real-time usage.

```
    score.sort;

    // again, options won't be needed for real time performance
//  options = ServerOptions.new.numOutputBusChannels_(1);

    score.play;
    // schedule the freeing of the buffer after the Score is done playing
    SystemClock.sched(11, {sndbuf.free; "Buffer resources freed".postln;});
    })
)
```

Figure 18.6
(continued)

commands. Those values (usually Strings, Symbols, and SimpleNumbers) have no way of knowing how they relate to the overall gesture. Consequently, if you want to alter the \freq parameter contained inside 1 or more Score events, there is simply no good way to do it. Accessing the data is tricky enough, but if you want to change the data from a scalar value to a time-varying one, even more problems arise. You either have to rewrite the SynthDef to include 1 or more EnvGens, or to add more OSC messages that create and map the output of a control-rate Synth onto the \freq parameter of the original.

Figure 18.3 is an excellent example of the problem encountered through the use of the server abstraction classes. These classes are simply not geared toward handling both real-time and NRT concerns, including parameters such as an event's start time and duration. These problems led to the development of the Composer's Tool Kit (Ctk, available as a Quark extension library). A basic goal of the system is to take the strengths of the server abstraction classes while also incorporating concepts of time and methods for setting an event's parameters that look and behave more like the rest of SuperCollider's object-oriented capabilities and language structure.

18.3   Object-Oriented Composition

18.3.1   Composer's Tool Kit

The Composer's Tool Kit (Ctk) is a library of objects that were designed from the beginning to be compatible with both real-time and NRT projects in SuperCollider. Ctk instances are created from the following classes:

CtkScore: Stores Ctk events for real-time or NRT performance.
CtkNote: The basic synthesis object.

CtkNoteObject, CtkProtoNotes, and CtkSynthDef: Objects for prototyping Ctk-Notes.

CtkBuffer: Memory and sound sample management.

CtkControl: Control Bus management and performance.

CtkAudio: Audio Bus management.

CtkEvent: Encapsulates and controls larger-scale gestures containing other Ctk objects.

A CtkScore may contain any number of Ctk Objects. Like Score, CtkScore can be played in real time or used for NRT rendering. Any Ctk Object can be used in real-time mode (and without the use of a CtkScore) through use of the play method. Since the system fully supports both approaches, Ctk can be used as an alternative to the server abstraction classes. While the Help files for the Ctk Objects (and the examples through the remainder of this chapter) show how the Ctk Objects are used, a couple of the system's features should be noted here.

In figure 18.7, a CtkNoteObject is used for prototyping CtkNotes. After an instance of CtkNoteObject is created, the new instance method will create new CtkNote objects using the SynthDef as a prototype. The resulting CtkNote instance automatically creates getter and setter methods for all of the SynthDef's arguments (including those created explicitly through calls to Control.names within the Synth-Def). In play mode, alterations to the control parameters respond in real time to scalars, Envs, or CtkControls. When CtkControls with time-varying signals are used, the system will manage the creation and mapping of additional CtkNotes to the controls.

For real-time performance, if a CtkScore contains CtkBuffers, all buffers are allocated before note events begin. In NRT mode, a CtkBuffer's messages are placed at the beginning of the CtkScore, ensuring that memory is properly prepared for notes that need to access it. Figure 18.7 shows some typical real-time uses.

CtkScores store the CtkObjects themselves, which allows you to easily change the contained objects later. Unlike Score, CtkScore uses the objects stored inside of it that have a start time and duration to calculate the total duration needed for a rendered sound file. CtkScore has the ability to store other CtkScores. As a result, you can store layers of events that you can then modify independently of other events. CtkEvent is another kind of structure that can encapsulate CtkObjects, allowing for large-scale gestural shaping. As a result, you are able to manipulate notes, gestures, and even entire pieces on a number of levels. Figure 18.8 shows examples of the power this approach and how it allows the kind of editing, shaping, and changing of material that we expect in a composition environment. In it, the basic melody initially stored in this instance of CtkScore ("Twinkle, Twinkle, Little Star") is expanded by taking a random chunk of the melody and reinserting it into itself. This

```
// environment variables are used for real-time examples of Ctk objects

n = CtkNoteObject(
    SynthDef(\NRT_grain, {arg gate = 1, freq, amp;
        var src, env;
        src = SinOsc.ar(freq, 0, amp);
        env = EnvGen.kr(Env([0, 1, 0], [1, 1], \sin, 1), gate, doneAction:2);
        OffsetOut.ar(0, src * env);
        })
    );

// create a new note based on 'n', start to play it in 0.1 seconds
a = n.new(0.1).freq_(440).amp_(0.1).gate_(1).play;
// the release method will set 'gate' to 0.0, and free this node
a.release;

// create another note
a = n.new(0.1).freq_(440).amp_(0.1).play;
// alter the freq argument in real time
a.freq_(550);
// alter the freq with a CtkControl that describes an Env
// CtkControl.env(Env)
a.freq_(CtkControl.env(Env([550, 440, 550], [1, 2], \exp)));
// apply a random control to the amp parameter, with an envelope applied to the
range.
// All parameters to the CtkControl can themselves be CtkControls
// CtkControl.lfo(KRUGen, freq, low, high, phase)
a.amp_(CtkControl.lfo(LFNoise2, 0.5, CtkControl.env(Env([0.1, 0.9], [5])), 0.1));
a.amp_(0.1);

// release the note
a.release;
```

Figure 18.7
Example real-time CtkScore usage.

```
// melodic expander
(
var note, keys, durs, now, score, chunk, expander, rangemap;

thisThread.randSeed_(123);

// a simple note player

note = CtkSynthDef(\NRT_dut, {arg key, amp, dur;
        Out.ar(0, SinOsc.ar(key.midicps, 0, XLine.kr(amp, 0.00001, dur)))
        });

// first, make a melody - these will be used as midikeynums (easier to alter later)

keys = [ 72, 72, 79, 79, 81, 81, 79, 77, 77, 76, 76, 74, 74, 72 ];

// a list of durations

durs = [0.25, 0.25, 0.25, 0.25, 0.25, 0.25, 0.5, 0.25, 0.25, 0.25, 0.25, 0.25, 0.25,
0.5];

// create a var to store 'now' in

now = 0.0;

// create a CtkScore with the above melody

score = CtkScore.new;

keys.do({arg thiskey, inc;
    var thisdur;
    thisdur = durs[inc];
    score.add(note.new(now, thisdur).key_(thiskey).amp_(0.2).dur_(thisdur));
    now = now + thisdur;
    });

// first, create a function that will return a chunk of the melody the duration of
the chunk
// sets the starttimes of the notes to a base of 0.0

chunk = {arg offset = 0;
```

Figure 18.8
Algorithmically fill and modify a CtkScore.

```
    var size, start, end, duration = 0, chunk, copies;
    // the size of the current melody - 1 (for array access)
    size = score.notes.size;
    // the beginning of the chunk can come from the beginning of the melody to the
second to
    // last note
    start = 0.rrand(size-1);
    end = start.rrand(size);
    chunk = score.notes[start..end].collect({arg anote;
        var newnote;
        newnote = anote.copy(duration + offset);
        duration = duration + anote.duration;
        newnote;
        });
    [chunk, duration];
    };

// now, create a function that will add those chunks to the score, and will keep
doing this
// until the score is at least the desired length. Then check the score size, and
truncate to
// desired size.

expander = {arg len;
    var curchunk, chunkdur, insert, inserttime, insertdur, cursize, newnotes;
cursize = score.notes.size;
    while({
        cursize < len
        }, {
        insert = 0.rrand(cursize - 1);
        inserttime = score.notes[insert].starttime;
        insertdur = score.notes[insert].duration;
        #curchunk, chunkdur = chunk.value(inserttime + insertdur);
        score.notes[(insert+1)..(cursize-1)].do({arg me;
            me.setStarttime(me.starttime + chunkdur)});
        score = score.add(curchunk);
        (score.notes.size > len).if({
            score.notes.do({arg me, i;
                (i > (len - 1)).if({score.notes.remove(me)});
                })
            });
        cursize = score.notes.size;
```

Figure 18.8
(continued)

```
        });
    };

// rangemap will place the melodic material within a certain range. The user passes
// in an envelope that will describe the center pitch in an octave range

rangemap = {arg center;
    score.notes.do({arg me;
        me.key_(me.key.mapIntoRange(12, center[me.starttime]));
        })
    };

// expand it to 100 notes
expander.value(100);

// describe a new range of pitches
rangemap.value(Env([60, 96], [20]));

// finally, play the CtkScore

score.play;
)
```

Figure 18.8
(continued)

process continues to repeat itself with each new iteration of the expanded CtkScore until the desired length is reached. After the creation of the expanded melody, the pitch material is mapped over time into a dynamic pitch range.

Figure 18.8 also demonstrates another important topic for composers of algorithmic music. Since there are random processes involved in these functions, seeding the randomness may be desirable. On the language side of SuperCollider, any thread can have a seed set. In Figure 18.8, the Thread that the entire SuperCollider interpreter is running is seeded through the `thisThread.randSeed_(seed)` line of code at the beginning of the figure, where "seed" is any integer. When this is set, all random language calls will advance the pseudo-random number generator from this seeded point. You can set the seed again later if you want to, and individual threads (such as Routine, which is a subclass of Thread) can also be seeded. An example of seeding a Routine is given in figure 18.9 while also showing another example of the power of CtkScore.

The example has been built from a basic gesture along with some functions that modify the gesture in a couple of simple ways. A Routine at the end of the code

```
(
var score, grain, now, thisdur;
var ampmap, double;

grain = CtkNoteObject(
    SynthDef(\NRT_grain, {arg freq, amp, dur, pan = 0;
        var src, env;
        env = EnvGen.ar(
            Env([0, 1, 0], [0.5, 0.5], \sin),
            timeScale: dur, doneAction: 2, levelScale: amp);
        src = SinOsc.ar(freq, 0, env);
        OffsetOut.ar(0, Pan2.ar(src, pan));
        })
    );

score = CtkScore.new;

now = 0;

// create a 3 second granular gesture

while({
    thisdur = 0.05.rrand(0.1);
    score.add(
        grain.new(now, thisdur).freq_(440.rrand(880)).amp_(0.05).dur_(thisdur).
pan_(0));
    now = now + 0.01;
    now < 3;
    });

// a function to later map the amplitude to a given shape
// envtimes should be scaled to 1
ampmap = {arg aScore, env;
    // scaled the envs times by the CtkScore's duration
    env.times = env.times * aScore.endtime;
    aScore.notes.do({arg thisNote;
        var curtime;
        curtime = thisNote.starttime;
        thisNote.amp_(env[curtime]);
        });
    };
```

Figure 18.9
Algorithmically build a granular gesture with Ctk for off-line rendering.

```
// returns a new copy of the CtkScore with notes
// double an octave higher
double = {arg aScore, shift = 2;
    var thisScore;
    thisScore = aScore.copy;
    thisScore.notes.do({arg thisNote;
        thisNote.freq_(thisNote.freq * shift)
        });
    thisScore;
    };

// a Routine to play the examples
Routine.run({
    var scoreDouble;
    // play the CtkScore;
    score.play;
    score.endtime.wait;
    // remap the amplitudes
    ampmap.value(score, Env([0, 0.2, 0], [0.1, 0.9], [4, -2]));
    1.wait; // pause for a moment
    // play it again!
    score.play;
    score.endtime.wait;
    // add the CtkScore that octaveDouble returns
    scoreDouble = double.value(score, 19.midiratio);
    ampmap.value(scoreDouble, Env([0, 0.25, 0], [0.6, 0.4], [4, -2]));
    score.add(scoreDouble);
    1.wait;
    score.play;
    score.endtime.wait;
    // don't like the second version? remove double
    score.ctkscores.remove(scoreDouble);
    ampmap.value(score, Env([0.15, 0.05], [1]));
    1.wait;
    score.play;
    }).randSeed_(123)
)
```

Figure 18.9
(continued)

plays, then alters, the gesture in steps for you to audition. The example shows how you are able to modify CtkNotes that are stored inside a CtkScore. In this case, a couple of functions treat the CtkScore and its contents as a single gesture. First, we create a simple granular gesture that lasts 3 seconds. Frequency is random, and the amplitude is flat. The ampmap function will iterate over the CtkScore's notes and alter each CtkNote's amp parameter according to an Env object. The modification is made in place, and once it is finished, we can play the CtkScore again to hear the changes. The second function, double, creates a copy of a CtkScore and scales the freq parameter of every note by a value. Then, this second CtkScore's amplitude curve is remapped to new values. This copied and altered CtkScore is added to the first one, and then the new version is performed. In the final step, we remove the second CtkScore and remap all of the CtkNote's amplitudes to the original level. While it is certainly possible to create and shape multiple layers of a piece in this fashion, the ideas of shaping the amplitudes of the event's objects or transposing a frequency over an entire CtkScore are far from specialized cases. Once we find ourselves treating an object and everything it contains in a unified way, then why not create objects that will do all of this for us?

18.3.2   Encapsulation

One of the fundamental elements of music, regardless of style, is varied repetition. The relationship between a subclass and its superclass is precisely this, a varied repetition. More than just a metaphor, object-oriented programming (OOP) codifies a set of general programming practices that can aid the computer musician in creating music. One of the basic elements of OOP is encapsulation (i.e., grouping related things together). In the score in figure 18.10, we have a group containing a simple oscillator that is controlled by a low-frequency oscillator (lfo) and an amplitude envelope.

These 4 objects are always together. Every time we have the oscillator, we have a group, an lfo, and an envelope.

Since these objects are related, we can group them together and give them a name, such as VSO (VibratoSinOsc). Then, whenever we want an oscillator, lfo, and an envelope, we just have to type something like

```
VSO.new;
```

Likewise, there are a number of parameters in common for every use of our combination group-oscillator-lfo-envelope: pitch, start, duration, vibrato depth, vibrato rate, peak amplitude, and decay amplitude. One clue that we can group these variables together into 1 object is that all their names have something in common: *first*Pitch, *first*Start, *first*Dur. Finally, anytime you see code that is copied and pasted (or

```
s = Server.local;
s.boot;

~sinosc = CtkSynthDef.new(\NRT_sinosc,
    {arg outbus = 0, freq = 622.254, phase = 0, amp = 1, offSet = 0;
        Out.ar(outbus, SinOsc.ar(freq, phase, amp, offSet));
    }
);

(
var score;
var baseNote = 75;
var slopeTime = 0.25;
var curve = \sine;
var firstPitch = (baseNote + 0).midicps;
var firstStart = 0.0;
var firstDur = 5.0;
var firstAttackTime = slopeTime * 0.5;
var firstDecayTime  = slopeTime - firstAttackTime;
var firstVibDepth = 0.21;
var firstVibRate = 2.3;
var firstPeakAmp = 0.25;
var firstDecayAmp = 0.01;
var secondPitch = (baseNote - 4).midicps;
var secondStart = 2.2;
var secondDur = 4.0;
var secondAttackTime = slopeTime * 0.5;
var secondDecayTime  = slopeTime - secondAttackTime;
var secondVibDepth = 0.15;
var secondVibRate = 1.7;
var secondPeakAmp = 0.25;
var secondDecayAmp = 0.01;
var thirdPitch = (baseNote + 7).midicps;
var thirdStart = 3.1;
var thirdDur = 3.75;
var thirdAttackTime = slopeTime * 0.5;
var thirdDecayTime  = slopeTime - thirdAttackTime;
var thirdVibDepth = 0.21;
var thirdVibRate = 4;
var thirdPeakAmp = 0.2;
var thirdDecayAmp = 0.25;

score = CtkScore.new(
    ~firstGroup = CtkGroup.new(firstStart, firstDur, server: s),
    ~sinosc.new(firstStart, firstDur, \tail, ~firstGroup, server: s)
```

Figure 18.10
Example of non-real-time Ctk usage.

```
            .freq_(CtkControl.lfo(SinOsc, firstVibRate,
                (firstPitch - ((firstPitch / (firstPitch.log2)) * (firstVibDepth *
    (1/3)))),
                (firstPitch + ((firstPitch / (firstPitch.log2)) * (firstVibDepth *
    (2/3)))),
                duration: firstDur, addAction: \head, target: ~firstGroup, server: s))
            .amp_(CtkControl.env(
                Env.new([0, firstPeakAmp, firstDecayAmp, 0], [firstAttackTime,
                    firstDur - (firstAttackTime + firstDecayTime), firstDecayTime],
    curve),
                addAction: \head, target: ~firstGroup, server: s)),
        ~secondGroup = CtkGroup.new(secondStart, secondDur, server: s),
        ~sinosc.new(secondStart, secondDur, \tail, ~secondGroup, server: s)
            .freq_(CtkControl.lfo(SinOsc, secondVibRate,
                (secondPitch - ((secondPitch / (secondPitch.log2)) * (secondVibDepth *
    (1/3)))),
                (secondPitch + ((secondPitch / (secondPitch.log2)) * (secondVibDepth *
    (2/3)))),
                duration: secondDur, addAction: \head, target: ~secondGroup, server: s))
            .amp_(CtkControl.env(
                Env.new([0, secondPeakAmp, secondDecayAmp, 0], [secondAttackTime,
                    secondDur - (secondAttackTime + secondDecayTime), secondDecayTime],
    curve),
                addAction: \head, target: ~secondGroup, server: s)),
        ~thirdGroup = CtkGroup.new(thirdStart, thirdDur, server: s),
        ~sinosc.new(thirdStart, thirdDur, \tail, ~thirdGroup, server: s)
            .freq_(CtkControl.lfo(SinOsc, thirdVibRate,
                (thirdPitch - ((thirdPitch / (thirdPitch.log2)) * (thirdVibDepth *
    (1/3)))),
                (thirdPitch + ((thirdPitch / (thirdPitch.log2)) * (thirdVibDepth *
    (2/3)))),
                duration: thirdDur, addAction: \head, target: ~thirdGroup, server: s))
            .amp_(CtkControl.env(
                Env.new([0, thirdPeakAmp, thirdDecayAmp, 0], [thirdAttackTime,
                    thirdDur - (thirdAttackTime + thirdDecayTime), thirdDecayTime],
    curve),
                addAction: \head, target: ~thirdGroup, server: s))
    );

score.play;
)
```

Figure 18.10
(continued)

copied and pasted with slight modifications, such as changing a variable name), that's a strong indication that such code can be grouped together, at least in a function, if not a class. For example, the bit of code (firstPitch – ((firstPitch/ (firstPitch.log2)) * (firstVibDepth * (1/3)))) occurs with every instance of our oscillator-lfo-envelope grouping, with changes only to the variable name. We can rewrite it as a function:

```
f = {arg pitch, vibDepth; pitch - ((pitch/(pitch.log2)) * (vibDepth *
(1/3)))};
```

Then, everywhere we have that bit of code, we can replace it with a call to our function:

```
CtkControl.lfo(SinOSsc, firstVibRate, f.value(firstPitch, firstVibDepth));
```

and similarly for the lfo's high argument.

When building a class (actually, when writing any code), it's good to have a clear idea of your goal. In this case we want a group-oscillator-lfo-envelope object that we can add to a CtkScore.

```
VSO {
    var < score, group, oscil, freqCntl, ampCntl;
}
```

We'll need a constructor with all of the parameters we want to allow the user to set:

```
*new {arg start = 0.0, dur = nil, freq = 622.254, ampPeakLevel = 0.707,
ampDecayLevel = 0.001, vibDepth = 0.21, vibRate = 3, addAction = 0, target
= 1, server;
    ^super.new.initVSO(start, dur, freq, ampPeakLevel, ampDecayLevel,
vibDepth, vibRate, addAction, target, server);
}
```

The constructor allocates memory for our objects (super.new) and then calls our initialization method, initVSO. Note the naming convention of our initialization method:

```
init<ClassName>
```

We strongly encourage this convention. For more details see the "New Instance Creation" section of the *Writing-Classes* Help file included in the SuperCollider distribution.

The initialization method is where most of the work is done, but before we dive into it, we have a couple of additional opportunities to encapsulate: the frequency and amplitude controls.

```
VSO_Vib {

    var <pitch, <depth, <rate, <control;

    *new {arg start = 0.0, dur = nil, freq = 1, vibDepth = 0.21, vibRate = 1,
        addAction = 0, target = 1, server;
        ^super.new.initVSO_Vib(start, dur, freq, vibDepth, vibRate, addAction,
            target, server);
    }

    initVSO_Vib {arg start, dur, freq, vibDepth, vibRate, add = 0, tgt = 1, server;
        server = server ?? {Server.default};
        pitch = freq;
        depth = vibDepth;
        rate = vibRate;
        control = CtkControl.lfo(SinOsc, rate, this.getLowerValue,
            this.getUpperValue, 0, start, dur, add, tgt, server: server);

    }

    getLowerValue {
        ^(pitch - ((pitch / (pitch.log2)) * (depth * (1/3))));
    }

    getUpperValue {
        ^(pitch + ((pitch / (pitch.log2)) * (depth * (2/3))));
    }
}
```

Figure 18.11
VSO_Vib class definition.

```
.freq_(CtkControl.lfo(SinOsc, firstVibRate,
        (firstPitch - ((firstPitch/(firstPitch.log2)) * (firstVibDepth *
        (1/3)))),
        (firstPitch - ((firstPitch/(firstPitch.log2)) * (firstVibDepth *
        (2/3)))),
        addAction: \head, target: _firstGroup, server: s))
```

Notice that every time we create a CtkControl for frequency, we have this little bit of code, and it occurs only when we create that control. Those facts make it a good candidate for encapsulation. We can group the CtkControl, the various data it requires (pitch, rate, depth), and the code that manipulates those data (the functions that give us our low and high values for our lfo) and call it something like VSO_Vib. (See figure 18.11.)

```
VSO_ADR {

    var <control, <attackDur, <releaseDur, <totalDur;

    *new {arg start = 0.0, dur =  nil, peak = 0.707, decay = 0.01,
attackDur = 0.125,
        releaseDur = 0.125, addAction = 0, target = 1, server;
        ^super.new.initVSO_ADR(start, dur, peak, decay, attackDur,
releaseDur, addAction,
            target, server);
    }

    initVSO_ADR {arg start = 0.0, dur =  nil, peak = 0.707, decay =
0.01, aDur = 0.125,
        rDur = 0.125, addAction = 0, target = 1, server;
        server = server ?? {Server.default};
        attackDur = aDur;
        releaseDur = rDur;
        totalDur = dur;
        control = CtkControl.env(Env.new([0, peak, decay, 0],
            [attackDur, this.decayDur, releaseDur], \sine),
            start, addAction, target, server: server, doneAction: 0);
    }

    decayDur {
        ^(totalDur - (attackDur + releaseDur));
    }

}
```

Figure 18.12
VSO_ADR class definition.

Like our VSO object, it has a constructor that allocates memory and calls our initialization method (initVSO_Vib) that does all the work of creating and initializing our CtkControl.lfo. Additionally, we've encapsulated our functions that determine the lower and upper limits of our lfo into the methods getLowerLimit and getUpperLimit, respectively. We can apply similar criteria to our amplitude control. (See figure 18.12.)

But doesn't all this belong to our VSO object? Well, yes, but perhaps not exclusively. We might want to apply vibrato to things other than an oscillator, such as the center frequency of a bandpass filter or another lfo. If we lock this code inside our VSO class, we'll have to rewrite it every time we want to apply vibrato to something

```
    initVSO {arg start = 0.0, dur = nil, freq = 622.254, ampPeakLevel = 0.707,
        ampDecayLevel = 0.01, vibDepth = 0.21, vibRate = 3, addAction = 0, target =
1,
            server;
        server = server ?? {Server.default};
        group = CtkGroup.new(start, dur, addAction: addAction, target: target,
            server: server);
        freqCntl = VSO_Vib.new(start, dur, freq, vibDepth, vibRate, \head, group,
server);
        ampCntl = VSO_ADR.new(start, dur, ampPeakLevel, ampDecayLevel, addAction:
\head,
            target: group, server: server);
        oscil = sinoscdef.new(start, dur, \tail, group, server)
            .freq_(freqCntl.control).amp_(ampCntl.control);
        score = CtkScore.new(group, oscil);
    }
```

Figure 18.13
VSO initialization method.

else. Later, if we decide we want to change the way we implement vibrato (say we want to add jitter to it, or use a different library), we'll have to update every class that implements vibrato. Conversely, if we separate the vibrato out, we can still use it in our VSO object and it will be available for use to any other class. If we decide to change our implementation of vibrato, we have to change it in only 1 place.

This raises another important life lesson in computer programming: "Write modular code!" Modular code isolates functionality into the smallest bit of code that has a practical use. By grouping together things that are closely related, and only things that are closely related, encapsulation promotes modular design. Likewise, practicing modular design leads to grouping together only the things that are really related to each other.

Now that we have our VSO_Vib and VSO_ADR classes, we can use them in our initVSO method. (See figure 18.13.)

Like our initialization methods for VSO_Vib and VSO_ADR, initVSO simply instantiates the objects for our instance variables score, group, oscil, freqCntl, and ampCntl. One interesting difference between VSO and VSO_Vib and VSO_ADR is its class variable sinoscdef and class method *initClass.[3] sinoscdef is the CtkSynthDef that describes our oscillator.

```
classvar <sinoscdef;

*initClass {
    sinoscdef.isNil.if({
```

```
sinoscdef = CtkSynthDef.new(\NRT_sinosc,
    {arg outbus = 0, freq = 622.254, phase = 0, amp = 1, offset =
    0;
        Out.ar(outbus, SinOsc.ar(freq, phase, amp, offset));
    })
});
}
```

Since we don't change this for any instance of VSO, we can define it once at the class level, so it is available for all VSO objects. It is even available to other objects without creating an instance of VSO:

```
a = VSO.sinoscdef;
```

So now we have our completed class definition. (See figure 18.14.)

"That's a lot of code!" you might say. Well, it is more than our initial short score, but let's take a look at that score after substituting our new class. (See figure 18.15.)

Notice that we've taken advantage of the fact that we can nest instances of Ctk-Score within a CtkScore. We've reduced the number of lines in our score by nine tenths, from 30 in the first example (figure 18.10) to 3 lines in our last example (figure 18.15). Now imagine that you want to create 100 vibrato-oscillators. What if you want to add lfo's to modulate the phase and frequency as well? But the benefits don't stop with less typing. Look at how much easier it is to read our last example than the first. Only the necessary details are present in the last example: that we have 3 objects that produce a vibrating sine wave. We don't need to know the specifics of CtkGroup, CtkSynthDef, and CtkControl; too much detail simply clutters up the score.

Encapsulation is a very simple idea: group together related objects and treat then like 1 thing. Yet it is a very powerful way to organize code that you use repeatedly and to make your code more readable.

18.3.3   Polymorphism

As an exercise we can encapsulate some information that is common to Ctk objects: start time and duration.

```
NRT_TimeFrame {

    var <>starttime, <>duration;

    *new {arg starttime, duration;
        ^super.newCopyArgs(starttime, duration);
    }

}
```

```
VSO {

    classvar <sinoscdef;
    var <score, group, oscil, freqCntl, <ampCntl;

    *new {arg start = 0.0, dur = nil, freq = 622.254, ampPeakLevel = 0.707,
ampDecayLevel = 0.01,
        vibDepth = 0.21, vibRate = 3, addAction = 0, target = 1, server;
        ^super.new.initVSO(start, dur, freq, ampPeakLevel, ampDecayLevel,
            vibDepth, vibRate, addAction, target, server);
    }

    *initClass {
        sinoscdef.isNil.if({
            sinoscdef = CtkSynthDef.new(\NRT_sinosc,
                {arg outbus = 0, freq = 622.254, phase = 0, amp = 1, offSet = 0;
                    Out.ar(outbus, SinOsc.ar(freq, phase, amp, offSet));
                })
        });
    }

    initVSO {arg start = 0.0, dur = nil, freq = 622.254, ampPeakLevel = 0.707,
        ampDecayLevel = 0.01, vibDepth = 0.21, vibRate = 3, addAction = 0, target =
1,
            server;
        server = server ?? {Server.default};
        group = CtkGroup.new(start, dur, addAction: addAction, target: target,
            server: server);
        freqCntl = VSO_Vib.new(start, dur, freq, vibDepth, vibRate, \head, group,
server);
        ampCntl = VSO_ADR.new(start, dur, ampPeakLevel, ampDecayLevel, addAction:
\head,
            target: group, server: server);
        oscil = sinoscdef.new(start, dur, \tail, group, server)
            .freq_(freqCntl.control).amp_(ampCntl.control);
        score = CtkScore.new(group, oscil);
    }

}
```

Figure 18.14
Complete VSO class definition.

```
s = Server.local;
s.boot;


(
var score;
var baseNote = 75;
var firstPitch = (baseNote + 0).midicps;
var secondPitch = (baseNote - 4).midicps;
var thirdPitch = (baseNote + 7).midicps;

score = CtkScore.new(
    (a = VSO.new(0.0, 5.0, firstPitch, 0.25, 0.01, 0.21, 2.3, server: s)).score,
    (b = VSO.new(2.2, 4.0, secondPitch, 0.25, 0.01, 0.15, 1.7, server: s)).score,
    (c = VSO.new(3.1, 3.75, thirdPitch, 0.15, 0.3, 0.21, 4, server: s)).score
);
score.play;
)
```

Figure 18.15
Example CtkScore from figure 18.10 with VSO substitution.

We could also add a common Ctk message: end time.

```
endtime {
    ^starttime + duration;
}
```

Now we can clean up that timing code we had earlier. (See figure 18.16.)

Notice that the relationship between the start of the first note and the start of the second note is clearer. It's certainly true that we could simply specify a start time of 2.4 for the second note. After all, it's not that hard to add 0.0 and 2.4, but that misses the point. It's better to identify the relationship and let the computer fill in the details. The fewer details you provide explicitly, the less work it takes to make changes later on.

While we expect the user to fill in the start time and duration with a SimpleNumber (i.e., an Integer or a Float), it might be interesting to support other types of objects, such as Functions.

```
d = [2.4, 1.7];
a = NRT_TimeFrame.new(0.0, 11);
b = NRT_TimeFrame.new({a.starttime + d.at(0)}, {a.endtime - (a.starttime +
d.at(0))});
c = NRT_TimeFrame.new({b.starttime + d.at(1)}, {a.endtime - (b.starttime +
d.at(1))});
```

```
s = Server.local;
s.boot;

(
var score;
var baseNote = 75;
var firstPitch = (baseNote + 0).midicps;
var secondPitch = (baseNote - 4).midicps;
var thirdPitch = (baseNote + 7).midicps;

d = [2.4, 1.7];
a = NRT_TimeFrame.new(0.0, 11);
b = NRT_TimeFrame.new(a.starttime + d.at(0), a.endtime - (a.starttime + d.at(0)));
c = NRT_TimeFrame.new(b.starttime + d.at(1), b.endtime - (b.starttime + d.at(1)));

score = CtkScore.new(
    (a = VSO.new(a.starttime, a.duration, firstPitch, 0.25, 0.01, 0.21, 2.3, server:
s)).score,
    (b = VSO.new(b.starttime, b.duration, secondPitch, 0.25, 0.01, 0.15, 1.7,
server: s)).score,
    (c = VSO.new(c.starttime, c.duration, thirdPitch, 0.15, 0.3, 0.21, 4, server:
s)).score
);
score.play;
//N.B. You may notice three "Node not found" warnings.
// This is expected behavior for this version of Ctk
)
```

Figure 18.16
Example CtkScore from figure 18.15 using NRT_TimeFrame.

However, we wouldn't want to add a start time function to a duration function in our end time method.[4] One way to handle this would be to check the type for start time and duration before we return a value:

```
endtime {
    var start, dur;
    if((starttime.isKindOf(Function)), {
        start = starttime.value;
    }, {
        start = starttime;
    });
    if((duration.isKindOf(Function)), {
        dur = duration.value;
```

```
}, {
    dur = duration;
});
    ^start + dur;
}
```

However, there is a better way. We can take advantage of the fact that Object implements a value method. Consequently, everything in SuperCollider, regardless of type, responds to value.[5] This is an example of polymorphism. When different objects implement the same method, we can write code that doesn't depend on the type of object at hand. It may mean something entirely different for a SimpleNumber to respond to a value message than for a Function to do so, but because they both respond to it, we don't have to overly concern ourselves with those details. We know that we can call value on anything that is passed in, so we can discard all that type checking and just get to work.

```
endtime {
    ^starttime.value + duration.value;
}
```

But end time is not the only thing to use start time and duration. The user is likely to access them, too, so in this case we can build our own getter methods.

```
starttime {
    ^starttime.value;
}

duration {
    ^duration.value;
}
```

Now, within the end time method we can call the getter methods rather than accessing the instance variables directly. We get the same results the user would get for start time and duration, and what's more, we protect the implementation of end time from any changes we make to the getter methods.

Another consideration is that the user might want to leave the start time and/or the duration empty (i.e., nil). nil responds to value, just like everything else in Super-Collider, but if we try to add nil to something else, that will throw an error. So we probably want a little bit of error checking to make sure that we don't try to add nil when we want to determine the end time. Figure 18.17 shows the completed class definition.

Polymorphism can be defined simplistically as differing objects implementing a method of a given name. But this glosses over many of the profound and extensive impacts it has on computer programming. The best we can do here is to offer some

```
NRT_TimeFrame {

    var >starttime, >duration;

    *new {arg starttime, duration;
        ^super.newCopyArgs(starttime, duration);
    }

    starttime {
        ^ starttime.value;
    }

    duration {
        ^ duration.value;
    }

    endtime {
        ^(this.starttime != nil).if({
            (this.duration != nil).if({
                //call the getter methods rather than accessing
                // the variables directly
                this.starttime + this.duration;
            }, {nil})
        }, {nil});

    }

}
```

Figure 18.17
Complete NRT_TimeFrame class definition.

introductory examples. As you spend more time with SuperCollider and programming for computer music, it will be worth your while to seek out more detailed examples and how to apply them to your work to make your life easier. Some suggested readings are listed at the end of this chapter.

18.4   A Customizable Object-Oriented Approach to Music Composition

SuperCollider is a versatile language supporting a wide variety of compositional approaches, from live coding, interactive installations, and other real-time techniques to computationally expensive algorithmic pieces and old-fashioned, fixed, studio works more suited to NRT techniques. Its support for object-oriented programming sets it apart from many of its predecessors and is the major reason most people find it so appealing. All the same, most of us still find it challenging to use. In this chapter, we've looked at ways to leverage OOP concepts and third-party libraries such as the Composer's Tool Kit to make our lives easier.

Object-oriented programming has been developed over several decades. Many books and college courses are devoted to the topic, and some of the earliest examples of its application to music can be found in the work of Henry Lieberman, Stephen Pope, and many others dating back to the late 1980s and early 1990s. As noted earlier, the best we can do here is to offer some introductory examples. As you spend more time with SuperCollider and programming for computer music, it will be worth your while to seek out more detailed examples and consider how to apply them to make your work easier. Some suggested readings include *Object-Oriented Design Heuristics* by Arthur J. Riel, *OOP Demystified* by James Keogh and Mario Giannini, and *An Introduction to Object-Oriented Programming* by Timothy Budd, the author who gave us *A Little Smalltalk,* which is recommended in the SuperCollider Help file *Streams-Patterns-Events1.html.*

Likewise, Ctk is a sizable library rich in functionality. We've only scratched the surface here. Check out the additional NRT materials on the supplemental Web site for some more examples.

Although we have focused on NRT approaches such as algorithmic composition and fixed, studio works, the figures we've presented are not meant as a prescription for any particular compositional method, nor are the tools and techniques we've described limited to NRT usage. Rather, we present these figures as opportunities to explore ways to codify the relationships inherent in music. It is of course up to you to define the relationships that are significant to you, the programming techniques that best represent those relationships, and the tools that are most useful to you. Good luck!

References

Budd, T. 2001. *Object-Oriented Programming*. Reading, MA: Addison-Wesley.

Budd, T. 1987. *A Little Smalltalk*. Reading, MA: Addison-Wesley.

Keogh, J., and M. Giannini. 2004. *OOP Demystified*. McGraw-Hill Osborne Media.

Pope, S. T., ed. 1991. *The Well-Tempered Object: Musical Applications of Object-Oriented Software Technology*. Cambridge, MA: MIT Press.

Riel, A. J. 1996. *Object-Oriented Design Heuristics*. Reading, MA: Addison-Wesley Professional.

Notes

1. It is important to be familiar with the specialized implementation of OSC that SuperCollider uses. There are some examples in this chapter that may provide a basic introduction to how OSC works in SuperCollider, but the *Server-Command-Reference* Help file that is linked from the main SuperCollider Help page gives a more complete overview.

2. Score started out as an extension put together by Josh Parmenter for reading event listings from the CommonMusic library extension to LISP. This was later greatly improved by Scott Wilson, Julian Rohrhuber, and James McCartney before becoming a part of the standard distribution and is one of the main tools for NRT work.

3. *initClass* is called by *Class:initClassTree* in *Process:startup* for everything that inherits from Object.

4. Actually, it is possible to add Functions. See the SuperCollider Help documentation on Function for more information.

5. This is because everything in SuperCollider is a subclass of Object.

Projects and Perspectives

19   A Binaural Simulation of Varèse's *Poème Électronique*

Stefan Kersten, Vincenzo Lombardo, Fabrizio Nunnari, and Andrea Valle

This chapter presents a SuperCollider application that realizes a binaural spatialization of Varèse's *Poème Électronique.* The application is integrated into a reconstruction project that has regained the aural and visual experiences of the *Poème Électronique* with virtual reality techniques. The chapter first introduces the original artwork, which features Le Corbusier, Xenakis, and Varèse as contributors, then presents the overall system architecture, and finally focuses on the SuperCollider application for the rendering of the spatialized sound.

19.1   The *Poème Électronique*

The *Poème Électronique* was a unique experience that originated from a request by Philips that the architect Le Corbusier design the company's pavilion at the Brussels World Fair in 1958 (see Petit, 1958; Xenakis et al., 1958; Treib, 1996; Lombardo et al., 2006). Le Corbusier conceived an electronic poem inside a building without particular facades (see figure 19.1a), a synthesis of sound, light, colors, and rhythm. He personally selected the sequence of black-and-white images that were projected onto the pavilion's walls. The pavilion was designed by Iannis Xenakis (who also composed the interlude music, *Concret PH*), and Edgard Varèse composed his well-known electroacoustic music for the occasion. The resulting 8-minute show can be considered the very first multimedia project involving a total experience of vision and sound, a real, immersive environment, since the space of the pavilion hosted the audio and the visual materials as integral parts of the architectural design (see figure 19.1b). The pavilion, notwithstanding the incredible number of spectators (ca. 2 million), was dismantled a few months after its inauguration, at the end of the exposition in 1959. The *Poème Électronique* remained in fragments, such as the stereo versions of Varèse's and Xenakis's music pieces, the original film of Le Corbusier's image sequence, archival photos, and project sketches.

The VEP (Virtual Electronic Poem) project[1] has reconstructed the *Poème Électronique* experience in a virtual environment (Lombardo et al., 2005, 2006; Dobson et

(a)

Figure 19.1
The original artwork: external of the Philips pavilion (a), a moment of the show (b), and loudspeakers along the internal surfaces (c).

al., 2005). The project has retrieved the original image sequence, the composition, and the control score for the visual effects, so as to render the visual component of the experience, as well as the original music tapes, Xenakis's drawing for sound spatialization, and the electronic equipment schema for sound motion, to render the aural component of the experience (see Lombardo et al., 2006).

All this material was arranged into a virtual reality reconstruction of the pavilion. The aural component is widely acknowledged as the most relevant: the 3 tracks of the "organized sound" composed by Varèse were delivered to 350 loudspeakers spread inside the pavilion's continuously curved surfaces (figure 19.1c). The speakers were grouped in clusters and sound routes; the control device that handled the activation/deactivation of the loudspeakers to simulate the sound motion on the pavilion surfaces operated through control signals that were recorded on magnetic tape and read in real time during the show. The reconstruction work of the aural

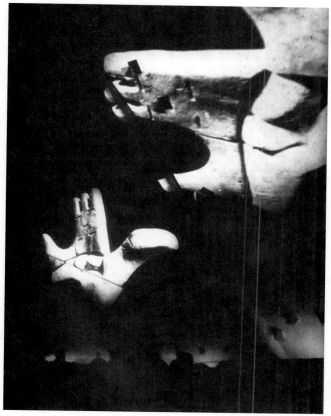

(b)

Figure 19.1
(continued)

component in the VEP project involved the definition of loudspeaker placement and grouping (figure 19.2c), the acoustic simulation of the architectural properties (building materials, the pavilion's geometry; see figure 19.2a), loudspeaker frequency response and radiance, the reconstruction of the control score (which existed only in fragments), and the simulation of the control mechanism for its performance.

The final result was a real-time installation with virtual reality techniques, allowing an immersive reconstruction of the disappeared masterpiece (figure 19.2b) with the use of a stereoscopic helmet for the visual elements and the simulation of the spatialized audio with binaural techniques. The application that implements the real-time binaural simulation was developed in SuperCollider.

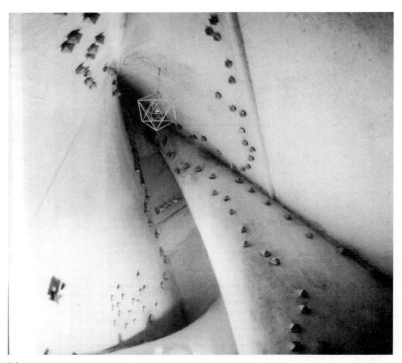

(c)

Figure 19.1
(continued)

19.2   The VEP Rendering System

Figure 19.3 shows the major components of the VEP application together with the information flow. The user receives the aural component over stereo headphones and the visual component over a stereoscopic head-mounted display (HMD), which includes a head-tracking device. The user sits on a rotating chair, and the tracking data (position and rotation of the head in the space) are sent to the VEP application.

This software consists of 3 modules: the core engine, the audio rendering engine, and the video rendering engine. The core engine controls the system by executing a strict real-time loop. It collects the tracking data, parses the Control Score (which contains the schedule of the visual and aural items), and pilots the audio and video rendering engines. The core engine was developed in Java and also includes a Java3D rendering engine that shows a simplified, lightweight version of the pavilion (via the Local video rendering engine), used mainly for navigation, control, and debugging purposes. The visual rendering engine was developed in C++, using the Ogre frame-

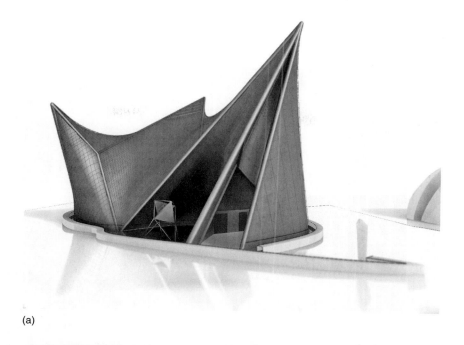

(a)

(b)

Figure 19.2
Reconstruction: 3D model (a), screenshot from the show (b), loudspeaker placement in the 3D model using photomatching (c).

(c)

Figure 19.2
(continued)

work.[2] It implements a 3-pass rendering: the first pass includes the base colors of the pavilion surfaces and the shadow maps; the second pass involves all the colored projective lights that formed the ambiences in which the black-and-white film was immersed; finally, the film is added on the third pass. The visual rendering features a high frame rate (over 30 fps) with prelighting and preloaded textures to ensure an appropriate speed in changing ambiences. The audio rendering engine was developed in SuperCollider after carefully modeling several contributions, as sketched in the previous section. It is addressed in detail in the next section.

The 3 modules run on 3 different machines (because of real-time computing constraints) connected through a dedicated Ethernet network. The core engine and the audio rendering engine communicate through the well-known OSC protocol; the communication between the core engine and the video rendering engine is based on an ad hoc protocol.

19.3   The Binaural Reconstruction

Physically, the binaural reconstruction process can be described as a superposition of 2 transfer functions—the head-related transfer function and the room-impulse

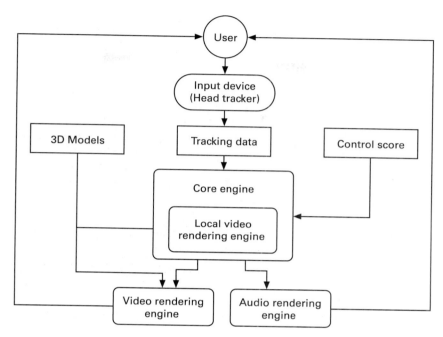

Figure 19.3
Overall architecture of the VEP application.

response — essentially describing a linear filter for each combination of sound source position and user head orientation, called binaural room impulse response (BRIR). In digital signal processing, the process of applying filter characteristics to an input signal is realized by means of convolution.

The binaural simulation of the original acoustic space of the *Poème Électronique* was complicated not only by the number of loudspeakers contributing to the acoustic image but also by the fact that many speakers were configured to sound simultaneously, in order to create peculiar spatial and temporal effects. The room modeling — reduced from the CAD model used for the visual reconstruction — and the impulse response rendering based on the loudspeaker positions were realized in the commercial software EASE[3] (figure 19.4). The 350 individual loudspeaker binaural impulse responses could, after a thorough investigation of the reconstructed control score, be combined into distinct groups of simultaneously sounding loudspeakers, thereby reducing the number of required binaural impulse response sets to 204. Each set consisted of 9720 separate binaural impulse responses for 360 horizontal degrees and 27 vertical degrees (−40° to 90° in 5° steps) of listener head-movement resolution, amounting to roughly 75 Gigabytes of data in total. Mainly due to the necessity of reducing the overall computation time for the BRIR sets, only

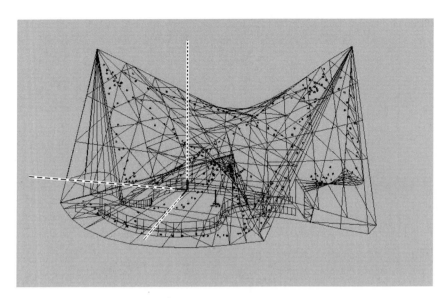

Figure 19.4
CAD model of the pavilion with reconstructed loudspeaker positions.

the first 130 milliseconds of early reflections were computed; the reverb tail comprised a single binaural impulse response of about 1.6 seconds' duration.

In the implementation of the audio rendering engine, SuperCollider provided the language for the application logic and the configuration facilities, while the actual rendering was implemented as a custom convolution plug-in for *scsynth* (Kersten, 2006). The object-oriented nature of the SuperCollider language and its extensive library support for both general-purpose programming and process scheduling in time substantially eased the development process from early prototyping to final deployment. The extensibility of the synthesis server in particular allowed the leveraging of huge amounts of architectural infrastructure that otherwise would have had to be re-created by other means. Figure 19.5 gives an overview of the audio engine's structure; in the following we provide a rundown of the overall algorithmic structure and describe some of the subsystems in more detail.

In the original realization of the *Poème Électronique*, audio was played back from 3 mono tracks; spatialization, room diffusion, and other effects were controlled by a separate control tape synchronized with the audio tracks.

For each track, the following pseudo code is executed in a loop:

```
// get horizontal/vertical head orientation
#alpha, beta = getTrackerInput;
```

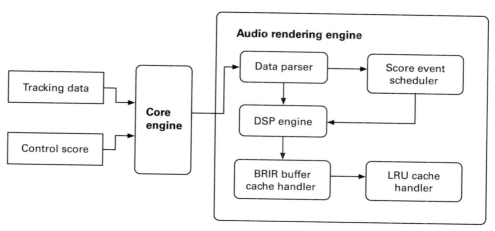

Figure 19.5
Control flow and aggregation structure of the VEP binaural renderer.

```
// get currently sounding speaker for this track
currentSpeaker = getScoreInput;
// discretize and encode position for cache lookup
posKey = encodePosition(alpha, beta)
// get buffer object from cache according to
//    - current position (encoded)
//    - current score speaker
buffer = caches[currentSpeaker].getBuffer(posKey)
if (buffer.isNil) {
    // cache miss: reuse previous buffer
    postln("cache miss");
} {
    // switch buffer in convolution process
    // (perform crossfade for smooth transition)
    convolution.switchBuffer(buffer);
}
```

The angles alpha and beta are translated into a single position code which, together with the currently active speaker as indicated in the score, contributes to the selection of the next BRIR buffer from the buffer cache. The routing of the audio signals through the convolution process is illustrated in figure 19.6 (which depicts in detail the DSP engine module of figure 19.5). The outputs of the 3 tracks are summed with the output of the reverb tail convolution and the low-frequency effects (LFE) signal, which is a lowpass filtered version of a mono sum of the tape tracks.

Low-latency convolution has been implemented within a dedicated unit generator plug-in; the algorithm uses nonuniform partition sizes and allows for very low

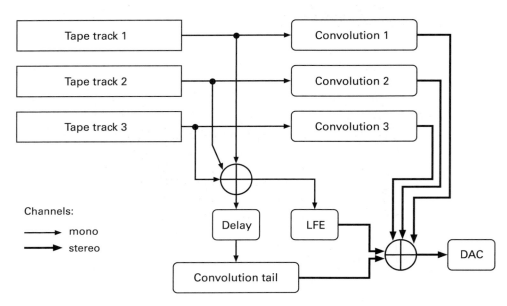

Figure 19.6
Audio signal flow of the VEP binaural renderer.

latencies while keeping computational demands within reasonable bounds (Gardner, 1995). When exchanging impulse responses, the plug-in performs a short crossfade in the time domain in order to minimize rendering artifacts during head movement. Impulse responses are stored in buffers on the synthesis server after being transformed to the frequency domain and partitioned for efficient convolution. The loading of time-domain impulse responses from disk and their transformation to the frequency domain are done asynchronously in a dedicated command plug-in, delegating the work to *scsynth*'s non-real-time thread (see chapter 26).[4]

An important consideration in the design of the VEP application was the amount of impulse response data — it was impossible to keep everything in memory on current off-the-shelf machines. Therefore, we designed a caching system for impulse responses in the 2-dimensional space of head movements (the tilt dimension was not taken into account). Impulse responses are loaded from disk asynchronously and stored in a least-recently-used (LRU) cache data structure in order to keep impulse responses in the proximity of current head orientation in memory. To minimize impulse response transition latency upon head movement, we implemented a look-ahead cache-filling strategy that predicts the motion vector of head movements and loads impulse responses along the trajectory ahead of time (figure 19.7):

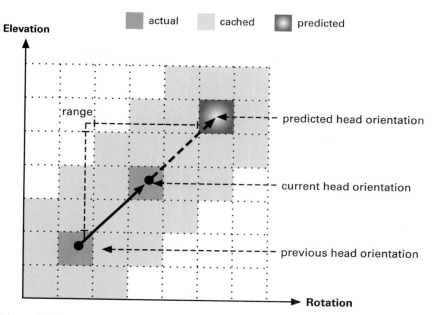

Figure 19.7
Asynchronous caching of listener head orientations. Each square represents head orientation as a region of angles/positions.

```
// for each position in the current position's "proximity"
proximity(currentPosition).do {| nextPosition |
    // get horizontal/vertical head orientation
    #alpha, beta = nextPosition;
    // encode position for cache storage/lookups
    posKey = encodePosition(alpha, beta);
    // if position not cached yet
    if (!cache.containsPosition(posKey)) {
        // alloc buffer and lock position
        // to prevent multiple updates
        buffer = cache.alloc(posKey);
        fork {
            // read BRIR from disk,
            // transform to frequency domain
            syncReadBuffer(server, buffer);
            // commit buffer and unlock position
            cache.commit(posKey, buffer);
        }
    }
}
```

Score events (i.e., commands for switching to another loudspeaker impulse response set for a given tape track) can be sent to the audio rendering application either in real time via *OpenSoundControl* (see chapter 4) or be read from a text file. In the case of real-time input, no caching apart from positional caching is performed, since the next speakers are unknown. Thus, when a command for switching to a new speaker is received, the buffer cache is invalidated. When rendering a known score, on the other hand, the series of speakers to switch to is known in advance at any point in time. In this mode, the VEP application maintains separate head position caches for a number of speakers farther ahead in the control score in order to perform a speaker switch as seamlessly as possible; those additional caches are updated asynchronously as described in pseudo code above.

19.4   Conclusions

This chapter has presented a SuperCollider application for the binaural rendering of the spatialization of the Varèses's *Poème Électronique*. The application has exploited both the language and the synthesizer modules of SuperCollider by implementing appropriate plug-ins. It features a careful design of caching and prediction structures for overcoming latency problems that can occur in strict real-time rendering.

References

Dobson, R., J. ffitch, K. Tazelaar, A. Valle, and V. Lombardo. 2005. "Varèse's Poème Électronique Regained: Evidence from the VEP Project." In *Proceedings of the 2005 International Computer Music Conference* (ICMC2005), Barcelona, pp. 29–36.

Gardner, W. G. 1995. "Efficient Convolution Without Input-Output Delay." *Journal of the Audio Engineering Society,* 43(3): 127–136.

Kersten, S. 2006. "A Fast Convolution Engine for the Virtual Electronic Poem Project." Master's thesis, Technical University of Berlin.

Lombardo, V., A. Arghinenti, F. Nunnari, A. Valle, H. Vogel, J. Fitch, R. Dobson, J. Padget, K. Tazelaar, S. Weinzierl, S. Benser, S. Kersten, R. Starosolski, W. Borczyk, W. Pytlik, and S. Niedbala. 2005. "The Virtual Electronic Poem (VEP) Project." In *Proceedings of the 2005 International Computer Music Conference* (ICMC2005), pp. 451–454.

Lombardo, V., A. Valle, F. Nunnari, F. Giordana, and A. Arghinenti. 2006. "Archeology of Multimedia." In *Proceedings of the 2006 ACM Multimedia Conference* (ACM2006), pp. 269–278. New York: ACM Press.

Petit, J. 1958. *Le Corbusier. Le Poème Électronique.* Paris: Edition Le Minuit.

Treib, M. 1996. *Space Calculated in Seconds: The Philips Pavilion, Le Corbusier, Edgard Varèse.* Princeton, NJ: Princeton University Press.

Xenakis, Y., C. G. J. Vreedenburgh, A. L. Bouma, F. K. Ligtenberg, H. C. Duyster, L. C. Kalff, W. Tak, and S. L. de Bruin. 1958. "The Philips Pavilion at the 1958 Brussels World Fair." *Philips Technical Review*, 20(1–3), pp. 1–49.

Notes

1. The VEP project was partially funded by the European Community under the Culture 2000 program and was featured the Virtual Reality & Multimedia Park (Torino, Italy), the University of Bath (UK), the Technical University of Berlin (Germany), and the Silesian Polytechnic School (Gliwice, Poland). See <http://edu.vrmmp.it/vep>. We thank all the people involved, in particular Sebastian Benser, who carried out the huge work of computing the pavilion impulse responses, and Stefan Weinzierl, who coordinated the Berlin unit.

2. Ogre 3D, open source graphics engine, <http://www.ogre3d.org>.

3. ADA, Acoustic Design Ahnert, Berlin: EASE Software 4.1, <http://www.ada-acousticdesign.de>.

4. The source code for the low-latency convolution plug-in VEPConvolution is available in the skUG Ugen library by Stefan Kersten, at <http://space.k-hornz.de/software/skug/>.

20   High-Level Structures for Live Performance: *dewdrop_lib* and *chucklib*

James Harkins

20.1   Introduction

SuperCollider excels at interactive programming. So much is possible by running short code fragments and accumulating their effects into a musical result that the organization of code might seem superfluous, one of those "best practices" frequently recommended but seldom followed. But music programming cannot stay simple forever. As Henry Lieberman observed, "Innovative applications in music constantly run up against the *complexity barrier*" (1991, p. 18), and complex problems benefit from organized responses. At the same time, creating music is an experimental process; structures that are too rigid get in the way of the free exploration of ideas. Strategies for structuring code should be able to absorb change easily.

I learned this the hard way. My earliest SuperCollider pieces used very simple processes, and I did not experience significant frustration or delays while composing. Expanding my work into processes that generate variations on input material—a pole vault in complexity—exposed several structural flaws that slowed composition. These problems cost hours of development time recompiling the class library and reloading the working environment from scratch for every debugging and refinement cycle, over hundreds of cycles. But, with new structures that better support interactive development practices, my work flow became much smoother.

This chapter describes 2 kinds of code organization. Utility classes can reduce intricate, often-performed activities to much simpler commands. My primary extension library, *dewdrop_lib*, offers several such enhancements.[1] I briefly introduce 3 devices here: MixerChannel for mixing and signal routing, Voicer for voice management and parameter control, and the MIDI Suite for MIDI input. A companion extension library, *chucklib*, attacks key structural problems related to composition and performance:

• Controlling object clutter: In performance, time is scarce, and it can become a burden to keep track of lower-level resources by hand. By encapsulating musical actions (Routines or Patterns) along with their resources in "process objects," performance is simpler because commands address the process container, trusting it to manage its own components.

• Real-time variations in behavior: A "process" can have a one-off, narrowly focused definition, or it can be general, parameterized, and reusable. The more complex the behavior, the greater the benefit of generalizing it so that it can adapt to future needs. Processes that expose parameters can be reconfigured while playing, making composition and performance more interactive and playful.

• Easy modifiability: Changing the definition of an object always incurs some cost. In artistic work, where changes are frequent, reducing the cost pays large dividends over time. *Prototype-based programming* supports the full range of object-oriented structures (including Design Patterns) while allowing object definitions to be created and selectively revised at runtime, without the expense of recompiling the class library.

• Object accessibility: A central, globally available, and easy-to-browse repository of process and component objects reduces confusion during a show ("Where did I put that thing?").

The bulk of the text outlines my own working method. Users may adopt some, all, or even none of the specific techniques described here. However, these general concerns can impact any programmer. New SuperCollider users may not yet need to explore these concepts in depth; it is more important to master the use of objects and SynthDefs and the scheduling of musical events. (The various objects in *dewdrop_lib* make many of these basic tasks simpler, however.) This chapter is mainly about what to do *after* learning the fundamentals, when the ambition to create more intelligent musical logic outstrips the capabilities of the simplest structures.

20.2   *dewdrop_lib* Toolbox: MixerChannel

Mixing is more than just scaling and summing signals. It also involves combining signals into meaningful groups (submixing), efficient deployment of effects, and arranging units so that downstream mixers are later in the server's execution chain than their sources are. MixerChannel handles all these tasks. Mono, mono-to-stereo, and stereo mixer definitions with standard level and panning controls come with the package, but the user can customize the controls, processing algorithm, and nearly every aspect of the GUI presentation for multichannel applications and non-standard configurations. Pre-fader and post-fader sends support shared effects and other common mixing arrangements.

Figure 20.1 creates a MixerChannel, displays it in a MixingBoard (depicted in figure 20.2), and plays a synth on it using m.play. Here, the SynthDef name is used,

```
// create the mixer: one channel in, two channels out
m = MixerChannel(\fig1, s, 1, 2);

// bring up a mixing board -- you can play with the level and panning controls
// closing the window, or freeing all of its channels, removes the MixingBoard
b = MixingBoard(\Fig1, nil, m);

// a SynthDef should include an outbus argument
// so that the MixerChannel can tell it where to write its output
(
SynthDef(\fig1, { |outbus, lowfreq = 220, hifreq = 1200, decay = 0.05|
    var trig = Impulse.kr(8);
        // Do not hard-code the outbus here!
        // Out.ar(0, ...) is not OK. Out.ar(outbus, ...) is good.
    Out.ar(outbus, SinOsc.ar(TExpRand.kr(lowfreq, hifreq, trig)) * Decay2.kr(trig,
0.01, decay));
}).add;
)

a = m.play(\fig1, [lowfreq: 100, hifreq: 2000, decay: 0.1]);

// automate panning - this is done with a control-rate synth
m.automate(\pan, { SinOsc.kr(LFNoise1.kr(0.5).exprange(0.4, 5.0)) });

// the GUI can show the automation
m.watch(\pan);

// add reverb using post-fader send
// auto-play the reverb synth in the completion function
(
r = MixerChannel(\rvb, s, 2, 2, level:1, completionFunc: { |chan|
    "creating reverb synth".postln;
    chan.playfx({ |outbus|
        var sig = In.ar(outbus, 2);  // read from channel's bus
        FreeVerb2.ar(sig[0], sig[1], 1, 0.6, 0.5)
    });
});

b.add(r);  // add to MixingBoard
)

// feed the signal into the reverb
```

Figure 20.1
MixerChannel creation, SynthDef conventions, Synth playing.

```
m.newPostSend(r, 0.6);

// prints out current state of all mixers in the board
// the board is accessible also through the MixingBoard.boards array
b.postSettings;

// fade to black
m.levelTo(0, 15);

// and release
// note that on m.free, the synth 'a' is removed also
// freeing the last MixerChannel in the MixingBoard closes the window
m.free;
r.free;
```

Figure 20.1
(continued)

but it could also be a Function to be treated in the manner of {...}.play or a crucial-library Instr. Control-rate synths can automate any MixerChannel control; the client can optionally "watch" the control to synchronize the GUI with the server-side changes.

A second MixerChannel houses a reverberation effect. Simply creating the reverb does not change the sound because nothing is passing through it yet. The reverb becomes audible after establishing the post-fader send with m.newPostSend(r, 0.6). According to the rules of server node ordering, m (the source) must precede r (the effect). MixerChannel automatically recognizes the relationship and sorts the MixerChannels into the right order.

20.3   Voicer

Voicer bridges the capabilities of a SynthDef and the behavior of a conventional synthesizer with the following features:

- Voice control: Capping the number of simultaneous notes
- Global controls: Sharing control values across all notes
- MIDI control: Playing a synth on a keyboard and changing parameters with continuous controllers
- Fingered portamento: Sliding between notes in a monophonic synth (with Mono-PortaVoicer).

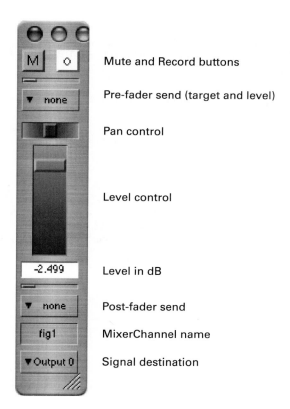

Mute and Record buttons

Pre-fader send (target and level)

Pan control

Level control

Level in dB

Post-fader send

MixerChannel name

Signal destination

Figure 20.2
MixingBoard screen layout.

The minimum Voicer setup, illustrated in figure 20.3, takes the number of nodes desired (which is also the maximum number of simultaneous synths the Voicer can play) and a SynthDef name (or Instr). Optionally, default values for SynthDef arguments may be supplied, as well as a bus and a target group. Specifying more than one SynthDef or argument list creates VoicerNode objects within the Voicer with different properties; potentially, each note could sound different.

The Voicer `trigger` and `release` methods start and stop a note; `gate` does both, releasing a specified amount of time after triggering (recommended for sequencing). All 3 methods take the note's frequency (or an array of frequencies, for a chord), which is passed to the synth's `freq` argument and used to identify every active Voicer-Node object. The caller does not need to know which node handles which frequency. It can ask to release a note by frequency, and the Voicer will look up the earliest corresponding VoicerNode.[2] In MIDI use, only the frequency (by way of MIDI note

```
// Voicer(voices, things, args, bus, target, addAction)
// target may be a Group, Server, or MixerChannel
v = Voicer(10, \default);

v.trigger(440, 1);  // v.trigger(freq, gate, args, latency)
v.release(440);

// v.gate(freq, dur, gate, args, lat) -- lat = latency
v.gate(440, 2.0, 1, [pan: -0.5]);

r = fork {
    loop {
            // play over a C major scale
        [60, 62, 64, 65, 67, 69, 71, 72].do({ |midi|
            v.gate(midi.midicps, 0.1, 1, [amp: rrand(0.05, 0.15)],
                lat: 0.1);
            0.125.wait;
        });
    }
};

r.stop;

v.free
```

Figure 20.3
Basic Voicer creation; triggering and gating notes.

number) is known at release time; thus, having Voicer perform the lookup greatly simplifies MIDI applications.

SynthDef arguments can be "mapped globally" in a Voicer (figure 20.4). Mapped arguments are associated with VoicerGlobalControl objects, which keep their values on control buses. Every time a VoicerNode creates a synth, it maps the global control names to their control buses. Parameter changes simply update the control bus, and all the synths follow suit, mimicking the behavior of a knob on a hardware synthesizer.

20.4   MIDI Suite

Out of the box, SuperCollider supports MIDI input as follows:

• MIDIIn: A hardware abstraction class with a single response function for each type of incoming MIDI message

```
// let's put a pan global control on the voicer

v = Voicer(10, \default);

// v.mapGlobal(name, bus, value, spec)
// \bipolar is a ControlSpec for the range -1..+1
v.mapGlobal(\pan, nil, 0, \bipolar);

v.gui;

// Pbind works with voicer, using 'voicerNote' event type
p = Pbind(
    \type, \voicerNote,
    \voicer, v,
    \degree, Pn(Pseries(0, 1, 8), inf),
    \amp, Pwhite(0.05, 0.15, inf),
    \dur, 0.125,
    \legato, 0.8
).play;

p.stop;

v.free;
```

Figure 20.4
Voicer global controls and GUI.

• MIDIResponder classes: Provide a separate class for each type of MIDI message, where each class may have any number of response functions. This is generally easier than using MIDIIn directly.

The *dewdrop_lib* MIDI Suite uses classes not for message types but for types of behavior; as a layer of abstraction, it focuses attention on what you want to do with the messages rather than on the messages themselves. "Socket" objects handle both note on and note off messages together. The AbstractMIDISocket class establishes basic connectivity and leaves specific behaviors, such as passing note messages to a Voicer or recording notes for later playback, to its subclasses. Continuous controller, pitchbend, and aftertouch fall under the category of "controller" messages; subclasses of AbstractMIDIControl implement those responses. The framework is extensible: a new response behavior requires only a subclass of 1 of these abstract classes. Also, BasicMIDISocket and BasicMIDIControl assign arbitrary response functions to MIDI inputs, such as the MIDIResponder classes, so there is no need to create a new class for every one-shot, custom action.

```
v = Voicer(10, \default);

// 0 = device 0, channel 0
// for a different device, use [device index, channel]
k = VoicerMIDISocket(0, v);

// modwheel to control pan
k.addControl(1, \pan, 0, \bipolar);
v.gui;

// a homegrown variety of just intonation
// release all notes before executing this!
k.midiToFreq = TuningRatios(12, tunings: [1, 135/128, 9/8, 6/5, 5/4,
4/3, 45/32, 3/2, 14/9, 27/16, 16/9, 15/8]);

// per-note argument generation using a Pbind
// here used to map velocity data onto the amp input
k.noteOnArgsPat = Pbind(\amp, Pkey(\velocity).linlin(0, 127, 0.01,
0.2));

// if you have a footswitch (controller number 64), this handles it
properly
l = VoicerSusPedal(0, 64, v);

// by default, freeing the voicer automatically frees the socket and
all attached MIDI controllers
v.free;
```

Figure 20.5
VoicerMIDISocket.

VoicerMIDISocket is the most powerful, and in figure 20.5 it illustrates how a MIDI socket can do more than a simple response function. It can add new global controls and automatically assign them to MIDI controllers (`k.addControl...`). The pattern supplied to noteOnArgsPat can generate synth arguments arbitrarily or, as shown here, transform note number or velocity values in the MIDI message into synth inputs. The VoicerMIDISocket also has a `midiToFreq` function to convert the MIDI note number into physical frequency, supporting custom temperaments. (*dewdrop_lib* includes some convenience classes for user-defined temperaments in the *ddwTemperament* quark. The example demonstrates TuningRatios for just intonation.)

Table 20.1
Structural Problems and *chucklib* Solutions

Problem	Solution in *chucklib*
Unable to access process objects quickly enough; rapid textural changes impossible	Global collections of processes and other objects, with convenient syntax for access; ability to address certain methods (e.g., `play`, `stop`, `reset`) to groups of processes
Changing process logic required destroying and rebuilding the entire work space, wasting time	Should be easy to rebuild a single process without affecting others. Processes should be as simple to use as possible, by creating and releasing resources automatically
Difficult to change behavior while playing, because some components were embedded in hard-to-reach places	Instead of hard coding components into process logic, embed *references* to components. Bundle references together with active logic in a unified process object
Difficult to reuse existing code for related, but different, behavior; too much copy-and-paste programming, not enough object-oriented inheritance and polymorphism	`Proto`, which supports runtime object definition and typical object-oriented modeling strategies; creation of generalized processes with details filled in by runtime parameters

20.5　*Chucklib*: Superstructures for Live Performance

The obstacles I faced while developing more complex musical behaviors stemmed from design decisions that seemed sensible at the time but turned out to cause unanticipated problems. For instance, at first it seemed easier to control a task (which I will hereafter call a *process*) with a dedicated GUI button. This made it harder to replace the process, however, because it was necessary to rebuild some or all of the user interface. Deleted processes also left behind unused server resources, which over time would clog the machine's performance. These factors called for frequent restarts of the interpreter, even for minor code changes.

Table 20.1 lists the factors that most influenced the design of *chucklib*. The third and fourth problems in particular have occupied computer scientists for decades. Code reuse is the Holy Grail of object-oriented programming; I raise the point in this context to emphasize the importance of a classlike structure that straightforwardly permits runtime changes. The issue of embedding components is another form of the general problem of designing an interface for a class: what to expose for manipulation and what to hide. Using *chucklib* does not exempt any user from these decisions; rather, it makes it easier to change the decisions on-the-fly.

Chucklib borrows its name from the ChucK language (Wang and Cook, 2003). In the code interface for performance, I wanted to unify many of the most basic operations into a simple notation that would decide which action to take based on the classes of both operands (i.e., multiple dispatch). ChucK introduces the *chuck operator* => as a general way to put something into something else. Chucking an object into a variable, a unit generator's output into an input of another unit generator, and even advancing the clock explicitly by chucking a time measurement into the special variable "now" (e.g., 10::ms => now) mean radically different things, but all are written using the same visually expressive notation: source => target. *Chucklib* likewise uses the => operator for assignment and instantiation of many object types, freeing the user from having to remember the difference between chucking a process definition and chucking a Voicer into a process object, for instance.

The next 3 sections introduce essential concepts before we make some noise in section 20.9.

20.6   Proto: Prototype-Based Programming

SuperCollider's class library is a solid foundation for object-oriented design, but in some ways it works against the demands of real-time, interactive composition. Henry Lieberman recognized the demands decades ago: "In fields like [artificial intelligence] and music . . . [the] nature of the problem often changes as work on the problem proceeds, and new control structures and data structures appear frequently. The AI or music programmer needs a programming environment in which new ideas can be tested quickly and easily" (Lieberman, 1991, p. 18). Since class definitions are frozen at the time of compiling, it takes extra effort to adapt them to new insights into a problem whose definition is not static, but "discovered" incrementally while addressing it.

Lieberman's work in the 1980s on actor-based languages, such as Act I, proposed *prototypes* as a more flexible alternative to fixed classes. As in object-oriented languages, prototype-based programming works with objects that have variables and methods. In class-based languages, a *constructor* method (new in SuperCollider) makes an instance of a class, but prototype-based languages do not have classes. All objects are prototypes; the same operation, copying, creates both "classes" and "instances." Adding new methods and variables to a copy of a prototype effectively produces a "subclass" of the original, and prototype objects handle state changes just as class instances do, by updating internal variables.

If an object is a set of variables and methods with unique names, it is generically a *namespace*. In SuperCollider, the Environment and Event classes are the best choices for arbitrary namespaces. Not only can they bind objects to symbolic names, but any given Environment can be assigned to the special `currentEnvironment` variable so that the items in its namespace can be accessed using the variable-like syntax `~variableName`. (See chapter 6 for a discussion of Events.) If an Environment's names do not conflict with the names of traditional methods defined in the class library, the Environment object can respond to messages (method calls) using objects held within it. Functions in the namespace may be called as if they were methods. Environments thus can act like other objects, as shown in chapter 8.

Standard class definitions obey *lexical variable scope*. Variables belonging to the object itself may be accessed "natively"; variables from other objects are accessible only through message-passing. By contrast, Environment variables are *dynamically scoped*, referring to whichever Environment is current at runtime. Proto, the cornerstone of *chucklib*, bridges the 2 kinds of scopes by pushing its Environment into the `currentEnvironment` variable on every method call. Environment variable references within a Proto use the variables belonging to that Proto object; external environments are not directly accessible.[3]

Figure 20.6 illustrates the creation and usage of a set of simple "Hello, World" prototypes. The function given to `Proto.new` sets default values and declares methods by assigning functions to Environment variables. "Subclasses" are created using the `clone` method, whose function may override values from the "superclass" and add new items. Copying a Proto (`copy`) creates a new instance; the copy may be manipulated independently of the original. Proto thus supports the key object-oriented concepts of inheritance and encapsulation.[4] Sending the message "sayhi" to a greeter — `~greeter.sayhi` — delegates to the greeter's `~sayhi` function, transparently mimicking normal object behavior.

One might ask, "Why use a mere 'prototype' when we have 'real objects'?" Indeed, classes have a small speed advantage, because looking up variables and methods in environments is slightly slower than using declared variables and methods in classes. Operations that require top performance may therefore be better as standard classes. (Proto can serve as another development option in the initial phase, to hash out the object's logic interactively. Once the behavior is stable, it is straightforward to make a class out of Proto with minor syntax adjustments.)

However, in terms of object design or program logic, Protos are no less functional than classes even though the word "prototype" has a connotation of something unfinished. "Unfinished" may actually be a desirable quality; a "finished" compositional algorithm can quickly become a dead algorithm, because it has nowhere to go. Since Protos are defined by running code in the interpreter, they can be changed in the interpreter; thus they absorb change more readily than classes fixed at startup, and they may be preferable when maximum flexibility is needed. (See table 20.2.)

```
// "Hello World" greeter classes

(
~greeter = Proto({
    ~sayhi = { |name|
        "%, %.\n".postf(~greeting.value, name ? ~name);
    };
    ~name = "Monique";        // default name
    ~greeting = "Hello";      // default greeting
});

// make a subclass with .clone
~frenchGreeter = ~greeter.clone({
    ~greeting = "Bonjour";
});

~timeAwareFrenchGreeter = ~frenchGreeter.clone({
    ~greeting = {
        var     hour = Date.getDate.hour;
        if(hour < 18) { ~dayGreeting } { ~eveningGreeting };
    };
    ~dayGreeting = "Bonjour";
    ~eveningGreeting = "Bon soir";
});
)

// Use the objects:
~greeter.sayhi;
~greeter.sayhi("Bob");
~frenchGreeter.sayhi("Isabelle");
~timeAwareFrenchGreeter.sayhi("Eric");
```

Figure 20.6
Classes and instances in prototype-based programming, with the Proto object.

Table 20.2
Comparison of Standard Classes against Prototypes

Standard Classes	Prototypes
Stable definition; runtime activities cannot break precompiled code	Flexible definition; good for behaviors that need to be changed frequently, even while executing
Less lookup overhead; better for heavy calculations	Slight performance cost; acceptable for sequencing where cost is amortized over streamed events
Minor changes require total reload of work space; time-consuming for experimental code	Objects can be selectively redefined without destroying other objects, minimizing downtime during the composition process

20.7 Keeping Track of Prototypes and Instances: PR and BP

Although prototype-based programming does not explicitly distinguish between "classes" and "instances," the distinction remains valuable. If a given prototype is the source of many other objects, its definition should remain consistent no matter what its copies do. Working copies of source prototypes contain instance-specific information that should be invisible to other instances. Accidentally putting these objects into a source prototype opens them up to all instances—a troublesome form of object pollution that is avoided by keeping a separate set of source prototypes.

Chucklib stores Proto objects in two repositories: PR (Process prototype) and BP (Bound Process, so named because specific data *bind* into a general prototype to create a unique behavior). The name "process" reflects their original usage for algorithmic sequencing (i.e., a musical process that unfolds over time). The PR repository may also hold nonplaying prototypes, such as data storage objects, for use by other prototypes. PR is like a class, and a BP is an instance of a PR.

In figure 20.7, the chuck operator => saves the greeter Proto into a PR slot. Once defined in this way, the PR can be chucked into a BP to create a working copy. The BP responds to method calls as its Proto would, and its state is independent of the original PR. Standard assignment syntax changes the values of variables, as in `BP(\greeter).name = "Zsa Zsa."` A longer form of chucking, using the chuck method, can override default values in the PR by inserting parameters into the copy before finishing initialization: `PR(\greeter).chuck(BP(\greetBob), parms: (name: "Bob"))` replaces the default ~name with "Bob."

```
(
    // define PR prototype - Proto(...) => PR(\name)
Proto({
    ~sayhi = { |name|
            // ~greeting.value is an internal pseudomethod call
        "%, %.\n".postf(~greeting.value, name ? ~name);
    };
    ~name = "Monique";          // default name
    ~greeting = "Hello";        // default greeting
}) => PR(\greeter);
)


// make working instance as BP
PR(\greeter) => BP(\greeter);
BP(\greeter).sayhi("Jacqueline");
BP(\greeter).name = "Zsa Zsa";
BP(\greeter).sayhi;
    // changing name in BP does not affect PR
PR(\greeter).name;

// override default at chuck time
// now this greeter belongs just to Bob
PR(\greeter).chuck(BP(\greetBob), parms: (name: "Bob"));
BP(\greetBob).name; // ~name variable is overridden
BP(\greetBob).sayhi;

// remove both instances from the repository
BP([\greeter, \greetBob]).free;
```

Figure 20.7
Greeter as a PR prototype, and usage through BP instances.

20.8   Library Storage and Retrieval

Functionally, figures 20.6 and 20.7 are nearly identical. In figure 20.6, however, the Protos are stored in the undifferentiated namespace of currentEnvironment. There is no way to tell which are source prototypes and which are working instances. Also, currentEnvironment cannot guarantee that all of its members are Protos; searching for processes and performing bulk operations on them is more difficult. Worse, pushing a different Environment into currentEnvironment prevents access to the Protos altogether.

The *chucklib* storage classes, of which PR and BP are 2, hold libraries of objects that are accessible at all times, using a consistent syntax (see table 20.3). They also

Table 20.3
Primary *chucklib* Storage Classes

Class Name	Full Name	Purpose
PR	Process prototype	Holds a Proto that defines behavior without executing it; its copies will perform the behaviors
BP	Bound Process	Binds a PR prototype to data to produce a musical result. PR is to BP as class is to instance
VC	Voicer	Holds a Voicer and its related resources
Fact	Factory	Holds instructions to create a complex Voicer or process with 1 simple command
Func	Function	A repository of reusable functions
ProtoEvent	Prototype Event	Event prototype for a BP event pattern

separate objects that have different purposes, so that each kind of object can have different convenience methods. BP is meant to play a process over time, so its interface includes scheduling and control methods. VC (which holds a Voicer) does not need such features, so it exposes a smaller interface supporting its Voicer's placement in the performance interface. Centralized storage also makes it easy to build a browser GUI, shown in figure 20.8. Storage classes appear in the left-hand pop-up menu, and existing objects can be chosen from the list. Buttons drag the selected object into other parts of the interface, and abbreviated text commands entered into the text field at the bottom simplify navigation.

20.9   Interactive Composition with *chucklib* Using Stream References

In practice, algorithmic composition is a matter of evolving musically rich behaviors from simple initial experiments. A Routine or Task is often the easiest starting point, but it can be difficult to adjust while running. If it is an unbroken block of code, the only way to change it is to throw it away and re-create it with an altered definition. Event patterns (Pbind and its companions) are inherently more modular—each sub-pattern is a self-contained module—but the way child patterns are embedded in their parents makes it impossible to replace them while playing. But if we embed *references* to components of the musical logic instead of the components themselves, it becomes possible to change the reference targets at any time. The behavior of the process updates immediately even as it continues to run. We can thereby try alternatives and refine behavior more rapidly. (Such reference strategies are not unique to *chucklib*. A Routine can call functions in variables outside the Routine itself, and the functions in those variables may be changed at any time. PatternProxies in JITLib

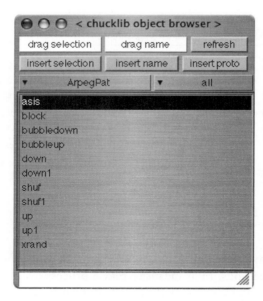

Figure 20.8
Chucklib browser GUI.

are pattern references that may be updated at will and used wherever a Pattern is valid.)

A *chucklib* process adds the ability to place a behavioral definition (whether Routine or Pattern), together with its replaceable references, into a single Proto object. Further, Patterns or Routines are usually not sufficient by themselves to realize a musical action. Often they depend on auxiliary resources: server-side buffers, buses, effects, and client-side data. It makes sense to store these resources along with the behavioral definition and, as an added convenience, automatically initialize the resources when instantiating the process. This is perhaps the most important way *chucklib* helps structure your code: by encouraging you to think of all the components of a behavior as a unified, self-managing package.

Consider a process to play randomized slices of a sound file loaded into a server buffer (figure 20.9). The buffer is an obvious candidate for automatic initialization; another, perhaps less obvious candidate, is a MixerChannel, since you might want to change the volume level interactively. A Pattern calculates the parameters for each slice and uses *chucklib*-style stream references to allow on-the-fly experimentation with the parameter streams.

A new process prototype begins as a clone (subclass) of an existing prototype; usually the source is PR(\abstractProcess) for its useful basic methods. Defining

```
(
SynthDef(\bufGrainPan, { |start, time, bufnum, pan, rate = 1, amp = 1,
        attack = 0.001, decay = 0.02, outbus|
    var sig;
    sig = PlayBuf.ar(1, bufnum, rate * BufRateScale.kr(bufnum), 1, start, 0)
        * EnvGen.kr(Env.linen(attack, time, decay), doneAction:2);
    Out.ar(outbus, Pan2.ar(sig, pan, amp));
}).add;

PR(\abstractProcess).clone({
        // BEHAVIORAL components
        // eventKey refers to ProtoEvent(\singleSynthPlayer)
    ~event = (eventKey: \singleSynthPlayer);
        // here, manufacture the pattern to play
    ~asPattern = {
        Pbind(
            \chan, ~chan,
            \instrument, \bufGrainPan,
            \bufnum, ~buf.bufnum,
            \delta, BPStream(\delta),        // reference to ~delta stream
            \time, BPStream(\tfactor) * Pkey(\delta),
            \start, BPStream(\startSec) * ~buf.sampleRate,
            \pan, BPStream(\pan),
            \amp, BPStream(\amp)
        )
    };
        // default Pbind streams
    ~delta = Pwhite(1, 5, inf) * 0.1;
    ~tfactor = 1;
    ~maxStart = Pfunc({ ~buf.duration }) - Pkey(\time);
    ~startSec = Pwhite(0.0, BPStream(\maxStart), inf);
    ~pan = Pwhite(-1.0, 1.0, inf);
    ~amp = 1;

        // ARCHITECTURAL components
    ~path = "sounds/a11wlk01.wav";  // default soundfile
    ~startFrame = 0;
    ~numFrames = -1;
        // constructor: auto-load soundfile and create mixer
    ~prep = {
        ~chan = MixerChannel(~collIndex, s, 2, 2);
        "loading %\n".postf(~path);
```

Figure 20.9
Interactive session to build a soundfile slicer.

```
            ~buf = Buffer.read(s, ~path, ~startFrame, ~numFrames,
                action: { "done loading buffer".postln });
    };
            // destructor, called on .free
    ~freeCleanup = {
        [~chan, ~buf].free;
    };
}) => PR(\bufSlicer);
)

// That was the definition. In performance you only need this to play it.

PR(\bufSlicer) => BP(\columbia);
BP(\columbia).play;

// change process's stream references while it is playing

BP(\columbia).tfactor = 0.25;

BP(\columbia).tfactor = sin(Pseries(0, 0.1, inf)) * 0.45 + 0.55;

BP(\columbia).delta = Pstutter(Pwhite(4, 12, inf), Pxrand((1..6) * 0.05, inf));

BP(\columbia).startSec = Pclutch(Pwhite(0.0, BPStream(\maxStart), inf),
Pdiff(Pkey(\delta)).abs > 0);


// also valid to chuck patterns into a BP
// ".pan" is an adverb indicating which variable to replace
sin(Ptime(inf)) =>.pan BP(\columbia);

BP(\columbia).stop;
BP(\columbia).free; // MixerChannel and Buffer go away also
```

Figure 20.9
(continued)

the new process takes the general form `PR(\abstractProcess).clone({ ... new definitions...}) => PR(\processName)`. Here, the `clone` function first adds the behavioral components: `~event` to set the pattern's event prototype[5] and the Pbind specification in `~asPattern`. The Pbind uses `BPStream` as a reference placeholder for the child patterns, which are populated immediately afterward with assignments to Environment variables. The definition concludes with architectural components: default values for loading the buffer, and the `~prep` and `~freeCleanup` methods that will be invoked to load the buffer automatically and release it later.

With the definition complete, only 2 commands (`=>` and `.play`) begin playing the process. From here, making the slices staccato is as simple as setting `tfactor` to a value less than 1.0, or the events can undulate between staccato and legato, using a sine function applied to a `Pseries` pattern. The randomized rhythm (`delta`) lacks shape; repeating some successive values with `Pstutter` adds occasional focal points for the ear. We can emphasize those focal points further by holding the same starting point in the buffer for repeated delta values via an interesting use of `Pclutch`. The result of each change is audible immediately, so the ear can rapidly drive the refinements to a better musical result.

Not every reader will be comfortable using patterns for general compositional needs, and not every algorithm can be expressed as a pattern. For those cases, `~asPattern` can define a `Prout`, which is a pattern class that treats a function just as Routine does. The resulting Routine has full access to the BP's Environment variables and methods, so that some portions of the logic may be split into separate Proto methods. These methods can be replaced at runtime, permitting kinds of rapid adjustment similar to those illustrated for patterns in figure 20.9.

Some behavioral changes require more extensive changes than child pattern replacement does. In such cases, the recommended procedure is to change the PR definition code as needed, recompile only the changed PR, free the BP, and rebuild it from the new definition. No other BP is touched; other processes may even continue playing while updating the definition.

20.10   Stability and Simplicity in Performance

The above code structures add some weight; the PR definition in figure 20.9 is longer than a stand-alone pattern, though it makes up for its length with increased power and flexibility. In performance, however, a lighter interface is essential. *Chucklib* simplifies performance use by separating complex definitions from their use in performance, and by automating intricate initialization sequences with Factories.

While performing, the details of process definitions are secondary; definition code need not appear alongside its performance usage. I use a multiple file structure: 1 or more files create PR and other object definitions, and a separate "performance script" file holds simple commands to instantiate BPs and Voicers, manipulate process behavior, and so on. Definition files load instantly, since they primarily store instructions in memory for future use, and the performance script is written at such a high level that it serves as a mnemonic for large-scale form, effectively an abbreviated Score. It is up to the user to decide how much detail to include in a performance script. My performance scripts tend to be exhaustive since I perform with acoustic instruments and live MIDI input in conjunction with automated processes, and have little time to type new commands during a show. But it is entirely feasible to improvise performance commands live, moving *chucklib* usage in the direction of live coding. The Web site includes a sample definition file and a performance script for a small, moody ambient sound track.

As process prototypes grow more complex and incorporate more and more parameters, the number of instructions to prepare a specific behavior increases to the point of cluttering the performance script. *Chucklib* borrows the Factory concept from Design Patterns to simplify the creation of objects that require more elaborate initialization.[6] A *chucklib* Factory is an Event object saved into the Fact storage class (figure 20.10). It must include at least a make function to construct and return the desired object and a type symbol to indicate what kind of object will be the result. In figure 20.10, the Factory reduces 9 lines of process initialization to a single short line to use in performance. Factories can thereby represent variants on existing PRs that are lighter in weight than spawning a new PR for every version. PRs define logic; Factories specify how to modify them for distinct uses; and BPs perform the behaviors. (Voicers also may comprise numerous objects, such as MixerChannels, buffers, effects, external controls, and other resources. A Voicer factory keeps the Voicer together with those objects and is just as easy to instantiate as a process factory.) In my usage, the definition file contains factory declarations and the performance script uses them.

20.11 Scalability

The ability to scale to longer durations and more complex algorithms was of prime importance in the design of *chucklib*.

Resource management is a key problem in long performances. In a 10–15-minute piece, it may not matter to keep careful track of buffers allocated on the server, audio or control buses, or long-running synths such as effects; the piece will be over long before supplies of memory or buses run out. A 2-hour performance increases the risk of shortages or of clogging the CPU with synths from long ago that are no longer doing anything useful. With the ~freeCleanup user hook, *chucklib* encourages the habit of writing every process to clean up after itself when released. Instead of track-

```
// In the definition file:
(
(make: { |name|
    PR(\bufSlicer) => BP(name);
}, type: \bp) => Fact(\basic);

(make: { |name|
    PR(\bufSlicer).chuck(BP(name), parms: (
        path: "sounds/a11wlk01-44_1.aiff",
        tfactor: sin(Pseries(0, 0.1, inf)) * 0.45 + 0.55,
        delta: Pstutter(Pwhite(4, 12, inf), Pxrand((1..6) * 0.05, inf)),
        startSec: Pclutch(Pwhite(0.0, Pfunc({ ~buf.duration }) - Pkey(\time)),
Pdiff(Pkey(\delta)).abs > 0),
        pan: sin(Ptime(inf)),
        quant: 1      // quantize to next beat
    ))
}, type: \bp) => Fact(\fancy);
)

// In the performance script:
Fact(\basic) => BP(\basic);

BP(\basic).play;

Fact(\fancy) => BP(\fancy);

BP(\fancy).play;

BP([\basic, \fancy]).stop;

BP([\basic, \fancy]).free;
```

Figure 20.10
Factories for two variants of the buffer slicer process.

ing possibly hundreds of disconnected resources, it is much easier to manage a few dozen processes that are responsible for handling their own resources. (Sometimes several processes need to share common resources, or it may be too expensive to load certain resources repeatedly when rebuilding individual processes during composition. In this case, a dedicated PR can load and store shared resources into a BP, and other processes can access its objects.)

Long performances likely divide into sections, such as tracks in a DJ-style set or movements of a multimovement composition. Sections can help reduce the impact of object loading by spreading initialization over time. Initialization takes place in 2 stages: loading definitions into memory and instantiating performance objects. Definition loading is fast enough that it is unlikely to interrupt active sequencing, so I do this in bulk, once at the beginning of each section. Creating BPs and Voicers adds new objects on the server and benefits from an incremental approach, making only a few at a time periodically during a section.

For cleanup at section's end, I exploit the subType property of *chucklib* storage objects. The subType is a Symbol that groups objects into one category. If all the objects that belong to a section have the same subType, a single command can free all of them when the section is over—a convenient way to make room, in both memory and CPU, for the next section's objects. The performance script on the Web site demonstrates this technique.

Ultimately, *chucklib*'s goal is to extend the "complexity barrier" of what is feasible to run in live performance. The most dramatic example is the generative melody prototype installed with *chucklib*, PR(\aiMel), whose logic runs close to 900 lines but can be configured for simple behaviors in as few as a half-dozen lines. More complicated actions require more parameters to be set, which may be done in a factory; in improvisational settings, the process may launch with simpler behavior and introduce more complexity with later parameter changes while the process is running.

This process also uses object-oriented modeling techniques. When an instance of this process receives melodic data, it splits the notes into phrases and subsegments, and stores the segments in Proto objects which hold the notes and calculate some analytical metrics to describe their shape. While the melody is playing, control passes through the phrase and segment Protos in turn to generate new variations and embed the notes into the outgoing sequence.

Objects that try to encompass too much functionality, to the point of collapsing under their own weight, are pejoratively called "God objects" and represent a common *anti-pattern*, or poor design choice (Laplante, 2005). Since Protos are self-contained objects, there is no reason not to divide a large problem into smaller objects and push the complexity barrier farther into the distance. Dividing a complex behavior into component objects raises the possibility of using behavioral design patterns, particularly Observers and Mediators,[7] to model true interaction between distinct musical actors and produce more sophisticated results.

20.12   Conclusion

This chapter demonstrates working methods that have been wholly successful for me since *chucklib* became performance-ready, and many users can benefit from the same techniques. More important, a larger proportion of users will, in 1 form or another, confront the categories of problems for which *chucklib* was designed. At root, the problems involve putting things in logical places and exposing parameters for real-time manipulation. Even if a particular user has not yet run into such problems, becoming familiar with them in advance can only help with devising effective solutions when the time comes. My hope is that this work inspires users to recognize when they have outgrown techniques that have become liabilities, and to press forward to discover more robust and flexible coding styles.

References

Gamma, E., R. Helm, R. Johnson, and J. Vlissides. 1995. *Design Patterns: Elements of Reusable Object-Oriented Software*. Reading, MA: Addison-Wesley Professional.

Laplante, P. A., and C. Neill. 2005. *Antipatterns: Identification, Refactoring and Management*. Boca Raton, FL: Auerbach Publications.

Lieberman, H. 1991. "Machine Tongues IX: Object-Oriented Programming." In S. T. Pope, ed., *The Well-Tempered Object: Musical Applications of Object-Oriented Software Technology*, pp. 18–31. Cambridge, MA: MIT Press.

Lieberman, H. 1986. "Using Prototypical Objects to Implement Shared Behavior in Object-Oriented Systems." In *Proceedings of the 1986 Conference on Object-Oriented Programming Systems, Languages, and Applications*, pp. 214–223. New York: ACM Press.

Wang, G., and P. Cook. 2003. "ChucK: A Concurrent, On-the-Fly, Audio Programming Language." In *Proceedings of the 2003 International Computer Music Conference*, Singapore, pp. 217–225.

Notes

1. The Web site accompanying this volume includes a copy of both *dewdrop_lib* and *chucklib* for SuperCollider. Updates are available in the Quarks extensions.

2. Release frequencies are matched by equality. Converting an abstract pitch representation (such as MIDI note number) into a physical frequency has proven to be reliable, provided the formula is deterministic—`notenum.midicps` may have some floating-point error, but it is the same floating-point error every time. If indeterminacy is needed per note, the `gate` method is preferred.

3. Proto represents a philosophy of object prototyping different from that described in chapter 6. Both are valid approaches intended for different tasks. If the prototype object is to interact freely with objects in the current environment, it is better to use Environment/Event's dynamic variable scope, as in the Shout discussion in chapter 8. Proto mimics the closed variable scope of conventional classes, and is recommended when objects should be more independent and interact in more carefully controlled ways.

4. Lieberman (1986) argues for delegation, rather than inheritance, as a better strategy in prototype-based systems to carry methods from one prototype into another. Delegation first tries to look up methods in the local object; if that lookup fails, it searches successively through ancestors until the responding method is found. In fact, *chucklib* implements delegation using Environment's parent variable. The standard at method automatically looks upward through parents recursively.

5. Ronald Kuivila's discussion of event patterns (chapter 6) explains the importance of the event prototype. In *chucklib*, event prototypes are saved in the ProtoEvent storage class; eventKey tells the process which ProtoEvent to use. Event prototypes are not the same as the object prototypes discussed so far in this chapter.

6. *Chucklib* Factories are more like the Builder design pattern (Gamma et al., 1995, p. 97).

7. Observers and Mediators facilitate communication between objects (Gamma et al., 1995, pp. 293, 273). As noted in chapter 5, an Observer listens to changes in another object. The dependency protocol implements this design pattern in SuperCollider: addDependant, removeDependant, changed to send a notification and update to receive it. A Mediator stands between many objects that need to communicate. Individual objects send messages to the mediator, which broadcasts to other registered objects. Both mechanisms are useful for processes to share intelligence and interact in musically meaningful ways.

21 Interface Investigations

Thor Magnusson

21.1 Introduction

An *interface* is a field of abstractions in which 2 systems interact with one another. We typically use this word for the locus where a human and a machine communicate. The interface can be as simple as an on/off button, or it can be multimodal: a mixture of different types of hardware used to input commands into a system that responds through the use of screens, speakers, motors, and haptic feedback. The computer is a metamachine with no *natural* interface, unlike physical machinery, where gears, buttons, and wheels are natural extensions of the mechanism itself. This fact is problematized when the computer is used for music, as we have innumerable arbitrary ways of representing an interface to the audio system of the computer. It could be anything from a simple "play" button to a custom-written class that encapsulates the digital signal processing of an audio unit generator. The question here is that of purpose: What intentional bandwidth do we—as software designers—give to the users of our system? What degree of control do we provide, and which interfaces do we present as affordances of the system, such that the cognitive processes of the user can be reflected in the machine signal?

21.2 The Machine as Musical Instrument and Tool for Thought

The more control parameters an acoustic instrument has, the more difficult it is to master. The sophistication of an instrument entails particulars of fine control designed through ages of evolution. Consider the difference in the learning curve of the kalimba or kazoo versus the violin or the piano (Jordà, 995). When designing a musical system on the *computer*, we are obviously concerned with the musical parameters of the composition or the tool, but we also have to decide which ones to make controllable by the user through some interface or another. In creating the interface, we decide upon the abstraction level and intensity of the system. Often it is quite arbitrary which parameters are made controllable, as such decisions could be dependent upon the piece, the hardware, or the specific group of people for which the system is made. A problem arises when the situation changes and the designer or the user of the system decides to change its internal variables. Not only will the piece be different, but the hardware will behave differently, causing regression of performance in the trained player and general distress in the user group.

The problems of human-computer interaction (HCI) in computer music are deep and wide. They are partly exemplified in the highly interesting field of research currently centered on the New Interfaces for Musical Expression Conference (NIME, nime.org). As much research in the field shows, the prominent issues with digital instruments tend to be those of the unnatural mappings between gesture and sound; dislocation of sound source and instrument; and the dynamic nature of the instruments. The megalomaniac's dream musical interface might be one in which all human gesture could be translated to music. It would consist of some amazing tactile, motion-capturing, haptic feedback device that would map movement to sound. The problem with this notion is that of bandwidth. Making full use of the capabilities of this interface would require a dedication to embodied practice that is rarely found in the field of computer music. Research has shown that people like constraints and limited scope. Designing musical instruments is akin to designing a game. We are therefore forced to face the dynamic nature of these tools and how their design is essentially a process of defining constraints.

What are we creating when we design a musical system on a computer? We hardly want to limit ourselves by imitating the world of acoustic instruments. The history of computer music shows that its strength comes from the unique qualities of the computer as a fast and general number cruncher. As opposed to humans, computers excel at calculations, complex pattern recognition, analysis, and creativity from generative rules. The unique strength and innovative power of the computer in music lies elsewhere than in simulations. It can be found in its nature as an "epistemic tool": a platform on which we can think about music—and think about ourselves thinking about music—due to its logical and self-referential nature. An environment like SuperCollider is in its own way a system of thought in which we can think about music. It is a perfect example of a musical environment in which the musician can externalize his/her thoughts, in order to sketch through the creation of musical systems that could become compositions (deterministic or generative), co-players (intelligent and adaptive), or instruments (for live or studio use).

21.3   Introduction to ixiQuarks

The ixiQuarks are the result of my decision, after having used SuperCollider for a long time, to write a modular system to produce patches for specific performances, on the one hand, and more complete instruments, on the other. The problem was that the patches didn't integrate well: each used its own buffer mechanism, effects, bus routing, and timers. The ixiQuarks are a way of modularizing work patterns through custom-built tools. These include buffer pools that take care of server buffer allocations, effect tools that include the most common effects (such as reverb, delays, filtering, etc.), and instruments that serve as pattern generators that allow for the automation of certain processes while the user is focusing on something else. The ixiQuarks are well integrated with SuperCollider. One could, for instance, write a Pattern in a live-performance situation and route it out through a prebuilt ixiQuark reverb effect in a matter of a few seconds. Many of the instruments even contain code windows as part of their GUIs. This makes their output more flexible, as the performers can write their own synthesis codes or even use the interface to communicate with other applications through protocols such as OSC or MIDI. Both the ixiViews and the ixiQuarks exist as Quarks libraries. They can also be found on the ixi audio Web site (<http://www.ixi-audio.net>), from which the ixiQuarks can be downloaded as a stand-alone binary. (See figure 21.1)

What interests me in regard to the task of building musical instruments are the conceptual engines we create when we program our tools (Magnusson, 2007). From what ground do we start, and where do we end? How does the environment lead us? For me, SuperCollider is the ideal environment by far: it has a fantastic sound engine

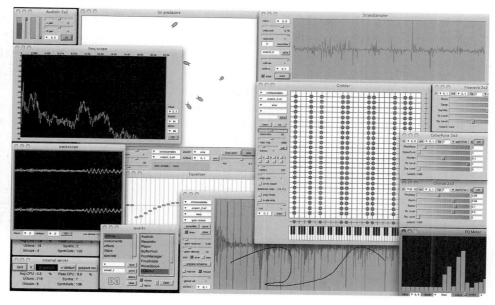

Figure 21.1
A screenshot of the ixiQuarks.

and a beautiful, object-oriented interpreted language; it is designed for music; it is open source; it has a good GUI tool kit (where for ixi, `Pen`, `UserView` and `SCImage` are the most important classes apart from the standard views); and last, but not least, it has a great developer and user community. That said, as in any environment, SuperCollider has its design strategies and vision of what music and musical practice are. It is not a neutral blank slate of freedom, although it is arguably freer than most musical tools.

21.4   Case Studies: Designing the Touch Surfaces of Our Systems

When musicians work with code as artistic material, they often tend to explore the expressive potential of an environment through a process of bottom-up exploration. Contrary to computer scientists, who frequently design software from a top-down approach before coding it, musicians who code typically explore the complex relationships between different code elements, unit generators, and the interface functionality of the environment. Instead of seeing the programming language as a tool for imperative instructions, they use it as artistic material that can be formed like clay to sculpt works of art. Often the environment leads or inspires musicians (who may or may not be conscious of it) onto paths that they would not take otherwise. Let us now look at a few case studies that exemplify how a tool can imply creative leads.

21.4.1   Study 1: Mapping the Frequency and the Amplitude

Say we want to design a simple synth with 10 harmonics and control its amplitude and frequency. We create the synth definition (see figure 21.2).

It has a variable `harmonics` so that we can set *at synthdef compile time* how many harmonics we want to have in our synth. This cannot be changed in real time nor when synths using this graph are instantiated. The `Mix.fill` mixes our 10 oscillators into a mono signal. Each oscillator has a frequency that is a harmonic (i.e., an integer multiple) of the fundamental. We divide the amplitude by i so that the higher frequencies are lower in amplitude than the ones below. (If we wanted the same amplitude in all of them, we could simply use the `Blip` UGen.)

We have created 2 inputs into the system of the simpleSynth. Its interface has 2 channels of control: frequency and amplitude. As these parameters can be changed in real time, we need to figure out a way to control them. Here practicalities and intentions come into consideration. What are we designing, and whom are we designing it for? Is this for one-time use or for wide distribution?

The most typical way to solve this is to use a slider (see figures 21.3 and 21.4).

```
SynthDef(\simpleSynth, {|freq, amp|
    var signal, harmonics;
    harmonics = 16;
    signal = Mix.fill(harmonics, {|i|
            SinOsc.ar(freq*(i+1), 1.0.rand, amp * harmonics.reciprocal/(i+1))
        });
    Out.ar(0, signal ! 2);
}, [0.15, 0.15]).add// lag times so the slider "sounds" better
)


// A line of code testing the synth definition that we created
Synth(\simpleSynth, [\freq, 440, \amp, 1])
```

Figure 21.2
A Synth Definition with 10 harmonics.

```
(
var synth, win;
// we initialize the synth
synth = Synth(\simpleSynth, [\freq, 100, \amp, 0]);
// specify the GUI window
win = Window("simpleSynth", Rect(100,100, 230, 90), false);
// and place the frequency and amplitude sliders in the window
StaticText(win, Rect(10,10, 160, 20)).font_(Font("Helvetica", 9)).string_("freq");
Slider(win, Rect(40,10, 160, 24))
    .action_({|sl| synth.set(\freq, [100, 2000, \exp].asSpec.map(sl.value)) });
StaticText(win, Rect(10,46, 160, 20)).font_(Font("Helvetica", 9)).string_("amp");
Slider(win, Rect(40,46, 160, 24))
    .action_({|sl| synth.set(\amp, [0, 1.0, \amp].asSpec.map(sl.value)) });
win.onClose_({ synth.free }).front; // we add a "onClose" message to the window
and "front" it.
)
```

Figure 21.3
A GUI with horizontal sliders to control the frequency and amplitude of our synth.

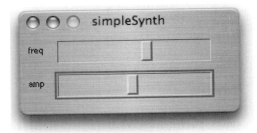

Figure 21.4
A screenshot of the GUI with horizontal sliders.

```
(
var synth, win;
synth = Synth(\simpleSynth, [\freq, 100, \amp, 0]);
win = Window("", Rect(100, 100, 94, 200), false);
StaticText(win, Rect(20, 170, 160, 20)).font_(Font("Helvetica", 9)).string_("freq");
Slider(win, Rect(10, 10, 30, 160))
    .action_({|sl| synth.set(\freq, [100, 2000, \exp].asSpec.map(sl.value)) });
StaticText(win, Rect(60, 170, 160, 20)).font_(Font("Helvetica", 9)).string_("amp");
Slider(win, Rect(50, 10, 30, 160))
    .action_({|sl| synth.set(\amp, [0, 1.0, \amp].asSpec.map(sl.value)) });
win.onClose_({ synth.free }).front; // we add a "onClose" message to the window and
"front" it.
)
```

Figure 21.5
A GUI with vertical sliders to control the frequency and amplitude of our synth.

We have now plugged the sliders into the 2-dimensional interface of the synth. But we have done so rather inconsiderately. Why are the sliders horizontal? If we look at the description of the synth above, we read sentences such as "We divide the amplitude by i such that the higher frequencies are lower in amplitude than the ones below." We use the *spatial* descriptors of high/low frequencies and high/low amplitude—yet we create sliders that go from left to right. Which metaphors are we working with here: Musical metaphors in which our language and musical notation encourage us to see pitch and amplitude as up/down, or mathematical/scientific metaphors in which negative numbers are on the left and positive numbers on the right? In fact, the GUI could just as well look like this (see figures 21.5 and 21.6):

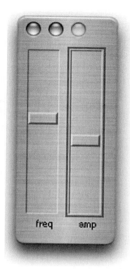

Figure 21.6
A screenshot of the GUI with vertical sliders.

21.4.2   Study 2: The GUI View as Inspiration and the ixiViews Quarks

Inspiration can come from anywhere. When working with GUI views, one often stumbles onto strange properties that can be used as a source for further work. It therefore makes sense to write GUI views that are as open and free as possible in terms of usage. A good example is the EnvelopeView. Below is a simple patch that came out of testing what happens when one connects all nodes in an envelope view. (See figure 21.7.)

The views of SuperCollider are basic and powerful, but there are limits to what can be done with them. This is where the Pen and the UserView classes can be useful, as they allow one to create custom GUI views. The ixiViews are examples of such custom views that afford functionality that the "native" GUI views of SuperCollider do not. The ixiViews are not the same as the ixiQuarks. They are used *in* ixiQuarks, but they are designed as general-purpose views to be used in various situations, and hence are not as eccentric and constrained as the ixiQuarks. Below are screen shots of the ixiViews (ParaSpace, Grid, BoxGrid, and MIDIKeyboard) in real-world usage situations. (See figures 21.8–21.10.)

The existence of views such as the ixiViews can encourage the production of alternative screen-based interfaces that encourage experimentation and improvisation. A good example is the Shooting Scales project, a collaboration between Shinji Kanki

```
(
var nNodes, envView, startStop, myWait, timeSlider, mouseTracker;
var xLoc, yLoc, mousedown = false;
var randLoc = 0.12.rand;

SynthDef(\irritia, { arg out=0, gate=1, freq=440, pan=0.0;
    Out.ar(out, Pan2.ar(LFSaw.ar(freq,0.4,0.05) * EnvGen.kr(Env.sine,
gate, doneAction:2), pan))
}).add;

nNodes = 10;
myWait = 0.033;

w = Window("irritia", Rect(200 , 450, 400, 400)).front;

envView = EnvelopeView(w, Rect(20, 20, 355, 300))
            .thumbHeight_(6.0)
            .thumbWidth_(6.0)
            .fillColor_(Color.grey)
            .background_(Color.white)
            .drawLines_(true)
            .selectionColor_(Color.red)
            .drawRects_(true)
            .resize_(5) // can be resized and stretched
            .value_([{1.0.rand}!nNodes, {1.0.rand}!nNodes]);

// connect all the nodes in the envelope view to each other
nNodes.do({arg i; envView.connect(i, {|j|j}!nNodes); });

// create a little interaction where mouseactions affect the activity
UserView(w, Rect(20, 20, 355, 300))
    .mouseDownAction_({|view, x, y| mousedown = true; xLoc = x/355;
yLoc = (-1+(y/300)).abs; })
    .mouseMoveAction_({|view, x, y| xLoc = x/355; yLoc =
(-1+(y/300)).abs; })
    .mouseUpAction_({mousedown = false});

r = Routine({
    inf.do({ |i|
        envView.select(envView.size.rand);
        if(mousedown.not, {
```

Figure 21.7
Irritia. A stochastic patch playing with the envelope view. The mouse can be used to interact with the patch.

```
                    0.05.coin.if({
                        0.5.coin.if({
                            myWait = rrand(0.028, 0.042);
                            xLoc = 1.0.rand;
                            yLoc = 1.0.rand;
                        });
                        randLoc = 0.12.rand2;
                    });
                    xLoc = envView.x+rand2(randLoc);
                    yLoc = envView.y+rand2(randLoc);
                }, {
                    xLoc = (xLoc + envView.x+rand2(0.1.rand))/2;
                    yLoc = (yLoc + envView.y+rand2(0.1.rand))/2;
                });
                envView.x_(xLoc);
                envView.y_(yLoc);
                Synth(\irritia, [\freq, (yLoc*200)+50, \pan, (xLoc*2)-1]);
                myWait.wait;
            });
        }).play(AppClock);

        w.onClose_({ r.stop });

    )
```

Figure 21.7
(continued)

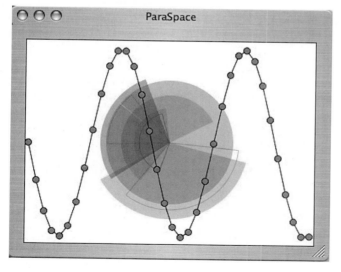

Figure 21.8
A screenshot of ParaSpace.

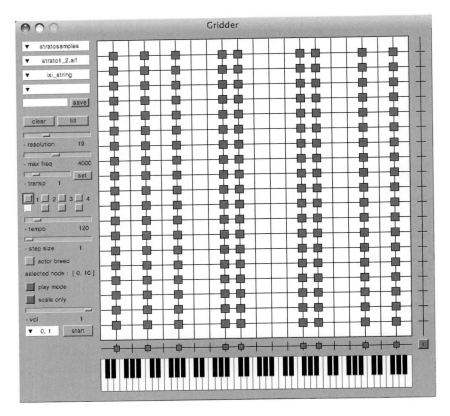

Figure 21.9
In the Gridder we see how the Grid view is used to map microtonal scales (the horizontal columns) to the octaves (the vertical rows). One can then play the Gridder with the mouse or a pen tablet as if the lines of active nodes were strings. Agents can be set to move in the system and trigger automatic performance. We also see how the MIDIKeyboard view is used to show the pitch of the node on the grid. (It is grey if it fits the equal tempered scale, but red if it is a microtone).

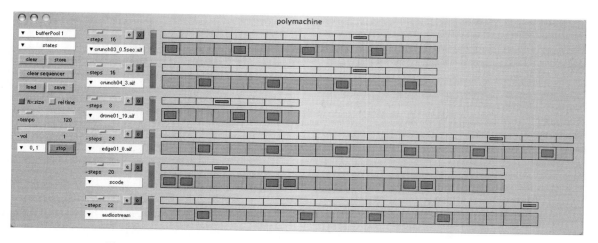

Figure 21.10
In the PolyMachine the BoxGrid is used for polyrhythmic step sequencers. It can have any number of columns and rows, but here it only has one row for each track and a row above for indicating which step the clock is at.

and myself. Here 6 virtuoso pianists from the Piano NYT group are given game pads connected to a USB hub read with the HIDDevice class of SuperCollider. Each player has his/her keyboard (represented by the MIDIKeyboard class) and can set up scales, chords, and arpeggios with the game pad. Their actions are then generalized in the GUI with a larger keyboard. In a performance, that keyboard is "connected" to a disklavier (a digital player piano) through MIDI. Thus, it is a 12-handed piece that is played by virtuosi pianists using an interface to the instrument that they may not be as accustomed to as the tactile keys of the physical keyboard. As SuperCollider supports networked communication, the disklavier can be played remotely through the Internet. (See figure 21.11.)

21.4.3   Study 3: From a Sketch to an Instrument

A look out the window on a cold winter day at the snowflakes may yield the desire to create a simulation of snow. In SuperCollider we can draw the snowflakes using Pen, but we can also check and see if the MultiSliderView could be enough (this would probably be more convenient in terms of processing power, as the MultiSlider-View is implemented as a primitive; see chapter 24). Below is a simple patch that has 4 layers of MultiSliderViews with transparent backgrounds, so one can see through to the next layer of snow. When the snow lands, it triggers a bell-like sound. (See figure 21.12.)

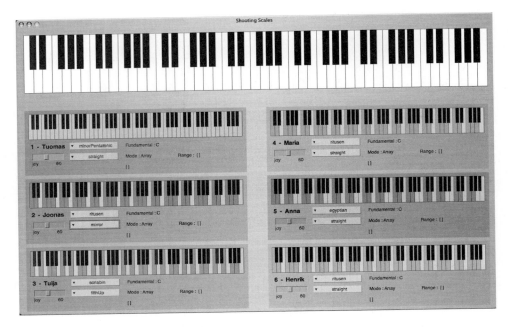

Figure 21.11
A screenshot of the Shooting Scales performance instrument.

I tend to work from this type of bottom-up approach. This sketch is interesting enough to explore a bit further. After adding some functionality, the sketch has turned into a full-blown instrument (called *sounddrops*) that is now distributed as part of the ixiQuarks. It makes use of the bufferPool tool of the ixiQuarks system, so when the drops land, they can trigger a sample, various synthesis types, code (allowing for live coding and morphing the instrument into something else in real time) or envelope an audio signal running through any audio bus (other ixi instruments could be outputting their signal on, say, audio bus 20 and the sounddrops would then listen to that). As seen from the example above, each slider in the array can have its own speed, and the Task takes care of recalculating the drop location according to another Array, speeds. We have thus taken a simple sketch and created a powerful tool that can be used for complex sequencing of polyrhythmic temporal structures that allow for ease of control, pitch mapping, and, most important, a graphical representation of the process that can inspire the musician. (See figures 21.13 and 21.14.)

All SuperCollider users eventually come up with their own design for organizing buffers, buses, effects, patterns, tools, and instruments. The ixiQuarks is but *one approach* to such organization. I decided to modularize the code so that instruments

```
(
SynthDef(\snowBell, { | freq=440, amp=0.4, pan=0 |
    var x, env;
    env = EnvGen.kr(Env.perc(0.001, Rand(550,650)/freq, amp), doneAction:2);
    x = Mix.fill(6, {SinOsc.ar(freq*Rand(-10,10), 0, Rand(0.1,0.2))});
    x = Pan2.ar(x, pan, env);
    Out.ar(0, x);
}).add;
)


(
var win, msl, trigAction, snowloc, speeds, speed, layers=4, snowcount = 62;

// fill an array with arrays (number of layers) of locations
snowloc = {{rrand(0.38,1.5)} ! snowcount} ! layers;
// fill an array with arrays (number of layers) of step size (speed)
speeds = {{rrand(0.01,0.018)} ! snowcount} ! layers;

speed = 0.1;

win = Window("snow", Rect(11, 311, 520, 240), border: false).front;
win.view.background = Color(0.14,0.17,0.24);

msl = Array.fill(layers, {|i|
        MultiSliderView(win, Rect(-1, -1, 522, 242))
            .strokeColor_( Color.new255(rrand(22,35),rrand(22,35),rrand(22,35)) )
            .fillColor_( Color.new255(rrand(222,255),rrand(222,255),rrand(222,255))
)
            .valueThumbSize_(rrand(2.8,3.8))
            .indexThumbSize_(rrand(2.8,3.8))
            .gap_(5)
    });

// when the snow falls this happens. (pitch is mapped to index and amplitude to
speed)
trigAction = {arg drop, amp; Synth(\snowBell, [\freq, 400+(drop*20), \amp, amp,
\pan, rrand(-0.8, 0.8)])};

t = Task({
    loop({
        snowloc = snowloc.collect({|array, i|
            array = array.collect({|val, j|
```

Figure 21.12
Snjókorn. A patch with 4 layers of MultiSliderView triggering sounds.

```
                    val = val-speeds[i][j];
                    if(val< 0.0, {val = 1.0; trigAction.(j, speeds[i][j]*10 )});
                    val
                });
                array
            });
            /*
            Task uses the TempoClock by default so we need to "defer" the GUI updating
            (Function:defer uses AppClock) This means that the Task is essentially using
            the SystemClock and therefore the timing is better on the sound front.
            The AppClock (used for GUI updates) has worse timing.
            */
            { layers.do({|i| msl[i].value_(snowloc[i]) }) }.defer;
            speed.wait;
        });
    }).start;

    // on stopping the program (Command/Ctrl + dot) the task will stop and the window
    close
    CmdPeriod.add({ t.stop; win.close; });
    )
```

Figure 21.12
(continued)

could make use of the same buffer pools, input signals from each other, and output on audio buses that contain effects and filters. When the system is modularized this way, the process of turning a sketch (such as the snowflakes above) into a full-blown instrument that works with ixiQuarks might not take more than a few hours.

21.5   Conclusion

In this chapter we have seen how the environment inspires innovation through play and exploration of its affordances. It has been argued that in artistic programming, the ability to work from a bottom-up design is important, and the fact that Super-Collider is an elegant, object-oriented, interpreted language makes it extremely well suited for such experimental coding. The more protocols, hardware, and graphics the environment supports, the more it lends itself to inspiration in which the creative mind and the tool interact in a way that can be seen as improvisation, sketching, exploring, building, and composing a complete piece or tool.

The ixiQuarks are GUI instruments built on top of SuperCollider. They can be seen as creative limitations that reside on top of an ocean of potential expression. As

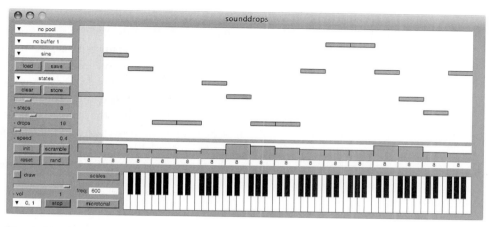

Figure 21.13

A screenshot of *sounddrops* in microtonal mode where each of the drops (there can be from 2 to 48 drops in the view) has properties such as sound function (sample, synthesis, code or audiostream), pitch, amplitude, speed, and steps. The microtonal keyboard under the multi-slider view has 7 octaves (vertical) and from 5 to 48 notes (equal tempered tuning) in an octave.

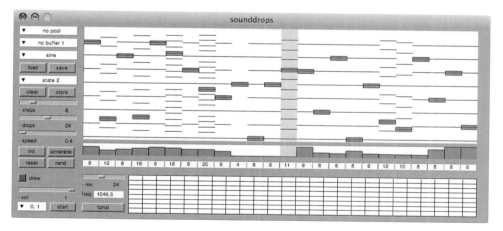

Figure 21.14

sounddrops in tonal mode. There are 2 pop-up windows as well, one is the coding window for live coding and the other is a window that contains various scales and chords that can be used to color the keyboard. These keys can then be used to assign the frequencies to the drops.

a recent survey has shown (Magnusson and Hurtado-Mendieta, 2007), people like to have constraints and limitations of all kinds when working in creative environments. This is true not only for tools or instruments but also for music or film theory. SuperCollider is an extremely open and expressive environment, perhaps the ideal intellectual partner for the musical freethinker. The ixiQuarks are on the other end of the spectrum: they focus, they concretize, and they constrain. They prime the user's mind into a certain way of thinking, a way that can be beneficial for the musical process or creativity. It is here that the power of the ixiQuarks lies: to be able to sketch and perform intuitively and quickly with tools that one has mastered but still be within the context and expressive scope of SuperCollider itself.

References

Jordà, S. 1995. "Digital Lutherie: Crafting Musical Computers for New Musics' Performance and Improvisation." PhD thesis, Department of Technology, Pompeu Fabra University, Barcelona.

Magnusson, T. 2007. "The ixiQuarks: Merging Code and GUI in One Creative Space." In *Immersed Music: Proceedings of the 2007 ICMC Conference*, Copenhagen.

Magnusson, T., and M. E. Hurtado. 2007. "The Acoustic, the Digital and the Body: A Survey on Musical Instruments." In *Proceedings of the 2007 NIME Conference*, New York, pp. 94–99.

22 SuperCollider in Japan

Takeko Akamatsu

22.1 Introduction

In the foreword to this volume, James McCartney has presented the origins and history of SuperCollider; I will present a specifically Japanese perspective. This chapter provides a case study of some Japanese users who have found SuperCollider a productive and empowering environment for audio art.

McCartney's aesthetic is demonstrated by SuperCollider's real-time capability, flexibility, and elegance as a programming language, which maximize the computer's potential. In turn, the combination of Japanese aesthetics with SuperCollider has made for some very interesting and exciting projects.

22.2 The History of SuperCollider in Japan

Let's trace the history of SuperCollider in Japan. According to McCartney, the first Japanese person to purchase a copy of SuperCollider 2 was Masayuki Akamatsu, a media artist. Among individual countries, Japan was the world's second-largest market after the United States' 50 percent, though other countries were close: the United States, 51.5%; Japan, 8%; United Kingdom, 7.6%; Germany, 6.1%; Canada, 3.8%; Australia, 3.4%; France, 3%; Italy, 3%; others, 13.6%.

Since SuperCollider 3 is now distributed free of charge, it's hard to tell how many people are currently using it in Japan, though many musicians and programmers are interested in SC and the forum is active. After tracing the history of SuperCollider in Japan, I will relate some of the activities of today's SC users.

The first known demonstration of SC in Japan was (ironically) Max Night, held at ICC (NTT Inter Communication Center) in Shinjuku on February 21, 1997, as the pre-opening event. ICC is at the vanguard of media art centers using progressive technologies in Japan. At the event, Masayuki Akamatsu gave a tutorial on programming and computer music. Though Max was featured in the lecture, Max had no audio synthesis capability at the time—so Masayuki Akamatsu introduced SC1 as a real-time audio synthesis tool and demonstrated it with a live performance. His band, gaspillage, featured SC in the CD *Maze and Lights* (1998), using it to generate abstract sounds clustered by Spawn and for sound morphing. While Masayuki Akamatsu was the first Japanese person to buy a copy of SC (purchased in London), the first to buy it in Japan was Yasuhiro Otani, the other member of gaspillage!

22.3 How I Discovered SC, and My Activities as an SC Maniac

After this event, many computer musicians became interested in SC; I was introduced to SC2 by a friend. I tried several sample programs and was attracted to the sounds. But I didn't even know what programming was, much less understand English, so I had to abandon learning it for the time being.

After this, I attended a progressive school of media arts, IAMAS (International Academy of Media Arts and Sciences). I gained some experience in programming and had good opportunities to learn English (IAMAS was the first school to buy academic licenses for SC in Japan). Yet at that time, no introductory books (such as tutorials) or information about SuperCollider was available in Japanese. English was difficult for me, and I also had to learn technical terms used in programming and audio synthesis. So it was very difficult for me to understand the Help files of Super-Collider. In addition, few people were using SC.

So I took a year to translate the Help files of the language and all the Help files for unit generators into Japanese. Through the process, I became fascinated with Super-Collider not only as a music production tool but also as SuperCollider itself. I published an e-mail newsletter and created a mailing list to increase users. I crafted socks with embroidered programming code to show that SuperCollider not only was a programming language for computer nerds, but also fashionable (figure 22.1). I held a small weekly workshop, SuperCollider Dame School, in Nagoya (2003) and a DSP Super School with James McCartney as a guest lecturer at IAMAS in Ogaki City (2004). I've continued with this kind of activity as an SC maniac, running the forum and wiki in Japanese (figure 22.2) and organizing SC user meetings.

22.4 SC Users in Japan

I'd like to introduce some remarkable SC users in Japan and their programming code. The code is provided with the book Web site.

SC is used as a tool for learning audio synthesis at a few schools. The most active place is Tama Art University, where professor Akihiro Kubota teaches. In his online book *Introduction to Code Composition* (<http://dp.idd.tamabi.ac.jp/dsc>), he in-

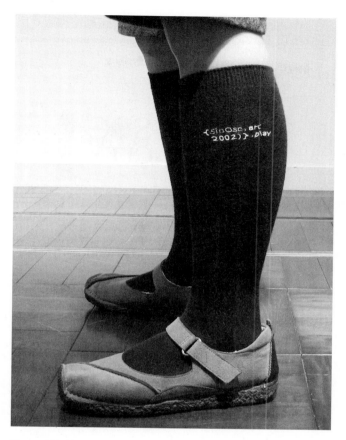

Figure 22.1
SuperCollider socks.

troduces compositional programming, algorithmic operation, and elements related to the aesthetics of digital music. He also shows how digital practice is connected to many historical methods concerning the sense and ideas of sound and music. He finds SuperCollider the most suitable tool to illustrate such ideas. Part of this material is included in the Akihiro_Kubota folder on the Web site.

Some of his students are working intensively with SuperCollider. Koichi Mori's recent audiovisual performance work, "Determinant Nonlinear Doom," focuses on generative music and images (the Koichi_Mori folder has an example Quicktime movie). He's interested in creating complex musical structures through simple repeated operations and rules. In this piece, L-systems are used to generate waveforms

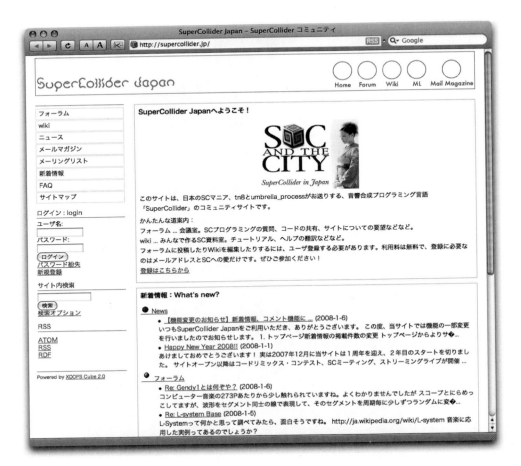

Figure 22.2
Top page of <http://supercollider.jp>, consisting of a wiki, forums, and more.

and visuals. The algorithm is written in Python and sends OSC messages to Super-Collider to generate sound; the animation is generated by OpenGL. A big advantage of SuperCollider is that it can communicate so easily with other applications via OSC commands.

SuperCollider is not used only by people with an academic background. Yamato Yoshioka is the youngest SC user I know in Japan (just 6 years older than SC!). During an interview he said that he studied programming by himself when he was a child in order to build computer games. He has since been making tools for music with SC (see the Yamato_Yoshioka folder). One of his works, "Fireworks," provided the

Figure 22.3
Playing SC with iPhone.

sound effects for a school play. Animation was added later. Some elements of the sound and animation (e.g., the size and location of fireworks) are synchronized. Another work, "GoodNose," is a rock guitar simulation, played from a laptop; he reflects on the possibilities and controversies raised by playing music from an audio programming language.

Takuro Hishikawa, aka umbrella_process, has been making music with SC since 2004 (see the Takuro_Hishikawa folder); he also helps me moderate the SuperCollider wiki and forums. In "Rainy Route 79," he obscures the perspective of time by means of sound. With increasing saturation of sound it is hard to know how much time has passed, like a boring drive on the highway on a rainy day. For this piece, it is important to make chords that have no relation to each other; for this purpose, SuperCollider is convenient for him. When I quizzed him on this, he justified this by the hard work required to write many unrelated chords by hand; using SuperCollider, variations of the ".rand" method are a natural way to proceed.

I myself also make synth pop using the pattern functions of SuperCollider. Recently I've been working with Apple's iPhone to control SC (figure 22.3). There are two important points in this work. One is that this wireless, small, and flexible device allows me to play anywhere, providing an alternative to staring at my laptop monitor when I'm doing live performance. The other is wanting to know what the essential elements and identity of my music are, which I explore by randomizing musical elements such as pitch, duration, and rhythm. SuperCollider's Pattern classes and functions are useful for implementing this, and it's also easy to write a program to control SC via these kinds of devices using SuperCollider's OSC message style (see the Takeko_Akamatsu folder).

SuperCollider has attracted an ever increasing number of users. Compared with my first encounter with SC, it's much easier for beginners to learn, especially here in Japan, with translated documents, tutorials, and the forum. Despite the high language barrier, we all wish for the wonderful unique music that can be made using SuperCollider.

23   Dialects, Constraints, and Systems within Systems

Julian Rohrhuber, Tom Hall, and Alberto de Campo

SuperCollider, like the layers of a Russian *matryoshka* doll, is a system of systems, containing an ever-increasing number of specialized subsystems that range from the general-purpose to the highly idiosyncratic. Extensions to a language add both new possibilities and new constraints. This chapter will explore this idea, looking at a variety of ways in which these possibilities and limitations can influence our practice and understanding of the process of programming and art. By discussing examples from different areas of research (e.g., language design, hardware, scheduling constraints, text manipulation, etc.), we will show how the restrictive potential of such systems can lead to an iterative and collective artistic process. Indeed, a SuperCollider composition can be regarded as a work of art within a work of art, or as a language within a language. We have chosen examples for their interesting idiosyncrasies as well as to convey an impression of the dimensions such systems unfold.

The benefits that these subsystems bring outweigh the initial difficulty of grasping their manner of operation. In programming (as in artistic activities in general), the need for constraints is at least as important as the desire for features — limitations are themselves features that require implementation. This consideration is revealed especially in the blurring of the distinction between a tool and its outcome, an application and an artwork or a model. The more general, generative, or aleatoric a work becomes, the more it becomes an environment, a system of axioms, or simply material for new works of art within its own world.

23.1   Dialects

It has often been stated that there is no essential difference between a language and a dialect; gradually one manner of speaking crosses over to another. Where languages end and dialects begin is a matter of perspective. Furthermore, languages are used heterogeneously: many people are multilingual, creole languages are abundant, and within a single language, domain-specific vocabularies exist to facilitate communication (or, of course, restrict it) within a given situation.

The extent to which a language or dialect constrains what is thinkable is a part of a long-standing debate within philosophy and linguistics (see, e.g., Wittgenstein, 1958; or Whorf, 1956). A language's structure and vocabulary define what we can say explicitly and how we make sense to others. Computer languages occupy a peculiar position here: on the one hand, they are an elaborate form of control instructions specifying what a machine should do, and on the other hand, they should also be human readable so as to make clear what the computer should do and how it should be achieved. A computer program is thus *doubly readable*. Donald Knuth, arguing in favor of programs as *literature*, puts it this way: "Instead of imagining that our main task is to instruct a computer what to do, let us concentrate rather on explaining to human beings what we want a computer to do" (Knuth, 1992, p. 99). Historically, the parallels to language were clear early on, but computer code itself was only rarely construed as art before the 1990s—even though computer code by both Max Mathews and Iannis Xenakis was included in a famous anthology of music notation edited by John Cage (Cage, 1969). How a particular notation may affect our human interpretation of a (here, computer) text is outside the scope of this chapter (see Hall, 2007), but we will return to text systems in a slightly different context in section 23.5

Wherever a program is not a *black box* (i.e., a closed system in which the user has access only to input and output), but an intermediate step in development or composition, the specific way in which a language is structured makes some things easy to express and do, and others harder; thinking within a given language, some ideas may never occur. On the other hand, computer languages not only intertwine process and description, doing and saying, but they also enable the construction of other languages, or systems, that in turn become the bases for new programs. In other words, if a program is something like a recipe for a cook, it resembles just as well a recipe for a recipe, or even a recipe for the construction of a cook.[1]

Historically, many programming languages evolved from being an extension of an existing one, adding new concepts until this extension became something quite different from the initial language. (SuperCollider, for instance, started as the MAX plug-in *Pyrite*. For many other examples, see Wexelblat, 1981.) Since the 1970s, many computer languages have been designed with this in mind, in order to make it easier to implement domain-specific subsystems—or even new languages with their own syntax. Code may produce code for other programs—a simple example is a *quine*, a program that returns its own source code; an example in SuperCollider is

```
(_ + '.(*' + quote(_) + '! 2)') .(* "(_ + '.(*' + quote(_) + '! 2)')" ! 2)
```

Programming an interpreter is programming a programming language. An interpreter is a program that executes instructions written in a specific language. For languages with a very simple syntax, such as Lisp, it is relatively straightforward to write such an interpreter in the original language itself (see, e.g., the *metacircular evaluator* in Abelson et al., 1996, ch. 4). The idea of object orientation takes this 1 step further: every object is in itself like a simple interpreter. The messages sent to such an object are actually small programs, instructions of behavior that can mean very different things depending on who receives them. This *polymorphism*—different objects responding to the same message in different ways—makes for one of the most interesting features of integrating systems within the system (see chapter 8 in this volume). In SuperCollider, it is trivial to write, for instance, a kind of List class that behaves like any other List, except that it responds to requests for 1 of its items with a blurring of boundaries between that item and its neighbors. Below we create a subclass of List that overrides the at message and modifies the index that is passed in as an argument.

```
VagueList : List {
    at {|index|
        ^super.at((index + 1.rand2).clip(0, this.lastIndex))
    }
}
```

The original message at is now understood differently by the object, which returns an element at or near the index that it was asked for. For example, a = VagueList[0, 1, 2, 3]; a.at(2); may return 1, 2, or 3. From this it becomes clear that a subclass of an object is like a very small sublanguage, or dialect, using the same syntax but with altered semantics. What is the constraint here? At first glance, we have introduced a kind of malfunction: when using this list to play a melody, some of the notes will be omitted and others repeated, without our knowing in advance which ones. This ignorance allows a different perspective on the musical material: while seen as *outside-time* material (Xenakis, 2001, pp. 155–161), the list of notes is identical; as *inside-time* it displays a characteristic degree of vagueness. (For a deeper exploration of vagueness, see Williamson, 1994). From a purely behavioral perspective, this state consists of truly ambiguous objects.

This discussion began with a shift from the unavoidable constraints implied in language and the variability of dialects to programming languages that encourage a formation of systems within systems. The above example of message-passing polymorphism demonstrated how we can shift the semantics of a program in order to change our idea of what we are working with, for instance, a melodic pattern. By constraining access, new meaning is created.

Before discussing a number of SuperCollider subsystems, we take a look at different levels at which such systems can come into play and show how apparent limitations in 1 area may reveal potential in another. From program text to sound, there are many intermediate levels at which interaction, but also conceptual constraints, may occur. The *code*, usually represented as a string object, is interpreted and results in a graph of connected *objects*. These objects specify a certain behavior: the *processes* of the running program that may create new objects, but also new code. In the current SuperCollider implementation, there are already 2 very different types of processes: the nodes in the sound synthesis tree on the SC server, and the streams and schedulers on the sclang side. Beginning with the former, we discuss a brief example of a constraint on each level.

23.2   Emulators, Deficient Synths, and Appropriating Protocols

The challenges of writing efficient code and inventing faster algorithms to run on current technology have often required clever "hacks" to get the most out of any given hardware. While scientific knowledge of algorithms is advanced through such efforts, some artists deliberately return to old hardware for other reasons. A game music specialist can often tell what computer was used for a piece, not only from its sound but also from the compositional strategy employed to work within the limited means available.

The aesthetic dimensions of such hardware constraints are well illustrated in a simulation of ENIAC, the first electronic computer, by Martin Carlé. The SuperCollider implementation uses the quasi-continuous synthesis model of UGen graphs to implement ENIAC's analog circuits. While one could encapsulate a universal machine entirely in a single UGen, the ENIAC model consists of a network of UGens simulating the hardware as the components change states in the process of running a program. In the example below, the ENIAC Cycling Unit (which was used for synchronizing the other units) is modeled as a CU_PulseLookUpTables UGen, which expects as input a periodic ramp from 0 to 80 (volts, as it were) to cycle through its "1 addition time" cycle and creates 10 synchronized clock signals, which in turn control the timing of all the other ENIAC components (see figure 23.1). These are also modeled as UGens and include multipliers, dividers, square-rooters, and accumulators (with 10 decimal places, thus running at the equivalent of 33.22 bits precision). All the UGens were first modeled in MATLAB/Simulink and from there exported for automatic conversion to SuperCollider UGens. The following demonstrates the use of the emulator.

```
// Eniac Cycling Unit with adjustable clock speed
(
{     var clockspeed = MouseX.kr(1, 300, 1);
      var clocksignal = LFSaw.ar(clockspeed).range(0, 80);
      var timingPulses = CU_PulseLookUpTables.ar(clocksignal); // 10
      channels.
      timingPulses * 0.2
}.scope;
)
```

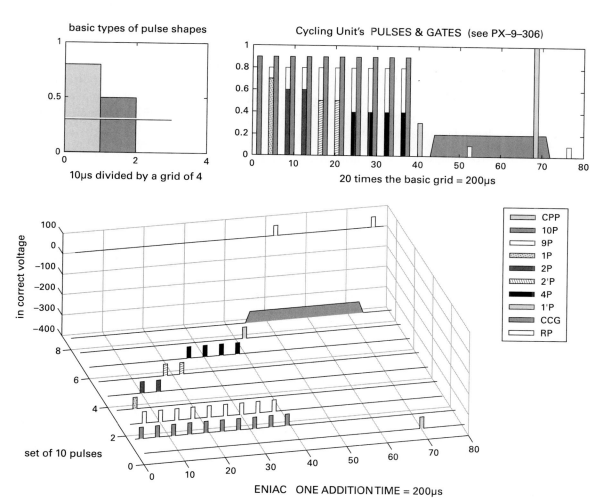

Figure 23.1
The ENIAC Cycling Unit and the structure of the 10 pulses it creates.

Hardware constraints have their equivalents in software. A program or a synth definition that has a peculiar parameter mapping, a specific trade-off, or some life of its own can be regarded as a constraint, or a system within the system. Within the graph of a synth, for instance, it is possible to derive boundary conditions or limits for some parameters from others, or to control several properties with a single one. To give a very basic example, when frequency and pulse width are coupled, timbre depends on frequency:

```
{var freq = MouseX.kr(20, 2000, 1); Pulse.ar(freq, freq.explin(20, 2000,
0.95, 0.05))}.play;
```

This dependency can become more intricate if a different mapping function is used.

```
{var freq = MouseX.kr(20, 2000, 1); Pulse.ar(freq, freq.explin(20, 2000,
0, 5pi).sin * 0.45 + 0.5)}.play;
```

Instead of trying to make as many parameters accessible for control as possible, we can thus find ways to reduce the entry points. On the other hand, we could supply both width and frequency inputs but still make them depend on one another, for example, by a limit that they pose for each other or by a mutual influence of their values when changed (figure 23.2).

With these simple prototypes in mind, we can easily see how compositions are made up of parts that set basic constraints or rules for other parts. While, for instance, this is not unlike a score for flute written with the idiosyncrasies of the instrument in mind, in a programming language like SuperCollider the relations become more complex. What used to be called *control* can be situated anywhere between rule definition (constraint) and navigation (exploration of consequences). In such a way, often initially unnoticed, a constraint turns into a subsystem. One such almost invisible subsystem in SuperCollider becomes apparent in the composition of synth definitions: the UGen graph is constructed by the operations within sclang, but its processes run on the server, which cannot access objects such as functions or dictionaries.

Another genre of constraint is the simulation of 1 computer by another, as discussed above in relation to ENIAC. Many other older chip sets also have been implemented in the virtual form of emulators in order to run old programs written with a very different set of features in mind. Examining such a system in SuperCollider demonstrates well how 1 part of a larger system can work with its own peculiar rules. Pokey, a UGen by Fredrik Olofsson, is an oscillator that implements an essential set of features of the 8-bit Pokey sound chip that formed part of the ATARI computer and served as sound source for many 1980s computer and arcade games.[2] While the floating-point inputs of the Pokey UGen can be modulated at control rate, they are truncated to integers that are then interpreted as binary numbers. Not only

```
(
{    var f = { | a, b | [a.min(1 - b), b.min(1 - a)] };
     var freq = f.value(MouseX.kr, MouseY.kr) * 400 + 500;
     SinOsc.ar(freq) * 0.1
}.play;
)


(
a = { |freq=100, width=0.5|
     var df, dw;
     df = freq - LastValue.kr(freq);
     dw = width - LastValue.kr(width);
     freq = freq + (dw * 100);
     width = width + (df / 100);
     Pulse.ar(freq, width.clip(0.01, 0.99).poll) * 0.1
}.play;
)

a.set(\freq, exprand(200.0, 600.0));
a.set(\width, 1.0.rand);
```

Figure 23.2
Two ways of constraining parameters.

does the resulting sound conjure up memories of "jump-and-run" games and the subsequent 8-bit or "chiptune" music genre, but its implementation also has another kind of cultural resonance; Pokey employs a very specific set of functions that bear a resemblance to the intersections of numerical sieves used by Xenakis in a number of his compositions (Xenakis, 2001, pp. 268–288; written in 1971). The sometimes surprisingly complex relation between addition and multiplication is used to generate a continuum between cyclic and pseudo-random movements — to this end both Xenakis and Pokey superimpose several layers of numerical regularities, resulting in interference patterns of common multiples.

A first glance reveals the abundant limitations within Pokey's functionality. There are only 4 sound channels for polyphony; each channel has 8-bit frequency resolution (256 steps), representing integer divisions of the sample rate, and 4-bit amplitude (16 steps). Also, each output channel is simply an amplitude-modulated pulse wave (figure 23.3). In its arcade game version, Pokey has been used for mimicking physical sound events, such as airplanes, Geiger counters, fires, cars, crashing buildings, and waterfalls, simply by supplying 2 bytes, one for frequency and one for the

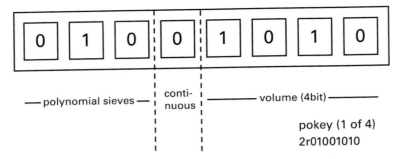

Figure 23.3
Overview of the registers for 1 Pokey channel.

sound. This type of constraint may resemble a bank of pre-sets or SynthDefs, which present us with no more than an arbitrary collection of choices. Yet this oscillator is different mainly for 2 reasons. First, the sounds have a quite specific relation to each other, as they are all produced by the same method: a high-frequency pulse train is subdivided (every *nth* trigger may pass, controlled by the frequency byte) and then is fed through a combination of numerical sieves that essentially consist of a pseudo-random pattern of holes. Because some of these (polynomial) pseudo-random patterns repeat fairly early, regular interfering beating patterns result—a small change in the frequency byte results in a sound that is almost entirely unlike the previous one (see figure 23.4).

As shown above, Pokey differs from a set of pre-sets in the way parameters closely interfere with each other to form a kind of inner sonic logic. The second reason for Pokey's difference is illustrated in figure 23.3—the graphic, which shows how, by using a binary numerical representation (e.g., 2r01001111 instead of the equivalent 79), some of this inner logic affects the way it is coded: by varying a certain bit in a number over time, for instance, we can multiply a binary number by the modulating unit generator. Addition attains a different meaning here, and the mapping becomes nonlinear: adding up to 4 bits increases the amplitude, but adding more than this will affect the sound in a different way. Someone who knows the intricacies of this chip can interleave its specific aesthetics with the rest of the system.

Pokey is an example of a metaphor of a specific chip within SuperCollider which demonstrates 2 things: how internally, a system within a system can be an interconnected space to explore compositionally, and also how externally, it may give rise to other ways of connecting it with other parts of the system.

MIDI, as Miller Puckette remarked, was "a huge step sideways" (Lyon, 2002). *General MIDI* in particular was an attempt to generalize a language for music making from the perspective of an existing music practice, but one which turned out to be excessively narrow. Nevertheless, MIDI provided a challenge to developers to ap-

```
// modulating the frequency input to a Pokey UGen results in great variance
(
{
    var rate = MouseX.kr(0, 255);
    var mod = LFPulse.kr(1);
    var amp = 2r1100; // 12 of 16
    Pokey.ar(rate + mod, audc1: 2r01000000 + amp);
}.play
);

// modulating the pure tone bit
(
{
    var rate = MouseX.kr(0, 255);
    var mod = LFPulse.kr(1);
    var amp = 2r1100; // 12 of 16
    Pokey.ar(rate, audc1: 2r00100000 + (mod * 2r00100000) + amp);
}.play
);
```

Figure 23.4
Modulating Pokey inputs.

propriate its standard into innumerable, partly "abusive" subsystems. A cluster of genres — MOD music — evolved from such slight extensions of the standard; Fredrik Olofsson's RedXM class is a SuperCollider implementation of tracker software worthy of mention in this context.[3] Also involving MIDI, but from a somewhat different perspective, we turn to Rohan Drape's *rd_ctl*, a "minimalist controller design" that integrates MIDI in a syntactically light way; the required classes are available as a Quark, and to install it, one evaluates "rd_ctl".include.

rd_ctl is a system within a system allowing easy access to a server's control buses either by software alone (a GUI and text code) or by using external MIDI hardware. The main class in the design is Controller, which maps individual control buses to Ctl instances, which are usually represented by GUI sliders. Figure 23.5 demonstrates using *rd_ctl* to control a frequency modulation synth by mapping the Ctls to the synth's controls.

If MIDI hardware is being used with the system, MIDI channels correspond to a Controller, and CC messages are mapped to Ctl indices. A typical chain of control would be MIDI control number –> a Ctl value –> control bus value –> synth control value. The Ctl GUI also corresponds to a typical MIDI controller setup, represented by a slider and a push-button, which can step through slider values determined by

```
(
SynthDef(\FreqMod, { |car=440, carFine=1, mod=100, modFine=1,
index=4, amp=0.3, pan=0|
    Out.ar(0, Pan2.ar(PMOsc.ar(car * carFine, mod * modFine, index),
pan, amp));
}).add;

c = Controller.new(s, 256);
c.makeInterface(2, 3, 0, "Freq Mod controller");

c[0].setup("carFreq", [50, 4800, \exp].asSpec, 440);
c[1].setup("carFreqFine", [0.95, 1.05, \exp].asSpec, 1);
c[2].setup("modFreq", [10, 4800, \exp].asSpec, 10);
c[3].setup("modFreqFine", [0.95, 1.05, \exp].asSpec, 1);
c[4].setup("mIndex", [0, 24, \lin].asSpec, 1);
c[5].setup("amp", [0, 1, \lin].asSpec, 0.2);
);

a = Synth(\FreqMod) // start the synth
6.do({|i| a.map(i, c[i].index)}); // map the synth control to the
controller.
a.free // when finished
```

Figure 23.5
Setting up Controller and mapping Ctls to a Synth's controls.

each Ctl's stateMap. Pre-sets allow returning to previous complete Controller states. Thus *rd_ctl* enables a direct "hands-on" approach to parameter control within SuperCollider, especially of use in performance contexts. Like Pokey, *rd_ctl* suggests a certain compositional approach while at the same time determining a number of internal and external configurations.

23.3   Scheduling Constraints: HierSch

Textbooks often claim that programming is about modeling aspects of the real world. As an approach to synthesis algorithms, physical models introduce material constraints into sound synthesis. By formalizing their parameters they allow for both exploration of their state space and for their combination with other entities (Cook, 2002). What we hear are the boundary conditions of human ideas about the physical environment.

Such models are plentiful among the default SuperCollider UGens, and more are available for download from the sc3 plug-ins project. *Sonification*, for instance, is a wide field at the borderline between reflection on models and exploration of the world (see chapter 13).

The next example shows a method for prioritizing simultaneous events. It models a common physical constraint of musical performers such as percussionists, namely, that they have a limited number of extremities with which to strike instruments.

A key aspect of any compositional system concerns the relations and constraints between its musical elements (Babbitt, [1961] 2003). Most systems, including tonal systems, are governed by a number of structural or perceptual hierarchies. Temporal relations between musical elements also form an important part of the constraints of the traditional tonal system in Western music; rules exist as to which simultaneities (chords) may follow which. Chords are in turn articulated within a metrical hierarchy, which in much Western music connotes "strong" and "weak" beats in the bar (Lerdahl and Jackendoff, 1983; Temperley, 2001). Where compositional systems are used for improvised or semi-improvised music, it can be a challenge to form a coherent system of (implicit or explicit) rules governing the articulation of the system's elements, especially where those elements (be they performed live or computer generated) have a degree of independence.

The HierSch class (*Hier*archical *Sch*eduler) of Tom Hall is designed to explore a real-time SuperCollider approach to such issues in the temporal domain. (HierSch is available on the book Web site and as a Quark.) A minimalist rule-based framework for priority-based scheduling, HierSch uses the same scheduling interface as TempoClock, but with an important difference: in HierSch, streams of functions, the events of which may or may not sound, can be independently scheduled according to their relation to other simultaneous events in other scheduled streams. This relation is expressed in the form of a number of simple rules centered on a numerical priority assigned to each stream (or individual tasks within a stream).

Priorities in HierSch range from 1 (highest) to 12 (lowest) — priority 0 is used to mark layers that always play. Once scheduled, by default an item with a given priority will be evaluated only if another item with a higher priority is not also scheduled to play at that moment. Results can be varied by inverting the priorities, increasing the number of priorities that can play simultaneously, and so on. HierSch has a number of scheduling methods, including schedAbs, whose syntax is similar to its namesake in TempoClock. One of the main syntactical differences is the addition of a number of extra arguments in HierSch's schedAbs, including priority and stream, which supply the control information for determining, together with HierSch's internal state, which events will play and which will be ignored.

Figure 23.6 illustrates a simple example of concurrent HierSch schedules, in which in 3 places simultaneous functions are considered by the system for evaluation, but only the highest (shown darkened in the figure) are evaluated.

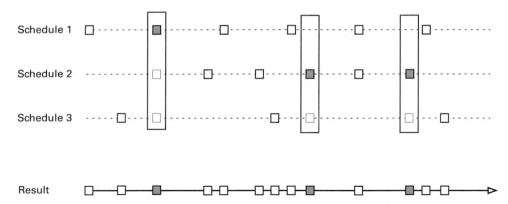

Figure 23.6
HierSch scheduling constraints and priority levels.

A simplistic diatonic example of the kind of scheduling constraints illustrated in figure 23.6 is demonstrated in figure 23.7. The example also demonstrates the use of the counter argument within the scheduling method. This is passed into the function and used to select the appropriate Array element pitch offset from the priority 1 and 2 functions. The VagueList class discussed in section 23.1 is used in the lowest voice for limited temporal pitch displacement.

23.4   Object Systems: Redirections and Constraints

Since this book provides many examples of class libraries and varieties of object semantics, we will take only a short excursion into 2 specific aspects of this topic. First, we will show how to use a redirection of access and assignment to create little worlds with rules of their own; second, we will show an example of a special syntax for declaratively formulating solutions to problems.

23.4.1   Redirecting Assignment: Maybe and LazyEnvir

As discussed in connection with the VagueList example, message passing is a way to change behavior polymorphically. By reinterpreting a message differently, we are able to smoothly integrate new functionality to propagate through the system. Two very basic things are excluded from this principle, though: a variable is not an object, and assignment is not a method. In other words, in the expression x + 1; the variable x is not itself passed the message +, but rather its *value* (whatever it is). Likewise, in the expression x = 1; the = is not a message but a sign for the binding of a value to

```
(
SynthDef(\ping, {
    arg out = 0, mfreq = 69, pan = 0, gain = 0.2, dur = 0.25;
    Out.ar(out, Pan2.ar(
    SinOsc.ar(mfreq.midicps, 0,
    EnvGen.kr(envelope: (Env.perc(0.01, dur)), doneAction: 2)),
    pan, gain));
}).add;

// function to play a synth
m = {|f, d=0.3, g=0.2, p=0| Synth(\ping, [\mfreq, f + 45, \pan, p,
\gain, g, \dur, d])};

// function to make a chord
c = {|a, b, c| [a, b, c].do{|i| m.value(i, 1.2, 0.075, rrand(-1.0,
1.0))}};

t = TempoClock.default.tempo_(116 / 60); // assign clock to t
b = HierSch.new(t); // start new HierSch, pass in clock
)

(
// HierSch schedules
b.schedAbs(t.beats.ceil + 48, 1, { var offset = [0, 5, 7, 12];
c.value(*[12, 16, 19]+ offset.choose)}, Prand(#[1.5, 3], 30)); //
enters last, priority highest

b.schedAbs(t.beats.ceil + 14, 2, {|b, p, d, c| m.value([0, 0, 7, 5,
4].at(c % 5) + [12, 24].choose, 0.4, 0.15, rrand(-1.0, 1.0))},
Pseq(#[2, 2, 2, 1], 15)); // enters middle, priority middle

b.schedAbs(t.beats.ceil, 3, { |b, p, d, c| m.value(VagueList[0, 12,
4, 7, 10, 10, 9, 9, 7].at(c % 9))}, Pseq(#[0.5, 0.5, 0.5, 0.5, 0.25,
0.75, 1, 0.5, 0.5], 17)); // enters first, priority lowest
)
```

Figure 23.7
Priority-based HierSch scheduling.

```
p = LazyEnvir.push;
~a = ~b * ~c;
~a.value;    // => nil
~b = Pseq([1, 2, 3]).asStream;
~c = 10;
~a.value;    // => 10
~a.value;    // => 20
~b = [1, 2, 3];
~a.value;    // => [10, 20, 30];
~a.postcs;   // => Maybe((Maybe([ 1, 2, 3 ]) * Maybe(10)))
p.pop
```

Figure 23.8
Maybe yes.

x. This provides the foundation of the object system: behavior is bound to variables by objects. Environments have a similar syntax; we can also write ~x = 1. In actual fact, however, we are implying something else: ~x = 1 is really equivalent to writing either \x.envirPut(1) or currentEnvironment.put(\x, 1). Within the just-in-time programming library (JITLib; see chapter 7), there is a simple class called LazyEnvir. Its superclass is EnvironmentRedirect (ProxySpace also derives from it). Instead of simply setting the value named "x" in the environment, a lazy environment returns a proxy, a placeholder instance of the class Maybe. In the programming language Haskell, a Maybe is something that, when used for calculation, returns either the result or, if it is not yet fully specified, simply returns nil. In SuperCollider, a Maybe works somewhat similarly: it allows us to write underspecified calculations within a lazy environment (see figure 23.8). More generally, this concept is called lazy evaluation.

Any object that responds to source_(arg) by keeping the argument in some internal representation and returning it when sent the message source, can be used in a LazyEnvir to modify how assignment and reference work. The proxy classes discussed in chapter 7 are examples of such objects.

23.4.2   Declaring Constraints: List Comprehensions

The SuperCollider language can be cryptic, but often, unusual syntax is simply a sign of a programming language influence from far outside the mainstream. Expressions such as _ + 1 ! 7 (i.e., Array.fill(7, {|i| i + 1})) have their own history and are yet another example that SuperCollider is already a system of systems drawing from many sources (in this case, APL). Some programming languages provide a way to

```
(
var x;
x = { |rates=#[1, 1]| Ringz.ar(Impulse.ar(rates) * 0.1, rates * 80, 1 / rates)
}.play;
fork {
    var str = {:[x, y],
        x<-(40..2),
        y<-(x + 1..40),
        gcd(x, y) == 1,
        x.isPrime.not and: y.isPrime.not
    };
    0.5.wait;
    str.do { |primes|
        x.setn(\rates, primes.postln);
        (primes.product / primes.sum / 20).wait;
    }
};
)
```

Figure 23.9
Co-primes as frequency and trigger rates.

pose constraints for solving problems, whereby after performing some algebraic and logic reformulations, the system returns solutions. One way of formulating such problems are *list comprehensions*, in which we supply a range of possible values for each variable (a domain) and a relation between these variables. For instance, to request all co-primes (all integer pairs that have only 1 as a common divisor) between 2 and 10 in SuperCollider, we write

```
f = {:[x, y], x <- (2..10), y <- (x..10), gcd(x, y) == 1}
```

where x <- (2..10) stands for all numbers between 2 and 10, and y <- (x..10) represents all numbers between each x and 10. To constrain this domain, we declare that the greatest common divisor of x and y must be 1. f can produce all the solutions step by step: f.next returns [2, 3] and so on. We might add an additional constraint such that the numbers should not be ordinary primes.

```
f = {:[x, y], x<-(2..10), y<-(x + 1..10), gcd(x, y) == 1 and: x.isPrime.
not and: y.isPrime.not}
```

Now the first solution is [4, 9]. Such sequences of solutions have many applications — and being essentially streams, they can be used in the SuperCollider pattern system (figure 23.9).

There are many musical subsystems that use constraints of a similar kind, albeit with different kinds of notations, some of which can be partly combined. To mention only a few, the *crucial library* provides constraint objects that could, for example, be used to select musical styles from databases. An event-based constraint system is used to experiment with Javanese music rules in the ethnomusicological research project *Virtual Gamelan Graz* (Schütz, Rohrhuber, and De Campo). Nick Collins's *Infno* synth pop generator uses constraint algorithms for interlocking multiple instrumental layers. Somewhat like a petri net, in Andrea Valle's *GeoGraphy* project sequences of sound objects are formalized and visualized as graphs of path constraints. Graphical interface constraints (discussed in chapter 21) form the basis of Thor Magnusson's *ixiQuarks*, a large collection of idiosyncratic performance interfaces.

23.5   Text Systems

Thus far we have discussed different levels at which to implement systems within systems: the levels of *primitive*, of *processes*, and of *object* semantics. A further possibility, perhaps for good reason less common in SuperCollider, is the *textual* level itself. Given that computers are ideal tools with which to manipulate and analyze text, it is not surprising to see early computer analysis and recent recompositions of Samuel Beckett's partly algorithmic text *Lessness*,[4] as well as John Cage's use of the computer to aid the creative "writing through" of a diverse range of existing texts. (Coetzee, 1973; Drew and Haar, 2002; Cage, 1990).

Before we show how to include other computer languages at the level of the text, we examine how strings can be used to express alphabetical constructions a little differently while remaining within the realm of standard code. A string such as "aggaca" or "what else?" may be given very different meanings—for instance, a = Pseq("aggaca".ascii) describes a stream that returns the number series 97, 103, 103, 97, 99, 97 (a.asStream.all); among other things, such a stream may be realized as a melody or a specification for a resonator bank. Using dictionaries (or in more advanced cases, finite state machines), strings may be split into parts with a meaning (e.g., to evaluate functions)—figure 23.10 shows how to do such a translation with a varying key size.

The possibilities for alternative notations, for file readers, and for string modification methods are many—regular expression methods such as findRegexp and matchRegexp may even be considered *little languages* in themselves. Implementations of *symbolic machines* such as simple finite state machines (e.g., the Pfsm pattern), instruction synthesis (Instruction, in Nick Collins's SLUGens), or Emil Post's *Tag-Systems* (e.g., Dtag UGen by Julian Rohrhuber) show that a simple syntax system may cause surprising and intractable behavior. For general-purpose programming

```
(
var dict, maxLength = 0;
dict = (
    ab: { (note: [4, 0, 7], legato: 0.1, dur: 1) },
    ba: { (note: [4, 9, 8], legato: 0.3, dur: 0.3) },
    aaa: { (note: 5, legato:1.5) },
    bbb: { (note: 0, legato:2.5, dur: 0.25) }
);

dict.keys.do { |key| maxLength = max(maxLength, key.asString.size) };

f = { |str|
    var i = 0, n = 0, substr, event;
    while { i < str.size } {
        substr = str[i..i + n];
        event = dict[substr.asSymbol].value;
        if(event.notNil) {
            substr.postln;
            i = i + n + 1;
            n = 0;
            event.postln.play;
            event.delta.wait;
        } {
            if(n + 1 < maxLength) { n = n + 1 } { n = n - 1; i = i + 1 }
        };
    };
};
)

// play some sequences
fork { f.value("abbbbaab"); }
fork { f.value("aaabbbabbaaaabbabaaaaba"); };
```

Figure 23.10
A very simple notation translater.

this is an unwanted constraint (a *Turing tar pit*), but the situation can be otherwise in experimental mathematics or sound synthesis.

Because everything is an Object in sclang, its own interpreted code is represented as a String object that also may be modified directly. In order to use a string of code in a program, we can define it (x = "1 + 2") and interpret it explicitly: x.interpret/3; returns the result 1. This also means we may, for example, replace the plus with a minus x = x.replace("+", "-"); so that the second part above would now return –1/3. We can easily replace plus with nonsense code so that the results will be difficult to understand or invalid—an obvious disadvantage of such self-modifying code. Nevertheless, such techniques are used wherever the notation syntax itself needs to be modified, for instance, in code art pieces, in which the form of representation is part of the meaning; for experiments with language syntax; and for the integration of other languages into SuperCollider code, as discussed below (Fredrik Olofsson's *redSnail, redSnake,* and *redWorm* are amusing examples that sonify open code documents, and can be found in the SuperCollider "examples/misuse_and_hacks" directory).

The integration of other languages with SuperCollider code is enabled through the existence of a *preprocessor* that allows the Interpreter to modify code before interpreting it. This kind of code for modifying other code may simply be a function that takes the compile string as argument and returns the modified code. Following on from our earlier example, this.preProcessor = {|str| str.replace("+", "-")} changes every plus to a minus in SuperCollider code. (Since this doesn't make much sense from a programming point of view, breaking as it does much existing code, it is useful to know how to return to standard behavior: this.preProcessor = nil.) Extending this principle on a less trivial level, the Quark named PreProcessor is designed to help embed multiple languages into SuperCollider ("PreProcessor".include. To activate it, evaluate this.preProcessor = PreProcessor.new). Using PreProcessor, the code between delimiters <% and %> is not evaluated directly, but instead returns a function that takes an environment in which both language and input values may be defined (see PreProcessor.help). Once evaluated, it stores the result in this environment. An interpreter for the Turing-complete esoteric programming language *brainfuck*[5] has been implemented (example in the book Web site), but PreProcessor is also expected to be useful as an interface with scientific systems such as *Octave* (octave.org). In line with our earlier discussion of dialects, the form, and especially the *syntax,* of notation is not neutral to the direction our thinking may follow. Problem-specific *little languages* (Bentley, 1986) often can be conveniently implemented within a host language simply by adding objects and methods, without any need to modify the host language syntax. Some little languages add very little new functionality but modify the general behavior of the host language. As an example, the little language GLOBOL (see Quarks directory) has a different syntax "look and feel" compared to sclang, and it introduces specific constraints and features. Mainly these are the constraint that global variables are always audio proxies and the feature that these audio proxies run on all networked machines. Thus, A = {SINOSC:AR(B) * 0.2} becomes a named global 8-channel audio proxy which can be made audible with A:PLAY. The global variable B can be set later with, for instance, B = 234, which will propagate to all networked computers running GLOBOL.

23.6   Systems Within Systems

Programmers tend to reinvent the wheel—perhaps simply because it takes longer to find a code that fits the purpose than to write new code. But if we consider what the nature of a "wheel" is in this case, we realize that synthesis algorithms, notation systems, useful classes, and idiosyncratic objects are less like engineering tasks than works of literature, formal science, and conceptual and performative art. Alan Newell, in his discussion of fair use and patentability of algorithms, doubts that we can draw a clear line between the discovery of a law of nature, a piece of literature (covered by copyright), and a novel technical idea (covered by patent law). One of his suggestions is to "[. . .] consider a model, in which inventions produce, not consumables, but 'inventibles'. That is, [to] suppose the primary effect of every product is to enable additional inventions" (Newell, 1986). Without doubt, the core of SuperCollider is a large conglomerate of such "inventibles"—whether fine-grained unit generators, design ideas such as multichannel expansion, or the Pattern library. From the perspective of art, every part and subsystem—even down to a simple method definition—may turn out to be as much a piece of art as a source of new art (McCartney, 2003); it is meta-art in the best sense. SuperCollider fuses not only sound synthesis with high-level programming paradigms, but also technical refinement with scientific and artistic invention, as if to remind us that these are just different aspects of culture.

Within the constraints of the GPL, every program published may at any time become the source of a new style—it may be quoted, appropriated, modified. Barthes's notion of the "death of the author" comes to mind here (Barthes, [1967] 1977), for at the very least, identity of invention can be seen as a continuum. Literal examples of this are the occasional *cadavres exquis* that have developed on the sc users mailing list, an example of which, *CadavreExquisNo2.scd*, can be found on the book Web site.

In an interview first published in 1968, John Cage discusses the 10 months of computer programming entailed in making the piece HPSCHD with Lejaren Hiller. Comparing subroutines to the traditional use of chords by composers, Cage states:

The notion that the chord belongs to one person and not to another tends to disappear, so that a routine, once constructed, is like an accomplishment on the part of society, rather than on the part of a single individual. And it can be slightly varied, just as chords can be altered, to produce quite other results than were originally intended. The logic of a routine, once understood, generates other ideas than the one which is embodied in it. This will lead, more and more, to multiplication of music for everybody's use rather than for the private use of one person. (Kostelanetz, 2003, p. 82)

Cage here highlights the important *social* aspect of computer programming implied above, as explicitly cultivated later within the open source movement, including the SuperCollider community. (Glenn Gould offers a related perspective in 1964 on the notion of multiple authorship and "implicit multilevel participation" in electronic culture; Gould, [1964] 1984, p. 93.) The term "community of practice" has been developed to explore how learning and sharing of knowledge happen within such communities (Lave and Wenger, 1991). A community of practice can be described as encompassing a *domain* of knowledge, a *community* that has an interest in this domain, and a *practice* that is developed in order to be effective in it (Wenger et al., 2002, p. 27). From this perspective, SuperCollider as software can be seen as a kind of "system within a system" *of learning* within the SC community itself, as well as being its primary focal point of practice (Wenger, 1998). At different levels discussed in this book, SuperCollider code—from little code components that carefully add a few concepts to large libraries that represent a whole way of thinking—forms a continuum of means and ends. Code written with a specific purpose in mind may inform the design of a musical composition, just as a piece of music may suggest a new programming concept.

References

Abelson, H., G. J. Sussman, and J. Sussman. 1996. *Structure and Interpretation of Computer Programs*, 2nd ed. Cambridge, MA: MIT Press.

Babbitt, M. [1961] 2003. "Set Structure as a Compositional Determinant." In S. Peles, S. Dembski, A. Mead, and J. N. Straus, eds., *The Collected Essays of Milton Babbitt*. Printceton, NJ: Princeton University Press.

Barthes, R. [1967] 1977. "Death of the Author." In Barthes's *Image-Music-Text*. London: Fontana.

Bentley, J. 1986. "Little Languages." *Communications of the ACM*, 29(8): 711–721.

Browne, R. 1981. "Tonal Implications of the Diatonic Set." *In Theory Only*, 5(1–2): 3–21.

Cage, J. 1990. *I–VI*. Cambridge, MA: Harvard University Press.

Cage, J. (ed.) 1969. *Notations*. New York: Something Else Press.

Coetzee, J. M. 1973. "Samuel Becket's *Lessness*: An Exercise in Decomposition." *Computers and the Humanities*, 7(4): 195–198.

Cook, P. R. 2002. *Real Sound Synthesis for Interactive Applications*. Natick, MA: A. K. Peters.

Drew, E., and M. Haar. 2002. "*Lessness*: Randomness, Consciousness and Meaning." Available online at <http://www.scss.tcd.ie/publications/tech-reports/reports.03/TCD-CS-2003-07.pdf> (accessed 10/16/10).

Gould, G. [1964] 1984. "Strauss and the Electronic Future." In T. Page, ed., *The Glenn Gould Reader*. New York: Knopf.

Hall, T. 2007. "Notational Image, Transformation and the Grid in the Late Music of Morton Feldman." *Current Issues in Music*, 1(1): 7–24.

Knuth, D. E. 1992. *Literate Programming*. CSLI Lecture Notes, no. 27. Stanford, CA: Center for the Study of Language and Information.

Kostelanetz, R. 2003. *Conversing with Cage*, 2nd ed. New York: Routledge.

Lave, J., and E. Wenger. 1991. *Situated Learning: Legitimate Peripheral Participation*. Cambridge: Cambridge University Press.

Lerdahl, F., and R. Jackendoff. 1983. *A Generative Theory of Tonal Music*. Cambridge, MA: MIT Press.

Lyon, E. 2002. "Dartmouth Symposium on the Future of Computer Music Software: A Panel Discussion." *Computer Music Journal*, 26(4): 13–30.

McCartney, J. 2003. "A Few Quick Notes on Opportunities and Pitfalls of the Application of Computers in Art and Music." In *Proceedings of the Ars Electronica "CODE" Symposium, Linz, Austria*, pp. 262–264.

Newell, A. 1986. "Response: The Models Are Broken, the Models Are Broken!" *University of Pittsburgh Law Review*, 47: 1023–1031.

Temperley, D. 2001. *The Cognition of Basic Musical Structures*. Cambridge, MA: MIT Press.

Wenger, E. 1998. "Communities of Practice: Learning as a Social System." *The Systems Thinker*, 9(5). Available online at http://www.ewenger.com/pub/pub_systems_thinker_wrd.doc (accessed 12/19/07).

Wenger, E., R. A. McDermott, and W. Snyder. 2002. *Cultivating Communities of Practice: A Guide to Managing Knowledge*. Boston: Harvard Business School Press.

Wexelblat, R., ed. 1981. *History of Programming Languages*. New York: Academic Press.

Whorf, B. 1956. *Language, Thought, and Reality: Selected Writings of Benjamin Lee Whorf*, J. B. Carroll, ed. Cambridge, MA: MIT Press.

Williamson, T. 1994. *Vagueness*. London: Routledge.

Wittgenstein, L. 1958. *Philosophical Investigations*, 2nd ed. Oxford: Basil Blackwell.

Xenakis, I. 2001. *Formalized Music*, 2nd ed. Hillsdale, NY: Pendragon Press.

Notes

1. Such programs may be either programs that output program text or programs that can read program text and interpret it. (Examples are on the book Web site; see Quines and others.)

2. In the U.S. patent application, the chip was described as "Apparatus for producing a plurality of audio sound effects." The UGen is based on a classic emulator by Ron Fries (1996–1998) that has been used in many applications.

3. Olofsson's SuperCollider Web page is <http://www.fredrikolofsson.com/pages/code-sc.html> (accessed 12/31/07).

4. Online at <http://www.random.org/lessness> (accessed 12/31/07). The simple algorithm to generate a further *Lessness* has also been implemented by the present authors in sclang.

5. <http://esoteric.voxelperfect.net/wiki/Brainfuck> (accessed 12/31/07).

Developer Topics

24 The SuperCollider Language Implementation

Stefan Kersten

24.1 Introduction

In this chapter we will have a closer look at the SuperCollider compiler and interpreter, its internal data structures, coding conventions, and inner workings. The last part of the chapter is devoted to writing language primitives in C++, which is necessary for interfacing to external C libraries and operating system APIs.

The SuperCollider interpreter is a complete implementation of an object-oriented language in the Smalltalk tradition that was written from scratch by James McCartney for SuperCollider 2 (McCartney, 1996). While some aspects, such as bytecode interpretation, class hierarchy, and object layout, can be recognized in similar existing interpreters, other features, such as its orientation toward audio and music, real-time garbage collection, and constant-time method lookup, are thus far unique to SuperCollider.

In general there are 4 key aspects to the design and implementation of a virtual machine: the layout of objects in memory; the virtual machine instruction set; the compiler; and the interpreter or virtual machine itself. The following sections are intended to give you a broad overview of all mentioned aspects and to enable you to dig deeper according to your interests and needs. To this end it would probably be beneficial also to have a look at other virtual machine implementations and design documents (Goldberg and Robson, 1983; Budd, 1987; Ingalls et al., 1997).

24.2 Coding Conventions

Before delving into the implementation details, we will introduce some coding conventions used throughout the source code which will (hopefully) help in better understanding the implementation.

SuperCollider is based on C as the main implementation language, using object-oriented features from C++ where appropriate (e.g., when sharing data in related hierarchies of implementation structures). Due to the inherently low-level nature of interpreters, high-level features of the host language usually don't map well to features in the target language, so it comes as no surprise that SuperCollider's virtual machine implementation is mostly restricted to pure C. Compilers, however, do benefit from high-level abstractions: that is why SuperCollider's byte-code compiler uses object-oriented features such as inheritance and polymorphism more intensively.

In the source code there are a few naming conventions that can be identified: class, structure, and union type names are often written in camel case (see <http://en.wikipedia.org/wiki/Camel_case>) and prefixed with a capital Pyr for historical reasons—the very first incarnation of SuperCollider was a *Max/MSP* object called *Pyrite*. Function and method names usually use camel case as well and start with a lowercase character (with some notable exceptions in low-level support code such as the storage allocator and the garbage collector). Functions implementing primitives are prefixed with pr; global variables visible across modules often start with a lowercase g; and certain constants are prefixed with k. Symbols (i.e., pointers to PyrSymbol) are usually prefixed with s or s_.

Indentation is by tabs of width 4 throughout the source code; this convention should be adhered to when adding code, in order to maintain a coherent code base.

24.3 Object Layout

The internal memory layout of objects is an important design consideration in any language implementation, as it constitutes the interface between compiler, interpreter, and garbage collector (figure 24.1). This section gives an overview of how objects (and pointers to them) are defined in SuperCollider and discusses some important object types in more detail.

In dynamically typed, garbage-collected languages that don't permit accessing and storing references to objects in raw memory, objects need to be enriched with additional run-time information, such as their type, memory layout, and garbage-collection state. Furthermore, it is often desirable to represent certain target language object types that see extensive usage—such as numeric values—not by a pointer to a heap-allocated object but directly encoded in a machine address. In SuperCollider, such tagged references reside in a special data structure called a slot (PyrSlot) that is bigger than a machine address (on 32-bit machines), allowing additional information to be stored along with a machine pointer. PyrSlot is a union holding either a 64-bit IEEE double value or a 32-bit integer tag followed by another union of 32-bit data (figure 24.2).

This allows the slot to be used either as a double value without any storage or dereferencing overhead or as a tagged value with data contained in the lower 32 bit of the 64-bit double word (figure 24.3). The tag is stored in the unused high-order

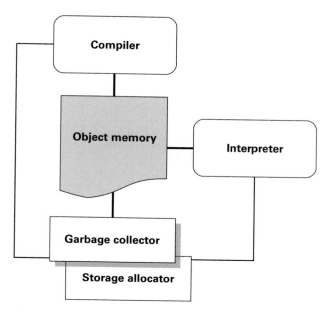

Figure 24.1
Overview of the SuperCollider language subsystems.

```
union PyrSlot
{
    double f;                  // double
    struct {
        int tag;
        union {
            int        c;      // character
            int        i;      // integer
            void       *ptr;   // raw pointer
            PyrObject  *o;     // object pointer
            PyrSymbol  *s;     // symbol pointer
            ...                // other object pointers
        } u;
    } s;
};
```

Figure 24.2
PyrSlot data struture.

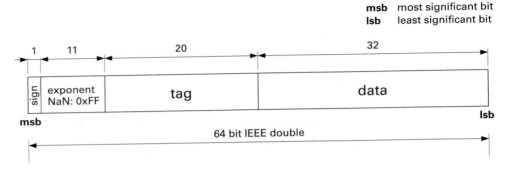

Figure 24.3
Slot memory layout.

Table 24.1
PyrSlot Tags

Tag	Description
tagObj	pointer to PyrObject
tagInt	32-bit integer
tagSym	pointer to PyrSymbol
tagChar	character value
tagNil	literal nil (no data)
tagFalse	literal false (no data)
tagTrue	literal true (no data)
tagPtr	pointer to memory not managed by SuperCollider

bits of an IEEE *not a number* (NaN) double (IEEE, 1985), so as not to limit the range of useful floating-point values. All the tags defined and their uses are listed in table 24.1. The data in the lower word may be a literal value (e.g., a character or a 32-bit integer) or a 32-bit pointer, or may remain unused when the literal value can be encoded using the tag itself (i.e., nil, false, true). This implementation strategy of encoding pointers and certain literal values in floating-point doubles is efficient, because floating-point values—presumably being used extensively in a language dealing with audio and music—do not have to be allocated on the heap, and dereferencing them does not require following a pointer indirection. However, a problem becomes apparent for 64-bit machines: here, 64-bit doubles are no longer big enough both to hold a machine address and to store tagging information, so another implementation strategy has to be found for a truly 64-bit address space.

PyrSlot members should rarely be manipulated directly, but rather by use of the convenience macros and functions defined in *PyrSlot.h*—note that some of the pre-

```
PyrObjectHdr
{
    // garbage collector links
    PyrObjectHdr   *prev;
    PyrObjectHdr   *next;
    // class pointer
    PyrClass    *classptr;
    // object size
    int     size;

    // indexable object format
    unsigned char obj_format;
    // object size class (power of two)
    unsigned char obj_sizeclass;
    // object flags
    unsigned char obj_flags;
    // garbage collector color
    unsigned char gc_color;
    ...
};
```

Figure 24.4
PyrObjectHdr data structure.

processor defines occasionally clash with symbols in system or third-party headers; thus it is often advisable to include *sclang*'s header files *after* any others.

Each object in SuperCollider includes a header with meta-information concerning the object's class, data format, size, and garbage-collector state, represented by the structure PyrObjectHdr (figure 24.4).

The prev and next fields hold object pointers used by the noncopying garbage collector *treadmill* (see section 24.6). classptr points to the object's class (a PyrObject itself), while size holds the number of slots or indexable elements contained in the object. The object's contents are further specified in the obj_format field, whose possible values are listed in table 24.2. obj_sizeclass is the object's power of two size class—obtained by a log2Ceil operation on the object's size—and is used by the storage allocator. obj_flags contains special flags concerning the object's state or interpretation; possible values are listed in table 24.3. Finally, gc_color is used by the garbage-collector graph-coloring algorithm.

PyrObject, defined in *PyrObject.h*, establishes the basic structure of any SuperCollider object and is nothing more than an object header followed by a variable number of *slots* representing the object's instance variables. The obj_format field is

Table 24.2
Object Formats

Format	Object Contents
obj_notindexed	nonindexed object
obj_slot	PyrSlots
obj_double	64-bit doubles
obj_float	32-bit floats
obj_int32	32-bit integers
obj_int16	16-bit integers
obj_int8	8-bit integers
obj_char	8-bit characters
obj_symbol	pointers to PyrSymbol

Table 24.3
Object Flags

Flag	Description
immutable	set if object may not be updated
finalize	set if object requires finalization
marked	used by garbage collector debug sanity check

used to describe the data type of objects contained in Arrays or RawArrays. All objects other than Arrays or RawArrays have obj_format set to obj_notindexed. Arrays can contain only pointers to PyrObject structures, whereas the contents of RawArrays can be symbol pointers or flat scalar data (integers of various sizes, 32-bit floats, and 64-bit doubles), effectively halving the memory requirements for arrays of those data types because the storage management overhead of PyrSlot can be dispensed with (figure 24.5).

Symbols—globally unique character strings that can be tested for pointer equality—are represented by a special structure, PyrSymbol (figure 24.6), that does not contain an object header and is treated specially by the garbage collector: memory allocated for a symbol is not reclaimed as long as SuperCollider runs. Symbols additionally point to associated information relevant for compilation and interpretation, such as the class object pointer for class name symbols or a selector index for method name symbols.

Most of the global information used by compiler and interpreter is stored in the structure VMGlobals (figure 24.7). An instance of this structure is held in the global variable gMainVMGlobals and is passed to primitives implemented in C; the most

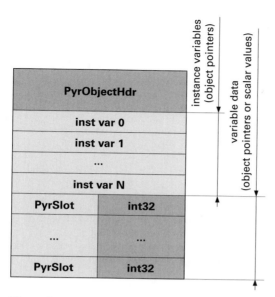

Figure 24.5
Object memory layout.

important members of this structure are pointers to the run-time stack, the garbage collector, the symbol table, and the current stack and instruction pointers.

24.4   The Compiler

The purpose of the compiler is to transform expressions given in textual form (e.g., in text files) to byte code for an instruction set that can be interpreted by the interpreter or the virtual machine.

24.4.1   The Compilation Process

The main entry point to the compiler is compileLibrary. It initializes the part of the run-time system needed during compilation (initPassOne), and in a first pass it processes SuperCollider source files found recursively in the main class library directory and the extension directories (passOne).

Each class definition found is parsed into a ClassDependancy structure that records the class's position in the hierarchy tree as well as the source file location of its definition (figure 24.8). It is stored in the classdep field of the PyrSymbol corresponding to the class name. In a first pass only the class symbols are stored in the

```
PyrSymbol
{
    // symbol name
    char    *name;
    // hash value
    long    hash;
    // special selector index
    short   specialIndex;
    // symbol flags
    uint8   flags;
    // length of symbol name
    uint8   length;
    union {
        // index in method table or primitive table
        long index;
        // pointer to class with this name
        struct PyrClass *classobj; name.
        ....
    } u;
    // class dependancy (used during compilation)
    ClassDependancy *classdep;
};
```

Figure 24.6
PyrSymbol data structure.

ClassDependancy because when the list is traversed, classes are not yet hierarchically ordered. buildDepTree then traverses the dependancy tree and records the actual links to the superclass dependancy, further constructing the subclass dependancy list. In traverseFullDepTree the dependancy tree is first flattened into an array of class dependancies (traverseDepTree). Finally, the serialized dependancy tree is compiled by compileDepTree (for regular classes) or by compileClassExtensions (for class extensions).

compileClass is the heart of the compiler: the parser generated from the bison grammar (Donnelly and Stallman, 2003) in *Source/LangSource/Bison/lang11d* parses each class according to its source location recorded in the class dependancy and returns a parse node in the global variable gRootParseNode of type PyrParseNode. A list of ParseNode subclasses, each representing a structural element found in SuperCollider source code, is given in table 24.4 (the Pyr prefix has been omitted for clarity). Each ParseNode subclass redefines the virtual method compile to emit code according to the structure it represents.

```
VMGlobals
{
    // global context

    AllocPool    *allocPool;
    // main thread context
    PyrProcess   *process;
    // global symbol table
    SymbolTable *symbolTable;
    // garbage collector for this process
    PyrGC        *gc;
    // class variable array
    PyrObject    *classvars;

    // next byte code is a tail call
    int       tailCall;

    // true when in 'main' thread
    bool          canCallOS;

    // thread context

    PyrThread    *thread;
    PyrMethod    *method;
    PyrBlock     *block;
    PyrFrame     *frame;
    PyrMethod    *primitiveMethod;

    // current instruction pointer
    unsigned char    *ip;
    // current stack pointer
    PyrSlot      *sp;

    // argument pointer for primitive
    PyrSlot       *args;
    // current receiver
    PyrSlot       receiver;
    // interpretation result
    PyrSlot       result;
    // number of args to pop for primitive
    int       numpop;
```

Figure 24.7
VMGlobals data structure.

```
        // current index into primitive table
        long        primitiveIndex;
        // random number generator state
        RGen        *rgen;
        // handler for unwinding C stack
        jmp_buf     escapeInterpreter;

        // scratch context
        long        execMethod;
    };
```

Figure 24.7
(continued)

```
ClassDependancy
{
    // next link in list
    ClassDependancy *next;
    // superclass dependency
    ClassDependancy *superClassDep;
    // subclass list (linked via 'next')
    ClassDependancy *subclasses;
    // class name symbol
    PyrSymbol       *className;
    // superclass name symbol
    PyrSymbol       *superClassName;
    // file name symbol
    PyrSymbol       *fileSym;
    // start character position of definition
    int         startPos;
    // end character position of definition
    int          endPos;
    // line number of definition
    int          lineOffset;
};
```

Figure 24.8
ClassDependancy data structure.

Table 24.4
Parse Node Classes

Parse Node Class	Description
ArgListNode	method or function argument list
AssignNode	variable assignment
BinopCallNode	method call (binary selector)
BlockNode	function definition
BlockReturnNode	return from function (last expression value)
CallNode	method call
ClassExtNode	class extension
ClassNode	class definition
CurryArgNode	curried function arguments
DropNode	drop expression result
DynDictNode	dynamic dictionary definition
DynListNode	dynamic array definition
LitDictNode	literal dictionary definition
LitListNode	literal array definition
LiteralNode	literal value
MethodNode	method definition
MultiAssignNode	multiple variable assignment
MultiAssignVarListNode	
PushKeyArgNode	keyword argument
PushLitNode	push literal value
PushNameNode	push object by name
ReturnNode	return from method (caret return)
SetterNode	method call (setter selector)
SlotNode	parse node representing named object
VarDefNode	variable definition
VarListNode	

The abstract syntax tree returned by the parser entry point yyparse is traversed by compileNodeList, which in turn calls the compile method for each ParseNode. The compiler holds state in a couple of global variables defined in *PyrParseNode.cpp*, most notably gCompilingClass and gCompilingBlock, that point to the currently compiling class object and the current block of compiled byte codes, respectively. Byte codes are appended to the current block by the compile methods of the ParseNodes in a method or function definition, which end up calling the low-level functions defined in *ByteCodeArray.cpp* that handle byte compilation as well as memory allocation.

Table 24.5
Virtual Machine Byte Codes with the Corresponding Constants from *Opcodes.h* Where Appropriate.

Primary Byte Code	Synopsis	Secondary Byte Code			
		1	2	3	4
0	push class	class index			
opPushInstVar 1	push instance variable	inst var index			
opPushTempVar 2	push temporary variable	temp var level	temp var index		
opPushTempZeroVar 3	push temporary variable from current frame	temp var index			
opPushLiteral 4	push literal selector	literal index			
opPushClassVar 5	push class variable	class var literal index	class var index		
opPushSpecialValue 6	push special class	class name index			
opStoreInstVar 7	store instance variable	inst var index			
opStoreTempVar 8	store temporary variable	temp var level	temp var index		
opStoreClassVar 9	store class variable	class var literal index	class var index		
opSendMsg 10	send message	num args	num key args	selector index	
opSendSuper 11	send super message	num args	num key args	selector index	
opSendSpecialMsg 12	send special message	num args	num key args	selector index	
opSendSpecialUnaryArithMsg 13	send unary arithmetic message	selector index			
opSendSpecialBinaryArithMsg 14	send binary arithmetic message	selector index			

Opcode	Description	Operand bytes
opSpecialOpcode 15	special opcode	(opgProcess) push thisProcess; (opgMethod) push thisMethod; (opgFunctionDef) push thisFunctionDef; (opgFunction) push thisFunction; (opgThread) push thisThread
opPushInstVar 16..31	push instance variable 0..15	
32	jump if true	jump length (high byte), jump length (low byte)
opPushTempVar 33..39	push temporary variable levels 1..7	temp var index
40	push literal constant	index (single byte)
41	push literal constant	index (byte 1), index (byte 0)
42	push literal constant	index (byte 2), index (byte 1), index (byte 0)
43	push literal constant	index (byte 3), index (byte 2), index (byte 1), index (byte 0)
44	push integer constant	single byte
45	push integer constant	byte 1, byte 0
46	push integer constant	byte 2, byte 1, byte 0
47	push integer constant	byte 3, byte 2, byte 1, byte 0
opPushTempZeroVar 48..63	push temporary variable 0..15 from current frame	
opPushLiteral 64..79	push literal constant 0..15	
opPushClassVar 80..95	push class variable	class var index
opPushSpecialValue opsvSelf 96	push self	

Table 24.5
(continued)

Primary Byte Code	Synopsis	Secondary Byte Code			
		1	2	3	4
opsvMinusOne 97	push 1 and subtract				
opsvNegOne 98	push –1				
opsvZero 99	push 0				
opsvOne 100	push 1				
opsvTwo 101	push 2				
opsvFHalf 102	push 0.5				
opsvFNegOne 103	push –1.0				
opsvFZero 104	push 0.0				
opsvFOne 105	push 1.0				
opsvFTwo 106	push 2.0				
opsvPlusOne 107	push 1 and add				
opsvTrue 108	push true				
opsvFalse 109	push false				
opsvNil 110	push nil				
opsvInf 111	push inf				
opStoreInstVar 112..127	push instance variable 0..15				

opcode	meaning	operand	operand
opStoreTempVar 128..135	store temporary variable levels 0..7	temp var index	
136	push instance variable, send special selector	inst var index	selector index
137	push all arguments, send message	selector index	
138	push all but first argument, send message	selector index	
139	push all arguments, send special selector	selector index	
140	push all but first argument, send special selector	selector index	
141	1 argument pushed, push all but first argument, send message	selector index	
142	1 argument pushed, push all but first argument, send special selector	selector index	
143	loop and branch byte codes	0..1 Integer-do 2..4 Integer-reverseDo 5..6 Integer-for 7..9 Integer-forBy 10 ArrayedCollection-do 11..12 ArrayedCollection-reverseDo 13..16 Dictionary-keysValuesArrayDo 17..18 Float-do 19..21 Float-reverseDo 22 method ? 23 method ?? 24 ifNil 25 ifNotNil 26 ifNotNilPushNil 27 ifNilPushNil 28 switch 29..31 Number-forSeries	

Table 24.5
(continued)

Primary Byte Code	Synopsis	Secondary Byte Code			
		1	2	3	4
opStoreClassVar 144..159	store class variable	class var index			
opSendMsg 160..175	send message with 0..15 arguments	selector index			
176	return from function (tail call)				
opSendSuperMsg 177..191	send super message with 1..15 arguments	selector index			
opSendSpecialMsg 192..207	send special message with 0..15 arguments	selector index			
opSendSpecialUnaryArithMsg					
opNeg 208	special unary message negate				
opNot 209	special unary message not				
opIsNil 210	special unary message isNil				
opNotNil 211	special unary message notNil				
212..223	Send special unary message with selector index 4..15				
opSendSpecialBinaryArithMsg					
opAdd 224	special binary message +				
opSub 225	special binary message –				
opMul 226	special binary message *				
227..239	send special binary message with selector index 3..15				

opcode	description		
opSpecialOpcode			
opcDrop 240	drop value on top of stack		
opcDup 241	duplicate value on top of stack		
opcFunctionReturn 242	return from function		
opcReturn 243	return from method		
opcReturnSelf 244	return self		
opcReturnTrue 245	return true		
opcReturnFalse 246	return false		
opcReturnNil 247	return nil		
opcJumpIfFalse 248	jump if false	jump length (high byte)	jump length (low byte)
opcJumpIfFalsePushNil 249	jump if false and push nil	jump length (high byte)	jump length (low byte)
opcJumpIfFalsePushFalse 250	jump if false and push false	jump length (high byte)	jump length (low byte)
opcJumpIfTruePushTrue 251	jump if true and push true	jump length (high byte)	jump length (low byte)
opcJumpFwd 252	jump forward	jump length (high byte)	jump length (low byte)
opcJumpBak 253	jump backward	jump length (high byte)	jump length (low byte)
opcSpecialBinaryOpWithAdverb 254	special binary message with adverb	selector index	
255	return from method (tail call)		

Class compilation is finished by `traverseFullDepTree2`, which first builds the final class tree with `PyrClass` objects (`buildClassTree`), then indexes it according to the number of classes defined and the number of methods defined in each class (`indexClassTree`), and finally assigns a unique index to each symbol selector (`setSelectorFlags`), information that is used in building the method dispatch table in the next step.

Method dispatch in SuperCollider is not based on method selector dictionary lookup, but is instead realized by indexing into a global dispatch table—the index is held in the class object and the selector symbol, respectively (see figure 24.6). In a simple implementation the 2-dimensional dispatch table, with rows representing classes and columns denoting selectors, would be largely empty because each class defines only a small subset of all method selectors. `buildBigMethodMatrix` builds a compressed table according to a row-displacement compression technique (Driesen and Hölzle, 1995), significantly reducing the table's size while retaining the advantages of low overhead *O(1)* method dispatch.

24.4.2   Byte Codes

The instruction set used in the SuperCollider virtual machine comprises variable-length byte codes. The primary byte code (8-bit) specifying the operation to be executed by the interpreter can be followed by up to 4 additional secondary bytes of 8 bits each, whose interpretation is dependent on the primary code.

In the following we will mention some broad groups of byte codes and their associated functionality. *Push byte codes* push a SuperCollider object onto the stack (e.g., instance and class variables, temporary variables, pseudo variables such as `self` (the current receiver) and literal values. *Store byte codes* store an object on top of the stack in an instance variable, class variable, or temporary variable location. *Send byte codes* send a message to a receiver on the stack (along with optional arguments) or execute a primitive function. *Jump byte codes* perform conditional (or unconditional) jumps by modifying the instruction pointer accordingly. Finally, *Special byte codes* are in-line implementations intrinsic to the interpreter and are generated by the compiler for certain message sends (e.g., `do`, `for`, `forBy`, `if`, `ifNil`, `switch`, etc.).

Table 24.5 lists all byte codes used by the interpreter with a short synopsis and the semantics of the corresponding extended byte codes. For extended byte codes with 1 operand, their argument is encoded in the opcode directly, if it fits into 4 bits, by shifting the byte code to the left by 4 and using the lower 4 bits for the operand value. In all other cases extended byte-code operands are compiled as separate byte codes following the primary one.

```
PyrBlock : PyrObjectHdr
{
    // pointer to PyrMethodRaw
    PyrSlot rawData1;
    // byte codes, nil if inlined
    PyrSlot code;
    // method selectors, class names, closures table
    PyrSlot selectors;
    // literal constants table
    PyrSlot constants;
    // temporary variable default values
    PyrSlot prototypeFrame;
    // defining block context
    // (nil for methods and toplevel)
    PyrSlot contextDef;
    // arguments to block
    PyrSlot argNames;
    // variables in block
    PyrSlot varNames;
    // source code (for closed functions)
    PyrSlot sourceCode;
};
```

Figure 24.9
PyrBlock data structure.

24.4.3   Byte Code Storage

Compile-time information for functions and methods is held in a PyrBlock structure (figure 24.9); the actual byte codes are stored in a byte array pointed to by the code field, unless the method is in-lined to a special byte code.

PyrMethodRaw is not a proper SuperCollider object and is stored as a raw machine pointer; its purpose is to record information regarding the type of a PyrBlock and the size and structure of its run-time activation frames (figure 24.10). The field specialIndex contains an integer index used in the special handling of run-time behavior such as primitive invocation and access of class and instance variables. Another type of optimization is realized by methType, denoting various special method types such as returning the receiver, returning and assigning instance variables, and so on (table 24.6).

Methods are a special case of ordinary code blocks, and they store some additional information such as class, method name, and source code location (figure 24.11).

```
PyrMethodRaw
{
    // special method index
    unsigned specialIndex;
    // method type
    unsigned methType;
    // prototype frame size
    unsigned frameSize;

    // number of arguments
    unsigned numargs;
    // 1 if has variable number of arguments
    unsigned varargs;
    // number of keyword and variable defaults
    unsigned numvars;
    // number of temporary (local) variables
    unsigned numtemps;
    // true when frame needs to be heap-allocated
    unsigned needsHeapContext;
    // numargs + varargs
    unsigned posargs;
}
```

Figure 24.10
PyrMethodRaw data structure.

Table 24.6
Method Type Enumeration Values

methNormal	normal method invocation
methReturnSelf	return the receiver
methReturnLiteral	return a literal value
methReturnArg	return a method argument
methReturnInstVar	return an instance variable
methAssignInstVar	assign an instance variable
methReturnClassVar	return a class variable
methAssignClassVar	assign a class variable
methRedirect	send a different selector to self
methRedirectSuper	send a different selector to self, start lookup in the superclass
methForwardInstVar	forward message send to an instance variable
methForwardClassVar	forward message send to a class variable
methPrimitive	execute a primitive
methBlock	denotes a function block

```
PyrMethod : PyrBlock
{
    PyrSlot ownerclass;
    PyrSlot name;
    PyrSlot primitiveName;
    PyrSlot filenameSym;
    PyrSlot charPos;
};
```

Figure 24.11
PyrMethod data structure.

24.5   The Interpreter

The interpreter's task is to execute — or *dispatch* — byte codes in a loop once they have been compiled into method and function definitions by the compiler. It maintains an instruction pointer (IP) indicating the currently executed byte code; after execution of a primary byte code the IP may point to a byte code in the same block or, in the case of function and method calls, to a totally different code block.

Arguments are passed through a global stack which is held in the VMGlobals structure described above. The interpreter maintains a pointer to the current top of the stack and increases or decreases the pointer as arguments are pushed and popped (the stack grows toward higher addresses). The receiver of a message is always pushed first, followed by the fixed-position arguments. Variable argument passing depends on the message being sent — normal message sends and function evaluation collect variable arguments in an Array that is passed as the last argument on the stack, while calls to primitives push variable arguments onto the stack directly (figure 24.12).

When a function or method is executed, all the run-time information that is needed for an activation frame is kept in a PyrFrame structure: the calling context, the closure context (for function activations), the enclosing method (*home*) context, the activation frame's instruction pointer, and storage for temporary variables (figure 24.13).

The functions executeMethod and blockValue are the principal means of executing methods and functions (*blocks*), respectively and are mostly identical in their operation, except for the closure context used by block activations, which captures a function's lexical environment. Here is a rundown of executeMethod's operation:

0. Receiver and arguments pushed onto stack, method already looked up via selector index by sendMessage

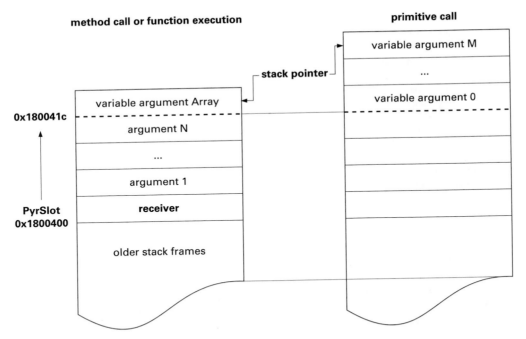

Figure 24.12
Stack layout for message sends and primitive calls.

```
PyrFrame : PyrObjectHdr
{
    // defining method
    PyrSlot method;
    // calling context
    PyrSlot caller;
    // closure context
    PyrSlot context;
    // method context
    PyrSlot homeContext;
    // instruction pointer
    PyrSlot ip;
    // temporary variable storage
    PyrSlot vars[1];
};
```

Figure 24.13
PyrFrame data structure.

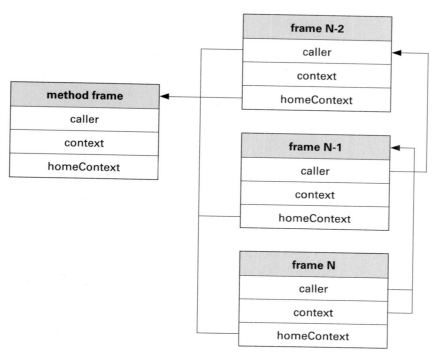

Figure 24.14
Activation frame call chain.

1. Create new frame, record calling context and home context
2. Save caller IP
3. Update interpreter state: SP, IP, current frame, and current code block
4. Process default and keyword arguments
5. Return to interpreter and resume at new IP.

When returning from a method, the interpreter calls the function `returnFrom-Method` (except for some specially optimized cases). Its purpose is to unwind the call chain, represented as a list of activation frames linked by the caller field (figure 24.14) and to resume execution at the method context's calling context:

1. If the current frame's homeContext exists (i.e., it hasn't been returned from yet), unwind the call chain to the homeContext's caller, else unwind to the top-level interpreter frame
2. Set interpreter IP to returnContext's saved IP
3. Return to interpreter and resume at new IP.

The interpreter's main entry point is `Interpret` (defined in *PyrInterpreter3.cpp*), which expects the interpreter state to be correctly initialized and the stack and instruction pointer to be set up for execution. The stack and instruction pointer are first copied to function local storage (in the hope that the compiler puts them into registers), and then the byte code pointed to by the IP is dispatched in a big switch statement.

A higher-level interface to the interpreter is `runInterpreter`, which takes care of interpreter initialization and cleanup and sends a selector symbol to the receiver that is expected to be pushed on the stack, followed by the message arguments:

```
void runInterpreter(VMGlobals *g, PyrSymbol *selector, int numArgsPushed);
```

Figure 24.15 shows the most important structures and classes used by the interpreter and their relationships. In the C code representation, all structs representing language objects have `PyrSlot` members lacking any type information. In the class diagram the following approach has been chosen instead: attribute types are named according to the corresponding language entity unless the class has a different name in the C code (UML comments signify the correspondence). For clarity, the prefix `Pyr` has been omitted in the class diagram.

24.6   The Garbage Collector

SuperCollider uses an incremental noncopying garbage collector (Wilson and Johnstone, 1993; Wilson et al., 1995) that can guarantee an upper bound for the amount of collection proportional to the amount of memory allocated per time interval, which is necessary in real-time applications that require an upper bound on GC pauses, such as audio synthesis and algorithmic composition.

A small and bounded amount of garbage collection is done whenever a storage allocation request is handled. Objects are not copied during collection but are kept in circular lists—the *treadmills*—that are incrementally traversed by the collector. The `PyrObjectHdr` fields `prev` and `next` links an object into the treadmill. Incremental collection is seen as a graph-coloring problem: the `gc_color` field of `PyrObjectHdr` contains 1 of the 3 colors *white, gray, black* or the special tag *free*, denoting the state of garbage collection a given object is currently in:

• *White* objects have not yet been considered by the incremental traversal
• *Gray* objects are known to be reachable, but their contained pointers have not yet been fully inspected
• *Black* objects are known to be reachable, and all of their fields have been scanned and colored *gray*
• *Free* objects are free to be reused by subsequent allocations.

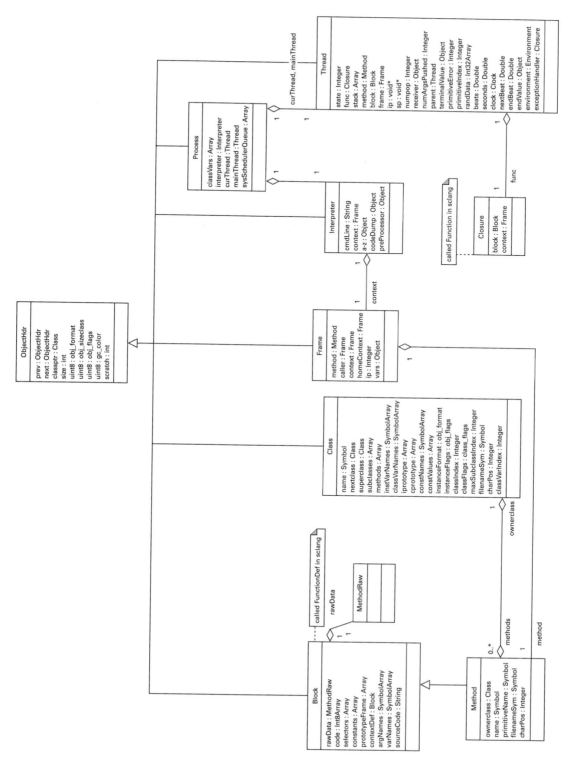

Figure 24.15
Interpreter implementation entities.

As the collector colors objects, they are moved to a linked list corresponding to the respective color; incremental collection finishes when the *gray* list does not contain any objects to scan. At this point, the *white* list contains objects that can be freed—they are appended to the *free* list in an *O(1)* operation—and the *black* list contains all live objects.

Because the mutator—the running program—might change the object graph between incremental collections, those updates have to be communicated to the garbage collector. In particular, the following invariant must be maintained. An object known to be reachable (*black* object) may point only to other *black* objects or ones that are currently under consideration by the garbage collector (*gray* objects). Storing a *white* object directly into a *black* object and discarding all other references would result in a dangling pointer, because the *white* object's storage space will be reclaimed at the end of a complete garbage-collection pass.

The above invariant is maintained by a *write barrier* (i.e., the garbage collector is notified whenever a pointer to a *white* object is stored in a *black* object). The method GCWrite, defined in *GC.h*, implements the write barrier by coloring the child *gray* when it is currently *white* and the parent is *black*.

```
void GCWrite(PyrObjectHdr* parent, PyrObjectHdr* child);
```

Variants of this method provide an optimized write barrier when the parent is known to be *black* (GCWriteBlack) and when the child is known to be white (GCWriteNew), such as when it was allocated by the preceding call to the garbage collector (newly allocated objects are colored *white*).

24.7   Writing Primitives

Sometimes it is necessary to add methods implemented in C to the SuperCollider language in order to interface to third-party libraries, access operating system services, or simply implement an operation as efficiently as possible. SuperCollider already contains a large number of primitive method implementations, which are an invaluable resource in writing your own primitives.

At the time of this writing, the SuperCollider language (as opposed to the synthesis server) does not support primitives to be loaded from plug-in modules or dynamic libraries. This means that a primitive implementation has to be included as a module in SuperCollider's source code and be added to the build system; the details of how to do this are platform-dependent and will not be explained here. Because of the "intrusiveness" of primitive implementations, the first question to answer when trying to implement a particular primitive (or set of primitives) is whether it is needed. Often the increase in performance is negligible to an implementation in pure *sclang* or there are alternative solutions that might be better suited to the problem at hand, such as communicating with external processes through *OpenSoundControl* (see chapter 4) or reading external command output (see systemCmd, unixCmd, and Pipe).

Primitives are implemented by registering a primitive *handler* function with the SuperCollider run-time system. definePrimitive is the main means of registering new primitives with a fixed or variable number of arguments:

```
int (*PrimitiveHandler)(VMGlobals *g, int numArgsPushed);
```

```
int definePrimitive(
    int base, int index, char* name,
    PrimitiveHandler handler,
    int numArgs, bool varArgs
);
```

base is a unique base index for a primitive module or collection of primitives; its initial value should be obtained by a call to nextPrimitiveIndex. index is an index for a particular primitive in the same module and should be incremented for each primitive registered. name is the identifier that is introduced to the run-time system and is also used by the compiler when encountering a primitive reference in the source code; the convention is to have primitive names begin with an underscore _ and a capital character. handler is a C function pointer with the signature of PrimitiveHandler above that is called by the interpreter upon primitive execution. numArgs specifies the number of fixed arguments a primitive is expected to be called with (including the receiver self), and varArgs should be true when the primitive expects a variable number of arguments after the fixed-positional arguments.

At a minimum the following header files need to be included in each source module with primitive definitions — more might be needed for additional functionality:

```
#include "GC.h"
#include "PyrKernel.h"
#include "PyrPrimitive.h"
```

Primitive definitions usually start by extracting arguments from the stack into a C representation, returning an appropriate error code when invalid arguments are encountered. Extracted arguments are then passed to a C library or operating system function that carries out the desired low-level operation. The result is converted back to a SuperCollider object and stored on the stack before control is passed to the interpreter by returning from the primitive.

The receiver (self) of the current primitive invocation can be found on the stack below the pushed arguments (i.e., at g->sp - numArgsPushed + 1), and the argument slots are at the subsequent numArgsPushed stack locations. *PyrSlot.h* defines a number of utility functions for extracting values from PyrSlot values and converting them to a representation compatible with C, as well as modifying slot tags and data (table 24.7). The returned value should replace the first argument pushed on

Table 24.7
PyrSlot Access Functions

Modifying Slots (tags and data)

SetInt	set slot to 32-bit integer value
SetObject	set slot to object pointer
SetSymbol	set slot to symbol pointer
SetChar	set slot to character
SetPtr	set slot to raw pointer
SetObjectOrNil	set slot to object pointer (or nil for NULL)
SetTrue	set slot to true
SetFalse	set slot to false
SetBool	set slot to Boolean value
SetNil	set slot to nil
SetFloat	set slot to 64-bit floating point value

Querying slots

IsNil	whether slot is nil
NotNil	
IsFalse	whether slot is true or false
IsTrue	
IsInt	whether slot is integer value
NotInt	
IsFloat	whether slot is floating-point value
NotFloat	
IsObj	whether slot is object pointer
NotObj	
IsSym	whether slot is symbol pointer
NotSym	
IsPtr	whether slot is raw pointer
SlotEq	whether 2 slots are equal (same tag and data)

Accessing slot data

`int slotIntVal(PyrSlot* src, int* dst);`	get integer value return error if src is not a number
`int slotFloatVal(PyrSlot* src, float* dst);`	get float value return error if src is not a number
`int slotDoubleVal(PyrSlot* src, double* dst);`	get double value return error if src is not a number
`int slotStrVal(PyrSlot* src, char* dst, int dstlen);`	get NULL-terminated string value return error if src is not a String or Symbol
`int slotPStrVal(PyrSlot* src, unsigned char* dst);`	get string value with byte count prefix (Pascal string) return error if src is not a String or Symbol
`int slotSymbolVal(PyrSlot* src, PyrSymbol **dstptr);`	get symbol pointer return error if src is not a Symbol
`inline void slotCopy(PyrSlot* dst, PyrSlot* src, int num);`	copy num slots from src to dst

```
#include <math.h>
#include "GC.h"
#include "PyrKernel.h"
#include "PyrPrimitive.h"

// Primitive implementation of atan2,
// calling the function from libm.
static int prAtan2(struct VMGlobals *g, int numArgsPushed)
{
    // Pointer to arguments
    PyrSlot *args = g->sp - numArgsPushed + 1;
    // Pointer to receiver (self)
    PyrSlot* self = args + 0;
    // Pointer to argument
    PyrSlot* arg  = args + 1;

    double x, y;
    int err;

    // Get receiver value
    err = slotDoubleVal(self, &x);
    // Signal error for invalid input type
    if (err != errNone) return err;

    // Get argument value
    err = slotDoubleVal(arg, &y);
    // Signal error for invalid input type
    if (err != errNone) return err;

    // Compute result
    double result = atan2(x, y);

    // Set top of stack to return value
    SetFloat(self, result);

    // Signal success
    return errNone;
}

// Call this function during initialization,
// e.g. from initPrimitives() in PyrPrimitive.cpp
void initMyPrimitives()
```

Figure 24.16
Implementation of an example primitive for atan2.

```
{
    // Initialize primitive indices
    int base = nextPrimitiveIndex(), index = 0;

    // Define primitive with two arguments (self, operand)
    definePrimitive(base, index++, "_MyFloatAtan2", prAtan2, 2, 0);
    // ... define more primitives here ...
}
```

Figure 24.16
(continued)

Table 24.8
Language Implementation Headers and Sources

File	Description
GC.h	garbage collector implementation
GC.cpp	
PyrInterpreter.h	interpreter interface functions
PyrInterpreter3.cpp	virtual machine implementation
PyrKernel.h	core object structures
PyrLexer.h	lexer implementation and parser interface
PyrLexer.cpp	
PyrMessage.h	message send interface, method execution, and return
PyrMessage.cpp	
PyrObject.h	object header and core object structure definitions
PyrObject.cpp	class tree and method table construction, basic constructors and primitives
PyrParseNode.h	parse node structure definitions, compilation function
PyrParseNode.cpp	implementations
PyrPrimitive.h	primitive interface
PyrSlot.h	PyrSlot definition and interface functions
PyrSymbol.h	symbol structure definition
PyrSymbolTable.h	symbol table interface
PyrSymbolTable.cpp	
SC_LanguageClient.h	abstract interpreter interface
SC_LanguageClient.cpp	
SC_LibraryConfig.cpp	library configuration file handling
SC_TerminalClient.h	command line interpreter interface
SC_TerminalClient.cpp	
VMGlobals.h	VMGlobals structure definition

the stack (i.e., the receiver), where the interpreter expects it after the primitive returns.

Let's have a look at a simple primitive implementation of the atan2 C math library function in figure 24.16.

First, the arguments are extracted from *PyrSlot.h* with the function slotDoubleVal, which returns an error when the slot argument is not a number object. Then the return value pointed to by the first pushed argument is set to the result of the library call before returning to the interpreter.

Primitives can get much more complicated than that—the primitive implementations in *Source/Lang/LangPrimSource* provide an excellent source of example code.

24.8   Source File Overview

Table 24.8 gives a short overview of the most important source and header files of the core language implementation.

References

Budd, T. 1987. *A Little Smalltalk*. Reading, MA: Addison-Wesley.

Donnelly, C., and R. M. Stallman. 2003. *Bison Manual: Using the YACC-Compatible Parser Generator*. Boston: GNU Press.

Driesen, K., and U. Hölzle. 1995. "Minimizing Row Displacement Dispatch Tables." In *OOPSLA '95: Proceedings of the Tenth Annual Conference on Object-Oriented Programming Systems, Languages, and Applications*, pp. 141–155. New York: ACM Press.

Goldberg, A., and D. Robson. 1983. *Smalltalk-80: The Language and Its Implementation*. Reading, MA: Addison-Wesley.

IEEE Standards Board. 1985. *IEEE Standard for Binary Floating-Point Arithmetic*. ANSI/IEEE Std 754-1985.

Ingalls, D., T. Kaehler, J. Maloney, S. Wallace, and A. Kay. 1997. "Back to the Future: The Story of Squeak, a Practical Smalltalk Written in Itself." *ACM SIGPLAN Notices*, 32(10).

McCartney, J. 1996. "SuperCollider: A New Real Time Synthesis Language." In *Proceedings of the 1996 International Computer Music Conference*, Hong Kong, pp. 257–258.

Wilson, P. R., and M. S. Johnstone. 1993. "Real-Time Non-copying Garbage Collection." In *ACM OOPSLA Workshop on Memory Management and Garbage Collection*. New York: ACM Press.

Wilson, P. R., M. S. Johnstone, M. Neely, and D. Boles. 1995. "Dynamic Storage Allocation: A Survey and Critical Review." In *Proceedings of the International Workshop on Memory Management*, Kinross, UK, pp. 1–116.

25 Writing Unit Generator Plug-ins

Dan Stowell

Writing a unit generator (UGen) for SuperCollider 3 can be extremely useful, allowing the addition of new audio generation and processing capabilities to the synthesis server. The bulk of the work is C++ programming, but the API (Application Programming Interface) is essentially quite simple—so even if you have relatively little experience with C/C++, you can start to create UGens based on existing examples.

You're probably already familiar with UGens from other chapters. Before creating new UGens of your own, let's first consider what a UGen really is, from the plug-in programmer's point of view.

25.1 What Is a UGen, Really?

A UGen is a component for the synthesis server, defined in a plug-in, which can receive a number of floating-point data inputs (audio- or control-rate signals or constant values) and produce a number of floating-point data outputs, as well as "side effects" such as writing to the post window, accessing a buffer, or sending a message over a network. The server can incorporate the UGen into a synthesis graph, passing data from 1 UGen to another.

When using SC language, we need to have available a representation of each UGen which provides information about its inputs and outputs (the number, type, etc.). These representations allow us to define synthesis graphs in SC language (SynthDefs). Therefore, each UGen also comes with an SC class; these classes are always derived from a base class, appropriately called UGen.

So to create a new UGen you need to create both the plug-in for the server and the class file for the language client.

25.2 An Aside: Pseudo UGens

Before we create a "real" UGen, we'll look at something simpler. A *pseudo UGen* is an SC class that "behaves like" a UGen from the user's point of view but doesn't involve any new plug-in code. Instead, it just encapsulates some useful arrangement of existing units. Let's create an example, a simple reverb effect:

```
Reverb1 {
    *ar {| in |
        var out = in;
        out = AllpassN.ar(out, 0.05, 0.05.rand, 1);
        ^out;
    }
}
```

This isn't a very impressive reverb yet, but we'll improve it later.

As you can see, this is a class like any other, with a single class method. The *ar method name is not special — in fact, you could use any method name (including *new). We are free to use the full power of SC language, including constructs such as 0.05.rand, to choose a random delay time for our effect. The only real requirement for a pseudo UGen is that the method returns something that can be embedded in a synth graph. In our simple example, what is returned is an AllpassN applied to the input.

Copy the above code into a new file and save it as, for instance, *Reverb1.sc* in your *SCClassLibrary* or *Extensions* folder; then recompile. You'll now be able to use Reverb1.ar within your SynthDefs, just as if it were a "real" UGen. Let's test this:

```
s.boot;
(
x = {
    var freq, son, out;
    // Chirps at arbitrary moments
    freq = EnvGen.ar(Env.perc(0, 0.1, 10000), Dust.ar(1));
    son = SinOsc.ar(freq, 0, 0.1);
    // We apply reverb to the left and right channels separately
    out = {Reverb1.ar(son, cutoff: 2500)}.dup;
}.play(s);
)
x.free;
```

You may wish to save this usage example as a rudimentary Help file, *Reverb1.html*.

To make the reverb sound more like a reverb, we modify it to perform 6 similar all-pass delays in a row, and we also add some LPF units in the chain to create a nice frequency roll-off. We also add parameters:

```
Reverb1 {
    *ar {| in, wet = 0.3 , cutoff = 3000|
        var out = in;
        6.do{out = LPF.ar(AllpassN.ar(out, 0.05, 0.05.rand, 1), cutoff)};
```

```
                   ^(out * wet) + (in * (1 - wet));
        }
    }
```

This is on the way toward becoming a useful reverb unit without having created a real plug-in at all.

This approach has definite limitations. It is of course confined to processes that can be expressed as a combination of existing units — it can't create new types of processing or new types of server behavior. It may also be less efficient than an equivalent UGen, because it creates a small subgraph of units that pass data to each other and must maintain their own internal states separately.

Now let's consider what is involved in creating a "real" UGen.

25.3   Steps Involved in Creating a UGen

1. First, consider exactly what functionality you want to encapsulate into a single unit. An entire 808-drum machine, or just the cymbal sound? Smaller components are typically better, because they can be combined in many ways within a SynthDef. Efficiency should also be a consideration.

2. Second, write the Help file. Really — it's a good idea to do this before you start coding, even if you don't plan to release the UGen publicly.

As well as being a good place to keep the example code which you can use while developing and testing the UGen, it forces you to think clearly about the inputs and outputs and how the UGen will be used in practice, thus weeding out any conceptual errors.

A Help file is also a good reminder of what the UGen does — don't underestimate the difficulties of returning to your own code, months or years later, and trying to decipher your original intentions!

The Help file will be an HTML file with the same name as the UGen. There is a "Documentation Style Guide" in the SC Help system which includes tips and recommendations for writing Help documentation. But, of course, during development the Help file doesn't need to be particularly beautiful.

3. Third, write the class file. You don't need to do this before starting on the C++ code, but it's a relatively simple step. Existing class files (e.g., for SinOsc, LPF, Pitch, Dwhite) can be helpful as templates. More on this shortly.

4. Fourth, write the plug-in code. The programming interface is straightforward, and again existing plug-in code can be a helpful reference: all UGens are written as plug-ins — including the "core" UGens — so there are lots of code examples available.

We now consider writing the class file and writing the plug-in code.

25.4 Writing the Class File

A class file for a UGen is much like any other SC class, with the following conditions:

It must be a subclass of UGen. This is so that methods defined in the UGen class can be used when the language builds the SynthDef (synth graph definition).

The name of the class must match the name used in the plug-in code — the class name is used to tell the server which UGen to instantiate.

It must implement the appropriate class methods for the rates at which it can run (e.g., *ar, *kr, and/or *ir). These method names are referenced for rate checking during the SynthDef building process.

The class methods must call the multiNew method (defined in the main UGen class), which processes the arguments and adds the UGen correctly to the SynthDef that is being built.

The class file does not have any direct connection with the C++ plug-in code — after all, it's the server that uses the plug-in code, while the class file is for the language client.

Let's look at a well-known example:

```
SinOsc : UGen {
    *ar {
        arg freq = 440.0, phase = 0.0, mul = 1.0, add = 0.0;
        ^this.multiNew('audio', freq, phase).madd(mul, add)
    }
    *kr {
        arg freq = 440.0, phase = 0.0, mul = 1.0, add = 0.0;
        ^this.multiNew('control', freq, phase).madd(mul, add)
    }
}
```

As you can see, SinOsc is a subclass of UGen and implements 2 class methods. Both of these methods call multiNew and return the result, which is 1 or more instances of the UGen we are interested in. The methods also call madd, which we'll discuss shortly.

The first argument to multiNew is a symbol to indicate the rate at which the particular UGen instance will be operating: this could be "audio," "control," "scalar," or "demand." The remaining arguments are those that will actually be passed to the C++ plug-in — here freq and phase. If any of these arguments are arrays, multiNew performs multichannel expansion, creating a separate unit to handle each channel. Indeed, this is why the method is called multiNew.

Note that the mul and add arguments are not being passed in to multiNew. This means that the actual plug-in code for SinOsc will never be able to access them. Instead, this UGen makes use of the `madd` method, which is essentially a convenience for multiplication and addition of the unit's output. As well as avoiding the programmer's having to implement the multiplication and addition part of the process, the `madd` method performs some general optimizations (e.g., in the very common degenerate case of multiplying by 1 and adding 0; no processing is really required, so the UGen is simply returned unaltered). It is the convention to add `mul` and `add` arguments to UGens as the final 2 arguments, as is done here; these 2 arguments are often very useful and are supported by many UGens. (Due to their commonness, they are often undocumented in Help files.)

Let's start to draft the class file for a UGen we can implement. We'll create a basic "flanger" which takes some input and then adds an effect controlled by rate and depth parameters:

```
Flanger : UGen {
    *ar {
        arg in, rate = 0.5, depth = 1.0, mul = 1.0, add = 0.0;
        ^this.multiNew('audio', in, rate, depth).madd(mul, add)
    }
    *kr {
        arg in, rate = 0.5, depth = 1.0, mul = 1.0, add = 0.0;
        ^this.multiNew('control', in, rate, depth).madd(mul, add)
    }
}
```

Save this as *Flanger.sc* in your extensions directory. If you recompile, you'll find that this is sufficient to allow you to use `Flanger.ar` or `Flanger.kr` in SynthDefs, which the SuperCollider language will happily compile—but of course those SynthDefs won't run yet, because we haven't created anything to tell the server how to produce the Flanger effect.

25.4.1   Checking the Rates of Your Inputs

Because SuperCollider supports different signal rates, it is useful to add a bit of "sanity checking" to your UGen class to ensure that the user doesn't try to connect things in a way that doesn't make sense: for example, plugging an audio-rate value into a scalar-rate input.

The `UGen` class provides a `checkInputs` method which you can override to perform any appropriate checks. When the SynthDef graph is built, each UGen's `checkInputs` method will be called. The default method defined in `UGen` simply passes through to `checkValidInputs`, which checks that each of the inputs is really something that can be plugged into a synth graph (and not some purely client-side object such as, say, an `SCWindow` or a `Task`).

The BufWr UGen is an example which implements its own rate checking. Let's look at what the class does:

```
checkInputs {
    if (rate == 'audio' and: {inputs.at(1).rate ! = 'audio'}, {
        ^("phase input is not audio rate:" + inputs.at(1) + inputs.at(1).
        rate);
    });
    ^this.checkValidInputs
}
```

If BufWr is used to write audio-rate data to a buffer, then the input specifying the phase (i.e., the position at which data is written) must also be at audio rate—there's no natural way to map control-rate index data to a buffer which is taking audio-rate data. Therefore the class overrides the checkInputs method to test explicitly for this. The rate variable is the rate of the unit under consideration (a symbol, just like the first argument to multiNew). The inputs variable is an array of the unit's inputs, each of which will be a UGen and thus will also have a rate variable. So the method compares the present unit's rate against its first input's rate. It simply returns a string if there's a problem (returning anything other than nil is a sign of an error found while checking input). If there's not a problem, then it passes through to the default checkValidInputs method—if you implement your own method checking, don't forget to pass through to this check.

Many UGens produce output at the same rate as their first input—for example, filters such as LPF or HPF. If you look at their class definition (or their superclass, in the case of LPF and HPF—an abstract class called Filter), you'll see that they call a convenience method for this common case called checkSameRateAsFirstInput. Observe the result of these checks:

```
s.boot;
x = {LPF.ar(WhiteNoise.kr)}.play(s); // Error
x = {LPF.ar(WhiteNoise.ar)}.play(s); // OK
x.free;
x = {LPF.kr(WhiteNoise.ar)}.play(s); // Error
x = {LPF.kr(WhiteNoise.kr)}.play(s); // OK
x.free;
```

What happens if you don't add rate checking to your UGens? Often it makes little difference, but ignoring rate checking can sometimes lead to unusual errors that are hard to trace. For example, a UGen that expects control-rate input is relatively safe, because it expects less input data than an audio-rate UGen—so if given audio-rate data, it simply ignores most of it. But in the reverse case, a UGen that expects audio-rate data but is given only control-rate data may read garbage input from memory that it shouldn't be reading.

Returning to the `Flanger` example created earlier, you may wish to add rate checking to that class. In fact, since the Flanger is a kind of filter, you might think it sensible to use the `checkSameRateAsFirstInput` approach, either directly or by modifying the class so that it subclasses `Filter` rather than `UGen`.

25.5   Writing the C++ Code

25.5.1   Build Environments: Xcode, scons . . .

UGen plug-ins are built just like any other C++ project. To make things easier for yourself as a developer, you can use and adapt 1 of the project files which are distributed along with SuperCollider's source code:

On *Mac*, the Xcode project file *Plugins.xcodeproj* is used to build the core set of SuperCollider plug-ins. It's relatively painless to add a new "target" to this project in order to build your own plug-ins—this is the approach used in the SuperCollider Help document "Writing Unit Generators," which has more details about the Xcode specifics.
On *Linux*, the scons project file *SConstruct* is used to build SuperCollider as a whole. You can edit this file using a text editor to add your plug-in's build instructions. Alternatively, the "sc3-plug-ins" SourceForge project provides an SConstruct file purely for building UGens—you may find it easier to start from that as a template.
On *Windows*, Visual Studio project files are provided to compile plug-ins, including a *UGEN_TEMPLATE_VCPROJ.vcprojtemplate* file which you can use as a basis.

You can, of course, use other build environments if you prefer.

25.5.2   When Your Code Will Be Called

The server (scsynth) will call your plug-in code at 4 distinct points:

When scsynth boots, it calls the plug-in's `load()` function, which primarily declares which UGens the plug-in can provide.
When a UGen is instantiated (i.e., when a synth starts playing), scsynth calls the UGen's *constructor* function to perform the setting up of the UGen.
To produce sound, scsynth calls each UGen's *calculation* function in turn, *once for every control period*. This is typically the function which does most of the interesting work in the UGen. Since it is called only once during a control period, this function must produce either a single control-rate value or a whole block's worth of audiorate values during 1 call. (Note: Demand UGens don't quite fit this description and will be covered later.)

When a synth is ended, some UGens may need to perform some tidying up, such as freeing memory. If so, these UGens provide a *destructor* function which is called at this point.

25.5.3   The C++ Code for a Basic UGen

The code in figure 25.1 shows the key elements we need to include in our Flanger plug-in code.

Here is what this code does:

First, the #include command calls the main header file for SuperCollider's plug-in interface, *SC_PlugIn.h*. This is sufficient to include enough SuperCollider infrastructure for most types of UGen. (For phase vocoder UGens, more may be needed, as described later.)

The static InterfaceTable pointer is a reference to a table of SuperCollider functions such as the ones used to register a new UGen.

We define a data structure (a "struct") which will hold any data we need to store during the operation of the UGen. This struct, which needs to be remembered or passed from 1 audio block to the next, must be stored here. Note that the struct inherits from the base struct Unit—this is necessary so that scsynth can correctly write information into the struct, such as the rate at which the unit is running.

We declare our UGen's functions, using the extern "C" specifier so that the scsynth executable is able to reference the functions using C linkage. In a given plug-in we are allowed to define 1 or more UGens. Each of these will have 1 constructor ("Ctor") function, 1 or more calculation ("next") functions, and optionally 1 destructor ("Dtor") function.

Our constructor function, Flanger_Ctor(), takes a pointer to a Flanger struct and must prepare the UGen for execution. It must do the following 3 things:

1. Initialize the Flanger struct's member variables appropriately. In this case we initialize the delaysize member to a value representing a 20-millisecond maximum delay, making use of the SAMPLERATE macro which the SuperCollider API provides to specify the sample rate for the UGen. For some of the other struct members, we wish to calculate the values based on an input to the UGen. We can do this using the IN0() macro, which grabs a single control-rate value from the specified input. Here, we use IN0(1)—remembering that numbering starts at 0, this corresponds to the second input, defined in the Flanger class file as "rate." These macros (and others) will be discussed later.

2. Tell scsynth what the calculation function will be for this instance of the UGen. The SETCALC macro stores a reference to the function in our unit's struct. In our example there's only 1 choice, so we simply call SETCALC(Flanger_next). It's possible

```
#include "SC_PlugIn.h"

static InterfaceTable *ft;

// the struct will hold data which we want to "pass" from one function to another
// e.g. from the constructor to the calc func,
// or from one call of the calc func to the next
struct Flanger : public Unit  {
    float rate, delaysize, fwdhop, readpos;
    int writepos;
};

// function declarations, exposed to C
extern "C" {
    void load(InterfaceTable *inTable);
    void Flanger_Ctor(Flanger *unit);
    void Flanger_next(Flanger *unit, int inNumSamples);
}


void Flanger_Ctor( Flanger *unit ) {

    // Here we must initialise state variables in the Flanger struct.
    unit->delaysize = SAMPLERATE * 0.02f; // Fixed 20ms max delay
    // Typically with reference to control-rate/scalar-rate inputs.
    float rate  = IN0(1);
    // Rather than using rate directly, we're going to calculate the size of
    // jumps we must make each time to scan through the delayline at "rate"
    float delta = (unit->delaysize * rate) / SAMPLERATE;
    unit->fwdhop = delta + 1.0f;
    unit->rate  = rate;

    // IMPORTANT: This tells scsynth the name of the calculation function
    // for this UGen.
    SETCALC(Flanger_next);

    // Should also calc 1 sample's worth of output -
    //ensures each ugen's "pipes" are "primed"
    Flanger_next(unit, 1);
}
```

Figure 25.1
C++ code for a Flanger UGen. This code doesn't add any effect to the sound yet, but contains the key elements required for all UGens.

```
void Flanger_next( Flanger *unit, int inNumSamples ) {

    float *in = IN(0);
    float *out = OUT(0);

    float depth = INO(2);

    float rate    = unit->rate;
    float fwdhop  = unit->fwdhop;
    float readpos = unit->readpos;
    int writepos  = unit->writepos;
    int delaysize = unit->delaysize;

    float val, delayed;

    for ( int i=0; i<inNumSamples; ++i) {
        val = in[i];

        // Do something to the signal before outputting
        // (not yet done)

        out[i] = val;
    }

    unit->writepos = writepos;
    unit->readpos = readpos;
}


void load(InterfaceTable *inTable) {

    ft = inTable;

    DefineSimpleUnit(Flanger);
}
```

Figure 25.1
(continued)

to define multiple calculation functions and allow the constructor to decide which one to use. This is covered later.

3. Calculate one sample's worth of output, typically by calling the unit's calculation function and asking it to process 1 sample. The purpose of this is to "prime" the inputs and outputs of all the unit generators in the graph and to ensure that the constructors for UGens farther down the chain have their input values available so they can initialize correctly.

Our calculation function, `Flanger_next()`, should perform the main audio processing. In this example it doesn't actually alter the sound — we'll get to that shortly — but it illustrates some important features of calculation functions. It takes 2 arguments passed in by the server: a pointer to the struct and an integer specifying how many values are to be processed (this will be 1 for control-rate, more for audio-rate — typically 64).

The last thing in our C++ file is the `load()` function, called when the scsynth executable boots up.

We store the reference to the interface table which is passed in — note that although you don't see any explicit references to `ft` elsewhere in the code, that's because they are hidden behind macros which make use of it to call functions in the server.

We must also declare to the server each of the UGens which our plug-in defines. This is done using a macro `DefineSimpleUnit(Flanger)`, which tells the server to register a UGen with the name *Flanger* and with a constructor function named *Flanger_Ctor*. It also tells the server that no destructor function is needed. If we did require a destructor, we would instead use `DefineDtorUnit(Flanger)`, which tells the server that we've also supplied a destructor function named *Flanger_Dtor*. You must name your constructor/destructor functions in this way, since the naming convention is hard-coded into the macros.

So what is happening inside our calculation function? Although in our example the input doesn't actually get altered before being output, the basic pattern for a typical calculation function is given. We do the following:

Create pointers to the input and output arrays which we will access: `float *in = IN(0); float *out = OUT(0);` The macros `IN()` and `OUT()` return appropriate pointers for the desired inputs/outputs — in this case the first input and the first output. If the input is audio-rate, then `in[0]` will refer to the first incoming sample, `in[1]` to the next incoming sample, and so on. If the input is control-rate, then there is only 1 incoming value, `in[0]`.

We use the macro `IN0()` again to grab a single control-rate value, here the "depth" input. Note that `IN0()` is actually a shortcut to the first value in the location referenced by `IN()`. `IN0(1)` is exactly the same as `IN(1)[0]`.

We copy some values from the UGen's struct into local variables. This can improve the efficiency of the unit, since the C++ optimizer will typically cause the values to be loaded into registers.

Next we loop over the number of input frames, each time taking an input value, processing it, and producing an output value. We could take values from multiple inputs, and even produce multiple outputs, but in this example we're using only 1 full-rate input and producing a single output. Two important notes:

If an input/output is control-rate and you mistakenly treat it as audio-rate, you will be reading/writing memory you should not be, and this can cause bizarre problems and crashes; essentially this is just the classic C/C++ "gotcha" of accidentally treating an array as being bigger than it really is. Note that in our example, we assume that the input and output are of the same size, although it's possible that they aren't—some UGens can take audio-rate input and produce control-rate output. This is why it is useful to make sure your SuperCollider class code includes the rate-checking code described earlier in this chapter. You can see why the `checkSameRateAsFirstInput` approach is useful in this case.

The server uses a "buffer coloring" algorithm to minimize use of buffers and to optimize cache performance. This means that any of the output buffers may be the same as 1 of the input buffers. This allows for in-place operation, which is very efficient. You must be careful, however, not to write any output sample before you have read the corresponding input sample. If you break this rule, then the input may be overwritten with output, leading to undesired behavior. If you can't write the UGen efficiently without breaking this rule, then you can instruct the server not to alias the buffers by using the `DefineSimpleCantAliasUnit()` or `DefineDtorCantAliasUnit()` macros in the `load()` function, rather than the `DefineSimpleUnit()` or `DefineDtorUnit()` macros. (The Help file on writing UGens provides an example in which this ordering is important.)

Finally, having produced our output, we may have modified some of the variables we loaded from the struct; we need to store them back to the struct so the updated values are used next time. Here we store the `rate` value back to the struct—although we don't modify it in this example, we will shortly change the code so that this may happen.

The code in figure 25.1 should compile correctly into a plug-in. With the class file in place and the plug-in compiled, you can now use the UGen in a synth graph:

```
s.boot
(
x = {
    var son, dly, out;
    son = Saw.ar([100, 150, 200]).mean;
    out = Flanger.ar(son);
```

```
    out.dup * 0.2;
}.play(s);
)
```

Remember that Flanger doesn't currently add any effect to the sound. But we can at least check that it runs correctly (outputting its input unmodified and undistorted) before we start to make things interesting.

25.5.4   Summary: The Three Main Rates of Data Output

Our example has taken input in 3 different ways:

Using `INO()` in the constructor to take an input value and store it to the struct for later use. Since this reads a value only once, the input is being treated as a *scalar-rate* input.

Using `INO()` in the calculation function to take a single input value. This treats the input as *control-rate*.

Using `IN()` in the calculation function to get a pointer to the whole array of inputs. This treats the input as *audio-rate*. Typically the size of such an input array is accessed using the `inNumSamples` argument, but note that if you create a control-rate UGen with audio-rate inputs, then `inNumSamples` will be wrong (it will be 1), so you should instead use the macro `FULLBUFLENGTH` (see table 25.2).

If the data that one of your UGen's inputs is fed is actually audio-rate, there is no danger in treating it as control-rate or scalar-rate. The end result is to ignore the "extra" data provided to your UGen. Similarly, a control-rate input can safely be treated as scalar-rate. The result would be crude downsampling without low-pass filtering, which may be undesirable but will not crash the server.

25.5.5   Allocating Memory and Using a Destructor

Next we can develop our Flanger example so that it applies an effect to the sound. In order to create a flanging effect, we need a short delay line (around 20 milliseconds). We vary the amount of delay and mix the delayed sound with the input to produce the effect.

To create a delay line, we need to allocate some memory and store a reference to that memory in the UGen's data structure. And, of course, we need to free this memory when the UGen is freed. This requires a UGen with a destructor. Figure 25.2 shows the full code, with the destructor added, as well as the code to allocate, free, and use the memory. Note the change in the `load()` function—we use `DefineDtorUnit()` rather than `DefineSimpleUnit()`. (We've also added code to the calculation function which reads and writes to the delay line, creating the flanging effect.)

```
#include "SC_PlugIn.h"

static InterfaceTable *ft;

// the struct will hold data which we want to "pass" from one function to another
// e.g. from the constructor to the calc func,
// or from one call of the calc func to the next
struct Flanger : public Unit  {
    float rate, delaysize, fwdhop, readpos;
    int writepos;

    // a pointer to the memory we'll use for our internal delay
    float *delayline;
};

// function declarations, exposed to C
extern "C" {
    void load(InterfaceTable *inTable);
    void Flanger_Ctor(Flanger *unit);
    void Flanger_next(Flanger *unit, int inNumSamples);
    void Flanger_Dtor(Flanger *unit);
}


void Flanger_Ctor( Flanger *unit ) {

    // Here we must initialise state variables in the Flanger struct.
    unit->delaysize = SAMPLERATE * 0.02f; // Fixed 20ms max delay
    // Typically with reference to control-rate/scalar-rate inputs.
    float rate  = IN0(1);
    // Rather than using rate directly, we're going to calculate the size of
    // jumps we must make each time to scan through the delayline at "rate"
    float delta = (unit->delaysize * rate) / SAMPLERATE;
    unit->fwdhop = delta + 1.0f;
    unit->rate = rate;
    unit->writepos = 0;
    unit->readpos = 0;

    // Allocate the delay line
    unit->delayline = (float*)RTAlloc(unit->mWorld, unit->delaysize *
sizeof(float));
    // Initialise it to zeroes
```

Figure 25.2
Completed C++ code for the Flanger UGen.

```
        memset(unit->delayline, 0, unit->delaysize * sizeof(float));

        // IMPORTANT: This tells scsynth the name of the calculation function
        //for this UGen.
        SETCALC(Flanger_next);

        // Should also calc 1 sample's worth of output -
        //ensures each ugen's "pipes" are "primed"
        Flanger_next(unit, 1);
}

void Flanger_next( Flanger *unit, int inNumSamples ) {

        float *in = IN(0);
        float *out = OUT(0);

        float depth = IN0(2);

        float rate     = unit->rate;
        float fwdhop   = unit->fwdhop;
        float readpos  = unit->readpos;
        float *delayline = unit->delayline;
        int writepos   = unit->writepos;
        int delaysize  = unit->delaysize;

        float val, delayed, currate;

        currate = IN0(1);

        if(rate != currate){
            // rate input needs updating
            rate = currate;
            fwdhop = ((delaysize * rate * 2) / SAMPLERATE) + 1.0f;
        }

        for ( int i=0; i<inNumSamples; ++i) {
            val = in[i];

            // Write to the delay line
            delayline[writepos++] = val;
            if(writepos==delaysize)
                writepos = 0;
```

Figure 25.2
(continued)

```
            // Read from the delay line
            delayed = delayline[(int)readpos];
            readpos += fwdhop;
            // Update position, NB we may be moving forwards or backwards
            //(depending on input)
            while((int)readpos >= delaysize)
                readpos -= delaysize;
            while((int)readpos < 0)
                readpos += delaysize;

            // Mix dry and wet together, and output them
            out[i] = val + (delayed * depth);
        }

    unit->rate = rate;
    unit->fwdhop = fwdhop;
    unit->writepos = writepos;
    unit->readpos = readpos;
}

void Flanger_Dtor( Flanger *unit ) {
    RTFree(unit->mWorld, unit->delayline);
}

void load(InterfaceTable *inTable) {

    ft = inTable;

    DefineDtorUnit(Flanger);
}
```

Figure 25.2
(continued)

Table 25.1
Memory Allocation and Freeing

Typical C Allocation/Freeing	In SuperCollider (using the real-time pool)
`void *ptr = malloc(numbytes)` `free(ptr)`	`void *ptr = RTAlloc(unit->mWorld, numbytes)` `RTFree(unit->mWorld, ptr)`

SuperCollider UGens allocate memory differently from most programs. Ordinary memory allocation and freeing can be a relatively expensive operation, so SuperCollider provides a *real-time pool* of memory from which UGens can borrow chunks in an efficient manner. The functions to use in a plug-in are in the right-hand column of table 25.1, and the analogous functions (the ones to avoid) are shown in the left-hand column.

`RTAlloc` and `RTFree` can be called anywhere in your constructor/calculation/ destructor functions. Often you will `RTAlloc` the memory during the constructor and `RTFree` it during the destructor, as is done in figure 25.2.

Memory allocated in this way is taken from the (limited) real-time pool and is not accessible outside the UGen (e.g., to client-side processes). If you require large amounts of memory or wish to access the data from the client, you may prefer to use a buffer allocated and then passed in from outside — this is described later.

25.5.6   Providing More Than 1 Calculation Function

Your UGen's choice of calculation function is specified within the constructor rather than being fixed. This gives an opportunity to provide different functions optimized for different situations (e.g., 1 for control-rate and 1 for audio-rate input) and to decide which to use. This code, used in the constructor, would choose between 2 calculation functions according to whether the first input was audio-rate or not:

```
if (INRATE(0) == calc_FullRate) {
    SETCALC(Flanger_next_a);
} else {
    SETCALC(Flanger_next_k);
}
```

You would then provide both a `Flanger_next_a()` and a `Flanger_next_k()` function.

Similarly, you could specify different calculation functions for audio-rate versus control-rate *output* (e.g., by testing whether BUFLENGTH is 1; see table 25.2), although this is often catered for automatically when your calculation function uses the `inNumSamples` argument to control the number of loops performed, and so on.

Table 25.2
Useful Macros for UGen Writers

Macro	Description
IN(index)	A float* pointer to input number *index*
OUT(index)	A float* pointer to output number *index*
IN0(index)	A single (control-rate) value from input number *index*
OUT0(index)	A single (control-rate) value at output number *index*
INRATE(index)	The rate of input *index*, an integer value corresponding to 1 of the following constants: calc_ScalarRate (scalar-rate) calc_BufRate (control-rate) calc_FullRate (audio-rate) calc_DemandRate (demand-rate)
SETCALC(func)	Set the calculation function to *func*
SAMPLERATE	The sample rate of the UGen as a double. Note: for control-rate UGens this is not the full audio rate but audio rate/blocksize)
SAMPLEDUR	Reciprocal of SAMPLERATE (seconds per sample)
BUFLENGTH	Equal to the block size if the unit is audio rate and to 1 if the unit is control rate
BUFRATE	The control rate as a double
BUFDUR	The reciprocal of BUFRATE
GETBUF	Treats the UGen's first input as a reference to a buffer; looks this buffer up in the server, and provides variables for accessing it, including float* bufData, which points to the data; uint32 bufFrames for how many frames the buffer contains; uint32 bufChannels for the number of channels in the buffer
ClearUnitOutputs(unit, inNumSamples)	A function which sets all the unit's outputs to 0
Print(fmt, ...)	Print text to the SuperCollider post window; arguments are just like those for the C function printf
DoneAction(doneAction, unit)	Perform a "doneAction," as used in EnvGen, DetectSilence, and others
RTAlloc(world, numBytes)	Allocate memory from the real-time pool—analogous to malloc(numBytes)
RTRealloc(world, pointer, numBytes)	Reallocate memory in the real-time pool—analogous to realloc(pointer, numBytes)

Table 25.2
(continued)

Macro	Description
RTFree(world, pointer)	Free allocated memory back to the real-time pool—analogous to free(pointer)
SendTrigger(node, triggerID, value)	Send a trigger from the node to clients, with integer ID, *triggered,* and float value *value*
FULLRATE	The full audio sample rate of the server (irrespective of the rate of the UGen) as a double
FULLBUFLENGTH	The integer number of samples in an audio-rate input (irrespective of the rate of the UGen)

The unit's calculation function can also be changed during execution—the SETCALC() macro can safely be called from a calculation function, not just from the constructor. Whenever you call SETCALC(), this changes which function the server will call, from the next control period onward.

The Help file on writing UGens shows more examples of SETCALC() in use.

25.5.7   Trigger Inputs

Many UGens make use of trigger inputs. The convention here is that if the input is nonpositive (i.e., 0 or negative), then crosses to any positive value, a trigger has occurred. If you wish to provide trigger inputs, use this same convention.

The change from nonpositive to positive requires checking the trigger input's value against its previous value. This means that our struct will need a member to store the previous value for checking. Assuming that our struct contains a float member prevtrig, the following sketch outlines how we handle the incoming data in our calculation function:

```
float trig = IN0(3); // Or whichever input you wish
float prevtrig = unit->prevtrig;
if(prevtrig<=0 && trig >0){
    // ... do something ...
}
unit->prevtrig = trig; // Store current value—next time it'll be the
"previous" value
```

The sketch is for a control-rate trigger input, but a similar approach is used for audio-rate triggering, too. For audio-rate triggering, you need to compare each value in the input block against the value immediately previous. Note that for the very first value in the block, you need to compare against the last value from the *previous* block (which you must have stored).

For complete code examples, look at the source of the Trig1 UGen, found in *TriggerUGens.cpp* in the main SC distribution.

25.5.8   Accessing a Buffer

When a buffer is allocated and then passed in to a UGen, the UGen receives the index number of that buffer as a float value. In order to get a pointer to the correct chunk of memory (as well as the size of that chunk), the UGen must look it up in the server's list of buffers.

In practice this is most easily achieved by using a macro called GET_BUF. You can call GET_BUF near the top of your calculation function, and then the data are available via a float pointer *bufData along with 2 integers defining the size of the buffer, bufChannels and bufFrames. Note that the macro assumes the buffer index is the *first* input to the UGen (this is the case for most buffer-using UGens).

For examples which use this approach, look at the code for the DiskIn or DiskOut UGens, defined in *DiskIO_UGens.cpp* in the main SC distribution.

Your UGen does not need to free the memory associated with a buffer once it ends. The memory is managed externally by the buffer allocation/freeing server commands.

25.5.9   Randomness

The API provides a convenient interface for accessing good-quality pseudo-random numbers. The randomness API is specified in *SC_RGen.h* and provides functions for random numbers from standard types of distribution: uniform, exponential, bilinear, and quasi-Gaussian (such as sum3rand, also available client-side). The server creates an instance of the random number generator for UGens to access. The following excerpt shows how to generate random numbers for use in your code:

```
RGen & rgen = *unit->mParent->mRGen;
float rfl = rgen.frand(); // A random float, uniformly distributed, 0.0 to
1.0
int rval2 = rgen.irand(56); // A random integer, uniformly distributed, 0
to 55 inclusive
float rgaus = rgen.sum3rand(3.5); // Quasi-Gaussian, limited to range ±3.5
```

25.5.10   When Your UGen Has No More to Do

Many UGens carry on indefinitely, but often a UGen reaches the end of its useful "life" (e.g., it finishes outputting an envelope or playing a buffer). There are 3 specific behaviors that might be appropriate if your UGen does reach a natural end:

1. Some UGens set a "done" flag to indicate that they've finished. Other UGens can monitor this and act in response to it (e.g., Done, FreeSelfWhenDone). See the Help files for examples of these UGens. If you wish your UGen to indicate that it has finished, set the flag as follows:

```
unit->mDone = true;
```

This doesn't affect how the server treats the UGen — the calculation function will still be called in future.

2. UGens such as EnvGen, Linen, Duty, and Line provide a "doneAction" feature which can perform actions such as freeing the node once the UGen has reached the end of its functionality. You can implement this yourself simply by calling the DoneAction() macro, which performs the desired action. You would typically allow the user to specify the doneAction as an input to the unit. For example, if the doneAction is the sixth input to your UGen, you would call

```
DoneAction(IN0(5), unit)
```

Since this can perform behaviors such as freeing the node, many UGens stop calculating/outputting after they reach the point of calling this macro. See, for example, the source code for DetectSilence, which sets its calculation function to a no-op DetectSilence_done function at the point where it calls DoneAction. Not all doneActions free the synth, though, so additional output is not always redundant.

3. If you wish to output zeroes from all outputs of your unit, you can simply call the ClearUnitOutputs function as follows:

```
ClearUnitOutputs(unit, inNumSamples);
```

Notice that this function has the same signature as a calculation function: as arguments it takes a pointer to the unit struct and an integer number of samples. You can take advantage of this similarity to provide an efficient way to stop producing output:

```
SETCALC(*ClearUnitOutputs);
```

Calling this would mean that your calculation function would not be called in future iterations. Instead, ClearUnitOutputs would be called. Therefore this provides an irreversible but efficient way for your UGen to produce silent output for the remainder of the synth's execution.

25.5.11   Summary of Useful Macros

Table 25.2 summarized some of the most generally useful macros defined for use in your UGen code. Many of these are discussed in this chapter, but not all are covered explicitly. The macros are defined in *SC_Unit.h* and *SC_InterfaceTable.h*.

25.6   Specialized Types of UGen

25.6.1   Multiple-Output UGens

In the C++ code, writing UGens which produce multiple outputs is very straightforward. The OUT() macro gets a pointer to the desired-numbered output. Thus, for a 3-output UGen, assign each one (OUT(0), OUT(1), OUT(2)) to a variable, then write output to these 3 pointers.

In the SuperCollider class code, the default is to assume a single output, and we need to modify this behavior. Let's look at the Pitch UGen to see how it's done:

```
Pitch : MultiOutUGen {

    *kr {arg in = 0.0, initFreq = 440.0, minFreq = 60.0, maxFreq = 4000.0,
        execFreq = 100.0, maxBinsPerOctave = 16, median = 1,
        ampThreshold = 0.01, peakThreshold = 0.5, downSample = 1;
    ^this.multiNew('control', in, initFreq, minFreq, maxFreq, execFreq,
        maxBinsPerOctave, median, ampThreshold, peakThreshold, downSample)
    }
    init {arg ... theInputs;
        inputs = theInputs;
        ^this.initOutputs(2, rate);
    }
}
```

There are 2 differences from an ordinary UGen. First, Pitch is a subclass of MultiOutUGen rather than of UGen; MultiOutUGen takes care of some of the changes needed to work with a UGen with multiple outputs. Second, the init function is overridden to say exactly how many outputs this UGen will provide (in this case, 2).

For Pitch, the number of outputs is fixed, but in some cases it might depend on other factors. PlayBuf is a good example of this: its number of outputs depends on the number of channels in the buffer(s) it is expecting to play, specified using the numChannels argument. The init method for PlayBuf takes the numChannels input (i.e., the first value from the list of inputs passed to init) and specifies that as the number of outputs.

25.6.2   Passing Arrays into UGens

25.6.2.1   The class file

As described earlier, the multiNew method automatically performs multichannel expansion if any of the inputs are arrays—yet in some cases we want a single unit to handle a whole array, rather than having 1 unit per array element. The BufWr and RecordBuf UGens are good examples of UGens that do exactly this: each UGen can take an array of inputs and write them to a multichannel buffer. Here's how the class file handles this:

```
RecordBuf : UGen {
    *ar {arg inputArray, bufnum = 0, offset = 0.0, recLevel = 1.0,
    preLevel = 0.0, run = 1.0, loop = 1.0, trigger = 1.0;
        ^this.multiNewList(['audio', bufnum, offset, recLevel, preLevel,
        run, loop, trigger] ++ inputArray.asArray);
    }
}
```

Instead of calling the UGen method multiNew, we call multiNewList, which is the same except that all the arguments are a single array rather than a separated argument list. This means that the inputArray argument (which could be either a single unit or an array), when concatenated onto the end of the argument list using the ++ array concatenation operator, in essence appears as a set of *separate* input arguments rather than a single array argument.

Note that RecordBuf doesn't know in advance what size the input array is going to be. Because of the array flattening that we perform, this means that the RecordBuf C++ plug-in receives a *variable number of inputs* each time it is instantiated. Our plug-in code will be able to detect how many inputs it receives in a given instance.

Why do we put inputArray at the *end* of the argument list? Why not at the beginning, in parallel with how a user invokes the RecordBuf UGen? The reason is to make things simpler for the C++ code, which will access the plug-in inputs according to their numerical position in the list. The recLevel input, for example, is always the third input, whereas if we inserted inputArray into the list before it, its position would depend on the size of inputArray.

The Poll UGen uses a very similar procedure, converting a string of text into an array of ASCII characters and appending them to the end of its argument list. However, the Poll class code must perform some other manipulations, so it is perhaps less clear as a code example than RecordBuf. But if you are developing a UGen that needs to pass text data to the plug-in, Poll shows how to do it using this array approach.

25.6.2.2 The C++ code

Ordinarily we access input data using the IN() or IN0() macro, specifying the number of the input we want to access. Arrays are passed into the UGen as a separate numeric input for each array element, so we access these elements in exactly the same way. But we need to know how many items to expect, since the array can be of variable size.

The Unit struct can tell us how many inputs in total are being provided (the member unit->mNumInputs. Look again at the RecordBuf class code given above. There are 7 "ordinary" inputs, plus the array appended to the end. Thus the number of channels in our input array is (unit->mNumInputs - 7). We use this information to iterate over the correct number of inputs and process each element.

25.6.3   Demand-Rate UGens

25.6.3.1   The class file
Writing the class file for a demand-rate UGen is straightforward. Look at the code for units such as Dseries, Dgeom, or Dwhite as examples. They differ from other UGen class files in 2 ways:

1. The first argument to multiNew (or multiNewList) is 'demand'.
2. They implement a single class method, *new, rather than *ar/*kr/*ir. This is because although some UGens may be able to run at multiple rates (e.g., audio rate or control rate), a demand-rate UGen can run at only 1 rate: the rate at which data are demanded of it.

25.6.3.2   The C++ code
The C++ code for a demand-rate UGen works as normal, with the constructor specifying the calculation function. However, the calculation function behaves slightly differently.

First, it is not called regularly (once per control period) but only when demanded, which during a particular control period could be more than once or not at all. This means that you can't make assumptions about regular timing, such as the assumptions made in an oscillator which increments its phase by a set amount each time it is called.

Second, rather than being invoked directly by the server, the calculation function calls are actually passed up the chain of demand-rate generators. Rather than using the IN() or IN0() macros to access an input value (whose generation will have been coordinated by the server), we instead use the DEMANDINPUT() macro, which requests a new value directly from the unit farther up the chain, "on demand."

Note: because of the method used to demand the data, demand-rate UGens are currently restricted to being single-output.

25.6.4   Phase Vocoder UGens

Phase vocoder UGens operate on frequency-domain data stored in a buffer (produced by the FFT UGen). They don't operate at a special "rate" of their own: in reality they are control-rate UGens. They produce and consume a control-rate signal which acts as a type of trigger: when an FFT frame is ready for processing, its value is the appropriate buffer index; otherwise, its value is −1. This signal is often referred to as the "chain" in SC documentation.

25.6.4.1   The class file

As with demand-rate UGens, phase vocoder UGens (PV UGens) can have only a single rate of operation: the rate at which FFT frames are arriving. Therefore, PV UGens implement only a single *new class method, and they specify their rate as "control" in the call to `multiNew`. See the class files for `PV_MagMul` and `PV_BrickWall` as examples of this.

PV UGens process data stored in buffers, and the C++ API provides some useful macros to help with this. The macros assume that the *first* input to the UGen is the one carrying the FFT chain where data will be read and then written, so it is sensible to stick with this convention.

25.6.4.2   The C++ code

PV UGens are structured just like any other UGen, except that to access the frequency-domain data held in the external buffer, there are certain macros and procedures to use. Any of the core UGens implemented in *PV_UGens.cpp* should serve as a good example to base your own UGens on. Your code should include the header file *FFT_UGens.h*, which defines some PV-specific structs and macros.

Two important macros are `PV_GET_BUF` and `PV_GET_BUF2`, one of which you use at the beginning of your calculation function to obtain the FFT data from the buffer. These macros implement the special PV UGen behavior: if the FFT chain has "fired," then they access the buffer(s) and continue with the rest of the calculation function; but if the FFT chain has not "fired" in the current control block, then they output a value of −1 and *return* (i.e., they do not allow the rest of the calculation function to proceed). This has the important consequence that although your calculation function code will look "as if" it is called once per control block, in fact your code will be executed only at the FFT frame rate.

`PV_GET_BUF` will take the FFT chain indicated by the *first* input to the UGen and create a pointer to these data called `*buf`.

`PV_GET_BUF2` is for use in UGens which process 2 FFT chains and write the result back out to the first chain: it takes the FFT chain indicated by the *first* and *second* inputs to the UGen and creates pointers to the data called `*buf1` and `*buf2`.

It should be clear that you use `PV_GET_BUF` or `PV_GET_BUF2`, but not both.

Having acquired a pointer to the data, you will of course wish to read/write that data. Before doing so, you must decide whether to process the complex-valued data as polar coordinates or Cartesian coordinates. The data in the buffer may be in either format (depending on what has happened to it so far). To access the data as Cartesian values you use

```
SCComplexBuf *p = ToComplexApx(buf);
```

and to access the data as polar values you use

```
SCPolarBuf *p = ToPolarApx(buf);
```

These 2 data structures, and the 2 functions for obtaining them, are declared in *FFT_UGens.h*. The name p for the pointer is of course arbitrary, but it's what we'll use here.

FFT data consist of a complex value for each frequency bin, with the number of bins related to the number of samples in the input. But in the SuperCollider context the input is real-valued data, which means that (a) the bins above the Nyquist frequency (which is half the sampling frequency) are a mirror image of the bins below, and can therefore be neglected; and (b) phase is irrelevant for the DC and Nyquist frequency bins, so these 2 bins can be represented by a single-magnitude value rather than a complex value.

The end result of this is that we obtain a data structure containing a single DC value, a single Nyquist value, and a series of complex values for all the bins in between. The number of bins in between is given by the value numbins, which is provided for us by PV_GET_BUF or PV_GET_BUF2. The data in a Cartesian-type struct (an SCComplexBuf) are of the form

```
p->dc
p->bin[0].real
p->bin[0].imag
p->bin[1].real
p->bin[1].imag
...
p->bin[numbins - 1].real
p->bin[numbins - 1].imag
p->nyq
```

The data in a polar-type struct (an SCPolarBuf) is of the form

```
p->dc
p->bin[0].mag
p->bin[0].phase
p->bin[1].mag
p->bin[1].phase
...
p->bin[numbins - 1].mag
p->bin[numbins - 1].phase
p->nyq
```

Note that the indexing is slightly strange: engineers commonly refer to the DC component as the "first" bin in the frequency-domain data. However in these structs, because the DC component is represented differently, bin[0] is actually the first non-DC bin—what would sometimes be referred to as the second bin. Similarly, keep in mind that numbins represents the number of bins *not including* the DC or Nyquist bins.

To perform a phase vocoder manipulation, simply read and write to the struct (which actually is directly in the external buffer). The buffer will then be passed down the chain to the next phase vocoder UGen. You don't need to do anything extra to "output" the frequency-domain data.

When compiling your PV UGen, you will need to compile/link against *SCComplex .cpp* from the main SuperCollider source, which provides the implementation of these frequency-domain data manipulations.

25.7   Practicalities

25.7.1   Debugging

Standard C++ debugging procedures can be used when developing UGens. The simplest method is to add a line into your code which prints out values of variables—you can use the standard C++ printf() method, which in a UGen will print text to the post window.

For more power, you can launch the server process, then attach a debugger such as *gdb* (the GNU debugger) or Xcode's debugger (which is actually gdb with a graphical interface) to perform tasks such as pausing the process and inspecting values of variables. On Mac, if you use the debugger to launch SuperCollider.app, remember that the local server runs in a process different from the application. You can either launch the application using the debugger and booting the internal server, or you can launch just the server (scsynth) using the debugger, which then runs as a local server. In the latter case you need to ensure your debugger launches scsynth with the correct arguments (e.g., "-u 57110").

When debugging a UGen that causes server crashes, you may wish to look at your system's crash log for scsynth. The most common cause of crashes is introduced when using RTAlloc and RTFree—if you try to RTFree something that has not yet been RTAlloc'ed, or otherwise is not a pointer to the real-time memory pool, this can cause bad-access exceptions to appear in the crash log. If the crash log seems to reveal that your UGen is somehow causing crashes inside core UGens which normally behave perfectly, then check that your code does not write data outside of the expected limits: make sure you RTAlloc the right amount of space for what you're doing (for example, with arrays, check exactly which indices your code attempts to access).

25.7.2 Optimization

Optimizing code is a vast topic and often depends on the specifics of the code in question. However, we can suggest some optimization tips for writing SuperCollider UGens. The efficiency/speed of execution is usually the number-one priority, especially since a user may wish to employ many instances of the UGen simultaneously. The difference between a UGen that takes 2.5% and another that takes 1.5% CPU may seem small, but the first limits you to 40 simultaneous instances, while the second will allow up to 66; a 65% increase. Imagine doing your next live performance on a 4-year-old processor — that's essentially the effect of the less efficient code.

Avoid calls to "expensive" procedures whenever possible. For example, *floating-point division* is typically much more expensive than multiplication, so if your unit must divide values by some constant value which is stored in your struct, rewrite this so that the *reciprocal* of that value is stored in the struct and you can perform a multiplication rather than a division. If you want to find an integer power of 2, use bit shifting (1 << n) rather than the expensive math function (pow(2, n)). Other expensive floating-point operations are *square-root* finding and *trigonometric* operations (sin, cos, tan, etc.). *Precalculate* and store such values wherever possible, rather than calculating them afresh every time the calculation function is called.

As a typical example, often a filter UGen will take a user parameter (such as cutoff frequency) and use it to derive internal filter coefficients. If you store the previous value of the user parameter and use this to check whether it has changed at all — updating the coefficients only upon a change — you can improve efficiency, since often UGens are used with fixed or rarely changing parameters.

One of the most important SuperCollider-specific choices is, for reading a certain input or even performing a given calculation, whether to do this at *scalar/control/audio rate*. It can be helpful to allow any and all values to be updated at audio rate, but if you find that a certain update procedure is expensive and won't usually be required to run at audio rate, it may be preferable to update only once during a calculation function.

Creating *multiple calculation functions*, each appropriate to a certain context (e.g., to a certain combination of input rates, as demonstrated earlier), and choosing the most appropriate, can allow a lot of optimization. For example, a purely control-rate calculation can avoid the looping required for audio-rate calculation and typically produces a much simpler calculation as a result. There is a maintenance overhead in providing these alternatives, but the efficiency gains can be large. In this tension between efficiency and code comprehensibility/reusability, you should remember the importance of adding comments to your code to clarify the flow and the design decisions you have made.

In your calculation function, store values from your struct as well as input/output pointers/values as *local variables*, especially if referring to them multiple times. This avoids the overhead of indirection and can be optimized (by the compiler) to use registers better.

Avoid `DefineSimpleCantAliasUnit` *and* `DefineDtorCantAliasUnit`. As described earlier, `DefineSimpleCantAliasUnit` is available as an alternative to `DefineSimpleUnit` in cases where your UGen must write output before it has read from the inputs, but this can decrease cache performance.

Avoid peaky CPU usage. A calculation function that does nothing for the first 99 times it's called, then performs a mass of calculations on the 100th call, could cause *audio dropouts* if this spike is very large. To avoid this, "amortize" your unit's effort by spreading the calculation out, if possible, by precalculating some values which are going to be used in that big 100th call.

On Mac, Apple's vDSP library can improve speed by vectorizing certain calculations. If you make use of this, or other platform-specific libraries, remember the considerations of platform independence. For example, use preprocessor instructions to choose between the Mac-specific code and ordinary C++ code:

```
#if SC_DARWIN
// The Mac-specific version of the code (including, e.g., vDSP functions)
#else
// The generic version of the code
#endif
```

`SC_DARWIN` is a preprocessor value set to 1 when compiling SuperCollider on Mac (this is set in the Xcode project settings). Branching like this introduces a maintenance overhead, because you need to make sure that you update both branches in parallel.

25.7.3 Distributing Your UGens

Sharing UGens with others contributes to the SuperCollider community and is a very cool thing to do. A SourceForge project, "sc3-plug-ins," exists as a repository for downloadable UGen plug-ins produced by various people. You may wish to publish your work either there or separately.

Remember that SuperCollider is licensed under the well-known GPL (GNU Public License) open-source license, including the plug-in API. So if you wish to distribute your plug-ins to the world, they must also be GPL-licensed. (Note: you retain copyright in any code you have written. You do not have to sign away your copyright in order to GPL-license a piece of code.) Practically, this has a couple of implications:

• You should include a copyright notice, a copy of the GPL license text, and the source code with your distributed plug-in.
• If your plug-in makes use of third-party libraries, those libraries must be available under a "GPL-compatible" copyright license. See the GNU GPL Web site for further discussion of what this means.

25.8   Conclusion

This chapter doesn't offer an exhaustive list of all that's possible, but it provides you with the core of what all UGen programmers need to know. If you want to delve deeper, you will find the online community to be a valuable resource for answers to questions not covered here; and the source code for existing UGens provides a wealth of useful code examples.

The open-source nature of SuperCollider makes for a vibrant online developer community. Whether you are tweaking 1 of SuperCollider's core UGens or developing something very specialized, you'll find the exchange of ideas with SuperCollider developers can be rewarding for your own projects as well as for others and can feed into the ongoing development of SuperCollider as a uniquely powerful and flexible synthesis system.

26   Inside scsynth

Ross Bencina

This chapter explores the implementation internals of scsynth, the server process of SuperCollider 3, which is written in C++. This chapter is intended to be useful to people who are interested in modifying or maintaining the scsynth source code and also to those who are interested in learning about the structure and implementation details of one of the great milestones in computer music software. By the time you've finished this chapter, you should have improved your understanding of how scsynth does what it does and also have gained some insight into why it is written the way it is. In this chapter sometimes we'll simply refer to scsynth as "the server." "The client" usually refers to sclang or any other program sending OSC commands to the server. Although the text focuses on the server's real-time operating mode, the information presented here is equally relevant to understanding scsynth's non-real-time mode. As always, the source code is the definitive reference and provides many interesting details which space limitations didn't allow to be included here.

Wherever possible, the data, structure, and function names used in this chapter match those in the scsynth source code. However, at the time of writing there was some inconsistency in class and structure naming. Sometimes you may find that the source file, the class name, or both may have an SC_ prefix. I have omitted such prefixes from class and function names for consistency.

Also note that I have chosen to emphasize an object-oriented interpretation of scsynth using UML diagrams to illuminate the code structure, as I believe scsynth is fundamentally object-oriented, if not in an idiomatically C++ way. In many cases structs from the source code appear as classes in the diagrams. Where appropriate, I have taken the liberty to interpret inheritance where a base struct is included as the first member of a derived struct. However, I have resisted the urge to translate any other constructs (such as the psuedo member functions mentioned below). All other references to names appear here as they do in the source code.

Now that formalities are completed, in the next section we set out on our journey through the scsynth implementation with a discussion of scsynth's coding style. Following that, we consider the structure of the code which implements what I call the scsynth domain model: Nodes, Groups, Graphs, GraphDefs, and their supporting infrastructure. We then go on to consider how the domain model implementation communicates with the outside world; we consider threading, interthread communications using queues, and how scsynth fulfills real-time performance constraints while executing all of the dynamic behavior offered by the domain model. The final section briefly highlights some of the fine-grained details which make scsynth one of the most efficient software synthesizers on the planet. scsynth is a fantastically elegant and interesting piece of software; I hope you get as much out of reading this chapter as I did in writing it!

26.1   Some Notes on scsynth Coding Style

scsynth is coded in C++, but for the most part uses a "C++ as a better C" coding style. Most data structures are declared as plain old C structs, especially those which are accessible to unit plug-ins. Functions which in idiomatic C++ might be considered member functions are typically global functions in scsynth. These are declared with names of the form `StructType_MemberFunctionName( StructType *s[, ...] )`, where the first parameter is a pointer to the struct being operated on (the "this" pointer in a C++ class). Memory allocation is performed with custom allocators or with `malloc()`, `free()`, and friends. Function pointers are often used instead of virtual functions. A number of cases of what can be considered inheritance are implemented by placing an instance of the base class (or struct) as the first member of the derived struct. There is very little explicit encapsulation of data using getter/setter methods.

There are a number of pragmatic reasons to adopt this style of coding. Probably the most significant is the lack of an Application Binary Interface (ABI) for C++, which makes dynamically linking with plug-ins using C++ interfaces compiler-version-specific. The avoidance of C++ constructs also has the benefit of making all code operations visible, in turn making it easier to understand and predict the performance and real-time behavior of the code.

The separation of data from operations and the explicit representation of operations as data-using function pointers promotes a style of programming in which types are composed by parameterizing structs by function pointers and auxilliary data. The use of structs instead of C++ classes makes it less complicated to place objects into raw memory. Reusing a small number of data structures for many purposes eases the burden on memory allocation by ensuring that dynamic objects belong to only a small number of size classes. Finally, being able to switch function pointers at runtime is a very powerful idiom which enables numerous optimizations, as will be seen later.

26.2   The scsynth Domain Model

At the heart of scsynth is a powerful yet simple domain model which manages dynamic allocation and evaluation of unit generator graphs in real time. Graphs can be grouped into arbitrary trees whose execution and evaluation order can be dynamically modified (McCartney, 2000). In this section we explain the main behaviors and relationships between entities in the domain model. The model is presented without concern for how client communication is managed or how the system is executed within real-time constraints. These concerns are addressed in later sections.

Figure 26.1 shows an implementation-level view of the significant domain entities in scsynth. Each class shown on the diagram is a C++ class or struct in the scsynth source code. SC users will recognize the concepts modeled by many of these classes. Interested readers are advised to consult the "ServerArchitecture" section of the Help files for further information about the roles of these classes and the exact operations which can be performed by them.

`World` is the top-level class which (with the exception of a few global objects) aggregates and manages the run-time data in the server. It is created by `World_New()` when scsynth starts up. An instance of `WorldOptions` is passed to `World_New()`. It stores the configuration parameters, which are usually passed to scsynth on the command line.

scsynth's main task is to synthesize and process sound. It does this by evaluating a tree of dynamically allocated `Node` instances (near middle-left of figure 26.1), each of which provides its own `NodeCalcFunc` function pointer, which is called by the server to evaluate the Node at the current time step. `Node::mID` is an integer used by clients to identify specific Nodes in server commands (such as suspending or terminating the Node, or changing its location in the tree).

There are 2 subtypes of `Node`: `Graph` and `Group`. `Graph` is so named because it executes an optimized graph of UGens. It can be likened to a voice in a synthesizer or an "instrument" in a *Music N*-type audio synthesis language such as Csound. The `Graph` type implements the SuperCollider concept of a *Synth*. `Group` is simply a container for a linked list of `Node` instances, and since `Group` is itself a type of `Node`, arbitrary trees may be constructed containing any combination of `Group` and `Graph` instances; readers may recognize this as the *Composite* design pattern (Gamma et al., 1995). The standard `NodeCalcFunc` for a Group (`Group_Calc()` in `SC_Group.cpp`) simply iterates through the Group's contained Nodes, calling each Node's `NodeCalcFunc` in turn. Although most code deals with Nodes polymorphically, the `Node::mIsGroup` field supports discriminating between Nodes of type `Graph` and of `Group` at runtime. Any node can be temporarily disabled using the `/n_run` server command, which switches NodeCalcFuncs. When a Node is switched off, a `NodeCalcFunc` which does

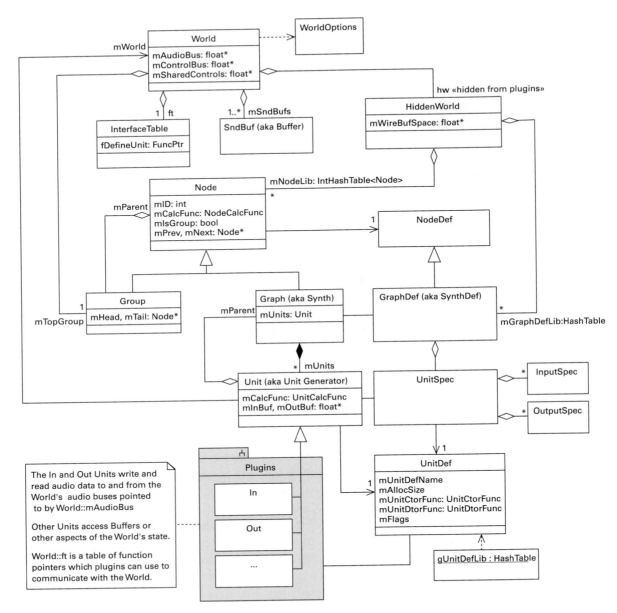

Figure 26.1
Class diagram of significant domain entities.

nothing is substituted for the usual one. Disabling a Group disables the whole tree under that Group.

A `Graph` is an aggregate of interconnected `Unit` subclasses (also known as Unit Generators or UGens). `Unit` instances are responsible for performing primitive audio DSP operations such as mixing, filtering, and oscillator signal generation. Each `Graph` instance is carved out of a single memory block to minimize the number of expensive calls to the memory allocator. Units are efficiently allocated from the Graph's memory block and evaluated by iterating through a linear array containing pointers to all of the Graph's Units. Each `Unit` instance provides a `UnitCalcFunc` function pointer to compute samples, which affords the same kind of flexibility as `NodeCalcFunc` described above. For example, many Units implement a form of self-modifying code by switching their UnitCalcFuncs on the fly to execute different code paths, depending on their state.

Graphs are instantiated using a `GraphDef` (Graph Definition), which defines the structure of a class of Graphs. The `GraphDef` type implements the SuperCollider concept of a *SynthDef*. A `GraphDef` includes both data for passive representation (used on disk and as communicated from clients such as sclang), and optimized in-memory information used to efficiently instantiate and evaluate Graphs. `GraphDef` instances store data such as memory allocation size for `Graph` instances, Unit initialization parameters, and information about the connections between Units. When a new GraphDef is loaded into the server, most of the work is done in `GraphDef_Read()`, which converts the stored representation to the run-time representation. Aside from allocating and initializing memory and wiring in pointers, one of the main tasks `GraphDef_Read()` performs is to determine which inter-Unit memory buffers will be used to pass data between Units during Graph evaluation.

The stored GraphDef representation specifies an interconnected graph of named `Unit` instances with generalized information about input and output routing. This information is loaded into an in-memory array of `UnitSpec` instances where each Unit name is resolved to a pointer to a `UnitDef` (see below), and the Unit interconnection graph is represented by instances of `InputSpec` and `OutputSpec`. This interconnection graph is traversed by a graph-coloring algorithm to compute an allocation of inter-Unit memory buffers, ensuring that the minimum number of these buffers is used when evaluating the Graph. Note that the order of Unit evaluation defined by a GraphDef is not modified by scsynth.

scsynth's tree of Nodes is rooted at a Group referenced by `World::mTopGroup`. `World` is responsible for managing the instantiation, manipulation, and evaluation of the tree of Nodes. `World` also manages much of the server's global state, including the buses used to hold control and audio input and output signals (e.g., `World::mAudioBus`) and a table of `SndBuf` instances (aka *Buffers*) used, for example, to hold sound data loaded from disk. An instance of `World` is accessible to `Unit` plug-ins via `Unit::mWorld` and provides `World::ft`, an instance of `InterfaceTable`, which is a table of function pointers which Units can invoke to perform operations on the World. An example of Units using World state is the `In` and `Out` units which directly access `World::mAudioBus` to move audio data between Graphs and the global audio buses.

`Unit` subclasses provide all of the signal-processing functionality of scsynth. They are defined in dynamically loaded executable "plug-ins." When the server starts, it scans the nominated plug-in directories and loads each plug-in, calling its `load()` function; this registers all available Units in the plug-in with the World via the `InterfaceTable::fDefineUnit` function pointer. Each call to `fDefineUnit()` results in a new `UnitDef` being created and registered with the global `gUnitDefLib` hash table, although this process is usually simplified by calling the macros defined in `SC_InterfaceTable.h`, such as `DefineSimpleUnit()` and `DefineDtorUnit()`.

Some server data (more of which we will see later) is kept away from Unit plug-ins in an instance of `HiddenWorld`. Of significance here are `HiddenWorld::mNodeLib`, a hash table providing fast lookup of Nodes by integer ID; `HiddenWorld::mGraphDefLib`, a hash table of all loaded GraphDefs, which is used when a request to instantiate a new Graph is received; and `HiddenWorld::mWireBufSpace`, which contains the memory used to pass data between Units during Graph evaluation.

26.3   Real-Time Implementation Structure

We now turn our attention to the context in which the server is executed. This includes considerations of threading, memory allocation, and interthread communications. scsynth is a real-time system, and the implementation is significantly influenced by real-time requirements. We begin by considering what "real-time requirements" means in the context of scsynth and then explore how these requirements are met.

26.3.1   Real-Time Requirements

scsynth's primary responsibility is to compute blocks of audio data in a timely manner in response to requests from the OS audio service. In general, the time taken to compute a block of audio must be less than the time it takes to play it. These blocks are relatively small (on the order of 2 milliseconds for current generation systems), and hence tolerances can be quite tight. Any delay in providing audio data to the OS will almost certainly result in an audible glitch.

Of course, computing complex synthesized audio does not come for free and necessarily takes time. Nonetheless, it is important that the time taken to compute each block is bounded and as close to constant as possible, so that exceeding timing constraints occurs only due to the complexity or quantity of concurrently active Graphs, not to the execution of real-time unsafe operations. Such unsafe operations include

• Algorithms with high or unpredictable computational complexity (for example, amortized time algorithms with poor worst-case performance)
• Algorithms which intermittently perform large computations (for example, pre-computing a lookup table or zeroing a large memory block at Unit startup)
• Operations which block or otherwise cause a thread context switch.

The third category includes not only explicit blocking operations, such as attempting to lock a mutex or wait on a file handle, but also operations which may block due to unknown implementation strategies, such as calling a system-level memory allocator or writing to a network socket. In general, any system call should be considered real-time unsafe, since there is no way to know whether it will acquire a lock or otherwise block the process.

Put simply, no real-time unsafe operation may be performed in the execution context which computes audio data in real time (usually a thread managed by the OS audio service). Considering the above constraints alongside the dynamic behavior implied by the domain model described in the previous section and the fact that scsynth can read and write sound files on disk, allocate large blocks of memory, and communicate with clients via network sockets, you may wonder how scsynth can work at all in real time. Read on, and all will be revealed.

26.3.2   Real-Time Messaging and Threading Implementation

SuperCollider carefully avoids performing operations which may violate real-time constraints by using a combination of the following techniques:

• Communication to and from the real-time context is mediated by lock-free First In First Out (FIFO) queues containing executable messages
• Use of a fixed-pool memory allocator which is accessed only from the real-time context
• Non-real-time safe operations (when they must be performed at all) are deferred and executed asynchronously in a separate "non-real-time" thread
• Algorithms which could introduce unpredictable or transient high computational load are generally avoided
• Use of user-configurable nonresizable data structures. Exhaustion of such data structures typically results in scsynth operations failing.

The first point is possibly the most important to grasp, since it defines the pervasive mechanism for synchronization and communication between non-real-time threads and the real-time context which computes audio samples. When a non-real-time thread needs to perform an operation in the real-time context, it enqueues a message which is later performed in the real-time context. Conversely, if code in the real-time context needs to execute a real-time unsafe operation, it sends the message to a non-real-time thread for execution. We will revisit this topic on a number of occasions throughout the remainder of the chapter.

Figure 26.2 shows another view of the scsynth implementation, this time focusing on the classes which support the real-time operation of the server. For clarity, only a few key classes from the domain model have been retained (shaded gray). Note that AudioDriver is a base class: in the implementation different subclasses of AudioDriver are used depending on the target OS (CoreAudio for Mac OS X, PortAudio for Windows, etc.).

Figure 26.3 illustrates the run-time thread structure and the dynamic communication pathways between threads via lock-free FIFO message queues. The diagram can be interpreted as follows: thick rectangles indicate execution contexts, which are either threads or callbacks from the operating system. Cylinders indicate FIFO message queue objects. The padlock indicates a lock (mutex), and the black circle indicates a condition variable. Full arrows indicate synchronous function calls (invocation of queue-member functions), and half arrows indicate the flow of asynchronous messages across queues.

The FIFO message queue mechanism will be discussed in more detail later in the chapter, but for now, note that the Write() method enqueues a message, Perform() executes message-specific behavior for each pending message, and Free() cleans up after messages which have been performed. The Write(), Perform(), and Free() FIFO operations can be safely invoked by separate reader and writer threads without the use of locks.

Referring to figures 26.2 and 26.3, the dynamic behavior of the server can be summarized as follows:

1. One or more threads listen to network sockets to receive incoming OSC messages which contain commands for the server to process. These listening threads dynamically allocate OSC_Packets and post them to "The Engine," using the ProcessOSCPacket() function, which results in Perform_ToEngine_Msg() (a FifoMsgFunc) being posted to the mOscPacketsToEngine queue. OSC_Packet instances are later freed, using FreeOSCPacket() (a FifoFreeFunc) by way of MsgFifo::Free(), via a mechanism which is described in more detail later.

2. "The Synthesis Engine," or "Engine" for short (also sometimes referred to here as "the real-time context"), is usually a callback function implemented by a concrete AudioDriver which is periodically called by the OS audio service to process and generate audio. The main steps relevant here are that the Engine calls Perform() on the mOscPacketsToEngine and mToEngine queues, which execute the mPerformFunc of any messages enqueued from other threads. Messages in mOscPacketsToEngine carry OSC_Packet instances which are interpreted to manipulate the Node tree, instantiate

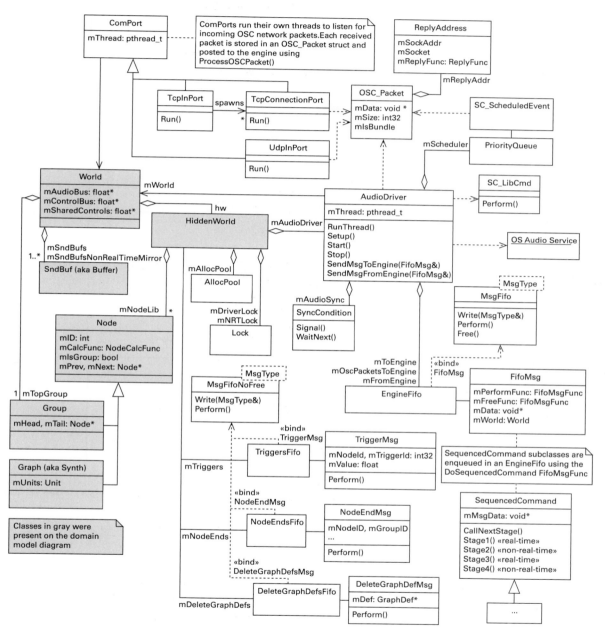

Figure 26.2
Real-time threading and messaging implementation structure.

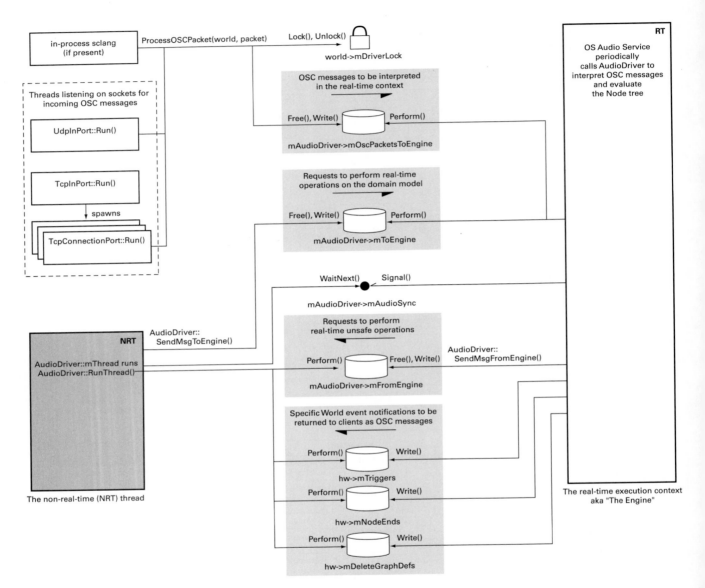

Figure 26.3
Real-time thread and queue instances and asynchronous message channels.

new Graphs, and so on. Whenever the Engine wants to perform a non-real-time safe operation, it encodes the operation in a FifoMessage instance and posts it to the non-real-time thread for execution via the mFromEngine queue. Results of such operations (if any) will be returned via the mToEngine queue. After processing messages from mOscPacketsToEngine, mToEngine, and any previously scheduled OSC messages in mScheduler, the Engine performs its audio duties by arranging for real-time audio data to be copied between OS buffers and mWorld->mAudioBus and evaluating the Node tree via mWorld->mTopGroup. When the Engine has completed filling the OS audio output buffers, it calls Signal() on mAudioSync and returns to the OS.

3. Before the server starts servicing OS audio requests, it creates a thread for executing real-time unsafe operations (the non-real-time or NRT thread). This thread waits on mAudioSync until it is signaled by the Engine. When the non-real-time thread wakes up, it calls Free() and Perform() on the mFromEngine queue to perform any non-real-time safe operations which the server has posted, then processes the mTriggers, mNodeEnds, and mDeleteGraphDefs queues. These queues contain notifications of server events. Performing the enqueued notification messages results in OSC messages being sent to clients referenced by ReplyAddress. After calling Perform() on all queues, the non-real-time thread returns to waiting on mAudioSync until it is next wakened by the Engine. Note that mAudioSync is used to ensure that the NRT thread will always wake up and process Engine requests in a timely manner. However, it may never sleep, or it may not process the queues on every Engine cycle if it is occupied with time-consuming operations. This is acceptable since the Engine assumes non-real-time operations will take as long as necessary.

The description above has painted the broad strokes of the server's real-time behavior. Zooming in to a finer level of detail reveals many interesting mechanisms which are worth the effort to explore. A number of these are discussed in the sections which follow.

26.3.2.1 Real-time memory pool allocator

Memory allocations performed in the real-time context, such as allocating memory for new Graph instances, are made using the AllocPool class. AllocPool is a reimplementation of Doug Lea's fast general-purpose memory allocator algorithm (Lea, 2000). The implementation allocates memory to clients from a large, preallocated chunk of system memory. Because AllocPool is invoked only by code running in the real-time context, it doesn't need to use locks or other mechansims to protect its state from concurrent access and hence is real-time safe. This makes it possible for the server to perform many dynamic operations in the real-time thread without needing to defer to an NRT thread to allocate memory. That said, large allocations and other memory operations which are not time-critical are performed outside the real-time context. Memory allocated with an AllocPool must of course also be freed into the same `AllocPool`, and in the same execution context, which requires some care to be taken. For example, `FifoMsg` instances posted by the Engine to the NRT thread with a payload allocated by `AllocPool` must ensure that the payload is always freed into `AllocPool` in the real-time execution context. This can be achieved using `MsgFifo::Free()`, which is described in the next section.

25.3.2.2   FIFO queue message passing

As already mentioned, scsynth uses FIFO queues for communicating between threads. The basic concept of a FIFO queue is that you push items on one end of the queue and pop them off the other end later, possibly in a different thread. A fixed-size queue can be implemented as a *circular buffer* (also known as a *ring buffer*) with a read pointer and a write pointer: new data are placed in the queue at the write pointer, which is then advanced; when the reader detects that the queue is not empty, data are read at the read pointer and the read pointer is advanced. If there's guaranteed to be only 1 reading thread and 1 writing thread, and you're careful about how the pointers are updated (and take care of atomicity and memory ordering issues) then it's possible to implement a thread-safe FIFO queue without needing to use any locks. This lock-free property makes the FIFO queue ideal for implementing real-time interthread communications in scsynth.

The queues which we are most concerned with here carry a payload of message objects between threads. This is an instance of the relatively well known *Command* design pattern (Gamma et al., 1995). The basic idea is to encode an operation to be performed as a class or struct, and then pass it off to some other part of the system for execution. In our case the Command is a struct containing data and a pair of function pointers, one for performing the operation and another for cleaning up. We will see later that scsynth also uses a variant of this scheme in which the Command is a C++ class with virtual functions for performing an operation in multiple stages. But for now, let's consider the basic mechanism, which involves posting `FifoMsg` instances to a queue of type `MsgFifo`.

Figure 26.2 shows that `mOscPacketsToEngine`, `mToEngine`, and `mFromEngine` queues carry `FifoMsg` objects. The code below shows the `FifoMsgFunc` type and the key fields of `FifoMsg`.

```
typedef void (*FifoMsgFunc)(struct FifoMsg*);

struct FifoMsg {
...
FifoMsgFunc mPerformFunc;
FifoMsgFunc mFreeFunc;
void* mData;
...
};
```

To enqueue a message, the sender initializes a `FifoMsg` instance and passes it to `MsgFifo::Write()`. Each FifoMsg contains the function pointer members `mPerform-Func` and `mFreeFunc`. When the receiver calls `MsgFifo::Perform()`, the `mPerformFunc` of each enqueued message is called with a pointer to the message as a parameter. `MsgFifo` also maintains an additional internal pointer which keeps track of which messages have been performed by the receiver. When `MsgFifo::Free()` is called by the sending execution context, the `mFreeFunc` is invoked on each message whose `mPerformFunc` has already completed. In a moment we will see how this mechanism is used to free SequencedCommand objects allocated in the real-time context.

A separate `MsgFifoNoFree` class is provided for those FIFOs which don't require this freeing mechanism, such as `mTriggers`, `mNodeEnds`, and `mDeleteGraphDefs`. These queues carry specialized notification messages. The functionality of these queues could have been implemented by dynamically allocating payload data and sending it using `FifoMsg` instances; however, since `MsgFifo` and `MsgFifoNoFree` are templates parameterized by message type, it was probably considered more efficient to create separate specialized queues using message types large enough to hold all of the necessary data rather than invoking the allocator for each request.

The `FifoMsg` mechanism is used extensively in scsynth, not only for transporting OSC message packets to the real-time engine but also for arranging for the execution of real-time unsafe operations in the NRT thread. Many server operations are implemented by the FifoMsgFuncs defined in `SC_MiscCmds.cpp`. However, a number of operations need to perform a sequence of steps alternating between the real-time context and the NRT thread. For this, the basic `FifoMsg` mechanism is extended using the `SequencedCommand` class.

26.3.2.3   SequencedCommand

Unlike `FifoMsg`, which just stores two C function pointers, `SequencedCommand` is a C++ abstract base class with virtual functions for executing up to 4 stages of a process. Stage 1 and 3 execute in the real-time context, while stages 2 and 4 execute in the NRT context. The `Delete()` function is always called in the RT context, potentially providing a fifth stage of execution. SequencedCommands are used for operations which need to perform some of their processing in the NRT context. At the time of writing, all SequencedCommand subclasses were defined in `SC_SequencedCommand.cpp`. They are mostly concerned with the manipulation of SndBufs and GraphDefs. (See table 26.1 for a list of SequencedCommands defined at the time of writing.)

To provide a concrete example of the SequencedCommand mechanism, we turn to the Help file for Buffer (aka `SndBuf`), which reads: "Buffers are stored in a single global array indexed by integers beginning with zero. Buffers may be safely allocated, loaded and freed while synthesis is running, even while unit generators are using them." Given that a SndBuf's sample storage can be quite large, or contain

Table 26.1
Subclasses of `SequencedCommand` Defined in *SC_SequencedCommand.cpp*

Buffer Commands	BufGenCmd, BufAllocCmd, BufFreeCmd, BufCloseCmd, BufZeroCmd, BufAllocReadCmd, BufReadCmd, SC_BufReadCommand, BufWriteCmd
GraphDef Commands	LoadSynthDefCmd, RecvSynthDefCmd, LoadSynthDefDirCmd
Miscellaneous	AudioQuitCmd, AudioStatusCmd, SyncCmd, NotifyCmd, SendFailureCmd, SendReplyCmd, AsyncPlugInCmd

sample data read from disk, it is clear that it needs to be allocated and initialized in the NRT thread. We now describe how the SequencedCommand mechanism is used to implement this behavior.

To begin, it is important to note that the `SndBuf` class is a relatively lightweight data structure which mainly contains metadata such as the sample rate, channel count, and number of frames of the stored audio data. The actual sample data are stored in a dynamically allocated floating-point array pointed to by `SndBuf::data`. In the explanation which follows, we draw a distinction between instance data of `SndBuf` and the sample data array pointed to by `SndBuf::data`.

In contrast to the client-oriented worldview presented in the Help file, `World` actually maintains 2 separate arrays of `SndBuf` instances: `mSndBufs` and `mSndBufsNonRealTimeMirror`. Each is always in a consistent state but is accessed or modified only in its own context: `mSndBufs` in the RT context via `World_GetBuf()` and `mSndBufsNonRealTimeMirror` in the NRT thread via `World_GetNRTBuf()`. On each iteration the engine performs messages in `mToEngine` and then evaluates the `Node` tree to generate sound. Any changes to `mSndBufs` made when calling `mToEngine->Perform()` are picked up by dependent Units when their UnitCalcFunc is called.

The code may reallocate an existing SndBuf's sample data array. It is important that the old sample data array is not freed until we can be certain no `Unit` is using it. This is achieved by deferring freeing the old sample data array until after the new one is installed into the RT context's `mSndBufs` array. This process is summarized in figure 26.4. The details of the individual steps are described below.

We now consider the steps performed at each stage of the execution of `BufAllocReadCmd`, a subclass of `SequencedCommand`, beginning with the arrival of an `OSC_Packet` in the real-time context. These stages are depicted in 4 sequence diagrams, figures 26.5 through 26.8. The exact function parameters have been simplified from those in the source code, and only the main code paths are indicated to aid understanding. The OSC message to request allocation of a Buffer filled with data from a sound file is as follows:

```
/b_allocRead bufnum path startFrame numFrames
```

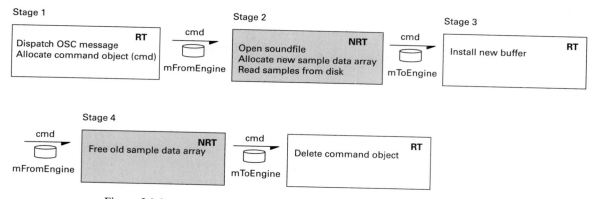

Figure 26.4
Overview of multithreaded processing of the /b_allocRead command.

Stage 1 (see figure 26.5): The real-time context processes an OSC packet containing the /b_allocRead message. The OSC dispatch mechanism looks up the correct function pointer to invoke from gCmdLibrary, in this case meth_b_allocRead(). meth_b_allocRead() calls CallSequencedCommand() to instantiate a new BufAlloc-ReadCmd instance (a subclass of SequencedCommand) which we will call cmd. Call-SequencedCommand() calls cmd->Init(), which unpacks the parameters from the OSC packet and then calls cmd->CallNextStage(), which in turn invokes cmd->Stage1(), which in the case of BufAllocReadCmd does nothing. It then enqueues cmd to the NRT thread, using SendMessageFromEngine() with DoSequencedCommand as the FifoMsg-Func.

Stage 2 (see figure 26.6): Some time later, the mFromEngine FIFO is processed in the NRT thread. The FifoMsg containing our cmd is processed, which results in cmd->Stage2() being called via DoSequencedCommand() and cmd->CallNextStage(). cmd->Stage2() does most of the work: first it calls World_GetNRTBuf(), which retrieves a pointer to the NRT copy of the SndBuf record for cmd->mBufIndex. Then it opens the sound file and seeks to the appropriate position. Assuming no errors have occurred, the pointer to the old sample data array is saved in cmd->mFreeData so it can be freed later. Then allocBuf() is called to update the SndBuf with the new file information and to allocate a new sample data array. The data are read from the file into the sample data array and the file is closed. A shallow copy of the NRT SndBuf is saved in cmd->mSndBuf. Finally, cmd->CallNextStage() enqueues the cmd with the real-time context.

Stage 3 (see figure 26.7): Similarly to stage 2, only this time in the real-time context, cmd->Stage3() is called via DoSequencedCommand() and cmd->CallNextStage(). A pointer to the *real-time* copy of the SndBuf for index cmd->mBufIndex is retrieved

Ross Bencina

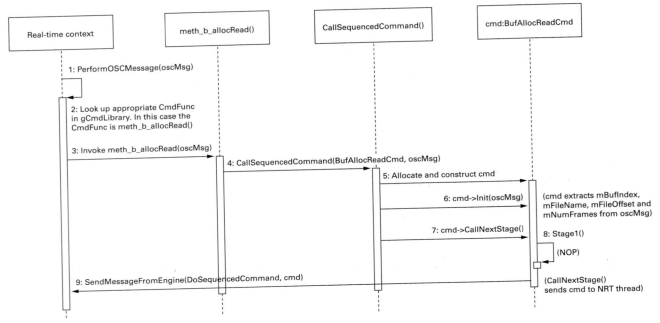

Figure 26.5
Stage 1 of processing the /b_allocRead command in the real-time context.

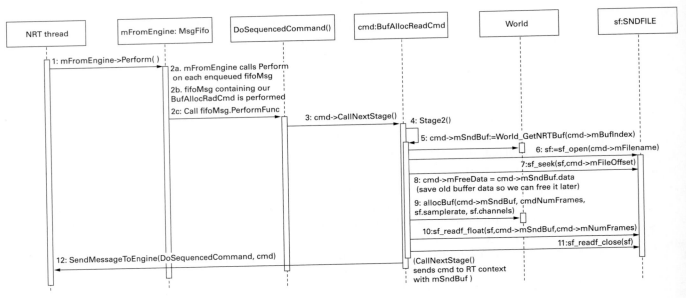

Figure 26.6
Stage 2 of processing the /b_allocRead command in the non-real-time (NRT) context.

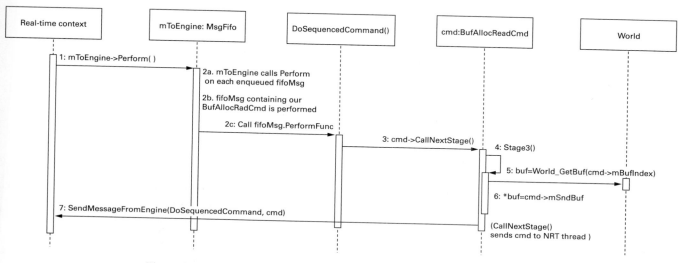

Figure 26.7
Stage 3 of processing the /b_allocRead command in the real-time context.

using World_GetBuf(cmd->mBufIndex), and the SndBuf instance data initialized in stage 2 is shallow copied into it from cmd->mSndBuf. At this stage the sample data array which was allocated and loaded in stage 2 is now available to Units calling World_GetBuf(). cmd is then sent back to the non-real-time thread.

Stage 4 (see figure 26.8): Once again, back in the non-real-time thread, cmd->Stage4() is invoked, which frees the old sample data array which was stored into cmd->mFreeData in stage 2. Then the SendDone() routine is invoked, which sends an OSC notification message back to the client who initiated the Buffer allocation. Finally, cmd is enqueued back to the real-time context with the FreeSequencedCommand FifoMsgFunc, which will cause cmd to be freed, returning its memory to the real-time AllocPool.

26.3.2.4   Processing and dispatching OSC messages

The ProcessOSCPacket() function provides a mechanism for injecting OSC messages into the real-time context for execution. It makes use of mDriverLock to ensure that only 1 thread is writing to the mOscPacketsToEngine queue at any time (this could occur, for example, when multiple socket listeners are active). To inject an OSC packet using ProcessOSCPacket(), the caller allocates a memory block using malloc(), fills it with an OSC packet (for example, by reading from a network socket), and then calls ProcessOSCPacket(). ProcessOSCPacket() takes care of enqueuing the packet to the mOscPacketsToEngine queue and deleting packets, using free(), once they are no longer needed.

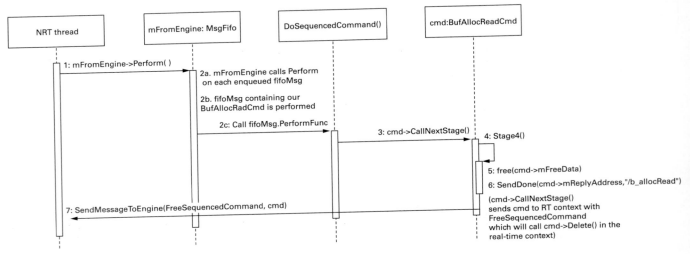

Figure 26.8
Stage 4 of processing the /b_allocRead command in the non-real-time (NRT) context.

Once the real-time context processes OSC packets, they are usually freed using the MsgFifo message-freeing mechanism; however, packets whose time-stamp values are in the future are stored in the mScheduler PriorityQueue for later execution. Once a scheduled packet has been processed, it is sent to the NRT thread to be freed.

scsynth dispatches OSC commands by looking up the SC_CommandFunc associated with a given OSC address pattern. At startup SC_MiscCmds.cpp wraps these functions in LibCmd objects and stores them into both the gCmdLib hash table and gCmdArray array.

OSC commands sent to the server may be strings or special OSC messages with a 4-byte address pattern in which the low byte is an integer message index. Command strings are compatible with any OSC client, whereas the integer command indices are more efficient but don't strictly conform to the OSC specification. When integer command indices are received, PerformOSCMessage() looks up the appropriate SC_CommandFunc in the gCmdArray array; otherwise it consults the gCmdLib hash table.

The mTriggers', mNodeEnds', and mDeleteGraphDefs' FIFOs are used by the real-time context to enqueue notifications which are translated into OSC messages in the NRT thread and are sent to the appropriate reply address by invoking ReplyAddress::mReplyFunc.

26.3.2.5 Fixed-size data structures
In real-time systems a common way to avoid the potential real-time unsafe operation of reallocating memory (which may include the cost of making the allocation and of

copying all of the data) is simply to allocate a "large enough" block of memory in the first place and have operations fail if no more space is available. This fixed-size allocation strategy is adopted in a number of places in scsynth, including the size of

- FIFO queues which interconnect different threads
- mAllocPool (the real-time context's memory allocator)
- The mScheduler priority queue for scheduling OSC packets into the future
- The mNodeLib hash table, which is used to map integer Node IDs to Node pointers.

In the case of mNodeLib the size of the table determines the maximum number of Nodes the server can accommodate and the speed of Node lookup as mNodeLib becomes full. The sizes of many of these fixed-size data structures are configurable in WorldOptions (in general, by command line parameters), the idea being that the default values are usually sufficient, but if your usage of scsynth causes any of the default limits to be exceeded, you can relaunch the server with larger sizes as necessary.

26.4 Low-Level Mechanisms

As may already be apparent, scsynth gains much of its power from efficient implementation mechanisms. Some of these fall into the category of low-bounded complexity methods which contribute to the real-time capabilities of the server, while others are more like clever optimizations which help the server to run faster. Of course the whole server is implemented efficiently, so looking at the source code will reveal many more optimizations than can be discussed here; however, a number of those which I have found interesting are briefly noted below. As always, consult the source code for more details.

- The Str4 string data type consists of a string of 32-bit integers, each containing 4 chars. Aside from being the same format that OSC uses, the implementation improves the efficiency of comparison and other string operations by being able to process 4 chars at once.
- Hash tables in scsynth are implemented using open addressing with linear probing for collision resolution. Although these tables don't guarantee constant time performance in the worst case, when combined with a good hashing function (Wang, 2007) they typically provide close to constant performance so long as they don't get too full.
- One optimization to hashing used in a number of places in the source code is that the hash value for each item (such as a Node) is cached in the item. This improves performance when resolving collisions during item lookup.
- The World uses a "touched" mechansim which Units and the AudioDriver can use to determine whether audio or control buses have been filled during a control cycle:

`World` maintains the `mBufCounter`, which is incremented at each control cycle. When a Unit writes to a bus, it sets the corresponding touched field (for example, in the `mAudioBusTouched` array for audio buses) to `mBufCounter`. Readers can then check the touched field to determine whether the bus contains data from the current control cycle. If not, the data doesn't need to be copied and zeros can be used instead.

• Delay lines typically output zeros until the delay time reaches the first input sample. One way to handle this is to zero the internal delay storage when the delay is created or reset. The delay unit generators in scsynth (see `DelayUGens.cpp`) avoid this time-consuming (and hence real-time unsafe) operation by using a separate UnitCalc-Func during the startup phase. For example, `BufDelayN_next_z()` outputs zeros for the first `bufSamples` samples, at which point the UnitCalcFunc is switched to `BufDelayN_next()`, which outputs the usual delayed samples.

• For rate-polymorphic units, the dynamic nature of UnitCalcFuncs is used to select functions specialized to the rate type of the Unit's parameters. For example, `BinaryOpUgens.cpp` defines UnitCalcFuncs which implement all binary operations in separate versions for each rate type. For example, there are separate functions for adding an audio vector to a constant, `add_ai()`, and adding 2 audio vectors, `add_aa()`. When the binary-op `Unit` constructor `BinaryOpUGen_Ctor()` is called, it calls `ChooseNormalFunc()` to select among the available UnitCalcFuncs based on the rate of its inputs.

This concludes our little journey through the wonderful gem that is scsynth. I invite you to explore the source code yourself; it has much to offer, and it's free!

References

Gamma, E., R. Helm, R. Johnson, and J. Vlissides. 1995. *Design Patterns: Elements of Reusable Design.* Reading, MA: Addison-Wesley.

Lea, D. 2000. "A Memory Allocator," <http://g.oswego.edu/dl/html/malloc.html> (accessed January 9, 2008).

McCartney, J. 2002. "Rethinking the Computer Music Language: SuperCollider." *Computer Music Journal,* 26(4): 61–68.

Wang, T. 1997. "Integer Hash Function," <http://www.concentric.net/~Ttwang/tech/inthash.htm> (accessed January 9, 2008).

Appendix: Syntax of the SuperCollider Language

Iannis Zannos

The following is not a formal exposition of the syntax rules but a summary to help the reader understand the code of the examples in this book.

A.1 Comments

Comments are written as in C++, Java, PHP, or similar languages

- Multiline comments are enclosed between /* and */
- Single-line comments start at // and run to the end of the line

A.2 Identifiers

Identifiers are sequences of alphanumeric characters and the underscore character _ that do not start with a capital letter. Such a sequence may be one of the following:

- The name of a variable or argument. Variables are declared in functions, methods, or classes, and arguments in functions or methods. Example: {arg freq; /* function code ... */}
- The name of a message. Message names must correspond to method names
- The variable and argument declaration keywords arg and var
- The special keywords this and super
- The constants pi, inf, nan, true, false

A.3 Literals

Literals are objects whose value is represented directly in the code (rather than computed as a result of sending a message to an object). Literals in SuperCollider are

- Integers (e.g., −10, 0, 123) and floating-point numbers (e.g., −0.1, 0.0, 123.4567), which can be in exponential notation (e.g., 1e-4, 1.2e4), alternate radices up to base 36 (e.g., 2r01101011, 12r4A.A), or combined with the constant pi (e.g., 2pi, −0.13pi)

- Strings, enclosed in double quotes: "a string"
- Symbols, enclosed in single quotes ('a symbol') or preceded by \ (\a_Symbol)
- Literal arrays: Immutable arrays declared by prepending the number sign (#)
- Classes: A Class is represented by its name. Class names are like identifiers but start with a capital letter
- Characters (instances of Char), a single character preceded by the dollar sign $ (e.g., $A, $a). Nonprinting characters (tab, linefeed, carriage return) and backslash are preceded by a backlash (e.g., $\n, $\t, $\\)
- Identifiers (as described in section A.2 above); see also the SuperCollider Help file on Literals)

A.4   Primitives

Primitives appear in the code of certain methods in class definitions and are identifiers that start with an underscore _. They call code that is compiled in C++ and perform elementary operations of the language, which cannot be coded in SuperCollider

A.5   Grouping Elements

Parentheses () are used to:

- Group expressions in order to specify order of execution: 1 + (2 * 3)
- Enclose arguments that accompany messages: 2.pow(3)
- Create numerical arrays from "Matlab type" series notation: (1..5)
- Create Events from keyword-value pairs: (freq: 440, amp: 0.1)

Brackets [] are used to:

- Create Arrays or other types of collections [1, 2, 5]
- Index into collections for reading or writing of values: aDictionary[\freq],
- anArray[0]

Braces {} are used to:

- Define functions: {arg a, b; a + b}
- Define Classes: Nil {/* class definition code */}
- Define methods: isNil {^true}

A.6   Binary Operators

Many arithmetic, logical, stream, and other binary operator symbols are used much as they are in C++.

A.7   Delimiters

- The dot . is used in the following senses
- To attach a message to the receiving object that it is sent to: `123.squared`
- To append an *adverb* to a binary operator. (Adverbs are identifiers or Integers that modify the behavior of an operator): `(1..15) *.f [1, 10, 100]`
- Triple dots . . . are used to collect multiple arguments into an array, in argument definitions: `{ |... args|` or in multiple variable assignments
- `#a, b ... rest = [1, pi, 10, true, inf];`
- Double dots are used in notation of arithmetic series: `(1..5), (0, 0.1 .. 10)`
- Comma is used to separate arguments `f.value(pi, 400)`, elements of Collections `[pi, \a, 5]`, or variables or arguments in declaration statements `{arg a, b;` or in multiple assignment statements `#freq, amp = #[440, 0.1]`
- Semicolon is used to separate statements. The last statement of a program (function) does not need to end in a semicolon. `a.postln; b = a.squared`
- Pipe signs `||` are used to delimit an argument declaration statement `{| a, b | a + b}`. This is alternative notation to `arg a, b;`

A.8   Special Characters

- `^` marks the statement that it precedes as a return value statement in a method: `^a * 2`
- `*` Has 2 uses:
- Preceding an argument in a message, it applies the collection's elements as separate arguments: `foo.value(*[1, 2, 10.rand]);`
- Preceding the name of a method in Class definition code, it indicates that this is a class method: `*initClass {all = IdentityDictionary.new}`
- `#` (number sign) is used as prefix in 2 cases:
- Multiple variable assignment: `#freq, amp = [400, 0.1]`
- Construction of immutable Arrays and closed Functions: `#[1, 5, 11], #{pi ! 3}`
- `$` precedes Character instances: `$a $. $A`
- `~` Tilde before an identifier treats it as an environment variable (see chapter 5, section 5.3.5: Environment Variables)
- `<` and `>` construct accessor methods for variables in classes: `var <>freq`

A.9   Construction of Specific Kinds of Objects, Abbreviations, Various Conventions

In addition to those covered above (`"string,"` `'symbol,'` `\symbol`) there are the following constructor elements:

- Braces {} construct Functions: `{|a, b| a * b}`
- Brackets [] construct Arrays (or other Collections when preceded by collection name): `[1, \a]` `Set[1, a]`, `Dictionary[\a->1, \b->2]`
- Parentheses () enclosing keyword-value pairs construct events: `(a: 1, b: 2)`
- "At" sign @ between 2 numbers constructs a Point: `-5@10`
- "At" sign @ between a collection and a number indexes into the collection: `[1, 5, 7]@1`
- Arrow -> between values constructs an association: `\freq->440`
- Underscore _ by itself in a message statement constructs a function: `_.isPrime` (see the "Partial Application" Help file)
- `element ! n` duplicates the element n times (evaluating it if it's a Function) and collects the result in an Array: `{10.0.rand} ! 12`
- The message `new` can be omitted between a Class name and arguments enclosed in parentheses: `Synth("sine")` is equivalent to `Synth.new("sine")`
- The message `value` can be omitted between a Function and arguments enclosed in parentheses: `foo.(n)` is equivalent to `foo.value(n)`. Also, `someFunc.()` is equivalent to `someFunc.value`.
- Functions as sole arguments need not be enclosed in parentheses: `10.do {"hello".postln}`
- Messages whose name ends in underscore _ can also be written in "variable assignment" format: `aPoint.x_(0)` is equivalent to `aPoint.x = 0`
- < or > prepended to a variable name in a variable declaration statement in a Class constructs corresponding methods for getting or setting the value of that variable. `var <>x, <>y;`

Subject Index

This index includes topics from the main body of the text. Ubiquitous topics have been limited to principal references. For messages and classes from the SC language, see the code index. For definitions of terms, see the syntax appendix.

Code Index

This index contains language elements of SuperCollider. While most terms are used throughout the text, this index is limited to initial references, typically from the tutorial chapters. Note that this index is divided into two sections: messages and classes.